India's Transition from Fossil Fuels to New Age Energy

A Quest for Energy Self-Sufficiency

India's Transition from Fossil Fuels to New Age Energy

A Quest for Energy Self-Sufficiency

KEDAR NATH SHARMA

authors
UPFRONT

Contents

SECTION III: ELECTRIC MOBILITY

Preface

Addressing a webinar on green growth in India on 23 February 2023, Prime Minister Narendra Modi described India's green energy potential—solar, wind and biogas—as "no less than a goldmine or oil field", and added that the country has been exploring every possible route to tap this potential to become self-sufficient in energy by 2047 - the year, when it will celebrate its independence centenary.

Renewables hold the key to the fulfilment of this mission. India is richly endowed with abundance of clean and renewable resources of energy such as sun, wind and water. All it needs is the application of appropriate technologies to exploit these endowments. Happily, India has taken multiple initiatives in this direction.

By moving away from fossil fuels, which drive the country's economy today and cost a fortune on imports—India hopes to, as they say, kill two birds with one stone: achieve energy self-independence and create a carbon-neutral pathway for sustainable development. India is richly endowed with an abundance of clean and renewable energy resources. All it needs is the application of appropriate technology to exploit these endowments.

The global energy landscape is undergoing a rapid and complete overhaul. The fast-changing world of clean energy technologies, electric mobility, innovations like hydrogen, battery and offshore wind technology, and the emerging environmental governance imperative are set to topple the traditional base of thermal energy.

As the energy transition toward low carbon resources continues, our dependence on oil, gas and coal is diminishing substantially. There is a greater awareness today than it was two decades ago that burning fossil fuels emits particulate matter, air pollution, carbon dioxide (CO_2) and greenhouse gases driving the planet to disastrous climate change. The former is strangling cities around the world with smog, and the later contribute to the climate crisis: the heat-trapping fossil fuel by-products are the single largest contributor to global warming.

In such circumstances, energy transition has become an existential necessity for the humanity, particularly for peoples, dependent on fossil fuel imports. They are faced with double-whammy of wild volatility in oil and gas prices, which plays havoc with their economies, and supply uncertainties in the event of geopolitical tensions in oil-producing regions. A transition to cleaner fuel sources, such as renewables and biogas, could play a critical role in whittling down is the overseas dependence of energy importing countries. The Nature has been generous enough to provide sunlight, wind, water and hydrogen to the entire humanity at no cost, and the technology has provided tools to tap these vast indigenous renewable resources.

The first part of this book is a modest review of the status of fossil fuels in India's energy mix. Later, the narrative moves on to India's efforts to develop the country's vast domestic potentials of renewable energy, biomass and thorium to secure a secure and sustainable future.

Introduction

❝ Energy is the only universal currency…", says energy historian Vaclav Smil. To get anything done, he says, one of the many forms of energy must be transformed. The universal manifestations of energy ranges from the enormous rotation of galaxies to thermonuclear reactions in stars. On Earth some of its transformations range from the terra-forming forces of plate tectonics that part ocean floors and raise new mountain ranges to the cumulative erosive impacts of raindrops. Humans depend on these for their survival. The distinct forms of energy are linked by numerous conversions, many of them universal, ubiquitous and incessant, and others highly localised, infrequent and ephemeral.[1]

But what is energy? Where did all the stuff in the universe come from in the first place? What was the universe like before the Big Bang? Scientists have developed a number of new ideas about what might have powered the Big Bang. One of the leading ideas is, 'The Inflationary Universe'. The key assumption of this model is that just before the Big Bang, space was filled with an unstable form of energy, whose nature is not yet known. At some instant, this energy was transformed into the fundamental particles from which arose all the matter we observe today. That instant marks what we call the Big Bang.[2]

The fundamental features of the universe are governed by gravitational energy, which orders countless galaxies and star systems. Gravity also keeps our planet orbiting at just the right distance from the Sun, and it holds a sufficiently massive atmosphere that makes Earth habitable. As with all active stars, fusion powers the Sun, and the product of those thermonuclear reactions reaches the Earth as electromagnetic (solar, radiant) energy. Its flux ranges over a broad spectrum of wavelengths, including visible light. About 30% of this enormous flow is reflected by clouds and surfaces, about 20% is absorbed by the atmosphere and clouds, and the remainder, roughly half of the total inflow, is absorbed by oceans and continents, that gets converted into thermal energy and is radiated into space. The geothermal energy of the Earth adds up to a much smaller flux: it results from the original gravitational accretion of the planetary mass and from the decay of radioactive matter, and it drives grand tectonic processes, which keep reordering oceans and continents and cause volcanic eruptions and earthquakes.[3]

Photosynthetic Conversion of Solar Radiation

Life on Earth—so far, the only life in the universe we know of—would be impossible without the photosynthetic conversion of solar energy into phytomass (plant biomass). Only a tiny part of the incoming solar radiation—less than 0.05%—is converted by photosynthesis into phytomass or new stores of energy in plants, providing the irreplaceable foundation of all higher life. Animate metabolism reorganises nutrients into growing tissues and maintains bodily functions and constant temperature in all higher species. Digestion also generates the mechanical (kinetic) energy of working muscles. In their energy conversion, animals are inherently limited by the size of their bodies and by the availability of accessible nutrition. A distinguishing characteristic of our species has been the extension of these physical limits through a more efficient use of muscles and the harnessing of energies outside our own bodies.

Controlled Combustion

Controlled combustion in fireplaces, stoves and furnaces turns the chemical energy of plants into thermal energy. This heat is directly used in households and in smelting metals, firing bricks as well as processing and finishing countless products. The combustion of fossil fuels made all of these traditional direct uses of heat widespread and more efficient. A number of fundamental inventions made it possible to convert thermal energy from the burning of fossil fuels to mechanical energy. This was done first in steam and internal combustion engines, then in gas turbines and rockets. We have been generating electricity by burning fossil fuels, as well by harnessing the kinetic energy of water, since 1882, and by fissioning a uranium isotope since 1956.

This created a new form of high-energy civilisation whose expansion now encompassed the whole planet and its primary energy sources now include small rapidly rising share of new renewable sources, especially solar (harnessed by photovoltaic devices or in concentrating solar power plants) and wind (converted by large wind turbines). Every form of energy can be turned into heat or thermal energy; no energy is ever lost in the process. Conservation of energy, the first law of thermodynamics, is one of the most fundamental universal realities. But as we move along conversion chains, the potential for useful work steadily diminishes. This inexorable reality defines the second law of thermodynamics. The epochal transition to fossil fuels has affected everything: agriculture, industry, transportation, weapons, communication, economics, urbanisation, quality of life, politics and even the environment.[4]

Energy Takes Different Forms

Energy is available in different forms such as coal, oil, natural gas, water, solar, wind, nuclear and in all matters in the universe. Coal, oil and natural gas are fossil fuels, while sources such as sunlight, wind, the flowing water and geothermal heat are renewables.

Fossil fuels are formed from the sustained exposure of organic matter, especially the dead remains of living organisms, buried under the Earth's crust to high pressure, heat and geologic processes over millions of years. Sun's radiation, which energises a habitable biosphere and produces all our food, animal feed and wood. The origin of fossil fuels is also in the transformation of solar radiation: peat and coal arose from the slow alteration of dead plants, hydrocarbons from more complex transformations of marine and lacustrine single-celled phytoplankton, zooplankton and some algae, invertebrates and fish.[5]

Renewables derive their energy from natural sources that are replenished at a higher rate than they are consumed. Sunlight and wind are examples of such sources that are constantly being replenished. Such sources are plentiful and all around us. Fossil fuels, on the other hand, are non-renewables that take hundreds of millions of years to form, and when burned to produce energy, cause harmful greenhouse gas emissions, such as carbon dioxide (CO_2). Generating renewable energy creates far lower emissions than burning fossil fuels.

The use of fossil fuels and electricity are the largest causes of anthropogenic pollution of the atmosphere and greenhouse gas emissions. The combustion of all fossil fuels entails rapid oxidation of their carbon, which produces increasing emissions of CO_2, while methane (CH_4), a more potent greenhouse gas, is released during the production and transportation of natural gas; small volumes of nitrous oxide are also released from fossil fuel combustion.

Here are some salient characteristics of fossil fuels and renewables:

Coal

Cheap, plentiful and easily extractable, coal has been the most dominant fuel used worldwide for generation of primary energy for ages. Historically, coal has been the main fuel of economic growth worldwide. It was responsible for the transition of Europe from the Middle Age to Industrial Age; the United States and Canada also owe their transformation to coal.

Coal combustion launched the thermal electricity generation during the 1880s and dependence on it increased greatly during the twentieth century as the leading transportation fuel and the fuel for power plants. During the 1950s, coal combustion provided the largest share of electricity generation globally. However, the combustion of coal is a large source of particulate matter, sulphur oxide (SO_x) and nitrogen oxide (NO_x). The acid deposition, created mostly by emissions of SO_x and NO_x from large coal-fired power plants in Europe and eastern North America, reached semi-continental scale and until the mid-1980s was widely seen as the most pressing environmental problem facing affluent countries.[6]

Oil

Oil is one of the world's most important primary sources of energy. It is a naturally occurring, unrefined petroleum product composed of hydrocarbon deposits in natural underground pools or reservoirs and remains liquid at atmospheric pressure and temperature. Often called 'black gold', crude oil has wide ranging viscosity and can vary in colour to various shades of black and yellow depending on its hydrocarbon composition. Crude oil can be refined to produce usable products such as gasoline, diesel, jet fuels, fuel oils, lubricants and various forms of petrochemicals. It is central to security, prosperity and the very nature of our civilisation. The development of the internal combustion engine, powered by gasoline, gave the oil industry a new life and a new civilisation was born.

Globally we get the largest amount of our energy from oil, followed by coal, gas and then hydroelectric power. According to *BP's Statistical Review of World Energy*, 2022, the share of fossil fuels in the world energy mix is slowly declining (82% in 2021, down from 83% in 2019 and 85% in 2017), but the absolute amount of fossil fuels used remains around the same, giving credence to the idea that energy sources are added to existing sources in the energy mix, rather than replacing them. Wind and solar together produced 10.2% of power generation worldwide in 2021, the first time the sources reached double digits combined, and the two outstripped nuclear power. Renewable primary energy (including biofuels but excluding hydropower) increased by 15% in 2021, with China adding around 36% of new solar and 40% of new wind power generation capacity.

BP report adds that the largest share of increase in energy consumption, 41%, was contributed by renewables. Natural gas contributed the second largest increment with 36%. However, as an overall share of energy consumption, oil remained on top with 33%, while the remainder of global energy consumption came from coal (27%), natural gas (24%), hydropower (6%), renewables (5%) and nuclear power (4%).

The majority of oil reserves in the world is in the Middle East—48% of the known and identified reserves—followed by North America, Africa, Central and South America, Eurasia, Asia and Oceania. Organisation of the Petroleum Exporting Countries (OPEC) accounts for about 75% of the world's proven oil reserves, and 55% of the oil traded internationally. There are almost 200 different varieties of oil available for sale today, but the three most common and most talked about are West Texas Intermediate (WTI), Brent Blend and OPEC Basket. WTI is the highest quality oil and, hence, more expensive than other types.

Natural Gas

Natural gas was unknown as a primary source of energy in Europe until it was discovered in 1659 in England, and even after the discovery it was not widely used. It was the gas obtained from carbonised coal (known as town gas) that was the primary fuel for illuminating streets and houses in much of Europe from 1790 onward. In North America the first commercial application of a petroleum product was the utilisation of natural gas from a shallow well in Fredonia, New York, in 1821. The gas was distributed through a small-bore lead pipe to consumers for lighting and cooking in a limited area. An important breakthrough came in 1890 with the invention of leakproof pipeline coupling that facilitated gas transportation through pipes.

For decades, natural gas remained a minor contributor to global energy supply. In 1900, it supplied merely 1% of all fossil energy, and by 1950 its share was still about 10%. But later, three major demand trends lifted its global share to nearly 25% of all fossil energies by the year 2000, and the twentieth century saw a 375-fold increase in total energy derived from it annually, making this the cleanest of all fossil fuels. Relatively, the smallest but a significant new market was the use of natural gas as both feedstock and fuel for ammonia—the most important nitrogenous fertiliser, now generally used as feedstock to produce solid urea—and for the production of plastics.

The largest new global market has developed in response to the high levels of urban air pollution experienced in most Western cities during the period of post-World War II industrialisation: replacement of coal and fuel oil by natural gas for industrial, institutional and household heating (cooking) that eliminated emissions of particulate matter and generation of sulphur dioxide (SO_2). The latest trend boosting natural gas use has been for generating electricity by gas turbines, and even more efficiently, by combined-cycle gas turbines.[7]

Renewables

Renewables are set to be major energy providers of the future such as solar, wind, hydropower, biofuels, biomass, geothermal, tidal power, even waste-to-energy. Unlike fossil fuels, they are not based on finite resources. They are widely distributed, and have very limited or no carbon footprint.

Solar Energy

Solar is by far the most promising of them all. Researchers have calculated that the Sun releases an estimated 384.6 yotta watts (3.846 × 10 × 26 times joule/second) of energy in form of light and other forms of radiation. The Earth receives 174,000 TW (terawatts) of incoming solar radiation (insolation) at the upper atmosphere. Approximately 30% is reflected back to space while the rest is absorbed by clouds, oceans and land masses.[8]

Solar radiation or just sunlight is a general term for the electromagnetic radiation emitted by the Sun, which can be captured and turned into useful forms of energy, such as heat and electricity, using a variety of technologies. The amount of solar energy that is available to us during an hour is more than the total amount of energy consumed worldwide in an entire year. But this is diffused, rather than concentrated energy. Instead of obtaining the Sun's energy from indirect sources like fossil fuels, researchers and organisations worldwide have developed and are developing various devices to tap this unlimited source of energy directly.

As of today, photovoltaic (PV) is the most preferred device to tap solar energy. By the end of 2016, cumulative PV capacity had increased by more than 75 GW (gigawatt) and reached at least 303 GW, sufficient to supply approximately 1.8% of the world's total electricity consumption. There were more than 24 countries with a cumulative PV capacity of more than 1 GW. The top installers of 2016 were China, United States and India.

Reducing costs of setting up solar PV projects have drawn developers, governments and consumers to this sector. For example, in India the costs have dropped by about 80% between 2010 and 2018. When the National Solar Mission was launched in 2010, the cost of solar power was Rs 17 per unit. In March 2019, the cost had fallen to Rs 2.44 per unit, with an average current price of solar electricity dropping to 18% below the average price of its coal-fired power.[9] By the end of September 2019, India had installed more than 82,580 MW of renewable energy capacity with around 31,150 MW of capacity under various stages of installation.[10]

People realised that it is cheaper to build and operate solar farms than run the existing coal-fired plants. In 2010, the installed solar power capacity stood at 10 MW. In March 2019, it had reached 30 GW, and six months later in November 2019, it was 32 GW, 32% of the 2022 target of 100 GW and it accounts for 38 of the renewable energy mix. India has established nearly 42 solar parks by making land available to the promoters of solar plants. In addition to its large-scale grid-connected solar PV initiative, India is developing off-grid solar power for local energy needs. Solar products have increasingly helped to meet rural needs. The International Solar Alliance (ISA) proposed by India as a founder member is headquartered in India.

Wind Energy

Wind power will be very important in the coming years, perhaps the most established renewable energy source, besides hydro. At the end of 2018, the installed capacity of wind turbines worldwide was 597 GW, according to World Wind Energy Association (WWEA) data. China was on the top with an installed capacity of 221 GW, US was second with 96.4 GW and Germany third, and highest in Europe, with 59.3 GW.

In India, wind power generation capacity has significantly increased in recent years. As of 31 March, 2020, it was over 40 GW, the fourth largest installed wind power capacity in the world. A recent study by National Institute of Wind Energy (NIWE) has shown India's wind energy potential at 302 GW at 100 m hub-height.

Decreasing cost of wind power generation has been behind its rapid growth. In December 2017, the tariff reached a record low of Rs 2.43 (US¢ 3.5) per kWh (without any direct or indirect subsidies) during auctions for wind projects before rising to Rs 2.82 (US$ 0.040) per kWh in the auction held by the Solar Energy Corporation of India (SECI) for 1,200 MW of four connected wind projects in 2019. Wind power capacity is mainly spread across the South, West, North and East regions.

Hydropower

Using the potential and kinetic energy of water hydropower is the second most important source of renewable energy, as it currently supplies around 8.25% of the world's power. India is the seventh largest producer of hydroelectric power. As of 30 April, 2017, India's installed utility-scale hydroelectric capacity was 45,399.22 MW. The state of Gujarat is at the top position in per capita installed electricity generation capacity followed by Maharashtra, Tamil Nadu, Andhra Pradesh and Uttar Pradesh.

The Indian government estimated its hydropower capacity at over 1,45,000 MW, but plagued by land acquisition problems, cost uncertainties and long construction periods (usually eight to nine years) this sector has fallen out of favour. Between 2008 and 2018, India's total installed hydropower electricity capacity declined from 25% to 13%, while thermal contribution remained the same, at two-thirds, and that of renewables more than doubled to a fifth. Globally also, hydropower seems to be losing its sheen: addition to hydropower capacity dropped from 43 GW in 2013 to 25 GW in 2017 and further to 21.8 GW in 2018, according to an International Hydropower Association Status Report published in January, 2019. Among those who added hydropower capacity were China (8,540 MW), Brazil (3,866 MW), Pakistan (2,487 MW), Turkey (1,085 MW), Angola (668 MW), Tajikistan (605 MW), Ecuador (556 MW), India (535 MW), Norway (419 MW) and Canada (401 MW).

Geothermal Energy

The Earth's interior is intensely hot as you go deeper towards the magma, while the shallow regions contain hot water, rock and steam. This heat can be harnessed to produce electrical energy to drive various applications.

Harnessing geothermal energy requires no fuel and minimal land. It is relatively cheap and a very sustainable source of energy since the amount of heat contained in the Earth's bed is so vast that even if we harness more energy than we require, it will still suffice for millions of years to come. Google-funded research revealed that geothermal could generate ten times the amount of power than that of all of our currently operating coal plants combined. Some analysts predict that geothermal projects will one day produce as much as one sixth of the world's energy.

Biomass

Biomass energy is generated from living or once-living organisms, the most common materials used for bioenergy are plants like corn and soy. Energy from these organisms can be burned to create heat or converted into electricity. Mankind has used biomass energy ever since the 'cave men' first made wood fires for cooking or keeping warm. Today, biomass is used to fuel electric generators and other machinery.

Biomass contains energy derived from the sun as plants absorb it through photosynthesis, and convert carbon dioxide and water into nutrients (carbohydrates). These are burned to create heat to generate direct energy or converted into electricity or processed into biofuel (indirect energy).

Biomass is the only renewable energy source that can be converted into liquid biofuels such as ethanol and biodiesel, which can be used to power vehicles. It is produced at industrial scale by gasification in countries like Sweden, Austria and the United States. Biofuels do not operate as efficiently as gasoline, but can be blended with gasoline to operate vehicles and machinery without emitting pollution associated with fossil fuels.

A Bengaluru-based Institute of Science study has shown that India produces around 120 to 150 mt of agricultural residues per annum which, it says, can be used to generate biomass energy to electrify homes. Cabinet Minister (Power, New and Renewable Energy) R K Singh says that India is already working on several schemes to generate around 18,000 MW by using biomass and 7,000–8,000 MW from bagasse cogeneration in sugar mills over the next few years.

Nuclear Energy

Amid growing concern with adverse consequences of climate change, the motivation to use nuclear power to generate carbon-free electricity is gaining increasingly greater impetus. As of April 2018, there were 449 civilian fission reactors in the world, with a combined electrical capacity of 394 GW, supplying about 10% of the world electricity. As many as 58 nuclear power reactors were under construction and 154 reactors planned, with a combined capacity of 63 GW and 157 GW, respectively. And, as of January 2019, another 337 reactors were proposed, most of them in Asia.

The United State and France are world leaders in the nuclear energy sector. The number of operation reactors in the US till 2022 are 93 (from 98), and currently only two new reactors under construction—Vogtle-3 and 4—in Georgia are expected to come online before 2023.[11] Another 15 units in the planning phase across the country are expected to be commissioned by 2025. Currently, nuclear reactors supply about 19% of US electricity.

France derives about 75% of its electricity from nuclear energy. In 2017, electricity production in France was 562 TWh (terawatt hours in gross), and of this, nuclear provided 398 TWh (71%), hydro 55 TWh (10%), coal 15 TWh (3%), gas 40 TWh (7%), solar 10 TWh (1.8%) and wind 25 TWh (4%). The country's installed nuclear energy capacity is 63.1 GW and power production 403.7 TWh.

China, India, Finland, Czech Republic, UK, Korea, Poland and Turkey are emerging as new leaders. They are implementing nuclear energy projects to partly decarbonise their coal-heavy power sector. Factors drawing governments towards the nuclear energy are: first, concerns about climate change and the need to reduce CO_2 emissions; second, improving energy security and independence, when compared with importing of oil and gas (almost most countries have neither uranium resources nor nuclear fuel making capabilities that they must import). In some cases, nuclear power can help keep electricity prices low, as in France which has the lowest electricity price in Europe. And finally, it ensures uninterrupted supply round-the-clock, as nuclear reactors, once started, cannot be stopped midway; if stopped, restarting them becomes heavily uneconomical.

Downsides are: 1. Nuclear plant takes a long time to build and is expensive; 2. shortage of uranium; 3. problem of waste management; 4. risk of radioactive material contamination in the surrounding area of nuclear plants.

However, studies have shown that nuclear power has one of the lowest levels of fatalities per unit of energy generated compared to other sources of energy. Coal, petroleum, natural gas and hydroelectricity each have caused more fatalities per unit of energy due to air pollution and accidents.[12] Accidents in nuclear power plants include the Chernobyl disaster in the

Soviet Union in 1986, the Fukushima Daiichi nuclear disaster in Japan in 2011 and the more contained Three Mile Island accident in the United States in 1979. In 2016, the US Energy Information Administration projected for its 'base case' that world nuclear power generation would increase from 2,344 TWh in 2012 to 4,500 TWh in 2040. Most of the predicted increase was expected to be in Asia.[13]

India plans to increase its nuclear power generation capacity by another 28,900 MW over the next few years, according to the state-owned Nuclear Power Corporation of India Ltd (NPCL). This will be in addition to 6,700 MW that will be provided by six reactors—KAPS-3 (Kakrapar, Gujarat); KAPS-4 (Kakrapar, Gujarat); RAPS-7 (Rawatbhata, Rajasthan); RAPS-8 (RAPS-8 (Rawatbhata, Rajasthan); KKNPP-3 (Kundankulam, Tamil Nadu) and KKNPP-4 (Kundankulam, Tamil Nadu)—already under advanced stages of construction. The proposed new plants are to be located in Jaitalpur (Maharashtra), Gorakhpur (Haryana), Mithi Virdi (Gujarat), Kowada (Andhra Pradesh), Chutka (Madhya Pradesh) and Bhimpur, Shivpuri (Madhya Pradesh).

As of March 2021, India has 22 nuclear reactors in operational in seven nuclear power plants, with a total installed capacity of 6,780 MW. Nuclear power plants produced a total of 35 TWh and supplied 3.22% of Indian electricity in 2017. In 2010, India had drawn up a plan to achieve a nuclear power capacity of 63 GW by 2032. But India's ambitious moves were handicapped by a lack of nuclear fuel. According to an International Atomic Energy Agency (IAEA) report, India has low uranium reserves of approximately 54,636 tonnes of 'reasonably assured resources' and 25,245 tonnes of 'estimated additional resources'. In addition, it is reported to have 15,488 tonnes of 'undiscovered conventional resources', and 17,000 tonnes of 'speculative resources'. The Nuclear Power Corporation of India says these reserves are only sufficient to generate about 10 GW for about 40 years.

But in 2011, it was reported that the Atomic Energy Commission of India had found a 'confirmed' reserve of 49,000 tonnes, with a potential of it rising to 150,000 tonnes, of uranium at Tummalapalle mine at Kadapa district of Hyderabad. This estimate was subsequently increased to 85,000 tonnes in 2014.[14] As recently as 14 December, 2019, the state-owned Uranium Corporation of India Ltd (UCIL) claimed that research had shown, "Several geographical regions in the country like Kadapa in Andhra Pradesh and

Chitral in Telangana have high concentrations of uranium occurring naturally under the Earth."[15]

Besides exploiting domestic sources, India also imports uranium to keep its seven nuclear plants running. The 48-nation Nuclear Suppliers Group (NSG) has granted a waiver to India—the only country with nuclear weapons which is not a party to the Non-Proliferation Treaty (NPT)—to access civilian nuclear technology and fuel from other countries. As of 2016, India had signed civil nuclear agreements with 14 countries: Argentina, Australia, Canada, Czech Republic, France, Japan, Kazakhstan, Mongolia, Namibia, Russia, South Korea, the United Kingdom, the United States and Vietnam. Currently, Kazakhstan is the largest supplier of uranium to India providing 5,000 tonnes. Meanwhile, Indian scientists have intensified studies on thorium which could eventually be used in place of uranium in the future nuclear plants. Independent studies have put Indian thorium reserves at 30% of the world reserves. According to the IAEA and the US Geological Survey India's thorium reserves could be 12 to 33% of the global reserves.

Finding a Balance

There may be various other ways of extracting energy from the Earth, but as of now hydrocarbons have been the main fuels for electricity generation and transportation all over the world, accounting for well over 80% of all energy. Supplies may be abundant today, but concerns about their adverse impact on the environment are more worrying than at any time in the past. At present, people in developed countries consume an average 14 barrels of oil per person per year, while it is only three barrels per person per year in developing nations.

Questions about the future of India's energy security are dominated by two topics: the strong rise in energy demand as the economy zooms at a rapid pace annually and a grim battle against climate change. At the base of both is energy, which is the principal source of economic growth as well as greenhouse gas emissions. That makes energy transition the topic of our time and a must if we want to keep our planet habitable for future generations. But striking a balance between fighting pollution and decarbonising the economy, while at the same time upholding economic growth, is an extremely hard task. Furthermore, we cannot afford to overlook social questions concerning affordability. Without affordability, there will not be public acceptance, and without public acceptance the energy transition will practically be impossible. Today, about 65% of the electricity consumed in India is generated by thermal power plants, 22% by hydroelectric power plants, 3% by nuclear power plants and the remaining 10% from other alternative sources like solar, wind, biomass, etc.

Striking a balance between the need to meet the rising energy demand of a growing population while at the same time reducing carbon emissions is one of the daunting challenges the country is facing. Forecasts suggest that the population is on way to touching 1.5 billion by 2030 from 1.3 billion today while domestic outputs of oil and gas continue to decline. In the first ten months of the fiscal year 2018–19, India's crude oil production declined by 3.6% to 23,075 tonnes from 23,943 tonne in the same period of 2017–18. Similarly, natural gas output dropped 0.67% to 21,783 million standard cubic metres in the same period. In order to improve domestic production, the government has opened up the oil and gas sector to enable foreign companies to invest in the sector. But barring two major discoveries in offshore Krishna-Godavari basin (operated by Reliance-British Petroleum) in Andhra Pradesh for natural gas and onshore Barmer Block (operated by Cairn Oil and Gas) in Rajasthan for crude oil, there has been little enhancement in domestic production. Uncertainties about the countries' ability to maintain its current 7–8% economic growth, which is needed to eliminate poverty, also looms large.

At the same time India has to grapple with an uphill task of fulfilling its international commitment, made in 2015 at the Paris Climate Summit, to significantly reduce greenhouse gas (GHG) emissions to mitigate climate change. The country's pledge envisages generating 40% of its electricity from renewable energy and reduce consumption of coal to 42% by 2030. The country has been ranked as the world's fourth largest emitter of carbon dioxide (CO_2) in the United Nations' Global Carbon Report submitted at the December 2018 session (24th session) of the Conference of Parties (COP) on Climate Change in Warsaw. The report said that India emitted 2.5 bt of CO_2 in 2017, with a projected growth of 6.7% for 2018. The latest '2018 Brown to Green' Report of Climate Transparency that partners with the Indian non-profit, The Energy and Resources Institute (TERI), predicted that based on implemented policies, India's GHG emissions was expected to increase from 4,469 tonnes to 4,570 tonnes of CO_2 equivalent by 2030, excluding forestry.

Doubts have been raised about the country's ability to meet its commitment to reduce its emission intensity, as most of its power sector is built around the heavy use of coal and the transport sector around oil. This means that most of the country's infrastructure is heavily dependent on fossil fuels. The government minces no words in acknowledging its overwhelming dependence on coal. It is only recently that the Prime Minister Narendra Modi-led government has shifted focus from India's coal-centric electricity generation to wind and solar-based power generation. However, the country cannot ignore its dependence on coal in the foreseeable future. Renewables could only be supplementary source to the main power source—the coal, which currently provides around 58% of India's energy. Efforts are also being made to reduce overdependence on imported oil by encouraging the use of electric vehicles. But it will be a long time before the price-sensitive Indian consumers would opt for the expensive electric cars in place of a relatively cheaper gasoline-powered (petrol, diesel or LPG) transport. The reliance on imported oil and gas is also likely to persist indefinitely.

The energy situation puts India on the stage for a great balancing act, as on one hand we have environmental protection and reduction of carbon and, on the other, economic growth and energy security. The book attempts to focus on multifarious challenges petroleum-deficient India is faced with to ensure the supply of energy to its growing population and to maintain its rapid economic growth without heavily replying on coal and jeopardising the environment. The book also looks into various sources from which the country draws its energy—coal, crude oil, natural gas, wind, sunlight, geothermal, biomass and nuclear. This volume attempts to inform the layman about the role of energy in their day-to-day life and how the transformation of energy to different forms keeps the engine of civilisation and economic prosperity chugging. The canvas is global. But the stress is on India, in particular.

The author seeks to explore answers of these problems in India's context and discuss the viability of measures adopted by the governments in different energy sectors (coal, oil, gas and renewables) to cope with the problem. In recent years, India has been importing more than 80% of its oil and 50% of its natural gas to power its rapid economic growth and has emerged as the world's third largest consumer of oil. Ironically, the country also imports coal, despite holding the third largest reservoir of coal in the world, because its own holdings are considered of poor quality.

India's energy consumption has been growing at more than 4.5% per annum—faster than all major economies of the world—and is set to overtake China as the largest growth market for energy in volume terms by 2030. At present, it is the third largest energy consumer behind the US and China. "We will use a combination of conventional fuel and other more sustainable options to create a balanced energy mix. We will also explore other new and sustainable sources of energy like hydrogen. Technology and innovations will play an important role in this," says Minister of Petroleum and Natural Gas, Dharmendra Pradhan.[16] He said that India is moving towards a gas-based economy and investments of about US$ 100 billion are underway in India's energy infrastructure, including renewables.

What Could Be the Ideal Source of Energy of the Future?

Surely, not the fossil fuels. Nuclear, solar, biofuels and wind are just a few of the promising alternatives for a cleaner and greener future source of energy. Other relatively new sources of energy such as fuel cells, geothermal energy and ocean energy are also being explored. But I do not see any single source of power to emerge to definitively take the place of hydrocarbons. In my opinion, most of the energy of the future would be drawn from a mix of all of the above plus a limited amount of fossil fuels. Wind, solar, geothermal, hydro, and nuclear power will probably play a major part, but fossil fuels cannot be banished altogether.

The volume is a narrative of the quest for energy self-sufficiency which India has been craving for decades to shake off its growing burden on energy imports. The first section deals with 'Old Age Energy' sources—biomass, coal, crude oil and natural gas—that still supply about 80% of the global energy. The second section is about renewable energy resources, energy transition, and the 'New Age Energy' sources—solar, wind, hydropower, hydrogen, geothermal and nuclear. In the third section, the main theme is electric transportation, while the fourth section deals with the energy of the future and the emerging geopolitics of energy.

This book, is a narrative of fossil fuels that supply most of the global energy at present, and what will be the main sources of energy supplies in the future.

References

1. Vaclav Smil, *Energy and Civilisation: A History*, p.3.
2. CFA Harvard, Universe Forum—Big Bang— What Powered It? https://lweb.cfa.harvard.edu.
3. Vaclav Smil, *Energy and Civilisation: A History*, pp.4–5.
4. Vaclav Smil, *Energy and Civilisation: A History*, p.7.
5. Vaclav Smil, *Energy and Civilisation: A History*.
6. Vaclav Smil, *Energy and Civilisation: A History*, p.381.
7. Vaclav Smil, *Energy and Civilisation: A History*, pp.279–80.
8. BeingToppr; toppr.com.
9. India's Solar Capacity to Cross 20 GW in Next 15 Months; Piyush Goyal, *The Economic Times*, retrieved 6 April, 2017.
10. Physical Progress (Achievements), Ministry of New & Renewable Energy, 18 July, 2019.
11. Markandya, A; Wilkinson, P (2007). 'Electricity Generation and Health'. Lancet. 370 (9591): 979–990. Doi:10.1016/S0140-6736(07)61253-7. PMID 17876910.
12. Nuclear Explained; U.S. Nuclear Industry; https://www.eia.gov/energyexplained/nuclear/us-nuclear-industry.php.
13. International Energy Outlook 2016, US Energy Information Administration, accessed on 17 August, 2016.
14. *The News Minute*, www.thenewsminute.com.
15. *The Times of India*, p.18; 14 December, 2019.
16. India to Be Largest Energy Growth Market by 2030: Dharmendra Pradhan, at a FICCI meeting; *PTI*, 21 December, 2019.

SECTION I

THE WORLD OF FOSSIL FUELS

Chapter 1

COAL

I. OVERVIEW

"Considering the limited reserve potentiality of petroleum and natural gas, eco-conservation restriction on hydel project and geo-political perception of nuclear power, coal will continue to occupy centre-stage of India's energy scenario."— Ministry of Coal, Annual Report 2017–18.

Despite a considerable pressure from several countries to raise its mitigation (emission reduction) goal by pledging either 'net-zero' target or 'peaking year' of its emission ahead of the 26th session of the UN Climate Conference (COP 26) in November 2021, India had categorically told the UN Climate Body that coal would indefinitely to be an 'integral part' of India's energy mix for its 'developmental needs'. However, the country has pledged to use coal 'responsibly' by applying latest technological advances to detoxify and make it a clean energy.

The message was conveyed through the country's biennial update report (BUR), submitted to the United Nations Framework Convention on Climate Change (UNFCCC). BUR is submitted by every country that has ratified the UNFCCC charter to assess the progress achieved by them in containing warming of the Earth below 2°C, preferably 1.5°C, by 2050. India holds the world's fifth largest proven reserves of coal (107 bt), behind the US (250.2 bt), Russia (160.3 bt), Australia (149 bt) and China (138.8 bt), according to 2019 estimates. But per capita coal consumption of India is one of the lowest at 0.7 mcf (million cubic feet), compared to most developed countries and other emerging economies—Australia (4.5 mcf), China (2.7 mcf), Germany (2.7 mcf) and the US (1.9 mcf). This shows that India still has enough leeway to exploit its coal reserves for its development needs.[1]

Cheap, plentiful and easily extractable, coal has been the most dominant fuel used worldwide for generation of energy for ages. In recent years its use has been discouraged in industrial countries, but in low-income countries it remains the single, largest source of energy. Its use ranges from serving as raw material for products like fertilisers, tar, benzol, naphthalene to by-products like toothpastes, dyes, nylon, aspirin, perfumes, explosives and disinfectants. Its crucial importance lies in its being a vital source of commercial energy. In 2022 it provided 55% of energy and 70% of electricity in India.

Commercial primary energy consumption in India has grown by about 700% in the last four decades since the coal industry was nationalised in 1973. The current per capita commercial primary energy consumption in India is about 350 kgoe per year (kilograms of oil equivalent per year) which is far below that of developed countries. However, driven by the rising population, expanding economy and a quest for improved quality of life, India's energy usage now is expected to increase by leaps and bound, and coal is likely to remain the pivotal source of energy indefinitely. Currently, the country produces around 700–800 mt per year of coal, while consumption exceeds a billion tonne, forcing it to meet the shortfall from imports. Around 50 GW of an additional capacity was already under construction in 2018 and many more were planned for the coming years.

India's industrial heritage has been built on coal. Oil and gas resources are sparse and the development of other options, like wind and solar power, would take years—even decades—to replace coal. Hard coal deposits are spread over 27 major coalfields, mainly in eastern and southern central parts of the country. India has more than 300 bt of proven reserves of coal. At the current rate of consumption, it is expected to meet the country's requirement for more than 100 years. Lignite reserves stand at a level around 36 bt, of which 90% occur in the southern state of Tamil Nadu. This makes India vastly dependent on coal to plan its energy expansion. An increased investment in the coal sector thus becomes unavoidable to fuel its rapid economic growth. However, due to local environmental concerns and global climate change movement the growth in the sector is expected to remain subdued.

Earliest Fossil Fuel

Historically, coal has been the main fuel of economic growth worldwide. Coal was responsible for the transition of Europe from the Middle Age to Industrial Age. United States and Canada also owe their transformation to coal. They switched to oil and natural gas sooner than Europe. Around the same period, the seventeenth and eighteenth centuries, Russia also became one of the largest producers of coal before slowly moving to exploit its vast and plentiful gas reserves for export. Asian and African countries, however, were slow to adopt coal as their main fuel, perhaps due to colonisation by the western countries.

Historical records reveal that the Chinese Han Dynasty (206 BCE–220 CE) were the earliest users of coal, they used it in iron production. European records show that Belgium was the first country in the region to extract coal in 1113, and London received its first shipment of coal in 1228. France received the first shipment of coal from the Tynemouth region in 1325. During the sixteenth and seventeenth centuries, England had become the first country to completely switch over to coal from phytomass, mainly due to rampant wood shortages and high prices of charcoal and lumber. The authorities answered the problem by opening up of almost all coalfields in the country.

The result was expeditious transition from biomass to coal in Wales, England, as a source of heat around 1620 or even earlier. By 1650, according to Smil, coal's share went up to 65% and by 1700 to about 75%. In 1800, it surged to about 90% and by 1850 more than 98%. British coal supremacy lasted for another century. By 1950, coal supplied 91% of the country's primary energy and 77% by 1960. Coal dominated (more than 75%) UK's energy use for 250 years, much longer than in any other country.

Outside England, France was a major producer of coal, especially in the northern regions of Liege and Ruhr, and from parts of Bohemia and Silesia, and it remained the country's dominant fuel until the late 1950s when imported oil overtook it. Coal mining started in colonial America in 1758 in Virginia, and by early nineteenth century in Pennsylvania, Ohio, Illinois and Indiana. By 1843, coal supplied only 5% the total primary energy, but gradually its share rose to 20% by early 1860s, 50% by 1901 and peaked to 77% by 1917.

Coal's greatest value as a prime fuel for heat and movement was realised during the eighteenth and nineteenth centuries when the first commercially successful steam engine, developed by Thomas Newcomen, was introduced in 1712, and later significantly improved by James Watt in 1769. The machine was the first practical, economic and reliable converter of chemical energy into mechanical energy and revolutionised industrialisation, urbanisation and transportation. Steam engines replaced sail for ships and steam locomotives operated in the railways. It was adopted in all sorts of manufacturing activity.

Coal Mining in India

India has been exploiting coal since antiquity, as archaeological relics from excavations at the Mohenjo-Daro and Harappan (5000–6000 BC) cities show the use of gold, silver, copper, tin, iron, lead, bronze, agate, amethyst, onyx, rock crystal, jasper, blood stone, jadeite, lapis-lazuli and gemstones by the people. The laws of *Manu* lay down that the king was the owner and guardian of mines, and was entitled to 20% of gold, silver and gems. During Kautilya's time, the *Arthashastra* states that mines are the source of wealth and lays down rules prescribing punishments from fines to death for theft and other crimes of mineral products and precious stones.[2]

The ruins of smithy furnaces and slack hips near coal deposits in eastern India indicate the use of coal for metallurgical processing 2000 years ago or even before. The names of some the places, like Angarpathra (firestone) and Kalipahari (black hills), near Asansol, or the rivers, such as the Damodar, on whose banks, large reserves of coal have been found, suggest that the people in ancient India knew of the existence of coal deposits in eastern India and they used it as a fuel for heating and melting iron.[3] The Ashoka Pillars bear standing testimony to the use of molten iron in India as long ago as during the emperor Ashoka's rule (268–232 BCE). In the Middle Age kings and emperors used molten iron to make cannons or leave their memoires by building monuments, like the Kutab Minar.

However, there has been no documented record of the early history of India's coal industry. It came only after 1774–75 when John Sumner and Suetonius Grant Heatly of East India Company started commercial exploitation in Raniganj coalfields along the western banks of the River Damodar in West Bengal, which is considered as the birthplace of coal mining in India. A survey conducted in 1845–46 and again in 1860 revealed that there were about 50 collieries in the area producing 28,200 tonnes of coal. But the real big boost to the industry came in 1853 when steam locomotives were introduced in India. This led to sharp increases in coal demand and consequent exploration and production of coal in Orissa and Madhya Pradesh, besides Raniganj. Within a short span, production soared, reaching

6.12 mt annually by 1900. Then came the First World War (1914–18), which gave another major boost to coal demand. According to estimates, India's production of coal rose to 21 mt in 1919, a year after the First world War. The trend lasted about a decade before it slumped due to the economic depression in 1930s. It rose again after the outbreak of the Second World War in 1939. By 1946, output had reached 30 mt per year.

Initially, the British and other European investors dominated the Indian coal industry. However, by end of the nineteenth century Indian entrepreneurs got involved in coal mining and well-established collieries at various locations, such as Khas Jharia, Jamadoba, Balihari, Tisra, Katrasgarh, Kailudih, Kusunda, Govindpur, Sijua, Loyabad, Dhansar, Bhuli, Bermo, Mugma, Chasnala-Bokaro, Bugatdih, Putki, Chirkunda, Bhowrah, Sinidih, Kendwadih and Dumka.

Seth Khora Ramji Chawda of Kutch was the first Indian to break the British monopoly by establishing a colliery in Jharia. In his book, *Diary of Golden Days at Jharia – A Memoir & History of Gurjar Kashtriya Samaj of Kutch in Coalfields of Jharia*, 1998, author Natwarlal Devram Jethwa of Kolkata says, "Khora Ramji in 1894 was working on a railway lines contract of Jharia branch line and with his brother Jetha Lira was also building Jharia Railway Station, when he discovered coal in Jharia belt. Names of the three collieries—Jeenagora, Khas Jharia and Gareria—which he established are mentioned in the 1917 Gazetteers of Bengal, Assam, Bihar and Odisha." Jharia was the most favoured area for the early entrepreneurs due to the multiplicity of coal seams of superior quality, easy mining conditions and low production costs.

Post-Independence

Realising the crucial role of coal and minerals in industrialisation and overall economic development, the government of independent India moved to set up or bring some industries under its control to ensure the supply of raw material and fuels for economic projects. Coal was one of them. The process started with the acquisition of a stake in Singareni Collieries Company Ltd (SCCL), a firm wholly owned by Hyderabad Nizam, which had been in operation since 1945, but later came under the control of, first, the government of Madras and, later, the government of Andhra Pradesh in 1956. SCCL is currently 49% owned by the Government of India, with the remainder being with the government of Telangana, a newly created state after the bifurcation of Andhra Pradesh.

In 1956, the Indian government also established the National Coal Development Corporation (NCDC) to modernise and increase coal production. The corporation brought all collieries owned and operated by the railways under its control. However, private collieries were allowed to operate outside the state control. But it was found that adequate capital investment was not forthcoming from private investors to meet the burgeoning energy needs of the country. Steel industry, which enjoyed great priority for reconstruction under the First Five Year Plan, was particularly hit due to low coal supply. Besides, obsolete mining practices and poor working conditions of labour in some private coal mines had become worrisome.

The government decided to nationalise private coal mines. It was accomplished in two phases. The Indira Gandhi-led government first nationalised the coking coal mines and plants in 1971–72 and put them under the newly-created Bharat Coking Company Ltd (BCCL) for management. However, Tata Iron and Steel Company Ltd (TISCO) and Indian Iron and Steel Company Ltd (ISCO), which also owned several coking plants were exempt from the purview of nationalisation and allowed to operate as private companies.

Then, in 1973, non-coking mines and plants were also nationalised and placed under the Coal Mines Authority of India. In 1975, Eastern Coalfields Limited, a subsidiary of Coal India Ltd, was formed to take over all private collieries in Raniganj Coalfields. This coalfield covered an area of 443.50 sq km and had coal reserves of 8,552.85 mt. The Eastern Coalfields had reserves of 29.72 billion metric tonnes, which made it the second largest coalfield in the country in terms of reserves.

But nationalisation failed to yield positive results. After liberalisation in the 1990s, the hunger for power increased significantly but the public sector was not able to keep up the pace with the supply of coal. The Coal Nationalisation Act was amended in 1993 to allow private sector participation in captive coal mining for generation of power, washing of coal and other end uses as notified by the government. After the re-introduction of the private sector, it was felt that coal supply constraints would ease but unfortunately that has not been the case. Currently, 117 coal blocks have been allocated between public sector units, state public sector units and the private sector for the power sector with an estimated geological reserve of

24.5 bt having the potential of producing 100 mt per year. Production from these mines now stands only at 25 mt (2009–10) as most of the blocks are not yet in operation due to several factors.

The end result of nationalisation was an increased bureaucratisation, exacerbated corruption and mafia culture in collieries. The state-owned coal mines in Bihar (now Jharkhand after the bifurcation of Bihar) were among the worst affected, with the emergence of mafia bands in the mining town of Dhanbad. It was alleged that trade union leaders formed mafia groups and indulged in pilferage and sale of coal in the black market. Cheating government by presenting inflated and fictitious supply bills, bogus worker contracts and expropriation and leasing of government land was rampant. A parallel economy had developed with a significant fraction of the local population employed by the mafia groups in manually transporting the stolen coal to illegal mafia warehouses and points of sale. In June 2012, the Bollywood epic, *Gangs of Wasseypur* was released portraying coal mafia in the area of Dhanbad. The movie received overwhelming response and was declared a hit, while another movie *Gunday* was also loosely based on Bihar's coal mafia.

Also, in 2012 a draft report by the Comptroller and Auditor General of India (CAG) pointed to various irregularities in allocating coal blocks between 2005 and 2009. It said the process adopted for allocation was not competitive. The report estimated a loss of Rs 10.7 lakh crore (US$ 213.47 billion) to the exchequer. This development certainly disrupted many coal blocks from coming into operation. The coal shortage estimated for the 2012–13 fiscal year was 60 mt, which included demand from imported coal-based projects as well. According to some companies, the demand for imported coal will increase on account of Coal India's inability to fulfil even their committed coal supply assurance. Many companies were looking to source coal from other countries. But how securing imported coal will ease the problem of shortages, especially in light of increased fuel cost that cannot be passed on to the final consumer is unclear.

II. DENATIONALISATION OF COAL

Concerned at the yawning gap between the rising demand and poor domestic supply, Narendra Modi government, which came to power in 2014, tried to reform the coal sector by denationalising and ridding it of malpractices. The first move in this direction was to revive the loss-making units operating under the state behemoth Coal India Ltd (CIL) or shut them down if they failed to return to proper health. In 2015, the government began denationalisation by permitting private companies to mine coal for use in their own cement, steel, power or aluminium plants. Finally, in January 2018 the Coking Coal Mines (Nationalisation) Act, 1972 and the Coal Mines (Nationalisation) Act, 1973, by which Indira Gandhi's government had taken over the private collieries and plants, were repealed. The amended Act now allows private firms to enter into commercial coal mining. Under the new policy, mines will be auctioned to firms offering the highest price per tonne of coal. This move has broken the monopoly of the state's Coal India Ltd over commercial mining.

Coal is the mainstay of India's energy sector, accounting for over 58% of the primary commercial energy supply. Around 74% of coal produced in the country is consumed by the power sector. India started using coal to generate power in 1920 with the commissioning of Hussain Sagar Thermal Power Station in Hyderabad. The country kept adding coal capacity at a gradual pace after that and had reached 71 GW of coal power generation capacity by 2007. Then, over the subsequent years, an explosion of capacity additions resulted in more than 130 GW of new coal plants coming online.

The last peak annual capacity addition was in 2015, when 19 GW of coal power plants were added. Annual net additions have been declining since then. In 2017, India added renewable power generation capacity at 11.778 GW as compared to the coal-fired capacity of 9.505 GW for the first time ever and is expected to repeat the same in the future. This is the beginning of a new era in the field of energy which will see renewables displacing coal power on an annual basis. On 31 March, 2018, India's installed generation capacity stood at 344 GW, comprising 223 GW of thermal, 45 GW of hydro, 7 GW of nuclear and 69 GW of renewables. Today, 196 GW of grid-connected coal-fired power stations supply about three quarters of the total electricity requirement in the country.

In its 2016–17 annual report, Central Electricity Authority (CEA), which oversees the development of the power sector, stated that the Indian industry consumed 841.56 mt of raw coal during the year. Of this, 527.26 mt was consumed by the power sector while the steel and washery plants consumed 54.15 mt, cement plants 6.43 mt and sponge iron industries 5.68 mt. In addition, the power sector also consumed 43.16 mt of lignite to generate electricity. Compared to this, Indian coal production totalled only 662.79 mt—78.75 mt less than the demand—forcing the country to import 190.95 mt to cover the deficit during the year.

Capacity Addition

The actual capacity addition during the Twelfth Plan from conventional sources, according to the CEA, as on 31 March, 2017 was 99,210 MW including 83,560 MW accruing from coal, 1,290 MW from lignite, 6,880.5 MW from gas, 5,479 MW from hydro and 2,000 MW from nuclear. This was 112% over the target of 88,537 MW. More than 56% of total capacity addition came from the private sector. Coal-based plants benefitted to the extent of 42% in their capacity addition from embedded supercritical technology. Capacity addition for renewable energy during 2012–17 was 32,741 MW, taking the total installed in the sector to 57,244 MW as on 31 March, 2017. For 2021–22, the renewable energy capacity target has been set at 175 GW.

Projecting the electricity demand growth at 6.18% per year through a period of five years from 2017–22, a CEA survey concluded that a capacity addition of 406 MW of gas, 6,833 MW of hydro, 3,300 MW of nuclear power, 1,17,756 MW of renewable energy and 6,445 MW of coal power will be needed. At the same time, it said, 22,716 MW of old and inefficient coal-based plants will be retired. The survey also revealed the need for another capacity enhancement of 6,800 MW of nuclear, 12,000 MW of hydro and 1,00,000 MW of renewable energy for 2022–27 years. But for this period, the CEA's survey does not see the need for any addition to the coal-based capacity, as 47,855 MW of coal-based capacity would already be under construction.

The government's National Electricity Plan (NEP), unveiled in 2018, reflects its commitment to steadily reduce coal power and increase installation of renewable power facilities over the coming years. Already starting from 2017, the installation of renewable energy capacity has outstripped coal's by two-to-one over two years up to 2018-end. Over the next years till 2027, there is a plan to retire 48.3 GW of 'end-of-life' coal plants. Of these, 22.7 GW of capacity is to be retired before 2022 and the remaining 25.6 of plants are slated to be closed by 2027. Taking these capacity retirements and planned new constructions worth 94.3 GW into account, the NEP sees the country's coal power capacity totalling 238 GW in 2027, which will be 11 GW lower than the forecast in 2016, and the share of thermal power declining to 42.7% of the country's installed electricity capacity in 2027, dramatically down from 66.8% in 2017.

Similarly, thermal coal imports are set to decline by two-thirds to 50 mtpa (million tonnes per annum) by 2022 and hold steady at that level or even lower through 2027, contrary to an increase in imports projected by the International Energy Agency (IEA). Despite being the world's fourth largest holder of coal deposits, with known reserves of 315.14 bt (as of March 2017), India needs to import coal, particularly coking coal, for use in the steel and aluminium industry. The low gross calorific value (GCV) of its own coal creates problems for power stations, including erosion of parts and material, difficulty in pulverisation, poor emissivity and flame temperature, low radioactive transfer and excessive amounts of fly ash containing large amounts of unburned carbons. Because of the poor carbon content and high ash content, an Indian power plant on an average consumes about 0.7 kg of coal to generate a kWh, whereas in the United States thermal power plants consume only about 0.45 kg of coal per kWh. Indian coal has an average GCV of about 4,500 Kcal/kg, whereas elsewhere in the world the quality is much better.

A recent study by researchers from ETH Zurich, published in the *Nature Sustainability* journal, has found that while China and the US are the two largest producers of coal power, Indian coal-fired plants took the highest toll on health. After calculating the side effects of coal produced power at 7,861 power plants across the world, the researchers concluded that a lack of sufficient flue gas treatment at Indian coal-fired plants produced high levels of particulate matter, sulphur dioxide, nitrogen oxide and mercury, which were more damaging to health and the climate than the similar plants in North America and central Europe.

In order to mitigate the impact of this problem, the government has introduced tighter environmental norms to curb the emission of suspended particulate matter and other pollutants at the thermal power plants. The new thermal plants as well as the existing ones are now required to install flue gas desulphurisation (FGD) systems at the plants to comply with the new environmental norms by 2022. The government has also proposed incentives worth Rs 835 billion (US$ 11.92 billion) to encourage coal-fired plants, whether run by private or public sector, to install emission-cutting devices.

The CEA has been asked to monitor the generation of fly ash at coal/lignite-based thermal power stations. Thermal power companies account for 80% of all industrial emissions of particulate matter, sulphur and nitrous oxides in India.

Notwithstanding, the harmful effects of thermal power plants on environment, India can ill afford to find an escape from coal. In the absence of sufficient oil or natural gas, coal is the only fuel to power its home, industries and economic growth in the foreseeable future. The Paris-based International Energy Agency (IEA) in its 2018 World Energy Outlook forecasted India to overtake Australia and the US in early 2020s to become the world's second-largest producer behind China. The agency estimated that growing at an annual rate of 3.9% per year, India's coal production will reach 955 mtce (mega tonnes of coal equivalent) by 2040 from 395 mtce in 2017 (the actual coal production number for 2017, if available, can be put here). But much of this would be steam coal, mired in ash and other pollutants. In view of this, the IEA projects that India would be importing more coal than the world's largest coal importer currently, China, through the 2020s.

The country has set an ambitious target to increase the domestic coal production; nonetheless, imports would rise, especially of coking coal to meet the growing demand from iron and steel industries. The Indian power ministry, however, refutes the IEA's claim. The ministry stresses that with accelerated coal plant closures and an anticipated surge in renewables, thermal coal requirement for power generation will be around 877 mtpa by 2027, which, according to the ministry, would require a domestic production of 827 mtpa of thermal coal—well under the 1,500 mtpa 'trumpeted'. The shortfall of 50 mtpa of coking coal would be made good by imports. The government expects that given the Indian economy's forecast growth at 7–8% per annum electricity requirement would double by 2027.

Renewables have now become central to India's electricity generation. The government has planned to increase their share to 40% in the power mix by 2030, yet, coal is to remain the largest single provider of fuel indefinitely. Currently, 69 GW of coal power plants are under construction, which will come online by 2022. In order to ensure the supply of coal for the under-construction projects, the government has allocated 51 of the 204 coal blocks, cancelled by the Supreme Court in 2014 because of irregularities in the previous allotment, to various power utilities: 42 of these blocks have gone to government power projects and nine allocated to the project sector through auction. They are expected to generate 62.33 GW. In addition, 14 other blocks have been allocated to central and state power PSUs.

Despite government's reliance on coal as a major source of energy, one cannot undermine the growing awareness of it being environmentally toxic, because of its sulphuric and nitrogenous contents. When coal burns, these impurities are released into the air. While floating in the air, these substances can combine with water vapour (for example, in clouds) and form droplets that fall to Earth as weak forms of sulphuric and nitric acid. Scientists call it the 'acid rain'. There are also tiny specks of minerals—including common dirt—mixed in coal. These tiny particles don't burn and make up the ash left behind in a coal combustor. Also, coal like all fossil fuels, is formed out of carbon. All living things, even people, are made up of carbon (coal started out as living plants.) But when coal burns, its carbon combines with oxygen in the air and forms carbon dioxide. Carbon dioxide is one of several gases that can trap Earth's heat in the atmosphere. Scientists believe this is causing the Earth's temperature to rise, and the altering its climate.

Environmental hazards, notwithstanding, every government has aggressively chased coal production to meet power generation targets. Looking to benefit from economy of scale and synergy, the Indian government has prioritised construction of ultra-mega power projects (UMPP), which are designed to generate 4,000 MW (megawatt) or more. The plants are built on public-private partnership or solely private model. Developers are selected through tariff-based international bidding. Two UMPPs, one each in Gujarat and Madhya Pradesh, have already started generating electricity and two others, Andhra Pradesh and Jharkhand, were under construction in 2018. The plan is to set up at least one UMPP in each of the 29 states in the country. For this, the government has formed a special purpose vehicle (SPV), Power Finance Corporation (PFC), to facilitate swift clearances from concerned agencies such as land, water, environment and forest, and transfer the facilities for successful bidders.

However, environmental compulsions and climate change issues force the government to slow its pace of implementation of the projects. The National Electricity Plan (NEP) 2018 indicates a fundamental shift in the government's approach. While unequivocally acknowledging that coal will continue to be used for electricity generation until sufficient power is generated from multiple zero-emission alternatives, the plan reinforces the government's intent to build 275 GW of renewable energy capacity by 2027, which would amount to 44% of the country's total energy mix capacity. But at the same it is also working on ways, including retrofitting and reengineering of the coal power plants, to ensure lower pollution emissions when coal is burnt to generate electricity. In addition, the government is also experimenting with new technologies developed by scientists, especially over the last 20 years, to capture pollutants trapped in coal before they escape into the air.

III. COAL GASIFICATION

Coal gasification—coal-to-gas—is one of the several options being tried to make coal environmentally less toxic to the air. It is a process of converting coal into synthetic gas (syngas), which is a mixture of carbon monoxide (CO), hydrogen (H_2), carbon dioxide (CO_2), natural gas (CH_4) and water vapour (H_2O), from coal and water, air and/or oxygen. During gasification, coal is blown with oxygen and steam while also being heated under high pressure. During the reaction, oxygen and water molecules oxidise the coal and produce syngas. Historically, the process had been used in the early 1800s to produce coal gas or 'town gas', in the US town of Baltimore for municipal lighting and heating.

Today, it is primarily used for electricity generation or for production of chemical feedstocks. The hydrogen obtained from coal gasification can be used for various purposes such as powering hydrogen economy or upgrading fossil fuels or converting the syngas into transport fuels like gasoline, methanol, naphtha and diesel and chemical fertilisers through additional treatment. Over the past 20 years, pushed by regulation and facilitated by the use of markets, the power industry and the equipment manufacturers that serve it have already done a remarkable job in eliminating pollution from coal. Some 99.9% of particulates, 99% of sulphur dioxide (SO_2) and 95% of nitrogen oxides (NO_x) emissions have been banished by new coal plants which use ultra-supercritical technology. But the amount of carbon, embedded in the carbon dioxide emitted by burning coal, is an altogether different and a much more intractable problem.[4]

Coal gasification is also a measure of capturing CO_2 emissions produced during the combustion of the fossil fuel in power generating or industrial manufacturing plants, and compressing and converting them into liquid form, and transporting them by pipeline to safe underground geological formation sites for storage or using them for another manufacturing or commercial activity. It is known as carbon capture and sequestration (CCS) or carbon capture, use and storage (CCUS) technology. "CCS is the critical future technology option for reducing CO_2 emissions while keeping coal's use above today's level," as stated in an MIT study, *The Future of Coal.*

Scientific consensus is that CO_2 can be stored with little or no leakage, as gases are already captured at various kinds of process facilities. It can later be transported by pipeline and pumped into ageing oil and gas fields to help boost output. But they are on a much smaller scale. The CCS system proposed by the Intergovernmental Panel on Climate Change (IPCC) or the United Nations Framework on Climate Change is an incredible enterprise, which is like creating almost a, "New energy industry, but one that works in reverse. Instead of extracting resources from the ground, transporting and transforming them, and then burning, the CCS, or the 'Big Carbon' industry, would nab the spent resource of CO_2 before it gets into the atmosphere, transform it, and transport and eventually put it back into the ground. This would truly be a round-trip," says the eminent energy historian and author Daniel Yergin. "If just 60% of the CO_2 produced by today's (2012) coal-fired power plants in the United States were captured and compressed into liquid, transported and injected into the storage site, the daily volumes of liquid so handled would be about equal to the 19 million barrels of oil, the United States consumes every day," he says.[5]

A few pilot projects integrating CCS with existing power plants are under way in the US. But it will take billions of research and development (R&D) dollars and several large-scale demonstration projects and a decade and a half or more to get to the point where CCS starts to become commercial, says Yergin. It is an engineering challenge, "Heavy-duty, large-scale process engineering, relentlessly squeezing cost and performance improvements out of large-scale chemical engineering facilities."[6]

Furthermore, the implementation of the CCS involves prohibitive costs. Estimates, based on experimental projects, suggest CCS could almost double the price of coal-fired electricity. However, advantages associated with the technology can potentially offset the investment. First, it can remove more than 90% of CO_2 from the emission stream; and second, it can provide a range of economic benefits and revenue streams in the energy and core sectors, according to experts. They say with policy support the implementation of a large-scale coal gasification project, along with CCUS, could be a game changer in the Indian context. It could spur carbon-neutral industries like methanol, ammonia/fertiliser, olefins, steel and power while enhancing India's oil production from the depleting oilfields. Carbon capture and coal gasification can be a game changer for India.[7]

Methanol from Coal

India is pushing thermal coal gasification for domestic production of methanol and urea. Coal to methanol is a proven technology and India can easily tap its large coal reserves to produce methanol as a substitute or drop-in fuel for gasoline and diesel. According to India's think-tank NITI Aayog, high methanol blends offer significant vehicle efficiency improvement potential of 25%. A fertiliser plant at Talchar in the eastern state of Odisha has already embarked on a project to produce 1.26 mtpa of neem coated urea through the coal gasification process. The plant is designed to use 3.3 mtpa of coal from Talcher mines. It is expected to be operational by 2023–2024. Coal India Limited is also working on setting up a coal-based methanol plant in Kolkata. It plans to produce 6.76 lakh tonnes of methanol per annum at Dankuni Coal Complex (DCC) of South Eastern Coalfields Ltd (SECL), a subsidiary of the state-run company.

According to energy consultant Atanu Mukherjee, "Methanol can be used for producing methanol-based chemicals and olefins for plastics and as a substitute for petrol, diesel and LPG. Close to 15% of petrol used today in vehicles can be substituted by methanol. Additionally, 20% of imported diesel and cooking gas can be substituted by domestically produced methanol. Over 15% of plastics/olefins feedstock based on imported crude oil heavy distillates can be replaced by coal gasification-based methanol saving over US$ 5 billion in imported naphtha." He says by enriching and exploiting Indian coal endowments through gasification and carbon capture, a clean coal-based economy for power, chemicals, fuels, steel, oil, and fertilisers can enable a US$ 50-billion direct increase in the gross domestic product (GDP) while creating employment for over half-a-million people, reducing imports by over US$ 30 billion and cutting the current account deficit by 50%.

China embarked on industrial scale coal gasification about ten years ago. Today, it is the world's largest methanol producer, and almost all of it is produced through the coal gasification route. Methanol accounts for close to 10% of Chinese fuel consumption and 30% of feedstock for plastics. South

Africa is the world's largest coal gasification-based economy. Sasol, which pioneered the technology, produces a wide range of commodities from coal-based gasoline to coal-based chemicals. Emirates Steel in Abu Dhabi captures 800,000 tonne of CO_2 per year and sells it to Abu Dhabi National Oil Company (ADNOC) for enhanced oil recovery (EOR). In India, a small-scale carbon capture and a plant running at Tuticorin Alkali and Chemicals captures 60,000 tonne of CO_2 per year and uses it for manufacturing baking soda. IPCC says that the economic potential of the CCS could be between 10% and 55% of the total carbon mitigation effort until the year 2100. Columbia University's Centre on Global Energy Policy says (26 March, 2019) policy shifts at the state and federal level in the US have created new markets for this clean energy technology, inspiring the launch of new projects in both the industrial and power sectors, extending into new enterprises (like direct air capture or CarbonTech).

Coal gas can also be produced by combusting coal underground where deposits are located deep in the ground and uneconomical to mine. Underground coal gasification (UCG) has multiple advantages. It eliminates the need for mining and transportation operations, thus leading to substantial savings in costs and reduced emissions of NO_x and SO_x, which are associated with coal if it is processed overground. Also, it makes carbon capture and sequestration operations more efficient. But UCG also has some flipsides: it is seen impacting the neighbourhood aquifers adversely and the process itself is fairly capital intensive. It can also be risky.

India started work on its first coal-to-gas liquefaction facility in September 2018 after Prime Minister Narendra Modi laid the foundation stone of a plant at Talcher in the eastern state of Odisha to produce 2.38 million standard cubic metres a day of synthetic gas. The project uses Fische-Tropsch technology and is expected to feed a fertiliser complex, designed to produce 2,200 tpd (tonne per day) of neem-coated ammonia and 3,850 tpd of urea, besides naphtha and sulphur. The coal gasification process will use clean coal technology, which is known to emit lower sulphur oxides and free particles, and makes the carbon capture easy during the operation. The promoters plan to recycle the captured carbon to produce urea. The project is a joint venture of Gas Authority of India Ltd (Gail), Rashtriya Chemicals and Fertilisers Ltd and Fertilisers Corporation of India, all state-run entities. The government sees it as an effective path to reduce the imports of chemical fertilisers and LNG, which cost tens of millions of dollars per annum. Syngas can also be used as LNG and CNG (compressed natural gas) to meet the fuel (diesel) requirement of the transport sector.

Supercritical/Ultra-Supercritical Technology

Other ways being adopted include growing use of sophisticated technologies to shore up thermal efficiency in power generation and carry out diffusion of cutting-edge emission-abatement equipment, even as increased share of renewables in the energy mix is actively sought. At present, the thermal efficiency of the majority of plants in the country is barely 30%. A National Thermal Power Corporation (NTPC) plant in Telangana has already started using ultra-supercritical technology, which has raised its thermal efficiency level to 45%. A new plant, coming up in Chhattisgarh, is also being fitted with advanced ultra-supercritical systems duly adapted for the Indian grades of coal. The adoption of supercritical technology helps generate 40–45% more power using the same amount of coal as a conventional sub-critical power plant. Another plus side is lesser carbon emission at coal power plants by its application.

Supercritical steam plant technology is today a choice for most new coal-fired power stations. It is acknowledged globally that if coal has a future, then supercritical technology will be the key. Indeed, the Organization for Economic Co-operation and Development (OECD) has introduced financial regulations that encourage the use of both ultra-supercritical and supercritical steam generator technology for new coal plants.

Here, it would be pertinent to figure out that a supercritical/ultra-supercritical technology coal power plant is different from a traditional sub-critical plant. We know that at the heart of coal-fired electricity generation lies the steam cycle. Typically, pulverised coal is fed into a giant industrial furnace surrounded by boiler tubes filled with water. The burning coal heats the water to create steam, which is transferred at high pressure to turbines linked to a generator.

As the generator spins, electrons are generated that are stepped up in voltage by transformers, while the turbine steam is condensed back into water and returned to the boiler for reheating. In ultra-supercritical steam power plants, the extreme boiler temperature and pressure heat the water so that it becomes a 'supercritical' fluid that exhibits properties of liquid and gas phases. In this state, supercritical steam is much more efficient at driving the giant turbines that spin the plant's generators. The upfront cost of such technology is 20–30% more expensive than a traditional subcritical unit, but that is offset by improved net thermal efficiency levels and reduced emissions.

A typical new subcritical plant will have a thermal efficiency of 38%, meaning that 38% of the thermal energy contained in the fuel is converted into electrical energy fed into the grid. A supercritical plant will have an efficiency of maybe 42% and a typical ultra-supercritical plant will achieve around 44% (designs going up to 47% are being developed).

Buoyed by the positive results of the technology, the Indian government has declared it is committed to adopt supercritical/ultra-supercritical technology in order to optimise coal usage. Now, new coal-fired power plant design prioritises operational efficiency and emissions reduction. In tandem with this, abatement equipment such as electrostatic precipitators, catalytic reducers and flue-gas desulphurisation units are being deployed, and older 210 MW and 500 MW units are being scrapped.

Coal Washing

Coal washing is another high-priority area which is being aggressively promoted in order to increase the thermal efficiency of domestic coal and curtail emissions. Indian coal has high ash content ranging generally between 15% and 45%. Various studies have shown that washed coal has higher calorific value than unwashed coal, and translates into better power generation efficiency and emits lower emissions. But in India, only 20% of coal produced is washed, compared to the global average of 50%. Coking coal washing has long been in vogue but now non-coking coal is also being washed due to environmental and efficiency concerns. Also, the government has prohibited the use of raw, blended or beneficiated coal with ash content of more than 34% on an average basis.

Currently, India, which uses more than 50% of coal to generate electricity, has only 19 coal washeries with a total capacity of 27.2 mtpa, which are mainly utilised to wash coking coals. Non-coking Indian coals, which contain more ash than imported coals, are fed into power plants unwashed, resulting in low thermal efficiency and more air pollution. The government has now decided to set up 20 new giant washeries with cumulated annual capacity of 111 mt to obtain higher value of its produce. The state-run Central Fuel Research Institute (CFRI) has developed three processes—Improved Froth

Floatation, Oleo Floatation and Oil Agglomeration—which new washery units will adopt to obtain better results from their operation.

These and other advanced technologies promise a prolonged shelf life of coal as the single largest source of power globally. But intensifying concerns about it being the most polluting of fossil fuels and the rapid resurgence of competing renewables like solar and wind power will keep its growth under heavy pressure. According to the CEA, for the second year running installations of renewable energy capacity, in 2018, were more than twice of net new installs of thermal power. Rapid deflation in the price for both wind and solar power is driving the trend, with tariffs down 50% since the start of 2016. Renewables are now clearly acknowledged as the low-cost source of new electricity capacity.

The Global Coal Plant Tracker, which keeps track of coal plants of more than 30 MW capacity, estimated that in the first six months of 2018, 26 GW of Indian coal-fired power plant proposals were shelved or cancelled. According to the US-based Institute for Energy Economics and Financial Analysis (IEEFA), this has raised the number of coal plant proposals cancelled since 2010 to 573 GW. The research institute estimates that renewables alone would represent 44% of installed system capacity by 2027.

Rising fuel costs, low fleet utilisation and air pollution regulations are making coal power economics unattractive. According to Energy Transition Commission (ETC) India, the cost of wind power will be between Rs 2.3–2.6 kWh (kilowatt per hour) and of solar power in the range of Rs 1.9–2.3 kWh by 2030. Transport alone, according to Bloomberg New Energy Forum (BNF), accounts for more than one third of the landed cost of coal supplied to the power plants. This is expected to rise further in future as costs of transport fuels like petrol, diesel and gasoline increase. This will escalate the cost of power generation from coal-fired plants. As for capacity utilisation factor (CUF), it dropped from 77.5% in fiscal 2010 to an average 56.5% capacity utilisation in 2018. A drop in CUF of a coal plant leads to an increase in the cost of power generation.

BNF estimates that the levelised cost of electricity (LCOE) of a new Indian coal power plant increases by 18% with a drop in CUF from 80% to 60%. In addition, new emission regulations from the government requiring installations of emission control equipment like flue gas desulphurisation plants, selective catalytic reduction units/low NO_x burners, electrostatic precipitators, etc., at power plants can increase the LCOE from coal by as much as 9%, depending on the choice of emission control technologies. Land acquisition difficulties and banks' reluctance to lend to coal power plants (for fear of delays and non-performance) further add to the cost.

Based on its forecasts of India's power system, BNF expects the share of coal to drop to just 14% in 2050 from 75% in 2017, and renewable energy sources (including hydro) to rise to 75% of India's total electricity needs by 2050. Solar and wind are expected to provide one third each of the total power demand. These developments indicate that India's transition from fossil fuel power generation to a clean and sustainable power mix will be faster than previously anticipated. As on 28 February, 2019, India had 63.9% of its 350 GW installed electricity capacity based on thermal sources, comprising coal (54.7%), lignite (1.8%), natural gas (7.2%) and oil (0.2%). Renewables sources (solar, wind, small hydro and biomass) accounted for 21.2%, large hydro 13% and nuclear 1.9%. Going forward the country's NEP envisages installing more wind, solar and biogas plants than coal plants to meet its electricity demand, growing at 7% annually. The IEEFA estimates that renewables alone would represent 44% of installed system capacity by 2027, with hydro and nuclear representing another 80 GW or 13% of the 619 GW total.

This means that India may be able to exceed one of its 2015 Paris Agreement commitments—reaching 40% of installed capacity from non-fossil fuel sources—according to the state's CEA, which has largely concurred with the IEEFA estimates with its own research. But in a report published in July 2019, it also sees annual carbon emissions from the power sector rising about 12% from levels expected in 2022 to 1.154 bt.

India Ratings and Research (Ind-Ra), a Fitch Group, expects coal-based capacity addition in the Indian power sector, which fell to a low of 3.6 GW in 2018–19, to remain subdued at 5–6 GW per year for another two fiscal years (FY 2020 and FY 2021). This is due to decommissioning of nearly 2 GW of coal capacity annually as the plants complete their useful life; difficulty in availability of funds, coal, power purchase agreements (PPA) and evacuation in nearly 85% of the private under-construction projects; and decline in fresh projects across central, state and private sectors.

Between FY 2013 and FY 2017, excess capacity in the thermal power sector had risen to an average of 42%, because of too many plants amid a lower-than-expected growth in power demand. The excess capacity touched a peak of 45% in FY 2016, and then declined subsequently back to around

42% in FY 2019. Power demand is likely to see a healthy growth during the period FY 2020 and FY 2024, and only a part of the incremental demand can be met by existing and upcoming renewable capacities. Considering the absence of any major alternatives to meet the growth in demand, the proportion of excess capacity in the thermal power sector would decline further during this period, as per Ind-Ra.

Kick-off of fresh thermal projects declined steeply to a mere 1.6 GW in FY 2019 from an average of 10 GW per year over FY 2015-FY 2018 period. The private sector's contribution to new projects was nil during FY 2019, signalling its lack of interest in the thermal sector. Greenfield project started by the state and central sector too have declined significantly owing to the gradual shift towards renewable capacity addition, given the single part tariff and the cost competitiveness of such tariffs.

As of FY 2018, of the total under-construction capacity of 24.7 GW in the private sector, 14.4 GW of capacity was uncertain or stressed or work-on-hold. This proportion increased to 20 GW (85% of the private under-construction capacity) at FY 2019, as the debt-servicing issues being faced by companies caused the supply of incremental credit from banks and equity markets to come to a standstill. The decline in fresh project starts on a yearly basis during FY 2017-FY 2019 clearly pointed to the likely decrease in thermal capacity addition over the medium term.

Another interesting trend is the shift from private sector to the state and the central sectors, with the bulk of fresh project starts coming in from the state sector. However, the intensity of capacity addition by the public sector too has been declining. Ind-Ra's analysis suggests that even in the public sector, the central sector is shying away from fresh project starts due to its increasing focus on renewable energy. The quantum of under-construction projects declined to 65 GW in FY 2019 from 95 GW in FY 2013. The decline was mainly driven by the private sector, which saw under-construction capacity falling to 24 GW in FY 2019 from 63 GW in FY 2013. Additionally, a bulk of the under-construction capacity in the private sector is stressed and is unlikely to be completed.

In view of the reduced capacity addition in the next few years and a significant decline in the building of fresh project, Ind-Ra believes that the capacity gap between the installed coal-based thermal capacity and the actual demand met by the coal-based thermal power plants will reduce in the coming years. The excess capacity increased to an average of 42% during

FY 2013-FY 2017 as capacity additions outpaced power demand growth during this period. However, the excess capacity will be reduced over FY 2020-FY 2024 due to decline in capacity addition intensity in FY 2018 and FY 2019 and Ind-Ra's expectations of capacity addition remains low over FY 2020-FY 2024.

According to a Global Energy Monitor report, India retired roughly 7.4 GW and added 82.3 GW of coal power plants under Prime Minister Narendra Modi's stint, while China retired 39.4 GW and added 290 GW worth of coal power plants during the helm of President Xi Jingping.

India's demand for coal in 2018 was 586 mt, which the IEA forecasts to rise to 938 million by 2030 and 1.16 billion by 2040. But in order to meet the sustainable development scenario it would need to reduce the use of coal to 546 mt, said the IEA.

India's demand is predicted to increase by 4.2% per year to 748 mtce in 2024 from 585 mtce in 2018, boosted by a rise in coal-fired power output. Coal consumption in China is projected to rise slightly over the next few years and plateau around 2022, said the IEA.

Minister of Coal Prahlad Joshi revealed in the Lok Sabha, the Lower House of Indian Parliament, in December 2019 that the state-run Coal India Ltd would add over 400 mt to its production capacity over the next five years. Around 92 mt of the new capacity will come from 55 greenfield projects and an additional 310 mt by expansion of the existing 193 brownfield projects, he added.

Privatisation

In January 2020, India privatised the coal sector by allowing private companies, both Indian and foreign, to participate in coal and lignite mining. Earlier it was open only to Indian firms engaged in iron and steel manufacturing, power generation and coal washing businesses.

A new law—Mineral Laws (Amendment) Ordinance 2020—first promulgated by ordinance and later enacted by parliament into Act, has scrapped a provision in the Mines and Minerals (Development and Regulation) Act 1957 and Coal Mines (Special Provisions) Act 2015, which barred companies from outside the iron, power and coal washing sectors and foreign entities from bidding for coal and lignite mining licences. The new Act effectively dismantles the monopoly of state-run Coal India Ltd, which produces 80% of India's coal and provides level playing field to global mining majors, like Peabody, BHP Billiton and Rio Tinto, which have offices registered in India, to bid for mining licences alongside domestic players, like Adani, ArcelorMittal India, Bharat Aluminium (Balco), NTPC, Jindal, GMR, Essar Power and others.

The decision to privatise coal mining, taken at the recommendation of a committee comprising senior government and NITI Aayog officials, was prompted by the declining domestic output and rising import of thermal coal. Data published by the government showed that India's thermal coal imports rose 12.6% to 197.84 mt in 2019, despite the government's efforts to cut imports. This was the second year of increase in thermal coal imports, despite the country possessing the fifth largest deposits of the fuel. The increase was attributed to low production by CIL. The government has resolved to end coal imports by power plants by 2024. Coking coal imports for iron and steel industry, however, cannot be avoided, as India lacks fine coking coal deposits. However, coking coal imports fell slightly in 2019 to 51.33 mt from 51.63 mt in 2018, after two years of increase. The participation of private companies, particularly foreign, is expected to bring in increased investment and latest mining technology to boost coal production in India.

The government plans to auction around 200 coal blocks for commercial mining by 2025 to bridge the demand-supply gap. The first tranche of coal auctions was held in May 2020 for the commercial sale of 40 blocks with peak mining capacity in the range of 1 mt to 50 mtpa. Some of the coal blocks on offer are fully explored blocks whose reserves are known; others are partially explored whose peak capacity is not yet known. The combined annual peak rated capacity of the explored blocks is 400 mt. The first to go for the auction are some 100 blocks which are large enough to produce in the range of 30–50 mtpa at their peak rated capacity. Two of the salient features of the auction this time around are: one, the blocks are being auctioned on a revenue sharing model, and two, that the government will not regulate prices, marketing or sale of coal. However, the government specifies a minimum production from the mines, given under the reformed system, accompanied by a bank guarantee. The revenue sharing model has been adopted at the recommendation of a committee after the tepid response to at least two rounds of auctions under the old system. It would be interesting to see how the industry responds to these auctions under the new system, especially as the 'dirty' coal is being priced out by renewable and reeling under an incessant assault by environmentalists and politicians all over the world.

Challenges Facing the Coal Industry

With free-fall in the cost of renewables, India has been aggressively pursuing rapid diversification of the electricity sector while pivoting away from coal-fired power plants towards electricity generated by solar, wind and other cleaner sources of power. The country had closed 170 old and polluting power stations to meet emission norms till 2019 and many more were in the process of either being upgraded with induction of new technology or being shut down. The plunging prices and the growing supply of electricity generated by solar and wind are displacing coal-fired generation, decreasing the load factor and decreasing their profitability. Over the past few years, especially since 2017, solar and wind energy prices have fallen to such levels that were previously unimaginable. A solar energy company in Rajasthan, for instance, has been generating electricity at the unheard-of, guaranteed wholesale price of Rs 2.44 kWh or US¢ 3. Now, this price level has become the sort of benchmark, as most investors since then have been offering solar power at Rs 2.40–3.00 kWh. This puts domestic renewable energy prices about 20–30% below the cost of existing domestic coal-fired power generation costs.

The coal power industry feels that it is 'under siege' because of the 'unfair fight' and faces a future of limited growth and eventual disbandment. "Coal-fired power in India is being increasingly priced out of the market by cheaper renewables such as solar, with the dirtier fuel abandoned by private capital, and only projects with government support being viable," delegates at an annual industry gathering, Coaltrans India, held in Goa in February rued. According to them, economic reasons were largely responsible for this state of affairs. Renewables could be offered in PPAs at around Rs 3 (US¢ 4.2) kWh, while existing coal generation comes in at around Rs 4 kWh and new-build coal between Rs 5–6 kWh. As a result, there are fewer takers of coal power, a fact that has led to India's coal fleet utilisation rate of around 52–55%, well below a level that would be considered economic in other countries. Diminishing return on investment has rendered coal-fired generation unviable. Already, coal plants make up the significant category of financially distressed assets of the Indian banking sector.

After a massive build-out of coal-fired plants between 2010 and 2016, construction has now slowed to a near trickle, while investment in renewables has soared. India added 106 GW of new coal-fired capacity between the said period, at an average of 15.2 GW per year, according to data collated by the Global Energy Monitor. Since then, the pace has slowed, with only 8.9 GW added in 2017, 8.4 GW in 2018 and 8.2 GW in 2019. While there is still some 36 GW of coal-fired power capacity under construction, this will come online over the next decade, and additions are likely to drop below 5 GW per year. Finance is the central driver for the renewable's surge. India's LCOE using solar photovoltaic had fallen to US$ 38 per mw/h in 2019, which was 14% cheaper than coal-fired power that has traditionally been the cheapest source of electricity generation until the rise of renewables.[8]

The country is, therefore, embracing renewables and new energy technologies due to the compelling economic benefits of the rapid expansion of a cheaper electricity supply. It's worth noting that coal-fired units under construction are overwhelmingly owned by the state-run NTPC, and are funded by state-owned banks. The private sector has withdrawn from the coal generation sector, and many lenders are sitting with assets that are likely worth less than half their stated value, given the struggles of the plants to sign PPAs at profitable prices. In FY 2020–21, India's coal production fell 2% to 716 mt, including 44.787 mt of coking coal. The private sector's share in the total production was a mere 30.13 mt, compared with 34.82 mt in the previous financial year.

IV. THE FUTURE OF COAL

However, the continuing surge of renewables doesn't mean the imminent death of coal in India. It is not. Even optimistic forecasts for renewables show that coal would still be generating about half of the country's electricity in 2030, and would be the dominant source of power for at least two decades. If coal is becoming unattractive today, it is only because it is too expensive relative to renewable energy alternatives. But the question is whether the intermittent source of power, which solar and wind represent, can be integrated onto the grid without installing sufficient storage in the form of costly batteries to ensure stability. This is where coal becomes an unavoidable source of uninterrupted electricity supply. However, coal's share of generation will slip, and power companies will have to do more to prepare for the increasingly likelihood that renewable energies are going to provide most of the new capacity in coming years. Data from the Global Coal Plant Tracker shows that as of January, 2020, India had 36.12 GW of coal capacity under construction and 220 GW operating. The data also shows, however, a total of 491 GW of planned capacity additions were cancelled in the past eight years, a fairly dramatic scale-back of India's coal-fired aspirations. According to the Institute for Energy Economics and Financial Analysis, 40.1 GW of Indian coal plants are currently assessed as 'stranded assets'.

However, amid this gloomy scenario, there is a glimmer of hope. The rising renewable energy capacity and broader changes in the power system are forcing corresponding changes in the coal sector, too, which are likely to narrow the yawning hiatus between renewable-coal tariffs. It is noteworthy that major coal power companies, perhaps in a desperate move, have started offering lower tariffs in bids for PPAs with buyers. At a tender invited by the Power Finance Corporation Consulting Ltd in February 2020 for the supply of 2,500 MW, a dozen companies like Adani Power, Jindal Power, GMR Energy and Essar Power quoted the tariff of Rs 3.26 kWh for supply to states, the lowest bid from coal, based power projects in years. The rate is valid for three years, with annual escalation allowed at 50% of the wholesale price index (WPI).

In addition, installation of carbon capture and storage (CCS) technology and flue gas desulphurisation (FGD) devices at the plants are expected to play an increasing role in extending the relevance of coal-fired power generation in the country. Most antipathy to coal stems from carbon emissions from it when it is burnt. CCS technology can capture up to 90% of the CO_2 emissions produced from the use of fossil fuels in electricity generation and industrial processes, thus preventing it from entering the atmosphere. Though CO_2 is a normal part of natural environment, at very high levels of concentration, it is poisonous. The scientific consensus is that CO_2 could be captured and stored with little or no leakage and could be put to industrial use. After all, gases are already captured at various kinds of process facilities. CO_2 is already transported by pipeline and pumped into old oil and gas fields to help boost production. The Massachusetts Institute of Technology (MIT) study on 'The Future of Coal' calls it, "The critical future technology option for reducing CO_2 emissions while keeping coal's use above today's level."[9]

But after a series of studies, the adoption of CCS technology at coal plants on a large scale in India has been found to be a very expensive proposition. Its use is limited to only oil and gas fields to enhance recovery. Even globally, it is not yet widely adopted, because of the prohibitive costs involved in its installation. Estimates today, based on experimental projects, suggest that CCS could raise the price of coal-fired electricity by 80–100%. Currently, there are only 19 large-scale CCS facilities in operation worldwide, with four more under construction. In India, finance minister Nirmala Sitharaman had announced a Rs 4,400 crore allocation in the 2020–21 budget to give away as subsidies to coal-fired plants for decarbonisation devices under the National Clean Air Programme (NCAP). Most of this fund is likely to be used for installing the FGD devices, which are used to remove SO_2 from exhaust flue gases using an alkaline reagent to produce a solid compound. In this chemical reaction, about 90% of SO_2 from the flue gas can be removed and the limestone converted into calcium sulphite ($CaSO_4$).

Despite International Chorus against Coal Power, Coal Is Still the King

The International Energy Agency has forecast that global coal demand would start flattening in 2025. Renewables are on track to surpass coal as the largest source of electricity in the world by 2025 overtaking coal, natural gas and oil as the source of primary, according to the IEA. But with coal demand, still expected to remain steady or to grow in key Asian economies, there is no sign that coal is going to fade away quickly.

The future of coal will largely be decided in Asia. Today, China and India account for 65% of global coal demand. With Japan, Korea, Taiwan and Southeast Asia included, that share rises to 75%. China, which currently accounts for half of the world's coal consumption, will be especially influential. By 2025, the European Union and United States will account for less than 10% of global coal demand, down from 37% in 2000. This will make the impact of any further change in demand in these markets very limited.

Coal producers are actively pursuing 2.2 btpa (billion tonne per annum) of new mine projects around the world, a growth of 30% from current production levels according to the Global Energy Monitor. While three-fourths (1.6 btpa) of the proposed coal mine capacity is in the early stages of planning, the remaining one quarter (0.6 btpa) of the proposed mine capacity is already under construction. India's single largest project, the Siarmal Open Cast mine in Sundergarh district in Odisha, has a capacity to produce 50 mtpa at peak, with an operational life of 38 years, making it the second largest proposed coal mine in the world after Australia's Carmichael Project (60 mtpa).

Coal will continue to be a significant contributor to development, both through its role in electricity and in producing the building blocks of our societies—steel and cement, says Michelle Manook, chief executive of the World Coal Association.

Prospects of Coal in India

Despite a dramatic rise in the adoption of solar, wind and other clean energy technologies, it is impossible India can ditch coal, which provides more than half of its electricity. Coal's use could plateau and even decline with the increasing induction of advanced technologies, but it is set remain the largest single source of power in the foreseeable future. As a percentage of total power generation, coal is expected to decline from 54% in 2020 to 48% over the next decade, according to India's Central Electricity Authority. But in absolute terms, its use will increase as India's overall energy demand grows.

The sector has been under financial distress for years due to bad loans and other business decisions that have saddled coal plants and distribution utilities with billions of dollars of debt. The Parliamentary Standing Committee on Energy previously identified 34 thermal coal power plants as stranded assets suffering from premature write-downs and devaluation. A December 2019 report published by the Institute for Energy Economics and Financial Analysis (IEEFA) found that an additional 12 plants could have moved out of the range of economic feasibility. The cost-competitiveness of renewable energy, air pollution regulations and water scarcity have also been putting pressure on the coal sector.

What India's energy mix will look like in the medium-term depends in large part on how the next phase of India's clean energy transition unfolds. Solar and wind have proven to be reliable and affordable energy resources, but a substantial market for energy storage and other advanced technologies, needed to balance the use of intermittent renewables on the grid, is yet to develop. Until clean energy is flexible enough to provide power whenever needed, experts say a significant role for coal will remain.

New Auctions for Coal Mines

In June 2020, Prime Minister Modi launched an auction process to open 41 coal mines to commercial mining for the first time. The move was designed to create competition for government-owned Coal India, reduce India's reliance on imported energy products and attract investment to help the country recover from the economic fallout of the Covid-19 pandemic. The auction brought new domestic players into the Indian coal sector. However, two-fifths of the mines opened up to private investment received no bids.

References

1. India's BUR-II to UNFCCC.
2. R Shama Sastri in his 'Evolution of Indian Polity', quoted by Ghosh, A.B., Coal Industry in India, Sultan Chand & Sons Publisher, New Delhi, pp.41–42.
3. Report of Coal Mining Committee, 1937, para 16, Cf. also MGMII volume, p.147.
4. The Future of Coal: Options for a Carbon-Constrained World, MIT, 2007, p.x.
5. Energy, Security, and the Remaking of the Modern World, Penguin Books, Yergin, Daniel, *The Quest*, London, p.405.
6. John Deutch, The Crisis in Energy Policy: The Godkin Lecture (Cambridge: Harvard University Press, 2011), Chapter 3; I CERA, Fueling North America's Energy Future: The Unconventional Natural Gas Revolution and the Carbon Agenda, 2010, pp.vii-2.
7. Atanu Mukherjee, MN Dastur & Co, published in EnergyWorld, 12 March, 2019.
8. Wood Mackenzie; LCOE comprises the cost of generating a mw/h of electricity, the upfront capital and development cost and the cost of equity and debt finance and operating and maintenance fee.
9. The Future of Coal.

Chapter 2
CRUDE OIL

*India's energy system is built around fossil fuels, in which coal
is the dominant fuel for power generation and industry, oil and
natural gas for transport, and natural gas and biomass
for residential cooking.*

I. OVERVIEW

Oil has been one of the world's most important primary sources of energy, and has also been a benchmark for determining prices of natural gas. It is a mixture of complex hydrocarbons whose refining produces gasoline, jet fuels, diesel, fuel oils, lubricants and paving materials. It is central to security, prosperity and the very nature of civilisation. It is the world's biggest and most pervasive business and the greatest of the great industries. Of the top ten companies in the Fortune 500 global ranking in 2008, six were oil companies. Today (2021), Saudi Aramco is the world's most valuable company (US$ 2,458 billion). According to a business intelligence group, IBISWorld, oil and gas drilling sector alone had total revenues of approximately US$ 2.1 trillion, making up 2.2% of global economy of an estimated US$ 93 trillion in 2021. The largest global producers of oil are the United States, Saudi Arabia and Russia. These three countries produced approximately 40 million barrels of oil per day in 2020, which was 43% of total world production.[1]

Until some alternative sources of energy are found in sufficient scale, oil will continue to have far-reaching effects on the global economy; major price movements can fuel economic growth or, contrarily, drive inflation and help kickstart recessions. It is a massive generator of wealth for individuals, companies and nations. At the end of the nineteenth century, John D Rockefeller had become the richest man in the United States by the sale of kerosene, derived from oil. Gasoline was then a useless by-product, which sometimes managed to be sold for as little as two cents a gallon, and when it could not be sold at all, it was run out into the rivers at night. The development of the internal combustion engine, powered by gasoline, gave the oil industry a new life and a new civilisation was born.[2]

Historical Development of Oil

Though the modern history of oil begins in the latter half of the nineteenth century, the substance has been well-known to mankind for millennia from seepages, bitumen pools and 'burning pillars', especially common in the Middle East (particularly in northern Iraq), but also found elsewhere. Bitumen seeps to the surface had been tapped for back into antiquity—in Mesopotamia, back to 3000 BC. The most famous source was at Hit, on the Euphrates, not far from Babylon (and the site of modern Baghdad). In the first century BC, the Greek historian Diodor wrote enthusiastically about the ancient bitumen industry, "Whereas many incredible miracles occur in the Babylonian country, there is none such as the great quantity of asphalt found there." Some of these seepages, along with escaping petroleum gases, burned continuously, providing the basis for fire worship in the Middle East.

Bitumen was a trade commodity in the ancient Middle East. It was used as a building mortar. It bound the walls of both Jericho and Babylon. Noah's Ark and Moses' basket were probably caulked, in the manner of the time, with bitumen to make them waterproof. It was also used for road making, and, in a limited and generally unsatisfactory way, for lighting. And bitumen served as a medicine too, it checked bleeding, said Roman naturalist Pliny in the first century BC, healed wounds, treated cataracts, provided a liniment for gout, cured aching teeth, soothed a chronic cough, relieved shortness of breath, stopped diarrhoea, drew together severed muscles and relieved both rheumatism and fever. It was also, "Useful for straightening out eyelashes which inconvenienced the eyes."[3]

Curiously, its application was not known to the West for many centuries, perhaps because the major sources of bitumen lay beyond the boundaries of the Roman Empire and there was little intercourse between the two regions. However, according to Daniel Yergin, a small oil industry had developed in Eastern Europe well before oil was first drilled in Pennsylvania in 1859, first in Galicia, which was variously part of Poland, Austria and Russia, and then in Rumania. Peasants dug shafts by hand to obtain crude oil, from which kerosene was refined. A pharmacist, with the help of a plumber, invented a cheap lamp suited to burning kerosene. This marked the beginning of oil as a source of lighting. By 1854 kerosene was a major commerce in Vienna, and by 1859 it was a thriving business in Galicia, with over 150 villages engaged in oil mining. European crude oil production in 1859 had been estimated at 56,000 barrels, mainly from Galicia and Rumania, but the East European industry lacked the technology for drilling.

In North America oil was collected from natural seeps in western Pennsylvania in the late eighteenth century and sold as medicinal 'Seneca oil', while in France, oil sands were exploited since 1745 in Alsace, near Merkwiller-Pechelbronn, where the first small refinery was built in 1857. But there was only one place in the preindustrial world with a long history of collecting crude oil, Baku's Absheron Peninsula on the Caspian Sea in today's Azerbaijan.

The American search for crude oil was motivated by a quest for an alternative to expensive whale sperm oil rendered on board ships. During the early 1840s more than 700 American vessels delivered 160,000 barrels of sperm oil to New England ports annually. The world's first oil well, which was drilled in America, rather than dug, was 1859. Edwin Drake, a former train conductor, is credited with drilling the first oil on 27 August, 1859 at a tiny, impoverished village of Titusville, tucked away into the hills of north-western Pennsylvania. The date is seen by oil historians as the beginning of the modern oil era.

Drake worked for Pennsylvania Rock Oil Company, an outfit set up by George Henry Bissell, an entrepreneur, and James Townsend, a banker. He reached Titusville in 1857 and chose a site at Oil Creek, near Titusville for drilling. He hired some 'salt borers' (drillers), the labourers who operated derricks, a kind of crane with a movable pivoted arm over an oil well that held the drilling machine. But the borers turned out to be an unprofessional, undependable lot. Disappointed, Drake tried to erect the steam engine himself to power the drill bit. Finally, he found a driller in spring 1859. He was a blacksmith named William A Smith—'Uncle Billy Smith'—who knew something about what needed to be done, as he used to make the tools for saltwater drillers. 'Uncle Billy' built the derrick and assembled necessary equipment with his two sons. It was assumed that they would have to go hundreds of feet into the Earth. The work was slow and the investors were getting restive. Towards the end of August 1859, Townsend sent a letter, along with a remittance, to Drake asking him to pay his bills and wind up the operation.

Drake had not received the letter when, on Saturday afternoon 27 August, 1859, at 69 ft (feet), the drill dropped into a crevice and slid another six inches. Next day, Uncle Billy came out to see the well. He peered down into the pipe. He saw a dark fluid floating on top of the water. He used a tin rain spout to draw up a sample. As he examined the heavy liquid, he was overcome by excitement. On Monday, when Drake arrived, he found Uncle Billy and his boys standing guard over tub, washbasins and barrels, all filled with oil. Drake attached a common hand pump and began to pump the liquid. He had hit oil. Farmers along Oil Creek rushed into Titusville, shouting, "The Yankee has struck oil." The news spread like wildfire and triggered a sort of gold rush. Within 15 months after Drake's discovery, some 75 wells were producing oil in and around Titusville. Bissell, who had conceived the idea of drilling for oil, rather than collecting it from seeps, became wealthy overnight, but it was not the same for others involved in the development of a new industry. Townsend, who had taken the biggest financial risk, was unhappy that he was denied credit and Drake died in 1873 a semi-invalid person, living in penury.

Within less than three years of Drake's ingenuous discovery, oil production in western Pennsylvania climbed to three million barrels in 1862 from about 450,000 barrels in 1860. But the demand did not grow correspondingly resulting in prices plunging as low as US¢ 10 a barrel at the end of 1861 from US$ 10 a barrel at the beginning of that year. But the demand picked up soon, and by the end of 1862 prices surged to US$ 4 a barrel and then to US$ 7.25 a barrel by September 1863. Those were the years of the Civil War in America, but oil market was hardly affected. On the contrary, the War added a boost to the oil market, as the shipments of turpentine from the South were cut off, driving the people to move to oil for lighting. By the end of the War, prices rose to US$ 13.75 a barrel.

The impact of Drake's discovery was not confined to western Pennsylvania. It was followed by drilling, exploration and discovery of various oil fields in other countries as well—in the Russian Empire, around Baku, on the Caspian Sea and in the Caucasus; in the Dutch East Indies; and in Galicia, the Austro-Hungarian Empire. But Pennsylvania was the Saudi Arabia of the day. During the 1860s three countries, the United States, Canada and Russia, had new, growing oil industries. By 1890 Russia was producing more oil than coal to meet its energy needs, and in 1899, before the discovery of giant oil fields in southern Texas, it was the world's largest producer of crude oil, just over nine million barrels per year. Other substantial pre-1900 oil discoveries were made in Rumania, Indonesia (Sumatra in 1883) and Burma (now Myanmar). Mexico joined the rank of oil producers in 1901. In India, the first oil was discovered in 1889 in the little-known town of Digboi in Assam, but it was not a major find. In the Middle East, first major discovery came in 1908 at Masjid-e-Soleiman in Iran, while Trinidad started oil production in 1913 and Venezuela in 1914.

Most of these discoveries were hydrocarbon fields containing both crude oil and associated natural gas, but gas was mostly flared, as it could not be moved over long distances in the absence of compressors and steel pipes in the early years of the hydrocarbon industry. In contrast, gasoline, kerosene and fuel oils, refined from crude oil, were easy to move and store, ideal for transportation and with the invention of internal combustion engines, they found a huge new market for their use. When George Bissell and Edwin Drake began their crude oil extraction efforts, their motive was to find an abundant and more affordable source of energy to replace expensive whale oil and other fluids used in oil lamps. There was no commercial electricity generation, light bulbs or commercial internal combustion engine at that time.

The primary market for oil for the first 40 years was illumination. The commercial electricity generation (see Chapter on Electricity) and light bulbs came 25 years after the first oil extraction at Titusville and internal combustion engines after another 25 years between 1886 and 1905, when two German engineers, Gottlieb Daimler and Wilhelm Maybach built their first practical automotive engines. The combination of Daimler's high-revolution engine, Benz's electrical ignition, Maybach's float-feed carburettor supplied the key components of modern road vehicle. The arrival of the motor car turned oil from an illuminant into the fuel of transportation. Warring nations during World War I used oil as strategic item to boost their capability; it powered their trucks, cars, tanks and planes. Describing the strategic importance of oil at the end of the war, British foreign secretary Lord Curzon said, "The Allied cause had floated to victory upon a wave of oil." World War II also ended, like the World War I, with great recognition of the strategic significance of oil. As it stands today, there is virtually no mobility without oil and no Internet age without electricity, and energy to generate that electricity.

Oil Discovery in India

In India, oil was first found in the swamps of river valleys of Assam during the British colonial rule. Prospecting for coal in Upper Assam, according to India's Directorate General of Hydrocarbons (DGH), geological surveyors of

British India had seen oil seepages on the banks of the River Dihing in Upper Assam at different times, but they had made no attempt to ascertain the cause of the seepages. It was only seven years since Edwin L Drake drilled the world's first oil well in 1859 at Titusville, Pennsylvania, that Mr Goodenough of McKillop, Stewart & Company, Calcutta, in 1866 hand-dug a well of 102 ft at Nahorpung near Jaipur area of Upper Assam, but failed to establish a satisfactory production of oil. In his second attempt on 26 March, 1867, he was able to strike oil at 118 ft (35.97 m) in Asia's first mechanically drilled well at Makum near Margherita area of Upper Assam.

However, the development of oil was not undertaken until 1889 when the Assam Railways and Trading Company Ltd (AR&TCL), registered in London, dug a well at Digboi in the dense forests of Assam and found oil in commercial quantity at a depth of 662 ft. This find is deemed as the first commercially successful discovery of oil in India. It produced 200 gallons a day of oil. AR&TCL created a colourful legend around this successful discovery. It said that during the construction of a railway line by AR&T, in 1867, a herd of logging elephants returned to the camp after a night time excursion to find food and water with their feet covered with oil. This aroused curiosity among men there and prompted them to trail to the salt lick where seepages were prolific. Looking at this, the elated English owner cried out to his men, "Dig boy, Dig." Probably the name Digboi came from those words. Subsequently AR&T acquired a 77.7 sq km (square kilometre) petroleum-rights concession in the Makum area of Assam, and by 1893 drilled 10 wells at Digboi producing 757.08 litres per day. AR&T established Assam Oil Company (AOC) in 1899 with a capital of British Sterling Pound £ 310,000 to take over the petroleum interests of AR&T, including the Digboi and Makum concessions and set up a small refinery at Margharita (Upper Assam) with a capacity of 500 barrel of oil a day to refine the Digboi oil. In 1901 the company set up Asia's first oil refinery at Digboi, which is still functional and is the world's oldest operating oil refinery.

At its peak Digboi oil field produced close to 7,000 barrels per day (1,100 m^3/d) of crude oil during the World War II. The field was pushed to produce the maximum amount of oil with little regard for reservoir management, resulting in production declining almost immediately after the war. Currently, the fields produce about 240 barrels per day (38 m^3/d) from over 1,000 wells. Today, though the crude production is not high, Digboi has the distinction of being India's oldest, continuously producing oil field. Digboi refinery, now part of the state-run Indian Oil Corporation, has a capacity of about 0.65 mmtpa (million metric tonnes per annum), and is the headquarters of Assam Oil Division of the Indian Oil Corporation. In 1989, the Department of Posts, issued a stamp commemorating the 100 years of the Digboi fields.

As for the AOC, which had first developed the Digboi fields, the failure to utilise geologic reasoning, promiscuous wild catting, misguided investment and nonchalance of the management towards technical support led to compounding of errors that made the company technically and financially impotent in the course of time, and forced it to gradually sell its petroleum interests to Burma Oil Company (BOC) by 1921. The UK-based BOC had arrived in Upper Assam (Surma Valley) in 1911, and in 1915, after acquiring oil interest from Budderpore Oil Co. Ltd (formed by a syndicate of Budderpore Tea Garden during 1911–13) began testing option in the Badarpur structure in the Surma Valley (Upper Assam).

Torsion balance which was successfully adapted for geophysical surveys of oil was used at Bordubi (Assam) by a team in 1925. The Indian Co. 'TATA Engineering Co' has also drilled several wells in Jagatia, Gujarat and produced small amount of gas in 1930s. In 1937, BOC jointly with British Petroleum (then Anglo-Iranian Oil Co) and Shell proposed to the Government of India to carry out a geophysical survey of the important plain areas of India. The proposal was accepted, and a new form of grant known as geophysical license was issued by the Assam Government. In Assam, successful seismic survey was carried out in Naharkatiya during 1937–39, triggering new enthusiasm in oil search and it became the forerunner of discoveries in Assam basins and others also. The successful outcome of well NHK-1 in 1937 was vindication for geophysical method in oil exploration.

Post-Independence Development of Oil

In 1947, India achieved independence from the British rule, and realising the crucial role of oil and gas in the country's economic and industrial development and national security, the new government took the task of developing the hydrocarbon resources on a priority basis. Earlier it was controlled by two British companies, Assam Oil Company and Attock Oil Company, who produced as much as the Imperial government needed to keep the administration running. Assam was the only state that produced oil and the total production was just around 2,50,000 tonnes per year that came from the Digboi field, operated by Assam Oil Company and Oil India Ltd, a 50–50 joint venture between the erstwhile Government of India and Burma Oil Company. The latter was mainly active in Naharkatiya and Moran oil fields of Assam. For exploration, Indo-Stanvac Petroleum, a joint venture of the erstwhile Government of India and Standard Vacuum Oil Company of the USA, was the only company that was engaged in the task in West Bengal. Beyond that, the vast sedimentary tract in other parts of India and adjoining offshore areas was left largely unexplored.

The dismal state of the hydrocarbon industry under the British called for urgent measures for solution. While formulating its industrial policy in 1948, the new Indian government gave top priority to the development of petroleum industry, and by 1948, the Geological Survey of India (GSI) started geophysical surveys. The first oil discovery in independent India was made by the AOC in 1953 in Naharkatiya and then in Moran in 1956, both in Upper Assam. But the development had to wait.

In 1956, the government adopted another Industrial Policy Resolution, placing the mineral oil industry amongst the Schedule 'A' industries, which meant that all future development of the petroleum industry would be reserved exclusively for the state undertakings. Thus, collaborations with Anglo-American oil companies were ruled out. However, as foreign technological and financial assistance were essential inputs (which the newly-independent state lacked) the government sought help from foreign experts from the USA, the erstwhile Soviet Union, West Germany and Rumania to develop the Indian petroleum industry and train its professionals for exploring and developing potential hydrocarbon reserves. Efforts were made to forge government-to-government co-operation for promoting oil projects and developing expertise, but it did not seem feasible with the US and West Germany, which followed free-market economies, with private companies mainly involved in exploration, production and marketing of energy.

In 1955–56, a delegation led by the then Minister of Natural Resources, KD Malviya, toured several European countries and invited foreign experts to share their know-how. Finally, the Left-leaning Indian government invited Soviet experts to draw up a detailed plan for geological and geophysical surveys and drilling operations. And, thus, the Soviets experts took charge of independent India's nascent oil industry. But over time their influence diminished, as US companies and multilateral funding agencies like World Bank started playing a significant role in the Indian oil sector.

Meanwhile, in 1955 India had set up a separate Oil and Natural Gas Directorate (ONGD) under the Ministry of Natural Resources and Scientific Research to intensify and expand exploration activities in various parts of the country. The department was constituted with a nucleus of geoscientists from Geological Survey of India. But soon after its formation, it was realised that the directorate could not function efficiently with its limited financial and administrative liberty. Hence, in early 1956, its status was upgraded to a commission, with necessary financial and administrative powers and renamed as Oil and Natural Gas Commission (ONGC). In 1959, the commission was made a statutory body by an Act of Parliament, but still placed under the Ministry of Natural Resources and Scientific Research. Its job, as defined in the Act, is, "To plan, promote, organise and implement programmes for development of petroleum resources and production and sale of petroleum and petroleum products produced by it, and to perform such other function as the central government may, from time to time, assign to it."

Within a year of its formation, ONGC systematically conducted geophysical surveys on area considered prospective based on global analogy. Special thrust was laid on areas of Himalayan foothills and adjoining Ganga plains, alluvial tracts of Gujarat, Upper Assam and Bay of Bengal. The exploratory drilling in Himalayan foothill during 1957 yielded no discovery. But those in the Cambay area of Gujarat yielded giant oil fields of Ankleshwar in 1960 and Kalol in 1961. In Assam, new oil discoveries were made in Lakwa in 1964 and Geleki in 1968, and a gas discovery in Manhartibba, Rajasthan in 1969.

At around the same time a new company, Oil India Private Ltd (OIL), formed in 1961 with Assam Oil Company, Burma Oil Company and the Government of India with each holding one third of the stake, discovered the Kusijan oil field in 1969 and Jorajan oil field in 1972. OIL also found some gas deposits in Tengakhat fields of Assam in 1973. Pursuing an aggressive exploration policy, the ONGC extended geo-scientific surveys to Uttar Pradesh, Bihar, Rajasthan, Jammu and Kashmir, Kutch, Tamil Nadu and Andhra Pradesh, and found one of India's biggest gas concentrations of 283.17 bcm (billion cubic metre) in the Bassein areas off Mumbai coast. The year 1972 was marked by the momentous discovery of Bombay High Offshore that continues to hold the largest amount of India's domestic oil even today. In 1976, ONGC discovered three other gas fields—Mid Tapti, South Tapti and B-55. Encouraged by this success, ONGC further extended exploration to entire western offshore including Kerala-Konkan basin and eastern offshore area, leading to significant discoveries of Bassein and Neelam in western offshore and PY-3 and Ravva in Eastern offshore. By the mid-1980s, it had found prospects of hydrocarbon reserves in the Cauvery and KG basin. Meanwhile, OIL, which was active in the North-East, found the Kharsang oil field in Arunachal Pradesh, about 50 km east of Digboi Refinery, at around the same time, and ventured out of Assam into Orissa (now Odisha) offshore and onshore and Andamans offshore. By the end of the 1980s, ONGC and OIL had together drilled nearly 3,100 wells totalling 4.9 million metres.

Nationalisation of Oil Industry

In the early 1970s, the government took over the refining and marketing facilities of foreign companies Burmah–Shell, Caltex and Standard Vacuum. It was the first step towards nationalisation of the oil industry. Caltex and Standard Vacuum left after shutting down their operations in India, but Burmah-Shell tried to continue its presence even as a junior partner in a joint venture with an Indian national oil company—ONGC, OIL or Indian Oil Corporation. The government declined, but allowed it to continue as a crude oil supplier.

Post-nationalisation, efforts were intensified on offshore exploration in order to increase oil resources (although substantial areas of onshore sedimentary basins remained unexplored). The new policy led to a growing involvement of US companies which had superior exploration technologies compared to the Soviets'. The result was a steep erosion of Soviet dominance in India's hydrocarbon industry in the 1970s and 1980s.

In 1974, the government offered offshore exploration and production rights in 7 million acres of the Bay of Bengal to Natamas Carlsburg Company, US. Soon thereafter another large acreage was offered to Readings and Bates, US, in the Kutch basin of Gujarat. Both exploration- and production-sharing contracts (EPSCs) were signed by the ONGC on the government's behalf. The EPSCs envisaged that the foreign companies would have a 61% interest in the joint ventures, while the remainder would be taken by the ONGC. Secondly, 40% of the crude, if produced, would go to the US companies as 'Cost Oil' towards the recovery of their expenses. Of the remaining the ONGC would take 65% and the US companies' 35% in their respective projects. The price of crude would be based on the prices of Indonesian and Persian Gulf crudes. But the projects did not go ahead as the companies failed to find oil in their sanctioned blocks.

In 1980s the government relaxed the terms of offer to attract foreign oil majors to India's exploration and production, such as royalty payments were waived and the provisions of a minimum expenditure commitment, normally associated with EPSCs, were removed. ONGC and OIL were allowed to take a 40% stake in joint ventures formed by foreign oil companies, if oil were found in commercially viable quantities. By the end of 1986, the government invited foreign companies to participate in its third round of international bidding for exploration blocks, but only few participated in it and there was no 'breakthrough' discovery. However, ONGC and OIL continued their efforts in several parts of India and by 1989 the ONGC had discovered south Heera oil field in Mumbai offshore and OIL a natural gas field in Tanot (Mata Temple), Rajasthan. By the end of 1986, third round of international bidding for exploration block were offered. OIL and ONGC were offered 40% stake in JV, if the field was found viable. Few foreign companies participated but there was no committed exploration or breakthrough discovery. The foreshore terminal of IOC was commissioned in Madras (Chennai).

This was the time when global oil prices were in a free fall. However, ironically oil-deficient India, instead of taking advantage of falling oil prices, continued to raise its domestic crude production until, in the words of a commentator, oil-bearing wells were 'flogged to death'. The country's oil production surged to 34 mmtpa in 1989–90 from 10.51 mmtpa in 1980–81. As a result of ill-considered exploitation of natural resources, domestic crude production fell sharply to 26.92 mmtpa in 1992–93. One reason advanced for this was that the country was facing a severe foreign exchange crunch which ultimately forced the government to mortgage gold reserves to raise funds to pay an International Monetary Fund (IMF) loan instalment in 1990–91.

Economic Liberalisation Opens Door to Private Investment

In 1991, the Narasimha Rao government reversed the decades-old Soviet-style command-and-control economic policy to attract private players, including foreign oil companies, to participate in oil exploration and production. The liberalised economic policy led to delicensing of several core industries, including petroleum, and a partial disinvestment of government holding in them. ONGC was reorganised as a limited company and renamed as Oil and Natural Gas Corporation Ltd, to run under the Indian Companies Act, 1956, instead of Oil and Natural Gas Commission, which was governed by the Act of Parliament. Following the incorporation of the Oil and Natural Gas Corporation Ltd under the Companies Act, in 1993 the government disinvested 2% of its shares through competitive bidding, while the reorganised ONGC expanded its equity by another 2% by offering shares to its employees. In 1999, ONGC, Indian Oil Corporation (IOC), a state-run downstream firm and Gas Authority of India Limited (GAIL), a state's gas marketing company, agreed to have cross holding in each other's stock. This paved the way for long-term strategic alliances for the domestic and overseas business in the energy value chain, amongst themselves. Consequent to this the government sold off 10% of its shares in the ONGC to IOC and 2.5% to GAIL. With this, the government's holding in ONGC came down to 84.11%. In 2004, the government divested another 10% of its shares through initial public offering (IPO). In March 2019, ONGC's shareholding structure stood as: Promoters 64.25%; Other Institutions 10.73%; Foreign Institutional Investors (FII) 6.47%; Mutual Funds 5%; Individuals 13.55%.

Liberalisation of the economy opened the door to private investment—both private and public—in the country's hydrocarbon developmental activities. This necessitated the establishment of a regulator to oversee the activities of the companies, hence, in 1993 the government set up the Directorate General of Hydrocarbon (DGH) to fulfil the need. The government was keen to attract major international firms with advanced technology and funds in India's hydrocarbon development either solely or in JV with local companies. To start with, the government awarded contracts for the development of 5 medium-sized and 13 small fields where oil or gas had already been discovered by national oil companies, ONGC and OIL.

The companies that benefitted from this first round included Enron Oil and Gas (USA, now defunct), Reliance Industries Ltd (India), Command Petroleum Ltd (Australia), Videocon Petroleum Ltd (India) and Ravva Oil Pte Ltd (Singapore). ONGCL and OIL's share in those JVs were limited to 40% only. A cumulative oil production from these fields was estimated at 360 billion barrels and gas output at 50 bcm. The consortium of Enron-Reliance was the luckiest beneficiary as it had bagged the most promising of the fields given away. (It had got Panna, Mukta and Mid and South Tapti, which had been explored earlier by ONGC. But no exploration expenditure incurred by the state explorer had been reimbursed). The consortium also benefitted from the purchase deal with the government which undertook to buy the consortium crude at the international price plus a US$ 4 per barrel premium for its low sulphur content.

II. OIL RESERVES AND RESOURCES

India's prognosticated conventional hydrocarbon resource potential is estimated at around 42 bt of oil equivalent (unrisked), of which about 28%, or 12 bt of oil equivalent, is converted into in-place volume through discoveries. However, production is done only at five locations—Barmer in Rajasthan; Gulf of Khambhat in Gujarat; Mumbai High Sea; Godavari-Krishna Basin and in Assam. It's surprising that India splurges billions of dollars enriching the sheikhs of Arabia, but does not monetise its hydrocarbon resources available in its backyard.

Based on British Petroleum's Statistical Review of World Energy and the U.S. Energy Information Administration (EIA) data, Worldometer had put India's proven oil reserves in 2019 at no more than 4,728.8 million barrels, and warned that sans imports India's domestic oil resources may not last beyond three years at the rate of consumption 4.5 mbpd (million barrels per day) in 2020. Other sources had put India's estimated crude oil reserves at 618.95 mt (4,536.9 million barrels), with the largest ones (40%) in Western offshore (Mumbai High, Krishna-Godavari Basin) and 27% in Assam.[4] During the same period, natural gas reserves were estimated at 1,339.57 bcm including 38.13% located in the Eastern offshore and 23.33% in the Western offshore.[5]

The above statistics present a grim picture of India's oil base. But the situation has not been as precarious as presented. The figures cited by the above agencies appear to have been loosely quoted from sources that have not been involved in any geological study of India's sedimentary basins. Even government agencies have cited the country's oil reserve figures randomly without citing the sources. For example, the *Minerals Yearbook*, 2012, issued by the Ministry of Mines, states India's total crude oil reserves at 759.59 mt (328.88 mt onshore and 430.71 mt offshore), and natural gas at 1,330.26 bcm (337.93 bcm onshore and 992.33 bcm offshore).[6] Another government agency, the Ministry of Petroleum and Natural Gas, gives two different figures of oil and gas reserves—763.476 mt of crude oil and 1488.73 bcm of natural gas as on 1 April, 2015, and 618.95 mt of oil and 1,339.57 bcm as of 31 March, 2019.

First Geophysical Survey (1995–96)

However, all these figures were mere guess-estimates. India's first scientific geophysical survey of sedimentary basins was carried out in 1995–96, which covered half of the country's 26 sedimentary basins, spread over an aerial extent of 3.36 million sq km. Of the total basinal area, only 22% was well explored, while 44% of the area was under initial exploration stage and 34% was either poorly explored or totally unexplored. At the conclusion of this survey, the DGH of India estimated the total oil and gas reserves at 28.1 bt of oil equivalent (205.13 billion barrels). Most of the reserves came from five of the seven basins presently under production. Other basins including compressional fold thrust belt and fore-deeps (Himalayas, Ganga/Punjab) and older rift basins (Proterozoic, Gondwana) are yet to be fully explored.

According to the DGH, five petroliferous basins of peninsular India, such as Cauvery, Krishna-Godavari, Mahanadi, Barmer, Cambay, offshore regions of Bombay, Saurashtra and Kutch invariably had thick units of Basalt, interlayered with sediments ranging from the beginning to the end of the Cretaceous period. Peri-cratonic rift basins and aulacogens formed in divergent set up are favourable locales for generation and accumulation of oil and gas, for example, Niger, Gabon, Chad, Angola shelf and Syrte basin of Africa, Campos basin of Brazil, Gulf of Mexico and Atlantic Margin basins of the US. However, the 1995–96 survey lacked advanced technologies for geoscientific-engineering data acquisition and methods of interpretation.

Second Survey (2017)

After more than two decades, India undertook another hydrocarbon re-assessment study in 2017, which covered all the 26 sedimentary basins, including the deep-water areas of respective basins. Improvised assessment tools were used for basins with intensive datasets and the assessment extended into hydrocarbon play level for a more refined insight into stratigraphic make-up. The project pooled in a huge amount of geo-scientific data, close to 4,500 wells, 50,000 LKM of 2D seismic and 750,000 SKM of 3D seismic data, along with vast amount of laboratory data of bio-stratigraphy, sedimentology and geochemical information—all adequate in building comprehensive geological models. In basins where limited data were present, information was gathered from public domains and analogous basins based on commonality of geological parameters. The new resource estimate of conventional hydrocarbons is a data-driven comprehensive assessment where the geological intricacies on hydrocarbon prospectivity have been mapped at 'play' level through adept use of industry-standard sophisticated petroleum system modelling tools. Continuous supervision by international domain specialists and Indian basin experts ensured data synthesis and quality-check of the assessment methodologies, leading to accuracy, reliability and global benchmarking of the results.

The result of the reassessment showed the 'unrisked' (proven) presence of 'conventional hydrocarbons of 42 bt of oil equivalent (305 billion barrels) 'in-place'. This is 49.1% more than 28.1 bt of oil equivalent estimated in 1995–96. At this level of reserve, if transformed into proven reserves, India becomes the world's largest holder of oil and gas resources, zooming past the current toppers, Venezuela, which is believed to hold 303 billion barrels, and Saudi Arabia, which has 297.7 billion barrels.

DGH attributes the increase in discoveries in the 2017 reassessment study to significant upsides in the producing basins (Krishna-Godavari, Mumbai Offshore, Assam Shelf, Assam-Arakan Fold Belt, Cauvery, Rajasthan and Cambay). On the basis of new discoveries reported, the new sub-basins, like Vindhyan, Saurashtra and Kerala Konkan have been upgraded to Category II.

However, hydrocarbons present in Indian sedimentary basins are largely 'prospective resources', which in the event of discovery will mature into 'contingent resources' and later on commercial viability transform into 'reserves'. As on 1 April, 2019, the upstream companies operating in India—ONGC, OIL and foreign companies in JV with Indian firms—had 'established' 11,238.37 mtoe (million tonnes oil equivalent) (82.37 billion barrels) of hydrocarbons in-place, and ultimate reserves of 4,322.25 mt (31.682 billion barrels) in their exploration areas. After accretion in ultimate reserves, the recoverable balance left on that date stood at 1981.92 mtoe (14.53 billion barrels), according to the DGH.

The total basin area of the 26 sedimentary basins of India is close to 3.36 million sq km with on land area of 1.63 million sq km (49%), shallow water of 0.41 million sq km (12%) and deep water of 1.32 million sq km (39%). During the 1995–96 exercise, deep water areas were separately assessed without geological linkage to respective basin areas. In the 2017 study, deep water areas were pushed deeper to 400 m bathymetry and the same geologically linked to respective basins falling into deep water. In terms of exploration potential, the reassessment of all 26 Indian sedimentary basins has shown quite a large undiscovered in-place, which is about three-fourths of total in-place reassessed for entire sedimentary cover.

Technology has undoubtedly improved the assessment of hydrocarbon reserves to the point of near accuracy. But the estimates of quantum of a discovery still remains intuitive, or at best speculative, and sometimes divorced from reality. According to BP's figures, the world has pumped just over 1 trillion barrels of oil since 1980, the year when the oil major started its study of world oil reserves and production. Proven reserves back then stood at only 684 billion barrels. Reserves at the end of 2018 were 1.73 trillion barrels, up 2 billion barrels from 2017. The ratio of reserves to production—how much oil is left at current rates of output—rose from less than 30 years to 50 years, while production having jumped by half. That clearly shows that quite a lot more oil has been found.

History is replete with such instances. Around the middle of the last century Admiral Hyman Rickover, 'father of the nuclear navy', had predicted end of the 'Fossil Fuel Age' (President Jimmy Carter once described him as, 'the greatest engineer of all time').[7] Rickover's central point was that fossil fuels would run out sometime after 2000, and most likely before 2050. He did not think that renewables—wind, sunlight, biomass—could ever get much above 15% of total energy. "It will be wise to face up to the possibility of the ultimate disappearance of automobiles," he said. But the resource endowment of the mother Earth has turned out to be nowhere near as bleak as Rickover thought. Oil production today is five times greater than it was in 1957, and renewables have established a much more secure foundation than Rickover imagined.

Hydrocarbon-Bearing Sedimentary Basins of India

Based on conventional resource potential, seven basins are grouped under Category I covering 30% of total basinal area and holding 85% of the total unrisked conventional hydrocarbon in-place of 41.8 bt of o+oeg (oil and oil equivalent gas). These seven basins are namely Krishna-Godavari (KG), Mumbai Offshore, Assam Shelf, Rajasthan, Cauvery, Assam-Arakan Fold Belt and Cambay. These are fairly appraised to the extent of 47% of country's total appraised area (1.6 million sq km) with 65% of country's total active operational area (0.3 million sq km).

Similarly, Category II basins cover 23% of total basinal area, holding 9% of the total hydrocarbon in-place. Five basins fall in this category and those are namely Saurashtra, Kutch, Vindhyan, Mahanadi and Andaman. These basins are moderately appraised to the extent of 22% of country's total appraised area with 26% of country's total active operational area.

Further, Category III basins cover 47% of total basinal area, holding 6% of the total hydrocarbon in-place. Fourteen basins fall in this category and those are namely Kerala-Konkan, Bengal-Purnea, Ganga-Punjab, Pranhita-Godavari (PG), Satpura-South Rewa-Damodar, Himalyan Foreland, Chattisgarh, Narmada, Spiti-Zanskar, Deccan Syneclise, Cuddapah, Karewa, Bhima-Kaladgi, and Bastar. These basins are appraised to the extent of 31% of country's total appraised area with 9% of country's total active operational area.

The grouping of the basins under different categories is dynamic, as a basin grouped under a lower category can be upgraded to a higher category if there is a new discovery of oil or gas in commercial quantity in that basin, or if discoveries are developed for commercial production. Instances are of Bengal-Purnea basin which was recently upgraded from Category III to Category II after the discovery of new hydrocarbon deposits in that basin; and that of Kutch/Saurashtra basin, which is expected to go into commercial production in partnership with some foreign companies in the near future. For unconventional resources, the above category will have completely different basin grouping. For example, CBM gas is currently produced from Damodar sub-basin of Satpura-South Rewa-Damodar, which is a Category III basin for conventional resources, however by virtue of commercial gas production, the basin will be deemed Category I for unconventional resources.

Under redrafted revenue sharing contract for Hydrocarbon Exploration Licensing Policy, contractors operating in Category II and Category III basins for respective conventional and unconventional resources are now exempt of revenue sharing with the government.

Oilmen insist that there are still abundant hydrocarbon resources left in India's vast, underdeveloped and unexplored sedimentary basins. According to BP's Bob Dudley India may be having more than a trillion cubic feet of natural gas in its deepwater sediments alone. But these have been sparsely explored. BP partners with Reliance Industries Ltd to operate India's largest and most prolific non-associated gas field, the KG-D6. Dudley's views are echoed by other oilmen and bodies, including the DGH, which admits that the country's 49% basins are still untapped. The Ministry of Petroleum and Natural Gas, in its 2018–19 annual report states, "As of now, 1 April, 2018, only 48% of the basinal areas have been appraised. About 4% of the sedimentary basinal area has been declared as 'NO GO' by the Ministry of Defence and Ministry of Environment and Forest which remains unapprised. This means, about half of the Indian sedimentary basins have the undiscovered potential of hydrocarbons."

In order to nudge upstream companies, both Indian and foreign, to intensify search for potential oil and gas resources in about 2.8 million sq km of unexplored area in the country's sedimentary basins, the government is offering various lucrative incentives, such as freedom to carve blocks of their choice to bid for, instead of bidding for only those blocks the government puts on offers for auctions. Under this scheme, called open acreage licensing policy or OALP, companies are allowed to put in an Expression of Interest (EoI) for prospecting of oil and gas in any area that is presently not under any production or exploration licence. The EoIs can be put in at any time of the year but they are accumulated twice annually and put on auction on 30 June and 31 December of each year.

The new policy has replaced the old system of government carving out areas and bidding them out. It guarantees marketing and pricing freedom and moves away from production-sharing model of previous rounds to a revenue-sharing model, where companies offering the maximum share of oil and gas to the government are awarded the block. For basins under Category I, bids are evaluated with 70% weightage on Minimum Work Programmes (MWP) and 30% on revenue share to the government. The MWP is further assessed based on 80% weightage on wells and 20% on seismic survey. Basins under Category II and III are offered with no revenue shared with the government. Contractor bidding for blocks in these basins are now required to pay only statutory levies including royalties and no revenue to be shared with government until there is any windfall gain. Till April 2019, three rounds of OALP auctions had been held under the scheme in which mostly Indian companies, except for BP in partnership with

Reliance, vied for 101 blocks on offer. Oil Minister Dharmendra Pradhan said the auctions brought investments of Rs 149,000 crore in prospecting of oil and gas.

The reforms implemented by the government has encouraged increased investment in exploration and production (E&P) activities. Pradhan told the Indian Parliament in December 2019 that the state-run ONGC and Oil India would spend Rs 1.77 lakh crore over a five-year period till 2025. He said the planned spending was based on the assessment of existing acreages made by the two companies aimed at raising oil production to 38.91 mt and natural gas output to 55.68 bcm by 2023–24 from 34.2 mt and 32.4 bcm in 2018–19 respectively. According to Pradhan, the three rounds of bidding for exploration under the OALP and two rounds of bidding under the Discovered Small Fields (DSF) policy garnered investment of US$ 58 billion between 2017 and 2018. Pradhan states that India expected investments of around US$ 118 billion in its oil and gas sector by 2023. This includes US$ 58 billion in oil exploration, as stated above, and US$ 60 billion in building pipelines, import terminals and city gas distribution networks.

Vedanta's upstream arm Cairn Oil and Gas has announced a spend of Rs 7,924 crore over the next decade to drill an additional 123 exploration and development wells along with ancillary infrastructure at the company's Ravva oil field, called PKGM-1, in Krishna Godavari basin off the Andhra coast. "With the proposed offshore development, enhancement from the currently declining oil and gas production levels will ensure that the production levels remain well within the approved plateau of 50,000 bpd (barrels per day) of crude oil and 2.32 mmscmd (million standard cubic meter per day) of gas as permitted by Andhra Pradesh Pollution Control Board," the company said in an application to the environment ministry.

In 2018–19, the central government extended Cairn Energy's Production Sharing Contract (PSC) for Ravva field by another 10 years, on the condition that it would increase the government's share of profit from petroleum by 10%. However, the company's average daily production from Ravva field dropped by 13% to 3,350 bpd from 3,869 bpd in 2017–18. An integrated contract for drilling development wells at Ravva field is currently underway. On completion, it is expected to enhance production from the field and maximise utilisation of the processing facility and other infrastructures within the already approved capacities. Apart from the main oil producing facility and satellite gas pools of Ravva Block, several small oil and gas discoveries had been made in the Ravva Block at various reservoir levels in different fault blocks.

Policy reforms and incentives offered by the government has seen both public and private explorers intensify their efforts to discover new reserves in their contract areas. As per the DGH data, volumes of oil and gas in-place have risen by 72% and ultimate reserves by 61% between 2008–09 (base year) and 2018–19 in production sharing contract and coal bed methane (PSC+CBM) areas. However, despite numerous incentives offered by the government, such as 100% foreign direct investment (FDI) and tax rebates, few foreign oil companies, barring BP, have invested in India's upstream sector, although quite a few like ExxonMobil, Shell, Adnoc and Aramco, have interest in marketing, refining and petroleum storage segments in India. BP has partnered with Reliance Industries Ltd in gas exploration and production at India's largest KG-D6 gas project. As a result of the geophysical surveys and exploratory drillings several conducted in unexplored and poorly explored areas at least 49 oil and 91 natural gas discoveries have been made, according to the DGH. Of these, 39 gas discoveries are in shallow offshore and 46 in deep water offshore. Still, some 52% of India's sedimentary basins remains unapprised.

Geological Structure of Sedimentary Basins

Assam Shelf and Assam-Arakan Fold Belt (AAFB)

The Assam-Arakan basin is situated in the north-eastern part of India, covering an area of 1,16,000 sq km. Major tectonic elements of the basin are Assam Shelf; Naga Schuppen Belt and Assam-Arakan Fold Belt. The Assam Shelf basin is comparatively more widely explored than Assam-Arakan Fold Belt which is part of a complex geology accentuated by difficult logistics. The basin is categorised as Category-I. Oil exploration in India commenced with the discovery of the Digboi oil field in Upper Assam more than 100 years ago, when, based on surface oil visibility, a well was drilled on an exposed anticline, associated with the Naga thrust. Other significant milestones in oil exploration in Upper Assam were the discoveries of the Nahorkatiya, Moran and Rudrasagar oil fields In 1953, 1956 and 1960, respectively. Subsequently, more than 100 oil and gas fields, including Jorajan, Kumchai, Hapjan, Shalmari, Lakwa, Lakhmani, Geleki, Amguri, Charali, Borholla, Khoraghat, Baghjan and Dirok were discovered.

The oil fields, discovered so far, are situated mainly in the areas south and southeast of the Brahmaputra river and a few in the thrust belts, associated with Naga-Patkai hills. However, the area to the north of the Brahmaputra river up to the Eastern Himalayan foothills has remained poorly explored. In the Naga Schuppen zone, apart from the Digboi oil field, two more major oil fields, namely, the Kharsang field, having oil accumulations in Upper Miocene to Pliocene reservoirs and the Champang field, having oil accumulations in fractured granitic basement rock of Precambrian age, have been discovered.

The prognosticated hydrocarbon resources (unrisked in-place) stand at 6,001 mmtoe, out of which 1,868 mmtoe has been established. Assam-Arakan Fold Belt basin covers the southern districts of Assam and the states of Tripura, Mizoram, Manipur and Nagaland and its area is 80,825 sq km. The unrisked hydrocarbon in-place stands at 1,633 mmtoe, out of which 178 mmtoe has been developed.

Cambay Basin

The Cambay is an intra-cratonic basin covering an area of about 53,500 sq km. Grouped under Category I basins it encompasses a narrow, elongated rift graben, extending from Surat in the south to Sanchor in the north. The prognosticated hydrocarbon resources of the basin are 2,586 mmtoe which are mostly established, with only 786 mmtoe remaining undiscovered.

In the north, the basin narrows, but tectonically it continues further north and merges beyond Sanchor into the Barmer basin of Rajasthan. On the southern side, it extends into shallow water and merges with the Mumbai Offshore basin in the Arabian Sea. Presence of oil in the basin was first seen in September 1958 from an exploratory well at Lunej in Anand district of Gujarat. This discovery dispelled the myth that there is no viable oil source in India, apart from some small ones in Assam.

The evolution of Cambay basin from petroleum point of view is well understood and hydrocarbon accumulations are known in all sequences ranging from Paleocene to Miocene. Major accumulations are known in Middle Eocene structural traps over block uplifts and block-edge folds. There are several petroleum systems in this basin; the most important one being the Cambay-Hazad Petroleum System.

The key fields in the Cambay basin are Ankleshwar, Kalol, Sobhasan and Gandhar, which have been actively explored since 1960, and production started in 1961 by ONGC. It is predominantly an oil-bearing area. The basin has an extensive transportation and processing network which has allowed ONGC to bring new fields onstream quickly. More than 2,318 exploratory wells have been drilled here. Out of 244 prospects drilled, 97 are oil and gas bearing.

Mumbai Offshore Basin

The Mumbai Offshore basin is the most prolific of all the hydrocarbon bearing provinces in India. Mumbai High field is approximately 160 km west of the coast and was discovered in 1974 by a joint team of Russia and India from seismic exploration vessel, 'Academic Arkhangelsky', while mapping the Gulf of Cambay between 1964 and 1967. The discovery of Bombay (Mumbai as earlier named) High with subsequent other discoveries of oil and gas fields in western offshore changed the oil scenario of India. It is spread over the area of 2,12,000 sq km.

Different oil and gas reservoirs (both carbonate and clastic) namely, L-I; L-II; L-III; L-IV; L-V; basal clastic and fractured basement from top to bottom, are encountered. L-II and L-III are primarily the limestone oil reservoirs of Miocene age, further classified into several layers.

Bounded by Diu and Narmada Faults and Deccan Trap outcrops to its north and east, the peri-cratonic Mumbai Offshore basin extends towards west parallel to the western continental margin of India up to the Western Margin Basement Arch. NE-SW trending Vengurla Arch separates the basin from the Kerala-Konkan basin to its south.

Based on structural elements and the nature of sediment fills, having influenced the hydrocarbon generation and entrapment patterns in different sectors, the basin is subdivided into a number of blocks, including Tapti-Daman block, Diu block, Heera-Panna-Bassein block, Mumbai High Deep Continental Shelf block, Shelf Margin block and the Ratnagiri block. Continued and sustained exploratory and development efforts in Mumbai Offshore basin since last four decades have shown remarkable results and led to conversion of nearly 50% of the prognosticated resource of 9,646 mmtoe into discovered volume of hydrocarbons.

Cauvery Basin

The Cauvery basin extends along the east coast of India, covering an area of 1.5 lakh sq km, including 25,000 sq km on land and 30,000 sq km shallow offshore. In addition, it spawns 95,000 sq km of deep-water offshore area.

Most of the offshore and on land basinal area is covered by gravity, magnetic and common depth point (CDP) seismic surveys. Geological map for the outcrop terrain shows the exposed formations. It is a peri-cratonic rift basin and comes under Category I (basins with established commercial production). It has been under hydrocarbon exploration since late 1950s. Application of CDP seismic in 1984 considerably increased the pace of exploration resulting in the discovery of several small oil and gas fields. The first deep well for exploration was drilled in 1964. The basin is endowed with 5 to 6 kms of sediments ranging in age from late Jurassic to recent (mainly thick shale, sandstone and minor limestone). The prognosticated resources of the basin are 700 mmt of oil and oil equivalent (430 mmt: on land and 270 mmt: offshore).

The Cauvery basin evolved due to rifting between India and Sri Lanka during the break-up of Eastern Gondwana land during late Jurassic-early Cretaceous and subsequent drifting (late Aptian) of Indian plate from Gondwana land along NE-SW oriented Eastern Ghat trend. The rifting has created several horsts and grabens. The present-day horst and graben picture of Mesozoic-Cenozoic stratigraphic column have been related to two principal tectonic episodes namely, extension stage during late Jurassic-early Cretaceous and thermal subsidence stage during late Cretaceous to Cenozoic. The basin has been divided into sub-basinal areas, called Ariyalur-Pondicherry, Tranquebar, Nagapattinam, Tanjore and Ramnad-Palk Bay separated by Kumbakonam-Madanam, Pattukottai-Mannargudi and Mandapam-Delft ridges.

Discovery from syn-rift sequence gave a major impetus to syn-rift play and chance of discovering large fields in the Cauvery basin. In Cauvery offshore, there is no much breakthrough except in the established PY and PH fields. Recent discoveries reported in Cauvery shallow water, deep waters and from Sri Lanka/Gulf of Mannar basins have rekindled the exploration interest in the Cauvery Offshore. Discovery by RIL (Dhirubhai-35) has opened a new corridor for exploration in Cauvery deep water. The Cauvery basin still has nearly 85% of total in-place resource in the undiscovered category.

Rajasthan Basin

Rajasthan basin forms the eastern flank of Indus geosyncline and comprises the sedimentary tract to the west and northwest of Aravallis up to Indo-Pakistan border. This peri-cratonic basin also forms a part of the great Thar

Desert. It is spread over 1,26,000 sq km on land between Aravalli mountains in the east and Pakistan in the west. It is divided into three sub-basins—Jaisalmer sub-basin on the north western slope of the Jaisalmer-Mari basement arch (45,000 sq km); Bikaner-Nagaur sub-basin on the northeast flank of the arch (70,000 sq km) and Barmer-Sanchor sub-basin south of the arch and northern extension of Cambay basin (11,000 sq km). The Pokhran High separates the Bikaner-Nagaur sub-basin from Jaisalmer sub-basin. Devikot-Nachna uplift separates Jaisalmer sub-basin from Barmer-Sanchor sub-basin. A string of discoveries of oil and gas has enhanced the perception of hydrocarbon potential of this basin. Available evidence indicates that the Cambrian sediments have generated both oil and gas. Oil is discovered in Cambrain dolomites in the well Karampur-1. Heavy oil is present in multiple zones within Cambrian sediments (Bilara Limestone and Jodhpur Sandstone) in Baghewala, Tavriwali and Kalrewara structures. Presence of light oil has been reported in an exploratory well drilled in an exploration block RJ-ON-90/5.

Barmer sub-basin comprises the sedimentary sequence ranging in age from Mesozoic to Cenozoic. High quality reservoirs are encountered in the Upper Cretaceous-Paleocene, syn-rift deposits. Number of oil and gas discoveries like Saraswati, Rageshwari, Kameshwari, Mangala, Aishwarya, Shakti, Bhagyam are some of the significant fields in Barmer sub-basin. Rajasthan basin has unrisked total petroleum in-place of 4,126 mmtoe, of which nearly 77% is undiscovered. As per expert's review, the basin has potential in Permo-Triassic and Jurassic plays in Jaisalmer part and Cretaceous Ghaggar-Hakra plays in Barmer area.

Krishna-Godavari (KG) Basin

The Krishna-Godavari basin is located in the east coast spreading over an area of 230,000 sq km and constitutes sedimentary sequences ranging in age from early Permian through Cenozoic. The basin has 31,456 sq km lying on land, 25,649 sq km in shallow water up to 400 m isobaths and 172,895 sq km in deep water. The unrisked total petroleum in-place of the basin is 9,555 mmtoe, out of which 7,578 mmtoe (79% of total petroleum in-place) undiscovered and this is the largest undiscovered potential among all sedimentary basins in India.

In KG deep waters mainly slope channel levee complex, debris flows, low stand wedge and basin floor fan complexes remain major targets. In shallow water growth fault related structures, channel fills combination traps, upper slope fans remain as attractive plays particularly in the delta-slope transition. In on land, the deeper syn-rift plays remain as major plays. As per expert's review, the basin has excellent subsurface database and exploration should focus on syn-rift and Eocene plays.

Extensive deltaic plain formed by two large east coast rivers, Krishna and Godavari in the state of Andhra Pradesh and the 16 adjoining areas of Bay of Bengal in which these rivers discharge their water is known as the Krishna Godavari basin. This is a proven petroliferous basin of continental margin located on the east coast of India. The on land part covers an area of 15,000 sq km and the offshore part covers an area of 25,000 sq km up to 1,000 m isobath. The basin contains about 5 km thick sediments with several cycles of deposition, ranging in Age from late Carboniferous to Pleistocene. The unrisked total petroleum in-place of the basin is 9,555 mmtoe, out of which 7,578 mmtoe (79% of total petroleum in-place) undiscovered and this is the largest undiscovered potential among all sedimentary basins in India.

The prospective area for oil and gas exploration in on land covers three coastal districts of East Godavari, West Godavari and Krishna and in offshore till 85 degrees east ridge. Efforts by both NOC's and private oil companies have unlocked huge hydrocarbon reserves. The major plays established in KG basin are Mandapeta (Permo-Triassic), Syn-Rift Gollapalli/Nandigama/Kanukollu (late Jurassic to lower Cretaceous), Raghavapuram (early-late Cretaceous), Pasarlapudi/Vadaparru (late Palaeocene to Eocene), Matsyapuri/Ravva (Oligocene to Miocene) and Godavari (Pliocene).

More than 225 prospects have been probed by drilling of more than 557 exploratory wells. Hydrocarbon accumulations have been proven in 75 of these prospects (22 oil and 53 gas). Notable oil discoveries are Kaikalur, Vadali, Mori, Bantumilli, Lingala, Suryaraopeta, Gopavaram, Kesanapalli and Kesanapalli West. The gas discoveries are Adavipalem, Elamanchili, Enugupalli, Narsapur, Razole, Tatipaka-Kadali, Pasarlapudi, Mandapeta, Chintalapalli, Nandigama, Endamuru, Penumadam, Ponnamanda, Achanta, Mullikipalle, Magatapalli, Gokarnapuram, Kesavadasapalem, Lakshamaneshwaram, Rangapuram and Sirikattapalli.

In onshore, so far 141 prospects have been probed by 375 exploratory wells by ONGC, out of which 11 oil and gas pools and 31 gas pools have been discovered and most of them are on production. In offshore, so far more than 84 prospects have been probed by 182 exploratory wells. Hydrocarbon accumulations have been proved in 33 of these prospects, 11 oil and gas and 22 gas prospects. About 19 discoveries have been made by Pvt/JV companies so far in NELP blocks (15 discoveries by RIL in blocks KG-DWN-98/3 and KG-OSN-2001/2, 3 discoveries by Cairn Energy in block KG-DWN-98/2 within Mio-Pliocene, 3 discoveries by ONGC in the block KG-DWN-98/2 within Plio-Pleistocene sandstone of Godavari formation and 1 discovery by GSPC in block KG-OSN-2001/3 within lower Cretaceous.

The Krishna Godavari basin is an established hydrocarbon province with a resource base of 1,130 mmt, of which, 555 mmt are assessed for the offshore region (up to 200 m isobath). Several oil and gas fields are located both in on land and offshore parts of the basin. The entrapments are to be expected from Permo-Triassic to Pliocene sediments. The tertiary hydrocarbon entrapments are so far observed only in offshore part of the basin while Paleogene to Permo-Triassic entrapments are discovered in East Godavari and West Godavari sub-basins in the on land part.

Both biogenic and thermogenic petroleum systems are present in the basin, and it has the distinction of reporting maximum number of discoveries in the last decade. As such, this basin has shown high potential of hydrocarbon, particularly in deep waters off the Godavari river mouth, essentially from Mio-Pliocene and Pleistocene formations. Similarly, recent discoveries of gas from Machilipatnam Bay area from Eocene-Pliocene formations from shallow water segment endorses for enhanced exploration. Based on trend of discoveries, there are good chances of discovering large fields, especially from deep water segment.

A number of gas fields are producing from Paleocene reservoirs, particularly in East Godavari sub-basin. Tatipaka, Pasarlapudi, Kadali and Manepalli fields are located on land, while, GS-8 is in the offshore part of the basin. The hydrocarbon generation centres in Paleocene indicate fair to rich organic content on the basinal side. The indications of gas and its pressure in this sequence justify good potential for Paleocene in the basin. Ten pools of hydrocarbon have already been discovered in this age group.

Bengal Basin

In December 2020, ONGC opened the eighth sedimentary basin, called Bengal basin, spread over 89,000 sq km, of which 57,000 sq km lies on land, and 32,000 sq km offshore up to 200 m bathymetry. It falls in the eastern Indian state of West Bengal and in the south extends into offshore region of the Bay of Bengal. The prognosticated hydrocarbon resources in Bengal basin have been estimated at 190 mt of oil and gas equivalents. The Bengal basin has now been elevated to Category I after it has gone on stream. The first oil shipment produced from Ashoknagar-I well at Bengal basin was delivered to Indian Oil Corporation's Haldia Oil Refinery.

The Bengal basin is extensively covered by geophysical surveys. Aeromagnetic and gravity surveys were carried out during the early stages of exploration (1963–1970). Many parts of the basin were extensively covered by 24- and 48-fold surveys from 1975 to 1988. 3D seismic data (4,217 LKM, equivalent to 210 SKM) was acquired in 1989–91 for confirming the presence and mapping the extension of reefs and other features/prospects which were inferred to occur in Amtala, Golf Green and Ichapur areas. Offshore areas were also covered by 24-fold seismic surveys conducted in 1975. This was followed by additional CDP survey in offshore areas and in the Sunderban estuaries during 1979–81. 3D seismic survey in offshore area measures 1,248 LKM (60 SKM).

The Bengal basin drew early interest of exploration teams of Standard Petroleum under Indo- Stanvac Petroleum Project (ISPP) when 10 wells were drilled by them during 1958–1960, and sedimentary sequences of Pliocene to Cretaceous age were encountered in these wells. Most of these wells are reported to have given hydrocarbon shows at various depths during the drilling.

The geological history of the basin began with the rift stage due to the mantle upwelling during the Gondwana period, as sedimentation took place in continental environment in the lakes. The Indian plate was located in the southern hemisphere. The continuing mantle upwelling resulted in the outpouring of Rajmahal basalts during upper Jurassic to lower Cretaceous period and final break of the Indian plate and due to the plate movement, its journey towards northern hemisphere. Thus, Indian eastern sea coast started forming during Cretaceous period and there was a sea transgression over Rajmahal basalts and Ghatal formation was deposited too. Paleocene period is marked by sea regression and sand shale deposition has taken place, which was known as Jalangi formation. During Eocene time, there was sea transgression but detrital influx was meagre and the sea was shallow and clear. Thus, widespread limestone deposition has taken place during this period. At this time, the Indian plate came into contact with Burmese plate in the east and Tibetan plate in the north. The Oligocene period was a regressive phase resulting in the deposition of Burdwan formation. Miocene period has several transgressive and regressive phases and the huge sediment supply was there due to the Himalayan uplift and deposition has taken place in deltaic environment. Finally in recent periods, the sea has regressed and alluvium is deposited in the flood plain environment.[8]

III. EXPLORATION AND PRODUCTION (E&P)

For years, India has relied on oil and gas production from major discoveries in the Krishna-Godavari, Barmer and Assam basins, leaving many of its 26 sedimentary basins virtually unexplored. Latest geophysical surveys have estimated around 42 bt (312.5 billion barrels) of hydrocarbon wealth lying under India's 3.36 million sq km of sedimentary basins. Most of India's crude oil and natural gas production comes from ageing wells that have become less productive over time. The government has reached out to major foreign players with incentives and asked ONGC to increase tie-ups with foreign players for extracting oil and gas from difficult oil and gas fields.

Although oil exploration has been occurring in India since the early 1880s, it gained accelerated momentum only after India gained Independence in 1947. Prior to this, it was believed that India had no significant oil and gas deposits. Kerosene was the main petroleum product, mostly imported from Britain, that was widely used in India for domestic lighting. British officials and Burmah-Shell regulated its supply in India. However, at the time of partition in 1947, India lost most of its major oil blocks to Burmah (now Myanmar) and Pakistan, and was left with only one oil producing field, located in northeast Digboi. Oil and gas exploration was not a significant activity during the British raj.

At the time of Independence, oil and gas industry was wholly controlled by international companies and domestic oil production was just about 2,50,000 tonnes per annum, all of it from the north-eastern state of Assam. International companies had written off India as far as any new discovery of petroleum reserve was concerned. In 1954, the new government of independent India announced its Industrial Policy that made petroleum exploration and production (E&P) one of its core concerns, and set up the Geological Survey of India to carry out extensive reconnaissance surveys and mappings to locate structures for exploration of oil and gas.

Around the same time, India had also set up other government-owned national oil companies (NOCs)—Oil India Ltd (OIL) and India Oil Corporation Ltd (IOC). OIL is an upstream company, which makes new oil discoveries, while IOC is a refining and marketing firm, which runs oil refineries and sells oil products. In the early 1970s, NOC supplied about 70% of the domestic requirement of oil and gas. In 1974, the discovery of oil in significant quantities in Bombay High opened up new avenues of oil exploration in offshore areas.

During the 1970s to mid-1980s, ONGC and OIL had made many exploratory attempts that yielded small to major discoveries of oil and gas in number of structures in Bassein, Tapti, Krishna-Godavari and Cauvery basins, and Cachar (Assam), Nagaland and Tripura. However, by the end of 1980, the supply reached at diminishing stage due to decline in production and steady increase in consumption of petroleum products. The domestic oil companies were able to meet only 35% of domestic requirement in India. This was further compounded by resource crunch in the beginning of the early 1990s. The Indian government had no money to give NOCs for the development of some of the newly discovered fields like Gandhar, Heera (Phase-II and III), Neelam, Ravva, Panna, Mukta, Tapti, Lakwa (Phase-II), Geleki and Bombay High Final Development schemes. Though, some of these fields were developed by ONGC (Gandhar, Neelam, Bombay High, Lakwa, Heera, Geleki, etc.), for others, there was no money available for indigenously developing fields.

Different factors such as the administered oil price, non-availability of appropriate technology, logistics were also a main problem. The situation forced the government to go in for petroleum sector reforms to attract funds and technology from abroad. This necessitated basic changes in the existing policy and regulatory framework and creation of a conducive environment to woo private capital, especially foreign and advanced technology, to modernise exploration and production and refining. The first change was made in the way Exploration and Petroleum Exploration licenses were granted.

Nomination Regime

Until the end of the 1970s, Indian E&P industry was dominated by the two NOCs, to whom licenses were granted on a nomination basis. Explorations those days were mainly confined to onshore and shallow offshore areas. But the rising demand of petroleum products amid depleting supply made it imperative to move away from the existing policy and opened the sector to both local and foreign capital. Initially, 17 offshore and 15 onshore blocks were offered to foreign companies through auction. Three rounds of auctions were conducted through 1980–86, but only a few foreign companies participated in the auctions. In 1990, the government permitted domestic companies also along with foreign entities to participate in the fourth bidding—hailed as the opening of the sector—otherwise reserved for the state-owned companies, to both foreign and Indian private companies, through a mechanism of competitive bidding.

Pre-NELP Era (1991–96)

The real opening up of this sector began only after 1991, when the government, then led by P V Narasimha Rao, dismantled decades-old Soviet-style command-and-control economy and the license raj. The government offered 126 blocks in five rounds of bidding between 1994 and 1996. Following liberalisation of the economy many foreign companies participated in auctions and were awarded contracts. Notable among them were Shell, Enron, Amoco and Occidental. The government signed 28 contracts for 29 discovered fields (1 PSC for Panna Mukta), 28 exploration blocks under Pre-NELP exploration regime. The liberalisation also spurred petroleum demand sharply, making it imperative for the government to increase production. To achieve this objective, India needed sufficient capital, geological knowhow, modern exploration and production technology and management practices, which major international oil companies possessed. Hence, the government came up with a New Exploration Licensing Policy (NELP) to lure international companies.

NELP Era (1997–2015)

The NELP policy was approved in 1997 and became effective from 1999. It was a historic move that ended state dominance in the oil and gas industry and created a competitive environment leading to liberalisation of the sector. It aimed at providing level playing field for all the investors, both private and public, in exploration and production activities for hydrocarbon resources, with the DGH acting as a nodal agency. At the time of launch, a mere 11% of the Indian sedimentary basin area of 3.36 million sq km was under exploration, which has increased considerably after the launch. Main features of the NELP are:

i)   Permission for 100% FDI.

ii)   No mandatory state participation through ONGC/OIL or any other body affiliated to the government.

iii)   Blocks to be awarded through open international competitive bidding.

iv)   ONGC and OIL to compete for petroleum exploration licenses on a competitive basis, rather than nomination basis.

v)   ONGC and OIL to get the same fiscal and contract terms as private companies.

vi)   Freedom to contractors for marketing of crude oil and gas in the domestic market.

vii)   Royalty at a rate of 12.5% on land areas and 10% for offshore areas.

viii) Royalty to be charged at half the prevailing rate for deep water areas beyond 400 m bathymetry for the first seven years after commencement of commercial production.

ix)   Cess to be exempted for production from blocks offered under NELP.

x)   Companies to be exempted from payments of import duty on the import of goods for petroleum operations.

xi)   No signature, discovery or production bonuses.

xii)   A Model Production Sharing Contract (MPSC), reviewable for every NELP round.

xiii) In 2021, the DGH further simplified the E&P process by reducing the number of statutory approvals for new exploration and production licenses. Earlier, investors needed 37 clearances at various levels for oil and gas blocks awarded under different rounds of the NELP and pre-NELP auctions. Now the number of clearances required has been reduced to 18, and in the case of extension of exploration phase or production sharing contract, abandonment of plan, transfer of participating interest in favour of a new entity, year-end statement and audited annual accounts presentation, just one approval by the DGH. The pre-NELP blocks include Panna/Mukta and Tapti oil and gas fields in the western offshore and Ravva field in the KG basin. The government undertook nine rounds of NELP that resulted in biggest oil and gas funds in the country outside nomination blocks with PSU oil explorers. The NELP blocks includes Reliance Industries' KG D6 block and several others held by ONGC and others.

The primary objective of NELP was to attract sufficient risk capital from local and foreign companies, latest technologies, new geological concepts and best management practices to explore oil and gas resources to meet the rising demand of the growing economy. Before the launch of NELP, a mere 11% of the Indian sedimentary basins had been explored and 29 fields discovered in 28 exploration blocks. After implementation of the NELP there was a dramatic surge in E&P activity, with the government awarding 254 blocks including 111 onshore, 62 shallow offshore and 81 deep water offshore. As a result, several unexplored and poorly explored areas, particularly in offshore and deep-water areas, had been appraised through geophysical surveys and exploratory drilling. According to the Ministry of Petroleum and Natural Gas, the NELP has not only accelerated the quest for hydrocarbon exploration, but also brought the state-of-the-art technology and efficiency in operations/management to India's oil industry.

During nine auction rounds held under the NELP, the number of bidding companies rose to 117, including 11 PSUs (public sector undertakings) and 58 private and 48 foreign firms as operators or non-operators or consortium partners. Major Indian private companies included RIL, Jubilant and Essar. Major foreign companies included British Gas, British Petroleum, Cairn Energy, ENI, Santos and BHP Billiton. The PSUs included Indian Oil Corporation (IOC), Gas Authority of India Ltd (GAIL), Bharat Petroleum Corporation Ltd (BPCL), Bharat Petro Resources Ltd (a subsidiary of BPCL), Prize Petroleum Company Limited (a subsidiary of Hindustan Petroleum Company Ltd). In addition to central PSUs, state PSUs like Gujarat State Petroleum Company (GSPC) participated in various NELP bidding rounds and were awarded exploration blocks. At the end of the NELP era in 2015, the government had awarded contracts for 254 exploration blocks, of which 166 are active, while 88 have been relinquished. Compare this with the number of companies working in E&P sector before the launch of the NELP—35, including 5 PSUs, 15 private and another 15 foreign.

However, despite the success, NELP had certain drawbacks, for example, investors needed different set of licence for each hydrocarbon contracts; that is, if an oil company carrying out E&P in a block found another hydrocarbon asset in that block or its vicinity, it required a separate set of licence to develop that asset. Secondly, fiscal terms differed from one acreage contract to another. The fragmented policy framework led to inefficiencies in exploiting natural resources. Thirdly, profit sharing issues arising from the production sharing contracts (PSCs) became the frequent source of disputes between private upstream operators and the governmental authorities under NELP. The PSC terms required operators to furnish complete details of every expense incurred by them at every stage in the course of development and production of the block to governmental authorities and seek approval from before starting work. This provision gave the authorities unlimited discretion and became a major source of disputes, and sometimes corruption. Many projects had been delayed for months and years due to disagreements between the authorities and contractors over the correctness of cost of items quoted by the latter.

There were also problems about the pricing of gas and royalties. Prices of gas, produced from domestic fields, are fixed by the government at every six months—a system which had led to multiple litigations. Producers found the prices fixed by the government unremunerative that undermined their operational efficiencies and investment strategies. As for royalties, the NELP did not distinguish between the shallow water fields, where costs and risks are lower compared to those in deep/ultra deep-water fields, where risks and costs are much higher. These drawbacks in the NELP failed to attract international oil majors like ExxonMobil, Chevron Corp and Shell to invest in large in India's E&P sector. The result was stagnating oil output, especially from ageing fields.

Hydrocarbon Exploration and Licensing Policy (HELP)

Concerned over the declining oil output amid spiralling demand and rising oil prices internationally, the government moved in 2016 to simplify licensing terms and offer more incentives to lure major oil companies, especially multinationals, to invest in E&P activities in India. A new Hydrocarbon Exploration and Licensing Policy, or HELP, thus, followed. Salient features of the new policy were:

1. A uniform license for exploration and production for all forms of hydrocarbon.
2. An Open Acreage Policy.
3. An easy to administer revenue sharing model.
4. Freedom to concessionaires to fix the price of oil and gas produced by them in their blocks and market them anywhere they choose.

The uniform licence was designed to enable the contractors to explore conventional as well as unconventional oil and gas resources including CBM, shale gas/oil, tight gas and gas hydrates with a single license. The concept of Open Acreage Policy was designed to enable E&P companies to choose any block/blocks from the designated areas for exploration. The NELP fiscal system of production sharing which was based on Investment Multiples and Cost Recovery/Production Linked Payment system was replaced by an easy to administer revenue sharing model. The NELP contracts were based on the concept of profit sharing where profits were shared between government and the contractor after the recovery of cost, which required the government to scrutinise cost details of the private participants and which led to delays and disputes in several cases. Under the new regime, the government is not concerned with the cost incurred by the contractor and just receives a share of the gross revenue from the sale of oil, gas and other products, as stipulated in the revenue sharing contract (RSC). This reduces the complexity of handling the contract.

Also, under the new system, a graded system of royalty rate had been introduced, in which royalty rates decreases from shallow water to deep water and ultra deep water. NELP did not distinguish between shallow water blocks, where the cost of exploration and risks are lower, and deep-water blocks, where the cost and risks are higher. However, the royalty rate for on land areas for both oil and gas have been kept unchanged to protect the revenues of the states from where oil and gas are produced. Similarly, no cess and import duty are imposed on blocks awarded under the new policy.

In order to facilitate the prospective bidders to know some technical details about Indian basins, the government created a National Data Repository (NDR) which stores integrated E&P data of all sedimentary basins. It can be bought for a low price, as it holds 160 terabyte information, which can help a bidder (Indian or foreign) to carve out a block to bid for exploration. NDR is regularly updated with geo-scientific data through the National Seismic Programme, an in-depth study of the 26 sedimentary basins. It is the cornerstone of the HELP. Companies, after studying geological data, can submit EOIs (expressions of interest) for hydrocarbon blocks of their choice.

HELP is implemented through innovative OALP, where continuous bidding rounds are conducted on the investor's selected blocks. The maiden bidding round under OALP received an overwhelming response with 55 blocks getting awarded covering an area of 60,000 sq km. As a further impetus to the sector the policy received a major overhaul in February 2019, when the government decided to forego the revenue share commitment from the operators at the time of bidding in case of Category II and Category III basins in India.

NELP regime saw Indian E&P sector opening to private and foreign players, however due to certain contractual bottlenecks, investor sentiments were impacted, with many global oil and gas majors deciding to forego the opportunities present beneath the Indian sub-surface. Taking cognizance of the issues arising out of the production sharing contracts, government made a paradigm shift towards revenue sharing contracts by introducing the DSF Policy and HELP. With recent impetus to the sector through policy interventions and facilitation of projects, Indian oil and gas industry is seeing a renewed global interest. The participation of global companies in recent DSF and OALP bidding rounds is a testimony to this fact.

Open Acreage Licensing Policy (OALP)

HELP is critically supported by Open Acreage Licensing Policy which allows prospective bidders to carve out a block of their own choice to bid for them. Launching the OALP in June 2017, Minister of Petroleum and Natural Gas Dharmendra Pradhan said that the scheme would open up 2.8 million sq km of sedimentary areas for E&P. Under this the upstream companies have discretion to select areas they consider attractive for exploration and submit their EoI to the Directorate General of Hydrocarbons (DGH). The DGH then collects EoIs submitted by other firms for that block and holds auctions with other blocks. A five-point advantage is given to the firm, on whose EoI the concerned block goes under hammer, but the main yardstick is the percentage of output the company offers to the government. Currently, auctions are held in June and December, but the DGH stated that the frequency could be increased as increasing number of companies come in to carve out their fields of choice for exploration and submit their EoIs. Tied to this is the NDR's centralised database of geological and hydrocarbon information that is available to all potential investors to enable them to make informed decisions about the field of their choice.

Under OALP, companies are welcome to submit their EoIs throughout the year and not during a time specified by the government. Also, it gives freedom to ask for auction of any block. Earlier, explorers were invited to participate in the auction of only those blocks offered by the government, which were often large swathes of land or sea in which only a small parcel had hydrocarbon reserve. The government hopes that these packages would entice oil companies to invest in India's hydrocarbon E&P activities. And, true to the government's expectations, the very first round of the auction under the OALP attracted investment commitments worth Rs 60,000 crore from nine companies—ONGC, OIL, GAIL India, IOCL, BPRL, Vedanta, Selan, HOEC and Sun Petro—in 55 blocks. The DGH had received 110 e-bids, of which 92 were for on land blocks and 18 for offshore, and the area covered was 60,000 sq km. OALP-II, which offered 14 blocks over an area of 29,333 sq km, attracted investment commitments of Rs 40,000, while OALP-III, which ran concurrently with OALP-II, generated an investment of US\$ 700 million. OALP-III offered 23 blocks in 12 sedimentary basins, covering an area of 31,000 sq km, and five of these were coal bed methane (CBM) blocks.

During the first round of the OALP auction, 49 EoIs had been submitted for the blocks falling under Category I basins, but none for Category II and Category III basins. The DGH itself carved out nine blocks from Category II and III basins and put them up for bidding in the second and third rounds of auction. Still there was a timid response, presumably due to insufficient geological data available about the two basins. In contrast, there was abundant data on the table about the seven Category I basins, which were known to hold 35,511 mtoe of the total 41,872 mtoe of proven commercial reserves across all of the 26 basins. The blocks on offer in the three rounds were spread across the states of Rajasthan, Gujarat, Tamil Nadu, Andhra Pradesh, Odisha, Assam, West Bengal, Nagaland, Tripura, Maharashtra, Jharkhand and Madhya Pradesh. There were also some blocks from the eastern and western offshores.

Notable among the contenders for E&P rights were Reliance Industries Ltd–British Petroleum (RIL-BP) consortium, ONGC, IOC, OIL, Vedanta and GAIL-SunPetro JV. Of them, the RIL-BP combine bid for only one block, while Vedanta for as many as 32 blocks and ONGC for 20. OIL bid for five blocks and IOC and GAIL-SunPetro for two each. Preliminary estimates by official agencies suggest that the 14 blocks on offer in OALP-II hold 12,609 mt of oil and gas equivalent in-place, while data for OALP-III were under study. ONGC said it was now focusing to carve out blocks in Categories II and III basins for E&P. Category II is made up of five basins and Category III of 14 basins.

The industry has enthusiastically embraced the OALP together with NDR—an initiative, explorers believe, will spur increased private participation in India's hydrocarbon E&P sector. By allowing potential explorers and operators to carve out their own blocks to bid for exploration, instead of them being forced for bidding for blocks chosen by the DGH, the government has made the system more attractive to investors, particularly foreign majors, who save on initial costs and time on collecting geo-scientific data. The UK-based Vedanta Cairn Oil and Gas described OALP as, "A fundamental shift and transformative step in India's E&P history." Sudhir Mathur, acting CEO of Vedanta Cairn Oil and Gas said, "The policy reiterates government's commitment to reduce administrative and regulatory burden, thus enhancing ease of doing business." While speaking with media he further added, "A single license to explore all forms of hydrocarbons, no oil cess, a reduced rates of royalty are just a few of the many enabling provisions which will stimulate investments in the sector."[9]

Since the launch of the OALP in 2018, the government has awarded about 120,000 sq km of sedimentary area for exploration, compared to 90,000 sq km under the NELP which was launched in 1998. However, oilmen insist that there is still an abundance of hydrocarbon resource left in India's vast, underdeveloped and unexplored sedimentary basins.

The DGH hopes that the regulatory modifications and multiple incentives would help attract international oil majors to participate in Indian exploration and production activities with both capital and modern knowhow to tap the virgin resources. According to the DGH, the introduction of the ready-to-use seismic data provided by NDR has proved a draw for big names in the international oil and gas industry like BP, Shell, Total, Saudi Aramco, Adnoc and Roseneft to participate in Indian E&P and upstream and downstream projects. But so far, barring the BP's, their presence in the upstream sector has been quite limited. Salient features of OALP are:

a. Single license for all hydrocarbons.
b. Revenue sharing model.
c. Pricing and marketing freedom.
d. Low royalty rates (varies from 2% in ultra deep offshore to 12.5% on land).
e. Further concession in royalty rates for early production.
f. Exploration rights on all retained area for full contract life.

g. Flexibility for multiple FDP revisions.
h. Simplified dispute resolution mechanism.
i. Management committee role revised to reduced number of approvals.

Up until January 2021, the government had awarded 105 blocks spread over 156,579 sq km (both on land and offshore through five rounds of auction under the OALP, and signed revenue sharing contracts (RSCs) with the licensees. RSC provides a basis for sharing the output of oil and gas fields between the government and operator. Introduced in 2020, it has replaced the traditional production sharing contract (PSC) model in vogue in the pre-NELP and NELP era. Quite a number of blocks awarded under the OALP were those which were chosen by operators themselves. According to the DGH, the government had received investment commitments of US$ 2.37 billion from contracting companies under the OALP. This sum is in addition to US$ 40 billion already invested, as of December 2019, according to DGH. For nearly six months, further auctions for large fields were deferred because of the outbreak of the second wave of Covid-19. It was resumed in August 2021, with an offer of 21 blocks in bid Round-IV of the OALP. These blocks were spread over 11 sedimentary basins and 9 states covering 35,346 sq kms—15 blocks on land, 4 in shallow waters and 2 in ultra deep sea.

Post-Liberalisation Period

The Indian oil and gas industry underwent major changes throughout the 1990s following the introduction of liberalised policies. In 1991, the government opened up the hydrocarbon sector and invited private companies, both foreign and Indian, to participate the E&P and refine and marketing (R&M) activities. Some of the global companies that entered India in the R&M segment were ExxonMobil, British Petroleum and Marathon while the companies in E&P were Shell, Geopetrol, Niko Resources Ltd, Cono Resources Ltd and Cairn Energy Plc. During 1991–1994, the government announced fourth, fifth, sixth, seventh and eighth rounds of exploration bidding.

Starting from the fourth round of exploration bidding, for the first time Indian companies were allowed to bid with or without previous experience in E&P activities. Lack of previous experience forced the Indian companies to seek foreign partner to work as operator and to share costs. In order to increase exploration activities, government formulated NELP in 1997–98 to provide level playing field on which all parties including private and public sector companies would compete in all fiscal and contract matters. NELP, conceived to address the increasing demand supply gap of energy, succeeded in attracting the interest of both domestic private sector players and some foreign players with eight rounds of bidding, with Reliance Industries and Cairn being particularly active in this arena. Since its operationalisation in 1999, NELP has completed eight rounds of bids and 239 production sharing contracts (PSC) have been signed.

In addition, 28 exploration blocks were signed prior to the NELP under various bidding rounds with private Indian and foreign companies and NOCs as licensee. After the implementation of NELP, India's oil and gas E&P scenario changed significantly in terms of both exploration and investment. NELP created a healthy competition between public and private sector companies, which proved beneficial to the Indian economy as well as upstream oil sector.

After Narendra Modi came to power in 2014, he initiated further with his eye fixed on bringing in foreign capital and advanced technology to modernise India's oil industry. He came out with HELP in place of NELP and fortified HELP with OALP and NDR. In 2018, E&P licensees were given freedom to sell their output to any customer (not necessarily to the government) in India and at a price agreed between them (not necessarily at the government-administered price).

Oil Production

Despite a dramatic rise in India's prognosticated in-place petroleum resources (see section, Oil Reserves and Resources) and considerable increases in in-place reserves in recent years, there has not been a corresponding spurt in oil production. Conversely, oil output has consistently declined. Annual oil production averaged 33–34 mtpa (242–249 billion barrels) from 2002 to 2009, which increased to 37.684 mt in 2010–2011 and in 2011–12 reached 38.090 mt on the back of start-up of production from the Barmer basin. Then it started declining, registering 37.862 mt in 2012–13; 37.788 mt in 2013–14; 37.461 mt in 2014–15; 36.950 mt in 2015–16; 36.008 mt in 2016–17; 35.684 mt in 2017–18; 34.203 mt in 2018–19 and 32.173 mt in 2019–20. This was the lowest in 18 years. Most recently, in 2020–21, oil production was further down by 5.2% to 30.5 mt and gas output by 8.1% to 28.7 bcm.

Statistics division of Ministry of Petroleum and Natural Gas attributed the shortfall in production to multiple reasons, most significantly to the natural decline of ageing fields and closure of wells in some producing basins. As a rule of thumb when a field is discovered in a basin, several wells are drilled, depending on the size of reserves, area field and techno-economic factors, to develop it and produce oil. If the field is developed quickly and brought onstream, it usually shows a rapid rise within two to three years; then a plateau within a few years; and lastly a long decline, lasting 30 years or more (for small fields, the duration of decline is sooner than 30 years). However, if the development wells are drilled slowly and build-up is slower, then the plateau lasts longer.

In Cambay basin, production of oil and gas began with the discovery and development of Ankleshwar field in Gujarat. Oil and gas output were ramped up and maintained by the discovery and development of Kalol, Nawagam, North Kadi, Balol-Lanwa-Santhal and Gandhar fields in the years in a quick succession. Since the discovery of Gandhar in 1982, there has been no significant discovery, but the level of oil and gas production was maintained by the discoveries of a large number of smaller fields. But in recent years, the discoveries of small fields have not been enough to maintain peak levels, resulting in declining oil production.

Crude output in Cambay basin built up from 1961 to 1989 and was maintained at a level of about 6 mtpa (44 million barrels) up to 2010. Since then, it has been in a decline phase, falling to 4.6 mtpa (34 million barrels) in 2017. In Cambay basin, gas production commenced in 1971, with production of 0.465 bcm (15.9 bcf [billion cubic feet] per annum) increasing to 3.11 bcm or 110 bcf per annum in 1997 and to 3.80 bcm (134 bcf) per annum in 2005. From that point, output has steadily declined, reaching 1.67 bcm (59 bcf) in 2017.

In Assam, production began with the discovery of Naharkatiya field and was ramped up and maintained by the discovery and development of Rudrasagar, Lakwa-Lakhmani, Geleki and several small fields. But barring Dikom group of fields, there has been no significant oil discovery in the last four decades. This has not been sufficient to sustain production at plateau levels, resulting in a steady decline in oil production. Assam oil production varied between 4.5 mt and 4.7 mt, or 33 million barrels and

34.5 million barrels per annum from 2002 to 2010, except in 2007, when oil production plunged to a low of about 4.3 mt or 31.5 million barrels. In 2011, production peaked to 5 mt, and after that it has started declining. Gas production in Assam basin increased gradually from 2.03 bcm in 2002 to 3.22 bcm per annum in 2017, the only basin showing an increasing trend.

Oil production from Bombay Offshore basin commenced with the discovery of Bombay High field and was maintained by the discovery and development of Bassein, Heera, Panna, Neelam, Mukta, Ratna, South Tapti, Mid Tapti and several small fields until 2010. Decline has kicked in since 2011. Oil production averaged between 17 and 18 mtpa (125–132 million barrels) from 2002 to 2010, and then it declined to 13.62 mtpa (100 million barrels) till 2013. Between 2015 and 2017 it rose again and averaged 15 mtpa. Gas production in the Bombay Offshore basin increased from 21.44 bcm per annum to 23.25 bcm in 2008. Since then, it has generally been in a decline phase, averaging 16.29 bcm per annum till 2016. However, it rose again to 17.70 bcm in 2017.

Production of oil from onshore fields in Cauvery and Krishna-Godavari basins ranged between 0.4 and 0.66 mtpa (3.0–4.8 million barrels) from 2002 to 2017, while offshore fields from those basins produced far more— 4.09 to 4.81 mtpa of oil from 2002 to 2007, and started declining thereafter, with the output averaging 1.93 mtpa until 2017. But gas production, which averaged at 0.83 bcm to 0.97 bcm per annum between 2002 and 2008 in the Eastern offshore, rose dramatically with the start-up of D1/D3 field in the KG-DWN-98/1 block in 2009. Output at D1/D3 began at 9.24 bcm in 2009 and peaked at 21.53 bcm in 2011, before declining due to water ingress and water cut, reaching a low of 4.48 bcm per year in 2017.

Barmer basin commenced oil production at Mangla, Bhagyam and Ashwariya fields in 2010, at an average of 3.7 mt (27 million barrels), while output increased to a maximum of 8.99 mt in 2014, before sliding into the decline phase. In 2017, production dropped to 7.23 mt.

A review of the oil and gas production profiles in almost all the basins clearly shows declining trends. Data sourced from the Ministry of Petroleum and Natural Gas show that there has been a consistent decline in crude oil output between FY 12 and FY 21. While cumulative crude oil production stood at 38.1 mt in FY 12, in FY 21 it went down to 30.5 mt, a decline of about 20%. The FY 21 figure was 5.65% lower than the target, set by the government. The biggest decline has been recorded since FY 19, which is continuing. According to Hong Kong-based CEIC Data, which claims to provide the most expansive and accurate data insights into both developed and developing economies around the world, historically, India's oil production averaged 620.754 barrels per day from 1960 to 2019, with an all-time high of 766.899 barrels per day in 2011 and a record low of 17.194 barrel per day in 1960.[10]

However, IEA projects India's crude oil production may increase marginally by 2024. The growth is expected to primarily come from state-run ONGC's KG-DWN98/2 deep water oil and gas project with output starting in 2020 and reaching 78,000 barrels per day of oil at peak production.

But for now, oil and gas output of Indian companies from overseas assets has also been declining side by side with plunging domestic production. In 2020–21 it was the second year of decline in production after peaking in 2018–19 at 24.7 mmtoe. In 2019–20 the output slipped marginally to 24.5 mmtoe, but in 2020–21 the drop was large—11% to 21.9 mmtoe. The shortfall in output was mainly in hydrocarbon fields in Russia, the UAE, Azerbaijan and South Sudan as these countries had cut production in compliance with the OPEC plus decision. At the same time, India's domestic production had fallen by 7% to 59.2 mmtoe. State-run Indian companies—ONGC, OIL, IOC and Bharat Petroleum—have poured in billions of dollars in overseas oil and gas fields in about 35 counties. But they scarcely bring their share of oil and gas output back home because shipping costs make it economically unviable. Therefore, they sell it where they produce.

Measures to Boost Production

With oil and gas output declining consistently since 2011–12, the worried Indian government is trying every policy measure it can think of to reverse the decline at ageing fields and bring discovered small and marginal and ultra deep offshore fields onstream. But the key to all measures is the modern technology and participation of foreign companies which possess such technology. In order to woo such companies, the government has allowed foreign companies to have a 100% stake in Indian oil and gas projects and carve out hydrocarbon blocks of their choice for E&P licences. The foreign companies can also enjoy all incentives and facilities (see section, Exploration and Production) available to local firms.

The government believes that much of the unexploited oil and gas available in India is in areas characterised by deep water/ultra deep water or high pressure/high temperature. Soon after coming to power in 2014, the Narendra Modi cabinet approved a mechanism for pricing of domestically produced natural gas. Recognising the need for incentivising gas production from deep water, ultra deep water and high pressure-high temperature (HPHT) areas on account of higher costs and higher risks involved in exploitation of gas, in principle approval was also given for a premium on the gas price for the gas to be produced from new discoveries from such areas.

ONGC and other operators have been requesting a higher price for producing gas from such fields. With the economy growing rapidly, demand for petroleum products including gas has been soaring. But with domestic oil and gas production falling, the gap between demand and supply has been widening, exacerbating the country's dependence on imports. The government has, therefore, allowed marketing and pricing freedom to producers to set the price of gas they produce from their new discoveries as well as existing discoveries which are yet to commence production. However, in order to protect user industries from market imperfections, this freedom would be accompanied by a price ceiling based on opportunity cost of imported fuels.

ONGC Seeks Foreign Partners

Another major initiative among various policy drives to ramp up the dwindling oil and gas production is the decision is to promote privatisation in the hydrocarbon sector. In a detailed 'Action Plan' given to ONGC, which holds most of the acreages allotted by the government on nomination basis in the pre-NELP days, has been directed to sell stakes in maturing oil and gas fields such as Panna-Mukta and Ratna and R-Series in western offshore and onshore fields like Gandhar in Gujarat, and forge partnership with global players in KG basin gas fields. According to government officials, there are at least 66 major fields that contribute over 95% of the domestic production where ONGC could bring in technically sound private partners to boost production.

The directive also asks the company to monetise existing infrastructure and hive off drilling and other services into a separate firm to increase production. It has set production targets of 40 mmt (million metric tonnes) of crude oil, and 50 bcm of gas by 2023–24 where ONGC is tasked to contribute 70%.

India's domestic crude oil production has been declining since 2011–12, mainly because ONGC, which contributes about 70% of the domestic output, has been unable to maintain production from existing fields and bring new fields on stream. As a result, ONGC's crude oil output fell to 20.34 mmt in 2019–20 from 23.09 mmt in 2011–12, and natural gas production to 19.423 bcm in 2019–20 from 20.202 bcm in 2011–12.[11] In the new action plan, ONGC has been given a target of 28 mmt of oil and 35 bcm of gas production by 31 March, 2024. To revitalise the company's operational efficiency, the Ministry of Petroleum and Natural Gas has asked it to create separate entities for drilling, well services, logging, work-over services and data processing and concentrate fully on E&P activities. ONGC produces oil and gas from 15 assets—10 onshore and 5 offshore.

ONGC Invites Private Partners to Operate Small Fields

Acting on the government directive, ONGC has grouped 43 small oil and gas fields into 11 contract units and invited bids from private players for partnership in boosting output at these fields. The main characteristics of these fields is that they are already producing oil and gas in small quantities. They are all land-based assets spread across Gujarat, Assam, Tamil Nadu and Andhra Pradesh. The estimated reserve of these fields is 160 mt of oil equivalent (1.7 billion barrels) in place. They were allotted to the state-run ONGC in the nomination regime, which operates them currently. The selected partner would have to be an entity firm with proven technology and ready to pump in capital. It will get a share of revenue from incremental production over and above the baseline output under the business-as-usual scenario. The partners will get a 15-year contract with an option of extending it by five years and have the right to explore for more oil and gas during the contract period. They will also have the incentive to enhance production beyond the committed incremental production. Output from these fields will have complete marketing and pricing freedom, meaning the partners will be free to sell the incremental output at their negotiated price (free from government control) to any buyer, within India.

Discovered Small Field (DSF) Policy

Accelerated exploration is a vitally important and continuing activity to boost hydrocarbon resources for ensuring energy security. But the immediate focus of the Modi government is monetisation of the existing discovered small oil and gas fields. In 2015, the government brought in a new initiative, called DSF Policy, to put onstream small and marginal discoveries made by ONGC and OIL under the nomination regime and relinquished discoveries under the production sharing regime. The declining oil and gas output added urgency to the need for an early utilisation of whatever resources are at hand to satisfy, if partly, the growing energy demand of the burgeoning population. The DSF policy envisages awarding of contract areas under revenue sharing model with an objective to provide faster development of fields and facilitate early production of oil and gas.

In 2018, the DGH had identified at least 149 small and marginal fields, discovered by the ONGC in the pre-NELP era, which have been lying untapped for decades. ONGC had not developed those fields because it was occupied with operating more prolific larger oil fields, and thought that they were not economically viable to be developed due to the fiscal regime in vogue then. The government now insists that they are valuable assets and cannot be left unmonetised indefinitely.

In order to lure private and foreign companies to participate in the country's E&P sector, the DSF policy offers a set of more liberal fiscal terms like no cess applicable on crude oil and gas production, no upfront signature bonus, no carried interest by state-run upstream companies or the state. Operators are given full freedom to determine price of their hydrocarbon produce in the domestic market through a transparent bidding process on arms-length basis. Exploration is allowed during entire contract period (maximum 20 years) with a single licence for conventional and non-conventional hydrocarbons.

The first auction under the DSF policy was held in 2016, offering 67 discovered small fields/discoveries clubbed into 46 contract area for international bidding. Total 30 contracts for 43 discovered small fields/ discoveries were signed in March 2017. It is expected that in-place locked hydrocarbons reserves of 44.7 o+oeg will be monetised over a period of 15 years.

The second round of bidding was held in 2018 with 59 discovered small fields/unmonetised discoveries holding an estimated 189.61 o+oeg in-place on offer. Of these, contracts for 57 discoveries were signed in March 2019 and one discovery in January 2021. The offer had received good response from companies with 145 submitted.[12]

Oil production from the areas awarded in the two rounds of the DSF auction is envisaged to reach 1.3 mt and gas output to 2.9 bcm by 2024. Further, it has been estimated that the indicative gross revenue over economic life of these fields would be approximately Rs 46,400 crore, of which royalty collection is expected to be around Rs 5,000 crore and government revenue share of Rs 9,300 crore.

Following the success of DSF I and DSF II and the assumption that there is still a slew of unexploited discoveries with good amount of hydrocarbon resources, the government launched DSF III in June 2021, offering 32 contract areas comprising 75 discoveries for international competitive bidding. The DSF III fields are spread over nine sedimentary basins covering more than 13,000 sq km with hydrocarbons reserves estimated at around 230 mt in-place.[13]

Production Enhancement Contract (PEC) Mechanism

In another major move to increase domestic production of oil and gas from existing fields, the government has asked ONGC and OIL to sell stakes in their maturing fields like Panna-Mukta and Ratna and R-Series in western offshore and onshore fields like Gandhar in Gujarat, get foreign partners in KG basin gas fields, and hive off drilling and other services into a separate firm to raise production. Fields identified for stake sale to global players include the gas-rich KG-DWN-98/2 block where output is slated to rise sharply by 2023, and the recently brought-into-production Ashoknagar block in West Bengal, Deendayal block in the KG basin and Daman in western offshore for stake sale. In October 2017, the DGH had identified 15 producing fields with a collective reserve of 791.2 mt of crude oil and 333.46 bcm of gas, for sale of its stake to private firms with improving baseline estimates and extraction.

Acting on the Ministry of Petroleum and Natural Gas directive, ONGC has started looking for foreign partners in its efforts to reverse declining output from its mature oil and gas fields through production enhancement contracts (PEC). In October 2020, ONGC invited bids from global firms with technical expertise, financial capability and resources to increase production by improving the recovery from such fields. The offer requires firms to commit investment in capital and operating expenditure for the duration of the contract, to run for 15 years or more. They will have to do reservoir modelling, reserves assessment and execution of a development plan to enhance production by injecting new technology. The ONGC undertakes to pay US$ 10 per barrel for an incremental oil produced and saved over the baseline. Initially, the fields offered are onshore assets located in Assam and Gujarat. Interested firms were asked to submit their EoIs by December 2020. There has been no headway on the project till July 2021 due to the second wave of Covid-19.

This is the second attempt by ONGC to induct partners in its 'mature' or ageing fields. On 28 December, 2018, it had invited PEC bids from three shortlisted companies, including Schlumberger Asia Services, Halliburton Offshore Services Inc and Baker Hughes Singapore, for Geleki field in Assam and Kalol in Gujarat. But only Schlumberger responded for Geleki and no bid was received for Kalol. Schlumberger sought deviations which ONGC turned down. ONGC re-launched the PEC process for Kalol and Geleki with a request for information (RFI) notice on 22 July, 2020. The government has been pushing ONGC to hire international oil service companies to raise output from its mature oil fields as it saw the foreign companies as the answer to declining production from ageing fields.[14]

Foreign Direct Investment Inflows

India allows foreign direct investment (FDI) in almost all segments of the hydrocarbon value chain—upstream, downstream and midstream—through automatic route. FDI allows 100% investment in oil and gas E&P and 49% in refining and other activities.

Areas open for 100% FDI via automatic route (where Reserve Bank of India's approval is not required) include exploration of oil and natural gas fields, infrastructure related to marketing of natural gas and petroleum products, petroleum product pipelines, natural gas pipelines, LNG (liquefied natural gas) regasification infrastructure, market study and formulation and petroleum refining in private sector, subject to the existing sectoral policy and regulatory framework in the oil marketing sector and the government policy on private participation in exploration of oil and the discovered fields of national oil companies.

The FDI limit is 49%, via automatic route, in the case of existing public sector refineries, but this can take place provided disinvestment or dilution of domestic equity does not happen. However, with effect from August 2021, the Department for Promotion of Industry and Internal Trade (DPIIT) has modified this restriction by an executive order allowing 100% FDI via automatic route for oil and gas public sector undertakings (PSUs), if the government has given in-principle approval for strategic disinvestment, such as in the case of Bharat Petroleum Corporation Ltd (BPCL). This modification has permitted to facilitate the sale of government's 52.98% stake in the BPCL. Many foreign entities like London-based Vedanta Resources, Apollo Management and Think Gas, promoted by I Squared Capital, have reportedly submitted EoIs to acquire BPCL. The modification opens the way for privatisation of other PSUs in the oil sector, which the government is expected to implement to bring in resources, the latest technology and best practices to push economic growth on to a higher trajectory.

In order to facilitate a single window clearance for approval of FDI projects, the government has set up a new Foreign Investment Facilitation Portal and issued standard operating procedure (SOP) for processing of applications by concerned ministries in a time-bound manner. The various path breaking reforms introduced by the government have resulted in increased FDI inflows in almost all sectors of the domestic economy. The country received FDI worth US$ 313 billion in five years from 2015 to 2019. FDI inflows in India stood at US$ 45.15 billion in 2014–2015, which increased to US$ 55.56 billion in 2015–16 and US$ 60.22 billion in 2016–17. In 2017–18 it rose to US$ 60.97 billion and in 2018–19 to US$ 62 billion. The country saw its highest ever FDI inflow of US$ 74.39 billion in 2019–20.[15] The DPIIT has not given sector-wise FDI inflow figures as these are total FDI figures for all sectors. But another government-sponsored organisation, Invest India, has given US$ 7 billion as amount of FDI in oil and gas during 2000 and 2019.[16]

IV. SUPPLY AND DEMAND

India's growing energy needs will make it more reliant on fossil fuel imports as its domestic oil and gas production has been stagnant for years despite government efforts to promote petroleum exploration and production and renewable energy. The reliance on overseas oil is expected to rise to 90% by

2030 and 92% by 2040 from 84% in 2022. This will mean that the rising oil demand would double India's oil import bill to about US$ 181 billion by 2030 and nearly treble it to US$ 255 billion by 2040, according to IEA.

India is the third largest energy consumer in the world after China and USA, and its need for energy supply continues to climb as a result of the country's dynamic economic growth, population growth and modernisation. Between 1990 and 2018 its primary energy consumption tripled, reaching an estimated 916 mtoe. Coal continued to supply most of it, 45.1% in 2018–19, followed by lignite at 1.6%, crude oil 33.2% (in terms of refinery other uses), natural gas 7.2% and electricity (including hydro, nuclear and other renewable sources) 12.9%.[17] The country has moved away from traditional biomass and waste over the past several years as the availability of electricity connections spread for the residential and commercial sectors. Although natural gas accounts for 7.2% of the country's energy consumption, the government has targetted to boost its share to 15% by 2030 as part of the country's plan to reduce air pollution and use cleaner-burning fuels. As on 31 March, 2022, total installed electricity capacity was 401 GW, of which 60.9% was supplied by thermal power and the remainder by gas, diesel, nuclear, hydro, solar, wind, biomass and urban and industrial waste.[18]

The outbreak of the coronavirus (Covid-19) in India at the start of 2020 and the ensuing national lockdown from late March through May 2021 adversely impacted industrial and economic activity, mobility and energy use. But by mid-2021 the energy demand had almost bounced back to pre-Covid level on the back of rejuvenated economic activities. Data from the Petroleum Planning and Analysis Cell (PPAC) of the Ministry of Petroleum and Natural Gas indicate that consumption of gasoline and diesel returned to pre-pandemic levels by September 2020 and continued through March 2021.[19] Rising at 4.59% compound annual growth rate (CAGR) since 2008–09, oil consumption reached 251.93 mt in 20217–18. High speed diesel oil constituted 39.3% of total consumption of all types of petroleum products in 2017–18, followed by petrol (12.7%), petroleum coke (12.4%), liquefied petroleum gas (11.3%) and naphtha (6.1%).

In FY 2021–22 India consumed 204.23 mt petroleum products and 63.9 bcm of natural gas, up 5.1% and 5% over the FY 2020–21. India's oil demand is projected to rise 50% to 7.2 million barrels per day in 2030 from 4.8 million per day in 2019 as against a global expansion of 7%. India's natural gas demand is projected to double to 133 billion cubic per day in

2030 from 64 billion cubic per day in 2019. India will make up the biggest share of energy demand growth at 25% over the next two decades, as it overtakes the European Union as the world's third-biggest energy consumer by 2030. "This is underpinned by a rate of GDP growth that adds the equivalent of another Japan to the world economy by 2040," says the International Energy Agency.[20]

The conventional hydrocarbon resources in India are currently estimated at approximately 42 bt of o+oeg, spread over 26 sedimentary basins covering an area of 3.36 million sq km. The total number of fuel retail outlets increased from 18,848 in 2002 to 77,094 in 2021 at a CAGR of 7.7%. This number had increased to 83,027 by June 2022.[21]

India Set to Overtake China in Oil Demand

Presenting a review of India's energy demand and supply, the IEA has projected that India is set to overtake China by mid-2020s as the largest source of global oil demand. Driven by rapid economic growth, oil demand in India has been growing for decades across all sectors and is expected to reach 6 mbpd by 2024 from 1,60,000 bpd in 2008, representing 3.9% growth per annum, well ahead of the global average of 1.2%. Currently, India is the world's third largest oil consumer, after the US and China, and the second largest oil importer, after China, who is now increasing the share of natural gas and renewables in its energy mix to fight climate change.

The IEA's India Energy Outlook 2021, projects the country's primary energy consumption to double to 1.1 bt of oil equivalent as its GDP expands to US$ 8.6 trillion by 2040 from about US$ 3 trillion in 2022. By 2040, India's power system will be bigger than that of the European Union, and the world's third-largest in terms of electricity generation; it will also have 30% more installed renewables capacity than the United States.

The report says that a five-fold increase in per capita car ownership will result in India leading the oil demand growth in the world. Also, it will become the fastest-growing market for natural gas, with demand more than tripling by 2040. Over the last three decades, India accounted for about 10% of world growth in industrial value added (in purchasing power parity [PPP] terms). By 2040, India is set to account for almost 20% of global growth in industrial value added, and account for nearly one-third of global industrial energy demand. Oil demand is seen rising by 74% to 8.7 mbpd by 2040 under the existing policies scenario. The natural gas requirement Is projected to more than triple to 201 bcm and coal demand is seen rising to 772 mt in 2040 from the current 590 mt. The dynamics look quite different for coal, where India's demand for imported coal is likely to remain subdued or reduce over the next decade, as the country gears up to boost domestic production.

Sectoral Demand

In India, oil demand for transport, the largest oil-consuming sector, has almost doubled in the past decade. Road transport is largely fuelled by diesel and gasoline. Up to 85% of India's gasoil demand comes from the road sector, with the country's massive transportation network of inter-state buses and freight trains fuelling much of gas oil demand. Over the past decade, oil use in transport has increased by 91%. The oil ministry's Petroleum Planning and Analysis Cell (PPAC) had forecast FY 2021–2022 gas oil consumption to a total of 83.677 mt, a 16.36% increase from 2020 and a 13.3% increase from its previous forecast for FY 2020–2021.

The buildings sector, including both residential and commercial, accounted for 19% of the total oil demand. In the residential sector, LPG accounts for a dominant share at around four-fifths of demand, mostly used for cooking and kerosene for the remaining one-fifth for heating. Industry is the third-largest oil consuming sector at 12% of the total demand, followed by the booming petrochemical sector at 9%.

However, the outbreak of Covid-19 rendered all forecasts infructuous. India closed the FY 2020–2021 with a 9% decline in overall fuel consumption over the last year. It was primarily due to Covid-19 lockdown-induced slump in economic activities. According to PPAC, total fuel consumption stood at 194.63 mt during the year, down from 214.13 mt a year before. It was the first overall decline recorded in India's fuel consumption. Petrol consumption stood 6.75%, down from 30 mt in 2019–2020 to 28 mt in 2020–2021. Diesel consumption plunged the most from 82.60 mt to 72.72 mt, reflecting a severe slowdown in economic activity. Diesel consumption in 2020–2021 was at a five-year low since 2014–2015. Aviation turbine fuel (ATF or jet fuel) consumption fell to less than half from a year ago.

Another interesting development in India's transport sector is biofuel. With an objective to reach 20% ethanol blend in gasoline and 5% biodiesel blend by 2030, the government introduced a new National Policy on Biofuels in 2018. This includes a new Ethanol Blending Programme that extends the scope of second-generation ethanol procurement to include oversupply of food grains such as maize and fruit/vegetable wastes. Previously, only excessive supply of sugarcane was allowed to be converted into ethanol, which restrained the feedstock availability to meet the blending target. The Indian government foresees that an increase in alternative fuels in the transport sector would help reduce the dependence on crude oil imports and promote low-carbon transition in transport.

Transport sector consumption, which already accounts for more than one-third of India's total oil consumption, is forecast to more than double over the next two decades, according to the IEA. Over half of the growth will come from diesel-based freight transport. An extra 25 million trucks will be travelling on India's roads by 2040 as road freight activity triples, and a total of 300 million vehicles of all types are added to India's fleet between now and then. Transport has been the fastest-growing end-use sector in recent years, and India is set for a huge expansion of transportation infrastructure—from highways, railways and metro lines to airports and ports. Today's policy settings are sufficient to prevent runaway growth in transport energy demand. And some parts of the system shift rapidly to less energy-intensive options, with one example being a strong increase in the use of two-or-three-wheeled vehicles for road transport. Nonetheless, India's oil demand is set to rise by almost 4 mbpd to reach 8.7 mbpd in 2040, the largest increase for any country. However, a much stronger push for electrification, efficiency and fuel switching would limit growth in oil demand to less than 1 mbpd.

Traditionally, diesel has been the largest oil product, consumed in India – almost 35% of the total petroleum consumption in the country. But over the past decade, its consumption growth rate has been slower than that of gasoline: 5% versus 10%. LPG, mostly used for cooking, has become the second-largest oil product consumed in India, but diesel still retains its top position. In 2022 India was the second-largest consumer of LPG, after China, with supplies coming from Saudi Arabia and the United Arab Emirates.

Rising Oil Imports

Speaking at an 'Urja Sangam' (Energy Conclave) in March 2015, Prime Minister Narendra Modi had vowed to bring down India's dependence on oil imports by 10% to 67% by 2022, from 77% in 2013–14. But instead of diminishing, oil imports have continued to climb, reaching 85% of the total supply in 2020. In FY 2019–20, India's crude oil import reached 227 mt against 202.9 mt in 2015–16, when the Prime Minister made the announcement of his target. Oil imports kept on increasing from 202.9 mt to 213.9 mt in 2016–17, 220.4 mt in 2017–18, 226.5 mt in 2018–19, 227 mt in 2019–20 and 198 mt in 2020–21.[22]

The lower import in 2020–21 was primarily due to a dramatic fall in consumption and declining domestic production of oil. According to PPAC, overall petroleum demand fell for the first time in 21 years as the Covid-19 pandemic forced businesses and factories to shut. Consumption plunged to a five-year low of 193.4 mt as demand for petroleum products including diesel, gasoline and jet fuel slid 10.8% from a year earlier, the first such annual contraction since 1999. But it was not going to be a lasting phenomenon. Demand started bouncing back in the second half of 2021. Gasoline demand hit pre-Covid levels and diesel sales were catching up fast. However, jet fuel sales were still subdued due to Covid restrictions of air travel.

According to the data from PPAC, India's demand for oil products rose 7.9% year on year to 4.3 mbpd in July 2021. It was 3% higher than the demand in June, an improvement for the second month in a row since April when the second wave of Covid-19 hit the country.

For the January-July period, demand for oil products rose by 9.3% to 119.4 mt, or 4.5 mbpd, over a year-ago period. Demand for diesel and gasoline rose by 11.9% and 15.6%, respectively, in the seven-month review period, while jet fuel demand was up 3%, and LPG and naphtha demand rose 2.4% and 6.5% respectively. These are signs of strong pickup in an economy, which registered a GDP growth of 20.1% year on year in the April-June 2021 quarter, according to the government data released on 31 August, 2021.

However, domestic oil production has consistently failed to keep pace with the rising consumption. Data released by the Ministry of Petroleum and Natural Gas show that India's crude oil output fell from 36.9 mt in 2015–16 to 36 mt in 2016–17. The trend of negative growth continued in the following years as well as output fell to 35.7 mt in 2017–18 and to 34.2 mt in the fiscal year that ended on 31 March, 2019. The 2020–21 plunge was more severe, as the output fell by 5% to 30.5 mt from 32.17 mt a year before. ONGC which accounts for about 70% of domestic output, produced 20.2 mt oil, over 2% less than the previous year, as a nationwide lockdown that lasted over two months shut some of its fields. The other major producer, OIL, produced 5.4% less, while fields operated by private firms such as Vedanta's Cairn Oil and Gas saw a 12.6% decline in output.

The net result 'f falling domestic oil output amid growing consumption has been an increased dependence on oil imports to meet our needs. In 2015–16, for instance, according to PPAC, India imported 80.6% of its oil, mainly from the Middle East countries. In 2016–17 it rose to 81.7%, in 2017–18 to 82.9% and further to 83.7% in 2018–19. In 2019–20 dependency jumped to 85%, but some of the imported oil was diverted for filling up caverns at strategic petroleum reserves (SPR). In the following fiscal year, 2020–21, Covid-19 disrupted energy use, with India's oil demand falling by 12.8% to 198 mt. This was a forced cutback. Otherwise, the IEA projects India's net dependence on oil imports—taking into account both the import of crude oil and the export of oil products to increase to more than 90% by 2040 as domestic consumption rises much more than production. Natural gas import dependency increased from 20% in 2010 to almost 50% in 2019 and is set to grow further to more than 60% in 2040. The IEA says that an expanding economy, population, urbanisation and industrialisation mean that India will see the largest increase in energy demand of any country over the next two decades.

Import Prices

Due to India's reliance on imports to meet its domestic demand, prices of crude oil and petroleum products in the international markets have a decisive influence on the domestic prices of petroleum products. After holding firm at over US$ 100 per barrel for more than three years, global crude oil prices started nosediving sharply in the second half of 2014. The global price decline had an immediate effect on prices of imported crude oil in India. The average price of Indian crude oil basket came down to US$ 46.17 per barrel in 2015–16 and US$ 47.56 per barrel in 2016–17. But it started warming up in 2017–18 and ended the year with an average basket price of US$ 56.43 per barrel. In 2018–19 it rose further to US$ 69.88 per barrel, before sliding back to US$ 60.47 per barrel in 2019–20.

This was the period when Covid-19 pandemic struck the oil market hammering oil prices to under US$ 20 per barrel in March-April 2020. On 27 March, 2020, Russian benchmark export grade medium sour Urals sold at US$ 18 per barrel and Saudi Arabia was selling its Arab Light in Europe for US$ 16 per barrel, according to *Reuters*. Canada's key Western Canada Select grade was worth US$ 15 per barrel on 16 March. The Organisation of Petroleum Exporting Countries (OPEC), which supplies around 40% of world's oil, saw its daily basket oil price tumbling to US$ 16.87 per barrel on 1 April, its lowest since 2005. Russian domestic oil prices fell by more than 75% from a month ago to ₽ 5,272 (Ruble) (US$ 67.2) per tonne or US$ 9.2 per barrel, according to *Reuters*. India used this decline to buy cheap oil worth Rs 5,000 crore (US$ 670 million) to strengthen its SPRs.

A lower crude oil price for a country like India (the third-largest importer of crude oil) is greatly beneficial, as it helps macroeconomic management. It results in lower inflation, gives comfort to the Reserve Bank of India in cutting interest rates and flexibilities in budget and fiscal management. Economists estimate that a 10% reduction in crude oil prices could reduce consumer price index-based inflation by around 20 bps (basis points) and bring about a 30 bps rise in gross domestic product (GDP) growth. A fall in oil prices by US$ 10 per barrel can help reduce the current account deficit by US$ 9.2 billion. This amounts to nearly 0.43% of the GDP.

Oil price affects the entire economy, especially because of its use in transportation of goods and services. A rise in oil price leads to an increase in prices of all goods and services. It also affects us all directly as petrol and diesel prices rise. As a result, inflation rises. Every US$ 10 per barrel fall in crude oil price helps reduce retail inflation by 0.2% and wholesale price inflation by 0.5%.

With low oil price, India's oil import bill, which normally constitutes around one-third of the total imports, plunged to US$ 62.7 billion in 2020–21 from US$ 101.4 billion in 2019–20. The lower bill was partly due to the reduced volume of imported oil but largely owed to the crash of global oil price. India bought 198 mt in 2020–21 following the fall in consumption in the wake of Covid-19 outbreak against 227 mt in the previous year. Pradhan at that time revealed that India saved Rs 25,000 crore in April 2020 when oil prices had dropped to their lowest level below US$ 20 per barrel. "We could fill up all the cabins by this time with this low oil price of April. India purchased around 9 mt of crude and we put that crude at high sea through some floating vessels and with inland product and crude oil in and around refinery and different terminals, we could store 25 mmt putting together around 38–40 mmt of oil or product we could save capturing the low oil price of April. That saved us around Rs 25,000 crore for the treasury. These are some strategies we could take," he said in an interview to *The Economic Times*.

India's Top Oil Suppliers

With continued strong growth in oil demand against falling domestic production, India has become more reliant on oil imports, which currently hovers around 80–85%. Until 2017 India's domestic oil production remained relatively stable at an average of 8,62,000 bpd, with an annual average growth rate of 0.3% per annum since 2008. But from 2018 onward, domestic output started declining, reaching 30.5 mt or 6,18,422 bpd in 2020, from 32.17 mt or 6,52,336 bpd, a year ago, according to data released by the Ministry of Petroleum and Natural Gas.

Until 2018 the top three suppliers were all from the Middle East—Iraq (9,70,000 bpd [barrel per day], 21%), Saudi Arabia (8,00,000 bpd, 18%) and Iran (5,21,000 bpd, 11%). Iraq has replaced Saudi Arabia as India's top crude oil supplier since 2017. Up to 2017, approximately 62% of India's imported crude oil came from the Middle East, passing through the Strait of Hormuz, while the rest came from Venezuela (8%), Nigeria (7%), the UAE (7%) and other countries.

In 2019, India moved to diversify its crude oil sources, which led to refiners tapping alternative supply sources. This resulted in the Middle East losing its dominance as crude oil supplier to India. In May 2021, India's oil imports from the Middle East fell to 52.7%, the lowest in 25 months since April 2019. To replace Middle Eastern oil, refiners hiked imports from Latin America, the United States and the Mediterranean. Indian refiners bought higher volumes of gasoline-rich US oil. Strong demand for light crude saw Nigeria. Private Indian refiners Reliance Industries and Nayara Energy, boosted their purchases of Canadian heavy oil to a record 2,44,000 bpd, equivalent to about 6% of India's overall imports. In 2020, India imported 8 mt of crude oil from Mexico and 1 mt from Canada, while Kuwait supplied 9.9 mt. However, the Middle East continues to hold its position as a main supplier because of its geographical proximity to India, which means lower shipping charges than if it imports oil from the US or Latin America or Africa.

Lower purchases of oil from the Middle East have dragged the share of OPEC in India's oil imports to a record low in at least two decades. Data obtained from industry and trade sources by the *Reuters* news agency in May 2021 showed that total crude imports by India from OPEC member-counties fell to 3.97 mbpd in FY 2021, down 11.8% from a year before. India bought more US and Canadian oil at the expense of Africa and the Middle East member countries of the OPEC. India's refiners are diversifying purchases to boost margins, having upgraded plants to process cheaper, tougher crude grades.

In 2021, the United States emerged as the fifth biggest supplier to India, up two places from 2019–20. Iraq remained India's top oil supplier followed by Saudi Arabia and the United Arab Emirates, while Nigeria replaced Venezuela as the fourth biggest supplier.

Issues with OPEC Contracts

Indian firms have been buying almost two-thirds of their crude oil on term or fixed annual contracts. The term contracts provide assured supplies of the contracted quantity but the pricing and other contract terms favour the supplier. The buyer has to indicate at least six weeks in advance of their intention to lift the quantity out of the contracted amount in any month and has to pay an average official price announced by the producer. While the buyer has an obligation to lift all of the contracted quantity, the producer has the option to reduce supplies if the OPEC decides to cut production to boost prices.

India needs pricing flexibility as well as the certainty of supply even during the time OPEC cuts production or reduces supplies for any other reason. Therefore, Indian refiners turn to spot market which provides both choice of flexibility and time of supply and advantage of fall, if any, of oil prices. The spot market operates like a stock market where shares can be bought or sold on a day and time when share prices are low or rise. The government has asked state-run refineries to make a joint strategy for buying their crude oil in coordination with private refiners such as Reliance Industries and Nayara Energy.

Oil Products Imports and Exports

Despite being the world's second biggest importer of crude oil, India is a net exporter of refined oil products, thanks to its large refining capacity. India produces significantly more diesel and gasoline than it needs for domestic consumption. In FY 2020–21, although badly affected by one of the strictest lockdowns due the Covid-19 pandemic, India could manage to export 42 mt of petroleum products worth Rs 2.9 billion, down from 66 mt worth Rs 32.6 billion in 2019–20. The country is the fourth largest refiner in the world and second largest refiner in Asia after China. With a refining capacity of 249 mtpa, it is emerging as a major refinery hub and plans to increase refining capacity to 400 mt by 2025. Crude oil processed during FY 2019–20 was 254.39 mt, down 1.1% from 257.20 mt in 2018–19 due to Covid-19, which struck India in the fourth quarter of FY 2019–20. Most of the exported oil products were road transport fuels, 43% diesel and 23% gasoline. The top five countries that imported India's petroleum products were the United Arab Emirates, Singapore, the Netherlands, China and Turkey.

The Indian Petroleum refining sector has come a long way since the first refinery was set up at Digboi in 1901. Till 1947, Digboi was the only refinery with a capacity of 0.50 mtpa. The present Mumbai Refinery of HPCL was the first modern refinery to be set up after independence by Esso in 1954, followed by Burmah-Shell and Caltex in Mumbai (BPCL) and Visakhapatnam (HPCL). Today, there are 23 refineries, 18 under public sector, 3 under private sector and 2 in a joint venture. IOC is the largest domestic refiner with a capacity of 70 mmtpa. Top three companies—IOC, BPCL and RIL—contribute around 66.3% of India's total refining production.

Simple refinery configuration was adopted in 1950s, comprising crude oil distillation, naphtha/kcrosene/ATF treatment and catalytic reforming for upgrading naphtha to petrol, with no secondary processing, low energy recoveries and high sulphur fuel oil as internal fuel. The refineries established in the sixties by the government undertakings were based on processing of indigenous crude oils of low sulphur origin available in North East and Gujarat basin. Indian PSU refineries started adopting state-of-the-art modern technologies to upgrade the configuration in line with the international trend and as per the product requirements and quality. Secondary processing facilities like fluid catalytic cracking (FCC) units to upgrade low value streams to high value middle distillates were installed in many of the refineries.

Configuration of Indian refineries further underwent a major change in late 1980s and early 1990s. There was increased emphasis on maximisation of middle distillates as well as better stability of products, with configurations showing shift from FCC towards hydrocracking process and a combination of both. The first hydrocracker in the country was commissioned in Gujarat refinery of IOCL in 1993. All new grassroots refineries started considering installation of hydrocrackers. This led to marked increase in investment requirements for refinery installations.

Refinery configurations in late 1990s were dictated by the product quality upgradation due to environmental considerations. These included lead-free gasoline, low sulphur diesel, fuel oil and other improvement in properties along with the ever-increasing demand for middle distillates. The configurations therefore were modified to include continuous catalytic reforming (CCR), hydrocracker, hydrotreating/hydrodesulphurisation facilities to generate low sulphur fuels and fuel oil for internal use, and INDMAX Technology for liquefied petroleum gas (LPG) maximisation.[23]

However, India is still import-dependent for certain petroleum products. In 2018, it imported 8,00,000 bpd of oil products, primarily petroleum coke and LPG. India stands as world's second-largest importer of LPG after China. The country's LPG imports have markedly increased over the last five years, surpassing the import volumes of Japan. According to state-owned IOCL, 50% of India's LPG demand will be met by imports until 2040.[24] The increased use of LPG as a cleaner cooking fuel, replacing firewood and kerosene, is expected to turn India into the world's largest LPG importer by 2040.[25] India also imports naphtha, for techno-commercial reasons rather than due to a domestic demand-supply gap.

References

1. IBISWorld, 'Global Oil & Gas Exploration & Production Market Size 2005–2025', 1 July, 2021.

2. Daniel Yergin, The Prize: The Epic Quest for Oil, Money and Power, Simon & Schuster UK Ltd, London, p.xiv.

3. Ibid, p.7, 8.

4. 'Energy Statistics 2020' (PDF), Ministry of Statistics and Programme Implementation.

5. 'Energy Statistics 2020' (PDF), Ministry of Statistics and Programme Implementation.

6. Indian Minerals Yearbook 2012 (Part- III: Mineral Reviews), 51st Edition, Petroleum and Natural Gas (Final Release), Indian Bureau of Mines, Ministry of Mines, Government of India, website: www.ibm.gov.in.

7. Daniel Yergin, *The Quest*, p.3.

8. National Data Repository, Directorate General of Hydrocarbons (DGH), Ministry of Petroleum and Natural Gas, Gov of India, https://www.ndrdgh.gov.in › NDR.

9. Govt. Unveils New Hydrocarbon Policy; *The Hindu*, 28 June, 2017.

10. CEIC Data. India Crude Oil: Production: http/ww.ceicdata.com/en/indicator/india/crude-oil-production.

11. ONGC Annual Report 2019–20.

12. Ministry of Petroleum and Natural Gas Annual Report 2020–21.

13. Press Information Bureau, Ministry of Petroleum and Natural Gas, 10 June, 2021.

14. 'ONGC Puts Mature Oil, Gas Fields on Block; Invites Bids from Global Firms', *PTI*, 8 November, 2020.

15. DPIIT Annual Report 2022–21; https://dpiit.gov.in/annual-report/anuual-report-year-2021-22.

16. Invest India website, FDI in India; https://www.investindia.gov.in/.

17. Energy Statistics 2019, Ministry of Statistics and Programme Implementation, Central Statistics Office, Government of India, www. Mospi.gov.in.

18. Ministry of Power.

19. Energy Information Agency (EIA), USA.

20. IEA, India Energy Outlook 2021.

21. Invest India, www.investindia.gov.in/sector/oil-gas.

22. Ministry of Petroleum and Natural Gas, Press Information Bureau.

23. MPNG: History & Evolution.

24. IOCL, 2018.

25. IEA, 2018c.

Chapter 3

NATURAL GAS

I. OVERVIEW

Natural gas accounts for about a quarter of global electricity generation, while in India it is just about 6.5% of the energy basket. The Indian government is trying to raise its share to 15% by 2030, which means tripling gas imports. In the medium-term, gas is seen playing a major role in supporting a transition to net zero energy systems; however, its long-term use is uncertain in a world dominated by renewable energies.

Natural gas is the third largest contributor to the global energy basket, after coal and crude oil, accounting for a quarter of the total primary energy consumption. Its storability, its ability to be delivered through pipelines or liquefied natural gas sent by ship, as well as the ability of gas-fired power plants to turn on and off quickly, allows it to respond to both seasonal and short-term demand fluctuations and to provide back-up to the growing use of variable renewables such as wind and solar power. It is also used as a raw material for chemical fertilisers, ammonia and urea, plastics, detergents and numerous organic chemicals. In a compressed form (compressed natural gas or CNG), it is used as a fuel for vehicles and piped natural gas (PNG) for cooking. It is an important ingredient in dyes, ink and rubber compounding operations. More than half of the world's ammonia is manufactured via a catalytic process that uses hydrogen derived from methane. Ammonia is used directly as plant food or converted into a variety of chemicals such as hydrogen cyanide, nitric acid, urea and a range of fertilisers.

Other end uses of natural gas include its conversion into other liquid products, such as gas-to-liquids (GTL)—gasoline, diesel or jet fuel. A variety of GTL technologies have been developed, including Fischer–Tropsch (F–T), methanol to gasoline (MTG) and syngas to gasoline plus (STG+). F–T produces a synthetic crude that can be further refined into finished products, while MTG can produce synthetic gasoline from natural gas. STG+ can produce drop-in gasoline, diesel, jet fuel and aromatic chemicals directly from natural gas via a single-loop process.[1] During the processing to remove water and impurities before its use as a fuel, natural gas produces several

92

by-products like ethane, propane, butane, pentane and higher molecular weight hydrocarbons, helium and hydrogen sulphide (which may be converted into pure sulphur), which are of great commercial value, along with some toxic gases like carbon dioxide and nitrogen.

Global consumption of gas has tripled over the last three decades, and it is expected to grow another 50% over the next two decades. Three decades ago, world consumption of gas on an energy-equivalent basis was only 45% that of oil; today it is about 70%. Technology is making natural gas more and more available, whether in terms of advances in conventional drilling, or, most recently, the revolution in unconventional natural gas (such as the 'shale gas' in North America).[2]

Relatively less carbon emitting than other fossil fuels, natural gas is seen as a fuel of the future. Burning natural gas for energy results in fewer emissions of nearly all types of air pollutants and carbon dioxide (CO_2) than burning coal or petroleum products to produce an equal amount. About 117 pounds of carbon dioxide are produced per million British thermal units (mmBtu) equivalent of natural gas compared with more than 200 pounds of CO_2 per mmBtu of coal and more than 160 pounds per mmBtu of distillate fuel oil.[3] Natural gas consumption has grown at a rate of 5.2% the last decade in India.[4]

However, as the combustion of all fossil fuels entails rapid oxidation of their carbon and methane, a compound with one carbon atom and four hydrogen atoms (CH_4), which is the largest component of natural gas, is a more potent greenhouse gas. But natural gas is considered less damaging to the environment than coal, which is seen as the largest source of particulate matter and sulphur (SOx) and nitrogen oxides (NOx). It produces 25–30% less carbon dioxide per joule than oil and 40–45% per joule less than coal,[5] and potentially fewer pollutants than other hydrocarbon fuels.[6] Despite fewer emissions, natural gas is still a source of greenhouse gases and like all fossil fuels, is a non-renewable resource. During drilling, natural gas can escape into the atmosphere and contribute to climate change. Natural gas leaks are also dangerous to nearby communities because it is colourless, odourless, highly toxic and highly explosive.

Evolution of Natural Gas

Natural gas was unknown in Europe until it was discovered in England in 1659. However, even then it did not come into wide use. Instead, gas obtained from carbonised coal (known as town gas) became the primary fuel for illuminating streets and houses throughout much of Europe from 1790 on. In North America the first commercial application of a petroleum product was the utilisation of natural gas from a shallow well in Fredonia, New York, in 1821. The gas was distributed through a small-bore lead pipe to consumers for lighting and cooking.

However, hydrocarbons (crude oil and natural gas) were well known for millennia from seepages, bitumen pools and 'burning pillars', especially in the Middle East and particularly in Iraq. But their use of combustion, including the heating of Constantinople's thermae during the late Roman Empire, was rare.[7] A remarkable exception was the Chinese burning of natural gas to evaporate brines in the landlocked Sichuan province.[8] Used at least since the beginning of the Han Dynasty (200 BCE) this process was made possible by the Chinese invention of percussion drilling.[9] Heavy iron bits attached to long bamboo cables from bamboo derricks were raised rhythmically by two to six men jumping on a lever. The deepest recorded boreholes started with only 10 m during the Han Dynasty, reached 150 m by the tenth century and culminated in the 1 km deep Xinhai well in 1835.[10] Natural gas, distributed by bamboo pipelines, was to evaporate brines in huge cast-iron pans.

But the wide-ranging, worldwide use of natural gas had to wait for more millennia. The discovery and identification of natural gas in the Americas happened in 1626. In 1821, William Hart successfully dug the first natural gas well at Fredonia, New York, US, which led to the formation of the Fredonia Gas Light Company. The city of Philadelphia created the first municipally owned natural gas distribution venture in 1836.[11] Based on an estimated 2015 world consumption rate of about 3,400 cubic km of gas per year, the total estimated remaining economically recoverable reserves of natural gas would last 250 years at current consumption rates. An annual increase in usage of 2–3% could result in currently recoverable reserves lasting significantly less, perhaps as few as 80 to 100 years.[12]

Throughout the nineteenth century, the use of natural gas remained localised because there was no way to transport large quantities of gas over long distances. Natural gas remained on the side line of industrial development, which was based primarily on coal and oil. An important breakthrough in gas-transportation technology occurred in 1890 with the invention of leakproof pipeline coupling. Nonetheless, materials and construction techniques remained so cumbersome that gas could not be used more than 160 km (100 miles) from the source of supply. Thus, associated gas was mostly flared (i.e., burned at the wellhead), and non-associated gas was left in the ground, while town gas was manufactured for use in the cities.

In the nineteenth century, natural gas was usually obtained as a by-product during the production of crude. Small, light gas carbon chains came out as the extracted fluids underwent pressure reduction from the reservoir to the surface, similar to the uncapping of a soft drink bottle when the carbon dioxide effervesces. It was an unwanted matter in an active oil field. If there was not a market for natural gas near the wellhead it was prohibitively expensive to pipe the gas to the end user. In the nineteenth century and early twentieth century, unwanted gas was usually burned off at the oil fields. Today, the unwanted gas (or stranded gas, as it is called) associated with oil extraction is often pumped back to the reservoir by 'injection' wells to repressurise the formation to enhance extraction rates from other wells. In petroleum production, gas is sometimes burned as a flare gas.

Natural gas forms naturally when layers of decomposing plants and animal matters are exposed to intense heat and pressure under the surface of the Earth over millions of years. The energy that the plants and animal matters receive from the Sun is stored in the form of chemical bonds in the gas, and when burnt, that energy is transformed into heat. Natural gas is mostly found in deep underground rock formations during extraction of crude oil and coal. There are two types of natural gas—biogenic or 'dry' gas, formed by bacterial decay at shallow depth such as marshes, bogs and landfills, and thermogenic or 'wet' gas, formed at high temperatures and pressures deep beneath the Earth. Biogenic gas has 95% or more of methane, while thermogenic has less than 95% of methane, the principal component of natural gas. 'Dry' gas is considered superior to 'wet' gas, because the latter contains water and impurities, in addition to methane, which lowers the energy efficiency of natural gas. Hence, it is processed before use, and during the processing many commercially valuable petrochemical products such as ethane, propane and butane are produced.

Most wells drilled to explore oil formations also yield a mixture of other hydrocarbons such as condensates, natural gas liquids and natural gas. Natural gas produced through this process is known as 'associated gas', for, it comes as a by-product from an oil well or field, while non-associated gas comes from a well or field that is primarily geared for gas production. For a long time, associated gas was considered as an unwanted by-product and was flared. Today, it is considered as one of the cleanest, safest and most environment-friendly fossil fuel available. The need to prevent global warming by reducing CO_2 emissions has made natural gas an increasingly acceptable source of energy worldwide. Factors like widespread distribution of natural gas reserves globally, better R/P ratios, better energy conversion efficiency, more stable prices vis-à-vis oil have also contributed to the growing popularity of natural gas.

Discovery and Early Application

The first discoveries of natural gas seeps were made in Iran between 6,000 and 2,000 BCE. Many early writers described the natural petroleum seeps in the Middle East, especially in the Baku region of what is now Azerbaijan. The gas seeps, probably first ignited by lightning, provided the fuel for the 'eternal fires' of the fire-worshipping religion of the ancient Persians.

The use of natural gas was mentioned in China in about 900 BCE. It was in 211 BCE that the first known well was drilled in China for natural gas, to reported depths of 150 m (500 ft). The Chinese drilled their wells with bamboo poles and primitive percussion bits for the express purpose of searching for gas in limestones dating to the late Triassic Epoch (about 237 million to 201.3 million years ago) in an anticline (an arch of stratified rock) west of modern Chongqing. The gas was burned to dry the rock salt found interbedded in the limestone. Eventually wells were drilled to depths approaching 1,000 m (3,300 ft), and more than 1,100 wells had been drilled into the anticline by 1900.

The world's largest gas field is the offshore South Pars/North Dome Gas-Condensate field, shared between Iran and Qatar. It is estimated to have 51,000 cubic kms (12,000 cu mi) of natural gas and 50 billion barrels (7.9 bcm) of natural gas condensates. In addition to conventional gas reserves, it is estimated that the world has about 9,00,000 cubic km of 'unconventional' gas such as shale gas, of which 180,000 cubic km may be recoverable. In turn, many studies from MIT, Black & Veatch and the Department of Energy (DOE) predict that natural gas will account for a larger portion of electricity generation and heat in the future.

Natural Gas in India

Although India had started producing and refining crude oil in Upper Assam in the 1880s, it took nearly seven decades to begin utilisation of natural gas. The natural gas industry in India began only in the 1960s with the discoveries of gas fields in Assam and Gujarat and South basin fields in the 1970s.[13] Data obtained from Indian Petroleum and Natural Gas Statistics 1994–95 show that recoverable reserves of natural gas in India in 1947–48 was 3 bcm, while the production was nil.

India produced its first natural gas in 1970–71, amounting to 1.45 bcm, of which 0.76 bcm was flared and 0.04 bcm was reinjected into oil wells to increase pressure. Things improved a little after the ONGC's Bombay High field went onstream in 1974. Still, the pick-up was quite slow, during ten years from 1970–71 to 1980–81, gas production increased from 1.45 bcm to only 2.36 bcm, of which 0.77 bcm was flared and 0.07 bcm reinjected. But the country's Seventh Five Year Plan (1985–89) saw a rapid increase in production by two-and-a-half times to 59.65 bcm from 23.86 bcm in the Sixth Plan. The Seventh Plan period also saw multiple applications of natural gas, as the government allowed it to be used in various industries, in addition to fertilisers. The increased production encouraged establishment of various gas-based power plants, petrochemical units and other gas-using chemical industries. Together with a partially liberalised economy in latter half of the 1980s, consumption of natural gas scaled up to 40 bcm during the Seventh Plan, and it was expected that if economic expansion continued apace, gas consumption would reach 80 bcm by the end of the Eighth Five Year Plan.

Post-Liberalisation

Under the liberalised policy smaller discovered fields were offered on a production sharing basis to private companies. Initially, there were 28 such fields. They were estimated to contain around 7,202 mcm of gas, of which 5,000 cubic metres were recoverable, besides 57.62 mt of oil, of which 11.52 mt were recoverable. The development of these fields was expected to cost around US$ 450 million. But an evaluation by the Planning Commission showed that predominantly small discoveries did not promise any substantial or sustainable incremental production of either gas or oil. The Planning Commission stated that if appropriate measures were not taken to make new discoveries, domestic production of both oil and gas may stagnate or even decline in the Ninth Five Year Plan. In order to ensure that the projects get implemented on a fast tract basis, the government needs to take policy and regulatory measures to boost investments in the gas chain including exploration leading to a sustained and healthy growth of the sector.

Current Status

Today, the natural gas sector is at the threshold of rapid growth supported by a soaring demand, increased exploration, large discoveries in the East Coast, establishment of a slew of LNG import terminals and, above all, positive policy initiatives, such as the development of a nationwide natural gas pipeline grid. However, the country's natural gas market still lacks depth, because of the presence of a small number of producers (that too mostly state-controlled), negligible number of shippers and a limited number of consumers in India. The Indian gas market is very small in terms of bilateral contracts between producers/marketers and consumers of natural gas. This affects the tiny spot market for gas that exists and that is perennially dogged by a lack of liquidity and transparency due to poor participation by players.

The natural gas pricing is moving towards a market determined pricing mechanism and Indian gas market is getting increasingly aligned with the global trends. Although this gets restrictive when volumes for gas produced locally gets allocated by the government which impedes the development of a gas market and deters imports as it limits the demand for LNG.

Equally important is the condition of sectors consuming gas, like power and fertilisers, which form the anchor load for any gas field or LNG terminal. The affordability of these two key user segments depends upon the policy directives and regulatory reforms in these sectors. The reform in the power sector has moved at a very slow pace which is burdened even today with high aggregate technical and commercial (AT&C) losses, tariffs charged which are not cost reflective and mounting losses to the State Electricity Boards (SEB) which are not bankable to sign power purchase agreements with power producers. In the fertiliser sector, the end product is subsidised with the government deciding the final price; thus limits the cost at which raw material like natural gas can be bought. Unless key reforms are not initiated in these two sectors it would keep affecting the development of the gas sector since the price signals will always be distorted.[14]

Tremendous Potential

The potential for growth of the natural gas market in India is tremendous; however, it is a very price sensitive market as the ability of customers to pay differs between sectors. The power generation and fertiliser sectors are the main consumers. Fertiliser producers are subsidised by the government and have limited ability to absorb higher prices. In the power generation sector, gas has to compete against coal for base-load generation. Any change in the power sector or in coal markets will have a huge impact on whether gas is used as a base-load option or for peak purposes, and therefore on future gas demand in the power sector. City gas and industrial users show greater price flexibility, but they are still emerging markets. Historically, gas had been allocated in priority to fertiliser and power plants, while city gas, compressed natural gas (CNG) and industrial had the remainder. Furthermore, fertiliser producers and power generators were allocated gas at low administrative price mechanism (APM) determined by the government. But the recent pricing reforms that took place mid-2010 mean the end of low APM, and that new gas supplies are likely to be more expensive.

The Indian gas sector, like the whole energy sector, is dominated by state-owned companies. ONGC and OIL have dominant upstream positions, and GAIL alone until 2006, was responsible for gas pipeline transportation. The state also has a very important role in the regulatory framework and gas policy, in particular the allocation and pricing of gas. Recent reforms have brought in more private investors in the upstream and downstream sectors, but a more transparent regulatory framework is needed to incentivise the future private investments.

Outlook

Natural gas contributes about a quarter to the global energy consumption. In India, however, it makes up only 6.2% of all energy consumed. To cut the dependence on polluting coal and liquid fuels, the government is targeting to raise its share to 15% by 2030, which means gas consumption has to rise to 600 mmscmd from the current 166 mmscmd. But the domestic production is unable to support this increase. Currently, only about 80–90 mcm, less than 50% of India's gas consumption, is supplied by the domestic output, while the remainder comes from imports. There is not much that the government can do beyond incentivising private and foreign investment to increase domestic production and on its own part, increasing gas imports and building distribution infrastructure to meet the shortage. Former oil minister Dharmendra Pradhan told a Federation of Indian Chamber of Commerce and Industry (FICCI) seminar in December 2019 that the government was spending US$ 60 billion on building LNG import terminals, laying pipelines and expanding city gas distribution network to boost the widespread use of natural gas in the country's economic life.

But, the use of natural gas also comes with its challenges. As India becomes dependent on imported gas, our fuel sources may be vulnerable to geopolitical issues. Further, land acquisition for laying gas pipelines is also a difficult challenge in the country. Subsidised rates of liquefied petroleum gas (LPG) and cheap coal also offer tough competition to the adoption of natural gas in the Indian gas market. Then, there is also the issue of subsidies. The fertiliser sector produces urea from natural gas at the cost of around Rs 900 per 45 kgs. However, the government subsidises this cost by almost 70% to a cost price of Rs 242 per 45 kgs. At the current rate of production, urea subsidies amount to US$ 7.51 billion per year. As the price of natural gas increases, the expenses from these subsidies will overburden the government. The researchers suggest implementing carbon tax for all the stakeholders such as power plants, fertiliser industries, and consumers (through pricing mechanism). They estimate that a carbon tax of US$ 10 per tonne of carbon dioxide released into the atmosphere will amount to US$ 3.31 billion collected per year, which would cover 44% of the total subsidy cost per year.

II. NATURAL GAS RESERVES

As of 1 April, 2021, India's proven natural gas reserves stood at 1,372.62 bcm (approximately 48.5 tcf [trillion cubic feet]), located largely in the Eastern Offshore (40.6%) and the Western Offshore (23.7%).[15] This is equivalent to 22.1 times its annual consumption, which means India has about 22 years of proven gas reserve (at current consumption levels and excluding unproven reserves), according to Worldometer, a reference website that provides counters and real-time statistics on diverse topics.[16]

But this is not full assessment of the reserves of all 26 sedimentary basins of India covering 3.36 million sq km on land and shallow and deep offshore areas. As stated in the Crude Oil chapter of this book, so far only 17% of these sedimentary basins have been explored. British Petroleum (BP), which partners with Reliance Industries of India to produce gas from one of India's most prolific gas fields, believes that India has about, "100 tcf of yet-to-be-discovered natural gas reserves that would be enough to meet half of the nation's gas demand till 2050." BP Chief Bob Dudley says, "But exploitation of gas reserves will depend a lot on how the economics works out as developing resources in the deep sea doesn't come cheap." Speaking at India Energy Forum of CERAWeek on 14 October, 2019, Dudley said, "It's going to take a lot of exploration and will require economics to be right. It's expensive deeper offshore, but once you get the networks and the pipelines in place, India is going to need every fuel it can get."

As of 1 April, 2018, 61% of India's confirmed recoverable reserves were offshore, mostly in Mumbai Bassein and Mumbai High and Krishna-Godavari basins, which provide two-thirds of the country's domestic gas. BP, with Reliance, is investing US$ 5 billion to bring about 1 bcf per day of new domestic gas onstream from mid-2020 from KG-D6, which is a shallow offshore field. The 2018–19 Annual Report of DGH puts prognosticated reserves of conventional hydrocarbon at over 300 billion barrels of oil and oil equivalent gas, with 70% of these in yet to be explored.[17]

On top of the conventional gas reserves, India holds an estimated 63 tcf of recoverable shale gas. While these reserves are considered to be a secondary energy option, Indian agencies are encouraging exploration, and leading companies, such as state-run ONGC and OIL have implemented pilot projects to assess the shale gas opportunities.

India's energy future remains hidden in unexplored, difficult-to-access basins across the country. Technological advancements make exploration and discovery of these reserves possible, though recent issues such as fuel-stranded power plants highlight logistical and infrastructure challenges. But in India, forecasting the discovery of oil and gas reserves is limited to prognostication of reserves. The estimation of reserves based on statistical methods has not yet been reported in or for India. Employing a 'rate-of-effort' approach, authors of an article titled, 'India's Oil and Gas Reserves and Production Potential', Sanjib Chowdhury and KC Sahu, for GE Corporation, have estimated India's ultimate recoverable reserves to be 1,900 mt of oil and 1,425 bcm of gas. They assert that the massive untapped natural gas reserves could help the country free up US$ 306 million per day on imported oil.[18]

Unconventional Natural Gas

In addition to the conventional gas reserves, India has a vast reservoir of unconventional gas. The one, which India has started exploiting currently, is coal bed methane.

Coal Bed Methane (CBM)

Coal bed methane is a form of natural gas formed during the process of coalification, the transformation of plant material into coal. It contains 90–95% methane, a highly flammable agent, which is used to generate electricity, and extracted from coal seams. Though a greenhouse gas, it is considered 'sweet gas' because it has fewer hydrogen sulphides. In recent decades it has become an important source of alternative energy. CBM is distinct from the typical sandstone or other conventional gas reservoir, as methane is stored within the coal by a process of adsorption. The methane is in a near-liquid state, lining the inside of pores within the coal, called the matrix. Unlike the natural gas from conventional reservoirs, coal bed methane contains very little heavier hydrocarbons such as propane or butane, and no natural gas condensate.

According to the Directorate General of Hydrocarbons, India holds around 92 tcf of prognosticated CBM reserves across 11 states—Andhra Pradesh, Assam, Chhattisgarh, Gujarat, Jharkhand, Madhya Pradesh, Maharashtra, Odisha, Rajasthan, Tamil Nadu and West Bengal. But being the fifth largest coal reserve in the world, India believes it could be holding more. Already, government statistics have shown tremendous increase in CBM reserves the past 11 years or so. Taking 2008 as the base year, the initial reserve of CBM has increased by approximately 97% and ultimate reserve by 170%. At present initial reserves are 280 mtoe and ultimate reserves at 108 mtoe.

In 1997, the DGH came out with a CBM policy to harness the potential of CBM resources on the lines of crude oil and conventional natural gas resources. The DGH carved out blocks in collaboration with the Ministry of Coal and Central Mine Planning and Design Institute to hold auction of CBM blocks for exploration and development. Four rounds of auction had been held till 2019 and 33 blocks, including two on nomination basis and one block through Foreign Investment Promotion Board (FIPB), were awarded. However, CBM is currently produced from only four—Jharia block in Jharkhand by ONGC; Raniganj East in West Bengal by Essar Oil Ltd; Raniganj South in West Bengal by Great Eastern Energy Corporation and Sohagpur West in Madhya Pradesh by RIL.

The total prognosticated CBM reserve of the awarded blocks is 62.4 tcf (1,767 bcm), of which, 9.9 tcf (280.34 bcm) has already been established. The awarded blocks cover 16,613 sq km of the total 26,000 sq km of the coal bearing areas available for CBM exploration. Most CBM exploration and production activities are currently carried out by domestic companies. But targetting a production level of 1 mmscmd of CBM by 2023–24, the state-run Coal India Ltd plans to outsource CBM production to global operators. India has been working for about two decades to tap its massive CBM reserves. But the output was still in a single digit, around 2–3 mmscmd in 2019, with just about three to four market players like Reliance Industries Ltd, Essar Oil and Gas, Great Eastern Energy and ONGC engaged in the sector.

In order to incentivise the private sector's greater involvement in tapping the country's massive CBM reserves, the government has formulated a new policy that allows investors marketing and pricing freedom in respect of their production. Contractors can now sell their CBM gas in the domestic market at 'arm's length' prices unhindered. CBM price is a major attraction for investors. While natural gas price is capped at US$ 2.89 mmBtu (per million British thermal unit) by the government, CBM gas fetches US$ 5.77-$ 10.64 per mmBtu. ONGC sold its gas from three coal bed methane blocks in Jharkhand in 2018 for a price ranging between US$ 5.77 mmBtu to US$ 6.12 mmBtu. Great Eastern Energy Corp Ltd (GEECL) sells its CBM gas at US$10.64 per mmBtu and Essar Oil's sale price is US$ 8.08 per mmBtu. ONGC has now fixed a price between US$ 5.7 per mmBtu and US$ 6.14 per mmBtu. The rise follows a 2017 government decision allowing oil and gas companies to sell their CBM at market prices. Among the companies ramping up their CBM output are Reliance Industries Ltd (RIL), Essar Oil Ltd, and GEECL.

As of March 2018, only 5 of the 33 awarded blocks were producing and their total average CBM production was around 2.01 mmscmd, which included test gas production from two CBM blocks and commercial production from three CBM blocks. By the end of 2019, two more blocks, Jharia and North Karanpura, were set to commence commercial CBM production, and with that, it was expected that the country's CBM production would reach 5.5 mcm by 2020, which would be about 5% of the total natural gas production in the country.

At present coal mine methane is not tapped and is blown out of the coal mines. Tight gas reservoirs in Eocene formations in Gujarat and Northeast India have been discovered. As per the study by the US, Oil Field Services Company, total reserves of tight gas at Cambay amount to 0.55 tcf, production of which at present is not economically viable but with the new technologies in place these reserves may be tapped in the future. Methane released by coal blocks remains trapped in seams and escapes into the atmosphere during the coal mining process. When extracted in concentrated form, it can be used as natural gas that can be transported through pipelines.

The Gondwana sediments of eastern India host the bulk of India's coal reserves and all the current CBM producing blocks. The vast majority of the best prospective areas for CBM development are in eastern India, situated in Damodar Koel valley and Son valley. CBM projects exist in Raniganj South, Raniganj East and Raniganj North areas in the Raniganj coalfield, the Parbatpur block in Jharia coalfield and the east and west Bokaro coalfields. Son valley includes the Sonhat North and Sohagpur east and west blocks. Currently, commercial production has commenced from Raniganj South, Raniganj East and Sohagpur West CBM blocks operated by GEECL, Essar and RIL respectively. Damodar valley coalfields currently have the maximum potential for CBM. Jharia coalfields hold reserves of 25 bcm and Raniganj coal block holds around 3 bcm of CBM trapped in coal seams.

Shale Gas

Shale gas is another form of unconventional natural gas, besides coal bed methane, tight sandstones, and methane hydrates, whose development has revolutionised the petroleum industry. It is more widespread and abundant than oil and conventional gas. It is found trapped in shale rocks. It is estimated that there are about 9,00, 000 cubic km of 'unconventional' gas such as shale gas, of which 1,80,000 cubic km may be recoverable. Shales are fine-grained sedimentary rocks formed of organic-rich mud at the bottom of ancient seas. Subsequent sedimentation and the resultant heat and pressure transformed the mud into shale and also produced natural gas from the organic matter contained in it. Over long spans of geologic time, some of the gas migrated to adjacent sandstones and was trapped in them, forming conventional gas accumulations. The rest of the gas remained locked in the nonporous shale.

However, extraction of shale gas is a difficult and a tardy process mainly because of less permeability of the shale rocks, which does not allow significant fluid flow. Due to low permeability, commercially viable production of shale gas needs fracturing of the rocks for it to provide permeability. For many years, this gas was produced from natural fractures, but as there was development of modern technologies such as horizontal drilling/hydraulic fracturing (fracking); more and more artificial fractures around the well bores were created. This skyrocketed the production of shale gas and led to the so-called Shale Gas Boom in United States. In 2000, shale gas provided only 1% of US natural gas production; by 2010 it was over 20% and in 2020 it was 35%. The US government's Energy Information Administration (EIA) predicts that by 2035, around 46% of the United States' natural gas supply will come from shale gas.[19] The US, which was a net importer of oil and gas until the first decade of this century, is now a major exporter of shale gas.

The success story of US has inspired other countries to follow suit, as global shale gas resource base is vast. Although the estimates will likely change over time as additional information becomes available, a study by EIA showed the world's proven shale gas reserve was 6,609 tcf, as on 1 January, 2010, and technically recoverable resource 16,000 tcf.[20] Thus, adding the identified shale gas resources to other gas resources, increases total world technically recoverable gas resources by over 40% to 22,600 tcf.[21] China is estimated to have the world's largest shale gas reserves (1,115 tcf), followed by Argentina (802 tcf), Algeria (707 tcf) and the US (665 tcf).

In a 2013 report, the EIA estimated the quantity of technically recoverable shale gas for 41 countries. North America leads the worldwide production of shale gas, with the US and Canada having significant levels. Beyond the two countries, shale gas is so far produced at a commercial scale only in Argentina and China. While the shale gas potential of many nations seems promising, there are several obstacles spanning several economic, environmental, technical and social issues grouped in major categories such as access to resources, infrastructure and governance.

Shale Gas/Oil Resources in India

It is estimated that a number of sedimentary basins (Gangetic plain, Gujarat, Rajasthan, Andhra Pradesh and other coastal areas), including the hydrocarbon bearing ones (Cambay, Assam-Arakan and Damodar) have large shale deposits. Various agencies have estimated the shale gas/oil resource potential in selected sedimentary basins/sub-basins in India. Oil field service provider Schlumberger has estimated India's shale gas resources at 300 to 2,100 tcf, while the Ministry of Petroleum and Natural Gas's Central

Mine Planning and Design Institute at just around 45 tcf. Schlumberger says its figure was arrived at based on the information available in the public domain, which varied drastically. Central Mine Planning and Design Institute's estimate was based on its own assessment of shale gas potential in six sub-basins namely, Jharia, Bokaro, North Karanpura, South Karanpura, Raniganj and Sohagpur.

The EIA had made two assessments. Its first assessment made in 2011 had put India's technically recoverable shale gas resources at an estimated 290 tcf in four onshore basins—Cambay on land, Damodar, Krishna Godavari on land and Cauvery on land—and the second, in 2013, at 584 tcf. The second assessment had also indicated the presence of 87 billion barrels of oil in those same basins. The United States Geological Survey (USGS) had also estimated the potential of shale oil in three onshore fields—Cambay on land, Krishna Godavari on land and Cauvery on land—and 6.1 tcf of technically recoverable shale gas reserve in Cambay and Krishna-Godavari basins. ONGC's estimate puts shale gas resource of five basins of Cambay on land, Ganga Valley, Assam and Assam Arakan, Krishna Godavari on land and Cauvery on land at 187.5 tcf. As per the NITI Aayog Report, India has 96 tcf of recoverable shale gas resources.

Based on the studies carried out by various national and international agencies for the identification of shale oil and gas resources, it has been concluded that India held promising reserves of shale gas and oil resources that can help it mitigate the drastic impact of energy deficiency. Most potential resources are deemed to be located in Cambay, Gondwana, Krishna-Godavari, Cauvery, Indo-Gangetic, Assam and Assam-Arakan basins. Basins of preliminary interest identified by Indian geologists are the Cambay basin in Gujarat, the Assam-Arakan basin in northeast India, and the Gondwana Basin.

In 2013, the government announced a shale gas and oil policy for the state-run upstream companies to explore and exploit shale gas and oil resources in nomination areas. ONGC was assigned 50 blocks and OIL 6 blocks in the first phase which ended in April 2017. ONGC said in its 2018–19 annual report that it had completed drilling of 26 wells (of which 8 were exclusive wells and 18 dual objective wells) in 21 blocks across four basins of Cambay, KG, Cauvery and Assam and Arakan Assam basins. Some indications of the presence of oil have been observed during the activation of the zones while hydro-fracturing wells of JMSGA and GNSGB in Cambay basin and WGSGA in KG basin. ONGC has reported, 'flowback of 0.7 cubic metre of oil and about 69 cubic metre of flow back water, thus establishing presence of shale oil system', in the West Godavari PML block. OIL has reported, 'poor shale prospectivity' in its nomination blocks.[22]

However, India doesn't seem to be in a hurry to exploit its shale gas/oil resources. As already stated, shale gas is found in shale rocks of low permeability, originally deposited as clay and silt, at about 2,500 to 5,000 m beneath the Earth's surface. In contrast, conventional natural gas is trapped in sandstone rocks having high permeability at around 1,500 m and can be easily extracted by traditional vertical drilling. The technique used for shale gas production requires first drilling a vertical well to the targetted rock followed by horizontal drilling. This makes it more difficult and more expensive to extract because of high upfront costs. Recent innovations implemented in the US, have cut the costs of fracking and made shale oil and gas competitive vis-à-vis conventional oil and gas.

The most common way to extract shale gas from the Earth's surface is 'hydraulic fracturing' or fracking, which involves pumping high volumes of pressurised water, mixed with certain chemicals and sand to break the low permeable rocks to unlock the shale gas reserves. The process requires around 5 to 9 million litres of water per extraction or an average 15,000 cubic metre per well. This makes the exploitation of shale oil/gas an imponderable proposition for India to adopt fracking. Hydraulic fracturing also has other negative consequences as it depletes water resources for agricultural irrigation and human consumption. Fracking has other impacts such as increase in air pollution and greenhouse gases and seismic activity. There have been instances of underground water pollution in the US and Canada. Restrictions have been imposed on shale gas production in many countries largely because of the environmental risks and social concerns due to hydraulic fracturing. The US experience shows that several chemical substances used in fracking are toxic to fresh water organisms and are carcinogenic.

However, Indian companies are not shying away from taking substantial stakes in the US shale oil/gas projects. State-run GAIL has taken a 20% stake in Eagle Ford Shale of Carrizo Oil and Gas. As part of the deal, GAIL will pay US$ 63.7 million in cash and will fund US$ 31.3 million of Carrizo's drilling and development costs. GAIL will also invest up to US$ 300 million in assets, which cover around 20,000 acres, over the next five years. They will secure access to around 4,000 acres in La Salle County, Texas, and a 20% interest in eight existing horizontal wells, which Carrizo says produce 1,700 bpd of liquids and 3.8 bcf per day of natural gas. The area has reserves of 13.8 million barrels of oil equivalent, of which 2.5 million barrels of oil equivalent are classified as proved developed, according to Carrizo.

Another state-run Indian Oil Corporation (IOC) has acquired 10% interest in the integrated upstream and LNG project, Pacific North West LNG, in British Columbia, Canada. The project will produce natural gas from its shale gas acreages. Supply of IOCL's share of 1.20 mmtpa of LNG was slated to commence from 2019.

The third state-run company, Petronet LNG, signed an agreement with Tellurian to acquire an 18% stake in the US company's US$ 28 billion Driftwood LNG terminal project in Louisiana. According to the deal, Petronet will pay US$ 2.5 billion for the stake and buy 5 mt of LNG per annum. The deal was signed during the visit of Prime Minister Narendra Modi to Houston in September 2019.

Private major Reliance Industries Ltd has invested around US$ 9 billion in shale gas assets in the US since 2010, but has been getting negative returns owing to low crude oil prices, which have made shale gas production unviable. Its upstream joint ventures in US shale include a 45% stake in Pioneer Natural Resources' Eagle Ford shale block and a 40% working interest in partnership with Chevron. RIL's third investment was a stake in a joint venture Carrizo Oil and Gas for US$ 392 million in Marcellus shale gas asset. But within a year it sold it at less than one-third of the purchase price to BKV Chelsea, an affiliate of Kalnin Venture, at US$ 126 million.

Gas Hydrates

The shallow sediments along the Indian continental margin are good hosts for gas hydrates, and the methane within it has been prognosticated as more than 1,500 times of India's present natural gas reserve. Production of even 10% from this natural reserve is sufficient to meet country's vast energy requirement for about a century.

Gas hydrate resources in India are estimated at 1,894 tcm (trillion cubic metres) and these deposits occur in Western, Eastern and Andaman offshore areas. The gas hydrates discovered are located in coarse-grained sand-rich depositional systems in the Krishna-Godavari basin and is made up of a sand-rich, gas-hydrate-bearing fan and channel-levee gas hydrate prospects.

India's oil ministry and USGS made the discovery of this large, highly enriched accumulations of naturally occurring, ice-like form of water, which contains gas molecules in its molecular cavities.

Scientists in the hydrocarbon field consider this form as the future source of natural gas; for, the carbon equivalent of methane hydrate is estimated to be twice that of all known conventional fossil fuels and more than 10 times the total reserves of conventional natural gas resources. However, the catch is, no country in the world has developed technology to extract gas from these hydrates.

Japan and Canada are two countries that have been working on the technology for a long time, and claim it would be possible to produce commercial gas from gas hydrates in the near future. ONGC has been an active participant in the National Gas Hydrate Programmes (NGHPs). To promote this, a Gas Hydrate Research & Technology Centre (GHRTC) was established in 2016 at Panvel in Maharashtra. This centre gives impetus to gas hydrate research and technology development and contributes to India's plan to commercialise it as energy resource at the earliest. The next steps for research will involve production testing in these sand reservoirs to determine if natural gas production is practical and economic.

Gas hydrates are crystalline form of methane and water, and exist in shallow sediments of outer continental margins. Its gas resources are 10 times more than global conventional gas reserves and twice the total carbon content in all the coal, petroleum and natural gas in the world combined, making them a potentially valuable energy resource. Under standard conditions, one unit of hydrate could contain approximately 180 units of natural gas. They are envisaged as a viable major energy resource for future.[23]

ONGC has struck gas hydrate reserves in the deep sea off the Andhra Pradesh coast. The reserves are located in the Krishna-Godavari basin, which came into the limelight about a decade ago and the fresh reserves are estimated to be around 134 tcf. ONGC reckons such a huge quantity of gas can turn India's fortunes in the future, by making the country self-sufficient in the energy sector.

The discovery was made during a comprehensive gas hydrate field venture, mounted by a team of scientists from India, Japan and the United States. It was led by ONGC in cooperation with the USGS, the Japanese Drilling Company and the Japan Agency for Marine-Earth Science and Technology. This was the country's second research expedition, called the

Indian National Gas Hydrate Program Expedition II, to carry out a joint exploration for gas hydrate potential in the Indian Ocean. The first expedition, also a partnership between the scientists from India and the US, discovered gas hydrate accumulations, but in formations that are currently unlikely to be producible.

In 2016, the Modi government established GHRTC at Panvel, Maharashtra, to develop the technology for exploitation of this massive resource. ONGC has been an active participant in this programme. Previous studies have shown that gas hydrate at high concentrations in sand reservoirs is the type of occurrence that can be most easily produced with existing technologies. Hence, the second expedition focused on highly concentrated gas hydrate occurrences in sand reservoirs and discovered gas hydrate located in coarse-grained sand-rich depositional systems in the Krishna-Godavari, Mahanadi, Gulf of Mannar and Andaman basins. The next step will involve production testing in these sand reservoirs to determine if natural gas production is practical and economic.

National Gas Hydrate Programme (NGHP), which carries out 'expeditions' to establish the physical presence of gas hydrates in various areas, says after completing two expeditions that the results of 42 holes drilled at 25 sites in Expedition II in 2015 revealed two distinct gas hydrate bearing areas in KG basin. Further extensive studies have been planned to assess the gas hydrate resource potential, reservoir characterisation, reservoir delineation and geo-mechanical modelling for seafloor and wellbore stability and identification of sites for pilot production for testing. The two KG deep offshore areas ('B' & 'C') that contain gas hydrate accumulations may be suitable sites for gas hydrate production testing under NGHP Expedition 03. But the technology for production of gas from gas hydrate is not yet matured and is at the R&D stage world over.

At present, collation and interpretation of all data is being done to identify sites for pilot production testing. The objective of NGHP Expedition III is to carry out pilot production testing at a suitable site identified during the NGHP Expedition II. Resource assessment of gas hydrates is planned to be carried by NGHP member organisations out in collaboration with international organisations.

The production technology is to be proved before venturing into the pilot production testing. For planning and execution of pilot production testing and assessment of gas hydrates exploitation commerciality in Indian offshore, member organisations are working on projects for the development of feasible production technology which should be helpful in gas hydrate extraction.

India Might Hold World's Second Largest Gas Hydrate Reserves

USA, Japan, Russia, China, Germany and Korea have been deeply involved in developing technology to exploit the proved gas hydrate reserves. Japan and Canada have been working on the technology for a long time, and claim that it would be possible to produce commercial gas from gas hydrates in the next four to five years. Japan said it plans to start commercial gas production from its offshore hydrates from 2020 after commercial testing was completed.

In 2010, the cost of extracting natural gas from crystallised natural gas was estimated to be as much as twice the cost of extracting natural gas from conventional sources, and even higher from offshore deposits.[24] In 2013, Japan Oil, Gas and Metals National Corporation (JOGMEC) announced that they had recovered commercially relevant quantities of natural gas from methane hydrate.[25]

III. SUPPLY AND DEMAND

Natural gas is the cleanest of all fossil fuels, and, as such, is seen as a suitable bridge fuel for the energy transition from coal and crude oil to a low carbon future. Worldwide natural gas consumption has been rising over the past 20 years. In 2021, worldwide natural gas consumption amounted to about 4.04 tcm. This was an increase of 4.8% over 2020,[26] representing a dramatic recovery from the Covid-induced declines in 2020. The recovery was mainly driven by fast-growing markets, primarily in Asia, where demand grew by 7% from 2020 levels and 8.5% from 2019 levels. China, India and other fast-growing Asian markets were driving this growth. China led the increase, with its demand zooming over 14% or 44 bcm, higher than 2019 levels.[27] India's natural gas demand rose by 4.5% to 32,360 mcm in 2021 over the 2020 level.

Natural gas enjoys broad policy support from all over the world as governments press ahead with the ambition to increase the share of clean energy in the primary energy mix and decarbonise economies, with natural gas as a transition fuel.

In India, natural gas is the third largest source of electricity, accounting for 8.7% of power generation, behind crude oil (10.34%) and coal (58%). In 2019, the country had 67 gas-based power plants of the combined capacity of 25,000 MW, of which 31 were either stranded or stressed, and those working were operating at an average plan load factor (PLF) of 24%. The combined production from gas-based plants had, hence, fallen to 11,000 MW. Of the 31 stranded plants, 24, with a capacity of 9,673 MW, are privately owned, while 6, with a capacity of 2,665.30 MW, are owned by states, 1 plant, of 1,967 MW capacity, belongs to the centre.

The stranded plants require 116.59 mmscmd of gas to run at their optimal levels, but government statistics (CEA) show that they had never got more than 30% of their requirement since 2013–14. In 2018–19 their share in the allocation of domestic gas was only 25.71 mmscmd. Part of the shortage is due to a drastic fall in the KG D6 field output in Andhra Pradesh, which has deprived the power sector of its gas supply. KG D6, operated by Mukesh Ambani-owned Reliance Industries, which went onstream in 2009, was expected to provide 80 mmscmd to the power sector, followed by increases in subsequent years. But gas production at the field declined to 5.5 mmscmd in 2017–18 from 55.35 mmscmd in 2010–11, and 'today the production is as good as nil', according to a parliamentary standing committee report on Petroleum and Natural Gas, submitted to the Parliament in December 2013.

The power sector received another setback in 2013, when it lost top priority, which it had enjoyed since 2010, in the allocation of cheap domestic gas to city gas distribution (CGD) systems. This change in the government further hit the power sector, which was already reeling under the gas shortage following the decline in KG D6 output. The standing committees of Parliament, which keep a critical eye on the functioning of various government ministries, warned in its 2013 report that the Ministry of Petroleum and Natural Gas's plan to cut gas allocations for the power sector was a major blow to the sector, and may make even the operating gas-based plants stranded. "This is a regulated sector which requires domestic gas allocation more than any other sector," the report noted.

At the end of 2019, India's total installed power capacity was 367 GW, of which 7.2% or 25 GW is from gas-based projects. But, with 14 GW gas capacity lying stranded, actual contribution from this sector did not exceed 11 GW. According to the parliamentary committee's observations, the 'normative' requirement to operate these gas-based power plants at 85%

PLF is 102 mmscmd, but total domestic gas supplied to them was only 30.72 mmscmd, which included 7.92 mmscmd of imported re-gasified liquefied natural gas (LNG), in 2013.

The share of natural gas in India's energy basket stands at 6.5% against a global average of 24%. The government wants to raise it to 15% by 2030 in order to replace coal and reduce pollution in as many sectors as possible. The International Energy Agency predicts that after a temporary slowdown in 2020, India is set to emerge as one of the primary drivers of growth in gas demand in Asia. The prospect is for an estimated 28 bcm per year increase in total consumption until 2019–25, thanks to a combination of supportive government policies and improved LNG and pipeline infrastructure. Currently city gas distribution receives the largest proportion of cheap domestic gas allocation followed by fertilisers and power generation, while refining, petrochemicals and other industries depend less on domestic gas supply.

As India builds out its gas infrastructure, natural gas can find multiple uses in India's energy system, including to help meet air quality and near-term emissions goals if supply chains are managed responsibly. But the sustainable development scenario also underlines that a long-term vision for gas needs to incorporate a growing role for biogases and low-carbon hydrogen, for which India has large potential. Natural gas is the cleanest of fossil fuels (coal and crude oil) that has wide-ranging use in the energy and non-energy sectors. It can be used for power generation, as raw material for fertiliser and petrochemicals manufacturing, as an alternative fuel for transportation, and for heating and cooking in the household sector. Demand has risen exponentially, especially since the massive expansion of the CGD programme in 2014. In recent years, India's gas demand has steadily increased across all sectors, including agriculture, industry, commercial and residential.

As elsewhere around the world, India too has embraced natural gas as a convenient transition fuel from coal to renewables to reduce carbon footprint and move to greener sources of energy. The country has committed to cut its CO_2 emission to 40% by 2030 from the 2005 level at the 2015 Paris Summit on Climate Change. As part of that pledge the Indian government has set the target of increasing natural gas' share in its energy mix to 15% by 2030 from 6.5% in 2020. To achieve this target, the government has adopted several measures to boost domestic gas production, increase LNG import and re-gasification facilities and expand distribution infrastructure. To increase domestic production, which has been declining since 2012, the government has thrown open the upstream sector for 100% FDI and allowed producers the freedom to market and price their gas produced from new discoveries across all regimes. Further, all E&P contractors, including even those currently operating in nomination, PSC and CBM regimes, have been allowed to explore and exploit unconventional hydrocarbons such as shale gas/oil and CBM from their awarded acreages with a single licence.

In order to strengthen capacity for gas imports to meet the rising demand, the government has already commissioned six LNG receiving and re-gasification terminals with a capacity of 38.8 mmtpa or 140 mmscmd[28] and plans to build another six or seven to raise the total capacity to 79 mmtpa by 2030. At present the operational facilities are on the western and southern coasts, while new facilities will come up on the eastern coast. The government aims to supply cooking gas to every household in the country by 2023 and set up LNG and CNG filling stations at major roads and highways throughout the country by 2030. To end this, it is implementing a massive expansion to its CGD programme.

Although natural gas has been used in households and industries in India for more than half a century, its rise in the primary energy mix has risen modestly. By 2011, its share in energy had reached merely 10% or an estimated 62 bcm per annum. By 2015, however, the share of natural gas in India's energy mix fell to around 6.2%, partly due to declining domestic production and sharp spike in LNG prices in the wake 2011 Fukushima disaster. Bombay High gas field, one of India's two main producing fields, reached peak production around 2010, while production from the other major field, the KG D6, remained well below the initial expectations due to smaller actual reserves.[29] Thanks to the poor availability of gas from KG D6, almost half of the 66 gas-fired power plants, which had been set up based on the anticipated supply from that field, remain stranded, leaving 25,000 MW of their capacity underutilised. Gas output from D1 (Dhirubhai 1) and D3 fields in KG D6 block was supposed to be 80 mmscmd but actual production was only 35.33 mmscmd in 2011–12, 20.88 mmscmd in 2012–13 and 9.77 mmscmd in 2013–14. The output continued to drop in the subsequent years and the fields ceased to produce in February 2020. Reliance-BP blamed unanticipated sand and water ingress for shutting down of one well after the other, leading to a drop in production.

Still, from 2007 to 2017, India's total primary energy supply increased by 55%, according to the IEA. Most of this was met by fossil fuels, coal accounting for over half of the total growth in energy supply, and oil 26 of the total growth in total primary energy supply (TPES). Natural gas, however lagged, with its share in the TPES falling from around 12% to 6%. Power and fertiliser industries are the two major consumers of natural gas, but in both sectors, it faced formidable challenges. While in power sector it struggled with coal, and to some extent with fuel oil, in price competitiveness, in the heavily subsidised fertiliser industry, which consumed about 25% of India's gas, it suffered extremely low returns.

Demand Forecasts

Experts and agencies are not surprised when presenting varying projections of gas demand in India. While the government's Petroleum and Natural Gas Regulatory Board (PNGRB) projects the growing natural gas demand to reach 746 mmscmd by 2029–30,[30] think tank NITI Aayog, predicts it will be 173 mtoe by 2047.[31] Energy consultancy Wood Mackenzie expects India's gas demand to double to 75 bcm by 2030, half of which will be in the form of LNG, while Elara Securities forecasts the gas demand soaring by 66% from 148 mmscmd to 250 mmscmd in 2025, with the bulk of incremental demand coming from CGD operations, being rolled out in 407 districts of 27 states. As much as 52 mmscmd of additional demand will come from the retailing of CNG to automobiles and piped natural gas to industries and households. Another 35 mmscmd is to come from the power sector and 15 mmscmd from fertiliser plants. This would serve an additional 3.8 million CNG vehicles, 33 million households, 0.3 million commercial units and 42,840 industrial units, says the securities firm.

The petroleum ministry's gas marketing arm GAIL, projects gas demand to rise from 174 mmscmd in 2021 to 550 mmscmd by 2030 as the government presses ahead with plans to boost the commodity's share to 15% in the primary energy basket by that year. Demand from city gas distribution is likely to rise to 140 mmscmd from 35 mmscmd in 2021 while gas use in refineries is expected at 58 mmscmd from about 14 mmscmd in 2021. At present 49% is met by domestic production and the rest through imports in form of liquefied natural gas.

In sum, while domestic natural gas demand is expected to grow at around 8–10% CAGR over FY 2022–2027, domestically available natural gas, which meets around 50% of the total demand currently, is expected to grow at around 7–9% in the same period. This is a key concern which will hinder growth in natural gas' share in the energy mix, as the end-user industries have to rely on expensive LNG imports to meet the demand. Domestic production of natural gas is projected to rise 50% to 48 bcm in 2030, which would be lower than India's output of 51 bcm in 2010. Gas imports will double to nearly 70 bcm by 2030 in the IEA scenario.

Demand Drivers

There are three main sectors that drive the most growth of natural gas consumption in India. The fertiliser sector is the largest consumer of natural gas today accounting for about 30% of consumption. The power sector which was expected to be the largest consumer of gas has fallen to third place accounting for only about 15% of consumption in 2021–22, while CGD which was expected to account for only about 9% of consumption has the second largest share in consumption accounting for about 20% in 2021–22. Different factors influenced consumption growth of natural gas in the fertilisers and CGD which account for 50% of consumption.

IEA forecasts industrial sector would emerge as the main driver of expansion in demand, with 36% of the incremental growth till 2025. Refining will contribute 10%, and the city gas distribution network, which is targetting more than 35 million additional household connections and over 7,000 new CNG filling stations by 2029, will account for 19% of the residential and 34% of the transport sector's incremental demand respectively.[32]

From 2020 onward, the petroleum ministry has nearly ended the power sector's entitlement to cheap domestic gas. The Cabinet is discussing a proposal to delist the power sector from the priority list for allocation of domestic gas, which is currently priced at US$ 3.23 mmBtu—less than half of what India pays for imported LNG. The ministry's contention is that domestic fuel remains insufficient to meet the needs of power producers. The ministry is of the opinion that the power companies should procure their required gas from the market or import LNG. Along with ending the power sector's priority entitlement to APM gas, the Cabinet is discussing setting up a national gas exchange that provides a competitive market-driven pricing for gas.

The gas, saved after the removal of the power sector from the priority list, is being diverted to fertiliser, CGD and petrochemical and small and medium industries (SMEs). More gas to the fertiliser industry is expected to ensure adequate and uninterrupted supply of fertiliser (ammonia and urea) to farmers at remunerative prices. City gas distribution entails supply of LPG and pressurised natural gas for household sector, and compressed natural gas for motor vehicles. This, it is felt, will incentivise the transport sector to use cleaner fuel and the country meet its commitment to cut the CO_2 emissions by 40% by 2030.

Fertiliser

The fertiliser sector is prioritised in gas allocation policy, a system of rationing scarce domestic natural gas. Though prioritisation continues, the volume of domestic gas that can be allocated to this industry (and other priority industries) has been declining because of the decline in the production of natural gas. In 2012–13, over 76% of total gas consumed by this industry was domestically produced. In contrast over 68% of the natural gas used for fertiliser production was imported LNG in 2021–22.

Fertiliser is sold to farmers at a 70% discount to the cost of production and the industry receives the difference as subsidy. Until 2015, the fertiliser industry was supplied with domestic natural gas at a price of US\$ 4.2 mmBtu (net calorific value basis) under the administrative price mechanism. When the government shifted to a new pricing formula for domestic natural gas in 2015 the price of domestic gas supplied to the fertiliser industry increased to about US\$ 4.66 mmBtu (on gross calorific value basis), but fell to about US\$ 2.99 mmBtu in March 2022. The formula-based price for domestic gas has since been increased to US\$ 6.10 mmBtu and the price of imported LNG is hovering around US\$ 20–35 mmBtu. As fertiliser production is critical for the agriculture sector gas price increases are absorbed by government subsidies. Pooling of gas prices (domestic and imported) for the fertiliser industry allows uniform price for all fertiliser plants irrespective of the share of LNG they use.

Many fertiliser plants that historically used naphtha as feedstock have switched, or are about to switch, over to natural gas use which will drive consumption of gas. Additionally, the investment of about Rs 500 billion for the revival of closed fertiliser plants and the investment in the 2,650 km Jagdishpur-Haldia and Bokaro-Dhamra natural gas pipeline, known as 'Pradhan Mantri Urja Ganga' for a 'second green revolution' as the government put it, is driving consumption of natural gas. Analysts highlight increase in fertiliser subsidies on account of increase in imported LNG prices and recommend a switch to greener options, but change is not likely in the near term given the complex strategic nature of food production.

City Gas Distribution (CGD)

India has embarked on a massive expansion of CGD to develop large-scale nation-wide infrastructure for making piped natural gas (PNG) available to domestic, commercial, industrial consumers, and compressed natural gas (CNG) for vehicles run on CNG instead petrol or diesel. The CGD project envisages marketing of PNG to customers in domestic, commercial and industrial segments and CNG to the automotive segment. As of 31 December, 2021, PNGRB had approved about 33,768 km length of natural gas pipeline network across the country, of which 20,334 km length of pipelines, including spur lines, had become operational and a total of 15,194 km length of pipelines were under various stages of construction.

In 2007, PNGRB planned to expand CGD networks from 30 to over 3,000 cities in India to supply CNG for transport and piped natural gas connections to households and industries. In October 2015, India had a total of 1,026 CNG stations and over 3 million PNG connections. In March 2022 there were 4,013 CNG stations (GAGR 21.51%) and over 9 million PNG connections (CAGR 17.16%). The national gas grid is to be expanded to about 35,000 km from the current 20,000 km. After completion of 11th CGD auction, 96% of India's population and 86% of its geographic area is expected to be covered under CGD network. The claim that 86% of the population is covered under CGD only implies potential access and not actual use. There are 300 million LPG connections compared to 9 million (or about 3%) PNG connections.

As of 31 March, 2022 India had a total of 93.02 lakh PNG connections and 4,433 CNG stations in 27 states and union territories, covering around 88% of the country's geographical area and about 98% of the country's population.[33] The outbreak of Covid-19 in the first quarter of 2020 negatively impacted the CGD market, as end-users suffered losses during prolonged lockdowns. But soon it recovered and now it is estimated to register a CAGR of over 15%, according to Bharat Petroleum, a PSU, engaged in marketing petroleum products. Lockdown restrictions imposed by the Government of India to stop the spread of Covid-19 infections in the country caused a drop in demand, which affected the market. For instance, the investment firm ICRA estimated that the city gas distribution sector's domestic gas volumes declined by 12% month-on-month to 15.2 mmscmd in April 2020, as the passenger and transportation end-user segments suffered the most during lockdowns.

Factors such as growing government initiatives to increase natural gas usage as a cleaner fuel than LPG and conventional fuels like wood, cow dung, etc., are likely to drive the market during the forecast period. However, the long waiting period for various ministries' approvals to lay pipelines and lack of awareness of the benefits of natural gas among people, especially in rural India, are expected to hinder the market growth. PNG connections are one of the prominent segments expected to dominate India's CGD market during the forecast period, which include domestic, commercial and industrial usages.

The government's intention of converting India into a gas-based economy is expected to increase the natural gas share in its energy mix from 6% in 2019 to 15% by 2030. The government also has plans to expand and cover untapped areas for natural gas access, which would create an opportunity for the market to grow in the near future.

Increasing PNG connections and CNG stations are expected to drive the market. It is estimated that upon the completion of work for the 11th bidding round, nearly 96% of India's population would have access to natural gas use.

In 2021–22, 48% of CGD consumption was sourced from LNG imports. Unlike the fertiliser industry the CGD industry can, in theory, pass on increase in the price of gas to consumers. However domestic consumers of PNG are price sensitive which limits the ability of CGD operators to allow full pass-through of increase in LNG import costs to consumers. Industrial consumers are also price sensitive, and they can switch to cheaper alternatives if pollution mandates are not enforced.

Liquefied Petroleum Gas (LPG)

According to a National Family Health Survey (NFHS) in 2019–2021, carried out by the Ministry of Health and Family Welfare, about 56.2% of the Indian population uses LPG or PNG as the primary cooking fuel, of this, about 88.6% are urban households users of both, while 42% rural households use only LPG, as the piped gas facilities are unavailable in rural India. Overall, thus, 43.3% of Indian households still continue to use solid biomass as the primary fuel for cooking, with rural households leading with 54.6% and urban households with 8.9% among solid fuel users.[34]

Modi government has vowed to extend cooking gas facility to every household in the country as part of its battle against pollution. LPG is a mixture of butane and propane, which is supplied in cryogenic cylinders. It is less polluting due to its low sulphur content, and provides energy efficiency as well as improved operational and environmental performance. The intrinsic qualities of LPG make it an ideal, consistent and exceptional source of energy that is mainly used for replacing biomass for cooking and heating. Pradhan Mantri Ujjwala Yojana (PMUY) is a flagship scheme to make clean cooking fuel such as LPG available to the rural and deprived households which were otherwise using traditional cooking fuels such as firewood, coal, cow-dung cakes, etc. Till October 2022, the government had given 32.6 crore LPG connections in country.

The marketing operations of LPG commenced in Mumbai in 1955 under the Burmah-Shell Oil Company, but it became a preferred kitchen fuel only after Indian Oil took charge of it. The Indian Oil released its first LPG connection in Kolkata under the brand name Indane in October 1965. In 2021–22, LPG consumption constituted about 13% of total petroleum product consumption. About 90% of LPG was consumed by households, 8% by industrial users and 2% by vehicles. Over 60% of LPG was imported and over 99% of domestic production was from public sector refineries. LPG consumption grew by over 84% from about 15.3 mt in 2011–12 to 28.3 mt in 2021–22. Most of the growth was accounted for by packaged LPG consumed by households and commercial entities. Domestic LPG consumption grew by over 76% between 2013–14 and 2021–22 while commercial consumption grew by over 108%. In the same period, bulk LPG consumption by industry grew by about 59% while consumption of LPG by the automobile sector decreased by over 37%. Direct import of LPG by the private sector declined by over 83% from a peak of 4,89,000 tonnes to 82,000 tonnes in 2021–22. Most of the growth in LPG consumption is driven by government policy to increase access to LPG.

Compressed Natural Gas (CNG)

Compressed natural gas is another type of gas, which is provided by PNGRB under the subsidised CGD scheme. It is generally used to fuel transport vehicles, like trucks, buses taxies, three-wheelers, small commercial vehicles and personal cars, as an alternative fuel in place of gasoline. Because of its environmental compatibility and cost-effectiveness vis-à-vis petrol and diesel, it is fast becoming a greatly preferred alternative fuel. Worldwide, there were around 28 million natural gas vehicles (NGV) in 2019. China had the highest number of NGVs, followed by Iran, India, Pakistan, Argentina, Brazil and Italy. In 2018, the CGD market in India was dominated by the rising demand of CNG. Just as PNG and LPG, which are used by households for cooking or heating, CNG emits lesser toxic gases and other pollutants than conventional gasoline.

Existing gasoline-powered vehicles may be converted to run on CNG or LNG only, or may be made bio-fuel vehicles to run on both diesel or petrol. Diesel engines for heavy trucks and busses can also be converted and can be dedicated with the addition of new heads containing spark ignition systems, or can be run on a blend of diesel and natural gas, with the primary fuel being natural gas and a small amount of diesel fuel being used as an ignition source. It is also possible to generate energy in a small gas turbine and couple the gas engine or turbine with a small electric battery to create a hybrid electric motor driven vehicle.

India is trying to expand the network of CNG and LNG filling stations in cities and highways to encourage motorists to use these natural gases to cut their vehicular pollutions. In February 2020, PNGRB unveiled plans to set up 8,181 CNG stations in 44 newly-created geographical areas to strengthen CNG and PNG dispensing facilities by 2024. As of September 2019, there were 1,815 CNG stations—most of them concentrated in Delhi, Gujarat and Maharashtra—and 3,500 new stations were under construction, and lay 58,000-inch kilometre of steel pipeline to provide 2 crore new PNG connections by 2024. Roads for setting up new gas distribution networks have been paved by the award of licenses to Indian Oil Corporation and Adani Gas Ltd In 2019. For the first time the government is providing Rs 10,000 crore as 'viability gap funding' for laying pipelines in eastern and north-eastern India. At the same time, the government is going ahead with plans to build 10,000 CNG stations throughout the country by 2030.

Impressed by the economic and environmental leverages and the ability of natural gas-operated vehicles (NGVs) to slash petroleum import bills the government has been working aggressively to expand CNG and LNG infrastructure in the country to make these fuels easily available in cities, roads and highways. Studies have concluded that India could save Rs 2 lakh crores oil imports if personal cars switched to CNG vehicles. The government's plan envisages strengthening CNG and PNG stations up to 10,000 to provide CNG to motorists by 2030. CNG pumps retailing the fuel to automobiles has expanded from 938 five years ago to 1,769. PNGRB expects the number of CNG-run vehicles to cross 2 crores, up from about 34 lakhs in 2020.

Natural Gas Vehicles (NGVs)

Natural gas vehicles cost 30–40% less than a vehicle run on petrol or diesel. For example, if you are driving a WagonR on petrol in a city like Delhi, you will get around 12 km of mileage, and petrol will cost you around Rs 75 per litre. But if you drive the same car, run on CNG, in the same traffic condition, it will deliver a mileage of 16–19 km, and CNG will cost you Rs 40 per kg, yielding a saving of Rs 35 and a mileage advantage of 4–7 km. As a rule of thumb, it is believed, CNG produces savings of 30–40% over gasoline on travelling.

Secondly, dedicated natural gas engines are superior in performance to gasoline engines because natural gas has an octane rating of approximately 130, whereas super and unleaded petrol or diesel have octane levels of 95 and 97 respectively. Additionally, CNG-run vehicles are safer than those run by gasoline. The ignition temperature of CNG is 600°C, which is higher than gasoline's 320°C and diesel's 285°C. This means that CNG vehicles are less likely to catch fire under any circumstances. In the event of a leak, CNG is lighter than air, meaning that it will dissipate into the atmosphere, unlike gasoline or diesel which pools on the ground and serves as a fire hazard.

Encouraged by the planned development of CNG infrastructure and growing customer acceptance automobile manufacturers, like Maruti and Hyundai, have also announced plans to increase the production of CNG-powered vehicles.

The country's largest carmaker, Maruti Suzuki, has discontinued manufacturing diesel vehicles 'due to steep increase in costs related to the transition to BS VI emission standards' from 1 April, 2020, and has said that it will make all its small cars in CNG variants. The company makes 16 models of cars, of which seven models—Alto, Alto K10, WagonR, Celerio, Dzire Tour S, Eeco and Super Carry mini truck—are available in both petrol and CNG options. But now they will only be available in CNG version.

Maruti intends to sell 2,00,000 CNG cars annually by 2022 and has asked its dealers to bid for licences to open their own CNG dispensing stations to keep pace with the company's plan. It also intends to introduce new models in the small car segment. India's second largest car manufacturer, Hyundai Motor India Ltd, has launched a new factory-fitted CNG version of Santro and Magna Trim.

CNG-powered vehicles currently constitute around 7% of the overall sales of the Maruti, but in states where CNG distribution outlets are available, the CNG variant of cars account for about 30% of the sales, according to Maruti chairman RC Bhargava (CNG distribution outlets currently are mostly located in Delhi, Mumbai and Gujarat). In FY 2018–19, Maruti increased production of CNG-powered vehicles by 40% and was in the process of raising it by another 50% in 2019–20.

Economic benefits of CNG have lured many buses, trucks and many personal cars, two-wheelers and most three-wheelers to retrofit their vehicles with CNG kits. In Delhi and surrounding areas, it costs about Rs 35,000 to Rs 45,000 to install CNG kits in passenger cars. Delhi Transport Corporation, which maintains one of the largest fleets in the world, runs 5,500 buses on CNG. According to the chairman of PNGRB, DK Sarraf, the transport sector currently consumes 3 mt of LNG and about 11 mcm of natural gas per day, and projects this volume to rise by five times in the next 8 to 10 years due to increasing awareness and cost advantage of the natural gas in mobility.

Foreign organisations, who smell good business opportunities in India, are more upbeat about the growth of NGVs in India. Japanese Nomura, for instance, says that NGVs are likely to account for 50% of the total new sales in three-wheelers and four-wheeler segments by 2030. Rapidly developing infrastructure and reduction in cost due to domestic manufacturing would tremendously impact the Indian mobility scenario. In a report on 'Transforming Mobility Through Natural Gas', released recently by the Nomura Research Institute (NRI Consulting & Solutions) said the implementation of BS-VI emission norms from 1 April, 2020, would significantly increase the price differential between CNG and diesel vehicles, making CNG vehicles more attractive. Nomura predicted that the increased number of CNG and LNG filling stations would catapult the sale of NGVs ten times in the next 10 years to 33 million by 2030 from 3.3 million in 2019. Nomura added that around 15 original engine makers (OEMs) were already offering CNG variants models in passenger, commercial and goods vehicle segments.

Meanwhile, the government has galvanised concerned ministries to expedite approvals needed for setting up new CNG and LNG filling stations along highways and intra-city corridors. Ministries are already in talks with commercial vehicle makers to encourage them to build trucks and buses that run on CNG and LNG as an alternative to diesel and petrol. Petronet LNG, the largest importer of the liquefied gas, too, is preparing to set up 20 LNG outlets, service stations and an LNG storage along the Delhi-Mumbai-Bengaluru-Chennai highways. In 2019, the state-run company had persuaded Gujarat State Road Transport Corporation and Kerala State Road Transport Corporation to run 20 and 10 buses respectively on LNG. Currently, around 76% of the 1,815 CNG stations and 80% of the 54.2 lakh domestic PNG connections across the country are concentrated in Delhi, Gujarat and Maharashtra.

Petrochemicals

Petrochemical industry is another major consumer of natural gas, which forms the basis of olefins (ethylene, propylene and butadiene) and aromatics (benzene, toluene and xylene), the raw material of wide range of agricultural and industrial products. Olefins and aromatics are the primary building blocks of numerous articles such as detergents, solvents and adhesives, polymers and oligomers used in plastics, resins, fibres, elastomers, lubricants and gels. Ethane, propane and natural gas liquids obtained from natural gas are other important feedstock used in the petrochemicals industry, as it plays a vital role in economic growth and development of manufacturing sector. The value addition in the petrochemicals industry is higher than most of the other industry sectors. Today, petrochemical products permeate the entire spectrum of our daily use items like clothing, housing, construction, furniture, automobiles, households, agriculture, horticulture, irrigation, packaging, medical appliances, electronics and electricals.

Presently, there are 11 crackers in operation with combined ethylene capacity of about 7.05 mtpa. Four of these operate on the feed of naphtha (hence, called naphtha crackers) and three are natural gas crackers. The remaining two use both naphtha and gas (called dual-feed crackers) to produce ethylene. In addition, there are six aromatic complexes in operation with a combined xylene capacity of about 5.5 mt. In recent years, unconventional gases like coal bed methane (CBM) have also been used as feed stocks. Based on the products of the olefin and aromatic complexes several downstream polymer and plastic industries have come up. The annual consumption of virgin grade polymers was more than 16 mt in 2018–19 and has been growing rapidly. Plastics consumption in the same year ran close to 46 mt, and was estimated to grow at 9% per year. At present there are more than 50,000 processing units in the organised and unorganised sector in India that produce 45 mt per year of diverse range of plastic products. To meet the rising future demand, investors have planned investment of US$ 10 billion to raise production capacity to 62.4 mt per year by 2022–23 and 86 mt per year by 2027–28.

Naphtha Crackers

Plastics and polymers units using naphtha as feedstock are well-supplied by naphtha cracker plants—Reliance Industries Ltd, Vadodara (Gujarat); Reliance Industries Ltd, Hazira (Gujarat); Haldia Petrochemicals Ltd, Haldia (West Bengal); and Indian Oil Corporation, Panipat (Haryana). But for natural gas users it is a different story. The reason is simple, while naphtha production by refineries in India exceeds the domestic demand and is exported, natural gas is in short supply and imported. The shortage of gas discourages investors from outside the oil and gas to set up natural gas-based plants, though gas is cheaper than naphtha, which is a by-product of oil or natural gas. At present, only three natural gas crackers are in operation—Reliance Industries Ltd, Nagothane (Maharashtra); Gas Authority of India Limited, Pata (UP); and Reliance Industries Ltd, Dahej (Gujarat)—and they are all owned by the oil companies, namely, Reliance Industries, Indian Oil and Gas Authority of India.

Natural Gas Supply

Over 80% of India's energy needs are met by three fuels—coal, oil and solid biomass. Coal has underpinned the expansion of electricity generation and industry, and remains the largest single fuel in the energy mix. Oil consumption and imports have grown rapidly on account of rising vehicle ownership and road transport use. Biomass, primarily fuelwood, makes up a declining share of the energy mix, but is still widely used as a cooking fuel. Natural gas is seen as an alternative to all three. However, despite the recent successes in expanding coverage of LPG in rural areas, 660 million Indians have not fully switched to modern, clean cooking fuels.[35] Relatively environmentally benign natural gas is now being promoted to replace all three.

Natural gas has been a part of India's energy mix since the 1960s, but it has never played a prominent role. But after the discovery a cluster of large deposits in the deep waters of the east coast of India in 2002, the view among the country's policy maker changed. The finds were the world's largest for that year and India's largest since the discovery of Bombay High in 1970. The DGH projected gas initially in place (GIIP) accretion of 7.35 tcf in 2002–2003 and 9.37 tcf in 2006–07. Assuming a reserve accretion rate of 1% per year, production in 2019–20 was estimated to be about 145 mmscmd which, if realised, would have met most of India's natural gas demand today. Under a 5% per year reserve accretion rate, production was estimated to exceed 1,000 mmscmd that would have generated exportable surplus of natural gas at current levels of gas consumption.

The Ministry of Petroleum and Natural Gas website said, "Natural gas has emerged as the most preferred fuel due to its inherent environmentally benign nature, greater efficiency and cost effectiveness... In India too, the natural gas sector has gained importance, particularly over the last decade, and is being termed as the fuel of the twenty first century." However, the reality did not play out as expected. In 2010 the share of natural gas in India's primary commercial energy basket (not including non-commercial energy sources) was 9.4% which fell to 6.2% by 2018. In 2012 natural gas accounted for roughly 10% of gross electricity generation but in 2018 natural gas accounted for less than 4% of gross generation.[36] In 2018–19, India produced just over 87 mmscmd of natural gas while it consumed 166 mmscmd of gas which means that about 78 mmscmd (just over 47%) of gas consumption was imported.[37]

The reason for decline in domestic production was that the ageing of Bombay High gas field, one of India's two main producing fields, which had reached peak production in around 2010, while production from the other major field, the KG D6, remained well below the initial expectations due to smaller actual reserves, technical challenges and slow government action.[38]

However, demand continued to grow and production continued to fall. Imports of liquefied natural gas, initially from Qatar and later from other countries, became available after 2004, when India's first LNG terminal was commissioned, with volumes rising from 10 bcm in 2004 to 24 bcm in 2016.[39] Thus, Gujarat today is one of the epicentres of natural gas consumption in India.

In recent years, growth in India's LNG imports has increased dramatically amid growing consumption, particularly in the industrial sector (where natural gas is used in the production of fertiliser) and expansion of CGD network. But domestic production of natural gas, 70% of which is located offshore, has experienced a steady decline, from 4.4 bcf per day in 2012 to 2.9 bcf per day in 2019, and it has limited potential of further growth. This has pushed up the share of costly LNG imports from 31% in 2012 to more than 50% currently in gas supply basket. India does not import natural gas by pipeline and has no plans to build natural gas pipelines through the deserts and mountains that form much of its northern borders.

In sum, while natural gas demand has been soaring exponentially because of the inherent environmentally benign nature, greater efficiency and cost effectiveness of the commodity, supply has been unable to keep pace with it. Small domestic gas production and inadequate infrastructure, particularly pipelines to wheel fuels to consumers, are to blame for the low share of gas in the country's energy basket. It is pity that the share of natural gas in India's energy basket is measly 6.2% against a global average of 24%. It has largely been due to a drastic fall in output from Reliance-BP operated D1-D3 fields of KG D6 offshore block due to issues related to reservoir pressure and water and sand ingress. D1-D3 was India's first deep water gas field which went onstream in April 2009 and marked a milestone in India's gas story. Production started declining from April 2010 after hitting a peak of 61.43 mmscmd in March 2010. In euphoria, consumption shot up from 43 bcm in 2009 to 59 bcm in FY 2010. But the story ended by 2012 after a precipitate decline in production. The operators tried to keep the dying field alive by investing US$ 1 billion and to recover a further 0.53 tcf of gas and 31.4 million barrels of oil and condensate. But in February 2020, D1-D3 was shut down for ever. It has no remaining reserves.

Ironically, when Reliance had found gas in the KG D6 block in 2002, it was touted as India's largest natural gas discovery in 30 years. Recoverable reserves were estimated at 10 tcf. But when production started falling sharply, it was alleged that the quantum of Reliance's finds had been overestimated. However, the D1-D3 and the smaller MA fields had produced around 3 tcf of gas equivalent from the fields before they were shut down. BP-Reliance are now investing another US$ 5 billion to monetise gas reserves from three other projects—R Cluster, Satellite Cluster and MJ fields in the KG D6 block. These fields are believed to contain reserves of 3 tcf. The first gas from R Cluster came onstream in mid-2020. The peak production from these fields is expected to reach 1 bcf per day, sometime in 2022.

Despite the rising demand natural gas production in the country has remained unchanged at around 30–32 bcm per year since 2013. Around three quarters of this production comes from Western offshore areas—Krishna Godavari and Mumbai offshore and the remainder from onshore fields in Gujarat, Assam and Andhra Pradesh. Some smaller quantities of gas also come from Tamil Nadu, Tripura and Rajasthan onshore fields. State-run ONGC and OIL are the main producers of India's domestic gas.

Natural gas was the third largest source of energy in India. In 2019, it accounted for 6.5% of the total primary energy supply (TPES) and 27.9% of electricity generation. Coal accounted for 44% of TPES and 74% of electricity generation, while crude oil provided 10.4% of TPES and 4% of total electricity generation.[40]

Most gas in India is used in the industrial and power generation sectors. Until recently, residential consumption was small, but of late it is expanding exponentially. Data from the Ministry of Petroleum and Natural Gas show that of the 148 bcm of natural gas consumed daily in 2018–19, 60.52% or 89.57 bcm per day, was by fertiliser and other industries like steel, petrochemicals and refineries, and 22.42% or 33.18 bcm per day, by the power sector. Consumption in the CGD sector, which covers residential and transport segments, was relatively small, at 17% (25.27 bcm per day) of the total daily consumption. Overall consumption rose in 2019–20 to 180–190 bcm per day, according to Dharmendra Pradhan, but it was still far from the increase in the rate of consumption required for achieving the target of 15% share of natural gas in the energy mix by 2030 from 6.5% in 2020. In an event organised by FICCI, Pradhan said that the rate of consumption must rise to 600 bcm per day in the coming years to reach the target. For this the government has launched a massive expansion of all sectors using natural gas, especially CGD, along with infrastructure to accelerate consumption and, in the process create a sustainable gas economy and curb CO_2 emissions.

Rising Imports

Two new projects, the first since 2013, started during 2019—the 5 mt per year Ennore terminal in Tamil Nadu and the 4.9 mt per year Mundra terminal in Gujarat—taking actual capacity to 39 mt per year. In FY 2018–19, India imported 21.7 mt of LNG. Growth in 2019–20 of 12% would lead to imports of 24.3 mt, implying LNG import capacity utilisation of 62%. So, import capacity per se will not be a constraint to further growth, though the locations of the terminals and the availability of pipeline connections across the country will be. Of the six operational terminals, five are on the west coast and only one on the east coast. Indeed, much of the capacity is in Gujarat, the state where Narendra Modi was chief minister before he became the nation's prime minister in 2014. The exceptional economic performance of Gujarat, where gas has a much higher share of primary energy consumption than elsewhere in India, was a factor in Modi's popularity during the campaign for the 2014 general election.

Four other terminals are under development, which along with the 3.3 mt capacity that will become available when the Dabhol breakwater is eventually completed, should boost the capacity by another 20.1 mt per year by the end of 2021, taking the total to 59.1 mt per year. That said, delays would not come as a surprise, given India's poor record of completing LNG import projects on time. Moreover, only 9.9 mt per year of this incremental capacity will be on the east coast. Various other projects have been mooted but have yet to reach final investment decision (FID).

This would considerably help revive stressed and stranded gas-based power plants in India to resume production and expand CGD services further. Driven by demand from city gas distribution services and transportation, India's LNG demand is expected to grow by 9 to 11% to about 25 to 26 mt in 2020, according to analysts from Wood Mackenzie and FGE. That would still put terminal utilisation at just over 60% at the year end. LNG accounts for nearly half of CGD consumption volume and a lower price augur well for both volumes and operating margins of distributors and project returns.

Differential Prices

Prices of domestic gas, which are distributed by the government, are fixed by PNGRB every six months (on 1 April and 1 October) to control the rates at which fertiliser manufacturers, gas-based power companies and CGD (CNG and PNG) service providers are required to supply their product to consumers. The PNGRB-fixed prices are based on volume-weighted annual average of prices prevailing in Henry Hub (US), National Balancing Point (UK), Alberta

(Canada) and Russia with a lag of one-quarter, but also heavily subsidised by the government. The cost of production of urea changes by around Rs 1,600–1,800 per tonne for every US$ 1 per mmBtu change. The price cut would reduce the subsidy outgo for the government by Rs 800 crore in the first half of FY 21, it is expected.

Responding to plunging gas prices globally, the PNGRB slashed prices of domestic gas by about 45%. Thus, India's domestic gas prices for the six months from 1 April to 30 September, 2020 was US$ 2 mmBtu, down from US$ 3.25 mmBtu in the previous six month-period, 1 October, 2019 to 31 March, 2020. The cut followed a corresponding decline in the US benchmark Henry Hub prices which had fallen to below US$ 2 mmBtu in early 2020, the lowest since 2016, and Dutch TTF gas hub where prices had also tumbled to under US$ 3 mmBtu, the lowest since September 2009. Asian prices were swinging between US$ 3 to US$ 4 mmBtu, thanks to a glut and reduced demand in the market, with no sign of improvement over the next two years as economic slowdown and incremental supplies from LNG producers, including the US, Qatar, Australia, East Africa and Russia, likely to continue to batter the market. The price of LNG supplies in India is determined, based on the cost of LNG imported in the country.

According to the Petroleum Planning and Analysis Cell (PPAC) of petroleum ministry's estimates the declining oil and gas prices were likely to reduce India's oil and gas import bills by 11.4% to US$ 101 billion, or even less than that, in 2019–20, from US$ 114 billion in the previous year, despite a 2.6% rise in the volume of imports. PPAC anticipates a further reduction in the bill, if crude oil prices, to which gas prices are closely linked, fell below US$ 50 per barrel. To its glee, benchmark Brent oil prices had crashed 30-year low to around US$ 30 per barrel and natural gas prices to around US$ 1.80 mmBtu in mid-March 2020, following the bitter Saudi-Russian price war.

In 2019 India's natural gas consumption stood at 166 mmscmd. The petroleum minister has said that consumption level has to increase to 600 mmscmd to achieve the target of 15% consumption in 2030. Concerned ministries and agencies are working to build new pipelines and pumping stations to supply CNG and LNG to motor vehicles and PNG to household for cooking and heating throughout the country.

Today, while domestic gas is priced at US$ 6.1 mmBtu (as of August 2022), contracted LNG is priced at around US$ 14 mmBtu and spot LNG at

US$ 35 mmBtu. Although LNG has historically been expensive vis-à-vis domestic gas, the realignment of global LNG trade structure post the Ukraine Crisis has led to skyrocketing LNG prices in the first half of 2022. While we expect the prices to correct in the second half, they will remain elevated as compared to historical levels next year as well, thus capping the growth of natural gas demand in the medium term, especially from the industrial segment.

While India's re-gasification capacity is further being increased to 61 mmtpa, the slow progress of the key projects under the national gas grid to 34,500 km has been slow, resulting in poor evacuation opportunities for LNG re-gas terminals and impacting their utilisation rates which stood around 60% in FY 22.

According to PNGRB,[41] it becomes easier for users in the power, fertiliser and city gas distribution sectors to switch to gas following the fall in gas prices. The regulatory body feels that the increased pace of substitution of oil by natural gas is set to alter the country's primary energy mix dramatically, with the share of natural gas rising expectedly to around 20%, more than the government's aspired target of 15% by 2030. A study by PNGRB has also projected a substantial increase in the country gas-based power generation till 2029–2030. A study by the government's think tank, NITI Aayog, has projected that the country's energy consumption will reach 2,300 mtoe by 2047, of which natural gas will contribute 173 mtoe.[42]

However, India's domestic production of natural gas can only partially fulfil the expected surge in demand in the coming years. The country will have to depend on increased imports to fill the gap. In FY 2018–19, for instance, the domestic production was 90 mmscmd against the bare minimum demand of 148 mmscmd to keep its existing CGD services and core industries like fertiliser, power, steel and petrochemicals running. The country had to import 22 mt of liquefied natural gas or 52% of the requirement, to fill the gap. Statistics available from different sources show LNG import was likely to increase, varying from 10 to 16% annually to 2030. Within nine months of FY 2019–20, LNG imports increased by 6.8% year-on-year to 23.58 bcm as domestic output declined by 3.2% and consumption climbed by 3.9%. The share of LNG in total domestic consumption expanded to 51.6% during this period from 47.9% in the year-ago period.[43]

After several years during which imports remained flat, they began to take off in 2015, and since then the compound annual surge rate has been at an average of 12%, with the volume up by 54% in 2018–19 from 2014–15. The numerous LNG terminal projects under development and being planned highlight expectations that strong growth will continue for the foreseeable future. At the start of 2019, India had four operational terminals with a nominal combined re-gasification capacity of 32.4 mt per year; however, actual capacity was 29.1 mt per year because the Dabhol terminal, with a capacity of 5 mt per year, was restricted to 1.7 mt per year as it lacked breakwater required to enable year-round deliveries. The Kochi terminal was under-utilised because of the slow development of evacuation pipeline capacity, with only a limited capacity for flowing gas.

Robust Expansion

In order to make gas available at highways and expressways, projects underway include building a strong network of LNG filling stations along the 6,000 km long Golden Quadrilateral highways which, it is expected, would encourage truckers to switch to this cleaner and less expensive fuel from the polluting diesel. State-run GAIL is putting together a plan and trying to get city gas distributors, gas suppliers, financiers, fleet owners and truck manufacturers onboard to build an effective ecosystem for LNG-fuelled vehicles in the country. The project entails building about 350 LNG fuelling stations, at a cost of Rs 3,000–3,500 crore, to cover the full length of the Golden Quadrilateral. Rules permit only CGD licence holders to set up LNG facilities in their specific areas.

GAIL has announced an investment of Rs 1.05 lakh crore over the next five years to expand pipelines and CGD networks and raise petrochemical production capacity to deliver gas to households and vehicles in the eastern, northeast and southern regions of the country. Around Rs 45,000 to Rs 50,000 crore will be spent on building new pipelines, Rs 40,000 crore for city gas distribution facilities and Rs 10,000 crore for petrochemical capacity expansion, according to Manoj Jain, GAIL Chairman. At present, GAIL operates 12,160 km of pipeline network and markets two-thirds of the total natural gas sold in the country. It will add about 7,000 km of pipeline length in the next five years. At the same time, it is raising its LNG import capacity by constructing a breakwater at its Dabhol LNG receiving and re-gasification terminal to ensure that it operates at its full 5 mt per year capacity. Presently, the operations are restricted during the monsoon as high tides pose risks to ships carrying gas In liquid form. Also, the company has booked capacity at Adani Group's upcoming terminal at Dhamra in Odisha. Currently, the company is building a 2,655 km gas pipeline from Jagdishpur in Uttar Pradesh to Haldia in West Bengal, passing through Bokaro in Jharkhand and Dhamra in Odisha. GAIL is looking to put up 400 CNG stations and provide PNG connections to 10 lakh household kitchens by 2025.

GAIL has planned to build 90 LNG stations in its own licence area to serve the fuel to heavy vehicles, and is in talks with ExxonMobil and Mitsui to explore whether they can partner with it as LNG supplier and financier. Initially it plans to serve about 10,000 LNG trucks. Natural gas in transportation and industrial applications holds significant potential for India in terms of lowering costs, reducing emissions and enhancing energy reliability. At present, Indian cities have about 3.5 million vehicles using CNG, but barely any that use LNG, which is natural gas super cooled to −162°C. Because of its lower energy density and slow refuelling time, CNG is seen as suitable for city transport, but not for haul drives. LNG contains 2.5 times more energy per unit volume compared to CNG and can fill fast, becoming appropriate for long-distance travel. In its plan to use LNG in transportation, India has taken cue from the immediate neighbour China (although the fuel is used everywhere in the US and Europe), where LNG-fuelled trucks have helped combat foul air. China's LNG heavy truck production reached nearly 7,00,000 units in 2020, according to International Gas Union.

According to PNGRB Chairman DK Sarraf, natural gas as vehicular fuel is 60% cheaper than petrol and costs 45% less than its diesel counterpart. In 2019, the transport sector was consuming 3 mt of LNG and about 11 mcm of natural gas every day. PNGRB has forecast these volumes to rise nearly five times by 2030, thanks to growing environmental awareness and cost advantages of the fuel. Although fervent efforts have been made to raise domestic gas production, rapid fat increases imports are unavoidable to meet the burgeoning demand. The trends had become evident in 2018–19 when the country's LNG import grew by 14% to 22 mt year-on-year, despite a modest 0.7% increase in domestic gas production, as gas consumption rose 7% to 54.5%, 56% of which was met through LNG imports. PNGRB expected the domestic gas production to increase from 2020 onward driven by deep water projects to 23 bcm in 10 years, and LNG processing and re-gasifying capacity to rise nearly double from 35 mmtpa to 69 mmtpa by

2025. In 2019–20, imports were expected to scale up further by 12% to 24.3 mt.[44] The CGD market in India is forecast to witness a CAGR of around 7.5% to grow from an estimated 9,100 mmscmd in 2019 to more than 28,500 mmscmd by 2035, on account of increasing demand from domestic, commercial, industrial and automotive segments.[45]

IV. THE FUTURE OF NATURAL GAS IN INDIA

According to IEA, consumption of natural gas in India is expected to grow by 25 bcm, registering an average annual growth of 9% until 2024. Industrial consumers are expected to account for 40% of net demand growth. The demand is also expected to be driven by other sectors such as transport, residential and energy. Transport and mobility sector, which comprises distinct modes such as railways, road, inland waterways, air and marine transport systems, had been the fastest-growing end-use system of energy. The sector is heavily dependent on petroleum fuels and contributes to half of India's oil and gas demand and 10% of its CHG emissions. In 2020, an estimated 60% of the country's energy consumption in transport arose from passenger transport and 40% from freight transport.

According to IEA, India's primary energy demand is expected to nearly double to 1,123 mtoe, as the country's gross domestic product is expected to increase to US$ 8.6 trillion by 2040.[46] Natural gas consumption is forecast to increase at a CAGR of 4.18% to 143.08 mt by 2040 from 58.10 mt in 2018. India's near-term goal is to increase the share of natural gas in the country's energy mix to 15% by 2030 from 6.5% in 2020. This requires more than tripling the consumption of gas to 600 mmscmd by 2030 from 190 mmscmd in 2020.

An expanding economy, rapid urbanisation and a growing population are fundamental drivers of India's energy demand, pushing the nation to become one of the most significant energy markets by 2040.[47] However, India's primary energy mix remains coal-dominated, which has been an impediment to the deep decarbonisation objectives of the country. The government has already recognised this issue and has adopted a multipronged approach to promote diversification of the primary energy mix with fewer carbon-emitting energy sources.[48] Indeed, India aims to become a natural gas-based economy by increasing its share to 15% of the primary energy mix by 2030.[49] But the share of natural gas in India's energy basket has been increasing at a much slower rate than anticipated, from 5.6% in 2012–13[50] to 6.5% in 2018–19,[51] despite a 6% increase in its consumption during the same period.[52]

In the immediate future, the use of natural gas in industries, transport and in homes will enable the move away from highly polluting coal, but it must be used as a 'transition fuel' only. However, investment in this transition must not be allowed to crowd out investment in greener technologies such as renewables, green hydrogen and storage capacity. After all, natural gas, though less polluting than coal, is a fossil fuel. A solution lies in planning ways that gas infrastructure can be repurposed for renewables such as green hydrogen, which will make India's energy systems emissions-free in the long term.

Currently, India's natural gas market has been grappling with three major challenges—lack of pipeline infrastructure to transfer natural gas across and to major demand centres, while unlocking the latent demand; the mandated domestic gas allocation policy for priority sectors; and the regulated wellhead prices of domestic gas production.

The gas allocation policy classifies consumer sectors in two tiers. Tier one includes priority sectors such as the city gas distribution sector for piped natural gas (domestic) and compressed natural gas (transport), fertiliser, power, LPG, etc., which receive the larger share of cheaper domestic gas. In contrast, tier two sectors have to rely on expensive LNG. The prioritisation is based on either the price-sensitive nature of consumers. For instance, fertiliser production is a priority considering the sensitivity of the agriculture sector, whereas the CGD sector is included as a consequence of a Supreme Court ruling to curb increasing air pollution in cities.

Reforms

In addition, as opposed to market-driven discovery, the gas market in India is governed by a controlled pricing mechanism. Currently, there are four major gas pricing regimes in the country: (i) Nomination regime (administered pricing mechanism or APM); (ii) Discovered Field regime (Pre-New Exploration Licensing Policy or Pre-NELP); (iii) New Exploration Licensing Policy (NELP); and (iv) Hydrocarbon Exploration and Licensing Policy (HELP).

Multi-billion dollar planned investments towards establishing 'One Nation, One Gas Grid' indicate the government's commitment to building a gas-based economy.[53] Also, considering the fast adoption of LNG in India, the focus on LNG infrastructure has become as important as that of the national gas grid. Overall, there is a 'chicken and egg' dilemma regarding natural gas uptake and the construction of supporting infrastructure. But infrastructure development is not the only factor that could accelerate gas penetration in India.

The price of natural gas in consumer sectors is an equally critical variable that influences gas uptake. Historically, gas prices have been high in countries worldwide, but a paradigm shift towards a low gas price regime is being observed. This shift can be attributed to several reasons such as the discovery of shale gas reserves in the US and the global supply glut. International gas prices started crashing in 2019 due to the supply glut, and amid the Covid-19 pandemic, the LNG price dropped to as low as US\$ 2 mmBtu.

LNG's low prices, especially for the spot, have triggered renegotiations of long-term contracts in India. Low gas prices offer great potential for uptake and corresponding benefits across sectors. But multiple associated nuances need to be explored before making a decisive push towards gas adoption. It is important to evaluate what a gas-based economy could offer in terms of jobs, growth and sustainability.

Also, high gas demand in India could facilitate further expansion of gas infrastructure in the country. The growing availability of infrastructure would increase employment opportunities. But gas will also replace other fuels, which could trigger job losses in associated value chains. Hence, the net impact of gas penetration on the jobs front remains uncertain. High gas penetration could also reduce oil import bills by substituting gas for oil in the primary energy mix. But conversely, it could also increase the expenditure on gas imports, which would have implications on planning for increasing energy security.

The idea of making India a gas-based economy has provoked discussions on the role of natural gas becoming a carbon neutral nation. One view favours natural gas adoption for decarbonisation, while the other opposes it due to its carbon-intensive nature. The view favouring gas adoption highlights natural gas as a cheap, plentiful, versatile and comparatively clean fuel, making it a viable option as a transition fuel between coal and renewables. On the contrary, people opposing it contend that greater gas penetration would hamper the government's measures taken to meet its decarbonisation targets.

In any case, at the end of the day, the key variable that will influence the outlook for the future of natural gas in India is its price. At the moment, gas appears priced out against other cleaner sources of generation such as solar and wind. As per the Central Electricity Authority report titled, 'Optimal Generation Capacity Mix' there could be a 2% share of gas in the gross generation in 2029–30.[54] The industry sector will also remain coal-dominated in 2050, and gas penetration is expected to make up about 13% of its total energy consumption.

References

1. In 2011, Royal Dutch Shell's 140,000 barrels (22,000 m3) per day F–T Plant went into Operation in Qatar.
2. Daniel Ergin, *The Quest*, p.331.
3. US Energy Information Agency, Natural Gas and the Environment.
4. BP Statistics, 2020.
5. 'Natural Gas and the Environment', NaturalGas.org, 3 May, 2009.
6. 'Natural Gas in Asia: History and Prospects,' Mikkal Herberg (PDF).
7. Vaclav Smil in *Energy and Civilisation: A History*, p.245.
8. Ibid.
9. Needham, 1964; quoted by Ibid.
10. Vogel 1993, Ibid.
11. 'A Brief History of Natural Gas – APGA', 18 February, 2019, www.apga.org.
12. 'World Energy Outlook 2009', International Energy Agency 2009 (PDF).
13. Natural gas scenario in India (PDF).
14. PNGRB, 'Vision 2030', Natural Gas Infrastructure in India, pngrb.gov.in.
15. 'Energy Statistics 2022', Ministry of Statistics and Programme Implementation.
16. India Natural Gas; https://www.worldometers.info/gas/india-natural-gas/.
17. DGI I, Annual Report, 2018–19.
18. Forecasting India's Oil and Gas Reserves and Production Potential, https://doi.org/10.1016/0040-1625(92)90017-N.
19. Stevens, Paul (August 2012). 'The 'Shale Gas Revolution': Developments and Changes. Chatham House.
20. Oil and Gas Journal, 2010.
21. Geology.com, 'World Shale Gas Resources'.
22. Directorate General of Hydrocarbons: India's Hydrocarbon Outlook, 2018–19.
23. Ministry of Earth Sciences, India.
24. Steve Hargreaves, 'Natural gas crystals: Energy under the sea', *CNN Money*, 9 March, 2010.
25. Tabuchi, Hiroko, "An Energy Coup for Japan: 'Flammable Ice'," *The New York Times*, 12 March, 2013.
26. Statista; www.statista.com/statistics/282717/global-natural-gas-consumption, 14 August, 2022.

27. IEA.

28. Natural Gas Scenario in India, Ministry of Petroleum and Natural Gas.

29. Columbia/SIP, Centre on Global Energy Policy.

30. PNGRB Vision: 2012/13 -2029/30.

31. 'India Energy Security Scenario', NITI Aayog, Government of India.

32. IEA Outlook.

33. Bharat Petroleum, bharatpetroleum.in/Our-Businesses/gas/city-gas-distribution.aspx.

34. Observer Research Foundation, 21 September, 2022.

35. IEA, India Energy Outlook.

36. Central Electricity Authority, 2018.

37. Observer Research Foundation (ORF), Natural Gas in India: From Cinderella to Goldilocks by Lydia Powell & Akhilesh Sati.

38. Charles Ebinger and Govinda Avasarala (2013), 'Natural Gas in India: Difficult Decisions', James A. Baker III Institute For Public Policy, Rice University, October 2013, http://belfercenter.hks.harvard.edu/files/CES-pub-GeoGasIndia-102513-3.pdf.

39. International Group of Liquefied Natural Gas Importers (GIIGNL), LNG Industry in 2016.

40. IEA, based on CEA Statistics, 2019.

41. PNGRB Vision: 2012–13-2029–30.

42. 'India Energy Security Scenario', NITI Aayog, Government of India.

43. *The Economic Times*, 29 January, 2020.

44. *The Economic Times*, 31 January, 2020.

45. TechSciResearch, Oil and Gas: January, 2020.

46. IEA, India Energy Outlook, 2021.

47. *PIB*, 2019.

48. IEA, 2020.

49. *PIB*, 2020.

50. MOSPI, 2014.

51. MOSPI, 2020.

52. PPAC, 2020.

53. MOPNG, 2020.

54. CEA, 2020.

SECTION II

RENEWABLE ENERGY

Chapter 4

RENEWABLE ENERGY

I. OVERVIEW

Climate change and global warming concerns, coupled with falling cost of solar panel and wing turbines are driving an irreversible shift from fossil fuels to renewable energy. Also helping the process are the growing adoption of electric vehicles (EVs), favourable government policies and spending priorities.

At least 47 countries across the world were already generating 50% of their electricity from renewable sources in 2022, according to the International Energy Agency (IEA). Iceland is the first country that draws 100% of its energy from renewable sources—87% from hydropower and 13% from geothermal. Costa Rica is another country among the top renewable energy users, which derives 99% of its electricity supplies from hydroelectric, geothermal and wind sources. Close behind is Norway, which generates 98% of its electricity from renewables, mostly hydropower. Other countries drawing most of their energy from renewables include Sweden, Costa Rica, Nicaragua, Scotland and Germany.

Renewables overtook fossil fuels as the main source of energy in the 27-country European Union in 2020. Renewables generated 38% of its electricity, as the share of natural gas and coal power shrank to 37%. Denmark received 61% of electricity from wind and solar, Ireland and Germany 35% and 33% respectively from these sources. Worldwide, renewables accounted for more than two-thirds of the newly installed electricity capacity in 2019.[1]

Oil Majors Suffer Massive Losses

However, the rise of renewable energy has not been good news for oil and gas companies. According to Wood Mackenzie consultancy, the global energy transition is creating uncertainty for an estimated US$ 14 trillion worth of oil and gas assets that have long depended on the humanity's insatiable demand for fossil fuels. In 2020, the world's top listed oil firms suffered unprecedented losses as the Covid-19 pandemic sent demand and prices tumbling, and cumulatively, BP, Chevron, ExxonMobil, Shell and Total reported US$ 77 billion in losses. Total's Patrick Pouyanne described 2020 as a landmark year that brought unexpected challenges and led to significant changes.

The spread of the pandemic and subsequent lockdowns caused massive slowdowns in economic activities, with international air travel coming to a near standstill. This dampened demand, triggering crash of oil prices. The crisis called further into question the financial model of oil majors, which already face a long-term threat from the ongoing shift away from fossil fuels to new age energy—solar, wind, nuclear and hydropower.

Energy transition, price volatility and weaker profitability are increasing risks for oil and gas producers, prompting S&P ratings agency to place shares of Chevron, ExxonMobil, Shell, Total and the Chinese oil company CNOOC on watch for a ratings downgrade. The oil majors are skating on ever-thinning ice and the pressure to diversify is rising as the effects of climate change combine with other events like the Covid-19 pandemic, says Professor David Elmes at the Warwick Business School.

European oil majors recognise the change and have begun to diversify their operations, including investing in renewable energy technologies. Total has even changed its name to TotalEnergies to better reflect its involvement in various energy sources, including renewables. It is followed by Norway's Statoil which has rebranded itself as Equinor.

US oil majors have, however, generally resisted moving into renewables. While ExxonMobil has moved to create a 'low carbon' unit, it will focus on carbon capture projects to reduce the emissions from its facilities. Once the world's most valuable publicly traded oil and gas giant, ExxonMobil lost its position, albeit briefly, to a Florida-based wind and solar energy player, NextEra, in October 2020 as its market capitalisation slipped to US$ 142 billion against the latter's US$ 145 billion. The event gave a glimpse of the profound changes convulsing the global energy system. Between January and November 2020, the mighty Exxon lost half of its market value and had been under pressure to write-down between US$ 17 billion and US$ 20 billion and cut its capital spending of up to one third in 2022–25. Two months later, Tesla joined the S&P 500 as the fifth-largest company on the index, after its stock skyrocketed in 2021, driving a lot of appetite for electric vehicles (EV) investment in general.

"The past 12 months (2020) brought new indignities," (for oil firms), said *The Economist* in January 2021. "All told, the big five (ExxonMobil, Royal Dutch Shell, Chevron, BP and Total) have lost US$ 350 billion in stock market value. They talk of slashing jobs, by up to 15%, and capital spending. Shell cut its dividend for the first time since the World War II. BP said it would sell its posh headquarters in London's Mayfair."[2] Shell wrote down up to US$ 4.5 billion in oil and gas assets following a string of impairments in 2020 as it adjusted to a weaker outlook. This followed a US$ 16.8 billion write-down in the second quarter and a sharp cut in its price outlook,[3] *Reuters* reported in August 2020.

More than 50 oil and gas firms filed for bankruptcy since oil prices crashed in March 2020, led by exploration and production companies with 29 filings. The amount of debt held by these companies, US$ 49.69 billion, was nearly twice the debt held by energy bankruptcy filers all of last year, the law firm's data showed, it said. Oil prices had fallen by about one third from above US$ 60 a barrel at the start of the year as the Covid-19 pandemic crushed fuel demand. They briefly turned negative in April 2020.[4]

Momentum Shifts to Renewables

Renewable energies offer more stable revenue than oil and gas, which are volatile. But stability is not the only reason attracting the oil majors. The reasons for diversifying today are also the climate change policies and pressure from investors, shareholders and even clients who are pushing the oil firms to decarbonise.

There are strong pressures on private companies to keep oil and gas portfolios in check. Despite higher prices, major oil companies kept their aggregate oil and gas spending flat in 2021, and their share of overall upstream spending is now at 25%, compared with nearly 40% in the mid-2010s. The shale sector is, for the moment, sticking to its newfound commitment to capital discipline, using higher revenues in 2021–22 to pay down debt and return money to shareholders rather than to increase output.

So far, investment by oil and gas companies outside their core business areas has been less than 1% of total capital expenditure. For the moment, there are few signs of a major change in company investment spending. For those companies looking to diversify their energy operations, redeploying capital towards low-carbon businesses requires attractive investment opportunities in the new energy markets as well as new capabilities within the companies.

Oil and gas companies are also coming under increasing pressure to adapt their investment strategies to the needs of clean energy transitions. This takes different forms, including commitments to reduce emissions resulting from oil and gas supply or to invest into new areas such as clean electricity or sustainable fuels. In 2020, clean energy investments by the oil and gas industry accounted for only around 1% of total capital expenditure. However, the IEA's tracking suggests that commitments to diversify investment, led by large European companies, are starting to have an impact. The share of capital investment by the oil and gas industry going to clean energy investments may have risen to more than 4% in 2021. Project financing for offshore wind—closely aligned with industry strengths—was considerably higher in the first quarter of 2021 than in the whole of 2020.

British Petroleum (BP)

European oil majors believe that the age of fossil fuels is fading; hence, they are leaving their reserves buried and preparing for a future in which governments enact tougher environmental policies for the net zero emissions era. BP has been the leading proponent of this strategy since 1980s. Formerly known as the British Petroleum Company, it rebranded to Beyond Petroleum (BP) in 2001 with a look towards other energy sources beyond oil. In the aftermath of the 2010 Deep Water Horizon oil spill incident in the Gulf of Mexico, BP closed most of its previous green energy investments, believed to be worth about US$ 8–10 billion. But the company still has more than 2200 MW of wind capacity in the US and has started to re-invest in renewables in recent years. It spent US$ 200 million in 2017 on acquiring a 43% stake in Lightsource, which has been rebranded to Lightsource BP and is Europe's largest solar power project developer.

In 2021, BP announced plans to increase its investments in low-emission businesses tenfold, to US$ 5 billion per year, while shrinking its oil and gas production by 40% over the next years until 2030. Royal Dutch Shell, Eni of Italy, Total of France, Repsol of Spain and Equinor of Norway have set similar targets. Several of these companies have cut their dividends to invest in new energy.

Shell

Shell's investment target for green energy projects was set between US$ 4 and $ 6 billion for the period from 2016 until the end of 2020, but according to *The Guardian,* the sum spent was well below those figures. The Anglo-Dutch firm's 2016 New Energies strategy covers several areas including electricity, wind and solar, electric vehicle charging and initiatives to encourage the adoption of hydrogen fuel cell electric vehicles. It spent a reported US$ 2 billion on setting up a low-carbon energy and electricity generation business in 2016, ensuring it was on course to meet its targets at the time. In 2018, Shell bought a 44% stake in US solar power firm Silicon Ranch for US$ 200 million and made a US$ 20 million equity investment in India-based renewable power company Husk Power Systems.

TotalEnergies

France's Total even changed its name to TotalEnergies to reflect its expanded operations covering all streams of energy. The company has plans to invest US$ 500 million per year in clean energy technologies. This is about 3% of the French oil major's total capital expenditure, with plans in place to ramp that up to 20% over the next 20 years. Over the past 10 years, it has made a number of strategic investments, including acquisition of a 60% stake in the US firm Sun Power for US$ 1.4 billion.

Total is aiming to become a global integrated leader in solar power. Already, it has a 1.6 GW solar capacity, which it plans to increase to 5 GW over the next five years. In 2016, it purchased the French battery manufacturer Saft for US$ 1.1 billion and Belgian green power utility Lampiris for US$ 224 million. It also acquired a 74% stake in the French electricity retailer Direct Energie for US$ 1.7 billion in 2018, propelling the company to one of the top utility providers in France.

Italian oil major, ENI, in 2014, launched the world's first conversion of a traditional refinery to a biorefinery that produces jet fuel, green diesel, green naphtha and liquid petroleum gas. With an eye on growing its onshore and offshore wind capacity, ENI has formed partnerships with France-based GE Renewable Energy and Norwegian energy company Equinor. Clean energy sources play a key role in the firm's corporate strategy. The company is investing US$ 1.3 billion to set up an installed renewable power capacity of 5 GW by 2025.

Switching to Renewables Is a Folly: Chevron

In contrast to European firms, American oil majors, which generally favour high returns on investment, consider the switch to renewables as a folly as they see it a low-profit business best suited to utilities and alternative companies. They prefer to stay put with their traditional business—oil and gas exploration and production and trading—and decarbonise their existing assets in a cost-effective way and consistently bring in new technology and new forms of energy.

Chevron says it is increasing its own use of renewable energy to power its operations. It also says it is reducing emissions of methane, a powerful greenhouse gas, as the company has invested more than US$ 1.1 billion in various projects to capture and sequester carbon so it isn't released into the atmosphere. Its venture capital arm, Chevron Technology Ventures, is investing in new energy start-ups like Zap Energy, which is developing modular fusion nuclear reactors that release no greenhouse gases and limit radioactive waste. Another, Carbon Engineering, removes carbon dioxide from the atmosphere to convert into fuel. Chevron Technology Ventures has two funds with a total of US$ 200 million, about 1% of the company's capital and exploration budget in 2020. The company has a separate US$ 100 million fund to support a US$ 1 billion investment consortium that aims to reduce emissions across the oil and gas industry.

ExxonMobil

Exxon has also largely steered away from renewables and has instead invested heavily in carbon-capture capacity. It spends about US$ 1 billion per year on research and development, much of which goes to developing new energy technologies and efficiency improvements that reduce emissions. One of its projects involves directing carbon emitted from industrial operations into a fuel cell that can generate power. That should reduce emissions while increasing energy production. In a separate experiment, Exxon recently announced a 'big advance' with scientists at University of California, Berkeley, and the Lawrence Berkeley National Laboratory for developing materials that help capture carbon dioxide from natural gas power plants with less heating and cooling than previous methods.[5]

Renewables Heading Towards Boom

Energy consultancy Wood Mackenzie forecasts that renewables are set to provide 60% of world energy demand by 2030. Scaling up and commercialising hydrogen produced from renewable energy for carbon capture and storage (CCS) will help many heavy industries such as green steel, fertiliser and cement, as well as heating, to decarbonise. All projections point to the fact that renewable energy is headed towards a boom in coming years, as concern for climate change and support for environmental, social and governance (ESG) considerations grow and demand for cleaner energy sources intensify. In 2021, only the renewable energy industry remained remarkably resilient. Rapid technological improvements and decreasing costs of renewable energy resources, along with the increased competitiveness of battery storage, have made renewables one of the most competitive energy sources in several areas. Despite suffering from supply chain constraints, increased shipping costs, and rising prices for key commodities, capacity installations of renewables remained at an all-time high. Wind and solar capacity additions of 13.8 GW in the first eight months of 2021 were up 28% over the same period in 2020. Many cities, states and utilities set ambitious clean energy goals, increasing renewable portfolio standards and enacting energy storage procurement mandates.

Activity is also heating up in next-generation technologies, and renewable energy industry stakeholders are considering investments in them, which can eventually help to more confidently integrate variable renewables such as wind and solar into the electric grid. For an industry that has largely focused on solar and wind, private investment and pilot projects combined with research support could help expedite commercialisation of emerging technologies such as green hydrogen, advanced batteries and other forms of long-duration storage.

These technologies can provide zero-carbon electricity and long-term seasonal electricity storage, ease grid congestion, stem renewable curtailment, boost reliability and facilitate integration of solar and wind into the grid while supporting goals for 100% clean energy. The industry is also exploring new long-duration energy storage solutions to help smoothly integrate renewables into the electricity grid. In August 2021 alone, private investments of about US$ 650 million were made in a number of energy storage companies exploring new technologies. One such company was Form Energy, which recently unveiled a breakthrough, long-duration energy storage iron-air battery that can provide over 100 hours of energy at a cost of US$ 20 per kWh—about one-tenth the cost of the more common lithium-ion batteries in use today. It received a US$ 240 million financing round with investors, including steel company ArcelorMittal.

A major driving force behind the rise of green hydrogen has been the decreasing costs of renewable energy—a critical input in the production process of hydrogen. In 2022, as renewable energy penetration on the grid increases, green hydrogen development is also expected to grow, owing to its potential to act as long-duration and seasonal storage of fuel available on demand to generate power.[6]

Renewables' Returns Are Seven Times Higher than Fossil Fuels

According to a report published by the Centre for Climate Finance at Imperial College Business School and the International Energy Agency in March 2021, renewable power generated significantly higher total returns over the last 10 years, at 422.7% against 59% for fossil fuels or over seven times the return. The report, Clean Energy Investing: Global Comparison of Investment Returns, says that renewables are likely to outperform the fossil fuels as increasing numbers of countries set net zero emission targets and growing concern amongst investors and the public about the negative impacts of energy generation. Over five years the performance is lower but still more than three times higher than fossil fuels. Annualised volatility was lower than fossil fuel portfolios in the global and advanced economies and higher than the fossil fuel portfolios in emerging markets and developing economies.

The findings show a superior risk/return profile for renewable power portfolios in both typical market conditions and during global economic imbalances. This was for a number of reasons: first, the global renewables portfolio is less correlated to the wider market than fossil fuels; second, the existing correlation fell during the recent economic downturn, highlighting the potential for diversification opportunities; recent economic volatility has resulted in deteriorating fundamentals within the energy sector, with renewables showing greater resilience.[7]

World Energy Investment Rebounds

According to the IEA, after staying nearly flat in 2020, global energy investment rebounded by about 10% to US$ 1.9 trillion in 2021, bringing the total volume of investment back towards pre-pandemic levels. However, the composition shifted towards power and end-use sectors, and away from traditional fuel production. The upswing in investments was a mixture of a cyclical response to recovery and a structural shift in capital flows towards cleaner technologies. The transition to a low carbon world requires a range of other energy sources and technologies, including low carbon hydrogen, modern bioenergy and carbon capture, use and storage (CCUS). CCUS plays a central role in supporting a low-carbon energy system: capturing emissions from industrial processes, providing a source of carbon dioxide removals and abating emissions from fossil fuels. A range of carbon dioxide removals—including bioenergy combined with carbon capture and storage, natural climate solutions and direct air capture with storage—may be needed for the world to achieve a deep and rapid decarbonisation.

This means a realignment of investment in the energy sector, requiring a total of US$ 131 trillion by 2050, or an annual investment of US$ 4.4 trillion.[8] These funds will need to be invested not just in renewables but also in other low carbon energy technologies, and the enabling technologies that underpin the energy transition. These include energy efficiency, end-use electrification, power grids, flexibility innovation (hydrogen) and carbon removal measures. In the 1.5°C scenario, fossil fuel production should decline by more than 75% by 2050, with total fossil fuel consumption continuously declining from 2021 onwards.

The International Renewable Energy Agency (IRENA) says that in anticipation of the upcoming energy transition, financial markets and investors are already directing capital away from fossil fuels and towards other energy technologies including renewables.[9] According to the JP Morgan Bank, the energy transition will transform the investment landscape beyond equity markets. For renewable energy to replace fossil fuels in the energy mix, global investment in clean energy and energy efficiency will need to triple by 2030 to US$ 2.3 trillion per annum. In 2021 the global green bond market surpassed the US$ 1 trillion milestone and is likely to grow steadily in the coming years as a preferred funding source for many green investments.[10]

Solar Championing New Configurations

After an 85% cost decline over the past decade, solar photovoltaic (PV) systems are among the most cost-competitive energy sources in the market. Efforts are underway to explore new configurations and business models, and 2022 could well see the industry growing solar-plus-storage buildouts, exploring floating solar PV modules and expanding community solar projects to new markets.

Pairing storage with solar offers cost synergies, operational efficiencies and the opportunity to reduce storage capital costs with the solar investment. We will likely see increasing demand for solar paired with energy storage for multiple use, including minimising curtailment risk and enabling solar to look more like baseload power. Similarly, the share of solar projects co-located with battery storage would increase from 3% to 14%. This is well supported in a Deloitte survey, where 62% of the power and utility executive respondents in the US are either building or procuring grid-scale solar that includes storage. Although a nascent technology, floating solar photovoltaics (FSPV) are gaining attention. Several developers are exploring these projects either separately or as hybrids with hydro, which could benefit from a shared substation and transmission.

Renewable investment has thrived in markets with well-established supply chains where lower costs are accompanied by regulatory frameworks that provide cash flow visibility, and where lenders and financiers that understand these sectors well are seeking sustainable projects to support. Demand from the corporate sector for clean electricity to meet sustainability targets has also played a significant role. The energy transition will transform the investment landscape beyond equity markets. In 2021 the global green bond market surpassed the US$ 1 trillion milestone and is likely to grow steadily in the coming years as a preferred funding source for many green investments.

Much of the spending resilience in 2020 was concentrated in a handful of markets, most notably China, which saw a remarkable year for wind power investment, as well as the US and Europe. Electrification was also a major driver of investment spending by final consumers. Electric vehicle sales continue to surge along with a proliferation of new model offerings by automakers, supported by fuel economy targets and zero emission vehicle mandates. For the sixth consecutive year, capital spending in the power sector in 2020 was higher than for oil and gas supply.[11]

According to BP, the levels of investment in wind and solar power capacity has been accelerating markedly in recent levels. Despite the falling cost of wind and solar capacity, the average annual investment consistent with these two scenarios over the outlook is US$ 500–800 billion. This is two to three times greater than recent investment levels, with around 65–70% of that implied investment occurring in emerging economies. This significant increase in the pace of investment in wind and solar power would need to be supported by corresponding investment increases in critical enabling technologies and infrastructure, including transmission and distribution capacity.[12]

II. RENEWABLE ENERGY IN INDIA

With about 300 clear, sunny days a year with powerful horizontal irradiation and abundant wind power potential and numerous waterways, India is one of the few most promising renewable energy resource-rich countries in the world. The country is among the leading regions having good direct normal irradiance (DNI), which depends on its geographical location, Earth-Sun movement, tilt of the Earth, rotational axis and atmospheric attenuation due to suspended particles. India is estimated to have huge potential for solar energy which is about 5000 trillion kWh per year.[13] The solar radiation incident over India is equal to 4–7 kWh per square meter per day[14] with an annual radiation ranging from 1200–2300 kWh per square metre.[15] It has an average of 250–300 clear sunny days and 2300–3200 hours of sunshine per year.[16] Theoretically, India's electricity needs can be met on a total land area of 3,000 sq km which is equal to 0.1% of total land in the country. Therefore, technologies for conversion of solar radiation into heat and electricity, namely, thermal and PV, can successfully be exploited for providing enormous scalability in India.

India is also endowed with vast wind energy potential—302 GW at 100 m hub height and 695 GW at 120 m, all commercially exploitable. This estimate has been arrived at given the 2% land availability for all states, except Himalayan states, north-eastern states and Andaman and Nicobar Islands.

Globally, the long-term technical potential of wind energy is believed to be five times the current total energy production, or 40 times the current electricity demand. This would require wind turbines to be installed, particularly in areas of higher wind resources, such as offshore, since wind speeds there are an average 90% greater than that of land, so offshore resources can yield substantially more energy than land-stationed turbines.

India's hydropower potential is largely untapped. The International Hydropower Association estimates that the total hydropower potential in India is 6,60,000 GWh per year, of which 5,40,000 GWh per year, or 79% is still undeveloped. The Indian government, however, estimates the current exploitable potential of hydropower resources at 145.3 GW, excluding small hydropower potential. In central India, the hydroelectric power potential from the Godavari, Mahanadi, Nagavali, Vamsadhara and Narmada river basins has not been developed on a major scale due to potential opposition from the tribal population. India ranks fourth largest among the countries with installed hydropower capacity, after Russia, China and Canada.

The government has set a target of developing renewable energy generation capacity up to 175 GW by 2022 and 500 GW by 2030 and has expressed confidence of achieving both targets well in time. Nearly Rs 5 lakh crore, or US$ 64 billion, was invested during 2014–20 to develop the renewable energy sector. The Modi government's motive behind large spending on this sector has been—one, to reduce the oil and gas imports, and, two, to cut greenhouse gases (GHG) emissions to meet the climate norms set by the 2015 Paris Climate Summit. In the process, the development of a new energy sector is expected to create lakhs of new jobs for both investors and people, which India needs to achieve a US$ 5 trillion economy by 2025. At present, it is over a US$ 3 trillion economy.

Renewables are Indigenous Industry

Renewable energy is an absolutely indigenous industry for all countries. But it has special salience in India, because this is a fast-developing giant (population-wise) with pigmy fossil fuel resources. It has more clear sunny days and windy provinces than many industrial nations and a fairly well-developed solar industry. Renewables are the cheapest of all other sources of energy—coal, oil, gas and nuclear—abundant and inexhaustible. It doesn't require shipping, refining, pipelines or vehicular transport costs, power station and pump stations to deliver the product to consumer, unlike the fossil fuels. Solar rays and wind are absolutely free for all. All a developer needs is to set up a network of solar panels to harness the sun's radiation in the case of solar energy and turbines in the case of wind to generate energy and transfer directly to the distribution system.

According to Union Minister for New and Renewable Energy (MNRE) Raj Kumar Singh, renewables are set to be the main source of India's energy provider in the twenty first century. Over the past six years since 2014 the installed capacity of renewables has grown by about 72%, from 80.8 GW in 2014 to 138.9 GW in April 2020, while another 62.4 GW clean energy capacity was under various stages of implementation and 34.07 GW under bidding. Globally, India stands third in terms of installed renewable power capacity, fourth in terms of wind energy capacity and fifth in terms of solar power installed capacity. During 2014–2019, solar energy grew by 1208%, from 2.6 GW to 34.4 GW; wind energy by 79%, from 21 GW to 37.7 GW; biomass, small hydro and waste energy by 24%, from 11.9 GW to 14.9 GW; and nuclear by 42%, from 4.8 GW to 6.8 GW.[17]

Meanwhile, a pre-budget economic survey of the country (2018–19) presented by the government in the Parliament has estimated that the country would need to invest an additional US\$ 80 billion up to 2022 (without transmission lines) and US\$ 250 billion between 2023–2030 to increase renewables capacity to achieve its target of 175 GW by 2022 and 450 GW by 2030. On annualised basis, it would mean an investment of US\$ 30 billion per year. As of 2020, US\$ 64 billion had been invested in the renewable energy, of which around US\$ 6.1 billion was in foreign direct investment (FDI).

Renewable Energy Resources in India

As stated in the introduction to this book, Sun is the basic source of all energy. The Earth is blessed with enormous energy, both conventional and non-conventional—all derived from the Sun. The Sun gives us 1,000 times more power than we need. Conventional sources of energy are fast depleting, but non-conventional or renewable sources have unlimited reservoir of energy to meet the increasing global electricity demand till eternity. Direct solar energy is believed to have the highest potential which can be harnessed for our use in different forms.

Mankind can use these inexhaustible and environmentally friendly renewable resources, rather than dirty fossil fuels that emit greenhouse gases leading to the climate change. Renewable resources are natural resources which are replenished to replace the portion depleted by usage and consumption, either through natural reproduction or other recurring processes in a finite amount of time in a human time scale. For example, sunlight or wind keep shining and blowing, even if their availability depends on time and weather. [18]

Renewable energy resources exist everywhere, in contrast to fossil fuels, which are concentrated in geographically limited regions and countries. They derive their energy from the Sun, either directly or indirectly, such as hydro and wind, and are expected to be capable of supplying energy for the humanity for almost another one billion years, at which point the predicted increase in heat from the Sun is expected to make the surface of the Earth too hot for liquid water to exist.[19]

While renewable energy is often thought of as a new technology, mankind has been using nature's energy for heating, lighting, farming, transportation and various other activities since antiquity. Wind has powered boats to sail the seas and windmills to grind grain. The Sun has provided warmth during the day and helped kindle fires to last into the evening. But over the past 500 years or so, humans have increasingly turned to cheaper, dirtier energy sources such as coal and fracked gas. Now that we have increasingly innovative and less-expensive ways to capture and retain wind and solar energy, renewables are becoming a more important power source and driving a clean energy revolution.

Albert Einstein's Law of Photovoltaic Effect

Credit for commercialisation of renewable energy, particularly, must go to Nobel laureate physicist Albert Einstein who laid out the theoretical foundations of the photovoltaic industry through his discovery of Law of Photovoltaic Effect. Scientists and engineers before him had observed the photoelectric effect—that in some circumstances light could produce an electric charge—but they could not explain it. It was Einstein who explained the why.[20] Light, said Einstein in his paper on photovoltaic effect, was made up of tiny particles, called quanta, also known as photons, that moved at 1,86,000 miles per second and were indivisible. When sunlight descends on photovoltaic cells, the photons are absorbed. They dislodge and displace electrons within the semiconductor. These loose electrons flow out of the silicon along minute channels, almost like water flowing through a canal, as electric current. The photons are one form of energy, and electrons another form.

Einstein received the Nobel Prize in 1922, not for the paper that laid the basis for nuclear energy, but rather for his paper on photons and quantum mechanics for his discovery of the Law of Photoelectric Effect, in the words of the award.[21]

But it took half a century after Einstein's paper for a real breakthrough to put his theory into practical use. That happened in 1953 when two scientists Gerald Pearson and Calvin Fuller at AT&T's Bell labs in New Jersey after much experimentation unveiled, 'the first solar cells capable of producing useful amount of power'. "Vast Power of the Sun is Tapped by Using Sand Ingredient," trumpeted the *New York Times*, which reported that this invention, "may mark the beginning of a new era" and "the realisation of one of mankind's most cherished dreams—the harnessing of the almost limitless energy of the sun for the uses of civilisation."

Today no part of the renewable industry attracts as much research focus as the quest to directly harness the power of the Sun, especially PV cells, also known as solar cells. Most industrial countries have joined the race, resulting in the development of multiple technologies for making PV cells. Some are cheaper to make than others but less efficient, while others are expensive, but more efficient at converting sunlight into energy. There are solar cells in which the semiconductors are made from silicon form or crystalline silicon. Then there are solar cells in which the semiconductor is made using a thin film manufacturing process in which just a very thin layer of PV material is employed. Another key thin film technology does not use silicon at all, but cadmium-telluride, which involves coating a sheet of glass with a thin film of cadmium-telluride to produce the PV effect.

There are various ways of taking advantage of the sunlight, and the objective of each innovative process is to achieve higher efficiency with lower costs. Scientists are still working on ways to make the process more efficient and reduce the cost. The solar industry has received tremendous boost after the 2015 Paris Climate Summit where countries gave their commitment to cut greenhouse gases (CHG) emissions to bring down the Earth's temperature to below 2°C by 2050 to prevent climate change. There has been huge surge in the solar deployment in the world as the cost of making PVs has plummeted dramatically. Within just 12 months, the world added nearly 100 GW of grid connected solar power capacity (China alone installed 53 GW) in 2017, with a 34% growth year-on-year of new installations. The deployment of solar in that year was twice as much capacity as wind. Solar also out performed traditional energy generation technologies, with almost three times as much solar compared to gas and coal, and around a factor of nine times more than nuclear additions. Solar alone installed more generation capacity than all fossil fuels and nuclear together. Cumulative installed capacity of solar exceeded 401 GW, sufficient to supply 2.1% of the world's total electricity consumption.

There are many reasons for solar energy's popularity, one of it being a potentially unlimited energy supply source and the convenience of generating one's own power directly from the Sun. But these attractions are outweighed by it being the lowest-cost power generation technology; a new normal is a low US¢ 2 per kWh tariff range in a high irradiation and stable policy framework. A tender in Saudi Arabia in 2017 brought down the tariff to US¢ 2.34 per kWh. One of the bids was still lower at US¢ 1.7 per kWh, but it was disqualified perhaps due to some formal discrepancies. This bid reportedly included bifacial technology, which enables power generation on both sides of a solar module and promises yield improvements of 10 to 30%. Bifacial solar is a simple and outstanding technology, though just one of many fascinating innovations in the solar field.[22] A prime reason for the fall in costs is a dramatic plunge in the price of silicon, the raw material of PV cells. Other reasons are government subsidies and intense competition in the solar market.

The year 2017 was a record year for PV in India, too. Cumulative installed capacity exceeded 19 GW, with net yearly additions of 9.6 GW, a staggering 127% growth from 4.3 GW in 2016. This growth could have been even stronger, if it were not for the price hikes of modules from China over the course of the year, a lagging rooftop segment and uncertainty regarding import taxes. Solar installations were the largest source of the new capacity additions, constituting 45% of the newly added capacity. In 2017, India replaced Japan as the third largest market worldwide for solar capacity. By the end of 2018, global cumulative installed PV capacity reached about 512 GW, of which 180 GW (35%) was utility-scale.[23] Solar power supplied about 3% of global electricity demand in 2019. China and India moved above the world average of 2.55%, while, in descending order, the United States, South Korea, France and South Africa are below the world's average.[24]

The IEA forecasts the combined share of solar PV and wind in global generation to rise to almost 30% in 2030 from 8% in 2019, with solar PV capacity growing by an average 12% per year. By 2050, it foresees solar PV to reach 4.7 TW (4,674 GW) in its high-renewable scenario, of which more than half will be deployed in China and India, making solar power the world's largest source of electricity.[25]

III. HISTORICAL DEVELOPMENT OF RENEWABLE ENERGY IN INDIA

It was during India's Third Five Year Plan (1961–66) that solar energy was first discussed as a technology which was being developed in different countries as a source of electricity generation. The electricity generation capacity commissioned during the Plan was 10,170 MW through thermal, hydro and diesel.[26]

After almost 20 years since 1961, it was the Sixth Five Year Plan (1980–85) which specifically addressed solar energy and its implementation. Developing solar energy was of particular interest for meeting the energy demand of decentralised rural areas and potential industrial uses. The Department of Non-Conventional Energy Sources was formed in 1982 under the Ministry of Energy. The objective of this department was to provide funding for strengthening research, development and demonstrations in the area of renewable energy technologies covering all important RES such as solar, wind, biomass, geothermal energy etc.[27]

In 1981, a commission for additional sources of energy was formed to promote and develop RES in the country by encouraging funding and R&D activities. The commission launched a programme for manufacturing and sale of 10,000 solar cookers through subsidy, which ran in twelve states and one union territory. Also, an agency, called Solar Thermal Energy Centre (STEC), was established to drive R&D, testing and demonstration activities for solar thermal to help devices and systems to achieve commercial production. During 1981–83 period, around 25 solar water heater systems were installed in industries like textile, dairy, bakery and brewery. Solar thermal pump was also developed jointly by Bharat Heavy Electricals Limited (BHEL) and Dornier Systems.

The National Solar Photovoltaic Energy Demonstration Program (NASPAD) was implemented through the Central Electronics Limited (CEL), which intended to bring down the cost per Watt peak of modules through development and demonstration of low-cost solar grade silicon material and improve the efficiency of solar cells for electricity generation. NASPAD also supported CEL in R&D project of Multi-Crystalline Silicon Solar Cells (MSSC) and develop Ultra-High Efficiency (UHE) solar cells. CEL was engaged in manufacturing solar PV cells and modules and it achieved a total capacity of 10.35 kW, 21.07 kW and 31.75 kW in the year 1980, 1981 and 1982 respectively. Along with it CEL also manufactured 60 solar pumps for irrigation, drinking and water supply purposes. They also manufactured Solar PV power packages for Indian Antarctica Expedition and Oil and Natural Gas Corporation (ONGC) for their offshore activities.

The Seventh Five Year Plan (1985–90) saw an important development of Amorphous Silicon Solar Cell (ASSC) technology. BHEL was given the responsibility to execute a plant with a capacity to manufacture 500 kW of modules per annum and to achieve the cell efficiency of 13–15% at laboratory level. It was also during this Plan period that the Rajiv Gandhi-led Congress government formed the Indian Renewable Energy Development Agency (IREDA) on 11 March, 1987, to operate a revolving fund for developing, promoting and commercialising new and renewable sources of energy. The fund was financially assisted by the Government of Netherland, World Bank, Asian Development Bank (ADB) and the Danish International Development Agency (DANIDA).[28]

During the Eighth Five Year Plan (1992–97), the Government of India showed the need to electrify 10,000 villages through decentralised and non-conventional methods of energy sources (such as solar PV). These villages were remotely located in far-flung areas where possibility for load development was very little. Further, the Plan laid importance on intensification and enlargement of low-grade devices to meet the needs of cooking and heating in rural areas of the country. In addition to this, a central budget was approved to develop a 1720 kW of capacity through solar PV, along with solar pumps, solar lightings and solar cookers.[29]

During the Ninth Five Year Plan (1997–2002) the government tried to encourage private sector to participate in power generation, transmission and distribution. Under this initiative the Independent Renewable Power Producers (IRPP) were given the right to wheel renewable power through existing transmission lines of the state electricity boards (SEBs) to sell to any third party on payment of a reasonable charges. All hurdles in this regard were needed to be resolved so as to encourage IRPPs to make their contribution in promotion of power generation from non-conventional energy sources. Policy permitted the private developers to set up power projects of any capacity of any type (wind or solar). Greater emphasis was laid on improving the reliability and quality of power. Special emphasis was laid on electrification of villages with due attention to decentralised energy resources.

In 1997 a Special Action Plan (SAP) was set up for rapid improvement of physical infrastructure, including the solar PV programme, to promote solar power in areas with distinct geo-physical structure and concomitant socio-economic issues, such as hill areas, Western Ghats, northeast, border areas and desert and drought prone areas. Solar energy programmes were implemented through subsidies. This plan also saw upgradation of indigenous technology for solar PV cells under a programme, promoted by the Department of Scientific Industrial Research. Encouraged, the government planned to install a 140 MW Integrated Solar Combined Cycle (ISCC) power plant at Mathania, Rajasthan, in the Tenth Five Year Plan (2002–2007). But the project was unduly delayed due to viability issues and availability of gas to run the hybrid plant during periods of low radiation.

During this Plan, 'Village Energy Security' programme was approved as part of the remote village electrification. MNES took up pilot projects to provide total energy security to villages, by promoting 900–3000 Wp (Watt peak) of capacity pumps which could be used in horticulture. The cost of a solar PV pump of 1800 W capacity was estimated to be Rs 2.7 lakh of which two-third of the cost was subsidised by the Ministry of Non-Conventional Energy Sources for general areas and 90% in case of special areas whereas IREDA was responsible for providing soft loans to meet the balance of cost. Further, in an effort to electrify 4,000 villages, a modest target of 5 MW Solar PV decentralised installations was set. In addition, 6 lakhs solar lanterns, 8,000 SPV pumps, 10,000 SPV generators, solar water heating systems, cookers and solar air heating systems were also encouraged. CEL developed Ultra High Efficiency (UHE) solar cells as planned under the Sixth Five Year Plan and further extended their R&D on 250 mm thick silicon wafers and manufacturing of 125 mm/150 mm pseudo square Multi Crystalline Solar Cells (MCSC).

This was in addition to R&D work in the area of thin film PV and cells. CEL had also set a target to achieve cumulative solar PV production capacity of 25 MW and produce 40,000 phased control modules per annum during the same plan. On the other hand, Council of Scientific Industrial Research (CSIR) was engaged in development of material technology for solar power and battery application in the power sector. Also, during this FY Plan, the government promoted community participation (people's participation) to meet and manage the energy requirements in the villages. This ensured the participation of panchayats, local bodies, cooperatives and NGOs, thus based on this initiative, Barefoot Solar Engineers, an NGO, was engaged.

In the Eleventh Five Year Plan (2007–2012), it was believed that solar power can be important in attaining energy independence which is clean in nature and can help the country to reduce GHG emissions. With increasing pressure of climate change and as a responsible developing country, India under its National Action Plan on Climate Change (NAPCC) officially launched Jawaharlal Nehru National Solar Mission (JNNSM) in January 2010. Through this mission, India envisions to promote solar energy in a big way to mitigate GHG emissions and map plausible ways to secure energy security by 2022. According to a 2017 estimate, total potential for renewable power generation in the country in that year stood at 1,001 GW which included a solar potential of 650 GW, wind power potential of 302 GW at 100 m hub height, small hydro potential of 21 GW, biomass power of 18 GW, 7 GW from bagasse-based cogeneration in sugar mills and 2.5 GW from waste to energy. But the policy envisioned only a modest installation of 22 GW through grid connections and off grid power plants by 2022. As of April 2014, India's total installed capacity through grid connected solar power plants stood at 2.2 GW with major contribution coming through grid connected solar PV power plants.

The growth of renewable energy has changed the energy business in India. It has, in many ways, democratised energy production and consumption in the country. Before the renewable sector became a significant player, the energy business was all about fossil fuel-based big companies and grid-connected power—they dominate even today. But today there is an alternate energy market in which thousands of small companies, NGOs and social businesses are involved in selling renewable energy products and generating and distributing renewables-based energy. This trend is likely to accelerate because of two key policies of the government. One is the Electricity Act, 2003, which has opened the rural electrification market to decentralised distributed generation systems. It promotes decentralised generation and distribution of electricity involving institutions like the panchayats, users' associations, cooperative societies and NGOs in rural India, which are not under the purview of distribution companies. In addition, private developers are free to set up renewable energy-based generators and sell electricity to rural consumers. The other impetus to decentralised renewables comes from rooftop solar policies of state governments. States like Gujarat, Andhra Pradesh, Uttarakhand, Karnataka and Tamil Nadu have policies to promote solar energy generation from rooftops of residential, commercial and industrial buildings. The response to these policies has been highly encouraging. Although the results of this policy are likely to be realised slowly, the stage for re-inventing electricity generation with power from rooftop installations has been set.

In the coming years we could see thousands of energy producers feeding the grid or supplying electricity to consumers through local mini-grids. We could also see millions of consumers generating their own electricity and feeding the surplus to the grid. The fact is we are just beginning to realise the potential of the renewables to open up the energy market and democratise energy generation and consumption.

However, the government were not seemingly quite optimistic about the significant role of renewable power in India's quest for energy supply. This is borne by projections made by both Integrated Energy Policy (IEP) and the Twelfth Five Year Plan documents about the share of renewable energy in the country's energy mix by 2031–32. The IEP, in its 2006 document, had projected that in the most optimistic scenario, by 2031–32, India will have 30,000 MW of wind and 10,000 MW of solar power and installation of 50,000 MW biomass power. The policy had put its faith in the biomass sector based on plantations and production of 15 mt of bio-diesel and ethanol every year, by 2031–32. But by 2014 the biomass sector was in big trouble as about 60% of the country's grid-connected power plants which were running on biomass had either shut down or were on the verge of shutting down.

The Twelfth Five Year Plan document projected a fourfold increase in the installation of renewable power by 2021–22, and the share of renewables in electricity generation will rise from around 6% in 2012 to 9% in 2017 and 16% in 2030. The resource allocation in the Twelfth Plan reflected the priority accorded by the government to renewable energy. The total Plan outlay for the energy sector during 2012–17 was Rs 10,94,938 crore, of which Rs 33,003 crore or about 3% was earmarked for the new and renewable energy, while the atomic energy, which contributed barely 2.5% of total electricity production in the country was provided Rs 66,590 crore, more than double that of the renewables.

Greater Push After 2014

All that changed after a Narendra Modi-led government came to power in 2014. He placed clean energy at the heart of a sustainable future and moved to implement a new energy strategy focused on rapid, but orderly transition from fossil fuels-based power system to predominantly renewables-based system.

Addressing the Fourth Annual India Energy Forum on 26 October, 2020, Prime Minister Modi highlighted seven key drivers of his energy strategy, "Greater reliance on domestic fuels; cleaner use of fossil fuels; greater use of renewable sources of power (such as wind, solar and biofuels); achieving the renewable energy target of 450 GW by 2030; accelerated move towards a gas-based economy; increasing the contribution of electricity to decarbonise mobility; and adoption of emerging fuels like hydrogen and digital innovation across all energy systems."

Modi shifted the very foundation on which India's power system was built—the polluting coal. In his energy strategy, coal, although indispensable for the next few decades, will be yielding its prime ground to less-polluting natural gas and zero carbon wind and solar. Indian planners envisage that by 2030 India will be drawing 50% of its energy from non-fossil fuels and 15% from natural gas. Coal's contribution in the total energy mix will diminish to 45% in 2030 from around 55% in 2020. By implementing this strategy, Modi aims at rapidly increasing energy access, while decarbonising generation sources, reduced oil and gas imports, and strengthen energy security. At present, energy consumption per head in India is at around 25 GJ (gigajoule), which is almost a sixth of that in most developed countries, even though it imports more than 80% of its oil and 50% of its gas.

Performance of the New Strategy

Has the Modi strategy delivered? A short answer is, Yes, to some extent. Let us take, for instance, the coal sector. In 2014, before the change of regime, much of the coal sector's narrative revolved around stories of coal shortages, opaque coal mine allocation policies and corruption. Under the Congress-led UPA regime, the sector became the ground for what is now remembered as the mother of all scams—the notorious Coalgate. Six years later, the narrative has shifted to excess coal availability on the back of continued output growth by state-run miner Coal India Ltd (CIL), and the stories of corruption are now a bad memory. The government has further opened up commercial coal mining, with revenue share arrangement, to boost the fuel's production in the country, and allowed 100% FDI in commercial coal blocks, with no restrictions on the end-use of the production.

As many as 19 commercial coal blocks were allocated to winners in November 2020 after a competitive bidding in which around 70 miners participated. The government has said there would be further reforms in the mineral sector, with no distinction between the captive and non-captive mines that will allow transfer of mining leases. In January 2021, the government launched the 'Single Window Clearance System', an online platform to obtain clearances for smooth operationalisation of coal mines, while other measures included promoting coal gasification through a rebate in revenue share. Modi said that India would invest Rs 20,000 crore to convert 100 mt of coal into gas by 2030.

PSUs' Pivot to Renewables

The country's largest power generator, the state-run National Thermal Power Corporation (NTPC), has set up a wholly-owned subsidiary, the NTPC Renewable Energy Ltd, to generate 39 GW of power from renewable sources by 2032, the company said in a statement marking 45 years of operations in October 2020. Currently, the company has 2,404 MW of renewable energy projects under implementation, of which 237 MW is from floating solar projects, while 5 GW of renewable energy projects are in pipeline.

The group's ambition is to become a 130 GW company with diversified fuel mix and a 600 billion unit per annum power generation by 2032. Of the 130 GW capacity, 30 GW is to come from solar harnessing, 5 GW from hydropower, 2 GW from nuclear and another 2 GW from biomass and agricultural residues. The remainder will come from coal and natural gas. The groups says that around 20 GW of renewable, including 5 GW of solar projects, are already under construction.

At present, the group has an installed capacity of 64.1 GW, of which around 53 GW comes from its power stations and the remainder from joint venture stations. Currently, it has 46 power stations of its own and 25 stations in JV (9 coal, 4 gas, 8 hydro, 1 small hydro, 2 wind and 1 solar PV).

Coal India Ltd is another state-controlled public sector undertaking which is embracing renewable energy. The move by this US$ 11 billion company which accounts for 80% of the dirty commodity dug up in India is ironically significant as it is striving to find a place in a greener world. It has entered into a JV with NTPC, Solar Energy Corporation of India (SECI) and Coal Lignite Urja Vikas Private Ltd, with each of them separately to set up 14 rooftop and ground-mounted solar power to produce a total of 3 GW of solar energy by 2024. Coal India's strategy is to acquire land and rope in partners to provide technology and capital to generate solar power.

Indian Railways has planned to install 20 GW of solar plants on its vacant lands along the railway tracks to meet projected consumption requirements of over 33 billion units (BU) by 2030, Railways Minister Piyush Goyal told the lower house of the Parliament in August 2020. For a starter, the Railways Energy Management Company Ltd (REMCL), a JV of Indian railways and engineering consultancy RITES, floated tenders in three packages of 1,600 MW and 1,007 MW on build-own-operate (BOO) basis and a tranche of 400 MW on engineering, procurement, construction (EPC) mode. But the tenders failed to evoke a good response. Among major developers, the Tata group, was the only contender to have bid for about 300 MW in the first package. The other two tenders have seen multiple extensions and the bid submission remains pending.

According to industry sources, there were inherent risks in the tender, which would have resulted in higher tariffs than the prevailing rates. In September, RITES issued amendments to the tender, adding a domestic content requirement (DCR) clause which made it mandatory that only domestically manufactured solar cells and modules can be used for projects, and in the case of crystalline silicon technology, all process steps and quality control measures involved in the manufacture of solar cells and modules, starting from wafers until the final assembly of the solar cells into modules, should be performed in India. Land encroachment and connectivity, according to industry sources, were other issues. In many cases, land parcels roll across multiple states, with most sites offering scope for smaller units of up to 10 MW and have low solar radiation. Such small sites push up the project costs as well as operational and maintenance expenses, resulting in high tariffs.

Private Sector Investment in Renewables

As per the REN21 Renewables 2020 Global Status Report, the renewable energy projects and programmes attracted US$ 64.4 billion of investment in the years 2014 and 2019. Having seen a growing interest in the renewable energy sector, big business houses in India responded by changing track, turning their attention to cheaper, cleaner, reliable renewable energy. In July 2021, Tata Power announced it would not build new coal-fired generation projects and is aiming for carbon neutrality by 2050. One week later JSW, another leading thermal power producer, announced 20 GW of solar, wind and hydropower plants by March 2030 and an investment of Rs 750 billion (US$ 10 billion) with the aim of also becoming carbon neutral by 2050.

Investment in renewable energy in India reached a record US$ 14.5 billion in the last FY 2021–22, an increase of 125% compared to FY 2020–21 and 72% over the pre-pandemic FY 2019–20, according to the Institute for Energy Economics and Financial Analysis (IEEFA). The largest deal was SB Energy's exit from the Indian renewables sector with a sale of assets worth US$ 3.5 billion to Adani Green Energy Limited (AGEL). The other key deals included Reliance New Energy Solar's acquisition of REC Solar holding assets and a host of companies like Vector Green, AGEL, ReNew Power, Indian Railway Finance Corporation and Azure Power, raising money in the bonds market. Both companies—Reliance and Adani—have announced plans to invest up to US$ 70 billion each over the coming year to increase their renewable energy portfolio.

IV. FUTURE OF RENEWABLE ENERGY IN INDIA

Various structural disruptions, occurring in the wake of the Covid-19 pandemic, have accelerated the energy mix transition at a steady clip. First, there has been a disincentive for thermal power with projects getting priced out due to falling renewable tariffs, especially solar, as cheap as sub-Rs 2.5 per kWh. With solar tariffs expected to fall further and the emphasis on reducing pollution by thermal plants, there has been limited focus on new thermal capacity creation. This is a global trend. Renewable energy had another record-breaking year in 2019, as installed power capacity grew more than 200 GW, the biggest increase ever in a single year. Capacity installations and investment continued to spread to all corners of the world.

In most countries, producing electricity from wind and solar PV is now more cost effective than generating it from new coal-fired power plants. The cost declines have led to record-low bids in the tender processes, while attracting larger multinational energy companies in competitive auctions.[30]

The energy landscape in India is being reshaped in fundamental ways as a result of the structural disruptions. The lockdowns, clamped during the first and second waves of Covid-19, triggered about a 20% decline in power demand that was driven by a slump in the commercial and industrial (C&I) segment. As a result, coal PLF declined to 42% in April 2020 from 63% in the corresponding month 2019, largely due to the lower position of thermal in merit order dispatch. In contrast, PLF of renewables remained unchanged at 16% versus 17% in 2019.

With increasing cost competitiveness, renewables are expected to respond fastest to power demand recovery. However, a continued growth in renewables beyond 20% of total supply from current 11%, will necessitate substantial investment in transmission capacity for power evacuation as well as a smart grid infrastructure—both of which will be dependent on the health of power utilities. Renewable penetration should improve gas power plant utilisation from the existing 25% levels, enabled by a fall in gas prices.

As per India's commitment at the UN's 2021 Climate Summit (COP 26) in Glasgow, the nation will be producing 500 GW from non-fossil sources and meeting 50% of its energy requirement from it by 2030. India's oil consumption will cease to grow after rising to 6 mbpd in 2025, as per BP's Annual Energy Outlook 2020. At present it consumes 5 mbpd, about 85% of it being imported.

Slowly but steadily, India has been inching towards becoming a major force in the world for tapping and harnessing renewable energy with an increase in installed renewable energy capacity over the last five years across the country. Today, the country stands fifth globally in terms of installed renewable energy capacity. The increase in the solar power capacity started since 2014–15 after the Narendra Modi government revised the target of harnessing solar power across the country. The previous UPA government had set a target of achieving 20 GW of grid connected solar power by 2022, which was revised by the Modi government in 2015 to 100 GW for the same period. The capacity had been proposed to be achieved through the deployment of 40 GW of rooftop solar power projects and 60 GW of large and medium scale solar power projects. According to the Ministry of New and Renewable Energy in December 2021, the target had already been exceeded and crossed 110 GW.

Indian renewable energy sector is the fourth most attractive renewable energy market in the world. India is ranked fourth in wind power, fifth in solar power and fifth in renewable power installed capacity as of 2018.

Installed renewable power generation capacity has gained pace over the past few years, posting a CAGR of 17.33% between FY 16–20. With increased support from the government and improved economics, the sector has become attractive from investors' perspective. As India looks to meet its energy demand on its own, which is expected to reach 15,820 TWh by 2040, renewable energy is set to play an important role. The government is aiming to achieve 225 GW of renewable energy capacity (including 114 GW of solar capacity addition and 67 GW of wind power capacity) by 2022, more than its 175 GW target as per the Paris Agreement. The government plans to establish renewable energy capacity of 500 GW by 2030.

The renewable energy sector has also attracted significant amount of foreign investment over the years. FDI in the renewable energy sector has gone up from US$ 783.57 million in 2016–17 to US$ 1.2 billion in 2017–18 and then to US$ 1.44 billion in 2018–19. The last 10 years have witnessed an FDI inflow of more than US$ 8.8 billion in the renewable energy sector in India. According to the data released by Department for Promotion of Industry and Internal Trade (DPIIT), FDI inflow in the Indian non-conventional energy sector stood at US$ 9.22 billion between April 2000 and March 2020. More than US$ 42 billion has been invested in India's renewable energy sector since 2014.

References

1. Renewable Energy Now Accounts for a Third of Global Power Capacity; IRENA. 2 April, 2019.
2. Big Oil's Diverging Bets on the Future of Energy; *The Economist*, 19 December, 2020.
3. 'Shell Writes Down up to US$ 4.5 billion in Oil and Gas Assets'; *Reuters*, 21 December, 2020.
4. 'Shell Writes Down up to US$ 4.5 billion in Oil and Gas Assets'; *Reuters*, 21 December, 2020.
5. 'U.S. and European Oil Giants Go Different Ways on Climate Change', by Clifford Krauss, *The New York Times*, 21 September, 2021).
6. Deloitte: Analysis, 2022 Renewable Energy Industry Outlook, New Avenues are Opening.
7. Quoted by KMPG: 'Global Renewables Investment Return Seven Times Higher Than Fossil Fuels', 19 March, 2021.
8. World Energy Transitions Outlook, 2021.
9. IRENA: Energy investment needs realignment.
10. JP Morgan Outlook, 2021.
11. IEA, World Energy Investment, 2021.
12. BP Energy Outlook, 2022.
13. Pandey S, Singh VS, 'Determinants of Success for Promoting Solar Energy in India', Renewable Sustainable Energy Review, 16, pp. 3593–98, 2012.

14. Kumar A, Kumar K, Renewable Energy in India: Current Status & Future Potentials. Renew Sustain Energy Rev 2010; Vol. 14:2434–42.

15. MNRE. Annual Report, New Delhi; 2006.

16. Sharma NK, Tiwari PK. Solar Energy in India: Strategies, Policies, Perspectives & Future Potential. Renew Sustain Energy Review 2011; vol. 16:933–41.

17. Power Minister Raj Kumar Singh in reply to a question in Lok Sabha, April 2020.

18. Renewable Energy: The Clean Facts; https://www.nrdc.org/stories/renewable-energy-clean-facts.

19. Schröder, KP; Smith, RC (2008). 'Distant Future of the Sun and Earth revisited'. Monthly Notices of the Royal Astronomical Society. 386 (1): 155–163. arXiv:0801.4031; Palmer, J., 'Hope dims that Earth will survive Sun's death'. New Scientist, 24 March, 2008.; and Carrington, D., "Date set for desert Earth". *BBC News*, 31 March, 2007.

20. John Perlin, 'From Space to Earth: The Story of Solar Electricity. Cambridge: Harvard University Press, 2002, p.18 Siemens.

21. Albert Einstein, Nobel Prize in Physics, 1921, at http.//nobelprize.org/nobel_prizes/physics/laureates/1921/.

22. http.//www.epia.org

23. '12 Countries Leading the Way in Renewable Energy', Click Energy.

24. IRENA, Renewable energy and jobs, Annual Review 2015.

25. World Energy Assessment (2001).

26. Planning Commission. Third Five Year Plan, New Delhi; 1961.

27. Planning Commission. Sixth Five Year Plan, New Delhi; 1980.

28. IREDA. Background; 15 March, 2014; www.ireda.gov.in.

29. Planning Commission. Eighth Five Year Plan, New Delhi; 1992.

30. Renewable energy is now the least-cost option in the power sector, REVE, 9 August, 2020.

Chapter 5

SOLAR POWER

I. OVERVIEW

The Sun gives us unlimited energy in the form solar radiation than we can consume. According to energy historian Vaclav Smil, the Earth receives 174 PW (petawatts) of incoming solar radiation (insolation) in the upper atmosphere. Approximately 30% of this is reflected back to the space, while rest 122 PW, is absorbed by clouds, oceans and land masses. The spectrum of solar light on the Earth's surface is mostly spread across the visible and near-infrared ranges with a small part in the near-ultraviolet.[1] Most of the world's population live in areas with insolation levels of 150–300 watts/m^2, or 3.5–7.0 kWh/m^2 per day.[2]

Solar radiation is absorbed by the Earth's land surface and oceans, which cover about 71% of the globe and atmosphere, which keeps the surface at an average temperature of 14°C.[3] By photosynthesis, green plants convert solar energy into chemically stored energy, which produces food, wood and biomass from which fossil fuels are derived.[4]

The total solar energy absorbed by the Earth's atmosphere, oceans and land masses is approximately 122 PW per year or 3,850,000 EJ (exajoules) per year.[5] In 2019, this was more energy in one hour (one hour and 25 minutes) than the world used in one year.[6] Photosynthesis captures approximately 3,000 EJ per year in biomass.[7]

In 2000, the United Nations Development Programme, the UN Department of Economic and Social Affairs and the World Energy Council published an estimate of the potential solar energy that could be used by humans each year that took into account factors such as insolation, cloud cover and the land that is usable by humans. They found that solar energy has a global potential of 1,600 to 49,800 EJ (4.4×1014 to 1.4×1016 kWh) per year.[8]

The amount of solar energy that is available to us during an hour is more than the total amount of energy consumed worldwide in an entire year. But this is diffused, rather than concentrated. Instead of obtaining the Sun's energy from indirect sources like fossil fuels, researchers and organisations worldwide have developed and are developing various devices (such as PV) to tap this unlimited source of energy directly.

Solar Potential in India

India receives about 5,000 trillion kWh of solar radiation incident per year over its land mass. The average solar insolation ranges from 1200–2300 kWh per square metre, depending on the location, with an average 250–300 clear sunny days. Solar radiation varies geographically, annual radiation of solar energy is highest in the northern region, especially in Ladakh and the least in the north-eastern region.[9] It has been observed that some areas of Gujarat, Rajasthan, Madhya Pradesh, Andhra Pradesh and Maharashtra receive larger amount of solar radiation, compared to other parts of India. The lowest level of solar radiation received are in parts of Arunachal Pradesh and Sikkim. It has been assessed by IPCC that even with only a small fraction of the amount of this form of energy which we receive, we can meet our needs.[10] In other words, if we can use only 5% of this energy, it will be 50 times of what the world requires.[11]

National Renewable Energy Laboratory (NREL) has released 10 km resolution solar resource maps for India, which shows that most areas of the country have greater than 5 kWh/m^2 per day of annual average direct normal irradiance (DNI), with the states of Madhya Pradesh, Gujarat, Rajasthan, Chhattisgarh and Maharashtra receiving more than 5.5 kWh/m^2 per day of DNI.[12] The National Institute of Solar Energy has assessed India's solar potential at about 748 GW, assuming 3% of the waste land area covered by solar PV modules.[13] This means, theoretically, India's electricity needs can be met on a total land area of 32,000 sq km which is equal to 0.1% of total land in the country.

Solar power plants require nearly 2.4 ha (hectares) of land per MW capacity, which is similar to coal fired power plants if their life cycle coal mining, consumptive water storage and ash disposal areas are taken into account, and hydropower plants when the submergence area of the water reservoir is included. Large tracts of land that are unproductive, barren and devoid of vegetation exist in all parts of India, exceeding 8% of its total area. These are potentially suitable for solar power. It has been estimated that if 32,000 sq km of these waste lands were used for solar power generation, 2,000 billion kWh of electricity could be produced, which is twice the total power generated in the year 2013–14.

The Thar Desert holds the largest reservoir of solar energy. At a price of Rs 4 per kWh, this would result in a land annual productivity per yield of Rs 1 million (US$ 14,000) per acre, which compares favourably with many industrial areas and is many times more than the best productive irrigated agriculture lands.[14] Building solar power plants on marginally productive land offers the potential for solar electricity to replace all of India's fossil fuel energy requirements (natural gas, coal, lignite, nuclear fuels and crude oil),[15] and could offer per capita energy consumption at par with USA/Japan for the peak population expected during its demographic transition.[16]

Land acquisition is a challenge for solar farm projects in India. Some state governments are exploring innovative ways to address land availability, for example, by deploying solar capacity above irrigation canals.[17] This allows solar energy to be harvested while simultaneously reducing the loss of irrigation water by solar evaporation.[18] The state of Gujarat was first to implement the Canal Solar Power Project, using solar panels on a 19,000 km long network of Narmada canals across the state to generate electricity. It was the first such project in India.

Solar Power Plants

Solar energy is generally produced by using solar photovoltaic (SPV) or concentrated solar power (CSP) technologies. Solar power plants transform the energy of sunlight into electrical energy, by using either SPV or CSP. CSP system consists of lenses and tracking systems to concentrate on the sunlight of a large area into a small beam. PV effects are used for converting the energy of sunlight to electrical energy in case of SPV. The first SPV plant was built by Arco Solar at Lugo in California in 1982 with 1 MW power generation capacity. The largest SPV plant, Desert Sunlight Solar Farm, is situated in the US with a 550 MW generation capacity and was commissioned in 2015. In 1968, the first CSP plant was built in Santilario, near Genoa, Italy, and could generate 1 MW solar power with super-heated steam of 100 bars at 500°C. World's largest CSP plant Ivanpah Solar Electric Generating System, is situated in California, and can generate 392 MW power and can supply to 94,400 American homes at an average.

Solar also provides the ability to generate power on a distributed basis and rapid capacity addition with a short lead time. Off-grid decentralised and low-temperature applications are useful for rural electrification and meeting other needs for power and heating and cooling in both rural and urban areas.

From an energy security perspective, solar is the most secure of all sources, since it is abundantly available. As stated, time and time again by the science community, a small fraction of the total incident solar energy (if captured effectively) can meet the entire country's power requirements. But unfortunately, scant efforts have been made to exploit this vast reservoir of natural resource until the threatening challenge of climate change forced our hands.

Increased Target for Non-fossil Energy

Speaking at the 26th Summit of the United Nations Conference of Parties (COP 26) in Glasgow, in October 2021, Prime Minister Modi announced a further increase in the target of renewables capacity from 175 GW in 2022 to 500 GW by 2030. This is the world's largest expansion plan, but India is confident of achieving it. Addressing the 15th G20 summit via video conferencing on 22 November, 2020, Modi said that India would not only meet its Paris Accord targets but exceed them. "Now, we are taking a big step ahead by seeking to achieve 450 GW by 2030."[19] India has committed to generate 40% of its power from non-fossil fuels by 2030, for which it has already invested about US$ 64 billion between 2015 and 2020, and expects another US$ 80 billion investment till 2030. Most of the investment is directed towards harnessing solar power, which is abundantly available in one of the world's largest markets. India's solar tariff, too, is among the world's cheapest.

The government's policies are tailored to lure maximum international and private investment and technology in this crucial sector. The government has also sought the World Bank and International Finance Corporation's (IFC) help in fostering innovative public-private partnerships, managing risks and attracting investors. From 2015, the World Bank has been providing US$ 100 million in concessional financing to boost the solar energy in India. It consists of US$ 75 million in loans from IBRD and US$ 25 million from the Clean Technology Fund (CTF), of which US$ 23 million is provided in loans and US$ 2 million in technical assistance grants. IFC's Transaction Advisory team has facilitated around US$ 575 million in private investment by helping with project structuring and to negotiate with international investors. It has also provided a loan of US$ 128 million to solar developers and helped mobilise about US$ 309 million from other lenders. This is helping to establish two large solar parks in Madhya Pradesh and develop the infrastructure to connect them to the grid and distribute power to consumers.

The Rewa Solar Park, commissioned by Modi in June 2020, set a record low tariff for renewable energy—less than US¢ 5 per kWh. Competitive with power produced from non-renewable sources, the tariff has made new investments in coal plants far less attractive. This could not have been achieved without the efforts of IFC to create a bankable project for domestic and international investors, and support from the World Bank to make land and infrastructure available in a timely manner. Of the US$ 100 million, the World Bank is investing in establishing solar parks in India, US$ 18 million was dedicated for infrastructure setup in Rewa, which leveraged almost 32 times the amount in commercial investment (US$ 575 million). The project is expected to add 750 MW of solar capacity to India's grid.

IFC has also opened a new market for institutional purchasers of solar power in India by developing a sound power scheduling arrangement—one that enabled Delhi Metro to procure power alongside the utility. Rewa will supply 60% of Delhi Metro's daytime energy needs, reducing the carbon footprint of moving three million people each day and saving about a million tons of CO_2 emissions per year. Manu Srivastava, Principal Secretary for New and Renewable Energy, Madhya Pradesh, says Rewa Solar Park is the country's first project where renewable energy is procured entirely on commercial principles—without using the subsidy of viability gap funding—by an institutional investor, namely Delhi Metro. The World Bank and IFC have been partners since its inception, providing both concessional funds and transaction advisory services.

Under the 'SolaRISING India' programme, the World Bank group is working to replicate the success of Rewa by establishing at least three more parks, with a combined 1.5 GW capacity. Solar parks built and operated by the private sector are expected to contribute 40% of the government's 100 GW target for solar capacity by 2022. This will be crucial for India to achieve its NDC target of renewables contributing 40% of total electricity capacity by 2030 and will save about 30 million tons of CO_2 emissions per year.

Solar power has been growing at a tremendous speed since 2015, with the installed capacity having risen 10 times from around 4 GW in 2015 to over 40 GW by 2020-end and is continuing relentlessly. Tamil Nadu,

Gujarat, Andhra Pradesh, Karnataka, Telangana, Madhya Pradesh and Rajasthan have embraced the expansion of solar capacity with great zeal. The central government's budget for FY 2021–22 raised the allocation for power sector by 66.41% to Rs 2,606 crore, compared to Rs 1,566 in the previous year. Of this, the lion share of Rs 2,369 was provided for grid-interactive solar power projects. This constitutes 54.77% of the total budgetary allocation of Rs 4,325 for the grid-connected renewable energy projects. This is in addition to an unspecified amount of central financial assistance, which has been provided for capacity addition of 7,500 MW of solar power during the fiscal year. During the fiscal year, the government would also implement Phase-III of the off-grid solar PV programme, which covers installation of 3 lakh solar street lights, distribution of 25 lakh solar study lamps and installation of solar power packs of total aggregated capacity of 100 MW.

As a result of business-friendly policies and incentives offered by the government the share of solar power had reached around 40 GW, and was set to overshoot the target of 100 GW by 2022. The Solar Energy Corporation of India (SECI), which oversees the implementation of central solar projects, has awarded contracts for 47 large-scale solar parks with a combined capacity of 25 GW. Five of these are world-class solar parks in terms of power generation capacity and length and breadth of the area they are located in. These are:

1. **Bhadla Solar Park:** Claimed to be the largest solar power plant in the world, with 2,250 MW capacity, this park spans over 14,000 acres in Rajasthan's Jodhpur district. It was developed by multiple entities, such as Rajasthan Solar Park Development Company Limited, Saurya Urja Company (a JV of the government of Rajasthan and IL&FS Energy Development Company) and Adani Renewable Energy Park Rajasthan (a JV of Adani Enterprises and Government of Rajasthan). The project supplies about 10% of Rajasthan's total current power demand.

2. **Shakti Sthala Solar Power Project:** The 2,050 MW project in Tumakuru district of Karnataka, was developed by the Karnataka Solar Park Development Corporation Limited (KSPDCL) with help from the National Thermal Power Corporation (NTPC). Also known as Pavagada (a semi-arid sub-district of Tumakuru), the park spans more than 13,000 acres and cost Rs 14,800 crore (US$ 1.95 billion).

3. **Ultra Mega Solar Park:** Situated in Orvakal, Kurnool district, Andhra Pradesh, this park is 1,000 MW, spread over more than 5,932 acres, developed by a JV of Solar Energy Corporation, Andhra Pradesh Generation Corporation and New and Renewable Energy Development Corporation at an investment of over Rs 7,143 crore (US$ 943 million).

4. **Rewa Solar Power Project:** Madhya Pradesh's 750 MW project is spread over an area of 1,590 acres and is operated by Rewa Ultra Mega Solar Ltd. Developed by Mahindra Renewables, Solengeri Power and ACME Solar Holdings, this plant is one of the major power suppliers to the Delhi Metro. Riding on an investment of Rs 2,800 crore (US$ 370 million), the commissioning of this plant reportedly saved Delhi Metro Rs 1,400 crore (US$ 185 million) over its project life.

5. **Kamuthi Solar Power Plant:** Kamuthi, in Ramanathapuram district of the southern state of Tamil Nadu, houses the country's fifth-largest solar power plant. Developed at a cost of Rs 4,550 crore (US$ 601 million), in 2016, by Adani Group's Adani Green Energy (Tamil Nadu) Ltd, the 648 MW plant consists of 2.5 million solar panels, covering an area of 2,500 acres. The plant is connected to Tamil Nadu Transmission Corporation's 400 KV Kamuthi substation, which distributes power to around 2,65,000 homes.

The main idea of solar parks is to provide projects with a 'plug-and-play' interface such that developers can focus on other aspects of project development and reduce project risks. The MNRE has recently amended guidelines for competitive bidding with provisions to reduce offtake risk, address revenue shortfall from curtailment and minimise delays related to land acquisition. However, land acquisition, grid integration and connection concerns have caused delays in the SECI auctions.

In this context, February 2017 marked an important step for ensuring the financial viability of off-takers. SECI joined the tripartite agreement between the central government, state governments and the Reserve Bank of India (RBI). SECI is the counterpart for central auctions of variable renewables and then sells this electricity to Discoms via power supply agreements. The tripartite agreement ensures that SECI is compensated for any payment delays from Discoms via a mechanism guaranteed by the RBI, thus making it a low-risk off-taker. NTPC, which also holds auctions for renewables, is also party to this agreement and thus is a viable off-taker.

The reverse auctions, managed by SECI, have led to the accelerated deployment of SPV at utility scale, while wind auction volumes doubled from 2017 to 2018. Onshore wind and SPV auction prices are well aligned and have come down to the lowest levels discovered in India to date, with some bids down to US$ 26 per MWh for solar and US$ 24–28 per MWh for wind in 2019.[20]

II. INDIAN GOVERNMENT'S INITIATIVES

Thar Desert of Rajasthan and Rann of Kutch of Gujarat, which straddles about 2,00,000 sq km along the India-Pakistan border, holds enormous potential for solar energy, with more than 325 days of solar radiation in a year. The state-run Power Grid Corporation of India estimates that just about 15% of the approximately 57,000 sq km of the Great Desert of Thar can produce enough clean energy to satisfy our requirement. The so-called 'wastelands'—defined as barren, rocky, underutilised areas—of ice-clad mountainous Ladakh, Lahaul and the Spiti Valley in the northern India also hold vast renewable energy potential. Currently, around 35,000 sq km of the Thar Desert has been reserved for solar power projects. India plans to produce at least 30 GW of solar energy from the desert along its western borders of Gujarat and Rajasthan.

On 15 December, 2020, Modi laid the foundation stone of India's largest hybrid renewable energy park in the Kutch district, which is designed to produce 30 GW of solar wind hybrid power. Spread over an area of 70,000 hectares this project, at Vighakot village, is equivalent to land area of Singapore and Bahrain combined, and is estimated cost about Rs 1.5 lakh crore to build. It is claimed that power produced from it would eliminate 5 crore tonnes of carbon dioxide emissions every year, which is equal to planting 9 crore trees. The plant will have two zones—a 49,600 ha hybrid park zone that will accommodate wind and solar power plants of 24,800 MW capacity; and another an exclusively wind park zone, spread over 23,000 ha. The exclusive wind zone park has been entrusted to the Solar Energy Corporation of India (SECI) to invite tenders from private developers to set up the projects. The selected developers have to develop 50% of the total generation capacity in the next three years, and finish the project within five years. Power Grid Corporation of India will evacuate the power produced at the park.

The Gujarat government has allocated land to six developers to set up the projects—Adani Green Energy Ltd (19,000 ha), Sarjan Realities Ltd (Suzlon, 9,500 ha), NTPC Ltd (9,500 ha), Gujarat Industries Power Company Ltd (4,750 ha) and Gujarat State Electricity Corporation (6,650 ha). Adani Green will install a capacity of 9,500 MW; Sarjan Realities, 4,750 MW; GIPCL, 2,375 MW; GSECL, 3,325 MW and NTPC, 4,750 MW.

Rajasthan Investment Promotion Scheme 2020 offers competitive advantages to investors in the form of customised packages under the scope of the scheme to attract big-ticket projects. By February 2021, four solar companies had offered to put up 34 GW of solar projects and 2 GW of component manufacturing facilities in Rajasthan. Adani Renew Power and Greenco have offered to bring their projects onstream within 3–5 years, while JSW has sought 10 years to complete its project. Collectively, they have been given 80,000 ha of government-owned land. Greenco's project includes storage solutions, while ReNew Power's project includes a 2 GW solar cell and panel manufacturing in addition to power generation. Rajasthan government in its 2019–20 budget, had exempted solar energy from electricity duty and focussed on the utilisation of solar power in its agriculture and public health sectors. The Rajasthan government has also announced plans to offer land near its ports to companies for building solar equipment factories.

The Ministry of New and Renewable Energy (MNRE) decided to provide customs and excise duty benefits to the solar rooftop sector, which will lower the cost of setting up as well as generate power, thus boosting growth. The central government budget for FY 2021–22 has raised customs duty on solar inverters from 5% to 20% and solar lanterns from 5% to 15% to incentivise domestic manufacturing. Union Finance Minister Nirmala Sitharaman says the move would positively impact the rooftop and ground-mounted solar projects, and the distributed renewable energy sector.

The budget has also provided Rs 1,000 crore increase in allocation for the SECI and Rs 1,500 crore raise in the allocation for IREDA. A Hydrogen Energy Mission in 2021–22 was launched to promote production of hydrogen power from green energy sources.

Utility-Scale Renewables

For utility-scale renewables India has introduced renewable purchase obligations (RPOs), renewable electricity certificates (RECs), accelerated depreciation of renewable energy assets for commercial and industrial users and most recently competitive tenders. The RPOs require DISCOMs, energy producers and certain consumers to obtain a share of their electricity from renewable sources. Determination of RPO trajectories and monitoring of compliance are carried out by the State Electricity Regulatory Commissions.

In June 2018, the RPO requirement was raised from 17% to 22%, with 10.5% from solar, up from 6.75% and 10.5% from non-solar renewable sources by 2022, up from 10.25%. It needs to be raised to achieve the 450 GW target.

The RECs are used by the obligated entities to meet their RPO requirements. The CERC established voluntary RECs in 2010 and allowed their trading in March 2011 to address the discrepancy between the availability of electricity from renewable sources across the regional markets and the demand from obligated utilities and customers to meet their RPOs under the Electricity Act 2003. The REC programme is enforced by the CERC. However, the REC markets have been insufficient in encouraging large investments because of demand and investment uncertainty in the absence of long-term targets and poor compliance.

The government approved a number of measures in March 2019 to promote the hydropower sector in the country, including declaring all hydropower projects as renewable energy projects and providing for hydro purchase obligations (HPOs), similar to RPOs. HPOs will help improve the economic viability of hydropower projects.

The accelerated depreciation tax benefit for renewable energy plant developers was re-established in 2014 after a two-year long gap and was fixed at an 80% level until March 2017. As of April 2017, the benefit was lowered to 40%. Users of renewable energy can depreciate their investment in a renewable energy plant at a much higher rate than general fixed assets and can claim tax benefits on the value depreciated in a given year. The tax benefit is available for several renewable technologies, including flat-plate solar collectors, concentrating and pipe-type solar collectors, solar power generating systems, windmills and related devices, biogas plant and engines, electrically operated vehicles including battery-powered or fuel cell-powered vehicles, and agricultural and municipal waste conversion devices. In order to reach the 2022 target, the government launched competitive auctions for solar, PV (2010) and wind (2017) with long-term power purchase agreements containing fixed price contracts.

Rooftop Solar

Rooftop Solar (RTS) offers an inexpensive, non-polluting alternative to grid electricity. A survey conducted by the energy consultancy Bridge to India of diesel generator set usage in three Gurugram residential societies found an abrupt spike in air pollution levels in Gurugram (Haryana) just after three to four hours of DG (diesel generator) set operation and the effect lingered on. Average particulate matter (PM) 2.5 levels increased by 30–40% and average PM 10 levels by 20–50%. This meant that the average PM 2.5 level was more than twice and PM 10 thrice the safe limits. Further, rough estimates showed that DG sets were more expensive than rooftop solar (RTS) installations in the long run because of recurring fuel costs for DG sets. There is no fuel cost in RTS. DG sets are often used to supplement grid electricity.[21]

The RTS system comprises four main components—solar panel, solar inverter, solar battery, and solar charge controller. The solar panel is the primary component which converts the sunlight into electricity; the inverter converts the DC into AC; the battery is a power storing component that stores electricity and runs the load as the grid power is off; and, the solar charge controller converts a normal inverter into a solar inverter. In addition to these, there are various other components like panel stand, ACDB, DCDB, cables, conduits, earthing electrodes, lightning arrestor and earthing strips.

As a rule of thumb, the installation of a 1 kW solar system on a residential rooftop can cost from Rs 45,000 to Rs 85,000, excluding the cost of batteries. The cost of the rooftop solar systems largely depends on the price of modules and inverters used. An advanced technology module will cost more but it is also of premium quality, lasts longer, generates more energy in constrained roof spaces and requires low maintenance. When it comes to inverters, micro-inverters cost more than string inverters but have several advantages, particularly in partially shaded conditions.

The average capacity of rooftop systems installed at home ranges from 1 kW to 10 kW depending on the availability of ideal roof space and is the permissible capacity allowed by the distribution company (Discom). Most Discoms only allow 80% of the sanctioned load. That is, to install a 5 kW system, you need to have a sanctioned load of not less than 6 kW. This means a household has to shell out Rs 2,25,000 to Rs 4,25,000 for a cost-effective model of a 5 kW rooftop solar system. Though the upfront cost may seem large, especially for the households in rural India, it saves a lot of money in the long run as they don't have to pay any electricity bill and reduces carbon footprints. The RTS system comes for more than 20 years. A 5 kW system produces nearly 20 kWh of electricity on a good day and 600 kWh a month, earning Rs 3,300 per month if we consider a tariff of Rs 5.50 per kWh. On an average a rooftop solar system's cost can be recovered in five to six years.

Subsidies and Incentives

To encourage consumers to install the RTS system, both governments, at the centre and the states, offer subsidies and various other incentives. The central government pays 30% of the benchmarked installation cost and in the case of states in the general category, and 70% of the cost in special category states such as Uttarakhand, Sikkim and Himachal Pradesh and Union Territories, Jammu and Kashmir, Ladakh and Lakshadweep. In addition to this, state nodal agencies also offer subsidies in various states. RTS subsidies are available for institutional, residential and social sectors, but not for commercial, industrial and public sector undertakings (PSUs). Commercial and industrial sectors are eligible for accelerated depreciation, custom duty concession, excise duty exemption and tax holidays, while PSUs are eligible for incentives on the basis of energy generation. In addition to installation cost subsidies, general consumers planning to instal RTS system are entitled to a home loan or home improvement loan of up to Rs 10 lakhs on priority basis from nationalised banks, and the payment of a generation-based incentive of Rs 2 per unit of electricity generated. Furthermore, people can sell their excess electricity at a regulated cost per unit as per tariff set by the government.

It is clear that RTS systems provide multiple benefits—to households, to the grid and even to Discoms. Promoting them, therefore, is a desirable policy goal. RTS systems can offer reduced power bills for households; the gains may increase as tariffs are likely to increase. They provide environmentally friendly, inexpensive back-up supply of power (compared to DG sets), a big advantage, given the persistent supply interruptions in most places. They can result in lower transmission and distribution losses and improved grid management, since the generation is close to the point of consumption.

However, despite these multiple benefits, the growth of RTS system has not matched the spectacular rise in other segments of the renewable energy in the country. The MNRE data show only around 5.9 GW of RTS installations until June 2020. Even then a large proportion, 70%, of the installed rooftop systems was for commercial and industrial (C&I) customers, while residential consumers accounted for less than 20% of the total installed capacity, according to Bridge to India. There are clear economic considerations behind industrial and commercial consumers' preference for rooftop systems, as solar rooftop power is cheaper than grid-supplied electricity. These consumers have the financial resources to make the necessary investments, which are sizable, to install STS systems. Besides, they have access to the Renewable Energy Service Company (RESCO) model (in which developers install the system on the consumers' premises and sign a long-term contract to sell them electricity), under which they do not need to make any investments. The industrial consumers of Maharashtra, Tamil Nadu, Karnataka, Rajasthan, Uttar Pradesh, Gujarat and Haryana have the largest share in the RTS system. In Delhi, PSUs are the largest rooftop drivers.

Raising the rooftop solar capacity addition to reach the 40 GW target by 2022 would require close engagement with numerous small consumers. Concerted efforts are needed for raising consumer awareness about the benefits of the RTS systems and financial support offered by the government. The MNRE has come out with guidelines for the implementation of Phase-II of its Grid-Connected Rooftop Solar Programme, under which the target is supported by RPOs, rooftop auctions and programmes that facilitate the deployment of rooftop solar PV on government buildings throughout the country. In February 2019, the Cabinet Committee on Economic Affairs (CCEA) approved financial support of US\$ 6.5 billion by 2022 to promote the use of solar among farmers. Solar deployment is picking up given the rising electricity retail prices with the net metering programmes in 28 states with various tariff structures. In recent years, the government has taken steps to improve the availability of loans for RTS projects. The Reserve Bank of India has identified solar rooftop as a priority sector for lending. Eight public sector banks have included RTS systems under their housing or housing improvement loans. Multilateral banks are providing concessional loans against sovereign guarantee to public sector banks to support subsidised lending to the segment.[22]

Net Metering Versus Gross Metering

However, the introduction of a new regulation in the 'Electricity (Rights of Consumers) Rules, 2020', promulgated in December 2020, excluding larger rooftop systems from net metering has upset corporate consumers. The new enactment mandates net metering for loads up to 10 kW and gross metering for loads above 10 kW. Although this central government notification is not legally binding on state distribution companies, it is unlikely the state governments will allow net metering for corporate consumers. Reports suggest that some states have already started implementing the new regulation in different forms. West Bengal has allowed net metering for consumers with sanctioned loads of up to 5 kW and gross metering for contract demand above 5 kW. Karnataka has also proposed a gross metering arrangement for rooftop solar projects over 10 kW capacity at Rs 2.84 per kWh tariff.

The national solar energy federation of India has opposed the new regulation on the ground that it would render investment in rooftop solar industry uneconomical. Under the new mandate, gross metered consumers are compensated for the export of solar power to the grid at rates of Rs 2–4 per kWh. However, current rooftop power purchase agreements (PPAs) signed by Tier-1 developers have tariffs in the range of Rs 3.5–4 per kWh. Developers and corporates consider any tariff lower than the current PPA tariff unviable. And not only would corporates be reluctant to set up a rooftop solar system for just Rs 2–2.5 per kWh benefit, under gross metering they would not benefit commercially from using the power generated from their own system for self-consumption.

Corporate consumers have told the Power Minister RK Singh that the exclusion of corporate customers would adversely impact around Rs 1,500–2,000 crore of new investment in the rooftop solar industry in pipeline. But the government is not worried as commercial and industrial customers constitute a minuscule part of the Discoms' customer base and are expected to contribute no more than 3–4% of the country's rooftop solar target of 40 GW by 2022. Taking advantage of the government incentives and subsidies several corporate consumers are known to have installed rooftop solar facilities and used it as a lucrative business by selling power to Discoms at higher tariffs than the retail rates. Earlier, these consumers were earning around Rs 7 per unit by selling the surplus power generated from their rooftop solar plants to Discoms. After implementation of the new mandate, the return on their investments in rooftop plants would be significantly reduced, giving them no reason to spend money on installing new plants, says the national solar energy federation.

Turnaround in Solar Sector

The country's solar installed capacity was 60.302 GW (gigawatt) as of December 2022. Solar power generation in India, ranks fourth globally in

2021.[23] Growth in the solar power from 2.6 GW in 2014 to 60 GW at the end of 2022 was nothing short of a dramatic turnaround. Solar energy has taken a central place in India's National Action Plan on Climate Change with National Solar Mission (NSM) as one of its key missions. The Mission targets installing 450 GW grid connected solar power plants by 2030 to achieve India's Intended Nationally Determined Contributions (INDCs) target to install 50% of cumulative electric power capacity from non-fossil fuel-based energy resources and to reduce the emission intensity of its GDP by 45% by 2030 from the 2005 level. The government has launched several schemes to boost generation of solar power, such as solar parks, VGF, CPSU, defence schemes, bundling scheme and grid connected solar rooftop scheme.

Various policy measures undertaken include declaration of trajectory for renewable purchase obligation (RPO) for solar power; waiver of Inter-State Transmission System (ISTS) charges and losses for inter-state sale of solar and wind power projects commissioned up to March 2022; must run status, guidelines for procurement of solar power though tariff based competitive bidding process; standards for deployment of solar PV systems and devices; provision of roof top solar and guidelines for development of smart cities; amendments in building bylaws for mandatory provision of rooftop solar in new constructions, infrastructure status for solar projects; raising tax free solar bonds; and providing long-tenure loans from multi-lateral agencies.[24]

Generous government subsidies, coupled with the ease of doing business and falling capital costs of renewable projects, lured proliferation of investments in the field of wind and solar power, leading to a significant fall in tariffs, from an unsustainable Rs 5–10 per unit in 2015 to under Rs 2.50 per unit in 2020. Analysts predict further drops in tariffs in the future as battery storage technology takes root or solar-wind hybrid generation expands. In December 2020, three firms—ABC Renewables, Adani Renewables and Amp Energy—won SECI's hybrid tenders worth about 1.2 GW at a tariff of Rs 2.41 per unit. Of these, ABC Renewables will supply 380 MW, Adani Renewables 600 MW and Amp Energy 130 MW hybrid power at Rs 2.41 per unit. According to the tender document, the projects will set-up on a build-own-operate basis and the power generated will be sold to the SECI.

Tumbling Tariff

The credit for the incredible growth of the solar industry must go to the nosediving solar tariffs since 2017. In July 2020, solar power tariffs had dropped to a low of Rs 2.36 per unit in a Solar Corporation of India's (SECI) auction for 2 GW solar capacity. In November 2020, the bidding price fell to Rs 2 per unit when Saudi Arabia's Aljoemaih Energy and Water Co and Green Infra Wind Energy offered to install 200 MW and 400 MW capacities. The plunge continued further at a 500 MW auction conducted by Gujarat Urja Vikas Nigam Limited (GUVNL) in December 2020 when NTPC, Torrent Power, Aljoemaih Energy and Water Company and Aditya Birla Renewables won 200 MW, 100 MW, 80 MW and 120 MW respectively at a tariff of Rs 1.99 per unit.

The continuous decline in solar power tariffs since the start of the FY 2020–21 is being driven by a mix of structural and state-specific factors, which are likely to sustain over medium-term, says India Ratings and Research (Ind-Ra). Advanced and more efficient panel designs have led to higher capacity utilisation factor (CUF) and lower capital costs globally, resulting a tariff of 10 to 15 paise per kWh, according to Ind-Ra. State-specific factors include such concessions as tax rebates or other incentives given by states to promote solar energy investment in their region. For example, the exemption of a cess from safeguard duty on panel imports in Rajasthan resulted into savings of 10 to 12 paise per kWh.

As prices for solar technologies fall, demand for them rises, and as production expands to meet the demand, prices fall further, all of which contribute to accelerating adoption. When Bell Labs built its first solar PV panel in 1954, the panel cost US$ 1,000 per watt of electrical power it could generate. By 2008, the modules used in solar arrays cost US$ 3.65 per watt; now that figure has fallen to less than 40 cents. In India that year, solar power generation crossed an important threshold, becoming cheaper than coal (by 14% on a 'levelised' basis, which adjusts for the impact of subsidies, construction costs and financing). Fast-plunging costs have allowed India to increase its solar-power generation capacity more than ten-fold since 2015.

The future looks bright, as nearly 293 global and domestic companies have committed to generate 266 GW of solar, wind, mini-hydel and biomass-based power in India over the next decade, involving an investment of US$ 310–350 billion. Among the foreign establishments interested in investing in

India's renewable energy programmes is International Finance Corporation, the investment arm of the World Bank, which has planned to invest about US$ 6 billion by 2022 in a slew of Indian sustainable energy projects. According to India Brand Equity Foundation (IBEF), the Indian power sector has an investment potential of Rs 15 trillion over the next four to five years in power generation, distribution, transmission and equipment.

Growing Foreign Interest

Record low solar power tariffs, plunging solar module costs, low interest rates, backed by government security and 25-year power purchase agreements (PPAs) have emerged as the biggest draw for foreign investors to invest in India's solar industry. Canada Pension Plan Investment Board (CPPIB) and US investor KKR, the world's largest private equity firm, are now major foreign investors in the Indian renewable energy sector and are leading the way. In December 2020, CPPIB acquired an 80% equity stake in SB Energy India at a valuation of US$ 525 million, and KKR acquired major stakes in the IndiGrid InvIT (India Grid Trust – Invest India Trust) in 2019.

In 2021, the year began with the landmark US$ 2 billion investment by TotalEnergies of France to acquire a 20% stake in Adani Green. In addition to Total, oil majors such as BP Plc and Malaysia's Petroliam Nasional Bhd have invested in the sector before. West Asian investors looking to invest in Indian green power assets include Doha-based Nebras Power QSC and Investment Corp of Dubai. Abu Dhabi Investment Authority has already invested in ReNew Power Ventures Pvt Ltd and Greenco Group. Masdar, also known as Abu Dhabi Future Energy Co, acquired around 20% in Hero Future Energies Pvt Ltd last year.

India's low per capita energy use, which is a third of the world average, sends a strong signal about the vast scale of potential investment available in Indian energy projects with attractive relative equity risk-return metrics. The enormous size of the 1.3-billion strong consumer market holds promise of consistent demand growth, led by urbanisation, applications from homes to transport and a switch to green energy. These factors, coupled with various government incentives and potential of returns, compulsively attract global investors to deploy large capital in building low-cost infrastructure for clean energy in India. According to a new report released in February 2021 by the Institute for Energy Economics and Financial Analysis (IEEFA), investment in India's renewable energy and grid projects historically yielded around 14–16% returns. The IEEFA report says that India would need to deploy US$ 500 billion in investment to reach its 450 GW capacity target by 2030. This includes US$ 300 billion needed for wind and solar infrastructure, US$ 50 billion for grid firming such as gas-peakers, hydro and batteries, and US$ 150 billion for expanding and modernising transmission and distribution.

III. ATMANIRBHAR BHARAT

Impressed by the robust growth of the solar sector, Modi has extended his 'Atmanirbhar Bharat' (self-reliant India) drive to domestic solar industry to boost indigenous production of solar equipment. While commissioning a 750 MW solar power project at Rewa in Madhya Pradesh he said that solar energy would play a major role in achieving self-reliance. "This is because solar energy is sure, pure and secure. Sure, because other sources of energy can be exhausted, but the Sun will continue to shine. Pure, because instead of polluting the environment, it helps in protecting it. And secure because, it's a huge symbol, inspiration for Atmanirbhar Bharat." But, "We won't be able to use solar power entirely, unless we have within the country improved solar panels, improved batteries and best quality storage."

Solar cell is the pivot around which solar manufacturing revolves. Investment in other components like modules, wafers, ingots, back sheets, inverters, transformers, etc., follow after there is a large manufacturing capacity of social cells. But India has lagged behind in this respect. In 2020, there only were 16 solar cell manufacturers with a cumulative domestic production capacity of about 2 GW. This barely meets around 15% of the demand, forcing the country to import over 80% of the modules and solar cells worth US$ 12.4 billion over 2015–19, most of it from China. The domestic manufacturing of solar equipment in India is largely limited to downstream value chain which also depends on imports of ingots and wafers.

The heavy reliance on imports of upstream components results in foreign suppliers having substantial control on prices, restricting the ability of domestic manufacturers to cut costs and be price competitive in the global market. Over the years, Chinese solar PV equipment has been more competitively priced, and this market pressure has deterred new investors from entering the domestic manufacturing industry. According to the Boston

Consulting Group, more than 60% of the world's supply of polysilicon, wafers, cells and modules comes from China, while they account for only 20% of the demand. The Chinese supply is also most economically viable, with cost structures of modules in China being US¢ 5–10 per Watt lower than those in India, Malaysia, US and Germany. The cost structures have decreased by about 15% year-on-year over the last five years and are expected to decline further, on account of consistent efficiency gains by Chinese manufacturers, making China the factory of the world.

In recent months the prospects of imports have come under threat amid heightening geopolitical tensions in Sino-Indian relations that may lead to ban on Chinese products or imposition of heavy protection duties. India's Atmanirbhar Bharat programme has laid a clear-cut emphasis on breaking the chain of imports to create a self-reliant India. But as of 2022, Indian manufacturing capacities are sub-scale, with an average plant size of 0.5–1 GW compared to China's 3–5 GW, and, that too underutilised.

However, solar power developers have started cutting down their equipment imports and buying more from the local manufacturers. Data from JMK Research shows that in the first seven months of FY 2020–21, the import of solar equipment such as photovoltaic cells, panels and modules plummeted by about 79% in value terms to Rs 1,83,902 lakh in April-October from Rs 8,91,234 lakh in the same period of FY 2019–20. The decline may be largely attributed to Covid-19 pandemic-triggered lockdowns, but also due to the duty imposed by the government on imports of some foreign, read Chinese, solar equipment following the border tensions with China. The global fall in prices of solar equipment may have also contributed to the decline of Indian imports in value terms. But we may see an increase in imports once the pace of construction picks up on projects already awarded. Anticipating this happening, the government has avoided imposing a heavy basic customs duty, as demanded by local manufacturers, on imports of solar cells and module imports, barring extending the 15% safeguard duty, introduced in 2018 to 2029, on solar cells and modules imported from China, Thailand and Vietnam.

Solar PV Is Key to the Target

Solar photovoltaic (PV) is the key to Modi's energy policy and stepping stone to reaching the target of generating 450 GW of renewable power by 2030.

But unfortunately, India's domestic production of solar PV is inadequate to accelerate the pace of development to reach the target comfortably. Domestic manufacturing meets no more than 15% of the demand. Heavy reliance on imports of upstream components results in foreign suppliers having substantial control on the prices, restricting the ability of domestic manufacturers to cut costs and be price competitive in the global market. Over the years, Chinese solar PV equipment has been more competitively priced, and this market pressure has deterred new investors entering the domestic manufacturing industry.

Module manufacturing has low technological barriers and investment requirement. Up to 94% of the total cost of module assembly is contributed solely by solar cells and other raw material. As we start moving up the value chain, the process becomes technology and capital intensive.

Ramping Up Solar Cell Manufacturing

The government seems to have realised that restrictive initiatives like safeguard duty, domestic content requirement (DCR) and the approved list of models and manufacturers (ALMM), among other things, have failed to ramp up manufacturing of necessary PV components. With the launch of 'Atmanirbhar Bharat' programme, the primary objective of the government policy has shifted to boosting domestic manufacturing. As stated in previous paragraphs, solar cell is the foundation on which this industry stands, and unless it is available in large quantities, no investor is going to put his money in building other components required to install a solar PV. But currently, the cell manufacturing capacity in the country is woefully insufficient to meet the demand.

In February 2019, the government introduced the Kisan Urja Suraksha Evam Utthaan Mahabhiyan (KUSUM) Programme, which aimed to add a solar capacity of 25,750 MW by 2022, and in March 2019, the second phase of the Central Public Sector Undertaking (CPSU) programme was launched to set up 12,000 MW of grid connected solar power projects, also by 2022, for self-use or use by government entities. These programmes have a domestic content requirement (DCR) mandate and are mainly driving the demand for locally manufactured solar cells. In stark contrast, the installed cell production capacity in India is only about 3 GW. To promote the growth of the manufacturing value chain as a whole and create an all-encompassing ecosystem, industry sources insist, it is crucial to focus on bolstering domestic solar cell manufacturing capacity. This way, there is scope for backward integration into secondary component manufacturing avenues in the future as well.

However, large costs involved in setting up or expanding a self-sustaining manufacturing base is a serious challenge. Manufacturing cells is a complicated, multi-stage process and requires extensive capital investment. According to one manufacturer, a 100 MW cell manufacturing facility calls for an investment of Rs 800 million (US$ 10.53 million), excluding land and infrastructure costs. However, such a facility would not have the same economies of scale to compete with imported cell prices, especially Chinese cells. So, an optimum capacity of 500 MW is what would be profitable, for which one needs an investment of about Rs 4 billion (US$ 52.63 million). Solar cell technology is upgraded every eight to nine months, making the whole process even more capital intensive. China's Technology Top Runner Program incentivises the introduction of next generation technology for higher efficiency solar cells. As a result, Chinese manufacturers bring in the latest technology at a competitive price. Such programmes do not exist in India.

Another factor which increases the cost is that the cell and module manufacturers are expected to provide warranties for their products for 20–25 years. This means they have to set aside reserves equivalent to the value of the components supplied for the entire duration of the warranty. Small and medium enterprises may not have the financial depth to provide warranties for so long. The nature of the business is such that it requires deep pockets, larger investments, frequent tech upgradation and large working capital.

Adding to the cost is a fee, which the government levies for enlisting the name of component manufacturers in an 'Approved List of Models and Manufacturers of Solar Cells and Modules (ALMM)'. Only those models and manufacturers that are included in the list are eligible to participate in tenders under government programmes, including projects set up for sale of electricity to government. The fee serves as a sort of disincentive for manufacturers with multiple product lines who wish to update their technology, as they have to pay the fee every time, they release a new model with increased efficiency and better technology.

Indian module manufacturers are also facing issues with domestic content requirement (DCR) tenders. Many of them who want to bid for government projects cannot participate in tenders because of shortage of cells of DCR specifications. There aren't many players who are ready to supply cells or modules which meet the DCR requirements. For example, monocrystalline passivated emitter and rear cells (PERC) under the DCR category are still not available in the market. Besides, the Indian solar cells which are available are not cost-efficient or at par with Chinese cells in price, quality and technology. Indian solar are, on average, 20–30% more expensive than cells manufactured in China, according to market analyst group Mercom India Research. Mercom says that the government has been imposing DCRs oblivious to the lack of PV cell supply, and this widening gap in domestic demand and supply is neither helping the manufacturers nor the developers procuring it. Currently, the installed solar PV cell capacity stands at 3 GW per year and solar PV modules capacity at 10 GW per year in India. Production of other major components such as polysilicon, wafer, ingots has not started yet.

However, certain measures are considered necessary to protect the domestic market from being swamped and products priced out of the home market by imported PV components. At the same time, the government is taking various measures to incentivise cell manufacturing to increase supply and scale to compete with imported cells. Some of them include DCR programme which requires solar projects being installed under the auspices of the CPSUs, KUSUM and rooftop schemes to source their requirement of solar cells and modules from domestic sources. Other incentives include an assured offtake in the form of PPA and the implementation of RPOs which makes it mandatory on state electricity commissions to purchase a certain percentage of power from renewable energy sources. India also plans to offer land near major ports for setting up solar equipment manufacturing. In the FY 2021–22 budget, the government had set aside Rs 4,500 crore for the manufacture of high-efficiency solar cells and modules, besides the usual incentives provided by the Ministry of New and Renewable Energy to priority sector.

Production-Linked Incentive (PLI)

Under the production-linked incentive scheme, the government rewards manufacturers for building vertically integrated, ingot-to-module, PV production lines. The scheme aims to create 10 GW of production capacity by April 2023. Ingot and wafers are the building blocks for manufacturing solar cells and modules, and are essential to India's clean energy plans. Globally, solar wafer and ingot manufacturing is dominated by China. To encourage solar component manufacturers to set up shops for these essential materials the government has come out with a viability gap funding programme which provides financial assistance up to a maximum of 30% of capital cost of projects.

This is in addition to various tax and customs rebates and financial incentives which the government offers to both local and foreign manufacturers for setting up manufacturing facilities in 10 'critical sunrise sectors'. The financial outlay for the scheme is around Rs 1.97 lakh crore or US$ 20 billion per year over five years. Allocation for the high efficiency solar PV modules is Rs 4,500 crore per year. Other sectors included under the scheme and incentives earmarked for them are—advanced chemistry cell (ACC) battery (Rs 18,100 crore); electronics and technology products (Rs 5,000 crore); automobiles and auto components (Rs 57,042 crore); pharmaceuticals and drugs (Rs 15,000 crore); telecom and networking products (Rs 12,195 crore); textiles products (Rs 10,683 crore); food products (Rs 10,900 crore); white goods (Rs 6,238 crore) and speciality steel (Rs 6,322 crore) to both domestic and foreign manufacturers for building gigawatt scale, vertically integrated PV facilities. Incentives provided under the scheme are available to both domestic and foreign manufacturers, as it is likely to increase demand for locally produced materials like EVA sheets, solar glass, back sheets and junction boxes.

In 2020, an accelerated manufacturing plan was operationalised to incentivise the setting up of solar cell manufacturing capacity of 4 GW. This is besides a 3 GW greenfield solar cell capacity which already exists. This scheme also incentivises power project developers, again both local and foreign, to make their own PV equipment alongside their power plants in order to reduce imports. The government hopes that the successful implementation would increase demand for locally produced materials like EVA sheets, solar glass, back sheets and junction boxes, and attract private investment of Rs 14,000 crore.

The PLI scheme seems to have elicited good response from manufacturers. In November 2020, Minister for New and Renewable and Power Raj Kumar Singh revealed that the government had received an 'expression of interest' for setting up 20 GW of solar modules, 15 GW of solar cells and a similar quantity of ingots, wafers from manufacturers. If the bids materialised, India's solar module manufacturing would jump 100% and solar cell capacity seven times.

In fact, module manufacturing does not require high technology or large investment. But as we start moving up the value chain—cell, in particular—the process becomes technology and capital intensive. However, little attention has been paid to developing upstream activities. High capital investment and loan interest rates deter investors from entering the upstream sector. Besides, low production and utilisation capacities impose further limitations on the ability of Indian manufacturers to cut costs and be price competitive in the global market. The industry needs protection to compete with Chinese manufacturers. While India has taken measures in the past to promote the domestic industry, these have had limited impact to generate investor confidence.

The country has begun well with strong policy support and incentives for local manufacturers. But technology is changing rapidly and global companies with cutting-edge R&D are in the race to dominate the rapidly expanding sector. India will need to pivot its own competitive advantage on 'innovation efficiencies' (replicating the China model will not work), i.e., the ability to continuously drive down cost curves and build sustainable competitiveness, akin to European wind turbine manufacturers, who have sustained a competitive edge over the long term. Secondly, India should bring in the best of the world—not just domestic players, but the best-in-class global manufacturing companies—to come to India and participate in the solar manufacturing journey of the world's second largest market.[25]

Realising the necessity of developing cutting-edge technology to improve the quality and efficiency of Indian solar products, the Ministry of New and Renewable Energy has started funding research at technology and specialised institutions. Two institutions, the Indian Institute of Technology (IIT) Bombay and Bharat Heavy Electricals Ltd (BHEL), are currently working to develop high-efficiency crystalline silicon solar cells, including those with passivated emitter and rear contact structure, and perovskites, in addition to roll-to-roll perovskite solar cells (PSC). In terms of design and processes, PSC technology is very close to dye-sensitised and organic solar cells. There is more than one process to produce PSC. In its simplest method, these can be manufactured by roll-to-roll coating, including well-known technologies such as slot die, spray coating and ink-jet printing, or through evaporation. This process essentially eliminates the need for wafer manufacturing and other related processes used in crystalline silicon (c-Si) cells. The researchers aim to develop crystalline silicon solar cells with an efficiency of a minimum 21%, in addition to roll-to-roll PSC.

India Versus China

China is outperforming India in many areas, in both manufacturing and R&D, and thus offers high-efficiency yet cost-effective modules. While Indian manufacturers have to import many raw material inputs, Chinese players rely on their end-to-end domestic PV value chain. Free land parcels allotted by various state provinces, financing at negligible interest rates and cheaper electricity at very subsidised rates are the other benefits available to China's PV manufacturing facilities that lead to lower costs. Chinese players utilise between 1–3% of gross revenue for solar module R&D every year, in contrast, India's leading players provide little R&D investment.[26]

The report finds that in terms of profit margins, Chinese module suppliers are able to absorb larger shares of profit (on average 4.3%) from operational revenues than Indian suppliers who earn an average profit income of less than 3%. This is because the Chinese module manufacturers have large-scale production facilities and low dependence on imports. They also have fully integrated facilities producing modules, cells and wafers complemented by robust R&D and favourable government support. In terms of technology adoption trends, China's mono-Si PV modules reached two thirds of the share of the entire global PV production chain in 2019 by gigawatt volume, while the top seven Indian domestic module manufacturers of Si PV modules accounted for only 13% of PV production.[27]

One World, One Sun, One Grid Solar Alliance

Prime Minister Modi initiated the process for the formation of the International Solar Alliance (ISA) during his speech at Wembley in 2015, whose primary objective is to reduce dependence on fossil fuels by efficient exploitation of solar energy. The alliance is a treaty-based inter-governmental organisation with more than 121 countries, most of which are sunshine countries, lying completely or partly between the Tropic of Cancer and the Tropic of Capricorn. It is the biggest global body, after the United Nations, where India is a founding member. Modi sees the ISA playing the same role in the future as being played by the Organisation of Petroleum Exporting Countries (OPEC) currently. Addressing a meeting of the member states in June 2020, Modi said the role, being played by oil wells now, will be played by rays of the Sun in future. Based in Gurugram (Haryana, India), the Alliance is also called International Agency for Solar Policy and Application (IASPA).

The Alliance has partnered with the World Bank to launch Global Solar Atlas, a free online tool displaying annual average solar power potential at any location in the world. World Bank says, this tool will help governments save millions of dollars on their own research and provide investors and solar developers with an easily accessible and uniform platform to compare resource potential between sites in one region or across multiple countries.[28] In 2016, the Alliance entered into an understanding with the World Bank for accelerating mobilisation of finance for solar energy. The Bank will have a major role in mobilising more than US$ 1 trillion in investments that will be needed by 2030, to meet ISA's goals for the massive deployment of affordable solar energy.[29] The ISA seeks to play a four-fold role in establishing a global solar market, as an accelerator, an enabler, an incubator and a facilitator. Its vision is to help establish, 'One World, One Sun, One Grid'.

Recognised for his bold environmental leadership on the global stage, Modi has been awarded by the United Nations, 'Champions of the Earth' award in the policy leadership category. The award as per the global committee was in due recognition for Modi's initiative in founding the International Solar Alliance, besides other initiatives.

As per IEA's World Energy Outlook 2020, solar PV is more cost-effective in India than coal and gas fired power energy. Going forward, the deflating cost of solar modules and advances in technology are expected to further reduce the cost of generation and storage of solar power in the country. Currently 80% of the solar modules are imported from China and Malaysia. It is important to ensure that introduction of new policies to promote Atmanirbhar Bharat (self-dependent India) does not lead to increased generation cost. Another key requirement is some sort of guarantee for steady revenue and the streamlined payment process to investors, and the involvement of SECI as an intermediary where PPA is signed between investors and less credit worthy state Discoms. PPAs with SECI are backed by an equivalent PSA between SECI and the Discom.

References

1. Vaclav Smil, *Energy and Civilisation: A History*, 1991 edition, p.240.
2. Karuppu, Karthik; Sitaraman, Venk; NVICO (2019). Solar Assessment Guidance: A Guide for Solar Trainee, Trainer & Assessor Examination. Notion Press. ISBN 978-1646505227.

3. Somerville, Richard. 'Historical Overview of Climate Change Science' (PDF). Intergovernmental Panel on Climate Change; 29 September, 2007.

4. Vermass, Wim. 'An Introduction to Photosynthesis and Its Applications'. Arizona State University, 3 December, 1998.

5. Vaclav Smil, (2006), p.12.

6. Solar energy: A New Day Dawning? Silicon Valley sunrise'. Morton, Oliver; 6 September, 2006; *Nature*. 443 (7107): 19–22. Bibcode:2006.

7. 'Energy Conversion by Photosynthetic Organisms'. Food and Agriculture Organization of the United Nations. Retrieved 25 May, 2008.

8. 'Energy and the Challenge of Sustainability' (PDF). United Nations Development Programme and World Energy Council, September, 2000.

9. Indian Solar Resources: National Renewable Energy Laboratory (NREL), www.nrel.gov/rredc/solar_data.html.

10. Singhal SK, Varun, Development of Non-Conventional Energy Sources, 24 March, 2006, www.energymanagertraining.com/Journal/24032006/Developmentofnon-conventionalenergysources.pdf.

11. Rai GD. Non-Conventional Energy Sources. 4th ed., New Delhi, India: Khanna Publishers; 2000.

12. Journal of Solar Energy: Development of Solar Electricity Supply System in India: An Overview: Volume 2013, Article ID 632364, https://doi.org/10.1155/2013/632364.

13. Kumar A, Kumar K. Renewable energy in India: current status & future potentials. Renew Sustain Energy Rev 2010; vol. 14:2434–42.

14. 'Solar'. Ministry of New and Renewable Energy, Govt. of India, 25 February, 2014.

15. 'Wastelands Atlas of India, 2011', 30 May, 2014.

16. 'Population Pyramid of India'. PopulationPyramid.net. 29 July, 2015.

17. 'The 'Solar Canals' Making Smart Use of India's Space'. *BBC*. Retrieved 3 August, 2020.

18. 'India's Building A Huge Floating Solar Farm - Indian Power Sector', 29 July, 2015.

19. India Will Not Only Meet, but Exceed Paris Pact Targets: PM Modi at G20 Meet, TNN, 23 November, 2020.

20. IEA, NITI Aayog.

21. State of India's Environment, Make Power While the Sun Shines, Shweta Miriam Koshy, *Down To Earth*, p.91.

22. Renewable Energy in India: Why Rooftop Remains the Most Untapped Solar Source, *Down To Earth*, 18 January, 2019.

23. BP Statistical Review of World Energy, 2022, p.45 (PDF).

24. 'Renewable Power', 'Overview', Ministry of New and Renewable Energy, website.

25. Vishal Mehta and Sumant Wattas, Boston Consulting Group: 'How India can become "Atmanirbhar" in Solar PV Manufacturing', ETEnergyWorld, 9 September, 2020.

26. JMK Analyst and Report Co-author Jyoti Gulia.

27. PV Magazine.com.

28. New World Bank Tool Helps Map Solar Potential', World Bank Statement, 11 February, 2018.

29. 'International Solar Alliance Cell and World Bank Sign Declaration for Promoting Solar Energy', Press Information Bureau, Govt. of India. 30 June, 2016.

Chapter 6
WIND ENERGY

Wind is the kinetic energy of air in motion. Winds are generated by the spinning of the planet Earth, by irregularities of the Earth's surface, from mountains and valleys to oceans and by solar radiation. As air is heated by the Sun, it expands and becomes lighter and rises, creating a vacuum, and cooler air rushes in to fill the vacuum. That flow may be as gentle as a breeze or as powerful as a tempest. It is this impact of the Sun on the temperature of air that most explicitly qualifies wind as a form of wind energy. A traditional windmill captures the moving force of the wind, its kinetic energy and transforms it into mechanical energy. In an electrical turbine, the mechanical energy is further transformed by a generator into electricity. A large wind turbine is really a small power plant.[1]

Globally, the long-term technical potential of wind energy is believed to be five times total current global energy production, or 40 times current electricity demand. It is the second largest renewable energy source globally, after hydropower, for power generation. Many parts of the world have strong wind speeds, but the best locations for generating wind power are sometimes remote ones. In 2019, wind supplied 1,270 TWh of electricity, which was 4.7% of worldwide electrical generation,[2] with the global installed wind power capacity reaching more than 651 GW, an increase of 10% over 2018.[3] According to the International Renewable Energy Agency (IRENA), wind energy has been increasing at an average compound annual growth rate (CAGR) of more than 21% since 2000, it is one of the most mature and cost competitive (onshore) renewable energy technologies.

The total amount of economically extractable power available from the wind is considerably more than the present human power use from all sources.[4] Axel Kleidon of the Max Planck Institute in Germany, carried out a 'top-down' calculation on how much wind energy there is, starting with the incoming solar radiation that drives the winds by creating temperature differences in the atmosphere. He concluded that somewhere between 18 TW and 68 TW could be extracted.[5]

Cristina Archer and Mark Z Jacobson presented a 'bottom-up' estimate, which unlike Kleidon's are based on actual measurements of wind speeds, and found that there is 1,700 TW of wind power at an altitude of 100 m (330 ft) over land and sea. Of this, "Between 72 and 170 TW could be extracted in a practical and cost-competitive manner."[6] They later upped the estimates to 80 TW.[7] However, a research at Harvard University estimates 1 W/m^2 on average and 2–10 MW/km^2 capacity for large-scale wind farms, suggesting that these estimates of total global wind resources are too high by a factor of about four.[8]

Onshore wind is an inexpensive source of electric power, competitive with or in many places cheaper than coal or gas plants. Onshore wind farms have a greater visual impact on the landscape than other power stations, as they need to be spread over more land and need to be built away from dense population. Offshore wind is steadier and stronger than on land and offshore farms have less visual impact, but construction and maintenance costs are significantly higher. Small onshore wind farms can feed some energy into the grid or provide power to isolated off-grid locations.

Wind is an intermittent energy source, which cannot be dispatched on demand. Locally, it gives variable power, which is consistent from year to year but varies greatly over shorter time scales. Therefore, it must be used together with other power sources to give a reliable supply. Power-management techniques such as having dispatchable power sources (often gas-fired power plant or hydroelectric power), excess capacity, geographically distributed turbines, exporting and importing power to neighbouring areas, energy storage, reducing demand when wind production is low, are used to overcome these problems. As the proportion of wind power in a region increases the grid may need to be upgraded. Weather forecasting permits the electric-power network to be readied for the predictable variations in production that occur.

I. HISTORY

Wind power has been used since as long as humans have put sails into the wind. King Hammurabi's Codex (reign 1792–1750 BC) already mentioned windmills for generating mechanical energy.[9] The first windmill used for the production of electric power was built in Scotland in July 1887 by Professor James Blyth of Anderson's College, Glasgow (the precursor of Strathclyde University).[10] Blyth's 10 m (33 ft) high, the cloth-sailed wind turbine was installed in the garden of his holiday cottage at Marykirk in Kincardineshire and was used to charge accumulators developed by the Frenchman Camille

Alphonse Faure, to power the lighting in the cottage, thus making it the first house in the world to have its electric power supplied by wind power.[11] Blyth offered the surplus electric power to the people of Marykirk for lighting the main street, however, they turned down the offer as they thought electric power was 'the work of the devil'.[12]

Although he later built a wind turbine to supply emergency power to the local Lunatic Asylum, Infirmary, and Dispensary of Montrose, the invention never really caught on as the technology was not considered to be economically viable.[13] Across the Atlantic, in Cleveland, Ohio, a larger and heavily engineered machine was designed and constructed in the winter of 1887–1888 by Charles F Brush.[14] This was built by his engineering company at his home and operated from 1886 until 1900. The Brush wind turbine had a rotor 17 m (56 ft) in diameter and was mounted on an 18 m (59 ft) tower. Although large by today's standards, the machine was only rated at 12 kW. The connected dynamo was used either to charge a bank of batteries or to operate up to 100 incandescent light bulbs, three arc lamps and various motors in Brush's laboratory.[15]

With the development of electric power, wind power found new applications in lighting buildings from centrally generated power. Throughout the twentieth century, parallel paths developed small wind stations suitable for farms or residences. The 1973 oil crisis triggered the investigation in Denmark and the United States that led to larger utility scale wind generators that could be connected to electric power grids for remote use of power. By 2008, the US installed capacity had reached 25.4 GW, and by 2012 the installed capacity was 60 GW. Today, wind-powered generators operate in every size range between tiny stations for battery charging at isolated residences, up to near-gigawatt-sized offshore wind farms that provide electric power to national electrical networks.

Presently, the impact of Covid-19 has delayed some of the wind project, but they are not cancelled. The sector is set for record growth over the next five years. In total, some 348 GW of new onshore and offshore capacity are expected to come up by the end of 2024, which would take the cumulative global wind power capacity to almost 1,000 GW, according to Global Wind Energy Council (GWEC). Governments are also under pressure to cut carbon emissions, which is helping to shift investment away from fossil fuels and into renewable energy, such as wind. Over 50% of the onshore wind capacity added between 2020 to 2024 will be installed in China and the US, led by installation rushes to meet subsidy deadlines. The costs of wind energy have fallen rapidly over the last few years and are expected to continue to decrease.[16]

Wind and solar power were the most resilient to the Covid-19 lock down restrictions. While demand had fallen in other sectors, renewable electricity was largely unaffected. The share of renewables in global electricity generation jumped to nearly 28% in the first quarter of 2020 from 26% as compared to the first quarter of 2019. The increase in renewables came mainly at the cost of coal and gas, though those two sources still represent close to 60% of the global electricity supply. In the first quarter of 2020 variable renewables—in the form of solar PV and wind power—reached 9% of generation, up from 8% in the first quarter of 2019.

Wind energy acquired importance during the pursuit for alternative energy in the wake of the oil crisis of the 1970s. Starting with the first three-bladed wind turbine of 22 kW model at a Danish farm in 1982, it has become a significant growth industry with a strong constituency globally. As of 2017, installed capacity of wind power in the European Union (EU) was 169.3 GW, generating 336 TWh of electricity, enough to supply 11.6% of the EU's electricity consumption, and it is likely to continue to grow. According to a European Environment Agency report, wind energy can play a major role in achieving the European renewable energy targets.[17] The European Wind Energy Association (now WindEurope) had expected that 230 GW of wind capacity would have been installed in Europe by 2020, consisting of 190 GW onshore and 40 GW offshore. This would produce 14–17% of the EU's electricity, avoiding 333 mt of CO_2 per year and saving Europe € 28 billion per year in fuel costs.[18]

The Global Scenario

The year 2021 was the second-best year for the wind industry, with 93.6 GW of capacity added globally. It was only 1.8% below the record growth in 2020. Europe, Latin America, Africa and Middle East had a record year for new onshore installations. Offshore wind capacity commissioned in 2021 was 21.1 GW, three times more than in 2020. China made up 80% of offshore wind capacity added worldwide in 2021, bringing its cumulative offshore wind installations to 27.7 GW. Total global wind power capacity rose to 837 GW, helping the world avoid over 1.2 bt of CO_2 annually—equivalent to the annual carbon emissions of South America. GWEC expects further addition of 557 GW new capacity in the next five years by 2026. This means an addition of 110 GW of new installations each year until 2026. However, this growth needs to quadruple by the end of the decade if the world is to stay on-course for a 1.5C pathway and net zero by 2050.[19]

Offshore wind power capacity is set to increase by at least 15-folds worldwide by 2040. The promising outlook for offshore wind is underpinned by policy support in an increasing number of regions, as it holds the promise of driving energy transitions by decarbonising electricity and by producing low-carbon fuels.

Currently, Europe is the leader in offshore wind industry. European governments have supported offshore wind energy over the years with multiple incentives. Such a support is lacking in India. In 2019, Europe had a total installed offshore wind capacity of 22.1 GW from 5,047 grid-connected wind turbines across 12 countries, and plans to construct 1.4 GW of additional capacity in offshore wind, costing € 6 billion, as go-ahead was given to France, Netherlands, Norway and the UK. The average rated capacity of offshore turbines installed in 2019 was 7.8 MW.[20]

For the future, the European Commission has said in its offshore renewable energy plan that the EU's climate change targets required 60 GW of offshore wind by 2030 and 300 GW by 2050 (for all 27 EU members). The biggest offshore wind producer in Europe is Britain, with an installed wind capacity of about 10 GW. The North Sea has led the way, with Germany, the Netherlands and Denmark, among the EU's main offshore producers.

Worldwide, wind energy is accepted as one of the most developed, cost-effective and proven renewable energy technologies to meet increasing electricity demands in a sustainable manner. While onshore wind energy technologies have reached a stage of large-scale deployment and have become competitive with fossil fuel-based electricity generation, with supportive policy regimes across the world, exploitation of offshore wind energy is yet to reach a comparable scale. India has achieved significant success in the onshore wind power development, with over 40 GW of wind energy capacity already installed and generating power.

India is surely and steadily moving towards complying with its climate change commitments under the Paris Agreement (COP21). India's pledge at the climate summit stated the country's intention to follow, "A cleaner path than the one followed hitherto by others at a corresponding level of economic development." To this end, India has established goals to expand its use of renewable energy and more efficient technologies. But execution difficulties like land availability at reasonable prices, lack of the transmission network combined with rising market risks—power distribution companies' financial weakness, payment delays and curtailment—led to an increase in discovered tariffs.

II. WIND ENERGY IN INDIA

India has been a latecomer to the wind energy sector, compared to Denmark, US, Spain and Germany. But it has leapfrogged to the position of top fourth in the world, in terms of installed capacity, after China, US and Germany. As of 31 July, 2022, India had the total installed wind power capacity of 40.893 GW. Studies to explore the possibilities of harnessing wind power and investigating the available resources that could be practically utilised started in India as early as 1952, but work on the establishment of the first wind project began in 1985 in Veraval, Gujarat, in the form of a 40 kW Dutch machine (make Polenko) connected to the grid.

However, the decisive change came with the Electricity Act of 2003, which jumpstarted growth of the renewable energy industry. Rapid economic growth and soaring oil and gas import prices forced the government to look for developing indigenous resources to supplement fuel imports, and obviously one was the wind energy and the other solar energy. It was also a way to reduce the dependence on fossil fuels and cut pollution. But any significant move got delayed with a change in government leadership in 2004.

It was only in 2014, when a new government led by Modi, that India moved with determination to reshape the country's moribund energy system. Modi identified renewable energy as a key growth industry for the twenty-first century and gave it a strong policy support. The result was that within the eight years from March 2014 to July 2022, the installed wind power capacity jumped from 23.3 GW to 40.9 GW and solar from 2.6 GW to 60 GW, and overall renewable energy capacity grew to 160 GW, according to data presented by the Minister for Power and New and Renewable Energy RK Singh in the Parliament in reply to a question.

However, post-2017, wind power installations started deflating, while solar boomed. Only 2.3 GW of wind capacity was added in 2019, almost half of the 4.1 GW installed in 2017. Stringent tender conditions, low tariff caps, off-taker risks, unavailability of grid and land were chiefly responsible for waning developers' zeal in bidding for new projects. Almost one-third of 17 GW of capacity auctioned by various power purchasing agencies between

2017–2019, went unsubscribed or were cancelled post-award due to various factors. According to a 2020 study by Global Wind Energy Council (India) more than 80% of the awarded projects had been delayed by 6–12 months.

Clearly, the steep pricing competition has come at a cost. Central government tenders have lost steam, following a decision to use the extremely low price captured in the first six auctions of (Rs 2.4–2.8 per kWh) for a ceiling tariff in the last two auctions of 2017. Such tariffs were not feasible, as wind is region specific, and achieving a particular tariff rate becomes difficult. In addition, there are numerous other problems such as curtailment in power generation and delayed payments to energy producers. The government had realised the problem and came up with an announcement to remove the price caps in future auctions and strengthen its agencies to step-in for helping developers. It also announced plans to set up two new large renewable energy parks.

In 1986, demonstration wind farms were set up in the coastal areas of Maharashtra (Ratnagiri), Gujarat (Okha) and Tamil Nadu (Tirunelveli) with 55 kW Vestas wind turbines, with help from MNRE. Both the technical and economic viability of the wind energy industry and the wind-mapping programme, undertaken along with them, resulted in the identification of many sites suitable for wind power projects.

Since then, the expansion of the wind industry has resulted in a strong ecosystem, project operation capabilities and manufacturing. Currently, India's wind industry is a fairly developed indigenous industry, with more than 20 manufactures of 53 different wind turbine models exporting to Europe, the United States and other countries. Suzlon Energy Limited is ranked among the top five manufacturers of wind turbines worldwide. Others include, Regen Powertech Pvt Ltd, Inox Wind Ltd, Orient Green Power Ltd, Vestas India, Enercon India Pvt Ltd and Gamesa Wind Turbines Pvt Ltd. Almost 90% of the components are made in India by firms as varied as Suzlon Energy, Siemens Gamesa and GE Renewable Energy, besides a 2,000 strong MSME supply chain.

Policy Push

India's push for wind industry, together with solar, is driven by soaring demand of electricity amid rapid economic growth. It is also a way to reduce the dependence on polluting coal and import of costly oil and gas. National concerns about greenhouse emissions and climate change and the need for cost-effective generation of power have proved propulsion for the growth of the renewable energy industry in which private sector is taking an active part. The government, on its part, has provided various fiscal and financial incentives such as accelerated depreciation benefit; concessional custom duty exemption on certain components of wind electric generators and generation-based incentive (GBI) to promote this industry. Other supports provided by the government to investors include:

a. Technical support including wind resource assessment and identification of potential sites through the National Institute of Wind Energy, Chennai.
b. Waiver of inter-state transmission charges and losses in order to facilitate inter-state sale of wind and solar power and
c. Guidelines for tariff-based competitive bidding process for procurement of power from grid connected wind power projects with an objective to provide a framework for procurement of wind power through a transparent process of bidding.

Wind Power Potential in India

The first assessment of wind energy resources in India, made in 2011 by Professor Jami Hossain of The Energy and Resources Institute (TERI), had put India's wind power potential at over 2,000 GW, which was subsequently re-validated by Lawrence Berkley National Laboratory (LBNL), US, in 2012. However, a more realistic, new estimate made by the state-run National Institute for Wind Energy (NIWE) put India's wind potential at 302 GW at 100 m above the ground level and 695 GW at a higher hub height of 120 m. "All this potential is commercially realisable," says the Director-General of NIWE, K Balaraman. The NIWE has installed some 800 wind-monitoring stations all over the country and issued maps of wind potential at the sub heights of 50 m, 80 m, 100 m and 120 m above the ground.

Onshore

Around 97% of this potential is concentrated in seven states—Gujarat (84.4 GW), Karnataka (55.85 GW), Maharashtra (45.39 GW), Andhra

Pradesh (44.22 GW), Tamil Nadu (33.79 GW) Rajasthan (18.77 GW) and Madhya Pradesh (10.48 GW), with scattered potential in Kerala, Telangana and Jammu and Kashmir. There are also areas of medium wind potential in states like Punjab, Haryana, Bihar, West Bengal, Odisha, Bihar and the north-eastern states. Around 70% of wind generation occurs during the five months, from May to September, coinciding with the southwest monsoon.[21]

In a study published in February 2020, the NIWE has said that of the 695 GW installable wind potential in the country at the hub height of 120 m, nearly 347 GW of wind projects could be installed on cultivable lands and 340 GW capacity could be set up on wastelands. Cultivable land areas in India have the highest potential for wind energy projects. Nearly 70% of the wind farms in Tamil Nadu are on cultivable lands, and 25% of wind farms on wastelands. In Gujarat, 35% of wind farms are on cultivable lands and 60% on wastelands. But availability of land resources has been proving a major constraint. Local communities sometimes object to wind farms being set up on farm lands because they think wind turbines spoil rural landscapes.

The cost of onshore wind farms is relatively cheap, allowing for mass farms of wind turbines. The shorter distance between the windmill and the consumer allows for less voltage drop-off on the cabling. Onshore wind turbines are quick to install, unlike a nuclear power station, which can take over twenty years, a windmill can be built in a matter of months.

However, one of the biggest issues of onshore wind farms is that many consider them as an eyesore on the landscape. They don't produce energy all year round due to uncertain wind speed or physical blockages such as buildings or hills. The noise that wind turbines create can cause noise pollution for nearby communities.

Offshore

With about 7,600 km long coastline and exclusive economic zone, India has ample opportunity to harness offshore wind energy. The NIWE has found that there could be some problems in exploitation of this plentiful resource in eastern coasts because of frequent cyclones, but western coasts starting from Gujarat, Maharashtra, Karnataka to Tamil Nadu and Andhra Pradesh have larger potential in terms of a stable, steady and speedy wind flow. Based on the studies by NIWE, MNRE has informed the Parliamentary Standing Committee on Energy that India has an offshore wind energy potential of around 70 GW along the coast of Gujarat and Tamil Nadu. This could be a plausible alternative to land resource.

The absence of any kind of obstruction at sea provides flawless pace of wind at the sea and its conversion to electrical energy. Offshore stations experience mean wind speeds at 80 m that are 90% greater than on land; so, offshore winds can produce substantially more energy than land-based turbines. Researchers have calculated that the wind at 80 m above the sea level travels at 8.6 m/s (metre per second) over the ocean, compared to 4.5 m/s over land (20 and 10 miles per hour, respectively).

In September 2015, the union cabinet approved the National Offshore Wind Energy Policy to develop offshore wind energy in the Indian Exclusive Economic Zone (EEZ) along the coastline and in April 2018 issued a tender inviting expression of interest bids from developers to build the country's first 1,000 MW commercial scale offshore wind farm near the Gujarat coast. The proposed location of the offshore wind farm is to be 23–40 km off the coast from the Pipavav Port, Gulf of Khambhat, and covers about 400 sq km. The government has allocated Rs 10,000 crores as the initial seed money from clean energy fund for offshore wind power development.

Wind, like solar, costs nothing, but the cost of setting up infrastructure and an offshore wind plant is so high that it more than offsets the cheapness of the motive power. Offshore wind turbines are not simple machines. They are very large, almost similar to a small power plant. Yet while the power electronics, computer control and engineering of a modern 25-storey-tall wind turbine may be complex, the basic concept is not. The wind may be free, but that is not true of the system required to harness it in large volumes, put it through the grid and deliver it to consumers. For producing wind energy from offshore, a lot of investment is required in developing the supporting infrastructure. As of 2020, there were no offshore wind farms in India. However, an Offshore Wind Policy was announced in 2015 and presently weather stations and Light Detection and Ranging Systems (LIDARS) are being set up by NIWE at some locations. The first offshore wind farm is planned near Dhanushkodi in Tamil Nadu.[22]

Offshore wind turbines are much larger in size, in the range of 5 to 10 MW per turbine against 2–3 MW of an onshore wind turbine. While, the cost per megawatt for offshore turbines is higher because of stronger structures and foundations needed in marine environment, the desirable tariffs can be achieved on account of higher efficiencies of these turbines after development of the ecosystem. The locations of offshore farms are less intrusive to neighbouring countries, allowing for larger farms to be created per square mile.

However, the biggest disadvantage of an offshore wind farm is its cost. Offshore wind farms can be expensive to build and maintain, and because of their hard-to-reach locations. Also, they are vulnerable to damages from very high-speed winds during storms and hurricanes, and expensive to repair. The effect of offshore wind farms on marine life and birds have not yet been fully assessed. But if they are built close to coastlines (generally within 26 miles), they could be unpopular as they can affect property values and tourism.

Wind's Competitiveness

The proliferation of capital and technology has led to a precipitous fall in the installation cost of renewable energy, and are expected to fall further, due to decline in technology costs and operating expenses. Wind costs were expected to plummet by 7% and solar by 11% by 2022. Coal power, on the other hand, was likely to be 9% costlier because of increased cost of equipment, such as addition of flue-gas desulphurisation systems, mandated by the government to comply new environmental standards and escalating domestic raw material costs. According to GWEC analysis, the gap between the cost of generation from renewables and coal was to widen from 35% in 2019 to 43% in 2022.

However, despite the lucrative cost-competitiveness of wind energy, new installations have declined by about 50% since 2018. The decline was more pronounced in 2019 when the government fixed the upper benchmark price at Rs 2.4–2.8 per kWh. Developers found it too low and skipped participating in auctions. However, demand is partially driven by non-solar renewable purchase obligations (RPO), as wind is the most cost-competitive resource among non-solar renewable resources, and to meet this demand the government is expected to install 11–17 GW capacity between 2020 and 2022, taking the cumulative installed base of wind power to 54 GW by 2022. In India, the government has separate RPOs for solar and non-solar power for all states ensuring that both wind and solar have their individual demand drivers and do not compete. Wind, small hydro and biomass are typical resources used to meet non-solar RPOs, as compared to small hydro (Rs 6–7 per kWh) and biomass (Rs 8–10 per kWh), wind is the most competitive on the cost basis.

Beyond RPOs, there are three market mechanisms for the procurement of wind, each of which have separate drivers—central auctions, state auctions and the commercial and industrial (C&I) market auctions. Seven states which have sufficient wind resources (where average wind speed at 100 m hub height is above 6 m/s), do their own procurement. The remaining 22 states and 7 union territories follow the central government-initiated auctions for wind power. Central auctions are driving the market. Nearly half of electricity demand in India stems from 21 states which can only procure wind through central auctions. Of these, 14 states are major demand centres. The 2022 RPOs of these states vary between 6–9%, which translates to nearly 10 GW of new demand for wind procurement. Central government intermediaries aggregate this demand to conduct auctions towards fulfilment of these RPOs. Around 80–85% of new installations are expected to come from central procurement.

Central Auctions

On top of the demand for wind from states and central government, C&I are allowed to set up their own wind power plants. These entities usually have high demand and have the option of buying power from outside of Discoms, and will account for a small yet consistent market share of 5–10% between 2020 and 2022. State Discoms are responsible for procurement of power from generators and distributing it to the consumers.[23] Most states without wind resources have an average power purchasing cost (APPC) 30–40% higher for wind than in central auctions. The cost feasibility of these projects is ensured by the central government through waive-off of inter-state grid transmission charges for a period of 25 years. Substantial demand for wind procurement is visible towards 2022 in these states, which can be procured at pricing levels lower than APPCs. The central government has conducted nine auctions towards fulfilment of this demand. However, execution of awarded projects has been delayed due to infrastructural bottlenecks on the ground.

Plummeting Tariff

The growth of wind power is being boosted by the plummeting cost of turbines and proliferation of willing investors, the two main factors, which have made it competitive against coal and other fossil fuels-based power. In the last decade, this scale of activity attracted multinational utilities, investors and supply chain players to India's wind market. An influx of capital and technology initiated a downward slide in prices, with levelised cost of energy (LCOE) of wind declining by 40% from 2015 to 2019. As a result, wind is now the second most cost-competitive power source on the grid, after solar, reaching a low of around Rs 2.43 (US¢ 3.4) per kWh without any direct or indirect subsidies during auctions. Variation in wind's LCOE is seen across the country due to variable resource availability and development costs. (Optimal sites in the country have wind speed above 7.5 m/s, while wind-based plants are also located on sites with wind speeds between 6 to 6.5 m/s.) On average, wind LCOE is roughly 35% cheaper than the majority of coal plants present in the country. In 2019, wind power accounted for 10% of India's total installed power generation capacity, and generated 62.03 TWh, which was about 4% of total electricity generated in the country.[24]

However, steep pricing competition has come at a cost. Central government tenders have lost steam, following a decision to use the extremely low prices (Rs 2.4–2.8 per kWh) captured in the first six auctions as a benchmark for an upper price cap in the last two auctions. Such tariffs were not feasible to meet in the face of exhausted grid infrastructure and changes to local land use criteria for awarding new sites.

Furthermore, the seven states which manage wind procurement themselves have seen a major decline in activity. Orders by these states contracted by 60% from 2017 to 2019. Auctions were severely undersubscribed due to the off-taker risk associated with the weak financial position of state distribution companies (Discoms) and chronic payment delays to projects installed pre-2017. Facing financial pressure, most of these states have moved to central auctions to hedge their payments with federal guarantees. The impact can be seen as the Solar Energy Corporation of India Ltd had to postpone its latest 1.2 GW wind interstate transmission system programme for the fourth time as it could not attract developers.

Wind installations levels have significantly declined after the reverse auction mechanism was introduced in the wind sector after several years of growth. Before the auctions were introduced, wind projects were mostly developed by private companies for captive consumption or sale to the state. But all of this changed in 2017 when the reverse auction was introduced. From 2017 to 2018, auctions were oversubscribed by 30–35% on an average, and tenders fully awarded. However, the activity severely declined later with nearly 60–70% of volume unallocated in auctions.

Of the 12 GW awarded in auctions in the last three years, 80–85% have been delayed by 6–12 months, as of 30 January, 2020. These projects have either been granted extensions by government agencies or have applied for the same. On top of this, 1–1.5 GW of projects have been cancelled or are at a risk of cancellation due to issues related to availability of land, grid or PPA signing delays.

Misplaced Doubt about the Target

The slowdown has naturally caused doubt among a section of analysts about the prospect of India achieving the 60 GW target of wind power capacity by 2022. GWEC expects the cumulative capacity to reach 54 GW, 'in best case scenario', if a 11–17 GW capacity, which is expected to be installed between 2020 and 2022, is added to the installed base of wind power. The domestic research group CRISIL is more conservative as it expects that the wind power may reach only up to 45 GW by 2022.

However, this is too pessimistic a foresight. It doesn't take into account the potential of government's Solar Wind Hybrid Policy, launched in 2018, that combines home wind electric and home solar electric (photovoltaic) technologies and which offers several advantages over either single system, such as use of land, the unavailability of which hinders implementation of many renewable energy projects. Once the hybrid policy starts working full steam, the problem of finding separate sites for wind and power projects will disappear. A single site would be enough for both solar and wind projects. The main objective of the hybrid policy is to provide a framework for promotion of large grid connected wind solar PV hybrid system for optimal and efficient utilisation of wind and solar resources, transmission infrastructure and land. The government is confident of reaching the target well before 2022. According to MNRE, 38 GW wind capacity was already established till September 2020, while 13 GW projects were under different stages of development and another 10 GW projects were likely to be tendered in 2020–21.

Two fundamental drivers are in place to sustain market growth—rising energy demand and political ambition. Over the next 10 years, electricity demand is set to double in the country of 1.35 billion people. Accordingly, Indian government is targeting 450 GW of renewable energy capacity by 2030 of which 140 GW will be wind-based generation. As of September 2020, it accounted for 42.7% of the installed renewable capacity, followed by solar, with 40.4%, biomass with 11.4% and small hydro by 5.3%.

State Auctions

The seven states which have high wind resources contributed nearly 52% of India's electricity demand in 2019. They had the highest RPOs and target

9–13% of non-solar procurement by 2022. These aggressive targets were expected to generate demand for roughly 10 GW of wind procurement in state markets by 2022. Given the presence of competitive wind resource sites in respective states, wind power procurement is most suitable route to fulfilment of the non-solar RPO target. The average power procurement cost is 10–40% higher than the cost of wind in all seven states, apart from Madhya Pradesh. However, after central auctions were introduced in 2020, activity in state markets has slowed. Three of the seven states—Gujarat, Maharashtra and Tamil Nadu—tried their hand at conducting their own auctions, but apart from Gujarat they failed to generate developer interest. The biggest challenge for state markets has been their discoms' inability to make timely payments to developers. As a result, developers have steered away from state auctions. The remaining four states are now in a state of flux, and have procured no new power in the last two years.

Commercial and Industrial (C&I) Market

Small in size, but consistent in procurement, the C&I sector, including the private and public establishments like SAIL and ONGC, is the largest power consumer in India, contributing roughly 50% of the overall demand. Primarily the sector is dependent on grid power, however an estimated 35–39% of the power needs of this sector are fulfilled by self-procurement (MEC+ estimates based on data from CEA and other state and industry authorities). India had installed nearly 65 GW of captive and third-party PPA projects as of December 2019, of which 12 GW was renewable-based (excluding rooftop solar). Wind contributed about 8 GW of this capacity, most of which was derived from captive wind installations. Only 10–20% of the 65 GW came from third-party PPAs. Going forward, C&I procurement is expected to remain small yet consistent, varying between 0.7–1.4 GW till 2022.

Growing urbanisation and industrialisation will continue to drive demand of electricity in India. By 2027, electricity demand in the C&I sector is expected to increase by 66%, according to the national electricity plan, creating a strong driver for corporate procurement. The demand for corporate procurement is facilitated by presence of an open access (OA) regulation which enables all entities with demand greater than 1 MW to procure power on their own. Additionally, certain C&I consumers are bound to meet RPOs. Industrial consumers with thermal captive generation capacity above 1 MW (to 5 MW, dependent on the state) need to procure a certain percentage of their demand from renewable generation.

With renewables becoming the cheapest source of grid power, C&I consumers have a strong financial incentive to switch to clean energy. C&I consumers typically pay 30–40% more per unit as compared to the other consumers, and their tariff generally ranges from Rs 6–10 per kWh. With the cost of wind and solar dropping significantly, a head-to-head comparison of C&I tariffs and cost of generation from renewable energy indicates a substantial cost differential between the two.

Barriers to Wind Energy Development

While there is strong support from the central government for increased uptake of renewable energy, there remains a number of barriers to wind power reaching its full potential. A part of this is due to the fact that the power sector is a 'concurrent' subject, meaning that both central and state governments exercise control. The reality is that it is often the states and local utilities which play the larger role.

Most of the state level power sector utilities in India are not in good financial health and are unable to comply with the national RPOs announced in 2016. Delayed payments of up to six months or more by certain state utilities (Discoms) are also an ongoing concern. The government has floated the idea of a performance-based initiative which would be of particular use to financially distressed Discoms, where the Discom would receive payments from central government for the timely payment of tariffs and other performance related issues.

Further, recent interconnections between key southern states in India have at least created the wires which would facilitate the transfer of power from windy states to other parts of the country. More are needed, but in addition to wires there needs to be both a mechanism and an incentive to trade renewable power, to assist with overall system reliability as well as load balancing. A truly effective interstate market, properly incentivised, would be a major boost to the renewables sector and the Indian power system as a whole.

Land acquisition and title-clearing continues to be a challenge for most onshore installations in India, and the reform of this sector is long overdue. Sourcing affordable debt finance remains a challenge. High interest rates and limited availability of affordable debt are challenges for developers as well as original equipment manufacturers (OEMs) in the country. Until now, equity investors have filled the gap sufficiently, but there are limits, and having a healthy mix of debt and equity will put these projects in a stronger position.

Grid Availability Delays

Delays in grid availability for evacuation of wind power is a major problem of this industry. There are 26 substations countrywide allocated for the evacuation of wind electricity, out of these only six are viable for new bids as the rest are either at uncompetitive wind resource sites or are fully booked by the existing pipeline. Bhuj in Gujarat and Tirunelvelli in Tamil Nadu are the two most preferred sites by the developers. Bhuj is preferred because of the availability of high resource sites and cheap revenue land that allow them to engineer lowest cost bids in central auctions. Revenue land is typically 60–70% cheaper than privately held land in India. Currently, 5.6 GW of projects are connected or planned for connection at Bhuj, against the existing and planned evacuation capacity of 6 GW at the substation. However, planned grid augmentation has a gestation period of 36–48 months, which is longer than the project timelines of 18–24 months. As a result, the capacity scheduled for commissioning at Bhuj continues to exceed the available and planned augmentation capacity.

Financing rate and tenure: The availability of finance to projects is a challenge both in terms of the amount available and the tenure for which it is lent. The average tenure for a bank loan ranges between 6 to 10 years for a project of 25 years, creating a significant mismatch between asset and liability. At the same time, banks have become extremely cautious after facing twin setbacks of bad debts to infrastructure projects in the early 2000s and real estate firms in 2010s.

Tariffs reality: Discoms in India who buy the wind power have set their budgets at low tariffs. Most utilities budget renewable energy procurement two years in advance, wherein they budget both the number of units to be bought and the price at which they are to be bought. These estimates are based on their demand-supply situation, the average cost of procurement, and recent market prices of renewables. Several Discoms have budgeted prices at the lowest level (Rs 2.5 per kWh) of renewable projects. This causes a problem after auctions are held. If the prices discovered in auctions are higher than the tariff budgeted for procurement, Discoms dither in adopting the prices discovered during auctions. As of today, 20–30% of the projects auctioned in the last two years are awaiting tariff adoption or the signing of a power supply agreement.

Also, this situation is made complex by the central government's intense focus on reducing the cost of power in auctions, subsequently leading to non-recognition of the real cost of energy, including the transmission costs and balancing costs, which are socialised as of now. These combined costs are nearly 120% of the cost price for energy supply. This sudden increase could shock the market expectations.

Payment delays: Payment delays on existing renewable energy projects create uncertainty for investors to further invest in the market. The total payment delay currently is small due to intermediary agencies guaranteeing payment in auctioned projects. However, it remains unclear if the agencies will be able to mitigate the risk as India nears its 100 GW renewable energy target.

Access to wind quality sites: India has a large land base and a long coastline. However, the wind speeds available to most sites are low. The sites where wind speeds are suitable (above 6.5 m/s) are usually remote and far away from the existing and planned grid (up to 100 km). This increases the transmission cost as well as the complexity of securing the right of way, especially in states where local government is non-cooperative, consequently creating delays and lumpiness.[25]

Supply Side Bottlenecks

At 5.5 GW, wind energy installations peaked in 2016–17. However, new installations in the following FY 2017–18 fell sharply to 1.8 GW and 1.6 GW in 2018–19. The target for 2019–20 was set at 3 GW, but actual installations were only 2.07 GW. The slowdown since 2017–18 was driven by supply-side bottlenecks, mainly attributed to the sanctioning of grid and land. Unlike the markets in Europe and the US, where there is sizeable demand from corporate for PPAs, the total contribution of corporate customers is low in India. This is primarily due to the high charges levied on consumers by Discoms to dis-incentivise them from switching. Hence, this market will remain niche. The government is aware of these realities and has done multiple consultations to resolve the bottlenecks. Some evidence is seen in the resolution of the supply side bottlenecks with the announcement of two new large renewable energy parks, removal of price caps in future auctions and strengthening its agencies to step-in for helping developers.[26]

Way Forward

a) First, India needs to replace inefficient windmills at older sites with new windmills.

b) India needs to delink grid development with energy generation. The government needs to trust the market and allow the tariff to move up and down. It is the market which has led to low tariffs for solar or wind. The imposition of a ceiling, like the one in 2017, leads to arbitrary curtailment of free flow of market mechanism. In a competitive market situation, if prices go up, government should learn to live with it.

c) India should first fully exploit onshore potential of wind before investing in the offshore wind energy sector.

d) At each stage of harnessing energy from winds, India needs competitive private investment to drive the progress.

e) There is merit in developing solar and wind in a complementary manner. From grid security perspective, as compared to solar, wind is better in monsoon and at night. Also, such a system will require a lower investment.

f) The way India has developed its solar sector, it needs to think on those lines for the wind energy sector as well.

References

1. Daniel Yergin, Mystery of Wind, *The Quest*: Energy Security and The Making of the Modern World, p.596.
2. 'BP Statistical Review of World Energy 2020' (PDF), pp.55, 59.
3. 'Global Wind Report 2019', Global Wind Energy Council. 25 March, 2020.
4. Hurley, Brian. 'How Much Wind Energy is there?', Claverton Group, 8 April, 2012.
5. Ananthaswamy, Anil and Le Page, Michael, 30 January, 2012; 'Power paradox: Clean Might Not Be Green Forever'. New Scientist.
6. Ananthaswamy, Anil and Le Page, Michael, 30 January, 2012; 'Power paradox: Clean Might Not Be Green Forever'. New Scientist.
7. Jacobson, MZ; Archer, CL. 2012. 'Saturation wind power potential and its implications for wind energy'. Proceedings of the National Academy of Sciences. 109 (39): 15679–84.

Bibcode:2012PNAS.10915679J. doi:10.1073/pnas.1208993109. PMC 3465402. PMID 23019353.

8. Adams, AS; Keith, DW. 2013. 'Are Global Wind Power Resource Estimates Overstated?' (PDF). Environmental Research Letters. 8 (1): 015021. Bibcode:2013ERL.....8a5021A. doi:10.1088/1748-9326/8/1/015021.

9. Trueb, Lucien. 2015. Astonishing the Wild Pigs, Highlights of Technology, ATHENA-Verlag, p.119, ISBN 9783898967662.

10. Price, Trevor J. 2005. 'James Blyth – Britain's First Modern Wind Power Engineer'. Wind Engineering. 29 (3): 191–200, doi:10.1260/030952405774354921. S2CID 110409210.

11. Shackleton, Jonathan. 'World First for Scotland Gives Engineering Student a History Lesson'. The Robert Gordon University. Archived from the original on 17 December, 2008. Retrieved 20 November, 2008.

12. Price, Trevor J. 2005. 'James Blyth – Britain's First Modern Wind Power Engineer'. Wind Engineering. 29 (3): 191–200. doi:10.1260/030952405774354921. S2CID 110409210.

13. Price, Trevor J. 2005. 'James Blyth – Britain's First Modern Wind Power Engineer'. Wind Engineering. 29 (3): 191–200. doi:10.1260/030952405774354921. S2CID 110409210.

14. Anon. Mr. Brush's Windmill Dynamo, Scientific American, Vol. 63 No. 25, 20 December, 1890, p.54.

15. 'History of Wind Energy' in Cutler J. Cleveland (ed.) Encyclopaedia of Energy. Vol. 6, Elsevier, ISBN 978-1-60119-433-6, 2007, pp.421–22.

16. Global Wind Energy Set for Five Years of Record Growth-Research, GWEC forecast, *Reuters*, 5 November, 2020.

17. 'Europe's Onshore and Offshore Wind Energy Potential—EEA'. Eea.europa.eu. 8 June, 2009.

18. www.ewea.org/fileadmin/swf/factsheet/1_statisticsandtargets.pdf.

19. GWEC Report, 2022.

20. Wind Europe: Offshore Wind in Europe: Key Trends and Statistics, 2019.

21. NIWE.

22. 'Arichamunai to get India's First Offshore Wind Turbines', 20 March, 2018.

23. GWEC, Merc + India Wind Outlook Towards 2022: Looking Beyond Headwinds.

24. 'CEA Monthly Utility Electricity Generation' (PDF), 3 May, 2019.

25. GWEC and MEC.

26. Evwindes: 'Total Wind Energy in India are Expected to Reach between 48 GW to 54 GW by 2020', 31 March, 2020.

Chapter 7
HYDROPOWER

I. OVERVIEW

Hydropower supplies about 50% of electricity in 66 countries and 90% in 24 countries. In Norway, 99% of electricity comes from hydropower, while China is the largest producer of hydroelectricity. The Three Gorges Dam in China, which holds back the Yangtze River, is the largest hydroelectric dam in the world, in terms of electricity production. The dam is 2,335 m (7,660 ft) long and 185 m (607 ft) tall, and has a power generation capacity of 22,500 MW. Currently, it produces 80 to 100 TWh per year, enough to supply between 70 to 80 million households. Other top producers of hydropower around the world include the United States, Brazil, Canada, India and Russia.

Converting over 90% of available energy into electricity, hydropower is the most efficient source. By comparison, the best fossil fuel power plants operate at approximately 60% efficiency. Hydropower facilities have a very long service life, which can be extended indefinitely, and further improved. Hydropower produces no air pollutants and has ultra-low greenhouse gas emissions. It is cheaper as compared to electricity generated from coal and gas fired plants. It also reduces the financial losses due to frequency fluctuations and it is more reliable and inflation-free as it doesn't need fossil fuels to generate electricity. Hydropower uses and not consumes the water for generation of electricity, and the hydropower leaves this vital resource available for other uses.

Hydropower's contribution is 55% higher than nuclear energy and larger than that of all other renewables combined, including wind, solar PV, bioenergy and geothermal. In 2020, hydropower supplied 17% of global electricity generation, the third-largest source after coal and natural gas. Over the last 20 years, hydropower's total capacity rose 70% globally, but its share of total generation stayed stable due to the growth of wind, solar PV, coal and natural gas. In 2021, global hydropower generation amounted to 4,327 TWh, down 0.4% year-on-year. But the hydropower capacity is set to increase globally by 17% or 230 GW, between 2021 and 2030. The potential is particularly high in emerging and developing economies, reaching almost 60%. The 2022 Hydropower Status Report finds that global installed hydropower capacity rose by 26 GW to 1,360 GW in 2021.[1]

There are three types of hydropower plants— impoundment, diversion and pumped storage. The most common type of hydroelectric power plant is an impoundment facility, which is typically a large hydropower system, that uses a dam to store river water in a reservoir. Water released from the reservoir flows through a turbine, spinning it, which in turn activates a generator to produce electricity. The water may be released to meet changing electricity needs or other needs, such as flood control, recreation, fish passage and other environmental and water quality issues.

A diversion, sometimes called a 'run-of-river' facility, channels a portion of a river through a canal and/or a penstock to utilise the natural decline of the river bed elevation to produce energy. A penstock is a closed conduit that channels the flow of water to turbines with water flow regulated by gates, valves and turbines. A diversion may not require the use of a dam. Another type of hydropower, called pumped storage hydropower, or PSH, works like a giant battery. A PSH facility is able to store the electricity generated by other power sources, like solar, wind and nuclear, for later use. These facilities store energy by pumping water from a reservoir at a lower elevation to a reservoir at a higher elevation. When the demand for electricity is low, a PSH facility stores energy by pumping water from the lower reservoir to an upper reservoir. During periods of high electrical demand, the water is released back to the lower reservoir and turns a turbine, generating electricity.

II. HYDROPOWER IN INDIA

India has a history of about 120 years of hydropower generation, when the first small hydro project of 130 kW was commissioned in the hills of Darjeeling in 1897. The Sivasamudram project of 4,500 kW was the next to come up in Mysore district, Karnataka, in 1902, for supply of power to the Kolar gold mines. Following this, there were a number of small hydro projects set up in various hilly areas of the country. Till the Independence (1947), the country had an installed capacity of 1,362 MW, which included 508 MW hydropower projects, mainly small and medium. As per MNRE, the estimated potential of small hydropower plant is 20 GW across the country.

In 2019, India overtook Japan to become the fifth largest producer of hydroelectricity and installed power capacity exceeding 50 GW. As of 31 March, 2019, its installed utility-scale hydroelectric capacity was 50,071 MW or 12.75% of its total utility power generation capacity, including 4,786 MW of pumped storage capacity. The country generated 162 TWh of hydroelectricity (excluding small hydro).[2]

Going forward, India targets a hydropower capacity of 70 GW by 2030. More than 9,000 MW of large hydro projects are already under construction, in addition to 1,500 MW of pumped storage hydro projects which are also under construction. Apart from these, India is working on building 10 hydropower projects totalling 6.8 GW in Jammu and Kashmir and Himachal Pradesh to fully utilise its share of water under the 1960 Indus Waters Treaty with Pakistan. The projects being constructed by the state-run National Hydropower Corporation (NHPC) are the 1,000 MW Pakal Dul, 850 MW Ratle, 624 MW Kiru and 540 MW Kwar, all in Jammu and Kashmir.

India has adopted a similar approach on its eastern borders and plans to construct the country's second-largest dam at Yingkiong in Arunachal Pradesh to counter China's ambitious scheme to divert water from the river that feeds downstream into the Brahmaputra.

The IEA says that India is also tripling its pumped storage hydro fleet by 2030 to accommodate growing solar capacity. The government has recently awarded 1,200 MW of renewables and storage in a tender that included 900 MW of pumped storage, offering a weighted average price of Rs 4.04 per unit and a peak tariff of Rs 6.12 per unit, and 300 MW of battery storage at average Rs 4.3 per unit with peak tariff of Rs 6.85 per unit.

However, the share of hydropower in the overall energy matrix has fallen consistently since Independence. In 1947, hydropower capacity in India was about 37% of the total power generating capacity and over 53% of power generation. In the first two decades since Independence (1947–67), hydropower capacity addition grew by over 13% and power generation from hydro stations grew by 11.8%. In the following two decades (1967–1987), hydropower generation capacity grew by over 18% but hydropower generation grew only by 5.6%. The decline continued in the following decades (1987–2007) with both capacity addition and hydropower generation growth falling to just over 3%. In 2007–2019, hydropower capacity addition grew by just over 1% and power generation from hydro stations grew by under 1%.

Specific generation or power generated per unit of capacity (a measure of economic efficiency) declined from over 4.4 in the 1960s to less than 2.5 in the early 2000s. Specific generation has improved since then reaching 3.4 in 2019–20.[3]

The decline in hydropower's share in energy mix was not because of government's apathy toward this form of technology. Rather, it has in large part been due to the growing adoption of different alternative energy sources such as coal, oil and gas, and the rest to environmental litigations, local disturbances, financial stress and unwilling purchasers. Several hydroelectric projects (HEPs) in India have been languishing for years due to contractual conflicts and public agitations. Only about 10,000 MW of hydropower could be added over the last 10 years.

In 1998, the Government of India announced the 'Policy on Hydro Power Development' under which impetus is given to development of hydropower in the country. This was a welcome step towards effective utilisation of our water resources in the direction of hydropower development. In October 2001, Central Electricity Authority (CEA) came out with a study which prioritised and ranked the future executable projects. As per the study, 399 hydro schemes with an aggregate installed capacity of 1,06,910 MW were ranked in A, B and C categories depending upon their inter-se attractiveness. In May 2003, the Atal Bihari Vajpayee administration launched 50,000 MW hydro initiative in which preparation of pre-feasibility reports (PFR) of 162 projects was taken up by CEA through various agencies. The PFRs for all these projects were prepared and projects with low tariff (first year tariff less than Rs 2.50 per kWh) were identified for preparation of detailed project report (DPR). More than half the capacity identified was in Arunachal Pradesh and about a third was in the Himalayan and north-eastern states.

However, as of 2021, only one project of 100 MW capacity in Sikkim had been commissioned and about 4,345 MW capacity was under construction. Forty projects of 13,633 MW capacity have either been abandoned or delayed due to local opposition to the projects rooted in environmental concerns. In the last few years, many of India's newer hydropower projects on the Himalayan rivers (commissioned or under construction) have been damaged by floods and landslides. High precipitation in the Himalayas, coupled with the sudden fall in altitude in the mountains of that region results in large volume of water gushing down river channels.

Hydroelectricity Potential

As per the Central Electricity Authority's assessment, India's economically exploitable hydroelectric potential is 1,48,700 MW, located mainly in northern and north-eastern regions. Sikkim, Arunachal Pradesh, Assam, Meghalaya, Manipur, Mizoram, Nagaland and Tripura cumulatively account for nearly 40% of the total hydropower potential of the country.[4]

Brahmaputra basin has the highest potential—66,065 MW of installed capacity, followed by Indus basin (33,832 MW), Ganga basin (20,711 MW), eastern flowing rivers of southern India (14,511 MW), western flowing rivers of southern India (9,430 MW), and the central Indian river system (4,152 MW). In addition, 56 number of pumped storage projects have also been identified with probable installed capacity of 94,000 MW. In addition to this, hydro-potential from small, mini and micro schemes have been estimated at 6,782 MW from 1,512 sites. Thus, in totality India is endowed with hydro-potential of about 2,50,000 MW.

However, exploitation of hydro-potential has not been up to the desired level due to various constraints confronting the sector. According to the International Hydropower Association 540 GWh per year or about 82%, of the total hydropower potential of 6,60,000 GWh per year of India, is still undeveloped.[5]

Public sector companies produce around 92.5% of India's hydroelectric power through the National Hydroelectric Power Corporation (NHPC), Northeast Electric Power Company (NEEPCO), Satluj Jal Vidyut Nigam (SJVNL), Tehri Hydro Development Corporation (THDC) and NTPC-Hydro. Currently, the country has five major hydroelectric power plants operating from the states of Uttarakhand, Maharashtra, Andhra Pradesh, Himachal Pradesh and Gujarat. Topping the list is Tehri Dam in Uttarakhand, with an installed capacity of 2,400 MW, followed by Koyna Hydroelectric Project in Maharashtra (1,960 MW), Srisailam Dam in Andhra Pradesh (1,670 MW), Nathpa Jhakri Dam in Himachal Pradesh (1,530 MW) and Sardar Sarovar Dam in Gujarat (1,450 MW).

The private sector is not far behind in developing hydroelectric energy, as at present it accounts for only 3,200 MW of the total installed hydropower capacity. It is estimated that of the over 12,000 MW of hydropower under construction, nearly 4,200 MW is in the private sector.[6] In the private sector, nearly 2,700 MW are stranded projects. While geology, hydrology and topography issues are some of the leading reasons for slippage of hydro projects, delays in clearance, local issues and law and order problems have also resulted in significant delays in project commissioning in states like Himachal Pradesh, Uttarakhand, Jammu and Kashmir and north-eastern states.

There are a number of private firms actively involved in hydropower projects in the Himalayan ranges and in the northeast of India. Some of them have already constructed hydropower projects in Bhutan, Nepal, Afghanistan and other countries. Tata Power's hydro plants have an installed hydro capacity of 693 MW, of which 65% is generated for the domestic market. The company has entered into an exclusive partnership with Norway-based SN Power to develop hydropower projects in India and Nepal.

Tata Power also has a joint venture deal with the Royal Government of Bhutan under which it has commissioned a 126 MW Dagachhu Hydro Project with Druk Green Power Company in March 2015. The company has synchronised 186 MW Shuakhevi Hydro Project in Georgia, and has commissioned two units of 60 MW each of its 120 MW Itezhi Tezhi Hydro Power Project in Zambia, in which Tata Power has a 50% stake. Sajjan Jindal-led JSW Energy and Him Urja Pvt Ltd are other leading private company in the power sector operating hydropower projects in India.

Measures to Boost Hydropower

The Indian government has recently announced a series of measures to support hydropower development, including mandating regional Discoms to purchase a certain portion of their electricity from large hydropower projects (of more than 25 MW capacity). So far, only small hydro projects of less than 25 MW capacity were categorised as renewable energy and were eligible for benefits under a non-solar RPO directive. In March 2019, the Indian cabinet decided to create Hydropower Purchase Obligation (HPO) for large hydro projects, commissioned after notification of the new measure. The trajectory of annual HPO targets will be notified by the Ministry of Power (MoP) based on the projected capacity addition plans in hydropower sector. For 2021–22, the MoP has set the HPO at 0.18% and proposed an increase to 2.82% by 2029–30. This will increase the demand for hydropower (just as solar purchase obligations increased the offtake of solar power) though not all state distribution companies have notified the HPO target. It is estimated that incremental hydropower generation capacity would have to increase by 39% or 18 GW to meet HPO obligations by 2030.

Necessary amendments have been introduced in the Tariff Policy and Tariff Regulations to provide flexibility to developers to determine tariff by back loading of tariff after increasing project life to 40 years, increasing debt repayment period to 18 years and introducing escalating tariff of 2%. The government has also decided to provide budgetary support for funding flood moderation component of the hydropower projects on a case-to-case basis. The budgetary support envisages funding of enabling infrastructure such as roads and bridges as per actual cost, limited to Rs 1.5 crore per MW for up to 200 MW projects and Rs 1 crore per MW for above 200 MW projects.

The measures are expected to draw in private investors and reinvigorate the moribund hydropower sector. But it is early to assess their impact at this point of time, as two years 2020 and 2021, since the HPO and budgetary support incentives had been announced on 7 March, 2019, were lost due to the pandemic and none of the country's under-construction hydropower plants are close to completion.

Challenges to Hydropower Growth

There are two main issues hindering a speedy growth of hydropower.

Financial: According to a parliamentary standing committee report on hydropower presented to the Indian Parliament in 2019, an average cost for a greenfield hydropower project comes to around Rs 10 crore per MW compared to Rs 8 crore per MW for a coal-based power project, while a solar power project costs still cheaper, at Rs 6–6.5 crore per MW. Hydroelectric projects are costlier, because they are located in difficult and inaccessible sites, and require development of roads and bridges for project implementation. The government has addressed this issue by giving budgetary support.

But electricity produced by hydropower plants remains still costlier than that generated by coal and gas plants. This is because hydropower plants are typically financed by a debt-equity ratio of 70:30 and their tariff are designed to recover debt in the initial 12 years. This frontloading of tariff makes hydro energy expensive. The government has now extended debt repayment period to 18 years and project life to 40 years, and introduced an escalating tariff of 2% annually to reduce the initial tariff. These measures are expected to make the cost of power affordable.

Clearance: The second issue that hinders speedy implementation of hydroelectric projects arises from long delays in environmental clearance. Several HEPs were dropped or had their design and capacity modified due to environmental considerations. Thermal projects do not require techno-economic clearance (TEC) from the CEA, but for hydroelectric plants with a capital expenditure of above Rs 1,000 crore, the concurrence of the CEA is required. Parameters like e-flow, free flow stretch, eco-sensitive zone, impact on wild flora and fauna, and site-specific changes required during construction are closely examined. Clearance is given in consultation with the CWC, and takes an inordinately long time.[7]

Small Hydropower (SHP)

As large hydropower projects are often opposed by environmentalist and non-governmental organisations on the ground of flooding, desertification, relocation issues and various other reasons, small hydropower could be seen as a better solution for electricity generation on a small scale. SHP projects are usually clean, sustainable and environmentally friendly as most of these are canal based or run off river type which use running water to drive the turbines. The weir or barrage is small and no water is stowed; it is free from problems such as relocation of local inhabitants or deforestation which are usually associated with large hydropower.

Since SHPs are sustainable, they are exempt from forest and land clearance and are free from public sitting/plenary inquiry in India. They are economically feasible and the gestation period is rather low. SHPs are ideal for powering villages and far-flung or isolated areas. The accessibility of electricity in these areas can boost small-scale industries and thereby improve the socio-economic status of the people. The capacity of SHP is different in different countries; for instance, in China, capacity up to 50 MW is considered as SHP while in USA the capacity is up to 100 MW. In India it is 25 MW. The Indian government was promoting accelerated development of SHP and in the year 2019–20, 12 SHP projects were commissioned out of which 6 projects were in Himachal Pradesh with a generating capacity of 45.9 MW. The estimated potential is 21,133 MW from 7,133 sites.[8]

Pumped Storage Hydropower (PSH)

Pumped storage hydropower is a type of hydroelectric energy storage. It is a configuration of two water reservoirs at different elevations that can generate power as water moves down from one to the other (discharge), passing through a turbine. The system also requires power as it pumps water back into the upper reservoir (recharge). PSH acts similarly to a giant battery, because it can store power and then release it when needed. It is the most competitive and reliable way of storing electricity, enabling both the efficient use of surplus energy and the returning of a significant amount of energy back on the grid. It allows energy from intermittent sources (such as solar, wind) and other renewables, or excess electricity from continuous base-load sources (such as coal or nuclear) to be saved for periods of higher demand.

The pumped storage schemes also contribute to secondary, seasonal power supply at no additional cost when rivers are flooded with excess water. Pumped storage units can be used as pumping stations to supply river water for upland irrigation, industrial needs and drinking water. In a tropical country like India, abundant water for agriculture is needed due to a very high annual evaporation rate. The amount of water necessary to meet this demand can be harnessed from India's rivers via pumped storage units. Food security in India is improved with water security which in turn is possible from the energy security to supply the power needed for the pumped storage schemes. India plans to add 79 hydropower projects with a total capacity of 30 GW, including 11 pumped-storage projects totalling 8.7 GW up to 2030. Till the end of 2021, the country had an installed pumped storage capacity of 4.9 GW.

References

1. IEA Analysis 2022; www.iea.org/reports/hydropower-special-market-report/executive-summary.
2. 2022 Hydropower Status Report; https://www.hydropower.org/publications/2022-hydropower-status-report.
3. India, International Hydropower Association; www.hydropower.org/country-profiles/india.
4. Observer Research Foundation, https://www.orfonline.org/expert-speak/hydropower-in-india.

5. Power Potential of North East by North Eastern Electric Power Corporation, a Unit of NTPC.

6. 'World Energy Resources; Hydropower 2016' (PDF). World Energy Council.

7. Business Today Newspaper, PB Jayakumar, 12 October, 2018.

8. Verma, AK, Former Joint Secretary in the Ministry of Power, 'India's True Hydropower Potential Remains Untapped', 14 May, 2020.

Chapter 8
HYDROGEN

*"I believe that water will one day be employed as fuel,
that hydrogen and oxygen which constitute it, used singly
or together will furnish an inexhaustible source of heat
and light of an intensity of which coal is not capable...
water will be coal of the future."*—Jules Verne,
Mysterious Island (1876)

Hydrogen is the most abundant element in the universe (three times as abundant as helium, the next most widely occurring element), but it makes up only about 0.14% of the Earth's crust by weight. Its low density allows it to just float off the Earth's gravity into space more easily than denser gases like oxygen. It occurs, however, in vast quantities as part of the water in oceans, ice packs, rivers, lakes and the atmosphere. It is essential to our life—it fuels the Sun, which converts hundreds of million tonnes of hydrogen into helium every second.

However, hydrogen does not exist independently, it is always bonded chemically with another element in naturally occurring compound like water, which is a combination of two atoms of hydrogen and one atom of oxygen (H_2O), or biowaste, or wood, or fossil fuels like coal, natural gas and oil. Hydrogen is not a source of energy, but an efficient energy carrier.

There are four main sources for the commercial production of hydrogen—natural gas, oil, coal and electrolysis—which account for 48%, 30%, 18% and 4% of the world's hydrogen production respectively.[1] Fossil fuels are the dominant source of industrial hydrogen. Bulk hydrogen is mostly produced around the world today by the steam reforming of methane or natural gas and coal, which, according to the IEA, is responsible for 830 mt of annual CO_2 emissions, equivalent to the CO_2 emissions of Indonesia and the United Kingdom combined. In India, around 2.79 mt a year of hydrogen is produced by fertiliser industry and petroleum refineries for captive consumption. Also, about 0.36 mt of hydrogen is available from chloro-alkali industries.

Hydrogen fuel is categorised into three types based on the source from which it is derived. The one derived from fossil fuels is 'grey hydrogen'; almost 95% of the hydrogen fuel produced in the world today is grey hydrogen. Another type is 'blue hydrogen', as it is generated from fossil fuels with carbon capture and storage options (CCS). The third type, derived entirely from renewable power sources like the Sun or wind, is 'green hydrogen'. In this, electricity generated from renewable energy is used to split water into hydrogen and oxygen.

The green hydrogen has multiple advantages: one, it is a clean-burning molecule, which can decarbonise a range of sectors including iron and steel, chemicals and transportation; two, renewable energy that cannot be stored or used by the grid can be channelled to produce hydrogen. This is what the Indian government's Hydrogen Energy Mission, launched in 2021–22, aims at.

Applications of Hydrogen

Hydrogen's principal application is in the production of ammonia, which is a compound of hydrogen and nitrogen (NH_3), and hydrogenation of carbon monoxide and organic compounds. Hydrogen is also added to fats and oils, and, when combined with liquid oxygen it can make a rocket fuel, an example of such an application is NASA's 1969 flight to the Moon that used Hydrogen as rocket fuel. Today NASA uses it regularly for its space flights and exploration. Hydrogen is also required in oil and gas, petrochemical, electric vehicles and power generation because of its improved functionalities and distinct properties. Green hydrogen is one of the gases with an increase in demand from the petroleum refining industry due to its function in different refining processes. One of the most promising areas for green hydrogen is the electric vehicle market. A hydrogen vehicle is an alternative fuel vehicle that uses hydrogen as its primary fuel, which include space rockets, automobiles and other means of transportation.

The electric vehicles industry is another emerging application area for green hydrogen, which is widely seen as the fuel of the future mobility—land, air, sea, where ever, its potential is huge. This technology addresses most of the shortcomings of the existing battery chemistries and could play a key role in India's electrification journey. It takes just a couple of minutes for a hydrogen vehicle to be refuelled irrespective of size, compared to hours in the case of electric vehicles. For instance, Japanese auto major Toyota Motor Corporation which recently launched the Toyota Mirai in India can travel up to 650 km on a full tank of hydrogen and then be refilled in 2–3 minutes, while Tesla, which promises the fastest charging for its vehicles using the Tesla Supercharger, takes 15 minutes to charge a car up to 327 km. However, the cost of refuelling a hydrogen car does not come cheap as this technology and infrastructure are still being developed. As per estimates, refuelling a Toyota Mirai costs around Rs 2,500 and the cost of green hydrogen ranges from around Rs 400–500 per kg. Then there is the challenge of hydrogen storage, as it leaks easily and is highly flammable.

Hydrogen fuel cell cars have a near-zero carbon footprint, and are two to three times more efficient than petrol car, because electric chemical reaction is more efficient than combustion. The cost of automotive fuel cells has fallen by 70% since 2008, thanks to technological progress and growing sales of fuel cell electric vehicles (FCEVs). Thanks to the efforts by Korea, US, China and Japan, the number of FCEVs on the road grew more than sixfold from 7,000 in 2017 to over 43,000 by mid-2021. In 2017, practically all FCEVs were passenger cars. Today, one-fifth are buses and trucks, indicating a shift to the long-distance segment where hydrogen can better compete with electric vehicles. However, the total number of FCEVs is still well below the estimated 11 million electric vehicles on the road today. Several demonstration projects for the use of hydrogen-based fuels in rail, shipping and aviation are already under development and are expected to open new opportunities for creating hydrogen demand.

Hydrogen as Pillar of Decarbonisation

In the run-up to the 26th Conference of the Parties to the UN Framework Convention on Climate Change (COP 26), a growing number of countries announced targets to achieve net zero GHG emissions over the next decades. In turn, more than 100 companies that consume large volumes of energy or produce energy-consuming goods have followed suit. As pressed time and time again by the IEA, achieving net zero by 2050 requires immediate action to turn the 2020s into a decade of massive clean energy expansion. Hydrogen will need to play an important role in the transition to net zero emissions. Since the first Hydrogen Energy Ministerial (HEM) meeting in Japan in 2018, momentum has grown and an increasing number of governments and companies are establishing visions and plans for hydrogen. In 2020, hydrogen and hydrogen-based fuels accounted for less than 0.1%, but by 2030 they must meet 2% of the total fuel consumption and in 2050, 10%.

Nevertheless, this demand increase alone is not enough to make hydrogen a key pillar of decarbonisation. Hydrogen production must also become much cleaner than it is today. For instance, of the 90 mt of H_2 used in 2020, around 80% was produced from fossil fuels, mostly unabated. Practically all the remainder came from residual gases produced in refineries and the petrochemical industry. This resulted in almost 900 mt of CO_2 emitted in the production of hydrogen, equivalent to the CO_2 emissions of Indonesia and the United Kingdom combined.[2]

The development of green hydrogen, made from water and using renewable electricity, hence, has become a policy priority for many countries as they prepare to cut emissions to 'net zero' by 2050, 2060 or 2070. Big energy consumers, including the US, China, EU, Japan, India and South Korea, have already made hydrogen a major component of their energy plans. The focus of most government policies is on producing low-carbon hydrogen. Measures to increase demand are receiving less attention. Japan, Korea, France and the Netherlands have adopted targets for FCEV deployment. But boosting the role of low-carbon hydrogen in clean energy transitions requires a step change in demand creation. Governments are starting to announce a wide variety of policy instruments, including carbon prices, auctions, quotas, mandates and requirements in public procurement. Most of these measures have not yet entered into force. Their quick and widespread enactment could unlock more projects to scale up hydrogen demand.

Countries that have adopted hydrogen strategies have committed at least US$ 37 billion, and the private sector has announced an additional investment of US$ 300 billion. But putting the hydrogen sector on track for net zero emissions by 2050 requires US$ 1,200 billion of investment in low-carbon hydrogen supply and use through to 2030.

Hydrogen demand stood at 90 mt in 2020, practically all for refining and industrial applications and produced almost exclusively from fossil fuels, resulting in close to 900 mt of CO_2 emissions, according to the IEA Global Hydrocarbon Review 2021. But there are encouraging signs of progress. Global capacity of electrolysers, which are needed to produce hydrogen from electricity, doubled over the last five years to reach just over 300 MW by mid-2021. Around 350 projects currently under development could bring global capacity up to 54 GW by 2030. Another 40 projects accounting for more than 35 GW of capacity are in early stages of development. If all those projects are realised, global hydrogen supply from electrolysers could reach more than 8 mt by 2030. While significant, this is still well below the 80 mt required by that year in the pathway to net zero CO_2 emissions by 2050 set out in the IEA Roadmap for the Global Energy Sector.

Hydrogen is versatile. Technologies already available today enable hydrogen to produce, store, move and use energy in different ways. A wide variety of fuels are able to produce hydrogen, including renewables, nuclear, natural gas, coal and oil. It can be transported as a gas by pipelines or in liquid form by ships, much like liquefied natural gas (LNG). It can be transformed into electricity and methane to power homes and feed industry, and into fuels for cars, trucks, ships and planes.

Hydrogen has the potential to help with variable output from renewables, like solar PV and wind, whose availability is not always well matched with demand. Hydrogen is one of the leading options for storing energy from renewables and looks promising to be a lowest-cost option for storing electricity over days, weeks or even months. Hydrogen and hydrogen-based fuels can transport energy from renewables over long distances, from regions with abundant solar and wind resources, such as Australia or Latin America, to energy-hungry cities thousands of kilometres away.

Cost Considerations

However, a key barrier for low-carbon hydrogen is the cost gap between it and the hydrogen produced from unabated fossil fuels. At present, producing hydrogen from fossil fuels is the cheapest option in most parts of the world. Depending on regional gas prices, the levelised cost of hydrogen production from natural gas ranges from US\$ 0.5 to 1.7 per kg. Using CCUS technologies to reduce the CO_2 emissions from hydrogen production increases the levelised cost of production to around US\$ 1 to 2 per kg. Using renewable electricity to produce hydrogen costs US\$ 3 to 8 per kg.

There is significant scope for cutting production costs through technology innovation and increased deployment. The potential is reflected in the IEA's Net Zero Emissions Scenario (NZE Scenario) by 2050, in which hydrogen from renewables falls to as low as US\$ 1.3 per kg by 2030 in regions with excellent renewable resources (range US\$ 1.3–3.5 per kg), comparable with the cost of hydrogen from natural gas with CCUS. In the long term, hydrogen costs from renewable electricity fall as low as US$ 1 per kg (range US$ 1.0–3.0 per kg) in the NZE Scenario, making hydrogen from solar PV cost-competitive with hydrogen from natural gas even without CCUS in several regions.

I. HISTORY OF HYDROGEN

Hydrogen was first identified in 1776 as a distinct element by British scientist Henry Cavendish while evolving hydrogen gas by reacting zinc metal with hydrochloric acid. In a demonstration to the Royal Society of London, Cavendish applied a spark to hydrogen gas yielding water. This discovery led to his later finding that water (H_2O) is made of hydrogen and oxygen. In 1788, building on the discoveries of Cavendish, French chemist Antoine Lavoisier gave hydrogen its name, which was derived from the Greek words, 'hydro', meaning water, and 'genes', meaning 'born of'.

In 1800 English scientists William Nicholson and Sir Anthony Carlisle discovered that applying electric current to water produced hydrogen and oxygen gases. This process was later termed 'electrolysis'. In 1838 Swiss chemist Christian Friedrich Schoenbein discovered fuel cell effect by combining hydrogen and oxygen gases to produce water and an electric current, while in 1845 Sir William Grove, an English scientist and judge, demonstrated Schoenbein's discovery on a practical scale by creating a 'gas battery', and earned the title 'Father of the Fuel Cell' for his achievement. In 1889 Ludwig Mond and Charles Langer built the first fuel cell device using air and industrial coal gas.

In the 1920s, German engineer Rudolf Erren converted the internal combustion engines of trucks, buses and submarines to use hydrogen or hydrogen mixtures. In 1937 a dirigible inflated with hydrogen gas, Hindenburg, made 10 successful trans-Atlantic flights from Germany to the United States, but one of them crashed upon landing in Lakewood, New Jersey. A study concluded in 1997 that the explosion was not due to the hydrogen gas, but rather to a weather-related static electric discharge which ignited the airship's silver-coloured, canvas exterior covering which had been treated with the key ingredients of solid rocket fuel. Currently, NASA's space programme uses the most liquid hydrogen worldwide, primarily for rocket propulsion and as a fuel for fuel cells.

Francis T Bacon of Cambridge University in England built the first practical hydrogen air fuel cell, named 'Bacon Cell' in 1959. The 5 kW system powered a welding machine. Later that year, Harry Karl Ihrig, an engineer, demonstrated the first fuel cell vehicle—a 20-horsepower tractor. Hydrogen fuel cells, based upon Bacon's design, have been used to generate on-board electricity, heat and water for astronauts aboard the famous Apollo spacecraft and all subsequent space shuttle missions.

The development of hydrogen fuel cells for conventional commercial applications began in the 1970s in the wake of the OPEC oil embargo on the western countries. In 1974 two international organisations—the International Association for Hydrogen Energy (IAHE) and International Energy Agency (IEA)—were formed to promote the research and development of hydrogen energy technologies. In the erstwhile Soviet Union, the Tupolev Design Bureau converted a 164-passenger TU-154 commercial jet to operate one of the jet's three engines on liquid hydrogen. The maiden flight lasted 21 minutes.

In 1990, the world's first solar-powered hydrogen production plant at Solar-Wasserstoff-Bayern, a research and testing facility in southern Germany, became operational. Around the same time in the US, work on a methanol-fuelled 10 kW Proton Exchange Membrane (PEM) fuel cell began through a partnership including GM, Los Alamos National Laboratory, the Dow Chemical Company and Canadian fuel cell developer, Ballard Power Systems.

However, Europe moved faster than the US in developing the hydrogen technology. In 1994 German car manufacturer Daimler-Benz demonstrated its first NECAR I (New Electric CAR) fuel cell vehicle at a press conference in Ulm, and in 1999 Europe's first hydrogen fuelling stations were opened in the German cities of Hamburg and Munich. In 2004, the German Navy demonstrated the world's first fuel cell-powered submarine in deep waters. In 1998, Iceland unveiled a plan to create the first hydrogen economy by 2030 with Daimler-Benz and Ballard Power Systems. A consortium of Icelandic institutions, headed by the financial group New Business Venture Fund, partnered with Royal Dutch-Shell Group, DaimlerChrysler (a merger of Daimer Benz and Chrysler), and Norsk Hydro to form the Icelandic Hydrogen and Fuel Cell Company Ltd to further the hydrogen economy in Iceland. In 2000, Ballard Power Systems presented the world's first production-ready PEM fuel cell for automotive applications at the Detroit Auto Show.

The discovery of cheap oil pushed R&D in hydrogen to fringe. But mounting concerns about climate change and rising global warming currently has brought the focus back on hydrogen, which has the potential to help tackle various critical energy challenges. As an energy carrier, hydrogen is favoured for its efficiency and environmental compatibility. It offers ways of decarbonising wide range of sectors, including long-haul transport, chemicals and iron and steel, where it is difficult to significantly reduce emissions. Hydrogen can also help improve air quality and strengthen energy security. Despite ambitious international climate goals, global energy-related CO_2 emissions rose by 6% in 2021 to 36.3 bt, their highest ever level, as the world economy rebounded strongly from the Covid-19 crisis and relied heavily on coal to power that growth, according to new IEA analysis.[3] Outdoor air pollution also remains a pressing problem, with around three million people dying prematurely each year globally.

Hydrogen Energy in India

Hydrogen is at an early stage of entering the energy sector in India. Government as well as non-government funding agencies are engaged in R&D projects pertaining to hydrogen production, storage, utilisation, power generation and for transport applications. As early as in 2003, National Hydrogen Energy Board was formed and in 2006 the Ministry of New and Renewable Energy laid out the National Hydrogen Energy Road Map identifying transport and power generation as two major green energy initiatives. India is participating in Mission Innovation Challenge for clean hydrogen and shares the objective to accelerate the development of a global hydrogen market by identifying and overcoming key technology barriers to the production, distribution, storage and use of hydrogen at gigawatt scale. By 2050, India intends to produce three-fourths of its hydrogen from renewable resources.

The R&D projects in India focus on improving the efficiency of water-splitting reaction, and finding newer materials, catalysts and electrodes to accelerate the reaction. Presently, more than 100 research groups are focusing on fuel cell technology. There are a number of foreign and Indian companies that are involved in hydrogen production, storage or delivery in India, including Praxair (USA), Linde (global-member of hydrogen council), Inox (Indo-US JV), Air Liquide (France), SAGIM (France), Air Products (USA), Fuel Cell Energy (USA), H2Scan (USA), ITM Power (UK), Heliocentris

(Germany), Aditya Birla, Bhoruka Gases Ltd, Gujarat Alkalies and Chemicals Limited, Gujarat Heavy Chemicals Ltd, Air Science Technologies and Sukan Engineering Private Limited.

More than 7 mt of hydrogen (H_2) was used in India in 2020, with 45% used for refining, 35% for chemicals and almost 20% for iron and steel. India is the world's largest producer of steel using the DRI route, consuming one-quarter of global hydrogen demand for steel making through this process. Practically all hydrogen demand was met through domestic production based on fossil fuels, with natural gas accounting for three-quarters, coal for about 15% and by-product from refineries making up the rest. In the decade ahead, hydrogen use in the country is expected to rise substantially as population growth and greater prosperity necessitate increased food production (requiring ammonia) and new infrastructure (requiring steel). The country's Nationally Determined Contribution (NDC), presented at the COP 26 in October 2021 in Glasgow, forecasts hydrogen demand to grow close to 11 mt by 2030, with DRI-based steel making accounting for around 30% of this increase.

If electrolysis were deployed at scale and the potential for cost reductions materialises, India can produce green hydrogen at one of the lowest costs in Asia-Pacific. As early as 2030, hydrogen production from renewables could cost just US$ 1.4–3.7 per kg, competitive with production through unabated fossil fuel methods. Low production costs for renewable hydrogen could enable the export of low-carbon hydrogen and hydrogen-based fuels, particularly to other Asia-Pacific economies that are likely to require imports to meet national hydrogen demand (for example, Japan and Korea).

National Green Hydrogen Mission

Delivering his Independence Day address from the ramparts of the Red Fort on 15 August, 2021, Prime Minister Narendra Modi, announced the launch of the National Hydrogen Mission aimed at fast-tracking the production and adoption of carbon-free fuels from renewables, and achieve self-reliance in energy by 2047.

Hydrogen is the simplest and smallest element in the periodic table. The pathways to produce it are very diverse, and so are the emissions of greenhouse gases like carbon dioxide (CO_2) and methane (CH_4). However, no matter how it is produced, it ends up with the same carbon-free molecule. Currently, it is produced predominantly through Steam Methane Reforming (SMR), which utilises fossil fuels, such as natural gas or coal, and through Proton Exchange Membrane Electrolysis, which splits water into hydrogen and oxygen using a current of electricity. At present, all hydrogen consumed in India comes from fossil fuels. By its colour in the 'hydrogen taxonomy rainbow', it can be called as 'grey' hydrogen. This has increasingly been produced also from coal, with significantly higher CO_2 emissions, the main culprit for climate change, and H_2 per unit of hydrogen produced, so much that is often called brown or black hydrogen instead of grey. It is produced at industrial scale globally today, with associated emissions comparable to the combined emissions of UK and Indonesia. It has no energy transition value, quite the opposite.

Blue hydrogen follows the same process as grey, with the additional technologies necessary to capture the CO_2 produced when hydrogen is split from methane (or from coal) and can be stored for long term. It is not one colour but rather a very broad gradation, as not 100% of the CO_2 produced can be captured, and not all means of storing it are equally effective in the long term. The main point is that capturing large part of the CO_2.

It is none of this India wants. India's National Hydrogen Mission (NHM) is focused on green hydrogen, which is totally carbon-free. Hydrogen is Green when it is produced by splitting water into hydrogen and oxygen using renewable electricity. This is a very different pathway from grey and blue hydrogen. But at present, there is only one green hydrogen project with a production capacity of 1 tonne per day in Bikaner (Rajasthan) in the private sector. The government had so far kept away, but is supporting an R&D project, a 5 Nm3/h (normal cubic meter per hour) green hydrogen production plant based on solar energy-powered electrolysis at the National Institute of Solar Energy, Gurugram (Haryana). Now, following its commitment made at the COP 26, the nation is planning to produce three-fourths of green hydrogen by electrolysis by 2030. The National Green Hydrogen Mission envisages to start commercial production of green hydrogen from FY 2025–26 onwards. The draft proposes to undertake hydrogen production projects through a competitive bidding mode which would be open to participation from both private and public entities.

Hydrogen produced from renewable energy (green hydrogen) can go a long way in enhancing India's decarbonisation efforts and energy security. India has committed to reduce carbon emissions as a signatory to the Paris Agreement on Climate Change. Hydrogen has the potential to reduce and replace the demand for fossil fuels in industries such as steel, refineries and fertilisers and in the transport and power sectors, thus enhancing the country's energy security. The demand for hydrogen is expected to increase five-fold by 2050.

Green hydrogen produced via the electrolysis of water is a zero-carbon energy-vector and chemical feedstock and can deepen renewable energy markets across industries, sectors and geographies and can be used for both grid-scale supply and off-grid storage. Globally, green hydrogen production is at a nascent stage and accounts for only 1% of the global demand for hydrogen. It is also the most expensive hydrogen production process and is at least two times more expensive than grey hydrogen—largely because of high cost of electrolyser, the main catalyst of hydrogenising process. But the paramount importance of hydrogen in achieving zero carbon emissions is a matter of vital necessity.

India plans to manufacture 5 mt of green hydrogen to meet its climate targets and become a production and export hub for the fuel by 2030, according to the power ministry. The nation is setting up separate manufacturing zones, waiving inter-state power transmission charges for 25 years and providing priority connectivity to electric grids to green hydrogen and ammonia producers to incentivise production. The 5 mt of India's production target is equal to half of the European Union's 10 mt of planned production of hydrogen from renewable energy by 2030. India, with a population more than three time the EU's, has a much lower per capita energy consumption, but is one with the fastest growth rate of energy demand in the world.

The National Green Hydrogen Mission has an outlay of nearly Rs 20,000 crore for a start, aimed at building domestic capabilities in developing technologies to produce hydrogen. A bulk of this is geared towards developing domestic manufacturing of electrolysers and R&D activities with the aim of developing globally competitive technologies.

As elsewhere in the world, India faces the challenge of producing green hydrogen at an affordable cost. Green hydrogen produced by renewables is far from competitive compared to other fuels, costing nearly double the price of hydrogen produced from coal, India's main source of electricity generation. The good news is that the private sector has taken on the challenge. Indian companies have declared ambitious intentions to adopt hydrogen as a fuel as the country converts to carbon-free fuel, ranging from Mukesh Ambani's and Gautam Adani's businesses to state-owned oil refiner Indian Oil and power generator NTPC. These are some of the top companies that are going to invest in renewable energy and green hydrogen in 2022 or the near future.

Reliance Industries' energy business is about to undergo a change that will make it a carbon-free conglomerate by 2035. It plans to replace sales of road fuels like diesel and gasoline with cleaner alternatives as it seeks to hit a net zero target. According to a presentation made at a seminar, the firm revealed its plan for achieving a US$ 1 per kg green hydrogen production. The conglomerate will repurpose a US$ 4 billion plant that currently converts petroleum coke into synthesis gas to produce blue hydrogen for US$ 1.2–1.5 per kg. Blue hydrogen is made by using fossil fuels but captures the carbon dioxide formed during its production, and Reliance sees the conversion as a temporary measure until the cost of green hydrogen, produced from the electrolysis of water using renewable energy, becomes competitive. Green hydrogen produced with renewable resources costs between US$ 3–6.55 per kg, according to the European Commission's July 2020 hydrogen strategy report. Fossil-based hydrogen costs about US$ 1.80, and the commission estimated the cost of blue hydrogen at about US$ 2.40–3 per kg. In comparison, RIL thinks syngas has potential to produce hydrogen at a competitive cost of US$ 1.2–1.5 per kg.

"In the interim, till the cost of green hydrogen comes down, RIL can be the first mover to establish a hydrogen ecosystem, with minimal incremental investment, in India," says the company. Subsequently, as hydrogen from syngas is replaced by green hydrogen, the entire syngas will be converted to chemicals. Hydrogen production from gasification provides highly concentrated carbon dioxide (CO_2) stream which provides unique opportunity to capture 15 mt per annum of CO_2 at 30% of typical cost of carbon capture. This CO_2 can be monetised by sale to urea producers and other users. The gasification unit is proposed to be transferred, as a going concern on slump sale basis, by way of the proposed scheme, it said adding the scheme of arrangement has been presented to National Company Law Tribunal for approval.

RIL has also announced plans to invest US$ 75 billion over the next three to five years for transition from being the operator of the world's largest oil refining complex to a leading producer of clean energy (with 100 GW by 2030). It entails three parts—a Rs 60,000 crore investment in four giga-factory that will manufacture and integrate all critical components for the business; a Rs 15,000 crore infusion in building the value-chain, partnership and future technologies, including upstream and downstream industries and management repurposing the company's engineering, project management and construction capabilities toward clean energy. RIL has already started work to build four giga-factories, an integrated solar photovoltaic module factory; an advanced energy storage, a battery storage, an electrolyser factory for green hydrogen and a fuel cell factory for converting hydrogen into power.

Adani Group has followed RIL. The logistics-to-energy conglomerate has said that it will invest US$ 70 billion over the next 10 years to produce green hydrogen at one of the lowest rates in the world. The company is already largest solar power developer. Now, the Adani Green Energy Ltd (AGEL), a group subsidiary, is targeting 45 GW of renewable energy capacity by 2030 and will invest US$ 20 billion to develop a 2 GW per year solar manufacturing capacity by 2022–23. The group's another energy arm, Adani Transmission Ltd (ATL), India's largest private sector power transmission and retail distribution company, is looking to increase the share of renewable power procurement from the current 3 to 30% by FY 2023 and to 70% by FY 2030.

State-owned GAIL (India) also has ambitious plans concerning green hydrogen. The PSU plans to build India's largest green hydrogen plant. The company is testing the mix percentage before it scales it up. The hydrogen that GAIL plans to produce can be sold to fertiliser units. NTPC is diversifying its portfolio to include renewable energy, storage, distribution and electric car charging. In addition, NTPC is trying to promote the use of green hydrogen-based solutions in industries such as transportation, energy, chemical, fertiliser, steel and others.

Indian Oil Corporation, one of India's biggest oil and gas provider with a strong hold on the domestic market, plans to tap into the green hydrogen opportunity, starting with a standalone green hydrogen manufacturing unit in Kochi. Indian Oil has set a target of converting at least 10% of its hydrogen consumption at refineries to green hydrogen soon.

Private engineering major, Larsen & Toubro (L&T), has announced plans to set up a green hydrogen plant at its Hazira Complex. The company plans to spend between Rs 10–50 billion on its green initiatives, spread over several years.

Green Hydrogen Policy

On 17 February, 2022, the government announced a comprehensive Green Hydrogen and Green Ammonia Policy aimed at boosting the domestic production of green hydrogen to 5 mt through electrolysis of water by 2030. Under it, manufacturers may purchase renewable power from the power exchange or set up renewable energy capacity themselves or through any other developer anywhere in the country. Distribution licensees can also procure and supply renewable energy to the manufacturers of green hydrogen/green ammonia in their states at concessional prices which will only include the cost of procurement, wheeling charges and a small margin as determined by the state commission. This means that a green hydrogen producer will be able to set up a solar power plant in Rajasthan to supply renewable energy to a green hydrogen plant in Assam and would not be required to pay any inter-state transmission charges. The move is going to make it more economical for key users of hydrogen and ammonia such as the oil refining, fertiliser and steel sectors to produce green hydrogen for their own use. These sectors currently use grey hydrogen or grey ammonia produced using natural gas or naphtha.

At present, the headline cost of Rs 2 per kWh (unit) of solar power is actually the price of generating it at the main site. When it reaches the end user, it becomes Rs 4 to 7 per unit after adding different levies during its transit through transmission lines in different states. Following the 'open access' as a result of waiver of central surcharge and inter-state transmission charges the cost of green hydrogen will come down significantly by 40–50%. It would go down further if the electrolyser used to split water into hydrogen and oxygen atoms is indigenously manufactured rather than imported.

The green hydrogen/ammonia manufacturer can bank his unconsumed renewable power, up to 30 days, with distribution company and take it back when required. Manufacturers of green hydrogen/ammonia shall be allowed to set up bunkers near ports for storage of green ammonia for export/use by shipping. The land for the storage for this purpose shall be provided by the respective port authorities at applicable charges. The implementation of this policy will provide clean fuel to the common people of the country. This will reduce dependence on fossil fuel and also reduce crude oil imports. The objective also is for our country to emerge as an export hub for green hydrogen/ammonia.

The manufacturers of green hydrogen/ammonia and the renewable energy plant shall be given connectivity to the grid on priority basis to avoid any procedural delays. The benefit of RPO will be an incentive to the hydrogen/ammonia manufacturer and the distribution licensee for consumption of renewable power. To ensure ease of doing business, a single portal for carrying out all the activities including statutory clearances in a time bound manner will be set up by the Ministry of New and Renewable Energy.

For green hydrogen, however, we might witness a similar story to that of solar PV. It is capital intensive, therefore we need to reduce investment cost through scaling up manufacturing of renewable technologies and electrolysers, while creating a low-risk offtake to reduce the cost of capital. This will lead to a stable, decreasing cost of green hydrogen, as opposed to a volatile and potentially increasing cost of blue hydrogen.

Hydrogen and Fuel Cell Roadmap

India made an early start by unveiling its first Hydrogen and Fuel Cell Roadmap and R&D programme as early as 2006, but has lagged behind other countries, that had started hydrogen development around the same time or later, in setting up large-scale demonstration hydrogen projects. Europe and the US lead in electrolyser and fuel cell electric vehicle (FCEV) technologies; Japan and Korea are investing heavily to become global hydrogen-use champions; and Australia and Chile are building global green hydrogen production hubs to export liquified or pressurised hydrogen. Each of them is building green hydrogen ecosystems for hydrogen's potential as a fossil fuel replacement and its storage potential, marrying it with renewable energy and battery technologies.[4]

This is not to say that India has made no headway, at all, in the application of and research into hydrogen technology. Hydrogen is being extensively used in India as an industrial feedstock in ammonia manufacturing, but most hydrogen produced in India is through reforming methane (CH_4), resulting in large-scale carbon dioxide emissions. India has been using the world's first large-scale alkaline electrolyser facility to produce hydrogen from electricity at the Bhakra Nangal Dam (Punjab) since 1962. Of late, Indian universities and research institutions have been conducting research around electrolysis, photolysis and biogenic methods of producing hydrogen, but these low carbon technologies are yet to be deployed at scale. Green hydrogen is produced from water by renewables-powered electrolysis. Its green credentials will make it critical for difficult-to-decarbonise industries like steel, but in 2020 it only constituted 0.1% of global hydrogen production. The economics are a challenge.

Electrolysers

On the face of it, electrolysis may look like a school laboratory experiment with a few beakers, a few wires and a couple of batteries. But the impact of this process, which allows molecules to be broken down using electricity, in this case the water molecules into their constituent oxygen and hydrogen atoms, is the key to obtaining green hydrogen. Ironically, one of the world's largest electrolysers is located in Fukushima, Japan, the site of the well-known 2010 nuclear disaster, a tell-tell story of a paradigm shift in energy production as it is powered by solar panels. Most recently, in January 2021, Canada commissioned a far greater electrolyser than the Japanese one in Bécancour, which consists of a polymer membrane device with an output of 8.2 tonnes per day.

Global electrolyser capacity in 2020 was just 0.3 GW, which is expected to reach nearly 17 GW by 2026, according to IEA's Global Hydrogen Review published in December 2021. Around 350 projects currently under development could bring global capacity up to 54 GW by 2030. Another 40 projects accounting for more than 35 GW of capacity are in early stages of development. If all those projects are realised, global hydrogen supply from electrolysers could reach more than 8 mt by 2030. While significant, this is still well below the 80 mt required by that year in the pathway to net zero CO_2 emissions by 2050 as set out in the IEA Roadmap for the Global Energy Sector.

Electrolysis was first discovered in 1800. After the invention of the electric battery by Alessandro Volta in the same year, other chemists tried connecting their poles in a container of water. They discovered that the current flowed through the water and that hydrogen and oxygen were separated at the electrodes.

An electrolyser consists of a conductive electrode stack separated by a membrane to which high voltage and current is applied, which causes it to break down into its components: hydrogen and oxygen. The complete system also includes pumps, power electronics, gas separator and other auxiliary components such as storage tanks. The oxygen generated in parallel is released into the atmosphere or can be stored for later use as a medical or industrial gas in some cases. The hydrogen is stored as a compressed gas or liquefied for use in industry or in hydrogen fuel cells, which can power transport vehicles such as trains, ships and even aircraft.

Hydrogen can be produced from both fossil and non-fossil fuels (such as grey hydrogen, blue hydrogen, tortoise hydrogen and green hydrogen). But when hydrogen is burned, carbon dioxide generation is nil; instead, water vapour is produced. In this way, its use can drastically reduce the emissions responsible for the greenhouse effect and global warming. The difficulty lies in the fact that in order to obtain green hydrogen, abundant electrical energy is needed, and if this energy comes from fossil fuels, emissions would be generated. In contrast, the production of hydrogen from renewable energies to power the electrolysis process, does not produce any emissions. The machine in charge of this process is called an electrolyser. At present, there are different types of electrolysers depending on their size and function. The most commonly used are:

Alkaline Electrolyser: They use a liquid electrolyte solution, such as potassium hydroxide or sodium hydroxide and water. Hydrogen is produced in a cell consisting of an anode, a cathode and a membrane. The cells are usually assembled in series to produce more hydrogen and oxygen at the same time. When current is applied to the electrolysis cell stack, hydroxide ions move through the electrolyte from the cathode to the anode of each cell, generating bubbles of hydrogen gas on the cathode side of the electrolyser and oxygen gas at the anode. They have been in use for more than 100 years and do not require noble metals as a catalyst; however, they are bulky equipment that obtains medium purity hydrogen and are not very flexible in operation.

Proton Exchange Membrane (PEM) Electrolyser: These use a proton exchange membrane and a solid polymer electrolyte. When current is applied to the battery, water splits into hydrogen and oxygen and the hydrogen protons pass through the membrane to form hydrogen gas on the cathode side. They are the most popular because they produce high-purity hydrogen and are easy to cool. They are best suited to match the variability of renewable energies, are compact and produce high-purity hydrogen. On the other hand, they are somewhat more expensive because they use precious metals as catalysts.

Solid Oxide Electrolysis Cell (SOEC): These operate at high temperatures (between 500 and 850°C) and have the potential to be much more efficient than PEMs and alkaline electrolysers. The process is called high-temperature electrolysis (HTE) or steam electrolysis and uses a solid ceramic material as the electrolyte. Electrons from the external circuit combine with water at the cathode to form hydrogen gas and negatively charged ions. Oxygen then passes through the sliding ceramic membrane and reacts at the anode to form oxygen gas and generate electrons for the external circuit. Technologically they are less developed than the above.

There are other types of electrolysers that are not yet as efficient or cost-effective as the above, but have a lot of potential for development. One example is photoelectrolysis, which uses only sunlight to separate water molecules without the need for electricity. However, this device requires semiconductors that have not yet been sufficiently developed.

These electrolysers function in slightly different ways depending on the electrolyte material involved. Both alkaline and PEM electrolysers can deliver onsite and on-demand hydrogen, pressurised hydrogen without a compressor and 99.999% pure, dry and carbon-free hydrogen. Alkaline electrolyser uses a liquid electrolyte solution such as potassium hydroxide (KOH) or sodium hydroxide (NAOH) and water.

Solid oxide electrolysers must operate at temperatures high enough for the membranes to function properly (about 700°C-800°C, compared to PEM electrolysers, which operate at 70°C-90°C, and commercial alkaline electrolysers, which typically operate at less than 100°C), and have the potential to become much more efficient than PEM and alkaline. Advanced lab-scale solid oxide electrolysers based on proton-conducting ceramic electrolytes are showing promise for lowering the operating temperature to 500°C-600°C. The solid oxide electrolysers can effectively use heat available at these elevated temperatures (from various sources, including nuclear energy) to decrease the amount of electrical energy needed to produce hydrogen from water.[5]

PLI for Electrolyser Manufacturers

In 2021 the government was considering extending the benefits offered under production-linked incentive (PLI) scheme to the green hydrogen sector to encourage consumers to switch to non-polluting energy and investors to set up electrolyser manufacturing facilities in India. Electrolyser plays the most vital role in hydrogen production. It is a system that is used to produce green hydrogen using electricity generated from renewable sources such as solar and wind plants.

The scheme, launched in 2020, is seen as a game-changer for enhancing domestic production and creating jobs, as it covered 14 sectors, including the renewable energy sector and capacity addition to solar cell and module manufacturing, till the end of 2021. The incentives offered under PLI come in diverse form—subsidies, financial assistance, tax rebates, import and export duty concessions, or maybe easier land-acquisition terms. The incentive could vary between 4–6% of turnover for most categories and can go up to 10% for some products.

The government offers PLIs to both foreign manufacturers and domestic companies. While foreign manufacturers are encouraged to start production in India, domestic companies are asked to expand their operations and export. The government estimates that the minimum production in India as a result of the PLIs will reach Rs 37.5 lakh crore (US$ 500 billion) in five years on a total government spending of Rs 3.46 lakh crore on the 14 sectors covered under the PLI scheme. In addition, it will create one crore jobs in the next five years. In 2020, a Credit Suisse Report stated that the scheme will add 1.7% to India's GDP by FY 27 and highlighted that the bulk of additional US$ 144 billion sales across 14 sectors will be exported, thus shrinking the country's trade deficit by US$ 50 billion.

Given the strong performance of the renewable sector as a result of concessions offered under the PLI scheme, the government is inclined to extend the same to the hydrogen energy segment. The policy is focused on boosting non-fossil fuel-based clean energy capacity to 500 GW by 2030 and reducing emissions to 45% from 2005, also by 2030. In this context, India is placing a big bet on green hydrogen to transition away from fossil fuels.

To support an increased production of green hydrogen through electrolysis, Power Minister RK Singh has said that the government is considering imposing a green hydrogen consumption obligation to create a hydrogen value-chain in the country and bring down the cost of hydrogen production. They would be mandated to source 10% of their requirement through domestic green hydrogen to start with, later scaling up to 20% and 25%. The minister has estimated that even at 10% of green hydrogen consumption mandate, as much as need 8.8 GW of electrolyser capacity is required to meet the demand of the obligated industries. Though there are sufficient capacities of installed and upcoming renewable energy generation sources, the shortage of electrolysers becomes a roadblock for meeting the estimated requirement on green hydrogen. The PLI scheme can begin with a target of around 10 GW manufacturing capacity, which would, according to experts, require investment of between Rs 15,000–20,000 crore. The government is proposing to come up with a viability gap funding (VGF) scheme for green hydrogen.

To take advantage of the PLI offers, Indian Oil Corporation has announced to build a green hydrogen plant at its Mathura refinery and run it on electricity generated at its Rajasthan's wind power project. Electricity is the major cost in green hydrogen production, around 70%. NTPC also plans to produce green hydrogen on a commercial scale from part of the electricity generated by the solar panels to be installed in its upcoming 4,750 MW renewable energy park at Rann of Kutch, Gujarat. Currently, the power generator is running a pilot project in its Vindhyanchal unit, where the cost of hydrogen is estimated to be around US$ 2.8 to 3 per kg. JSW Future Energy has entered into a framework agreement with Australian Fortescue Future Industries to collaborate on green hydrogen production. A US-headquartered renewable energy start-up Ohmium International has launched a green hydrogen electrolyser giga-factory in Bengaluru, which will manufacture India-made PEM hydrogen electrolysers with an initial manufacturing capacity of about 500 MW per year and will scale it up to 2 GW per year in due course.

High Production Costs

A faster adoption of hydrogen is expected to lead to a drop in the costs of electrolysers, green energy production as well as FCEVs—moving down from US$ 4–6 per kg currently to US$ 2 per kg by 2030 without government incentives, and US$ 1.5 per kg with incentives. As per Wood Mackenzie Report, a sharp rise in electrolyser deployments in the 2020–25, 3.2 GW of new electrolyser capacity is going to be added globally (from 252 MW in 2019), leading to further drops in capital costs. Fuel cost is the largest component of hydrogen production, accounting for between 45–75%. It is the lowest in the Middle East, Russia and North America because of low gas prices, while costliest in gas importing countries like India, Japan, Korea and China. Hydrogen prices for consumers are highly dependent on the easy availability of refuelling stations, the frequency at which they are used and the quantity of hydrogen is delivered per day. Tackling this requires proper planning and coordination that brings together national and local governments, the industry and investors. As of 2020, green hydrogen in the US was estimated to have costed between US\$ 2.50–6.80 per kg and 'turquoise' or 'blue hydrogen' between US\$ 1.40–2.40 per kg, and high-carbon 'grey hydrogen' US\$ 1–1.80 per kg.

Wood Mackenzie expects green hydrogen to fall down the cost curve even faster than wind, solar and lithium-ion. The consultancy's report 2050, 'The Hydrogen Possibility', details how the project pipeline has grown nine-fold since October 2019 to a staggering 26 GW. National hydrogen strategies have set targets totalling 66 GW of electrolyser capacity, suggesting there is plenty more growth to come. The EU is targetting 40 GW of electrolyser deployment by 2030. France is eyeing 6.5 GW, and both the UK and Germany have set their own 5 GW goals.

Predictions on when green hydrogen might be competitive with existing high-carbon production methods abound. In January 2021, manufacturer Nel set a target of US\$ 1.5 per kg by 2025, a price level that would beat the traditional fossil fuel-based options. The current price is closer to US\$ 4 per kg. At the same time, major utilities like RWE and Iberdrola have joined oil majors like Shell, BP and Total in developing substantial early-stage green hydrogen projects.

India's premier research institute that specialises in energy, environment and sustainable development, The Energy and Resources Institute (TERI), predicts that the cost of hydrogen from renewables will fall more than 50% and will start to compete with hydrogen produced from fossil fuels. As of today, essentially all of the hydrogen consumed in India comes from fossil fuels. However, by 2050, nearly 80% of India's hydrogen is projected to be 'green', produced by renewable electricity and electrolysis. Based on a comprehensive assessment of possible production routes conducted by the institute, TERI in its report, 'The Potential Role of Hydrogen in India' says, "It is clear that green hydrogen will become the most competitive route for hydrogen production by around 2030. This is driven by dramatic cost declines in key production technologies such as electrolysers and solar PV."

For example, the cost of alkaline electrolysers is projected to drop from around Rs 6.3 crore per MW in 2022 to around Rs 2.8 crore per MW by 2030. The decline in electrolyser costs will be partly driven by large-scale deployment in India and globally, by a virtuous circle between falling costs and strengthening policy to promote hydrogen. Improving efficiencies of electrolysers, as well as increasing load factors of solar plants, will also play an important role in driving the costs of green hydrogen below Rs 150 per kg by 2030 (US\$ 2 per kg) versus Rs 300–440 per kg (US\$ 4–6 per kg) as of today. At this price, green hydrogen starts to compete with hydrogen produced from natural gas allowing it to make inroads into various end-use segments. India's lack of domestic natural gas supply and high cost of imports make green hydrogen competitive sooner than in other parts of the world, according to TERI.

The reduced costs will lead to rising demand for hydrogen. TERI expects demand could increase five-fold by 2050, with use in industry being the major driver. Currently, the demand is at around 6 mtpa, coming solely from industry sectors, such as fertilisers and refineries. This can increase to around 28 mt by 2050, driven by cost reductions in key technologies, as well as the growing imperative to decarbonise the energy system. Demand will continue to be largely focused in industry sectors, either expanding in existing sectors, such as fertilisers and refineries, or growing into new sectors, such as steel. Hydrogen will play some role in the transport sector in heavy-duty and long-distance segments, and a minor role in the power sector as a long-term storage vector. Beyond 2050, we can expect demand for green hydrogen to continue to grow, particularly in the steel and road transport sectors, as well as in shipping and aviation. Reaching a net zero target by 2060 could require around 40 mt of green hydrogen, a seven-fold increase over the level at present.

In 2016, MNRE published a report laying out a comprehensive plan for increasing R&D activity, which included significant funding for different electrolyser technologies and their integration with renewable electricity sources that has strong potential in India given the cost and availability of renewable electricity. Across Indian industry, there are considerable efforts to establish a hydrogen economy in India, not least, the work being taken forward by Indian Oil. Despite these positive moves by the government and industry, current activity is still an order of magnitude below where it needs to fully take advantage of a transition to hydrogen technologies, with manufacturing centred in India. In terms of the investment requirements, if India is to deploy green hydrogen as a clean energy solution for key sectors, including transport, industry and power, by 2050, this would require significant investment in electrolysers. Beyond this, additional investment in renewable electricity would be required, at a time when other demands for electricity in India will still be growing rapidly. This would clearly be a challenge to deliver, which is why it is imperative that India begins now in scaling-up activity.

India's National Hydrogen Mission, launched in 2021, primarily aims at promoting adoption of green hydrogen as an alternative fuel to curb CO_2 emissions that pollute the air from dirtier fossil fuels. Transport sector is one of India's top CO_2 emitter, accounting for 35% of the total CO_2 emissions of 2.5 bt as of 2019. The 2020 figure has not yet been released, but it is estimated that the emissions may have fallen by 30 mt thanks to the Covid-19 pandemic. The transport sector consumes 47% of India's total oil supply and accounts for 17% of the country's total energy consumption. India, which imports 85–90% of oil and 50% of gas, reckons fuel transition in the transport sector from oil and gas to hydrogen fuel cell a matter of utmost necessity to cut down carbon emissions for an 'Atmanirbhar Bharat'. India is one among the 182 of the 185 countries, which are party to the United Nations Framework Convention on Climate Change (UNFCCC) and have ratified the Paris Agreement 2015.

Hydrogen could be ideal as a synthetic energy carrier for transport sector as its gravimetric energy density is very high, abundantly available in combined form on the Earth and its oxidation product (water) does not contribute to greenhouse gas emissions. Hydrogen may be used as fuel for almost any application, where fossil fuels are used presently and would offer immediate benefits over the conventional fuels, if produced from renewable sources.

The development of hydrogen as an automotive fuel has gained momentum worldwide. Hydrogen-fuelled cars and buses are already in use in the United States, Japan, South Korea, China and Germany. Japan used fuel cell buses and cars for the Tokyo 2020 Olympics to promote the use of hydrogen. These countries are making investments towards cleaner production technology and expanding the network of hydrogen refuelling infrastructure.

A hydrogen fuel cell bus has been launched in India by Tata Motors in collaboration with the Indian Space Research Organisation (ISRO) and

Indian Oil (IOC). Further, Hyundai also seeks to launch its first fuel cell SUV in India by 2021 and plans on building the required infrastructure for it in and around Delhi-NCR area. It has further shown interest in introducing hydrogen powered trucks in India if the government demonstrates a positive stance in the promotion of hydrogen.[6]

Hydrogen Enriched CNG (H-CNG)

Indian Oil Corporation (IOC) has initiated a pilot project for using hydrogen enriched compressed natural gas (H-CNG) in vehicles. H-CNG has been found to be more efficient than CNG in terms of reducing emissions. The company has developed a single-step procedure for blending hydrogen with CNG, which is expected to lower the emissions. India's nodal policy think-tank NITI Aayog has also recommended the distribution of H-CNG through the existing piped-gas infrastructure in Delhi. It has further recommended that H-CNG be notified as an automotive fuel, standards for its use be issued by the Bureau of Indian Standards (BIS), and clearance for H-CNG storage cylinders on vehicles be issued by the Petroleum and Explosives Safety Organisation (PESO).[7]

Is Green Hydrogen the 'Energy of the Future' for India?

India is increasingly looking towards hydrogen as an alternative source of fuel to reduce its carbon footprint and to meet its growing energy needs. When Prime Minister Narendra Modi launched India's National Hydrogen Mission on 15 August, he said, "The thing that is going to help India with a quantum leap in terms of climate is the field of green hydrogen." About 40% of India's energy demand is imported currently at a cost of US$ 160 billion. By moving to a hydrogen economy, India can not only reduce imports of oil, coal and natural gas, but will also be able to export hydrogen to other countries in Europe and Asia. Thanks to its geography, India has the potential to produce 210 mtpa (598 mtoe) of hydrogen from solar and wind and meet 32% of Asia-Pacific's (APAC's) hydrogen demand.

Why hydrogen? Hydrogen, combined with air, produces energy and water vapour, packs more energy per kilogram than several fuels. Most importantly, apart from being a fuel, hydrogen acts as feedstock in the refining, fertiliser and chemical industries, and is gradually replacing carbon as a feedstock in the iron and steel industry too. Thus, just one hydrogen production plant can address the demand requirements of several applications.

However, unlike fossil fuels, which are readily available in natural form, hydrogen has to be extracted from feedstocks such as natural gas, water or biomass. To make zero emission hydrogen or green hydrogen competitive with fossil fuels, its price has to be brought down to around Rs 75–150 per kg. Grey hydrogen, produced from natural gas, is already available at Rs 150 per kg, but it leads to emission of 9.21 kg of CO_2 for every kilogramme of hydrogen produced, and hence is not a preferred choice. Alternatively, hydrogen can be produced by splitting water, but historically, this process has been hampered by electricity costs, accounting for about 50–60% of total hydrogen production. However, with renewable prices falling drastically and funds inflowing numerous, large-scale green hydrogen projects are coming up globally, including about 20 in India.

II. WHY DOES INDIA NEED HYDROGEN ENERGY?

For energy-deficit India, which is aiming for carbon neutrality by 2070, the path to energy security goes through a mix of oil, coal, blended fuels, natural gas, renewables and electricity. At present India's US$ 3.12 trillion economy needs 1,650 BU (billion units) of power, made from nearly 400 GW of capacity. Of this, green electricity is only 17%. When the economy touches US$ 5–7 trillion in the next decade, it will need at least 3,000–4,000 GW. Further, at current rate, the energy import bill will triple by 2040. The only way out of these massive challenges is tapping as many green and locally available energy sources as possible.

New Delhi-based climate and energy research firm, Council for Energy, Environment and Water Research (CEEWR) has estimated that net zero emissions by 2070 will require 5,630 GW solar capacity, 99% reduction in coal use between 2040 and 2060 and 90% fall in crude oil consumption between 2050 and 2070. By that time, green hydrogen should meet 19% of industry's needs. CEEWR's Centre for Energy Finance says, India requires US$ 10 trillion (Rs 750 lakh crore) energy investments, including US$ 8.4 trillion for augmenting renewable capabilities, another US$ 1.5 trillion will be required for creating a green hydrogen ecosystem in the industrial sector.

TERI estimates 23 mt hydrogen demand by 2050. India's current output is 6.7 mt, produced mostly from natural gas through steam-methane reforming process. The biggest consumers of this hydrogen are refineries, chemical companies and fertiliser plants.

However, the game changer will be green hydrogen, as other ways of generating this new-age fuel are not 100% carbon neutral. "Green hydrogen accounts for just 0.1% global hydrogen production. However, declining cost of renewable electricity (70% cost of producing hydrogen) and electrolysis technology indicates it could be the next best investment in the world of clean energy," says JP Gupta, Chairman, Expert Appraisal Committee (Industry-II), Ministry of Environment, Forest and Climate Change.

Pashupathy Gopalan, an investor in Ohmium, says production of 20 mt green hydrogen (at US$ 1 per kg) will be a US$ 20–25 billion opportunity. India can produce green hydrogen from 15–20 GW installed capacity by 2030. For that, it will need to invest US$ 4–5 billion in electrolysers, according to the India Hydrogen Alliance (IH2A), a grouping of industry stakeholders.

"Inclusion of hydrogen as an energy carrier in future energy portfolio presents a unique opportunity to address emerging energy vectors, including power to gas, power to power, power to mobility and even vehicle to grid applications," Dharmendra Pradhan, former Union Minister for Petroleum and Natural Gas and Steel said at a seminar. "We are working on a pilot on blue hydrogen, hydrogen CNG and green hydrogen. We are blending hydrogen with compressed natural gas for use as transportation fuel and industrial input in refineries," he added. The government is planning to blend piped natural gas for domestic, commercial and industrial consumption with 15% of green hydrogen.

In order to meet these goals, Union Budget 2021 earmarked Rs 800 crore for pilot projects, infrastructure, research and development, regulations and public outreach. The Ministry of New and Renewable Energy is also working on a policy document for the National Hydrogen Energy Mission.

Corporate Interest

Mukesh Ambani, Chairman, Reliance Industries Ltd (RIL), is anticipating a New Green Revolution. "India can set an even more aggressive target of achieving under US$ 1 per kg within a decade. This will make India the first country to achieve US$ 1 per 1 kg in 1 decade—the 1-1-1 target for green hydrogen," he said at the International Climate Summit 2021.

RIL has kicked off its green initiatives with a slew of deals in recent months and plans for setting up four giga-factories in Jamnagar at an investment of Rs 60,000 crore for making solar PV modules, advanced energy storage batteries, electrolysers and fuel cells. RIL's new renewable subsidiary, Reliance New Energy Solar, has partnered with Danish climate change technology company Stiesdal A/S to develop and manufacture hydrogen electrolysers at one of these four factories. It has also invested US$ 50 million in US-based energy storage company Ambri, besides acquiring Norwegian solar equipment maker REC Solar Holdings AS and a 40% stake in renewable project specialist Sterling & Wilson Solar. Bernstein Research analysts estimate that RIL is building a clean energy business worth US$ 36 billion but says it will have to master more fuel cell technologies to tap opportunities in hydrogen.

Gautam Adani plans to build the world's largest renewable energy company with 45 GW capacity by 2030. He is also aiming to become the largest hydrogen producer in the world. The group plans to spend 80% of its capital expenditure in green businesses, including US$ 20 billion in renewables, green component manufacturing and enabling infrastructure, over the next decade. The group's large capabilities in energy (both fossil and renewable), transmission and distribution infrastructure and logistics can make it a big green hydrogen player.

India's oil marketing companies are also in the game. The leader, Indian Oil Corporation (IOC), is working on plans to convert a part of the grey hydrogen it produces to blue hydrogen. The Mathura refinery will be turned into a green hydrogen-powered refinery. The company has floated an Expression of Interest (EoI) for setting up green hydrogen plants in Mathura and Panipat refineries. Mathura is envisaged as the largest plant in India with 40 MWh capacity, while the plant in Panipat will have a capacity of 15 MWh. The company has also tied up with L&T and ReNew to set up hydrogen plants.

Other state-run fuel companies are not far behind. Bharat Petroleum Corporation Ltd (BPCL) will soon float a tender for a 20 MW electrolyser at its Bina refinery, Madhya Pradesh, for building India's largest green hydrogen plant. "We will scale up after seeing the results. We are also exploring use of green hydrogen as a transportation fuel. Indian refineries are the first in the world to adopt green hydrogen," says Arun Kumar Singh, CMD, BPCL. Hindustan Petroleum Corporation (HPCL), is setting up a 370 mt green hydrogen plant at Vizag refinery.

While GAIL will build one of India's largest PEM electrolyser at Guna in Madhya Pradesh to produce green hydrogen by the end of 2023, India's largest integrated power generator, NTPC Ltd, has floated an EoI for a pilot on blending hydrogen with natural gas in city gas distribution networks. Its renewable energy subsidiary, NTPC REL, is setting up a green hydrogen fuelling station at Leh where it plans to begin with five fuel cell vehicles. The station will be powered by a 1.25 MW solar plant at Leh.

Even the Indian Railways Organisation for Alternate Fuels has invited bids to develop a hydrogen fuel cell-based hybrid power train for retrofitting the 700 HP diesel-hydraulic locomotives running on the Kalka-Shimla narrow gauge section. The initiatives have piqued the interest of global technology providers. Hyderabad-based cleantech firm Greenco teamed up with Belgian alkaline electrolyser maker John Cockerill to make electrolysers in India. Before that, Ohmium International had shipped its first PEM electrolysers to the US. Bengaluru-based Ohmium has a capacity to produce about 500 MW of electrolysis equipment per annum. This is eventually planned to be expanded to 2 GW per annum.

Once these companies manage to develop their capabilities, it's clear that green hydrogen will change the country's energy consumption patterns, especially in industries where hydrogen is a key input even today.

References

1. Press, Roman J, 'Introduction to Hydrogen Technology', John Wiley & Sons. p.249. ISBN 978-0-471-77985-8.
2. IEA Global Hydrogen Review, 2021.
3. IEA, 'Global CO_2 Emissions Rebounded to their Highest Level in History in 2021', 8 March, 2022, www.iea.org.
4. FTI (Forensic Technologies International) Consulting: India's Energy Transition Towards A Green Hydrogen Economy: White Paper on Building A Green Hydrogen Economy and Policy Roadmap for India, December 4, 2020.
5. Cummins: Electrolysers: How They Work and Where They Fit in a Green Economy, Nov 16, 2020.
6. Hyundai May Look at Entering Trucks Biz if India Focuses on Hydrogen Fuel, 26 August, 2019
7. Action Plan on Clean Fuels, NITI Aayog and Confederation of Indian Industry, 2018.

Chapter 9

NUCLEAR ENERGY

I. OVERVIEW

Notwithstanding some notable nuclear disasters, such as the Three Mile Island and Chernobyl, nuclear power is one of the least deadly sources of energy, only solar energy is less deadlier than nuclear. Coal is the deadliest because of the air pollution it causes, 1 TWh (terawatt per hour) of electricity from coal is linked to 24.6 deaths, while a TWh of electricity from nuclear energy is associated with 0.03 deaths (including indirect deaths from disasters and workplace accidents at the plants). That makes it even safer than wind energy, which is associated with 0.04 deaths per TWh, mostly from accidents during the installation process, drownings on offshore sites and helicopter collisions with turbines.[1]

Because of its green attributes, nuclear energy has become a preferred fuel, after solar, wind and hydro, in the fight against climate change. Nuclear technology plays an important role in medicine, industry, science, food and agriculture, as well as power generation. For example, doctors use radioisotopes to identify and investigate the causes of disease. They also use them to enhance traditional medical treatments. In industry, radioisotopes are used for measuring microscopic thicknesses, detecting irregularities in metal casings and testing welds. State-run Russian atomic energy corporation Rosatom, is tasked with building India's atomic reactors in Tamil Nadu. Archaeologists use nuclear techniques to date prehistoric objects accurately and to locate structural defects in statues and buildings. Nuclear irradiation is used in preserving food. It causes less vitamin loss than canning, freezing or drying.

In the six decades since the first nuclear power came online, it has become the world's fourth largest source of electricity and the second-largest low carbon source, after hydropower, in the global power mix, accounting for 10% of the world's electricity supply. According to the IAEA, 44 nuclear units, with a capacity of almost 40 GWe (gigawatts electric), are currently under construction globally, while, according to the World Nuclear Association, another 250 are proposed and 70 new units planned.

As of mid-2021, world operable nuclear capacity was around 394 GWe (from 442 units), and about 60 GWe (from 57 units) was under construction. The United States has the largest fleet of nuclear reactors, generating over 800 TWh of zero-emissions electricity per year with an average capacity factor of 92%. Average global capacity factor is 89%. Most new reactors under construction are generation III reactors in Asia.[2] In the World Nuclear Association's reference scenario, nuclear capacity is expected to rise to 439 GWe by 2030 and to 615 GWe by 2040, while in the upper scenario, it is predicted to go up to 521 GWe in 2030 and 839 GWe in 2040. The lower scenario shows a slight increase that becomes more pronounced after 2030 due to the commissioning of new reactors in China, India and several newcomer countries, compensating for reactor closures in the USA and Western Europe.[3]

Almost all reports on future energy supply from major organisations suggest an increasing role of nuclear power as an environmentally benign way of producing reliable electricity, alongside growth in other forms of low-carbon power generation, to create a sustainable future energy system. About 70 years past the startup of the first civil nuclear energy plant in the US, the commercial nuclear energy is experiencing a sort of rejuvenation that could make it a significant source of new age energy, alongside renewables, to replace fossil fuels in the world. Sceptics still harbour many of the objections that have slowed or stopped the construction of new nuclear power plants, but rising concerns about the cost and security of energy supplies and global climate change have reframed the debate in terms more favourable for nuclear power advocates.

As of 2020, the countries generating the most nuclear power are the United States, France, China, Russia and South Korea. The US is the largest user of nuclear energy, with a total installed capacity of 98.2 GW from 96 reactors in operation. Two new nuclear reactor units, Vogtle 3 and 4 with Westinghouse AP1000 reactors, were under construction in Georgia, due to be commissioned in 2021 and 2022, respectively, while two old reactors, Indian Point 2 and Duane Arnold with a combined capacity of 1.5 GW, were shut down in 2020. In 2019 the US produced 809 TWh of nuclear energy that represented more than 30% of global nuclear energy production.

France generates 70% of its electricity from nuclear plants. It has 58 operating reactors with a combined net capacity of 63.1 GW, while a new nuclear reactor, Flamanville 3 with a 1,650 MW capacity, is under construction. In 2019, France generated 382.4 TWh of nuclear electricity, including 17% from the recycled nuclear fuel. Low production cost makes France the world's largest net exporter of nuclear energy. The French government plans to reduce nuclear share in its electricity mix to 50% by 2035, by increasing renewable power generation.

China is the world's third largest producer of nuclear energy, with an installed capacity of 47.5 GW. In 2019, China produced 330.1 TWh of nuclear power, which accounted for 5% of its total production of electricity from all sources. China has 49 operational nuclear reactors, while 16 reactors with a combined net capacity of 15.9 GW are under construction, and 39 nuclear reactors with a combined capacity of 43 GW have been planned.

In addition to these three largest nuclear energy-producing states, there are 28 other countries which have operational nuclear power plants. Ten of them are: Japan (33 nuclear reactor, with a net installed capacity of 32 GW); Russia (38 reactors, with a combined net capacity of 28.5 GW); South Korea (24 reactors, with a combined 23.2 GW capacity); Canada (19 reactors, with a 13.6 GW installed capacity); Ukraine (15 reactors, with a combined installed capacity of 13.1 GW); UK (15 reactors, with a combined energy capacity of 8.9 GW) and Sweden (7 nuclear reactors, with a combined installed capacity of 7.7 GW).[4]

Many other countries get nuclear-generated power through regional transmission grids. For example, Italy and Denmark get almost 10% of their electricity from imported nuclear power. When the commercial nuclear industry began in the 1960s, there were clear boundaries between the industries of the East and West. Today, the separate American and Soviet spheres no longer exist, and the nuclear industry is characterised by international commerce. A reactor under construction in Asia today may have components supplied from South Korea, Canada, Japan, France, Germany, Russia and other countries. Similarly, uranium from Australia or Namibia may end up in a reactor in the UAE, having been converted in France, enriched in the Netherlands, de-converted in UK and fabricated in South Korea. The uses of nuclear technology extend well beyond the provision of low-carbon energy. It helps control the spread of disease, assists doctors in their diagnosis and treatment of patients, and powers our most ambitious missions to explore space. These varied uses position nuclear technologies at the heart of the world's efforts to achieve sustainable development.[5]

In 2019, twelve countries produced at least one-quarter of their electricity from nuclear plants. Slovakia and Ukraine get more than half from nuclear, while Hungary, Belgium, Sweden, Slovenia, Bulgaria, Switzerland, Finland and Czech Republic get one-third or more. South Korea normally gets more than 30% of its electricity from nuclear, while in the US, UK, Spain, Romania and Russia, about one-fifth of electricity is from nuclear. Japan was used to relying on nuclear power for more than one-quarter of its electricity before the Fukushima disaster and is now expected to return to that level soon. For countries with fast-growing economies such as China and India, nuclear energy has become a central component of energy policy. For example, to achieve its goal of generating 4% of electricity from nuclear power, China plans to add more than 30 new nuclear plants to the 11 currently in operation or under construction. India's goal is to supply 25% of its electricity from nuclear power by 2050.

IEA has projected growth of nuclear power capacity globally from 393 GW in 2020 to 630 GW in 2035, while in the net zero projection by 2050, released in May 2021, it has forecast nuclear capacity addition would double between 2020 and 2050.[6] The International Atomic Energy Agency's (IAEA's) high case projection indicates a faster increase in the global nuclear generating capacity: to 475 GWe by 2030, 622 GWe by 2040 and 715 GWe by 2050 from 392 GWe in 2020.[7]

History of Nuclear Energy

The question of whether nuclear energy should play a significant role in future electric power generation cannot be separated from its history. The idea of nuclear power began in the 1930s, when physicist Enrico Fermi in 1934 conducted experiments in Rome that showed neutrons could split many kinds of atoms. In the fall of 1938, German scientists Otto Hahn and Fritz Strassman fired neutrons from a source containing the elements radium and beryllium into uranium (atomic number 92). They were surprised to find lighter elements, such as barium (atomic number 56), in the leftover materials. These elements had about half the atomic mass of uranium. In previous experiments, the leftover materials were only slightly lighter than uranium. Hahn and Strassman contacted Lise Meitner in Copenhagen before publicising their discovery. She was an Austrian colleague who had been forced to flee Nazi Germany. She worked with Niels Bohr and her nephew,

Otto R Frisch. Meitner and Frisch thought that barium and other light elements in the leftover material resulted from the uranium splitting or fissioning. However, when she added the atomic masses of the fission products, they did not total the uranium's mass. Meitner used Einstein's theory to show the lost mass changed to energy. This proved fission occurred and confirmed Einstein's work.[8]

The Self-Sustaining Chain Reaction

In 1939, Bohr came to America. He shared with Einstein, the Hahn-Strassman-Meitner discoveries. Bohr also met Fermi at a conference on theoretical physics in Washington, DC. They discussed the exciting possibility of a self-sustaining chain reaction. In such a process, atoms could be split to release large amounts of energy. Scientists throughout the world began to believe a self-sustaining chain reaction might be possible. It would happen if enough uranium could be brought together under proper conditions. The amount of uranium needed to make a self-sustaining chain reaction is called a critical mass. Fermi and his associate, Leo Szilard, suggested a possible design for a uranium chain reactor in 1941. Their model consisted of uranium placed in a stack of graphite to make a cube-like frame of fissionable material.

Early in 1942, a group of scientists led by Fermi gathered at the University of Chicago to develop their theories. By November 1942, they were ready for construction to begin on the world's first nuclear reactor, which became known as Chicago Pile-1. The Pile was erected on the floor of a squash court beneath the University of Chicago's athletic stadium. In addition to uranium and graphite, it contained control rods made of cadmium, which is a metallic element that absorbs neutrons. When the rods were in the Pile, there were fewer neutrons to fission uranium atoms. This slowed the chain reaction. When the rods were pulled out, more neutrons were available to split atoms. The chain reaction sped up. On the morning of 2 December, 1942, the scientists were ready to begin a demonstration of Chicago Pile-1. Fermi ordered the control rods to be withdrawn a few inches at a time during the next several hours. Finally, at 3:25 pm, Chicago time, the nuclear reaction became self-sustaining. Fermi and his group had successfully transformed scientific theory into technological reality. The world had entered the nuclear age.[9]

Nuclear Energy for Peaceful Applications

In 1945, United States used the product of that technological reality, two atomic bombs, over the Japanese cities of Hiroshima and Nagasaki that brought the Second World War to an end. In the following post-war years, the US, with its ally Britain, held an atomic monopoly. But in 1949, 'in what was a stunning shock', the Soviet Union tested its first atomic bomb. To counter the Soviet bomb in 1952, US tested a prototype of 'Mike—the first full-scale thermonuclear device'—a far more powerful hydrogen bomb, 150 times more powerful than the atomic bomb. "The Pacific islands on which 'Mike' had been tested was now, (in the stark words of a document presented by President Eisenhower) 'missing', replaced by an underwater crater almost a mile in diameter."[10]

Then in August 1953, the Soviet Union tested another weapon, nicknamed 'Joe 4', that set off new alarms, since it seemed to indicate that the Soviet Union was also developing a hydrogen bomb. Eisenhower, who had been the Supreme Commander of the Allied Forces in Europe during the Second World War, was worried about the dangers of a nuclear conflict. Was there not a way to temper the arms race and move the 'atom' onto a more peaceful path? In his address at the United Nations in December 1953, where he presented his 'Atoms for Peace Doctrine', he called for US-Soviet cooperation to modulate the nuclear arms race and commit to the development of the peaceful atom for people around the world. That meant, primarily, the generation of electricity with nuclear power.[11]

The US Navy was the first to develop the now-widely used pressurised-water reactor for propulsion in submarines. This design became the basis for the first commercial nuclear plant at Shippingport, Pennsylvania, which began operation in 1957. In the Soviet Union, reactors designed for producing plutonium for weapons were modified and new ones developed to generate heat and electricity. The first such reactor began producing electricity for the city of Obninsk in 1954. The Shippingport plant used light water, which is another term for normal water, for coolant that flows around the core where radioactive material generates a controlled chain reaction, releasing a great amount of energy and heat. Core is at the heart of all of the reactor design. The light water is the basis for about 90% of the 437 nuclear reactors currently operational in the world. Canada's CANDU reactor uses heavy water, a variant of natural water that occurs rarely in nature, while a British design uses gas rather than water as a coolant.

The nuclear power industry in the US grew rapidly in the 1960s. Private sector became more and more involved in developing light water reactors after the Shippingport Atomic Power Station became operational. Utility companies saw this new form of electricity production as economical, environmentally clean and safe. In the 1970s and 1980s, however, growth slowed. Demand for electricity decreased and concerns grew over nuclear issues, such as reactor safety, waste disposal and other environmental considerations. Still, the US had twice as many operating nuclear power plants as any other country in 1991. This was more than one-fourth of the world's operating plants. Nuclear energy supplied almost 22% of the electricity produced in the US. Scientists are also studying the power of nuclear fusion. Fusion occurs when atoms join, or fuse, rather than split. Fusion is the energy that powers the Sun. On Earth, the most promising fusion fuel is deuterium, a form of hydrogen, which comes from water and is plentiful.

II. NUCLEAR ENERGY IN INDIA

India's nuclear programme, devised by the eminent nuclear physicist Dr Homi Jehangir Bhabha, is largely indigenous, aimed at achieving energy independence with the use of domestic resources—uranium and thorium reserves found in the monazite sands of coastal regions of southern India. It is mainly directed at generating nuclear power for civil use. Since building of two small boiling water reactors at Tarapur in the 1960s, India's nuclear strategy has proceeded largely without fuel or technological assistance from other countries. It adopted the pressurised heavy-water reactor (PHWR) design in 1964, since it required less natural uranium than the boiling water reactors (BWRs), needed no enrichment, and could be built with indigenous engineering capacity at that time—pressure tubes rather than a heavy pressure vessel being involved. Its power reactors to the mid-1990s had some of the world's lowest capacity factors, reflecting the technical difficulties of the country's isolation due to the trade embargo placed on it after its 1974 nuclear test because of its refusal to sign the Nuclear Proliferation Treaty (NPT), but rose impressively from 60% in 1995 to 85% in 2001–02. Then in 2008–10, the load factors dropped due to shortage of uranium fuel. India's nuclear energy self-sufficiency extended from uranium exploration and mining through fuel fabrication, heavy water production, reactor design and construction, to reprocessing and waste management. It has a small fast breeder reactor and is building a much larger one. It is also developing technology to utilise its abundant resources of thorium as a nuclear fuel.

The Three-Stage Programme

India embarked on its commercial nuclear power production in 1969, based on a three-stage closed fuel cycle roadmap, with each stage feeding into the other in such a way that the spent fuel from one stage of the cycle is reprocessed and used in the next stage to produce power. As per the roadmap drawn by Dr Bhabha, PHWRs is used in the first stage to produce energy from natural uranium. PHWRs do not just produce energy; they also produce fissile plutonium (Pu)-239. The second stage involves using the indigenous fast breeder reactor technology fuelled by Pu-239 to produce energy and more of Pu-239. By the end of the second stage the reactor produces more fissile material than it consumes, thus earning the name 'breeder'. The final stage of the cycle involves the use of Pu-239 recovered from the second stage, in combination with thorium-232, to produce energy and U-233, another fissile material, using thermal breeders. The production of U-233 from thorium-232 completes the process, which can then be used as fuel for the remaining part of the fuel cycle, creating a self-sustaining cycle of nuclear power generation.

While India has successfully completed the first stage of its nuclear fuel programme, the second stage is still in the works and has taken much longer than expected. The first 500 MW Pressurised Fast Breeder Reactor (PFBR), Bharatiya Nabhikiya Vidyut Nigam Ltd (BHAVINI), being set up in Kalpakkam, Tamil Nadu, has suffered significant delays of almost two decades and cost overruns of four-five times since the project was first approved in 2003. The latest news is that the Kalpakkam PFBR was commissioned and operationalised in December 2021, marking a major landmark and signalling the start of Stage II of India's three-stage nuclear power programme, a culmination of 50 years of work on fast reactors by the country's nuclear scientists and engineers.

In the meantime, India has commissioned the first of its 16 planned PHWR at Kakrapar Atomic Power Station in Gujarat. It is a 700 MW facility, based on the PHWR technology, mastered by Indian nuclear scientists and engineers. It was connected to the grid in January 2021. The Nuclear Power Corporation of India Ltd (NPCIL), which connected the reactor to the grid, expects to start five more units through March 2027, and has planned to place orders for another 10 to be commissioned by 2031. All future PWHRs will also be of 700 MW. Up to 40% of the fuel they would use will be slightly enriched uranium (SEU), about 1.1% U-235, to achieve higher fuel burn-up, about 21 GW d/t (depletion per ton), instead of one-third of this. Initially this fuel will be imported as SEU. The PWHRs will help balance the grid against growing intermittent renewable generation, but when they are used with natural uranium, they do not just produce energy; they also produce fissile Pu-239 as a by-product. This Pu-239 will fuel the indigenously-developed PFBR to produce energy and more of Pu-239 in a self-sustaining cycle of nuclear power generation.

The objective of the three-stage programme is to utilise the country's vast thorium resources, the third largest in the world. According to the Bhabha Atomic Research Centre (BARC), India has nuclear ores from which a total of about 78,000 tonnes of uranium metal and about 5,18,000 tonnes of thorium metal can be extracted. If the entire uranium resources are first used in natural uranium, fuelled PHWRs, it is estimated that about 420 GWe years of electricity can be produced. The resulting depleted uranium and separated plutonium from these PHWRs, if used in FBRs, could generate an additional 54,000 GWe years of electricity. In these FBRs, production of U-233 can also be achieved by loading thorium assemblies in their blanket and low-power zones. Eventually by transitioning to generations of Th-U-233 fuelled breeder reactors, India should be able to produce an additional 3,58,000 GWe years of electricity. Thus, even at an installed nuclear power capacity of 500–600 GWe, the country's nuclear resources will be able to sustain its electricity generation needs far beyond the extinction of its coal deposits.[12]

Thorium

Several independent studies have put India's thorium reserves at 30% of the total world thorium reserves.[13] In absolute terms it is around 4,00,000 tonnes. According to an official report tabled in the Indian Parliament in August 2011, the country can obtain 8,46,477 tonnes of thorium from 9,63,000 tonnes of ThO_2 (thorium dioxide, a radioactive crystalline solid compound used in a broad range of industrial applications), which in turn can be obtained from 10.7 mt of monazite occurring in beaches and river sands in association with other heavy metals. Indian monazite contains about 9–10% of ThO_2.[14]

Out of nearly 100 deposits of the heavy minerals, at present only 17 deposits containing about 4 mt of monazite have been identified as exploitable. Mineable reserves are 70% of identified exploitable resources. Therefore, about 2,25,000 tonnes of thorium metal is available for nuclear power program.[15] The Indian nuclear establishment estimates that the country could produce 500 GW equivalent of power for at least four centuries using just the country's economically extractable thorium reserves.[16]

There are many ways thorium could be applied to energy production. One way is to use solid thorium fuel in a conventional water-cooled reactor, similar to modern uranium-based power plants. Another prospect that has been exciting to scientists and nuclear power advocates is the molten salt reactor. In these plants, fuel is dissolved in a vat of liquid salt. The salts have a high boiling point, so even huge temperature spikes would not lead to explosions. In addition, molten salt reactors don't require a lot of cooling so they don't need a huge amount of water to operate. German physical chemist Otto Hahn was awarded the Nobel Prize for chemistry in 1944 for his discovery, with Fritz Strassmann and Lise Meitner, of the nuclear fission of uranium and thorium.[17]

However, thorium isn't a fuel like uranium. It is non-fissile, which must be bombarded with neutrons—or a small amount of radioactive material like uranium to jumpstart—so it can transmute into a uranium isotope (U-233/Th-232) for creating power. On the other hand, uranium is fissile that produces a runaway chain reaction if it is put in a place at one time. Thorium was used in a lot of early nuclear physics experiments—Marie Curie and Ernest Rutherford worked with it. Uranium became more heavily associated with the nuclear process during World War II, because uranium is better for making bombs, but for power generation, thorium has an advantage over uranium. Thorium is more efficient than uranium, and its reactors are less likely to melt down because they operate at lower pressures. In addition, less plutonium is produced during reactor operation. However, on the downside, thorium and its waste products are more dangerously radioactive in the short term than uranium, and, hence, can be harder to work with.

Uranium

Indian scientists chose thorium as ultimate fuel for nuclear power production, partly because of the limited availability of uranium, both by domestic reserves or by import. India's uranium resources are modest, with 1,83,600 tU (tonnes of uranium) in situ, with 1,60,000 tU identified as 'reasonably assured resource' and 23,600 tonnes as 'inferred resource', as of January 2015, according to the OECD NEA 'Red Book'. In July 2017, India's Department of Atomic Energy (DAE) claimed its uranium reserves at 2,29,499 tU. However, it woefully falls short of its needs. In 2013, it imported about 40% of its uranium requirements. Russia, Kazakhstan and France are main suppliers of India's uranium. India has also signed Civilian Nuclear Agreement with the US, Australia, Canada and the UK, but has not been able to import uranium because it has not signed the NPT.

India's Nuclear Power for Civil Use Is Well-Established

The Atomic Energy Establishment was set up at Trombay, near Mumbai, in 1957, and renamed as Bhabha Atomic Research Centre (BARC) 10 years later. Plans for building the first PHWR were finalised in 1964, and this prototype—Rajasthan 1, which had Canada's Douglas Point reactor as a reference unit, was built as a collaborative venture between Atomic Energy of Canada Ltd (AECL) and NPCIL. It started up in 1972 and was duplicated as subsequent indigenous PHWR development based on these units, though several stages of evolution can be identified: PHWRs with dousing and single containment at Rajasthan 1–2, with suppression pool and partial double containment at Madras, and later standardised PHWRs from Narora onwards having double containment, suppression pool and calandria filled with heavy water, housed in a water-filled calandria vault.

The Indian Atomic Energy Commission (AEC) is the main policy body. NPCIL is responsible for design, construction, commissioning and operation of thermal nuclear power plants. At the start of 2010 it said it had enough cash on hand for 10,000 MWe of new plant. Its funding model is 70% equity and 30% debt financing. However, it is aiming to involve other public sector and private corporations in future nuclear power expansion, notably NTPC, which is very much larger than NPCIL and sees itself as the main power producer. NTPC is largely government-owned. The 1962 Atomic Energy Act prohibits private control of nuclear power generation, and 2016 Amendments allowing public sector joint ventures do not extend to private sector companies, nor allow direct foreign investment in nuclear power, apart from the supply chain.

India's Nuclear Energy Programme 'Most Innovative'

India's nuclear energy programme is the brain-child of Indian scientist Dr Bhabha to overcome the unjustifiable restrictions imposed by the P-5 nuclear powers to deny other nations to develop nuclear energy for civilian use. It is largely based on indigenous resources and knowhow. Siegfried Hecker, a former director (1986–1997) of the Los Alamos National Laboratory in the United States, has described, "India's nuclear energy programme technically most ambitious and innovative nuclear energy programme in the world. The extent and functionality of its nuclear experimental facilities are matched only by those in Russia and are far ahead of what is left in the US."[18]

According to Dr HN Sethna, who succeeded Dr Bhabha as Chairman of India's Atomic Energy Commission (AEC), "India was among the seven or eight countries in the world, and the only developing country, to have the complete fuel cycle, right from uranium exploration, mining, extraction and conversion, through fuel fabrication, heavy water production and reactors, to reprocessing and waste management. The nation has reached a stage where its indigenously developed knowhow, can support all the required activities encompassing feasibility studies, site selection, detailed project design, construction, commissioning and operation of any plant in the entire fuel cycle chain. India is one of the few countries at present continuing with the development of natural uranium-fuelled reactors. The major reason has been our preference for a reactor system that can be operated using indigenous resources. This system also has the advantage of an efficient burnup, producing significant quantities of plutonium for use in fast reactors."

India is one of the few countries at present continuing with the development of natural uranium-fuelled reactors. The major reason is our preference for a reactor system that can be operated using indigenous resources. India's first nuclear power station at Tarapur consisted, of two boiling-water reactors to demonstrate the economic viability of nuclear power without delay by using a proven system. This station was a turnkey project awarded to General Electric of the US on the basis of a global tender. The involvement of Indian personnel was, however, substantially more than the usual turnkey project. Our scientists and engineers were responsible for all the preliminary work such as site selection, tender preparation and evaluation and also participated, to the extent possible, in the review of detailed designs, construction, inspection and testing of equipment and commissioning activities. Since 1975, the enriched uranium fuel elements for this station have been fabricated in India at the Nuclear Fuel Complex in Hyderabad from uranium hexafluoride imported from the US. We had not gone in for the development of indigenous enrichment capability primarily since a commercial scale enrichment plant would not be economically feasible for only one power plant for which, in any case, we had entered into an agreement for life-time fuel supplies.

About the same time as a commitment was made on the Tarapur plant, BARC decided to install a heavy-water power station at Kota, Rajasthan, consisting of two 220 MWe reactors. In this case, the project was a collaborative venture with Canada. India retained the responsibility for construction and installation activities while Canada undertook to supply the design and major equipment. India took the risks involved not only on the prices and schedule that such a procedure entailed but also in the capital investment on a system which was in its initial stages of development. While major equipment for the first unit of this station was imported, part manufacture of some of the major components was undertaken in India along with fabrication of many items of auxiliary equipment and half the initial fuel charge for the first unit. The efforts to rely on indigenous resources were intensified for the second unit of this station and major components such as the calandria, end shields, steam generators and fuelling machines were manufactured in the country.

The first unit of the Rajasthan station has been in operation since 1975 and the second unit is in an advanced stage of commissioning. The third atomic power station, consisting of two heavy-water reactor units of 235 MWe each, is being built near Madras in south India. The full responsibility for the execution of this project rests with BARC's engineers and scientists. Several design modifications and improvements have been introduced at this plant for reasons of economy and to take into account local conditions. The fourth power station under construction at Narora in Uttar Pradesh also consists of two 235 MWe heavy-water reactors. These reactors have several new design features and concepts, including earthquake resistant design of the buildings, reactor components, an integral calandria-end-shield assembly, two independent fast-acting shut down systems for safety and reliability and a simplified water-filled calandria vault. Efforts are under way to standardise the Narora design and propose to repeat this design for two additional projects of 500 MWe each before the construction begins.

As a result of intensified efforts at using indigenous resources, India has progressively reduced the import component of nuclear power projects. The import component of the first unit of the Rajasthan station was 45%, and this was reduced in the case of the second unit to 30%. The import component declined further to 12% for the Madras power station and it is only around 9% for the Narora plant now. Even this marginal import will be eliminated once the new manufacturing plants being set up in the country start operation. The establishment of design and manufacturing capability has helped us to reduce indirect costs of engineering, field management and commissioning, which usually form substantial part of a turnkey project. Dr Sethna says the BARC was able to reduce the cost of engineering as a percentage of cost per kilowatt installed from around 15% for the first unit of the Rajasthan station to less than 6% for the Narora plant. This is in spite the fact that extensive design modifications were carried out for seismic conditions and various new concepts introduced in the later plant.[19]

Advanced Heavy Water Reactor (AHWR)

Subsequent to the accidents at Three Mile Island in USA in year 1979 followed by Chernobyl in 1986, there was a radical change, says Dr Sethna, in the philosophy of design of new nuclear reactors. Passive safety systems became integral part in Gen-III and III+ reactors. This philosophy gave birth to the concept of Advanced Heavy Water Reactor (AHWR) being designed by BARC. The AHWR retained the pressure tube concept of PHWRs but adopted several passive systems in design, making the reactor safe enough to deploy close to the population centre. Apart from this, AHWR targetted to produce significant power (more than 60%) from thorium.

In February 2014, BARC presented its latest design for AHWR which, estimated that the reactor could function without an operator for 120 days. Validation of its core reactor physics was underway by late 2017. The design envisages a start up with reactor grade plutonium that breeds U-233 from Th-232. Thereafter, thorium is to be the only fuel.[20]

According to Dr RK Sinha, Chairman of the Atomic Energy Commission, "This will reduce our dependence on fossil fuels, mostly imported, and will be a major contribution to global efforts to combat climate change." Because of its inherent safety, they expect that similar designs could be set up 'within' populated cities, like Mumbai or Delhi.[21] Indian government is planning to build up to 62 reactors, mostly thorium-based. In 2017–18, it made a budget provision for the construction of 10 indigenous PHWRs of 700 MW. Of these, the Kakarapar Atomic Power Project being developed in Gujarat became the first one to achieve criticality. The Indian government has announced that seven more reactors with a cumulative capacity of 5,500 MW are under construction. It has also cleared the paperwork for 12 more reactors with a cumulative capacity of 9,000 MW.

While India has successfully completed the first stage of its nuclear fuel programme, the second stage is yet to be fully completed. The first 500 MW PFBR BHAVINI, built in Kalpakkam, Tamil Nadu, was commissioned only in December 2021 after missing many deadlines and cost overruns. Of the 10 PHWRs of 700 MW each, sanctioned in 2015, the first one, the Kakarapar Atomic Power Project in Gujarat, achieved criticality in 2022, while seven other reactors with a cumulative capacity of 5.5 GW are under construction.

NPT Embargo Hits India's Nuclear Programme

However, despite the 'most innovative nuclear programme', as cited by American scientist Siegfried Hecker, and abundant indigenous scientific expertise, production of nuclear power has been extremely slow in India. As of March 2021, the country was producing only about 6.7 GW power from nuclear fuel, mostly pressurised heavy water, at its 22 nuclear power plants, which contributed 1.8% to the total energy mix. This is far below the vision of the Department of Atomic Energy (DAE), which hoped to produce at least 20 GW of nuclear power by 2020, and 63 GW by 2032. One of the main reasons for this state of affairs has been the international embargo imposed on India's nuclear programme following its 1974 nuclear explosion at Pokhran (Rajasthan). To a certain extent some of India's crucial projects for the peaceful utilisation of atomic energy had been affected by restrictive trade practices, mandated by the Treaty on Non-Proliferation of Nuclear Weapons (NPT), and unilateral embargoes on nuclear supplies by certain countries. Such measures caused temporary delays and perhaps cost overruns. But in the long run, they only strengthened and accelerated India's programme for 'complete self-sufficiency in the nuclear field'. The innumerable hurdles that came along the way gave our scientists and engineers confidence that the difficulties, which may come in the future, can be surmounted. India has so far doggedly refused to sign the NPT because it considers it one-sided and discriminatory as it only allows the Permanent Five (P5) members of the UN—US, UK, France, Russia and China—to possess nuclear arsenal, while it denies other countries any access to nuclear technology, the supply of fuel, reactor and necessary equipment, to develop their nuclear capability.

In 1994, P5 nations convened a world conference in Geneva to start negotiations on a Comprehensive Nuclear Test Ban Treaty (CTBT). India walked out of this conference, and four years later it conducted five underground atomic tests on 11 and 13 May, 1998 for 'scientific purposes'. The CTBT is a multilateral treaty that bans all nuclear tests, for both civilian and military purposes, in all environments. It was adopted by the United Nations General Assembly on 10 September, 1996, but has not entered into force, as eight specific nations with nuclear bombs—United States, China, India, Israel, Iran, Pakistan, Egypt and North Korea—have not ratified the treaty. India considers this treaty, too, like the NPT, discriminatory against non-nuclear capable nations.

Notwithstanding the restrictions and embargoes imposed by the P5 nuclear powers on access to nuclear technology and material in the case of non-nuclear states, a number of countries have managed to develop their nuclear capability on their own. Such countries include India, Israel, Pakistan and North Korea. By 1998 India had conducted nuclear tests twice (first in 1974 and the second time in 1998) and possessed both nuclear weapons and extensive nuclear fuel cycle capabilities, even though it had remained and still remains in 2021 outside both, the NPT and the CTBT. However, its nuclear behaviour has been commensurate with what might be expected of a responsible nuclear power. Its standards of nuclear security and safety of nuclear materials and activities and declaratory policy on nuclear strategy, centred on restraint, have been in compliance with significant parts of the NPT. Just after the 1998 atomic tests, India had reiterated its stand on 'No First Use' of nuclear weapons in the event of conflict. Thus, many members of the international community, including the elite P5, have apparently found India's record as a responsible nuclear power, "Mixed, but increasingly positive when it comes to observable and measurable benchmarks of nuclear behaviour."[22]

In 2000, Russian President Vladirmir Putin visited New Delhi and signed agreements on defence and nuclear cooperation with India, however, this agreement did not unshackle India from the restrictive clauses of the NPT. But with this deal India was able to start construction of its largest nuclear power station at Kudankulam in the Tirunelveli district of the southern Indian state of Tamil Nadu with Russian help. The Kudankulam Nuclear Power Plant (KNPP) is scheduled to have six VVER-1000 reactors, with an installed capacity of 6,000 MW of electricity. Unit 1 was synchronised with the southern power grid in 2013 and since then, has been generating electricity at its warranted limit of 1,000 MW. Unit 2 was synchronised with the electricity grid in 2016. The ground-breaking ceremony for construction of Units 3 and 4 was performed in 17 February, 2016. NPCIL is building the complex in collaboration with Atomstroyexport, a Russian state company.

The construction work on Units 5 and 6 of KNPP began on 29 June, 2021, with the first concrete pouring by the state-run Russian atomic energy corporation Rosatom, which is tasked with building India's atomic reactors in Tamil Nadu, into the foundation plate of the reactor building. Rosatom and NPCIL have been building six power reactors of 1,000 MW each at Kudankulam, which is the country's largest nuclear power generation park. Units 1 and 2 have already been commissioned while work on Units 3 and 4 is in the advanced stage and is scheduled to be completed by 2026–27.

The Russian deal helped India gain a degree of acceptability in the international nuclear community as a responsible nuclear nation. However, real recognition came in 2008, India's nuclear agreements with United States and the International Atomic Energy Authority (IAEA) and Nuclear Suppliers Group (NSG) waiver, which places no restrictions on fuel supplies to India or the right to build strategic reserves. These agreements ended India's 34-year-old international nuclear apartheid and paved the way for integration into the international nuclear community. India has thus succeeded in winning recognition as a nuclear power from the international community. It is the only nuclear possessor and non-NPT signatory state that has won the right to engage in civil nuclear trade with other states.

However, India's entry into the nuclear club has come with certain strings: 1) It must separate civil and nuclear facilities in a phased manner and place civil facilities under IAEA safeguards; 2) Have in place an IAEA additional protocol on safeguards with respect to civil nuclear facilities; 3) Continue India's unilateral moratorium on nuclear testing; 4) Work towards conclusion of a Fissile Material Control Treaty (FMCT); 5) Refrain from transferring uranium enrichment and plutonium reprocessing technologies to states which do not have them and support international efforts to prevent their spread; and 6) Match India's export controls with that of the NSG.

Post-NSG Waiver

Following the Nuclear Suppliers Group agreement, which was signed in 2008, the scope for sourcing both reactors and fuel from suppliers in other countries opened up. Now India has civil nuclear cooperation agreements with US, Russia, France, UK, South Korea, Czech Republic, Canada, Australia, Argentina, Kazakhstan, Mongolia and Namibia. A further nuclear cooperation agreement was signed with UK in November 2015, with 'a comprehensive package' of collaboration on energy and climate change matters involving sterling £ 3.2 billion (US$ 4.9 billion) in programmes and initiatives related to energy security and energy access. Also in 2015, another landmark agreement was signed with Japan which allows India to import Japanese nuclear technology, and secures Japan's support for India to join the international NSG. A civil nuclear cooperation agreement was signed with Japan in 2016 and passed by its parliament in June 2017.

On the basis of the 2010 cooperation agreement with Canada, in April 2013, a bilateral safeguards agreement was signed between the DAE and the Canadian Nuclear Safety Commission (CNSC), allowing trade in nuclear materials and technology for facilities which are under IAEA safeguards. A similar bilateral safeguards agreement with Australia was signed in 2014 and finalised in November 2015; both apply essentially to uranium supply.

The initial two Russian PWR types at the Kudankulam site were apart from India's three-stage plan for nuclear power and were simply to increase generating capacity more rapidly. Now there are plans for eight 1000 MWe units at that site, and in January 2007 a memorandum of understanding was signed for Russia to build the next four there, as well as others elsewhere in India. Further such agreement was signed in December 2010, and Rosatom announced that it expected to build no less than 18 reactors in India. Then in December 2014 another high-level nuclear cooperation agreement was signed with a view to Russia building 20 more reactors plus cooperation in building Russian-designed nuclear power plants in third world countries, in uranium mining, production of nuclear fuel and waste management. India was also to confirm a second location for a Russian plant, Haripur in West Bengal being in some doubt. Most of the new units are expected to be large 1200 MWe AES-2006 designs.

Russia was earlier reported to have offered a 30% discount on the US$ 2 billion price tag for each of the Phase II Kudankulam reactors. This was based on plans to start serial production of reactors for the Indian nuclear industry, with much of the equipment and components proposed to be manufactured in India, thereby bringing down costs. However, at the end of 2015 the approved cost of Kudankulam Units 3 and 4 was Rs 39,747 crore (US$ 5.96 billion), according to the Minister for Atomic Energy, more than twice the costs of Units 1 and 2, due to liability issues. Between 2010 and 2020, further nuclear plant construction was expected to take total gross capacity to 21,180 MWe, though this timeline is now extended and less than half that was likely to be achieved by 2020. The nuclear capacity target is part of the National Energy Policy.

Looking beyond the Russian light water reactors, NPCIL had meetings and technical discussions with three major reactor suppliers—Areva, GE Hitachi and Westinghouse Electric Corporation—for the supply of reactors for these projects and for new units at Kaiga. These resulted in more formal agreements with each reactor supplier early in 2009. The benchmark capital cost sanctioned by DAE for imported units was quoted at US$ 1,600 per kilowatt. An important aspect of all these agreements is that, as with Kudankulam, India will reprocess the used fuel to recover plutonium for its indigenous three-stage civil programme, using a purpose-built and safeguarded integrated nuclear recycle plant. However, all three agreements beyond that with Russia were stalled due to liability concerns.

In late 2008, NPCIL announced that as part of the Eleventh Five Year Plan (2007–12), it would start site work for 12 reactors including rest of the eight 700 MWe PHWRs, three or four fast breeder reactors and one 300 MWe advanced heavy water reactor (AHWR) in 2009. NPCIL said that India was now focusing on capacity addition through indigenisation with progressively higher local content for imported designs, up to 80%. Looking further ahead its augmentation plan included construction of 25–30 light water reactors of at least 1,000 MWe by 2030. In the event, only four 700 MWe PHWR units started construction over 2007–12. Early in 2012, NPCIL projections had the following additions to the 10.08 GWe anticipated in 2017 as 'possible': 4.2 GWe PHWR, 7.0 GWe PHWR (based on recycled U), 40 GWe LWR, 2.0 GWe FBR. These projections also have not materialised.

In June 2012 NPCIL announced four new sites for twin PHWR units—Gorakhpur/Kumbariya near Fatehabad district in Haryana; Banswara in Rajasthan; Chutka in Mandla district and; Bhimpur, both in Madhya Pradesh. Initially these would add 2,800 MWe, followed by a further

2,800 MWe. Site work has started at Gorakhpur with Haryana state government's support. In mid-2015, NPCIL confirmed plans for Kaiga Units 5 and 6 as 700 MWe PHWR, costing about Rs 6,000 crore. In September 2019, India's Ministry of Environment, Forest and Climate Change (MoEF) approved NPCIL's plans. NPCIL is also planning to build an indigenous 900 MWe PWR, the Indian pressurised water reactor (IPWR), designed by BARC in connection with its work on submarine power plants. A site for the first plant is being sought, a uranium enrichment plant is planned, the reactor pressure vessel forging will be carried out by Larsen & Toubro (L&T) and NPCIL's new joint venture plant at Hazira, and the turbine will come from Bharat Heavy Electricals Limited (BHEL). Meanwhile, NPCIL is offering both 220 and 540 MWe PHWRs for export, in markets requiring small- to medium-sized reactors.

The NSG deal had a special strategic significance for India. Not only it helped India address its energy security concerns, it also opened the door for agreements with various countries in the field of civil nuclear energy, defence, nuclear technology and infrastructure. It enhanced India's international profile, and encouraged countries to invest in India in various fields, including nuclear energy, and sell nuclear reactors, enriched uranium and other nuclear material. It facilitated and strengthened defence ties with the US, France, Russia and UK.

Two months after the IAEA safeguards agreement, the NSG resolution and finally the US Congress approval of a bilateral trade agreement in October 2008, Russia's Rosatom and Areva from France contracted to supply uranium for power generation. The Russian agreement was to provide fuel for PHWRs as well as the two small Tarapur reactors. In February 2009 the actual Russian contract was signed with TVEL to supply 2,000 tonnes of natural uranium fuel pellets for PHWRs over 10 years, costing US$ 780 million, and 58 tonnes of low-enriched fuel pellets for the Tarapur reactors. The Areva shipment of 300 tonnes of uranium arrived in June 2009 for Rajasthan Atomic Power Station (RAPS-2), which is the first PHWR to be fuelled with imported uranium, followed by Units 5 and 6. In January 2009, NPCIL signed a memorandum of understanding with Kazatomprom for the supply of 2,100 tonnes of uranium oxide concentrate (UOC) over six years and a feasibility study on building Indian PHWR reactors in Kazakhstan. NPCIL said it represented 'a mutual commitment to begin thorough discussions on long-term strategic relationship'. The actual agreement in

April 2011 covered 2,100 tonnes by 2014. In March 2013 both countries agreed to extend the civil nuclear cooperation agreement past 2014.

In 2015 the DAE renewed its contract for supply of 5,000 tonnes from Kazatomprom over four years. In 2009, India signed uranium supply and nuclear cooperation agreements with Namibia and Mongolia. The latter was reaffirmed in May 2015, noting that Mongolian uranium 'could help power India's low-carbon growth'. In March 2010 Russia offered India a stake in the Elkon uranium mining development in its Sakha Republic, and agreed on a joint venture with ARMZ Uranium Holding Co. In August 2014, Navoi Mining and Metallurgical Combine (NMMC) in Uzbekistan signed a contract for supply of 2,000 tonnes of U-308 to India during the four years to 2018, its first export to India. A further contract was signed in January 2019, for long-term supply.

In September 2014, a bilateral safeguards agreement with Australia was signed, then came into force in November, enabling supply from there. In April 2013 a bilateral safeguards agreement was signed between the DAE and the Canadian Nuclear Safety Commission (CNSC), and in April 2015 Cameco signed an agreement to supply 3,200 tonnes of U-308 (UOC) to India up to 2020. The first Cameco shipment arrived in December 2015. In July 2015, the DAE reported to the Parliament that eight reactors (Kaiga 1–4, Madras 1 and 2, Tarapur 3 and 4) were using indigenous sources of uranium and 14 reactors were using imported uranium. This situation was confirmed in July 2016 and July 2017. In 2014 the DAE reported that India had imported 4,458 tU since 2008 (2,058 tonnes from TVEL, 2,100 tonnes from Kazatomprom, and 300 tonnes from Areva).

III. REACTORS UNDER IAEA SAFEGUARDS

In July 2017, eight reactors—2,400 MWe (gross)—of nuclear capacity was fuelled by indigenous uranium and being operated close to their rated capacity. The 14 units (4,380 MWe gross) under safeguards were operating on imported uranium at rated capacity. The two Tarapur 150 MWe boiling water reactors (BWRs) built by GE on a turnkey contract before the advent of the Nuclear Non-Proliferation Treaty were originally 200 MWe. They were downrated due to recurrent problems but have run reasonably well since. They have been using imported enriched uranium (from France and China in 1980–90s and Russia since 2001) and are under IAEA safeguards.

However, late in 2004 Russia deferred to the NSG and declined to supply further uranium for them. They underwent six months' refurbishment over 2005–06, and in March 2006 Russia agreed to resume fuel supply.

In December 2008, a US\$ 700 million contract with Rosatom was announced for continued uranium supply. In 2015 a further contract was signed with TVEL for pellets which will be incorporated into fuel assemblies at the Nuclear Fuel Complex in Hyderabad. The supply contract was renewed in January 2019. The two small Canadian (Candu) PHWRs at Rajasthan Nuclear Power Plant started up in 1972 and 1980, and are also under safeguards. Rajasthan 1 was downrated early in its life and has operated very little since 2002 due to ongoing problems. It has been shut down since 2004 as the government considers its future. It is still listed by NPCIL as operable though a parliamentary answer in August 2012 said, "It is under extended shutdown for techno-economic assessment on continuation of operations." In March 2017 the minister said a decision on reopening Rajasthan 1 will be made following the techno-economic assessment. Rajasthan 2 was downrated in 1990. It had major refurbishment 2007–09 and has been running on imported uranium at full capacity.

The 220 MWe PHWRs (202 MWe net) were indigenously designed and constructed by NPCIL, based on a Canadian design. The only accident to an Indian nuclear plant was due to a turbine hall fire in 1993 at Narora, which resulted in a 17-hour total station blackout. There was no core damage or radiological impact and it was rated 3 on the INES scale, a 'serious incident'.

The Madras (MAPS) reactors were refurbished in 2002–03 and 2004–05 and their capacity restored to 220 MWe gross (from 170 MWe). Much of the core of each reactor was replaced, and the lifespans extended to 2033/36. Kakrapar Unit 1 was fully refurbished and upgraded in 2009–10, after 16 years of operation, as was Narora 2, with cooling channel (calandria tube) replacement. In March 2016, Unit 1 was shut down due to a coolant leak, and repairs ran through to May 2019. Kakrapar 2 was shut down in July 2015 and restarted in September 2018. There was widespread corrosion in both Kakrapar units and coolant channels were replaced.

Following the Fukushima accident in March 2011, four NPCIL taskforces evaluated the situation in India and in an interim report in July made recommendations for safety improvements of the Tarapur BWRs and each PHWR type. The report of a high-level committee appointed by the Atomic Energy Regulatory Board (AERB) was submitted at the end of August 2011, saying that the Tarapur and Madras plants needed some supplementary provisions to cope with major disasters. The two Tarapur BWRs have already been upgraded to ensure continuous cooling of the reactor during prolonged station blackouts and to provide nitrogen injection to containment structures, but further work is recommended. Madras needs enhanced flood defences in case of tsunamis higher than that in 2004. The prototype fast breeder reactor (PFBR) under construction next door at Kalpakkam has defences which are already sufficiently high, following some flooding of the site in 2004.

Tarapur 3 and 4 reactors of 540 MWe gross (490 MWe net) were developed indigenously from the 220 MWe (gross) model PHWR and were built by NPCIL. The first, Tarapur 4, was connected to the grid in June 2005 and started commercial operation in September. Tarapur 4's criticality came five years after pouring first concrete and seven months ahead of schedule. Its twin, Unit 3, was about a year behind it and was connected to the grid in June 2006 with commercial operation in August, five months ahead of schedule. Tarapur 3 and 4 cost about US$ 1,200 per kW, and are competitive with imported coal.

Future indigenous PHWR reactors will be 700 MWe gross (640 MWe net). The first four are being built at Kakrapar and Rajasthan. They were due online by 2017 after 60 months of construction from first concrete to criticality, but this schedule has slipped by several years. Kakrapar 3 became the first of the four to achieve criticality in July 2020, and the unit was connected to the grid in January 2021.

Kudankulam 1 and 2: Russia's Atomstroyexport supplied the country's first large nuclear power plant, comprising two VVER-1000 (V-412) reactors, under a Russian-financed US$ 3 billion contract and Russia-India agreement with 1998 supplement. The cost was reported as Rs 17,270 crore or US$ 2.7 billion, in 2015 but at 'over Rs 22,000 crore' (US$ 3.3 billion) by NPCIL in mid-2016, including Rs 9,000 crore escalation due to delays. A subsequent figure was Rs 20,962 crore. A long-term credit facility covered about half the cost of the plant.

The AES-92 Units at Kudankulam in Tamil Nadu state have been built by NPCIL and also commissioned and operated by it under IAEA safeguards. The turbines were made by Silmash in St Petersburg and have evidently given some trouble during commissioning. Unlike other Atomstroyexport projects such as in Iran, there was only a maximum of 80 Russian supervisory staff on the project. This resulted in more problems than expected learning curve as Indian engineers adapted to the PWR design from Canadian-type PHWR experience. Construction started in March 2002. Russia is supplying all the enriched fuel through the life of the plant, though India will reprocess it and keep the plutonium for civil use. The first unit was due to start supplying power in March 2008 and go into commercial operation late in 2008, but this schedule slipped by six years. In the latter part of 2011 and into 2012 completion and fuel loading was delayed by public protests, but in March 2012 the state government approved the plant's commissioning and said it would deal with any obstruction. Unit 1 started up in mid-July 2013, was connected to the grid in October 2013 and entered commercial operation at the end of December 2014. It had reached full power in mid-year but then required turbine repairs for nearly six months. It generated only 2.8 TWh in its first year, at a cost of under Rs 4 per kWh (US¢ 6 per kWh). Unit 2 construction was declared complete in July 2015, it was grid-connected in August 2016, and commenced commercial operation at the start of April 2017. Each unit is 917 MWe net. The original agreement in 1988 specified return of used fuel to Russia, but a 1998 supplemental agreement allowed India to retain and reprocess it.

While the first core load of fuel was delivered early in 2008 there have been delays in supply of some equipment and documentation. Control system documentation was delivered late, and when reviewed by NPCIL it showed up the need for significant refining and even reworking some aspects. The design basis flood level was 5.44 m, and the turbine hall floor was 8.1 m above mean sea level. The 2004 tsunami was under 3 m. A small desalination plant is associated with the Kudankulam plant to produce 426 m^3/h for it using four-stage multi-vacuum compression (MVC) technology. Another reverse osmosis (RO) plant is in operation to supply local township needs. Output from Kudankulam 1 is being supplied to India's southern grid and in 2016 divided among five states: Tamil Nadu (56%), Karnataka (22%), Kerala (13%), Andhra Pradesh (5%) and Puducherry (3%). Kudankulam 3 and 4 are being built as the first stage of Phase-II at the site and AES-92 Units are also being built with Russian technical assistance 'within the scope of' the 1988 agreement. Their cost is expected to be Rs 39,747 crore and the project was officially launched in October 2016.

Kaiga 3 started in February, was connected to the grid in April and went into commercial operation in May 2007. Unit 4 started up in November 2010 and was grid-connected in January 2011, but was about 30 months behind original schedule due to shortage of uranium. The Kaiga units are not under UN safeguards, so cannot use imported uranium. Kaiga 4 was the last of the 220 MWe PHWRs to enter service.

Rajasthan 5 started in November 2009, using imported Russian fuel, and in December it was connected to the northern grid. RAPP 6 started in January 2010 and was grid connected at the end of March. Both are now in commercial operation.

Under plans for the India-specific safeguards to be administered by the IAEA in relation to the civil-military separation plan, eight reactors were to be safeguarded (beyond Tarapur 1 and 2, Rajasthan 1 and 2 and Kudankulam 1 and 2): Rajasthan 3 and 4 from 2010, Rajasthan 5 and 6 from 2008, Kakrapar 1 and 2 by 2012 and Narora 1 and 2 by 2014. In mid-2008 Indian nuclear power plants were running at about half of capacity due to a chronic shortage of fuel. Average load factor for India's power reactors dipped below 60% over 2006–2010, reaching only 40% in 2008. Some easing after 2008 was due to the new Turamdih Mill in Jharkhand state coming online (the mine there was already operating). Political opposition too delayed new mines in Jharkhand, Meghalaya and Telangana.

The 500 MWe PFBR started construction in 2004 at Kalpakkam near Madras. It was expected to function about the end of 2010 and produce power in 2011, but this schedule was delayed significantly. In 2014, 1,750 tonnes of sodium coolant was delivered. With construction completed, in June 2015 BHAVINI was 'awaiting clearance from the AERB for sodium charging, fuel loading, reactor criticality and then stepping up power generation'. In March 2020 the government said that commissioning would be in December 2021. The approved cost was Rs 5,677 crore (US$ 850 million). It was not under IAEA safeguards. The reactor was fuelled with uranium-plutonium oxide. It had a blanket with thorium and uranium to breed fissile U-233 and plutonium respectively. Initial FBRs would have mixed oxide fuel or carbide fuel but these would be followed by metallic fuelled ones.

In contrast to the situation in the 1990s, most PHWR reactors under construction in 2012 were on schedule (apart from fuel shortages 2007–09), and two, Tarapur 3 and 4, were increased in capacity. Future PHWR units would be nominal 700 MWe (630 MWe net). In 2005, four sites were approved for eight new reactors. Two of the sites, Kakrapar and Rajasthan, would have 700 MWe indigenous PHWR units, Kudankulam would have imported 1,000 MWe VVER light water reactors alongside the two being built there by Russia, and the fourth site was Greenfield for two 1,000 MWe LWR units, Jaitapur (Jaithalpur) in the Ratnagiri district, Maharashtra, on the west coast. The plan has since expanded to six 1,600 MWe EPR units. In April 2007, the government gave approval for the first four of eight planned 700 MWe PHWR units: Kakrapar 3 and 4 and Rajasthan 7 and 8, to be built by Hindustan Construction using indigenous technology. In mid-2009 construction approval was confirmed, and late in 2009 the finance for them was approved. Site works at Kakrapar were completed by August 2010. First concrete for Kakrapar 3 and 4 was in November 2010 and March 2011 respectively, after the Atomic Energy Regulatory Board (AERB) approval. The AERB approved Rajasthan 7 and 8 in August 2010, and site works then began. First concrete was laid in July 2011 and construction was expected to take 66 months to commercial operation.

In September 2009, L&T secured an order for four steam generators for Rajasthan 7 and 8, having already supplied similar ones for Kakrapar 3 and 4. In December 2012, L&T was awarded the US$ 135 million contract for balance of turbine island for Rajasthan 7 and 8. Their estimated cost was to be Rs 12,320 crore (US$ 2.6 billion) each pair. Both these projects were delayed apparently by the reluctance of supply chain companies to provide equipment without NPCIL giving indemnity under the 2010 Civil Liability for Nuclear Damage Act. Delays were also attributed to financial constraints. NPCIL said in July 2016 that delays in the supply of equipment including steam generators from Indian sources plus the nuclear liability issue have put the projects behind schedule, and the Minister of Atomic Energy said that Kakrapar 3 and 4 were only 75.5% complete and Rajasthan 7 and 8 were only 61.5% complete by then.

In March 2020, the government said that Kakrapar 3 and 4 and Rajasthan 7 and 8 were expected to be commissioned in October 2020, September 2021, March 2022 and March 2023, respectively. In July 2020, Kakrapur 3 achieved first criticality, and was connected to the grid in January 2021. Construction costs of reactors as reported by AEC are about US$ 1200 per kilowatt for Tarapur 3 and 4 (540 MWe), US$ 1300 per kW for Kaiga 3 and 4 (220 MWe) and expected US$ 1700 per kW for the 700 MWe PHWRs with 60-year life expectancy.

In April 2015 the government gave in principle approval for new nuclear plants at ten sites in nine states. Those for indigenous PHWRs are: Gorakhpur in Haryana's Fatehabad; Chutka and Bhimpur in Madhya Pradesh; Kaiga in Karnataka and Mahi Banswara in Rajasthan. Those for plants with foreign cooperation are: Kudankulam in Tamil Nadu (VVER); Jaitapur in Maharashtra (EPR); Chhaya Mithi Virdhi in Gujarat (AP1000); Kovvada in Andhra Pradesh (originally ESBWR) and Haripur in West Bengal (VVER), though this location had been in doubt. In addition, two 600 MWe fast breeder reactors are proposed at Kalpakkam. (All these are in line with the Twelfth Five Year Plan of 2012–17, with the addition of Bhimpur, which in 2017 was dropped in favour of two extra units at Mahi Banswara.) In mid-2016 the Kovvada site was allocated for AP1000 units instead of Mithi Virdhi, and the ESBWR prospects receded.[23]

IV. NUCLEAR ENERGY PARKS

In line with past practice such as at the eight-unit Rajasthan nuclear plant, NPCIL intends to set up five more 'nuclear energy parks', each with a capacity for up to eight new-generation reactors of 1,000 MWe, six reactors of 1600 MWe or simply 10,000 MWe at a single location. By 2032, 40–45 GWe would be provided from these five. NPCIL was hoping to be able to start work by 2012 on at least four new reactors at all four sites designated for imported plants, but this did not happen. In mid-2015 it was reported that an additional site could be assigned for a Japanese multi-unit plant. However, apart from the Russian projects under inter-governmental agreement, no overseas reactor vendor has been ready to proceed under India's unique liability arrangements.

Original plans were for widespread deployment of new nuclear capacity, but due to protests in Gujarat, Tamil Nadu, West Bengal and Maharashtra, some of the plans have relocated proposed developments to Andhra Pradesh. That state may now host six Russian reactors moved from Haripur in West Bengal to Kavali in Nellore district, six Westinghouse AP1000 moved from Mithi Virdi in Gujarat to Kovvada in Srikakulam district, as well as the original six GE Hitachi ESBWR units if they are ever approved. In addition, seven new energy parks have been planned, of which two—Kudankulam (KKNPP) 2, 3 and 4 and Kovvada in Andhra Pradesh's Srikakulam district— are proceeding, while the rest are on the drawing board. They include, Gorakhpur Haryana Anu Vidyut Pariyojana (GHAVP) in Fatehabad district of Haryana; J Mahi Banswara in Rajasthan; Markandi (Pati Sonapur) in

Orissa; Chhaya-Mithi Virdi in Gujarat's Bhavnagar district; and Chutka (CNPP) in Madhya Pradesh.[24]

Nuclear Fuel Fabrication

India's main nuclear fuel fabrication complex was established at Hyderabad in 1971. It has both the front end and back end nuclear fuel cycle facilities that include exploration, mining, milling, fuel fabrication, spent fuel reprocessing and other associated facilities. It also has six facilities under safeguards, listed in the Annex to India's Additional Protocol with IAEA, which includes facilities related to fuel fabrication, as part of the civil-military separation. The complex meets the fuel and zircaloy requirements of all the nuclear power reactors in the country. In addition, it manufactures stainless steel tubes for industrial applications.

The complex undertakes refining and conversion of uranium, which is received as magnesium diuranate (yellowcake) and refined to UO^2. The main 1,250 tonnes per year plant fabricates PHWR fuel (which is unenriched). A small (25 tonnes per year) fabrication plant makes fuel for the Tarapur BWRs from imported enriched (2.66% U-235) uranium. Depleted uranium oxide fuel pellets (from reprocessed uranium) and thorium oxide pellets are also made for PHWR fuel bundles. Mixed carbide fuel for FBTR were first fabricated by BARC in 1979.

Heavy water is supplied by DAE's Heavy Water Board. Some US\$ 16 million worth of heavy water was exported to the USA and France in 2013–14. A very small centrifuge enrichment plant—insufficient even for the Tarapur reactors—is operated by DAE's Rare Materials Plant (RMP) at Ratnahalli near Mysore, primarily for military purposes including submarine fuel, but also for research reactors. It started in 1992 as a unit of BARC, and is being expanded to 25,000 SWU (separative work unit) per year. A conversion plant is also being built there at RMP. Some centrifuge R&D is undertaken by BARC at Trombay. In 2011, the DAE announced plans to build an industrial-scale centrifuge complex, the Special Material Enrichment Facility (SMEF), in Chitradurga district, Karnataka, as part of BARC, to serve both civil and naval purposes. But construction had not started until mid-2020. India's enrichment plants are not under international safeguards.

The DAE is setting up a second Nuclear Fuel Complex (NFC)—a PHWR fuel plant at Kota in Rajasthan, next to the Rawatbhata Power Plant—to serve large new reactors. Each of the 700 MWe reactor is likely to need 125 tonne per year of fuel. A third fuel fabrication plant has been is planned, with 1,250 tonne per year capacity, in joint venture with a foreign entity, American, French or Russian or all three, to produce fuel for those reactors. Development of PFBR fuel and plutonium-based fuels and their characterisation has made further progress at Trombay, where high-density thorium oxide fuel pellets for flux flattening of all the new PHWRs are being fabricated. At Kalpakkam-based India Gandhi Centre for Atomic Research (IGCAR), studies have been conducted for the development of fast reactor fuels and cladding materials. Here, a laboratory scale facility was commissioned for the preparation of uranium oxide microspheres by sol-gel method.

Reprocessing

Used fuel from the civil PHWRs is reprocessed by BARC at Trombay, Tarapur and Kalpakkam to extract reactor-grade plutonium for use in the fast breeder reactors. The first 'plutonium plant' was commissioned in 1964 at Trombay, for weapons. Then the Power Reactor Fuel Reprocessing (PREFRE) facility at Tarapur was commissioned in 1979, and in 2010 a second PREFRE plant with 100 tonne per year capacity effectively replaced it. A new Kalpakkam plant (KARP) of some 100 tonne per year was commissioned in 1998 in connection with Indira Gandhi Centre for Atomic Research (IGCAR), though it was shut down over 2003–2009 due to an accident, then upgraded. It is being extended to reprocess FBTR carbide fuel. Apart from this, all reprocessing uses the Purex process. A P3A project is being built to increase the capacity at Kalpakkam.

Partitioning of Purex product in a multi-step solvent extraction process is being undertaken in a demonstration facility at Tarapur. Civil plutonium initially has gone into the FBTR, the amount being estimated at 200–250 kg. More recently most has been for the PFBR, which is expected to require 400 kg per year in full operation. India's civil plutonium stock at the end of 2014 is estimated at about 2.9 tonnes, mostly in connection with the PFBR.

Reprocessing capacity is understood to be about 100 tonnes per year each at Tarapur and at Kalpakkam, total 200 tonnes per year, but actually in operation is about 115 tonnes per year producing 400 kg per year plutonium, all related to the indigenous PHWR programme and not under international safeguards. An away-from-reactor (AFR) fuel storage and another store at

Tarapur are under safeguards from 2012 and 2014 and are listed in the AP Annex. The Power Reactor Thoria Reprocessing Facility (PRTRF) was under construction at BARC in October 2013, and is designed to cope with high gamma levels from U-232. The recovered U-233 will be used in the AHWR Critical Facility. India will reprocess the used PWR fuel from the Kudankulam and other imported reactors and will keep the plutonium. This will be under IAEA safeguards, in new plants.

In April 2010, it was announced that 18 months of negotiations with the US had resulted in agreement to build two new reprocessing plants to be under IAEA safeguards, likely located near Kalpakkam and near Mumbai, possibly Trombay. In July 2010, an agreement was signed with the US to allow reprocessing of US-origin fuel at one of these facilities. Since then, the first Integrated Nuclear Recycle Plant (INRP) with facilities for both reprocessing of used light water reactor fuel of foreign origin, and waste management has been designed. Hindustan Construction Company (HCC) in October 2015 won the Rs 943 crore contract to build this at BARC at Tarapur. The plant will process used fuel from new nuclear power plants, including Gorakhpur 1 and 2 at Haryana, Rajasthan 7 and 8, Kakrapar 3 and 4 and future PHWRs.

In 2003, a facility was commissioned at Kalpakkam to reprocess mixed carbide fuel using an advanced Purex process. In 2010 the AEC said that used mixed carbide fuel from the Fast Breeder Test Reactor (FBTR) with a burn-up of 155 GW d/t was reprocessed in the Compact Reprocessing facility for Advanced Fuels in Lead Cells (CORAL). Thereafter, the fissile material was refabricated as fuel and loaded back into the reactor, thus 'closing' the fast reactor fuel cycle for the FBTR.

Future Expansion

India's Integrated Energy Policy projects need 778 GW installed power capacity by 2032, of which 63 GW of capacity is envisaged to come from the nuclear source. The plan envisages an addition of 4.2 GW from indigenous PHWRs based on natural uranium, 7 GW from PHWRs based on reprocessed uranium from LWR spent fuel, 40 GW from LWRs and the balance through 500 MW/1000 MW FBRs. Other reactors like the Advanced Heavy Water Reactor (AHWR), a technology demonstrator for thorium utilisation and Indian LWR under development are also planned.

Beyond 2032, the main capacity addition is expected to come from metallic fuel-based FBRs that are currently under development. The first of these reactors is expected to come online in next two decades. The integration of 17 LWRs into the three-stage programme, when spent fuel of LWRs is reprocessed to fuel the down-the-line FBRs is crucial for meeting the long-term electricity requirements.

Fast Neutron Reactor

Fast neutron reactors are sodium-cooled pool-type fast nuclear reactors having two primary and two secondary loops, with four steam generators per loop. They produce significantly more energy from natural uranium than thermal reactors and provide big technological advancement in nuclear waste management. They are designed for a 40-year operating lifetime at 75% load factor. The World Nuclear Organisation sees them as being 'poised to become mainstream', because they offer the prospect of vastly increased efficient use of uranium resources and ability to burn actinides which are otherwise the long-lived component of high-level nuclear waste.

Several countries have set up research and development programmes to create improved fast neutron reactors. France has planned to replace half of its present nuclear capacity with fast neutron reactors by 2050. There are about 20 fast neutron reactors around the world, with some of them already supplying electricity commercially.

In India, a 500 MWe PFBR is being constructed at the Madras Atomic Power Station in Kalpakkam in Tamil Nadu. Work on the project had started in 2004, with start-up expected in 2010. But it has repeatedly missed deadline. The government has now told the Parliament that the inordinately delayed PFBR will be 'commissioned and operationalised' in December 2021. The website of BHAVINI, which is building it, has said that the overall construction of the PFBR and commissioning of individual systems has been completed and the integrated commissioning of various systems is steadily progressing. After establishing integrated commissioning of the systems, sodium will be filled in the main vessel and the primary loops. After purification of sodium and the starting of primary sodium pumps and isothermal operations, fuel loading in the core will commence towards the first approach to criticality.

This PFBR has been constructed indigenously with the involvement of some major Indian industries. It will be fuelled by uranium-plutonium mixed oxide (MOX) with a thorium blanket to breed fissile U-233 and uranium. The reactor-grade plutonium will be obtained from PHWRs (already operating in its neighbourhood) via Purex reprocessing. The plutonium content would be 21% and 27% in two different regions of the core. Initial fuel will be MOX pellets, later vibropac fuel may be used.

Its successful commissioning will lead to construction of two more FBRs, in the adjoining site of PFBR at Kalpakkam, and a fleet of future FBRs in other probable sites. Two more such 500 MWe fast reactors have been announced for construction at Kalpakkam, but slightly redesigned by the Indira Gandhi Centre to reduce capital cost. Then four more are planned at another site. Initial FBRs will have mixed oxide fuel or carbide fuel, but these will be followed by metallic fuelled ones to enable shorter doubling time. One of the last of the above six, or possibly the fourth one overall, is to have the flexibility to convert from MOX to metallic fuel (i.e., a dual fuel unit), and it was planned to convert the small FBTR to metallic fuel about 2013. With metal fuel, a 500 MWe unit is expected to produce 2 tonnes of reactor grade plutonium in 8–10 years. The reactor is not under international safeguards.

Following these will be a 1,000 MWe fast reactor using metallic fuel, whose design will be the main part of the Indian nuclear fleet post-2021. A fuel fabrication plant and a reprocessing plant for metal fuels are planned for Kalpakkam, as the Fast Reactor Fuel Cycle Facility (FRFCF) approved for construction in 2013 and contracted in August 2017. A December 2010 scientific and technical cooperation agreement between the AEC and Rosatom is focused on 'joint development of a new generation of fast reactors'.

The PFBR would take India's ambitious thorium programme to Stage 2, and set the scene for eventual full utilisation of the country's abundant thorium to fuel reactors. Six more such fast reactors are envisaged. FBR 1 and 2 of 600 MWe each with oxide fuel have been announced. Initial FBRs would have mixed oxide fuel but these would be followed by metallic-fuelled ones to enable shorter doubling time. They would have a homogeneous core with two enrichment zones of mixed oxide fuel, plus blanket and reflector. Burn-up will be 150 GW d/t and core breeding ratio will be 1:11.

NPCIL, on pattern of the eight-unit Rajasthan plant, intends to set up another five 'nuclear energy parks', each with a capacity for up to eight new-generation reactors of 1,000 MWe or six reactors of 1,600 MWe or

10,000 MWe at a single location by 2032. NPCIL was hoping to be able to start work by 2012 on at least four new reactors at all four sites designated for imported plants, but this did not happen. In mid-2015 it was reported that an additional site could be assigned for a Japanese multi-unit plant. However, apart from the Russian projects under inter-governmental agreement, no overseas reactor vendor has been ready to proceed under India's unique liability arrangements.

About 20 fast neutron reactors (FNR) have already been operating, some since the 1950s, and some supplying electricity commercially. Over 400 reactor-years of operating experience has been accumulated. Fast reactors more deliberately use the U-238 as well as the fissile U-235 isotope used in most reactors. If they are designed to produce more plutonium than the uranium and plutonium they consume, they are called fast breeder reactors (FBRs). But many designs are net consumers of fissile material including plutonium. Fast neutron reactors also can burn long-lived actinides which are recovered from used fuel out of ordinary reactors.

Carbide Fuel

India is also developing mixed carbide fuels for FNRs (U-Pu-C-N-O) that runs on mixed carbide fuel since 1985 (70% PuC and 30% UC). Carbide fuel in the FBTR has demonstrated 165 GW d/t burn-up without failure, and has been reprocessed at a pilot scale. A Demonstration Fast Reactor Fuel Reprocessing Plant (DFRP) is being established to process both MOX and mixed carbide fuels, and a dedicated co-located FRFCF for PFBR is under construction.

Natural uranium contains about 0.7% U-235 and 99.3% U-238. In any reactor some of the U-238 component is turned into several isotopes of plutonium during its operation. Two of these, Pu-239 and Pu-241, undergo fission in the same way as U-235 to produce heat. In an FNR, this process can be optimised so that it 'breeds' fuel. Some U-238 is burned directly with neutron energies above 1 MeV. Hence FNRs can utilise uranium about 60 times more efficiently than a normal reactor. They are however expensive to build and operate, including the reprocessing, and are only justified economically if uranium prices are reasonably high, or on the basis of burning actinides in nuclear wastes. The fast reactor has no moderator and relies on fast neutrons alone to cause fission, which for uranium is less efficient than using slow neutrons. Hence, a fast reactor usually uses plutonium as its basic fuel, since it fissions sufficiently with fast neutrons to keep going. At the same time the number of neutrons produced per Pu-239 fission is 25% more than from uranium, which means that there are enough neutrons (after losses) not only to maintain the chain reaction but also to continually convert U-238 into more Pu-239.

Furthermore, the fast neutrons are more efficient than slow ones during this breeding, due to more neutrons being released per fission. These are the main reasons for avoiding the use of a moderator. The coolant is a liquid metal (normally sodium) to avoid any neutron moderation and provide a very efficient heat transfer medium. So, the fast reactor 'burns' and 'breeds' fissile plutonium. While the conversion ratio (the ratio of new fissile nuclei to fissioned nuclei) in a normal reactor is around 0.6, it may exceed 1.0 in a fast reactor.

In the long term, the AEC envisages its fast reactor programme being 30 to 40 times bigger than the PHWR programme, and initially at least, largely in the military sphere until its 'synchronised working' with the reprocessing plant is proven on an 18- to 24-month cycle. This would be linked with up to 40 GWe of light water reactor capacity, the used fuel feeding 10 times that fast breeder capacity, thus 'deriving much larger benefit out of the external acquisition in terms of light water reactors and their associated fuel'. The 40 GWe of imported LWR capacity multiplied to 400 GWe via FBR would complement 200–250 GWe based on the indigenous three-stage programme of PHWR-FBR-AHWR. Thus, AEC is talking about 500 to 600 GWe of nuclear over the next 50 years or so.

V. NUCLEAR POWER RISKS

When arguing against nuclear power, opponents point to the problems of long-lived nuclear waste and the spectre of rare but devastating nuclear accidents such as those at Chernobyl in 1986 and Fukushima Daiichi in 2011. The deadly Chernobyl disaster in Ukraine happened when flawed reactor design and human error caused a power surge and explosion at one of the reactors. Large amounts of radioactivity were released into the air, and hundreds of thousands of people were forced from their homes. Today, the area surrounding the plant—known as the Exclusion Zone—is open to tourists but inhabited only by the various wildlife species, such as grey wolves, that have since taken over.

In the case of Japan's Fukushima Daiichi, the aftermath of the Tohoku earthquake and tsunami caused the plant's catastrophic failures. Several years on, the surrounding towns struggle to recover, evacuees remain afraid to return, and public mistrust has dogged the recovery effort, despite government assurances that most areas are safe. Other accidents, such as the partial meltdown at Pennsylvania's Three Mile Island in 1979, linger as terrifying examples of nuclear power's radioactive risks. The Fukushima disaster in particular raised questions about safety of power plants in seismic zones, such as Armenia's Metsamor Power Station.

Other issues related to nuclear power include where and how to store the spent fuel, or nuclear waste, which remains dangerously radioactive for thousands of years. Nuclear power plants, many of which are located on or near coasts because of the proximity to water for cooling, also face rising sea levels and the risk of more extreme storms due to climate change.

NPCIL Collaboration with Other State Entities

In February 2016, the government amended the Atomic Energy Act to allow NPCIL to form joint venture companies with other PSUs for involvement in nuclear power generation and possibly other aspects of the fuel cycle. Three joint venture companies involving major PSUs in the energy area have been incorporated and are able to come into effect under the revised legislation—Anushakti Vidhyut Nigam Ltd (NPCIL and NTPC), NPCIL-Indian Oil Nuclear Energy Corporation Ltd, and NPCIL-Nalco Power Company Ltd. NPCIL itself is reported to have about Rs 12,000 crore (US$ 1.8 billion) of investible surplus; three other PSUs, NTPC, IOC and Nalco, are able to contribute about Rs 10,000 crore (US$ 1.5 billion) each to new nuclear projects in which they will have 49% equity. Some of this will be in hard currency, which may be why the focus has shifted from indigenous PHWR plants (which can be paid for in local currency) to new plants with imported LWR technology.

National Thermal Power Corporation (NTPC) Plans

India's largest power company, NTPC in 2007 had proposed building a 2000 MWe nuclear power plant to be in operation by 2017. It would be the utility's first nuclear plant and also the first conventional nuclear plant not built by the 89.5% government-owned NPCIL. This proposal took the form of a joint venture in 2011 with NPCIL holding 51%, and possibly extending to multiple projects utilising local and imported technology, but pending amendment to the Atomic Energy Act. One of the sites earmarked for a pair of 700 MWe PHWR units in Haryana or Madhya Pradesh was considered prospective for the joint venture. NTPC said it aimed by 2014 to have demonstrated progress in 'setting up nuclear power generation capacity', and that the initial 'planned nuclear portfolio of 2,000 MWe by 2017' could be greater. However, in 2012 it indicated a downgrading of its nuclear plans.

NTPC planned to increase its total installed capacity to 70 GWe by 2017 and 128 GWe by 2032, from 47 GWe (74% coal) in 2016. In 2008 it also formed JVs in heavy engineering, with BHEL and Bharat Forge. The former is to explore, secure and execute EPC contracts for power plants and other infrastructure projects in India and abroad, as well as manufacturing and supplying equipment for them. With the 2011 JV with NPCIL, this was reported as also selling India's largely indigenous 220 MWe PHWR reactor units abroad, possibly in contra deals involving uranium supply from countries such as Namibia and Mongolia.

Agreement with Overseas Reactor Vendors

There have been a succession of agreements with Russia's Atomstroyexport to build further VVER reactors. In March 2010 a 'roadmap' for building six more reactors at Kudankulam by 2017 and four more at Haripur after 2017 was agreed, bringing the total to 12. The number may be increased after 2017, in India's Thirteenth Five Year Plan. Associate company Atomenergomash (AEM) set up an office in India with a view to bidding for future work there and in Vietnam, and finalising a partnership with an Indian heavy manufacturer, either L&T or another. A Russian fuel fabrication plant is also under consideration.

In February 2009, Areva signed a memorandum of understanding with NPCIL to build two, and later four more, EPR units at Jaitapur, and a formal contract was expected. This followed the government signing a nuclear cooperation agreement with France in September 2008. Areva says that the EPR has achieved Design Acceptance Certification in India.

In March 2009, GE Hitachi Nuclear Energy signed agreements with NPCIL and BHEL to begin planning to build a multi-unit power plant using

1,350 MWe Advanced Boiling Water Reactors. In May 2009 L&T was brought into the picture.

In April 2010, it was announced that the BHEL-NPCIL joint venture was still in discussion with an unnamed technology partner to build a 1,400 MWe nuclear plant at Chutka in Madhya Pradesh, with Madhya Pradesh Power Generating Company Limited (MPPGCL), the nodal agency to facilitate the execution of the project.

In May 2009, Westinghouse signed a memorandum of understanding with NPCIL regarding deployment of its AP-1000 reactors, using local components (probably from L&T). After a break of three decades, Atomic Energy of Canada Ltd (AECL) was keen to resume technical cooperation, especially in relation to servicing India's PHWRs (though this would now be undertaken by Candu Energy), and there were preliminary discussions regarding the sale of an ACR-1000.

In August 2009, NPCIL signed agreements with Korea Electric Power Co (KEPCO) to study the prospects for building Korean APR-1400 reactors in India. This could proceed following bilateral nuclear cooperation agreements signed in October 2010 and July 2011. The LWRs to be set up by these foreign companies are reported to have a lifetime guarantee of fuel supply.

Near Term Future Developments

In the last seven years, the installed nuclear power capacity has grown from 4,780 MW in 2014 to 6,780 MW by 2021, an increase of over 40%. On progressive completion of the reactors under construction, the nuclear power generation capacity is expected to reach 22,480 MW by 2031, catering 6–9% of India's immediate electricity requirements with comparable tariffs vis-à-vis those of contemporary base-load generating plants of other technologies. If this pace is maintained, nuclear energy can be part of the achievement pathways towards India's target to reduce emissions intensity of its GDP by 45% by 2030.

To give boost to nuclear power generation, the government has brought necessary amendments to the existing legal framework, allowed new industrial players to have joint ventures with NPCIL, and approved new reactor construction in fleet mode besides accelerated domestic uranium production and import from external partners.

Currently, 22 reactors with total capacity of 6,780 MW are in operation in India; 10 reactors, totalling 8,000 MW, are at various stages of construction. Meanwhile, the government has accorded administrative approval and financial sanction for 10 more reactors to be set up in fleet mode whose pre-project activities have commenced, which will add 7,000 MW. It is expected that by 2031, nuclear power generation in India will triple (22,480 MW) from the current level.

To ensure uninterrupted reactor operation, the government has made necessary arrangements to supply adequate quantity of fuel from both domestic and imported sources. The government has accelerated domestic uranium exploration and production process as the current production of uranium is not adequate to meet the annual fuel requirement of uranium-based reactors. The Atomic Minerals Directorate (AMD) for Exploration and Research is carrying out integrated and 'multi-disciplinary field exploration', "employing world's latest technology for airborne geophysical surveys," in around a dozen states in India to accelerate domestic uranium production.[25]

Fusion Breakthrough

The US government has made a breakthrough in the pursuit of producing fusion energy that powers the Sun in a laboratory by using 192 lasers to blast a small cylinder about the size of a pencil eraser that contained a frozen nubbin of hydrogen encased in diamond.

The experiment crossed a critical threshold for fusion as the energy that the fusion reaction generated, 3.15 million joules, exceeded the 2.05 megajoules the lasers pumped out to trigger the reaction. Fusion researchers denote the ratio of output energy to input energy with the letter Q, and this is the first time a fusion reaction surpassed Q = 1. Fusion reactors will have to reach a threshold of Q = 10 before energy generation is practical. This is what fusion experiments around the world, including the massive government-funded projects, ITER in France, and Joint European Torus (JET) in UK, aim for.[26]

Physicists have since the 1950s sought to harness the fusion reaction, but no one had been able to produce more energy from the reaction than it consumes, a milestone known as net energy gain or target gain. The scientific and engineering challenges of controlled fusion are formidable. The US scientists' first fusion reaction in a laboratory setting that actually produced more energy than it took to start the reaction is a high-water mark for fusion research. However, it doesn't mean a bountiful green energy is around the corner. It will still be years, even decades, before fusion power progress bears fruit, and it is still not clear if fusion will ever be cheap enough to radically transform our power grid. At this point it is simply an academic achievement.

Fusion energy is an emissions-free source of power, emits no carbon, produces no long-lived radioactive waste. It can help reduce the need for power plants burning coal and natural gas, which pump billions of tons of planet-warming carbon dioxide into the atmosphere each year. Fusion occurs when two lighter elements like hydrogen or helium merge into a single, heavier element. This nuclear reaction releases a lot of energy. Within the Sun and stars, fusion continually combines hydrogen atoms into helium, producing sunlight and warmth that bathes the planets.

But it's harder to get fusion to occur on Earth, because atomic nuclei are positively charged and therefore repel each other. The Sun's enormous mass produces tremendous pressure that overcomes repulsion, but on Earth, other forces are required. There are two general approaches to fusion: inertial and magnetic confinement. Inertial confinement usually uses lasers to zap a pellet with a lot of power, triggering an explosion that compresses the fusion fuel. That's the method, the US' National Ignition Facility (NIF), which produced the landmark fusion reactions in December 2022, uses. The other approach uses magnetic fields. It's more widespread among companies trying to commercialise fusion energy. NIF is a US$ 3.5 billion US national laboratory project funded to research nuclear weapons for the US. It is not a project designed to produce reliable energy for the grid at the competitive cost.

References

1. *The Economist*, 19 July, 2022.
2. Power Reactor Information System, IAEA, 17 August, 2022.
3. World Nuclear Association, The Nuclear Fuel Report, 2021.
4. Power Technology, 16 February, 2021.
5. World Nuclear Association: Nuclear Power in the World Today, March 2021.
6. World Energy Outlook, 2021.
7. IAEA, 31 August, 2022.
8. 'The History of Nuclear Energy', US Department of Energy/NE-0088 pdf.
9. 'The History of Nuclear Energy', US Department of Energy/NE-0088 pdf.

10. Daniel Yergin, *The Quest*, pp.364–5.

11. Ibid, p.365.

12. Bhabha Atomic Research Centre (BARC), Department of Atomic Energy, Government of India: barc.gov.in.

13. Bucher, RG; India's Baseline Plan for Nuclear Energy self-sufficiency stage, Argonne National Laboratory, 26 March, 2012.

14. Availability of Thorium, Press Information Bureau, Government of India, 10 August, 2011.

15. Thorium-Based NPP (PDF), Department of Atomic Energy, 21 March, 2012.

16. Subramanian, TS (December 1998), 'A Debate Over Breeder Reactors', Vol. 15, No. 25, Frontline, retrieved 8 April, 2012.

17. Niharika Tagotra, India's Ambitious Nuclear Power Plan – And What's Getting in Its Way, The Diplomat, 9 September, 2020.

18. Rahman, Maseeh, 1 November, 2011, 'How Homi Bhabha's Vision Turned India into a Nuclear R&D Leader', *The Guardian*, Mumbai, 1 March, 2012.

19. Dr Sethna, HN, BARC Activities for Indian Nuclear Power Programme.

20. Krivit, Steven; Lehr, Jay H (2011). Nuclear Energy Encyclopaedia: Science, Technology, and Applications. p.89. ISBN 978-1-118-04347-9. Archived from the original on 4 March, 2017.

21. 'Design of World's First Thorium based Nuclear Reactor is Ready', *India Today* magazine, 14 February, 2014.

22. Kate Sullivan, RSiS, 24 March, 2014.

23. Dr Sethna, HN; BARC Activities for Indian Nuclear Power Programme.

24. World Nuclear Association: Nuclear Power in India; January, 2021.

25. *The Times of India*; 6 November, 2022.

26. CNET; Stephen Shankland, 'What the Fusion Energy Breakthrough Really Means', 19 December, 2022.

SECTION III
ELECTRIC MOBILITY

Chapter 10

ELECTRICITY

I. OVERVIEW

Electricity is mother of the modern age. There can be no lighting, no television, no telephone, no computer, no fan, no air conditioning, no medical equipment without electricity. Electricity is all-pervasive in the modern society—it is essential for every kind of trade, commerce and industrial activity.

However, electricity is not a primary energy source like oil, natural gas, coal or renewables. It is a product generated by converting other resources, as it can be made from coal, oil, natural gas, water, wind, sun, even waste and garbage.

India is the world's third largest producer as well as the consumer of electricity. In October 2022, the country's national electric grid had an installed capacity of 405.76 GW, which generated 1,491.86 BU (billion units) against the demand of 1,379.81 BU. Fossil fuels made up 58.2% (204.1 GW) of the total capacity, while non-fossil fuels (including nuclear) contributed 41.8%.[1]

India's electricity sector is dominated by coal, which makes up nearly half of the country's installed electricity capacity. As of October 2022, its share in the total installed capacity was 50.3% (204.1 GW), followed by solar (14.6%), hydro (12.7%), wind (10.2%) and natural gas (6.1%).[2]

Growth of Electricity in India

Electricity was introduced in India by the British 10 years after it was introduced in London and after 17 years in New York. P W Fleury & Co used light bulbs to demonstrate electricity on the streets of Calcutta (now Kolkata) in 1879. But it was another British company, Kilburn & Co, which secured license from London-based Indian Electric Co for Calcutta electric lighting and electrify the Harrison Road (now MG Road) in 1889. This was the first street to have electric light bulbs in India. A month later the company was renamed as Calcutta Electric Supply Corporation. But the control of the company continued to rest in London even after India had attained

Independence from the British in 1947. It was only in 1970 that the company's control was transferred from London to Calcutta. The first generating station was Sidrabong Power Station set up by the Darjeeling municipality in 1896 with a capacity of 130 kW. It was a hydroelectric installation which powered the Darjeeling tea plantations.

Initially, electricity did not catch the imagination of the people. Advertisements in the newspapers, pamphlets and on blotting papers were used to promote the use of electricity for lighting and heating. Consumers of electricity were mainly public utilities, industries, banks, clubs and few private residences. By the early 1900s, electricity-operated trams were introduced replacing horse-driven carriages and ceiling fans started being used replacing hand-held punkahs (hand fans). Gas lighting became increasingly obsolete. The rate at which the company supplied electricity to consumers was Rs 1 per unit, which was comparable to the price in London at that time.

In Bombay, the municipality entered into an agreement in 1882 with the Eastern Electric Light and Power Company to provide electric lighting in the Crawford Market and on some roads. But the company went into liquidation in the following year after holding the first demonstration at Crawford Market. In 1899, Bombay Tramway Company Ltd, which had been running the horsecar tramway service in the city since 1874, applied for a licence to run electrically operated trams. But due to the high costs, the project was abandoned. In 1905, a newly-formed Bombay Electric Supply & Tramway Co Ltd (B.E.S. & T) was granted the monopoly for electric supply and running an electric tram service. It bought the assets of the Bombay Tramway Company for Rs. 9,850,000.[3] Two years later in 1907, the first electric tram debuted in the city. Later that year, a 4,300 kW (5,800 hp) steam power generator was commissioned at Wari Bunder. In 1916, the Tata Power group began purchasing power and by 1925 all power generation was outsourced from Tata.[4] In 1947, the B.E.S. & T became an undertaking of the Municipal Corporation and rebranded itself to 'Bombay Electric Supply & Transport (BEST)'. In 1995 the organisation was renamed to 'Brihanmumbai Electric Supply & Transport (BEST)' alongside Bombay being renamed as Mumbai. It now operates as an autonomous body under the Municipal Corporation.

Bangalore (now Bengaluru) got its first electric light in 1905. Hydroelectric power was harnessed from the Cauvery Falls at Shivanasamudra to power mining operations at Kolar Gold Fields (KGF). Transmission lines passing through Bengaluru to KGF supplied electricity to light up roads in the city. Before the arrival of electricity, kerosene lamps dotted the streets. In the same year, Delhi too got power from a set up by an English company, M/s John Fleming, with both generation and distribution responsibilities. Electricity generation in Madras (Chennai) was confined to a few tiny plants in tea estates run on water power and to a small hydroelectric station at Kattery near Coonoor until about 1908. In 1927 the government of the Madras Presidency created electricity department which built a bigger Pykara Hydroelectric Power Station. The initial installed capacity of the plant was 70 MW and it was commissioned in 1933.

The electricity sector in India was firmly controlled by the British colonialists. Foreign companies like P W Fleury & Co, Kilburn & Co and Calcutta Electricity Supply Corporation produced and supplied electricity to major cities, offices and ports. Electrification during the period was limited to only cities and urban areas. The Electricity Act, 1910, also framed by the British, provided the basic framework for the industry, like licensing rules for generating and distributing electricity and defining the relationship between the licensee and the consumer.

Post-Independence (1947-to Current Period)

In 1948, the independent India enacted the Electricity Act, 1948, creating state electricity boards (SEB) for each state in the Indian Union and entrusting them with the responsibility of building and managing generation, transmission and distribution facilities of power in their respective states. But SEBs fared miserably due to mismanagement, inefficiency, corruption and undue political interference in their operations, and started incurring losses by the 1970s. The politics of power subsidies for the agricultural sector became a favourite strategy of politicians to woo farmers' vote. This gimmick was first used during the 1977 elections in Andhra Pradesh, when the Congress party offered flat-rate tariffs (tariffs based on capacity of the pump rather than on measured consumption) to farmers as an election promise to help get re-elected. This opened the floodgate of freebies and handouts, including free power, being promised by competing political parties during elections. In recent years, agriculturally rich Punjab and Haryana states have been providing free electricity to farmers.

"The low tariffs for agricultural sector were sought to be covered through higher tariffs on industrial and commercial consumers (cross-subsidisation). But the distortions of such a high magnitude in cross-subsidisation, increasing theft and leakages, lack of accountability, loss of revenue and misreporting and mounting losses of the SEBs made them increasingly dependent on budgetary allocations from their respective governments reducing their ability to add generating capacity, and most importantly to carry out the periodic maintenance and upkeep of their distribution assets."[5]

Disappointed at the dismal performance and deteriorating financial state of the SEBs the Union Government set up two major public sector utilities, National Thermal Power Corporation Limited (NTPC), for thermal generation and National Hydro Power Corporation Limited (NHPC), for hydroelectricity generation. They were also expected to facilitate power sharing between different regions. This required setting up a pan-India transmission network interlinking different plants into a common web to transmit electricity from one state to another.

From this was born the idea of regional grids, which allowed the trade and free flow of electricity between states. Individual state grids were interconnected to form five regional grids covering mainland India—northern, eastern, western, north-eastern and southern. These links were established to enable transmission of surplus electricity between states in each region. In the 1990s, the Indian government began planning for a national grid. Regional grids were initially interconnected by asynchronous high-voltage direct current (HVDC) back-to-back links facilitating the limited exchange of regulated power. The links were subsequently upgraded to higher capacity synchronous links.[6] The first interconnection of regional grids was established in October 1991 when the north-eastern and eastern grids were interconnected. The western grid was interconnected with these grids in March 2003. The northern grid was also interconnected in August 2006, forming a central grid that was synchronously connected and operating at one frequency. The sole remaining regional grid, the southern grid, was synchronously interconnected to the central grid on 31 December, 2013 with the commissioning of the 765 kV Raichur-Solapur transmission line, establishing the national grid.[7]

1991 Reforms

In 1991, the government allowed domestic as well as foreign entrepreneurs to invest in power generation as part of Narasimha Rao's government historic economic reforms. Prior to this, except for a handful of private sector licensees operating in certain urban areas, SEBs and central government-owned NTPC and NHPC controlled generation and transmission of electricity. However, the power to fix tariff was vested in the government by an amendment to the 1948 Act. In mid-1990s, a decision was taken to split the generation, transmission and distribution activities into separate entities to allow the SEBs to address the problems of each wing in a focussed way.

The focus was to sell electricity like businesses sell their commodities. The generation aspect became analogous to manufacturing, the transmission was analogous to warehousing in bulk and similarly, the distribution would become analogous to the retail sale. This was a sharp evolution from the welfare model to the business model where electricity was earlier seen more as a necessity rather than a commodity when free electricity and subsidies were given, and currently it has to be packed and sold like a commodity with chances of prices increasing as well.[8]

In the late 1990s, the government offered a number of incentives to attract private capital in generation, but their response remained tepid, with independent power producers (IPPs) contributing less than 5% to the capacity expansion and power generation. The main reason for this was the failure of SEBs to pay the IPP's dues on time. In 1998, two regulatory commissions were set up to regulate generation and transmission tariffs of electricity at the central and state level. But quick-fix measures proved inadequate to shortage of electricity and remedy the woeful state of the SEBs.

In 2003, the Atal Bihari Vajpayee government came out with a comprehensive Electricity Act 2003 that repealed the Electricity Act of 1910, Electric Supply Act of 1948 and Electricity Regulatory Commission Act of 1998. The Act allowed, "Open access in transmission, phased open access in distribution, mandatory SERCs, license-free generation and distribution, power trading and mandatory metering." It also allowed new producers to construct captive generation plants (plants serving electricity to a plant constructed by that same company to meet their energy needs). The Act removed the biggest obstacle in the path of IPPs-obligatory power sales to SEBs and provided for appellate tribunals for disposal of appeals against orders of regulatory commissions. This led to a spurt in private sector participation in power generation and distribution sector. A 2014 Amendment to 2003 Act made it mandatory for coal and lignite based thermal generators to produce 10% of thermal power installed capacity as renewable energy. The statutory changes provided made in the Act encouraged almost all major business houses in the country to invest in the power sector. Some of the big names engaged in electricity generation, transmission and distribution business are Tata Power, Adani Power, Reliance Power (ADAG), Torrent Power, Suzlon, GVK Power, Calcutta Electric Supply Corporation (CESC) and Jaiprakash Power.

Impact of Reforms

The reforms had tremendous impact on capacity addition in the power sector. From 84 GW in 1996–97, the installed capacity rose nearly five times to 409.16 GW in November 2022. The private sector played a huge role in capacity addition; as of 30 November, 2022, it contributed 50.2% (205.23 GW) to the total installed capacity, while the central sector lagged behind with 24.2% (90 GW) and the state sector with 25.6% (104.9 GW) share. Renewables' contribution is growing rapidly; as on 30 November, 2022, the installed capacity of renewables, including large hydro, wind, solar, biomass and biomass waste, stood at 40.7% (166.32 GW) and nuclear at 1.7% (6.8 GW). The government aims to scale up the non-fossil fuels' share in the country's energy basket to 500 GW or 50% by 2030. A continuous decline in the plant load factor (PLF) has, however, been a matter of concern. From 77.5% in 2009–10 to 55.99% in 2019–20 it has been a huge slump, probably a result of erratic supply of coal to coal-fired plants and natural gas to gas-based plants. The fall has been more pronounced in the case of private and state sector plants wherein PLF has dived from 83.9% to 54.64% and 70.9% to 50.24% respectively between 2009–10 and 2019–20.[9]

Transmission

Prior to the launch of reforms, only regional grids existed, and they were the monopoly of the SEBs. In 1998, the transmission, generation and distribution were three distinct activities and private players were invited to invest in them. For a long time, entrepreneurs hesitated, but private players were working on dozens of transmission projects. In 2014, the national grid was launched, connecting all power stations and major substations of India through a high-voltage electricity transmission network and ensuring that electricity generated anywhere in mainland India could be used to satisfy demand anywhere. Today, the national grid of India is one of the largest operational synchronous grids in the world with the installed inter-regional transmission capacity of over 1,50,000 cKm (circuit kilometres).

The national grid is owned, operated and maintained by the Power Grid Corporation of India, a PSU, comprising roughly 1,53,635 cKm and 243 EHVAC and HVDC substations, that provide total transformation capacity of 3,67,097 mega volt ampere (MVA). Some of the major stations owned by it include the Vizag back-to-back HVDC converter station, the Chandrapur back-to-back HVDC converter station, the India-Sri Lanka HVDC Interconnection and the Talcher–Kolar HVDC system. There are also synchronous interconnections to Bhutan, and asynchronous links with Bangladesh, Myanmar and Nepal.[10] An undersea interconnection to Sri Lanka (India-Sri Lanka HVDC Interconnection) has also been proposed. A proposed interconnection between Myanmar and Thailand would facilitate the creation of a power pool and enable trading among all Bay of Bengal Initiative for Multi-Sectoral Technical and Economic Cooperation (BIMSTEC) nations.[11]

Work is now under way to increase the inter-regional power transfer capacity further to 1,18,050 MW and 3.8 lakh MVA of additional substations to cater to annual energy requirement of 1,566 BU and peak load demand of 226 GW by 2022. The creation of 175 GW renewable capacities, which are intermittent and unpredictable, is seen to necessitate a significant ramp up in power transmission infrastructure. Inadequate transmission infrastructure has been a longstanding impediment to renewable power developers, often delaying project commissioning. This has already forced the government to reduce capacities offered in wind auctions by more than 50%.[12]

Distribution

However, electricity grids could prove to be a weak link in the transformation of the power sector, with implications for the reliability and security of electricity supply. Power distribution is a crucial link in the electricity supply chain. It comes at the point where transmission leaves. It is responsible for supply and distribution of energy to consumers (industry, commercial, agriculture, domestic, etc.). India produces enough 24 x 7 'Power for All', but distribution companies (discoms) fail to buy it from generators and deliver to customers 24 x 7 adequately because of their poor finances, mismanagement, inefficiency, pilferage, low metering, under-recoveries, high transmission and distribution (T&D) losses and chronic debt burdens.

A March 2020 report of the ADB Institute reveals that thanks to the regulated price and general mismanagement of the network, India's distribution companies lose around Rs 360 (US$ 4.63) on every megawatt per hour of electricity they deliver—equivalent to roughly 10% of the retail price. Spread that across a market generating more than 1.5 billion MW hours per year, and the losses quickly mount up. Total debt in the sector now amounts to Rs 4.3 lakh crore. A Bloomberg survey adds that out of 45 Indian electricity companies, of which it had the data, just two were covering their cost of capital—KKV Agro Powers Ltd, a tiny renewables developer and PTC India Ltd, a power-trading business set up by the government.[13] The ailing state-owned power Discoms continue to hamper the efficient functioning of the generation and transmission sectors and also renewables. As of May 2020, the Discoms had accumulated massive overdue payments to generators of Rs 1,16,340 crore (US$ 16 billion), creating an immense liquidity crunch across India's entire power sector, which, in turn, has been undermining India's banking system integrity and foreign investment inflows.

II. UDAY: A WAY TO REJUVENATE DISCOMS

Over the years, governments have launched a number of schemes aimed at improving the operations and financial health of discoms, such as Accelerated Power Development Programme (APDRP 2001); Restructured-Accelerated Power Development Programme (R-APDRP); Integrated Power Development Scheme (IPDS 2008); Deen Dayal Upadhyay Gram Jyoti Yojana (DDUGJY); Sahaj Bijli Har Ghar Yojana (SAUBHAGYA) and National Smart Grid Management project (NSGM). But the segment continues to remain a resource drain on the economy. In its latest move, in November 2015, the Modi government launched an ambitious Ujjwal Discom Assurance Yojana (UDAY) to pull the Discoms out of their financial morass, improve PLF of generating plants and reduce operating losses. UDAY is by far, Modi government's most radical reform to breathe a new energy in the sector. Besides stipulating a phased takeover of Discom debt by state governments, the scheme targets improving their operational efficiency, reducing the cost of power purchase and enforcing fiscal discipline through alignment with state finances.

The scheme envisaged the states to take over 75% of the Discom debts by 30 September, 2015, in two tranches—the first 50% in FY 2015–16 and the second 25% in FY 2016–17—by issuing non-statutory liquidity ratio (SLR) and state development loan (SDL) bonds and transfer the proceeds to Discoms in a mix of grant, loan and equity. For the remaining 25 of the debts, the Discoms were supposed to issue their own bonds, backed by the home states or re-priced by banks/financial institutions at interest rates not exceeding bank base rates +0.10%. Balance losses were to be financed through state bonds or Discom bonds backed by state guarantees.[14]

As part of the UDAY's financial restructuring of Discoms, state bonds worth a total of Rs 5,01,219 crore had been issued to reduce the debts by saving on the interest burden amounting to Rs 250–300 billion per year. As a result of state takeover of Discom liabilities, there was a 'significant' surge in states' debts which were 'expected to reach Rs 52.58 trillion by the end of March 2020 or almost 25% of GDP', according to a Reserve Bank of India (RBI) report. The central bank, in its annual report on state finances, said the scope of debt restructuring was larger under UDAY than under earlier programmes as state governments took over 75% of the outstanding liabilities of Discoms in the form of grants or equity. (The earlier financial restructuring schemes were 'One Time Settlement (OTS)' launched in 2003 and the Financial Restructuring Plan (FRP) in 2012.) States have now been asked to reduce AT&C losses of their discoms and also reduce the average cost of supply-average revenue realised (ACS-ARR) gap which will earn them additional net borrowing space of 0.25% of the respective gross state domestic product in FY 2021.

Financial Losses

UDAY aimed to substantially reduce the overall Discom losses from Rs 514.80 billion in FY 2015–16 to Rs 200 billion by 2018 (as projected by the Ministry of Power), and Aggregate Technical and Commercial (AT&C) losses from 26% in 2015–16 to 15% in 2018–19. According to a Ministry of Power report on UDAY, state Discom losses came down from Rs 515.62 billion in FY 2016 to Rs 151.32 billion and AT&C losses from 20.81% in FY 16 to 18.8% in FY 18. ACS-ARR per unit of power gap fell from Rs 0.6 per unit in FY 16 to Rs 0.17 per unit in FY 18. Billing efficiency rose from 81.57% to 83.86%, but collection efficiency slid from 97.09% to 96.84%. Power purchase cost came down slightly from Rs 4.22 to Rs 4.19 during this period.

However, losses started to rise again from 2019. Overall losses grew again to Rs 280.36 billion in FY 2019 from Rs 151.32 billion in FY 2018 (85.3%)

and ACS-ARR gap to 0.27 per unit from 0.17. Power purchase cost rose to Rs 4.42 per unit from Rs 4.19 during this period. According to the UDAY portal, AT&C losses were 18.9% and ACS-ARR gap was Rs 0.42 per unit at the end of FY 20. The only silver lining was an improvement in billing and collection efficiency (84.31% and 97.03% respectively), which may be attributed to the introduction of smart metering.[15]

Aggregate Technical & Commercial Loss (AT&C)

The UDAY scheme ran from November 2015 to March 2019. It was projected that a reduction of AT&C losses from 26% in 2015–16 to 15% for March 2019 would yield around Rs 550 billion in these four years, which would substantially wipe out the past losses. But this did not happen as the AT&C loss at all-India level was just 18.19% in FY 2019, far short of the targetted 15%.

At the state-level, in 2018, 14 Discoms reported loss reduction below the target level of 15%, eight of which were in Gujarat, Karnataka and Andhra Pradesh. But Discoms in Uttar Pradesh, Haryana, Madhya Pradesh, Punjab and Rajasthan either recorded increase or maintained significantly high AT&C losses.[16]

ACS-ARR (Average Cost of Supply-Average Revenue Realised) Per Unit of Power Gap

The January 2019 newsletter on UDAY website shows that the ACS-ARR gap of Rs 0.58 per unit in 2015–16 came down to Rs 0.17 per unit in 2017–18, with an estimated reduction of Rs 360 billion in book loss overall. However, the national dashboard of UDAY website depicts the ACS-ARR gap to be Rs 0.33 per unit as on December 2018 after tariff revisions for 25 out of 27 states.[17] These are the tariff revisions by respective state regulators that resulted in 0.33 per unit ACS-ARR gap—timing of regulatory orders is during the year up to December 2018. According to Policy Research Studies (PRS, an independent institute to make MPs and MLAs better informed about the Indian legislative process) the national average for AT&C losses has now come down to around 19% in 2019–20 from 25% in 2012–13. In countries such as UK and US, AT&C losses are about 6–7%. The Modi government wants to bring it down to 15% by 2021–22.

Revenue

- The improvement of 1% in the billing efficiency resulted in an increase of Rs 54.03 billion in revenue (including subsidised consumers) at national-level in FY 2018. It contributed only 8% to the total revenue increase, but indicates improvement in the internal operations of Discoms.
- Tariff hikes contributed Rs 225.3 billion, a 34% revenue increase in FY 2018. This can be attributed to proactive actions of both regulators and Discoms across states, but this does not reflect the improved operational efficiency of Discoms.
- Higher energy supply contributed Rs 280.53 billion, an increase of 42%, in the total revenue of FY 2018. The Discoms supplied 824 billion units in FY 2018 compared to 694 billion units in FY 2016. However, the cost of higher sales was not fully recovered due to tariffs being below cost, reflective level (ACS-ARR gap widening).

The total outstanding dues of Discoms as of February 2019 stood at Rs 418.81 billion, according to data from 58 Discoms as per 17 participating generation companies (GENCOs). This included Rs 267.55 billion overdue amounts. Around 51.84% of the overdue amounts were payable to private generators and 38.71% to NTPC.[18] Among the state Discoms lagging in their payments (average 600 days), were Uttar Pradesh, Rajasthan, Madhya Pradesh, Punjab, Haryana, Karnataka, Andhra Pradesh and Tamil Nadu. States making timely payments are Gujarat, West Bengal, Jharkhand, Orissa, Chhattisgarh and Himachal Pradesh. The payment delays create liquidity crunch for Discoms, who, in turn, fail to pay GENCOs.

A Fresh Bailout

The festering problem led the government to come out with yet another bailout package worth Rs 90,000 crore (US$ 11.94 billion) in May 2020 to enable Discoms to pay off their outstanding dues to generators and transmission companies (transcos). The Discoms owed Rs 1,08,387 crore to central public sector power generation companies, transmission companies, independent power producers and renewable energy generators at the end of April 2020. This was one-time emergency liquidity injection infusion. The state-run Power Finance Corporation (PFC) and Rural Electrification

Corporation (REC) raised the cash from the market and gave it to Discoms against their receivables and state government guarantees. The state government were also made to commit that they would take concrete action to reform their power sector by introducing direct subsidy transfer, reducing cross-subsidies and rolling out smart metres. Union Power Minister RK Singh told the Rajya Sabha that as of mid-September 2020, loans totalling Rs 70,590 crore out of the package had been sanctioned and Rs 24,742 crore disbursed.

This is not the first bailout for Discoms to pull them out of their financial mess. In the past two decades, at least four bailout packages had been launched by the Centre to enable to manage their finances. But they have failed to sort out their mess, and continue to remain in heavy debts. The situation is worse in respect of state-run Discoms. A CEA report issued in September 2022 showed the net worth of all public sector Discoms put together stood at a negative Rs 61,757 crore, while that of the private sector, it was a positive Rs 24,965 crore.

III. WHAT AILS THE DISCOMS?

It is a peculiar situation. The crux of the problem, which continues to ail discoms despite the various measures taken in the past is revenue deficit. The cost at which discoms procure power is almost always higher than the revenue that they make from tariff charged to consumers. There are two reasons for this—technical losses and gap between average cost of power supplied and average realisable revenue. The former is caused because of loss of energy while transmission through dissipation in conductors, transformers and other equipment, and the latter because of the uneconomic tariff that does not cover even cost of procurement of power.

Improving these two measures (that is, reducing the technical losses and ACS-ARR gap), along with other operational indicators like feeder metering were part of the UDAY bailout. States even adhered to tariff hikes to an extent that were mandatory to be eligible for relief under the UDAY scheme. The inherent problem is the lopsided nature of the tariff structure. Domestic consumers are charged a tariff lower than industrial or commercial consumers. Agricultural consumers are not charged tariff in many states across India. The states also remit money to Discoms to bear the subsidy burden.

The thing to keep in mind is the share of power consumption by different types of consumers. Industrial consumers make up nearly 42% of India's power consumption, followed by domestic consumers (24%) and agricultural consumers (18%). Commercial consumers make up 9% of India's total power consumption. During Covid 19-induced lockdown, domestic consumption led to an increase in power consumption in May-July 2020. But this was insufficient to make up for the loss of revenue which resulted from the unprecedented slowdown in industrial consumption due to the lockdown. The Discoms finances that were already at the edge, deteriorated further making matters worse for power developers. The latest bailout package was a much-needed help to tide over the crisis. But it barely scratches the surface on issues plaguing the beleaguered electricity sector. Unless the state governments move to radically reform the way the Discoms operate, they will continue to run on losses no matter how much financial aid is provided.

Under-Utilised Capacities

While power producers are sitting on thousands of megawatts of under-utilised capacities, consumers are facing frequent power cuts, load shedding and fluctuating supplies. Historically, inadequate generation capacity had been the key contributor to the power deficit. However, now after the participation of private investors in the sector following the Electricity Act of 2003, which opened the sector to private players, has led to the buildout of surplus generation capacities. During 2008–2018 capacities grew at a CAGR of 11% compared to demand at 6%. As of July 2020, India had an installed generation capacity of 372 GW and peak demand of just about 190 GW, meaning it could produce enough power to supply 26,303,084 households and tens of millions industrial and commercial consumers and offices in the country. But ironically India is one of the poorest electricity-served countries in the world, with low per capita electricity consumption of 1,181 kWh, compared with the world average consumption of 2,674 kWh.[19]

Reason for low consumption is certainly not the lack of inadequate generation capacity. An overzealous buildout by both public and private firms, lured by easy bank credits (70% debt and 30% being the norm) led to creation of 99,209 MW of additional capacity surpassing the target of 88,537 MW between 2012 and 2017. The new capacities developed by India over the five years through 2018 were equivalent to 50 nuclear power stations, accounting for 13% of the increase in generation worldwide.[20] Private sector's share in the overall installed capacity rose from just 13% in 2007 to 48% in 2020. Renewable energy capacity also doubled since 2015 to almost 23% of the installed capacity of utilities in 2020, and is now poised to reach about 50% by 2030. The greatest push to the renewable energy sector comes from Modi's commitment at the November 2021 UN Climate Summit (COP 26) at Glasgow that India would increase its non-fossil fuel production capacity to 500 GW to meet up to 50% of its energy demand by 2030. Power Minister RK Singh speaking at a conference of the Confederation of Indian Industries (CII) that India would far exceed the target set by the prime minister and would, in fact, have 65% of its installed power capacity from non-fossil fuel sources by 2030. "We already have 170 GW of renewable energy capacity and 80 GW capacity is under construction."[21] The under-construction capacity would be ready to generate power by 2026, according to CEA estimates.

However, actual production has not been commensurate with the increased capacity of power. Numerous bottlenecks plaguing the sector have kept power plants from operating at their capacity, resulting in frequent load-shedding and intermittent and unreliable electricity supplies. Millions of households use battery storage UPS as back-ups in case of load shedding. The government claims that every business and household has been grid-electrified through its rural electrification and 'Power for All' programmes, but still billions kilo-watt of electricity is generated annually by diesel generator sets that consume nearly millions of tonnes of diesel oil.

Key reasons for low utilisation of generation capacity:

(a) **Coal:** Lack of fuel is one of the main causes of the stress in the power sector. India draws more than 70% of its electricity from coal. But according to a top government bureaucrat, secretary at the Ministry of Power SC Garg, about Rs 5 trillion investment in coal-based power plants in India was in jeopardy due to the dry fuel shortage. "Many of our coal-based power plants in power sector are today gasping for breath. Some of them are in National Company Law Tribunal (NCLT, is a court where companies are dragged by banks for defaulting on repayment of debts for bankruptcy proceedings), many are producing just 15 to 20% of their capacity and others are not producing at all."[22]

As per the Ministry of Power, the PLF has significantly dropped over the past 10 years from 77.5% in 2009–10 to 56% in 2019–20, with the private power plants having much lower PLFs of 55.69% which they blame on poor coal supplies. At least 31 GW of potential coal power were sitting idle due to lack of supply or purchasing agreements with state distribution companies. This paradigm shift is one of the reasons for the reduction in demand for thermal assets. Rating agency CRISIL in a report last year notified of 60% fall in capacity addition in thermal power generation over the next five years. The government has to be more realistic while establishing more coal plants. It should ensure adequate coal supplies and 100% PLF.

The government believes that close to 290 mt of coal could be produced annually from the mines allotted to the power sector. But they are producing just about 15 to 20 mt. This has created a wide hiatus between the demand and supply, forcing the country to import coal, both thermal and coke. According to government statistic, coal is one the five top commodities imported by India. In 2019–20, the import of thermal coal, mainly for power generation, jumped 12.6% to 197.84 mt. However, coking coal import, which is used mainly for steel production, fell marginally to 51.33 mt from 51.63 mt in 2018–19, reflecting a similar decline in steel output. India produces around 730–740 mt at home and imports about 230–250 mt to satisfy a demand of close to 1 bt of coal annually. In 2019–20 the total production of coal of the country was 729.10 mt and imports 249.2 mt.[23]

(b) **Natural gas:** Shortage of natural gas is another major factor crippling the operation of gas-based power plants. More than half of India's capacity to generate power from natural gas is not being used due to lack of gas, putting plants on the verge of becoming non- performing assets, according to a parliamentary panel. The Power Ministry has classified 31 of the country's 64 gas-based power plants in 'stranded', of which one is owned by the central government, with a capacity of 1,967 MW, six by states (2,665.30 MW) and 24 by private developers (9,673 MW). Based on the assumption that there would be plenty of cheap domestic gas available after the start-up of Mukesh Ambani's Reliance Industry's Krishna-Godavari-D6 (KG-Dhirubhai 6) gas project, governments and private investors had poured in billions of dollars to set up 25 GW of gas-fired capacity. According to a parliamentary standing committee report on energy, investments ranging from Rs 4–5 crore per MW had been made into these stranded gas-based projects, out of which around 70–80% of the capital cost was financed by banks.

However, none of the gas-fired plant operated at its economically viable capacity (85%) due to the shortage of gas. The average domestic gas supplied to gas-based power plants during 2017–18 was only 25.71 mmscmd, which is 70% short of the allocation. Due to this shortfall, gas-based power PLF has shrunk 43% points since 2009–10 to 24% in 2017–18. PLF measures a power plant's output to its capacity. KG-D6 was expected to provide 80 mmscmd by the end of 2009, followed by subsequent increases. But production declined to 5.5 mmscmd in 2017–18 from 55.35 mmscmd in 2010–11, and now the field is shut down. Thus, dozens of gas-based power plants with a capacity of 14,305 MW remain 'stranded' due to the non-availability of domestic gas and high cost of imported supply. The recent collapse of the international oil and gas market has thrown a lifeline to these plants. Plant operators are looking to revive their plants.

(c) **Transmission bottlenecks:** Transmission forms a critical link in the power sector value chain. But it has failed to grow in tandem with the growth of generation capacity due to inadequate investment. As a thumb rule, for every dollar invested in power generation, at least 50 cents should be invested in power transmission.[24] Over the last five- or six-years India's power generation rose more than 50% to 372 GW, but transmission capacity grew by less than 30% to 60,790 MVA. One of the major reasons for the shortage electricity supply or erratic supply is the inadequate transmission capacity, not matching the generation capacities and load requirements.

As of August 2019, the total transmission line length stood at 4,17,944 cKm, the alternating current (AC) substation capacity at 9,21,118 MVA and the high voltage direct current (HVDC) substation capacity at 22,500 MW. Between 2011–12 and 2018–19, the line length grew at a CAGR of 7% and AC substation capacity at about 11.9%. The interregional transmission capacity also grew significantly over the years to 99,050 MW as of March 2019. Significantly, 24,000 MW of this capacity was added in the past two years. As a result, interregional power transfer increased from 138 BUs in 2016–17 to 182 BUs 2018–19.

In recent years, private participation in the transmission segment has also increased significantly, with a share of 7.4% in total line length during 2018–19, up from 3.3% in 2011–12, and a share of 3.7% in substation capacity, up from a mere 0.5%. That said, Power Grid Corporation of India Ltd (Power Grid) continues to dominate the country's transmission sector with 1,58,833 cKm of lines and 3,48,356 MVA of capacity. Over 99% of people who have gained access in India since 2000 have done so as a result of grid extension, the focus of government measures. The government has more recently been targetting mini-grid and standalone solar home systems to deliver access to some of the hardest-to-reach homes.[25]

Going forward, an investment of Rs 2.6 trillion is required in transmission alone to meet the future peak load, which is expected to reach 234 GW by 2021–22. Grid expansion will also be driven by the government's ambitious plan to scale up renewable energy to 175 GW by 2022. The private sector is expected to play an important role in achieving the country's grid expansion targets as competitive bidding gains momentum at both interstate and intra-state levels.

Advanced technologies are being deployed at various levels to make the grid smarter and robust. The strengthening of power system operations has become paramount for dealing with the intermittency associated with large-scale renewable energy integration into the grid as well as the altered load profiles likely to be triggered by the government's e-mobility programme. Power Line provides an overview of the recent trends and developments in the power transmission segment.

Green Energy Corridors (GEC)

For the integration of 175 GW of renewable energy by 2022, Power Grid along with other involved state utilities is undertaking the Green Energy Corridors (GEC) project to connect new solar and wind capacity. Under GEC I, where Power Grid received long-term access applications for 12 GW, about 9,400 cKm and 19,000 MVA of substation capacity is targetted to be added at the intra-state level and 3,200 cKm and 17,000 MVA (across six substations) at the interstate level. Most of the schemes under GEC I have been commissioned at the interstate level while several intra-state lines are under construction.

Under GEC II, transmission schemes for evacuation from 34 ultra-mega solar power parks with capacity totalling 20 GW have been planned. Of these, 13 solar parks (9.2 GW) have been identified for evacuation through the Inter-State Transmission System (ISTS). Further, Power Grid is responsible for the implementation of the transmission system for eight solar parks (7.2 GW) entailing 1,870 cKM of lines and five substations of 13,500 MVA. So far, the implementation has been completed for three solar parks (4,250 MW) by Power Grid.

Apart from this, the central government has approved transmission schemes of around Rs 432 billion for renewable energy zones with a potential capacity of 66.5 GW. These will be implemented in two phases. Under Phase-I, transmission projects for 28 GW of renewable capacity will be developed at an investment of Rs 168 billion. The remaining 38.5 GW will be developed under Phase-II at an investment of Rs 264 billion. Transmission projects under the first part of Phase-I were completed in March 2020.

Technology Focus

In July 2018, Power Grid in collaboration with GE T&D India Ltd commissioned the wide area monitoring system (WAMS) for the northern region (NR) grid. This marked the first leg of a mega grid stabilisation project (unified real time dynamic state measurement) and will enable Power Grid to monitor power flow across 110 substations in the NR grid and respond to fluctuations within a fraction of a second. Once fully commissioned in all five regional grids, the WAMS solution will be the world's largest, comprising of 1,184 phasor measurement units and 34 control centres, with 350 substations. Meanwhile, to ensure the availability of uninterrupted quality power, Power Grid commissioned a 400 kV static synchronous compensator (STATCOM), with a dynamic swing range of 600 MVAr (megavolt ampere reactive power) and 250 MVAr mechanically switched components, at its substation in Rourkela, Odisha, during 2018.

To ensure system stability and grid security, 11 renewable energy management centres are being set up at the regional, state and national levels. Further, 14 STATCOMs (11,350 MVAr), four static VAR (volt-amps reactive power) compensators (2,500 MVAr) and 48 fixed series capacitors and thyristor-controlled series compensators are planned to be deployed.

Strengthening Cross Border Links

In January 2019, India and Nepal agreed to set up an 'energy banking' mechanism to facilitate a two-way exchange of electricity between the two countries. Nepal can export surplus power to India during the monsoon season and import it during its lean period in the winter season. The energy banking agreement will be initiated with the newly constructed 400 kV

Dhalkebar-Muzaffarpur transmission line. Besides this, India has agreed to extend the capacity of the 132 kV Raksaul-Parwanipur and Kataiya-Kusaha transmission lines to strengthen Nepal's electricity system. The two countries are also working on funding and implementation modalities for the proposed 400 kV Butwal (Nepal)-Gorakhpur (India) link.

In August 2018, the 500 MW second block of the HVDC back-to-back link in Bheramara, Bangladesh, was commissioned as part of the capacity upgrade of the existing 104 km Bangladesh (Bheramara)-India (Baharampur) interconnection to meet the increasing demand for electricity in both countries.

Challenges and Outlook

Several challenges need to be resolved to ensure the timely implementation of grid expansion plans. Due to the lack of harmonisation of policies and regulations across states, securing right of way remains a key concern for all project developers. Environmental and forest clearances continue to be the leading challenges in project development. The large-scale capacity addition and connection of millions of new consumers to the grid requires robust grid planning. Further, system operators and regulators need to be empowered to ensure effective implementation of relevant policies and regulations.

The augmentation of transmission infrastructure, particularly GECs at the intra-state level, must be accelerated to ensure that the government's renewable energy and Power for All goals are met. This coupled with the implementation of power system operation reforms at the state level will help in building a more flexible and robust grid equipped to support the shift in generation mix and distribution loads.[26]

(d) **Unviable tariff:** In 2013–14, the average cost of supplying power was Rs 5.9 per kWh whereas the average tariff was Rs 4.8 per kWh. In the same year, across consumer categories, the average tariff was highest for commercial (Rs 7.6 per kWh) and industrial (Rs 6.3 per kWh) consumers. Average tariff was the lowest for agricultural consumers at 1.8 Rs per kWh (due to direct subsidies received from the state government and cross-subsidisation by commercial and industrial consumers). It is primarily because tariff is driven by political compulsion at the state level as successive governments announce freebies and lack the will to fix the issues.

The differential tariff and accumulated losses of state-owned Discoms (without subsidies) rose from Rs 11,699 crore in 2004–05 to Rs 71,271 crore in 2013–14. These losses have resulted in state Discoms relying more on short-term loans to fund their operations. Borrowings by state Discoms rose from Rs 1,58,003 crore in 2007–08 to Rs 5,45,922 crore in 2013–14. Interest cost on these loans further worsened the finances of state Discoms, affecting their ability to buy power, leading to power deficits.

Tariff hikes have been few and far between in the power sector. The tariffs charged for certain consumer categories do not match the actual cost of power generation. Unless tariffs are revised and regulated, Discoms will continue to run on losses no matter how much financial aid is provided. It is imperative that they are allowed to charge prices that are reflective of the cost. The proposed reforms of calculating tariffs without taking subsidies into account will help Discoms regain their financial health to a large extent.[27]

Smart Meters

Smart meters are known to help increase billing efficiency by 80–100%, according to the Union Power Secretary SC Garg. Speaking at a conference of state power ministers in Ahmedabad in March on 'Smart Meter National Programme', Garg said that the government had started work on retrofitting all the existing 250 million conventional analogue meters with prepaid smart meters in the country to eliminate billing losses and inefficiencies from the power supply system. The work is being carried out by a specially-created vehicle Energy Efficiency Services Limited (EESL) under the Union Ministry of Power. The EESL had already installed about 1.1 million smart meters till January 2020 and was working aggressively to complete the installation of all 250 million smart meters 'within a few years'. The EESL says it has set to install 1,00,000 meters a day.

Smart meters provide a digital link between electric companies and their customers and open the door to new and expanded services, such as time-based pricing, load control, budget billing, high-usage alerts, push notifications and web services for energy management. They measure and record electricity use hourly and feed that data to utilities and consumers. Traditional meters only record energy consumption for billing purposes. Information from smart meters can help consumers save money by letting them manage energy use in real-time, while utilities save money because they no longer need to send meter readers to every home in a service area on a monthly basis and despatch electricity bills on paper and maintain staff for payment collection.

A Council on Energy, Environment and Water (CEEW) study conducted in collaboration with Initiative for Sustainable Energy Policy (ISEP) has found that only 17% of billed consumers pay their bills digitally (27% in urban India and 12% in rural India). This is despite the fact that 70% of Indian households own a smartphone. According to the study, 93% of households had grid-electrified metered connections, while 91% were billed regularly for consumption.[28]

With prepaid smart meters, consumers top up their meters up-front, failing which their power is disconnected. This ensures timely payments to Discoms, which help them fund their working capital. But what about government departments and politicians who have been the largest defaulters in a number of regions? In October 2020, Tata Power, which distributes electricity in a part of the Delhi, told the Delhi government that it had no option but to switch off 65,000 street lights in north and northwest Delhi from October 15 for non-payment of outstanding bills of Rs 22 crore and unpaid maintenance charges by Delhi State Industrial and Infrastructure Development Corporation for 32 months. Will Discoms be willing to disconnect them? The matter was resolved, with the Delhi Power Minister Satyendra Jain ordering payment of Rs 8.7 crore immediately and the rest by March 2021. But the non-payment of bills and subsidies on time remains a perennial problem with grave consequences for all Discoms throughout the country. Will Discoms then make pre-paid meters mandatory for government establishments? Discoms will also have to resolve the problem of how they will offer differential tariffs for users with prepaid smart meters? However, despite all scepticism smart meters are a valuable tool for improved Discoms. If utilities are to come out of their financial mess in this country, there is no better option.

Subsidies

Twenty-seven states and union territories of India spent around Rs 1.32 trillion in 2020–21 in providing power supply subsidies to customers, according to data from the Ministry of Power. At the all-India basis, agricultural consumers account for 75% of the total subsidies, followed by domestic consumers at 20% and industries at 4%.

A study, conducted by the Council on Energy, Environment and Water (CEEW) in collaboration with International Institute for Sustainable

Development (IISD), about the financial performance of Discoms, from FY 2016 to FY 2019—before and after the implementation of Ujjwal Discom Assurance Yojana (UDAY) scheme—reports that direct tariff electricity subsidies from state governments in India increased 32% since FY 2016 to FY 2019 amounting to Rs 1,10,391 crore (US$ 14.96 billion). This was 4.52% of the total budget outlay for FY 2019, and 37.36% of the budget allocated for defence expenditure in FY 2019. In addition to direct tariff subsidies, cross subsidies increased 11% to Rs 75,027 crore (US$ 10.2 billion) in 2019 from Rs 67,785 crore (US$ 9.2 billion) in 2016.

Between FY 2016 and FY 2019, the revenue deficit on account of domestic and agriculture consumers has grown 48% from Rs 1,17,824 crore (US$ 16.1 billion) to Rs 1,74,391 crore (US$ 23.7 billion). Electricity distribution companies in 24 out of the 31 Indian states showed a revenue gap in FY 2019. Sales revenue as a share of total expenditure had fallen 3% from FY 2016 to FY 2019, despite the fact that UDAY required Discoms to increase revenue recovery. In FY 2019, 19 of 31 states and UTs had a higher supply cost as compared to FY 2016. Higher supply cost is mainly driven by high power purchase costs, which include inefficient planning and forecasting of demand, fixed cost commitments going up while demand has not, increasing fuel costs or increasing system costs (such as transmission).

Under the UDAY scheme, states had to reduce AT&C losses to 15% by FY 2019, but at least 25 out of 31 states and UTs had not reduced losses in line with the target. Poor collection is typically the biggest contributor to these losses. According to a high-level empowered committee set up by the Power Ministry in 2018, the total overdue amount of generating companies was Rs 22,313 crore[29] as on 22 July, 2019. The top six states in terms of overdue amount at the end of May 2019 were Uttar Pradesh (Rs 4,982 crore), Karnataka (Rs 3,351 crore), Tamil Nadu (Rs 3,330 crore), Telangana (Rs 2,119 crore), Jammu and Kashmir (Rs 1,862 crore) and Rajasthan (Rs 1,541 crore) contributing together about 77% of the overdue amount. This did not include the disputed amount and the amount overdue against PPAs signed between the generators and power trading companies for power sale to Discoms through back-to-back PPAs. Across generating companies, IPPs had the highest overdue amount of Rs 14,472.55 crore from Discoms at the end of May 2019. Amongst the public sector generating companies, the highest overdue amount in May 2019 was for NTPC (Rs 4,661.16 crore) followed by NHPC (Rs 1,973.90 crore).

As recently as on 8 August, 2022, Prime Minister Modi asked the states to clear dues to power utilities amounting to Rs 2.5 trillion, and termed the culture of subsidies as 'a serious disorder' in Indian politics. "People will be surprised to know that different states have outstanding dues of over Rs 1 lakh crore. They have to give this money to power GENCOs. Power distribution companies are owed more than Rs 60,000 crore. These companies are unable to get even the money committed for subsidy on electricity in different states. This arrear is also more than Rs 75,000 crore," he said.

IV. IMPACT OF POWER SUBSIDIES ON STATE FINANCES

The state governments have been lending to the power sector specially to fund capital expenditure of transmission and Discoms, plus to cover the mounting financial losses accrued by them. In addition to direct lending, the state governments have been providing support to the state Discoms in the form of grants and subsidies. The state governments also provide guarantees for the borrowings of state Discoms from financial institutions. The Reserve Bank of India (RBI) has noted that these contingent liabilities are a risk to state governments owing to the large outstanding debt and rising losses of Discoms, given the state governments act as guarantor for them.

Subsidies have increased in India for several reasons. In particular this proliferation can be attributed to the expansion of governmental activities, weak determination of governments to recover costs from the users of subsidy, even when this may be desirable on economic grounds and generally low efficiency levels of governmental activities. For example, the net costs of coal are much larger than the revenues. An analysis of the data of a few states reveals that while government is lending 6.2% of the budget to the energy sector, the outstanding liabilities of the energy sector as a proportion of the state Gross State Domestic Product (GSDP) are quite high. The fiscal deficit as a proportion of GSDP exceeds the permissible limit of 3% if just the energy sector is included. A few state governments with better performing state Discoms, such as Maharashtra, Gujarat and Karnataka, have less risk exposure. But for states like Rajasthan, Uttar Pradesh and Tamil Nadu it is high. This limit has now been increased to 5% in light of shrinking revenues on account of the Covid-19 pandemic. Subsidies have a direct impact on the fiscal health of state finances since a large part of them emanate from the budget. They directly increase fiscal deficits. Indirectly, they affect the budget by drawing resources away from tax-yielding sectors to sectors which have little tax-revenue potential.

Culture of Subsidy

The so-called 'culture of subsidy' is not bad as long as it softens prices and boosts consumption. It is given to promote a social good or an economic policy. While this helps consumers, it tends to erode efficiency and competitiveness among producers. By subsidising a certain sector, it puts other sectors at a disadvantage, thus distorting the market and generating losses to the economy. In India, subsidies also become prey to misuse, and, nowhere is misuse more pronounced than it is in fuel subsidies. In a report on how subsidised fuel eluded the targeted beneficiaries, a Washington-based non-profit research and advocacy group, Oil Change International (OCI), says that in developing countries such as India, it is common for a prized commodity to be diverted to uses other than for which the subsidy is intended. Referring to a ground survey by Delhi-based non-profit Vasudha Foundation, OCI points out that almost every policy design, subsidies and budgetary allocations intended to benefit the poor, end up benefiting primarily the well-off sections of the society.

Prime Minister Modi recognises this when he says that the need of the hour is to plug the leakages in the subsidiary chain, not the policy per se. According to the International Institute for Sustainable Development (IISD) and the Council on Energy, Environment and Water (CEEW), state-level under-priced electricity is the costliest individual subsidy policy, estimated at Rs 63,778 crore (US\$ 9.5 billion), in India. But evidence suggests it is not well targeted. It has been found that almost every policy design, subsidies and budgetary allocations intended to benefit the poor, end up benefiting primarily the well-off sections of the society. Gasoline and diesel subsidies, for example, benefit people who own cars or other vehicles. In this case, poorer households simply cannot afford the car, let alone the fuel. A United Nations Development Programme 2017 report says that the richest 20% of the Indian population received US\$ 16 billion in subsidies in 2014 on cooking gas, railways, power, aviation fuel, gold and kerosene.[30] The Modi government has reoriented the focus of subsidies towards the deprived and the rural population. There are at least a dozen subsidies meant for farmers (such as fertiliser, irrigation, equipment, credit subsidy, seed subsidy, diesel, kerosene, LPG and minimum support price (MSP).

Subsidies to transmission and distribution (T&D) doubled between FY 2014 to FY 2019, from Rs 41,252 crore to Rs 79,671 crore. The largest T&D subsidy was under-pricing of electricity, worth Rs 63,778 crore or 33% of all energy subsidies and 80% of all T&D subsidies. Renewable energy subsidies increased three-fold between FY 2014 and FY 2019, from Rs 3,224 crore to Rs 9,930 crore. In FY 2019, subsidies for electric vehicles (EVs) increased over 400 times to Rs 1,673 crore from Rs 3.8 crore in FY 2014. According to IISD and CEEW, India's total energy subsidies amounted to Rs 1,51,480 crore (US$ 23 billion) in FY 2016–17, a 36% decrease since financial year 2013–14.[31]

Delayed Payment of Subsidies

Subsidies constitute 10 to 30% of discoms' revenue. But they are barely able to keep pace with the rise in average cost of supply in many states. Long delays in payment of subsidies are frequent, resulting in increased working capital borrowings by discoms to meet the operating expenses. There are also numerous instances of states failing to pay struggling distribution utilities for free power supplied to farms and unmetered consumers (mostly rural consumers), and, even if they pay, such payments are often done through book adjustments against the electricity duty the electricity board owes to the government. Power supply to the agricultural sector is unmetered, which most utilities write off as transmission and distribution losses. This puts additional stress on cash-strapped discoms. A timely payment of committed subsidies could make a vast impact on discoms finances, which possibly may not need frequent rescue packages as is the case at present. With the rising cost of supply for discoms and the increasing demand from newly electrified and poor households, the need for subsidies will only increase. With the growth in open access and captive consumption, discoms may not have the ability to raise enough cross subsidy, which further underlines the need for increased subsidy support.

Despite strong legal and policy mandates to ensure timely payments, state governments seldom pay the committed subsidies in a timely manner. Delays in receiving the subsidy reimbursements from governments have weighed down distribution companies for a long time. Setting aside the fact that tariffs have so far been calculated based on promised subsidies, which are seldom reimbursed, how subsidies have been reimbursed has also led to new issues. As of August 2020, discoms had accumulated outstanding over dues of Rs 1.33 lakh crore to generators, creating an immense liquidity crunch across the entire power sector, which is, in turn, undermining the country's banking system integrity and foreign investment inflows. Discoms in Rajasthan, Maharashtra, Uttar Pradesh, Jammu and Kashmir, Telangana, Andhra Pradesh, Karnataka and Tamil Nadu accounted for a major portion of dues to GENCOs, according to data released by PRAAPTI. Outstanding to independent power producers amounted to 32.07% of the total overdue of Rs 1,33,062 crore, and to central government owned GENCOs 36.61%. Non-conventional energy (like solar and wind) producers' bills not paid by Discoms even after the 45-day grace period stood at Rs 10,908.65 crore.

The Electricity Act, 2003, states that subsidy declared for any consumer or class of consumers must be paid by the state government in advance to the distribution licensee. However, this has not been practised by state administrations. The soaring subsidy costs have left state governments with little money to pay their discoms. According to a World Bank report titled, *'In the Dark: How Much Do Power Sector Distortions Cost South Asia'*, released in December 2018, India loses tens of billions annually to power sector distortions (it cites the loss of US$ 86.1 billion or roughly 4.13% of GDP in 2015–16). According to the report, subsidies to discoms amounted to US$ 8.8 billion (0.42% of GDP) in 2015–16.[32]

Privatisation

Having failed to rejuvenate the state of perpetually debt-ridden Discoms, despite a raft of bailout packages and reforms, the union power ministry is now pushing state governments to seek privatisation of their loss-making discoms, modernise their operations and cut electricity losses. Discoms in the eight union territories, which are directly administered by the central government, are set to be privatised by early 2024, and others run by states (there are 27 states which are served by 54 public and private discoms) are being nudged to offer their discoms to private players through competitive biddings. The central power ministry has issued a standard bidding document (SBD) to guide the process.

According to the SBD, the states are supposed to hand over their power distribution firms to the highest bidder, 'with a clean balance sheet, free of accumulated losses/unserviceable liabilities'. It also provides that the existing assets of the discom, other than land, shall also be transferred to the highest bidder at the rate determined by the state power regulator. The government expects the private sector to own 100% of electricity distribution operations in urban areas and 74% in mixed rural-urban areas. This is a significant reform in a sector which has largely been 100% state controlled.

Power distribution in India is a combination of commercial business and public service, operating in a highly regulated environment. Many state-owned discoms have improved their performance and reduced losses, like in Gujarat and Kanpur, while licensed privatisation in Odisha and franchising in MP or Bihar did not work. Ownership per se does not matter as much as management style. Mismanagement of utilities over time resulted in lack of accountability, distorted internal communication, role obscurity amongst employees, management apathy towards capacity building of staff, obsoleteness of technology and inefficiency in business processes.

At present, the power distribution market has a few established private players with hands-on experience in turning around distribution utilities, but they cannot stretch to cover entire rural-urban electricity supply requirements of the country. New entrants could not pull off similar success stories in various parts of the country leaving consumers in lurch. Empowering employees or even employee ownership might lead to another option to get out of this quagmire; the country needs several innovative models to resurrect the flagging distribution sector.

We need to lay the ground for a similar transformation in distribution. International experience suggests that distribution companies in India may be too big. For example, there are over 3,000 distribution utilities in Unites States. Smaller ones (municipal) serve 2,000 customers (median) and the larger one (investor-owned) serve about 4,00,000 customers each. Network is a scale business and India's population is four times that of the US. Nevertheless, the 70-odd distribution companies are too few and far. Their large size, customer base and heterogeneity of terrain lead to inefficiencies, slow decision-making and poor customer service. It is hardly surprising that employees disengage, and customers have low willingness to pay.

Private sector distribution utilities have been successful in delivering better quality of power supply and customer service in relatively high-income urban settings with concentrated and relatively heterogeneous load. Smaller distribution entities will create similar heterogeneity, enhance ownership and engagement, and bring localisation and continuity to their management. Furthermore, they will be easily approachable and accountable to customers.

Universal Electrification

In 2014 when Narendra Modi came to power, one of his election promises was that he would electrify all villages within 1,000 days. There were as many as 18,452 villages (an additional 1,275 villages were added to the list later) that were without electricity at the time. On 28 April, 2018, Leisang village in Senapati district of Manipur became last of the country's 5,97,464 census villages to be electrified—12 days ahead of the deadline. The development was described by the International Energy Agency (IEA) as, 'one of the greatest achievements in the history of energy'. The agency highlighted as a bright spot for energy access in its Energy Access Outlook 2017, and said, 'India is clearly a success story'. Since 2000, around half a billion people have gained access to electricity in India, with political effort over the last five years significantly accelerating the progress. The country is already on track to achieving universal household electricity access by the early 2020s it said.[33]

Undoubtedly, the electrification of all census villages was a great feat for a country that had begun rural electrification with a total power generation capacity of just 1,362 MW and a T&D network of 23,238 km and with an almost negligible per capita electricity consumption of 16 kWh (power was mainly available to colonial rulers and the privileged section of the Indian society) at the time of Independence.[34] Successive Indian governments continued the mission which saw the total generation capacity reaching 409.16 GW in November 2022 and a per capita electricity consumption of 1,010 kWh.

But 100% electrification of a village does not mean does not mean 100% household electrification. According to the government criteria, a village is considered electrified even if just 10% of its households or a public place such as school, health centre, medical dispensary and panchayat building is grid-connected. This implies that even if 90% of the households are left without electricity access, the village can be deemed as electrified. The definition has led to criticism by some activists, policy think-tanks and socio-economic organisations. The official view is not much different from the critics. But the government thinks that this is only the first step in delivering power across India and it must go on. In the process the government prepares the people for universal electrification, including 100% household electrification.

In order to complete the process, the Modi government has rolled out two flagship schemes—Deen Dayal Upadhyay Gram Jyoti Yojana (DDUGJY) and Pradhan Mantri Sahaj Bijli Har Ghar Yojana (Saubhagya). Launched in 2015, DDUJY was designed to provide uninterrupted power supply to all villages by May 2018 (the goal was achieved 12 days ahead of the target). DDUGJY laid down the physical infrastructure for providing round-the-clock power to rural households and adequate power to agricultural consumers. The feeder separation for rural agricultural and village households was aimed at preventing load shedding by distribution utilities and help improve crop yield and socioeconomic development of rural areas.

However, there remained a bigger challenge of providing power to every household in the country. DDUGJY was soon followed by Saubhagya, which aims at providing free electricity connections and low-cost power supply to every single 'willing' household under the BPL category. According to official estimates, there were about 3.14 crore rural households or 17% of the total 17.99 crore rural households, which did not have any access to electricity at the time the scheme was launched in 2017. Saubhagya has also envisaged strengthening of sub-transmission and distribution system and metering at all levels of distribution network.

In its 2018 report, the World Bank says that between 2010 and 2016, India had provided electricity to 30 million people each year, more than any other country.[35] Eight new states have achieved 100% saturation in household electrification under Saubhagya namely, Madhya Pradesh, Tripura, Bihar, Jammu and Kashmir, Mizoram, Sikkim, Telangana and West Bengal as of March 2018. With these, 15 states in the country now have 100% household electrification.[36]

However, as of 31 August, 2020, there were still about 3.2 lakh or about 10.5% of the rural households left unconnected to the power grid, with most of them in Chhattisgarh, Assam, Uttar Pradesh and Jharkhand, according to a statement made by Power Minister Raj Kumar Singh in the Lok Sabha.[37] The Saubhagya percentages does not count the households who have 'willingly not taken connections' as not electrified. In an interview to the Rajya Sabha TV, Singh said that the parts of Chhattisgarh left out are the ones that fall in the Bastar region where the Naxals hold sway.

Universal household electricity access was a central political commitment in India's 2014 national elections and the government placed a high priority on following through. India is also taking these lessons onboard as it tackles a related problem—access to clean cooking facilities. Globally, nearly three billion people are forced to cook with wood and other fuels that produce smoke, resulting in 2.8 million premature deaths each year. This is more than twice the number of deaths related to malaria and AIDS combined. Despite these staggering figures, clean cooking rarely features on the agendas of policy makers, and as a consequence the number of people cooking with unhealthy fuels has not changed since 2000.

Uninterrupted Supply a Bigger Challenge

Now, more than access, a bigger challenge for the government is to provide uninterrupted and affordable electricity. Across the country, there are significant disparities in the number of hours households get electricity. For instance, a CEEW survey revealed that while West Bengal households get 20 hours of power supply on average, Jharkhand households receive only 9 hours. As of August 2018, 91% of the total households are electrified in India. Rural areas in India are electrified non-uniformly, with richer states being able to provide a majority of the villages with power while poorer states still struggling to do so.

Data from the Mission Antyodaya, a nationwide survey of villages conducted by the Ministry of Rural Development, also points to these differences. Around 20% of India's households received less than 8 hours of electricity and only 47% received more than 12 hours, suggesting that another NDA promise—24x7 power for all households by 2019—is still a mirage in 2022. A big reason for low-quality electricity supply is the financial health of the Discoms, which are responsible for distributing electricity.

Consumer Rights

Frequent blackouts and outage have led the central government to bring in a consumers' rights law, making it obligatory on power distribution companies to pay a penalty for deficient services such as disruptions in electricity supplies, faulty metering and delayed connection. The Electricity (Rights of Consumers) Rules, 2020, empowers the state electricity regulatory commission (SERC) in each state to fix average number and duration of outages for different segment of consumers, such as agriculture and rural households (for example, UP provides power for irrigation and rural households at night). SERCs shall also specify the maximum period within which distribution utilities would provide new electricity connections. However, defective meters will have to be replaced within 24 hours.

According to the new rules, power distribution companies are required to supply 24x7 electricity supply to all customers, except those specified by the SERC, failing which they will have to compensate customers for the duration of the disruption in form of a rebate in next bill. It provides that no power connection shall be given without a meter, and the meter shall be a 'smart prepayment' or 'prepayment' meter. Any exception to this provision shall be duly approved by the SERC, which shall record proper justification for allowing the deviation from installation of smart prepayment or prepayment meter.

The Electricity (Rights of Consumers) Rules, 2020, have been built upon the Consumer Charter under the Electricity Act, 2003, that provides a synopsis of rights of consumers which most states have not implemented. The new rules now make it mandatory for states to implement them.

The Energy Conservation (Amendment) Bill, 2022

In December 2022, the Indian Parliament passed an amendment to the Energy Conservation Act of 2001 seeking to empower the central government to specify a carbon credit trading scheme and mandating designated consumers to meet a proportion of their energy needs from non-fossil sources. Other highlights of the new amendment include the scope of the Energy Conservation Code, provided in 2001 Act, to office and residential buildings with a connected load of 100 kW or above, and energy consumption standards for vehicles and ships.

Carbon credit implies a tradeable permit to produce a specified amount of carbon dioxide or other greenhouse emissions. The central government or any authorised agency may issue carbon credit certificates to entities registered and compliant with the scheme. The entities will be entitled to trade the certificates. Any other person may also purchase a carbon credit certificate on a voluntary basis. Reports suggest that India will set up a stabilisation fund to keep credit prices above a certain threshold so that they remain attractive for investors. The credit market is expected to become fully operational by 2026.

Under the obligation to use non-fossil sources of energy, different consumption thresholds may be specified for different non-fossil sources and consumer categories. Designated consumers include: (i) industries such as mining, steel, cement, textile, chemicals and petrochemicals; (ii) transport sector including railways and (iii) commercial buildings, as specified in the schedule. Failure to meet this obligation will be punishable with a penalty of up to Rs 10 lakh. It will also attract an additional penalty of up to twice the price of oil equivalent of energy consumed above the prescribed norm.

The 2022 Bill replaces the Energy Conservation Code for buildings, provided under 2001 Act, with 'Energy Conservation and Sustainable Building Code' and provides norms for energy efficiency and conservation, use of renewable energy and other requirements for green buildings. Under the Act, the Energy Conservation Code applies only to commercial buildings, built after the notification of the Code and having a minimum connected load of 100 kW or contract load of 120 kVA (kilo volt ampere). It will also apply to the office and residential buildings meeting the above criteria. The Bill empowers the state governments to lower the load thresholds.

Similarly, the 2022 Bill has expanded the scope of the 2001 Act to include vehicles (as defined under the Motor Vehicles Act, 1988), and vessels (including ships and boats) for the observance of energy consumption standards. The Act specified for only equipment and appliances which consume, generate, transmit or supply energy. The failure to comply with new standards will be punishable with a penalty of up to Rs 10 lakh. Non-compliance in case of vessels will attract an additional penalty of up to twice the price of oil equivalent of energy consumed above the prescribed norm. Vehicle manufacturers in violation of fuel consumption norms will be liable to pay a penalty of up to Rs 50,000 per unit of vehicles sold.

The objective of the 2022 Bill is to introduce concepts such as mandated use of non-fossil sources and carbon credit trading to ensure faster decarbonisation of the Indian economy. During the COP 26 summit in 2021, India had committed to reducing the carbon intensity of its economy by 45% till 2030, over the 2005 level and cutting total projected carbon emissions by 1 bt. The Bill seeks to consolidate multiple sources/aspects related to energy transition, efficiency and conservation under one legislation to avoid overlap and confusion between multiple legislations. It introduces initiatives which are necessary for energy transition and conservation.

In India, the energy sector is responsible for 75% of CO_2 emissions, of which, energy industries contribute 43%, manufacturing industries and construction 14%, transport 10%, agriculture 14%, industrial processes and products 8% and waste 3%—total CO_2 emissions 2,839 mt. The Bill is expected to receive the presidential assent to become an Act in early 2023 as it has already been passed the both houses of Parliament.

References

1. Ministry of Power, Government of India.
2. Ibid.
3. 'Electricity Arrives in Mumbai', BEST Undertaking. Archived from the original on 11 October, 2006.
4. 'Electricity Arrives in Mumbai', BEST Undertaking. Archived from the original on 11 October, 2006.
5. Vasant Surdeo, Power Sector Policies in India: History and Evolution, p.117, reproduced in Jindal Journal of Public Policy, Vol. 3, Issue 1.
6. 'Indian Power System becomes Largest Operating Synchronous Grid in the World'. *The Times of India*, retrieved 2 December, 2016.
7. 'Indian Power System becomes Largest Operating Synchronous Grid in the World'. *The Times of India*, retrieved 2 December, 2016.
8. Vasant Surdeo, Power Sector Policies in India: History and Evolution, p.117, reproduced in *Jindal Journal of Public Policy*, Vol. 3, Issue 1.
9. All figures are from CEA.
10. Central Electricity Regulatory Commission.
11. "BIMSTEC Needs a 'Power Tool'; Here's Why it is Time for a Green Energy Revolution." *The Financial Express*, 3 January, 2017.
12. Power Grid Corporation of India; www.powergridindia.com.
13. 'Why India's Booming Power Market is Bad for Business', by David Fickling, Bloomberg, 3 April, 2020.
14. Government of India, Ministry of Power; https://powermin.gov.in.
15. Ministry of Power, Financial Performance States Under UDAY, website. www.uday. gov.in.
16. UDAY, website. www.uday.gov.in. (State Health Cards); accessed on 29 April, 2019.
17. January 2019 Newsletter and Consolidated All India Data; accessed on 29 April, 2019: UDAY website. www.uday.gov.in.
18. The Ministry of Power website www.praapti.in, Payment Ratification and Analysis in Power Procurement for bringing Transparency in Invoicing of Generators.
19. EIA 2019 fact sheet.
20. 'Why India's Booming Power Market is Bad for Business', David Fickling, Bloomberg, 3 April, 2020.

21. Power Minister RK Singh at CII Conference of 'Green Energy', 17 October, 2022.

22. Power Secretary SC Garg at a Round-table Conference on India Energy Forum, 24 September, 2019.

23. Ministry of Coal website: https://coal.nic.in, August, 2019–20.

24. Infra Woes Trip Transmission Despite Power-surplus Oases, *The Financial Express*, 2013.

25. IEA, Electricity in Every Village in India, by Bruce Murphy, India Programme Manager, and Hannah Daly, WEO Energy Analyst, Commentary, 1 June, 2018.

26. PowerLine, Transmission Trends Strengthening the Grid to Support Renewable Integration, by Swarna Kesavan, September, 2019.

27. Data Sources: Ministry of Power; Ministry of Statistics and Programme Implementation; Central Electricity Authority; Lok Sabha Questions; Power Finance Corporation; PRS.

28. Over 90% Families have Electricity Meters, Billed Regularly: CEEW study, *PTI*, 8 October, 2020.

29. Source: PRAAPTI Portal; Payment Ratification and Analysis in Power Procurement for Bringing Transparency in Invoicing of Generators: http://praapti.in.

30. 'Human Development Report 2016' (PDF). UNDP. p.118, 21 March, 2017.

31. Energyworld, New Delhi, 20 December, 2018.

32. ETEnergyWorld, India Loses $86 billion Annually to Power Sector Distortions: World Bank, 17 December, 2018.

33. IEA, Electricity in every Village in India, by Bruce Murphy, India Programme Manager, and Hannah Daly, WEO Energy Analyst, Commentary, 1 June, 2018.

34. CEA, 1948.

35. Jha, Lalit K, 'India doing Extremely well on Electrification: World Bank', *Mint*, 29 August, 2019.

36. 'India Likely to Achieve 100% Household Electrification by January end', *Business Today*, 29 August, 2019.

37. 3.2 lakh Households Remain Un-electrified Till August-end under Saubhagya Scheme: Govt, *PTI*, 31 August, 2020.

Chapter 11

ENERGY STORAGE

I. OVERVIEW

Ever since the discovery of electricity, the world has sought effective methods to store that power for use on demand. The energy storage industry has, thus, continued to evolve, adapt and innovate in response to changing energy requirements and advances in technology. Given the urgency of climate change mitigation, it has become crucial to increase the practical utilisation of renewable energy. However, high uncertainty and large fluctuation of variable renewable energy create enormous challenge to increasing the penetration of the renewable energy in the mix. Power storage is a major part of India's clean-energy mission.

The IEA forecast that the global installed storage capacity would expand by 56% in the next four years to reach over 270 GW by 2026. The main driver is the increasing need for system flexibility and storage around the world to fully utilise and integrate larger share of variable renewable energy (VRE) into power systems. Utility-scale batteries are expected to account for the majority of storage growth worldwide. Their installed capacity is expected to increase six-fold by 2026, driven by incentives and an increasing need for system flexibility, especially where the share of VRE covers almost all demand in certain hours of the day. Hybrid auctions combining wind or solar PV with storage have emerged in India and Germany, with contracts in the range of US$ 40–60 per MWh over 2020.

With India having targeted a 500 GW of electricity production from non-fossil fuels to meet 50% of its demand by 2030 and mitigate climate change, it will need more energy storage capacity than any other country in the world. According to the IEA, over the next 20 years, India will need to add a power system the size of the European Union to what it has now, to satisfy the growth in electricity demand. As such, India could have energy storage capacity of between 140–200 GW, the largest of any country, by 2040. Energy storage is a critical element in the process of smoothing the variability of wind and solar PV and supporting the integration of grid.[1]

Grid-scale batteries have proven to be an important grid management tool to deal with frequency fluctuations. One GWh (1,000 MWh) of battery capacity is considered sufficient to power about one million homes for an hour and around 30,000 electric cars. Should battery prices fall significantly, coupling solar PV with affordable batteries will become an attractive bargain to meet the growing electricity demand and flexibility in India. This combination would become competitive with new coal power plants in the near future and enable the deployment of larger amounts of cost-effective solar PV.

A Wide Array of Technologies

Energy storage systems provide a wide array of technological approaches to manage the power supply to create a more resilient energy infrastructure and bring cost savings to utilities and consumers. However, as no single energy storage technology has this capacity, these systems will comprise combinations of technologies such as electrochemical supercapacitors, flow batteries, lithium-ion batteries, superconducting magnetic energy storage (SMES) and kinetic energy storage. The evolution of the electrochemical supercapacitor is largely dependent on the development of optimised electrode materials (tailored to the chosen electrolyte) and electrolytes. Some of the technologies widely used today are—batteries, thermal storage, mechanical storage, hydrogen and pumped hydropower. By far, the world's most popular battery on the market today is the lithium-ion (Li-ion) battery.

Lithium-ion technology has significant potential, and a step-change is required in order to promote the technology from the portable electronics market into high-duty applications. Flow-battery development is largely concerned with safety and operability.[2] However, opportunities exist to improve electrode technology yielding larger power densities.

Lithium-ion (Li-ion) Batteries

Italian physicist and chemist, Alessandro Volta, is credited with the invention of the first battery in 1800. On its most basic level, a battery is a device consisting of one or more electrochemical cells that convert stored chemical energy into electrical energy. Each cell contains a positive terminal or cathode, and a negative terminal or anode. Electrolytes allow ions to move between the electrodes and terminals, which allows current to flow out of the battery to perform work.

Advances in technology and materials have greatly increased the reliability, output and density of modern battery systems, and economies of scale have dramatically reduced the associated cost. Continued innovation has created new technologies like electrochemical capacitors that can be charged and discharged simultaneously and instantly and provide an almost unlimited operational lifespan.

After Exxon chemist Stanley Whittingham developed the concept of lithium-ion batteries in the 1970s, Sony and Asahi Kasei introduced lithium-ion batteries for the first time in 1991 in their consumer electronics. These smaller and more powerful batteries enabled laptop computers to run faster and longer. Since then, the growth of Li-ion has been phenomenal, enabling the rise of smartphones, and other personal electronics that revolutionised the way we interact with people and exchange information. From the early 2010s, the Li-ion batteries started powering electric vehicles (EVs), and from 2018 being installed in electricity grids to smooth the variability of wind and solar farms. Li-ion batteries have been deployed in a wide range of energy storage applications, ranging from energy-type batteries of a few kilowatts per hours in residential systems with rooftop photovoltaic arrays to multi-megawatt containerised batteries for the provision of grid ancillary services.[3]

Lead Batteries

Lead batteries are most extensively used rechargeable battery technology in the world. They have an unrivalled track record for reliability and safety, which together with a well-established worldwide supplier base, make them the dominant battery in terms of MWh of production. Lead batteries are widely used in cars and trucks, in virtually all vehicles, supporting increased vehicle hybridisation and electrification, all the way from start-stop technology to full electric vehicles. In addition, lead batteries are widely used in industrial applications, where they provide energy for telecommunications, uninterrupted power supply, secure power, electric traction and for energy storage for utilities as well as domestic and commercial applications.

Redox Flow Batteries (RFB)

RFB represent one class of electrochemical energy storage devices. The name 'redox' refers to chemical reduction and oxidation reaction employed in the RFB to store energy in liquid electrolyte solutions which flow through a battery of electrochemical cells during charge and discharge.

Nickel-Cadmium (NI-CD) Batteries

In commercial production since the 1910s, nickel-cadmium (Ni-Cd) is a traditional battery type that has seen periodic advances in electrode technology and packaging in order to remain viable. While not exceling in typical measures such as energy density or cost, Ni-CD batteries remain relevant by providing simple implementation without complex management systems, while providing long life and reliable service.

Sodium Sulphur (NaS) Batteries

NaS were originally developed by Ford Motor Company in the 1960s and subsequently the technology was sold to the Japanese company NGK. NGK now manufactures the battery systems for stationary applications. The systems operate at a high temperature, 300 to 350°C. The round-trip efficiency is in the 90% range which provides an efficient use of energy.

Electrochemical Capacitors (ECs)

ECs are referred to as 'electric double-layer' capacitors, and also appear under trade names like 'Supercapacitor' or 'Ultracapacitor'. The phrase 'double-layer' refers to their physically storing electrical charge at a surface-electrolyte interface of high-surface-area carbon electrodes. There are two types of ECs, symmetric and asymmetric, with different properties suitable for different applications. Markets and applications for electrochemical capacitors are growing rapidly and applications related to electricity grid will be part of that growth.

Iron-Chromium (ICB) Flow Batteries

ICBs were pioneered and studied extensively by NASA in the 1970s-1980s and by Mitsui in Japan. The iron-chromium flow battery is an RFB. Energy is stored by employing the $Fe^{2+} - Fe^{3+}$ and $Cr^{2+} - Cr^{3+}$ redox couples. The active chemical species are fully dissolved in the aqueous electrolyte at all times. Like other true RFBs, the power and energy ratings of the iron-chromium system are independent of each other, and each may be optimised separately for each application. All the other benefits and distinctions of true RFBs compared to other energy storage systems are realised by iron-chromium RFBs.

Zinc-Bromine (ZNBR) Flow Batteries

The zinc-bromine battery is a hybrid redox flow battery, because much of the energy is stored by plating zinc metal as a solid onto the anode plates in the electrochemical stack during charge. Thus, the total energy storage capacity of the system is dependent on both the stack size (electrode area) and the size of the electrolyte storage reservoirs. As such, the power and energy ratings of the zinc-bromine flow battery are not fully decoupled. The zinc-bromine flow battery was developed by Exxon as a hybrid flow battery system in the early 1970s.

Phenomenal Growth of Utility Scale Batteries

According to the IEA, globally growth of batteries is set to outstrip that of any other flexibility option available to electricity systems over the next two decades. Global battery production is expected to increase 20-fold by 2040 under today's stated policies, driven by rising sales of electric vehicles. Most of the advances leading to battery cost declines have occurred and are expected to occur through the deployment of electric vehicles. Under stated policies, the World Energy Outlook 2019 projects the number of electric cars to grow from 5 million in 2018 to 330 million in 2040. Battery deployment in cars and other means of transport (bikes, scooters, etc.) creates spill over effects for stationary battery storage systems, helping to cut their costs further by 2040. These trends will drive a significant increase in the use of battery storage, led by India, which is projected to account for more than one-third of total deployment by 2040.[4]

Long Duration Energy Storage (LDES)

Among the various energy storage technologies in use across the world, Li-ion batteries are by far the most popular battery currently, but they present various challenges. They have a complicated international supply chain with three key battery materials—lithium, nickel and cobalt. They are expensive and limited, keeping costs high, increasing dependence on foreign suppliers and delaying supply chain ramp-up to meet rapidly growing demand. Li-ion batteries also have performance limitations for some applications. They cannot discharge at full power for more than four to six hours. And they cannot reach the high-energy densities required to power long-haul trucks, rail, marine shipping and aviation, which requires two to three times the energy density of Li-ion. In our climate-constrained world, we must search beyond Li-ion batteries to meet these energy storage needs.[5]

However, currently we have no commercial battery storage technology to stabilise a renewable power grid for several days in the event of consecutive cloudy or calm days. The Joint Centre for Energy Storage Research (JCESR) is working on next-generation organic redox flow batteries for 10-plus hour applications, and we need new chemical energy carriers such as green hydrogen, ammonia or other hydrogen-rich, carbon-free carriers.[6]

LDES can help address these issues by increasing the flexibility of the power systems and national grids. It has the potential to deploy 1.5 to 2.5 TWh of power capacity by 2040 and the flexibility required for net zero power systems. It is estimated that the world will require 4–8 TWh of LDES by 2030, and by 2040 the requirement could be 85–140 TWh. Deploying such storage capacities may require US$ 3 trillion in investment.[7]

II. OTHER TECHNOLOGIES

Energy storage can be achieved in vastly different ways, including mechanical, thermal, electrochemical or chemical storage. But pumped hydro storage (PHS) is a proven mature technology which is cost-effective and suitable for many developing countries if they have a reasonably integrated grid. As of December 2021, the installed generation capacity of the country stood at 393 GW, comprising 235 GW of thermal, 151 GW of renewable (wind, solar, hydro and biomass) and 6.78 GW of nuclear. India saw its peak electricity demand surpass 200 GW in 2021. As per a study done by CEA, our storage requirement by 2030 is forecast at 41 GW and this aim is getting much-awaited attention in the country.

Pumped Storage Hydro

Among the various energy storage technologies, PHS is the oldest and most mature large-scale storage technology, accounting for 96% of installed global energy storage capacity. Around 169 GW of pumped storage capacity is installed worldwide, with China leading with 32.1 GW, followed by Japan with 28.5 GW, and United States with 24.2 GW.

PHS is a type of hydroelectric energy storage which uses a two-reservoir system (upper and lower) to store energy and generate electricity. It is of two types: open loop', which has an associated natural water source (like a river) for one or both the reservoirs; and 'closed loop' (or off-river PHS), which does not have a connected natural water source and the same water is cycled between the two reservoirs for pumping and generation.

Unlike battery storage technology that uses expensive and critical materials such as lithium, nickel and cobalt (lithium-based), or polluting materials such as lead (lead acid), PHS uses the potential energy of water as the storage medium. Also, batteries have a much shorter lifespan, making their replacement and disposal a hassle. Thus, PHS is best suited for complementing India's storage needs. India's draft National Electricity Policy (NEP) 2021 underpins the need for large-scale adoption of PHS for supporting the electricity grid.

PHS can generate power continuously for 6–10 hours, depending on the storage capacity of the reservoir. It has a lifetime of over 40 years, with an efficiency of 70–80%. Also, as compared to the conventional thermal generator, PHS has a higher ramping capability, the ability of quick start-stop.

But there are challenges too, including a high initial investment (US$ 600–2,000 per kW), topographical requirements like the range for elevation (20–1,000 m) between the two reservoirs, proximity to a large water body, and environmental impacts like loss of wildlife habitats and issues of resettlement and rehabilitation of human population. As a result of the high investment cost and long gestation for a PSH project, private participation has been low. Most of the current PSH plants are owned by state governments and centre-state joint venture power generation utilities, except one project being developed by an independent power producer.

Although PHS dominates the global storage-capacity scene, its growth in India has been tepid. The Central Electricity Authority of India has estimated a PHS potential of 96 GW, but only 3.3 GW is currently operational in India. This slow pace can be attributed to the high cost associated with the commissioning of PHS plants, the long gestation period due to delays in obtaining environmental clearances, and the low recovery from the existing pricing mechanism of PHS.

Only nine plants with an installed capacity of 4,785 MW have been commissioned so far, and three with a capacity of 2.7 GW are under construction, while three of 1,480 MW capacity are yet to be operated in pumping mode, for various reasons. Apart from these, about 17 PSH projects with a capacity of 16.5 GW in different states are under various stages of implementation (which include pre-feasibility studies, detailed surveys, investigations and project reports and clearances).

Thermal Energy Storage

Thermal energy storage is used particularly in buildings and industrial processes. It involves storing excess energy—typically surplus energy from renewable sources or waste heat—to be used later for heating, cooling or power generation. Liquids, such as water, or solid material, such as sand or rocks, can store thermal energy. Chemical reactions or changes in materials can also be used to store and release thermal energy. Water tanks in buildings are simple examples of thermal energy storage systems.

In its 2020 Innovation Outlook: Thermal Energy Storage update, the International Renewable Energy Agency predicted that the global market for thermal energy storage could triple in size by 2030, from 234 GWh of installed capacity in 2019 to more than 800 GWh.

Mechanical Energy Storage

Mechanical energy storage harnesses motion or gravity to store electricity. For example, a flywheel is a rotating mechanical device that is used to store rotational energy that can be called up instantaneously. Other mechanical systems include compressed air energy storage, which has been used since the 1870s to deliver on-demand energy for cities and industries. The process involves storing pressurised air or gas and then heating and expanding it in a turbine to generate power when this is needed.

Sodium Hydroxide

A Danish manufacturer of molten salt nuclear reactors claims to have developed a storage system that uses molten salt to provide large-scale storage solution for wind and solar energy. Seaborg Technologies, which has developed this technology which was originally developed for nuclear power, says that its first pilot manufacturing facility should be operational by second half of 2023.

The proposed storage system uses renewable energy to heat the salt using electrical heaters. It is based on two-tank molten salt storage designs developed for concentrated solar power (CSP) plants. It has a scalable storage capacity from 250 MWh to 5 GWh. A 1 GWh facility with sodium hydroxides is expected to be able to store heat to produce power and heat for around 1,00,000 households for 10 hours of discharge. The two tanks are able to store electricity as heat at 700°C. The high temperature provides large flexibility for how energy can be extracted back out.

The immersion heaters are used to store excess electricity as heat, while pumps control the flow for discharging through salt to steam heat exchangers for producing steam to drive steam turbines for co-generation in the simplest setup. Seaborg said this storage system may have a maximum heat loss down to 0.5 to 1% per day and its charge and discharge are freely scalable. Its costs should be between 30–50% lower than conventional molten salt storage.

The company said sodium hydroxide can be produced at low cost from seawater as a by-product from chlorine production. It is six times cheaper than standard salts used for storage. Hydroxides can contain more heat per salt unit, making it more efficient and reducing the amount of salt needed compared to current salt uses, which reduces the cost of salt as a storage medium by approximately 90%.

III. STATUS OF ENERGY STORAGE SYSTEMS IN INDIA

Currently, the demand for energy storage batteries in India is modest. However, it is expected to increase several folds in the coming years because of the ambitious renewable energy targets. As of the mid-2022, India had an installed renewable energy capacity of 160 GW, leaving it only a short distance from hitting its 2022 target of 175 GW. This capacity constituted around 40% of the total installed power capacity of 400 GW, comprising 234 GW of thermal, 160 GW of renewables (wind, solar, hydro and biomass) and 6.78 GW of nuclear. The country is on the way to increase its renewables capacity further to 450 GW by 2030 to meet 50% of its requirement. But while we are racing ahead with the target of generation expansion, we lag behind in providing adequate energy storage solutions to support the integration of renewables in the power mix. As per a CEA study, India would require 41 GW of storage capacity to provide supply-side flexibility to integrate 450 GW of renewables to the grid by 2030. In mid-2022, however,

India had just about 20 MW of installed battery storage capacity, with 1.7 GW of battery capacity in the pipeline.[8]

Manufacturing: A Costly Affair

The Ministry of Power has stressed on the essentiality of adequate energy storage systems, including battery energy storage systems (BESS), pumped hydro energy storage (PHES) or other technologies like green hydrogen or green ammonia storage to integrate the large volumes of variable renewables into the grid. The CEA has modelled that this could need around 27 GW/108 GWh of energy storage by 2030. But it costs dearly to set up a fully integrated battery energy storage system that includes the thermal management system, battery management systems and power conversion system, as well as fire prevention and suppression technology, Supervisory Control and Data Acquisition (SCADA) and metering.

Based on its analyses, Lawrence Berkeley National Laboratory (LBNL) has estimated that capital investment required for building a 50 GWh facility would be about Rs 30,000 crore (US$ 4.6 billion). This includes equipment, land and building costs. The equipment cost would constitute the major share (85%) in the total capital expenditures (CAPEX).

Li-ion battery manufacturing is a working capital-intensive industry, costing an average Rs 16,231 crore (US$ 2.5 billion) annually. The cost of Li-ion battery comes to around Rs 9,614 per kWh (US$ 148 per kWh). The raw material is the biggest cost component in a Li-ion battery (66%) of the total cost. Within the raw material category, the separator comprises the major share (24%) in the total cost of a battery. Once the Li-ion battery manufacturing facility has been established, and an ecosystem developed, technological innovation, dedicated R&D efforts and economies of scale can be helpful in lowering the cost of the separator. Consequently, the cost of manufacturing the Li-ion battery would further reduce. Graphite and Li contribute 10% and 5% of the cost share, respectively.

Currently, China dominates the market for supply of battery-grade graphite to the Li-ion battery industry. India is the second largest producer of graphite, globally, but lacks the processing technology required to make battery-grade graphite suitable for LIB applications. Advancements in processing technology can help the industry to include Indian graphite in the Li-ion battery value chain. The other major part of raw material cost comes from Manganese (Mn), Ni and Co which are part of the cathode component. Together, these materials contribute 7% to the total battery cost. Apart from these, Al, Co and Ni foil, Polyvinylidene fluoride (PVDF), N-Methyl-2- pyrrolidone (NMP), etc., comprise 20% of the total cost of a battery. These materials can be manufactured indigenously. Thus, there is a scope for cost reduction.

The operating expenses would initially be high in this facility. However, with a better understanding of the technology, domestic or global demand and market dynamics, the efficiency of operations can be enhanced and these expenses would reduce. Therefore, the Li-ion battery cost can be further lowered. As per the LBNL analysis, the cost of Li-ion batteries (US$ 148 per kWh) in India would be globally competitive. The cost of Li-ion batteries is estimated to decline further considering the subsidies from the government, economies of scale and introduction of cost-effective battery materials. Globally, a sharp decline in prices of lithium-ion (Li-ion) batteries is expected to transform how electricity from renewable sources, such as solar and wind, is integrated into the grid.[9] The Energy Transition Commission (ETC) of India projects the levelised cost of storage systems to decline from US$ 0.41 (Rs 30.8) kWh in 2018 to US$ 0.17 (Rs 12.8) kWh in 2030.

Production-Linked-Incentives for Advanced Chemistry Cells (ACC)

The government is trying to take advantage of the downward pressure on prices of battery storage systems to boost domestic manufacturing of advanced chemistry cell (ACC), a key component of storage batteries. The ministry of industries has launched a 'National Programme for ACC Battery Storage' that offers cash incentives and tax concessions to investors, both domestic and overseas, to setup giga-scale ACC manufacturing facilities. The programme aims to achieve 50 GWh of advanced chemistry cells and 5 GWh of niche advanced chemistry cell manufacturing capacity. Investors are selected through a competitive bidding process to obtain a competitive price. The emphasis is on maximum value addition, quality output and achieving pre-committed capacity level within a defined period. Selected firms are expected to setup manufacturing facilities in India within 24 months, conduct research and development, invest around US$ 6.1 billion in ACC battery storage manufacturing projects and facilitate demand creation for battery storage in the country. The ACC programme is part of the bigger production-linked-incentives scheme and expected to cost around Rs 18,100 crore (US$ 2.47 billion) in pay out over five years.

In March 2022, the government announced that it had selected four companies for the ACC Battery Storage projects and placed another five companies on the wait list. The selected firms are: Reliance New Energy Solar Ltd, Ola Electric Mobility Pvt Ltd, Hyundai Global Motors Company Ltd and Rajesh Exports Ltd. They will receive production-linked incentives under the plan. The wait listed companies include Mahindra & Mahindra (M&M), Exide Industries, Larsen & Toubro (L&T), Amara Raja and India Power Corporation.

Each selected ACC Battery Storage manufacturer will to setup an ACC manufacturing facility of minimum 5 GWh capacity, achieve a domestic value addition of at least 25% and incur the mandatory investment Rs 2.25 billion (US$ 31.02 million) per GWh at 'Mother Unit Level' within two years. The ACC battery manufacturer will need to ensure a minimum 60% domestic value addition at the project level within five years. The incentive will be disbursed over a period of five years. It will be paid out on the basis of energy efficiency, sales, battery life cycle and localisation levels. The scheme proposes that the relevant state government, central government and manufacturer enter into a tripartite agreement where the state government will support the private sector by providing land for setting up the facility, assisting in procuring permits and licenses, providing trunk infrastructure, etc.

Expected Benefits of Local Manufacturing of ACC

ACC battery manufacturing represents one of the leading economic opportunities for several industrial growth sectors in India, such as consumer electronics, EVs and renewable energy. The rapidly growing EV industry, in particular, stands to benefit from this PLI scheme. One of the major factors contributing towards higher costs of EVs in India is the import of ACC batteries, which display the capability of energy storage, and will be the key to achieving the goal of round-the-clock supply of power from renewable energy. Benefits include:

a. Facilitate demand creation for battery storage in India.
b. Facilitate 'Make-in-India' and 'Atmanirbhar Bharat', thereby emphasising domestic value capture and reduction in import dependence.
c. Facilitate demand for EVs, which are proven to be significantly less polluting. One of the key agendas for ACC battery storage will be to reduce India's Greenhouse Gas (GHG) emissions.

d. Import substitution of around Rs 200–250 billion (US$ 2.76–3.45 billion) every year, on account of oil imports as this scheme is expected to accelerate EV adoption in India.

e. Impetus to research and development to achieve higher specific energy density and cycles in ACC.

f. Promote newer and niche cell technologies.

IV. WIND-SOLAR HYBRID POWER PROJECTS

Simultaneously, along with its battery programme, the government is implementing wind-solar hybrid power projects to decarbonise the power sector and build a sustainable ecosystem for transitioning towards a greener future. Hybrid systems combine two or more modes of electricity generation together, usually renewable technologies such as solar photovoltaic (PV) and wind turbines. As both solar radiation and wind speed vary throughout the year, neither solar nor wind-based system can provide reliable electricity individually. Hybrid systems provide a high level of energy security through the mix of generation methods, and often incorporate a storage system (battery, fuel cell) or small fossil fuelled generator to ensure maximum supply reliability and security.

It is fast emerging as a viable new renewable energy structure in India due to the high potential of both wind and solar resources across various locations and the provision of enhanced grid stability and reliability. To promote the setting up of win-solar hybrid power plants, the Ministry of New and Renewable Energy adopted the National Wind-Solar Hybrid Policy in 2018 which also provides certain waivers and incentives to developers. Various state governments have also come up with their own WSH policies including Gujarat, Andhra Pradesh and Rajasthan. Renewable hybrid projects are a game changer as they can generate round-the-clock power with high reliability level.

The main objective of the policy is to provide a framework for promotion of large grid connected wind-solar PV hybrid system for optimal and efficient utilisation of transmission infrastructure and land, reducing the variability in renewable power generation and achieving better grid stability. Policy also aims to encourage new technologies, methods and way-outs involving combined operation of wind and solar PV plants.

SECI tenders for wind-solar hybrids without storage have attracted low tariffs to the tune of Rs 2.67 per kWh (US¢ 3.7 per kWh) which are comparable to solar tariffs. Adani Green Energy, SB Energy, Greenco and ReNew Power are the key active participants across wind-solar hybrid tenders.

However, a financial model developed by JMK Research and Analytics for a 250 MW wind-solar hybrid project has revealed that for solar and wind blended at a ratio of 80:20 respectively for a 250 MW WSH plant, the levelised tariff comes to Rs 2.49 per kWh (US¢ 3.32 per kWh), while blending solar and wind at a ratio of 50:50 results in a tariff of about Rs 2.57 per kWh (US¢ 3.43 per kWh). But on analysing the impact of adding a storage component to the WSH project, for a two-hour battery back-up, the levelised tariff increases substantially to Rs 4.59 per kWh (US¢ 6.12 per kWh). Clearly, adding battery storage is not a feasible option at present because it significantly increases project costs and hence the tariffs. However, the declining trend in the battery prices will make these projects viable within a few years and provide more stable power.[10]

References

1. IEA.
2. ScienceDirect: Energy-Storage Technologies and Electricity Generation.
3. Energy Storage Association, now American Clean Power.
4. IEA's World Energy Outlook 2020, 'India is Going to Need More Battery Storage than any other Country for its Ambitious Renewables Push', 23 January, 2020.
5. George Crabtree, an Argonne National Laboratory Senior Scientist and Distinguished Fellow and Director of the Joint Centre for Energy Storage Research, in an Interview with *Lab Manager* magazine, 2 May, 2022.
6. Ibid.
7. World Economic Forum: How Long Duration Energy Storage can Enable India's Net-Nero Transition, 6 December, 2021.
8. Mercom India Research.
9. LBNL: Estimating the Cost of Grid-Scale Lithium-Ion Battery Storage in India, April 2020.
10. JMK Research & Analytics, Wind-Solar Hybrid: India's Next Wave of Renewable Energy Growth.

Chapter 12

ELECTRIC VEHICLES

I. OVERVIEW

Oil has been the king in the realm of transportation for centuries. But no longer. The carbon dioxide (CO_2) emissions coming out of the auto tailpipes when the engines burn petrol or diesel have triggered worldwide concerns about climate change, and are thus driving efforts to find an engine that does not require fossil fuel to run. Electricity is now being seen as the future fuel of transportation, instead of gasoline which has been held culprit for a third of the emissions on roads threatening the planet.

The consumer acceptance of electric cars is growing, albeit slowly, as companies roll out more models. Almost every major automaker is working on battery-electric vehicles, which require recharging from the power grid, and cars that produce their own electricity from compressed hydrogen gas. Toyota, Honda and Hyundai already have begun marketing fuel cell vehicles, although a lack of hydrogen fuel stations has confined initial sales to select cities. It is hoped that cars with small onboard generators, advanced batteries or tanks of hydrogen will one day be as plentiful as gasoline vehicles are today.

Electric vehicles (EVs) are the means of transport that operate by electricity instead of conventional fuels such as petrol, diesel or CNG. They may be powered by a collector system by electricity from off-vehicle sources or maybe inbuilt with a battery, solar panels, fuel cells or an electric generator to convert fuel to electricity. Electric bikes, electric cars, electric rickshaws, electric buses and electric trucks etc., are some examples of electric vehicles. Most of the trains including metros are already running worldwide by electricity.

There are three types of electric vehicles—battery electric vehicles (BEV), hybrid electric vehicle (HEV), plug-in hybrid electric vehicles (PHEV) and fuel cell electric vehicles (FCEV). BEVs are powered by electricity stored in a battery pack. They use electric motors and motor controllers instead of internal combustion engines (ICEs) for propulsion. They derive all power

345

from battery packs and thus have no internal combustion engine, fuel cell or fuel tank. These include motorcycles, bicycles, scooters, skateboards, railcars, watercraft, forklifts, buses, trucks and cars. As of October 2020, the world's top selling all-electric car in history has been the Tesla Model 3, followed by the Nissan Leaf. In India, Tata Motors' Nexon and Tigor were the top selling EVs, followed by MG's ZS EV, Hyundai's Kona EV and Mahindra's eVeritos EV. In April 2022, Indians bought a total of 2,150 electric cars which was a gain of 260% year-on-year, compared to the same period in April 2021.[1]

HEV uses both the internal combustion (usually petrol) engine and the battery-powered motor powertrain. The petrol engine is used both to drive and charge when the battery is empty. HEVs have both engine and electric motor. The engine gets energy from fuel, and the motor gets electricity from batteries. The transmission is rotated simultaneously by both engine and electric motor. This then drives the wheels.

PHEV uses both an internal combustion engine and a battery charged from an external socket (they have a plug). This means the vehicle's battery can be charged with electricity rather than the engine. PHEVs are more efficient than HEVs but less efficient than BEVs. They are also known as series hybrids. They have both engine and a motor. One can choose between fuels, conventional fuel (such as petrol) or alternative fuel (such as bio-diesel). It can also be powered by a rechargeable battery pack. The battery can be charged externally.

FCEVs split electrons from hydrogen molecules to produce electricity to run the motor. They employ fuel cell technology to generate the electricity required to run the vehicle. The chemical energy of the fuel is converted directly into electric energy. FCEVs generate electricity using a fuel cell stack powered by hydrogen, which is stored on-board. FCEVs are among the cleanest modes of transportations as they release no harmful tailpipe emissions, and only emit water vapour and warm air.

Rationale behind the Use of EVs

Electric vehicles have a smaller carbon footprint than gasoline-powered cars, no matter where their electricity comes from. EVs are more efficient in converting energy to power cars and trucks and cleaner and cheaper, even when the electricity that is used to charge them comes from the dirtiest grid.

EVs are widely seen as the future of transport. There were 16 million electric cars on the world's roads at the end of 2021, and the numbers were increasing through the pandemic, even during a worldwide downturn in overall car sales electric, according to the International Energy Agency (IEA). China, with 4.5 million electric cars, had the largest fleet, and Europe, with 3.2 million electric cars, had the second largest. BEVs accounted for two-thirds of the 6.7 million new electric cars sold worldwide in 2021.

India's thrust on EVs stems from two factors. One, to fight back the rising menace of air pollution, which kills hundreds of thousands of people every year in the country. According to a Lancet study, pollution led to more than 2.3 million premature deaths in India in 2019. Of this, about 1.6 million deaths were due to air pollution and 500,000 due to water pollution.

According to an IEA report, published in 2018, transport carbon footprint accounted for 37% of CO_2 emissions from end-use sectors because transport has the highest reliance on fossil fuels of any sector. But in 2020, CO_2 emissions from the global transport sector fell by over 10%, as Covid-19-related restrictions and lockdowns altered personal mobility patterns, global supply chains and domestic and international travel.

India has a massive and diverse transport sector, which is also the third most CO_2 emitting sector. Data from the Ministry of Environment Forest and Climate Change suggest that the transport sector is responsible for 13.5% of India's energy-related CO_2 emissions, with road transport accounting for 90% of the sector's final energy consumption within the transport sector.[2] Through various policy measures and initiatives, the government is working towards the decarbonisation of road transport, with a major focus on the adoption of EVs. NITI Aayog has been at the helm of the promotion of EVs and sustainable mobility through the National Mission on Transformative Mobility and Battery Storage.

The problem can be solved by transitioning to renewable energy sources, phasing out diesel and petrol cars, and building public transport. Given the promising progress of electrification of this sector in recent years, India has an unprecedented opportunity to maximise the electrification of all modes of transport. Both the rail and road focused scenarios feature rates of close to 100% electrification by 2050. India's rail infrastructure is already largely electrified with a share of 54% of conventional passenger demand and 65% of freight transported on electrified trains. However, significant underinvestment over recent years has not enabled the full electrification of the network. Road transport, as is the case in almost all regions in the world, is only just beginning to electrify, with buses and two-wheelers showing the most significant trends in India.

But decarbonising heavy duty vehicles (HDVs), and particularly long-range trucks, poses a much larger challenge. While studies have demonstrated that efficiency improvements already lead to cost savings today, the case for BEV or hydrogen fuel cell HDVs is currently not as compelling. Electric HDVs, primarily buses, have seen some growth in Indian cities for use in urban routes over shorter distances, but electric or hydrogen HDV use for medium to long distance has not seen any uptake. A comprehensive HDV refuelling/charging network—for instance built around major freight corridors—could be developed throughout India, and concerted marketing campaigns put in place to help disseminate the technology.

Electric Vehicles (EVs) Sales Soar

Despite global car markets struggling with Covid-19 restrictions and chip shortages, EV sales rose 109% in 2021, according to market research firm Canalys, as nearly 6.7 million EVs, including fully electric and plug-in hybrid passenger cars, were sold worldwide, with Tesla leading with 14% share. Nearly 85% of EVs sold globally were delivered to customers in Mainland China and Europe. In comparison, while demand is growing, just 4% of new cars sold in the US in 2021 were EVs, some 5,35,000 units. China is the fastest-moving EV market, which accounted for nearly half of the 3.2 million EVs sold worldwide in 2021. Many new models are launching every month in each important market segment, from tiny, inexpensive city cars to mainstream and premium sedans and SUVs. The Tesla Model 3 was the best-selling electric car in Europe in 2021, but Volkswagen Group was the leading manufacturer of EVs, with several models from Audi, Skoda and VW selling well. Demand for EVs continues to be strong in Europe. In fact, in many European countries EVs represented more than a quarter of new cars sold, with customers waiting for 9 to 12 months for a new EV delivery.

II. EV SALES IN INDIA

The number of EVs plying on road has seen a considerable rise since 2020. A total of 1.19 lakh EVs were sold in 2020, which increased to 3.11 lakh in

2021 and 4.19 lakh in 2022, as per data tabled in the Parliament by the Minister of State for Heavy Industries Krishan Pal Gurjar. However, the sale of gasoline-driven and diesel-driven vehicles far outnumber the EVs; as against 6.3 crore non-electric vehicles, only 10 lakh EVs were sold in the country during the last four years, said the minister.

India's national mission for electric mobility as well as faster adoption and manufacturing of EVs have fast-paced the adoption of these vehicles. The government hopes that around 30% of private cars, 70% of commercial vehicles and 80% of two and three wheelers plying on the road will be EVs by 2030. Electric vehicles have surged in the last five years, leading India to become one of the largest markets for it in Asia, behind China and ahead of Japan. If India achieves its true potential of 50% electrification, every tenth EV sold globally could be manufactured in India. EV manufacturers in India have announced a significant increase in production, the big corporations are choosing EVs to deliver goods and services, consumers are slowly adopting and preferring electric and hybrid variants evidenced by the rise in demand, but there is still a long way to go for the industry to reach a sizeable scale compared to internal combustion engine (ICE) automobiles.

The government has taken several initiatives to accelerate the implementation of the Electric Mobility Mission Plan which targets producing 6–7 million electric and hybrid vehicles in the country by 2025. Another initiative is the FAME Scheme (Faster Adoption and Manufacturing of Hybrid and Electric Vehicles) which aims at providing financial support for technological growth. The 'Green Urban Transport Scheme (GUTS)' aims at introducing high-tech features that minimises carbon emissions and facilities in public transport to encourage more people to make use of public transports rather than preferring individual or private mode of transport.

The first phase of the FAME I scheme, which incentivised vehicle manufacturers to produce EVs increasingly, became operational in 2015. Self-reliance and localisation have, therefore, become high on national priority. The government already has rolled out subsidy and charging infrastructure-based incentive programmes called FAME. The scheme focused on four areas in this phase—demand creation; technology platform; pilot project and charging infrastructure. Demand creation entailed incentivising the manufacturing and adoption of electric two-wheeler, three-wheelers, four-wheeler passenger cars, light commercial vehicles and buses. The government supported about 2.8 lakh EVs (electromotive vehicles such as hybrid electric vehicles, plug-in hybrid electric vehicles and fuel-cell electric vehicles) through demand incentives of about Rs 359 crore, according to the Ministry of Heavy Industries, in the first phase. In addition, 425 electric and hybrid buses were deployed across various cities in the country, and incentives for 520 charging stations were sanctioned. Total budget outlay for FAME I was Rs 895 crore.

In 2019, the government introduced FAME II for five years which focused on subsiding public-shared vehicles such as e-rickshaws and buses alongside personal vehicles such as scooters and cars. Besides giving financial assistance, the central government has reduced GST on electric vehicles from 12% to 5%; and setting up of charging infrastructure to promote the development of EV charging stations. Several state governments too have announced their respective EV policy to promote the sales of electric vehicles by offering subsidies and incentives to the manufacturers and charging infrastructure developers to create the complete ecosystem for electric vehicles. These factors have been playing a key role in the growth of EV sales in India. Additionally, sky-high prices and unpredictability of petrol and diesel availability are fuelling demand for battery-operated electric vehicles across India.

What Drives the Trajectory of EVs?

A short answer is climate change. The transition to electric mobility is a promising global strategy for decarbonising the transport sector, which is a significant contributor to the global energy demand and associated emissions. It is responsible for 24% of direct carbon dioxide (CO_2) emissions due to the burning of fossil fuels, according to the International Energy Agency (IEA), with three-quarters of these emissions being produced by road vehicles. Currently, the CO_2 emissions in the transport sector are about 30% in the case of developed countries and about 23% in the case of the total man-made CO_2 emissions worldwide. There is widespread agreement to reduce CO_2 emissions from transport by a minimum of 50% at the latest by 2050.[3]

Countries worldwide have been devising strategies to mitigate emissions from this sector. To meet the net-zero ambitions, energy efficiency milestones and emissions trajectory, announced by various countries at COP 26 Climate Summit at Glasgow in October-November 2021, road transport electrification continues to expand globally. Governments across the world spent US$ 14 billion on direct purchase incentives and tax deductions for electric cars in 2020, a 25% rise year-on-year. EV fleets are expanding at a fast clip in several of the world's largest vehicle markets. The costs of batteries and EVs are dropping. Charging infrastructure is expanding. This progress promotes electrification of transport modes such as two/three-wheelers, light-duty vehicles (LDVs) (cars and vans), taxis and shared vehicles, buses and heavy-duty vehicles with short range requirements such as urban deliveries. Manufacturers are continuing to expand the number of EV models available to customers.

In India, although the transport sector accounts for less than a fifth of India's final energy use and almost 11% of India's energy sector related carbon dioxide emissions, its GHG emissions are growing at a faster rate compared to other sectors. In 2020, direct emissions (tailpipe emissions) by the transport sector (excluding international aviation and international shipping) stood at 272 mt of CO_2. The road sector, including passenger and freight, dominate transport emissions, accounting for a share of more than 92%. It also significantly contributes to India's air pollution problem. Emissions produced by road transport are growing faster than in any other sector and are expected to be a significant challenge to decarbonising India's energy sector.[4]

The transport sector accounts for about 50% of the oil demand in India.[5] It accounts for a significant share of the total energy in demand in India, with only three other countries dedicating a larger share of their energy to transport—the US, China and Russia.[6] While the growth of transport energy demand in these countries is declining, India's transport demand is set to increase, given that it is currently a growing economy with a low per capita energy consumption for transport.[7] The demand for transport will continue to grow in parallel with accelerating economic growth, making the transport sector in India critical from an energy use and decarbonisation perspective.

Going forward, as India's economic growth accelerates, emissions from this sector are expected to grow at an even faster pace. Currently, India is the fifth largest car market in the world and has the potential to become one of the top three in the near future—with about 40 crore customers in need of mobility solutions by the year 2030. The motor vehicle fleet has been growing rapidly, and expected to almost double to over 200 million by 2030. The current trajectory of adding ever more cars running on expensive imported fuel and cluttering up already overcrowded cities suffering from infrastructure bottlenecks and intense air pollution are bound to worsen the situation further.

As the nation gears towards its 2070 'zero-emission' target, the government has, therefore, intensified efforts to decarbonise the transportation and power generation, the key two sectors, that emit most of India's carbon emissions. As a jumpstart, around 80% of two-wheelers and three-wheelers, 40% of buses and 30–70% of cars are likely to be electric vehicles by 2030, according to the government think tank, NITI Aayog.

India is one of the largest car and two-wheeler manufacturers in the world. It also has the fourth-largest railway network and the fastest-growing aviation market. Between 2019–2020 and 2020–2021, the number of electric two-wheelers had risen by 422% and three-wheelers by 75%. Four-wheeler EVs had increased by 230%, according statistics submitted by Road Transport and Highways Minister Nitin Gadkari in the Parliament in reply to a question in March 2022.

The Society of Manufacturers of Electric Vehicles (SMEV) of India expects EVs sales to hit 10 lakh units in a single year in 2022, which, it said, was equal to the cumulative sales of EVs in the last 15 years. India's electric vehicle market is expected to grow at a CAGR of 94.4% and reach 152.21 billion units by 2030.

Electric two-wheelers have been leading the EV market, accounting for 98% of the total EV sales in the country. This is because a two-wheeler is usually the first vehicle owned by an average middle-class Indian family. Electric two-wheelers, which cost roughly Rs 1–2 lakhs (US$ 1,300–26,000), will see faster adoption in India than smartphones, according to Goldman Sachs Group, whose base-case scenario is for EV penetration in the segment to swell to 38% by 2030 from 2% in 2022.

Other Advantages

Low running costs: The running cost of an EV is much lower than an equivalent petrol or diesel vehicle. EVs use electricity to charge their batteries instead of using fossil fuels like petrol or diesel. They are more efficient, and that combined with the electricity cost means that charging an EV is cheaper than filling petrol or diesel for your travel requirements. Using renewable energy sources can make the use of electric vehicles more eco-friendly. The electricity cost can be reduced further if charging is done with the help of renewable energy sources installed at home, such as solar panels.[8]

Low maintenance cost: Electric vehicles have very low maintenance costs because they don't have as many moving parts as an internal combustion vehicle. The servicing requirements for these are lesser than the conventional petrol or diesel vehicles.[9]

Zero tailpipe emissions: Driving an EV can help reduce carbon footprint because there are zero tailpipe emissions in these.

Tax and financial benefits: Registration fees and road tax on purchasing EVs are lesser than petrol or diesel vehicles. There are multiple policies and incentives offered by the central and state governments, such as purchase incentives, interest subventions, road tax exemption, registration fee exemption, income tax rebates and scrapping incentives.[10]

Eco-friendliness: Toxic emissions from petrol and diesel vehicles lead to long-term, adverse effects on public health. The emissions impact of EVs is much lower than petrol or diesel vehicles. From an efficiency perspective, electric vehicles can covert around 60% of the electrical energy from the grid to power the wheels, but petrol or diesel cars can only convert 17–21% of the energy stored in the fuel to the wheels. Fully electricity-powered vehicles have zero tailpipe emissions, but even when electricity production is taken into account, petrol or diesel vehicles emit almost three times more carbon dioxide than the average EV. To reduce the impact of charging electric vehicles, India is ambitious to achieve about 40% cumulative electric power installed capacity from non-fossil fuel-based energy resources by the year 2030.

Easy to drive: Electric vehicles don't have gears and are very convenient to drive. There are no complicated controls, just accelerate, brake and steer. When you want to charge your vehicle, just plug it in to a home or public charger.

No noise pollution: Electric vehicles have the silent functioning capability as there is no engine under the hood. No engine means no noise. The electric motor functions so silently that you need to peek into your instrument panel to check if it is 'ON'. EVs are so silent that manufacturers have to add false sounds in order to make them safe for pedestrians.

Government help: Central and state governments in India have been providing incentives to encourage consumers to make the switch to EVs. These include a tax exemption of Rs 1.5 lakh plus discount of interest if you buy an electric car on loan. The Goods and Service Tax (GST) for EVs has been cut down to 5% from 12%, with zero cess, compared to 18–28% for other goods. One-time registration fee applicable on new vehicle purchase is waived off. Other incentives include interest-free loans, top-up subsidies, special incentives on electric three-wheelers. And, if you are de-registering an old petrol and diesel vehicle, you can claim a scrapping incentive.

Cash incentives include: For two wheelers (2 kWh)—Rs 15,000 per kWh up to 40% of the cost of vehicle; for three wheelers (5 kWh)—Rs 10,000 per kWh; for four wheelers (15 kWh)—Rs 10,000 per kWh; for e-buses (250 kWh)—Rs 20,000 per kWh; e-trucks—Rs 20,000 per kWh. It is intended to bring about purchasing price parity with ICE vehicles, coupled with the benefits of long-term operational costs advantages of EVs, and to boost the latter's adoption rate. In addition to financial reasons, the rise of conscious Indian buyers who are aware of their environmental responsibilities is also driving the growth of EVs in India.

The government is also prioritising the shift towards clean mobility, and recent moves to amend the FAME II scheme to make electric two-wheelers more affordable, is a case in point. Under phase two, about 1,65,000 EVs have been supported, as on 25 November, 2021, by way of demand incentive amounting to about Rs 5.64 billion (US$ 75.16 million). Further, under the scheme, approvals have been granted for 6,315 electrical buses, 2,877 EV charging stations amounting to Rs 5 billion (US$ 66.63 million) in 68 cities across 25 states/union territories and 1,576 charging stations amounting to Rs 1.08 billion (US$ 14.39 million) across 9 expressways and 16 highways.

India's EV Revolution Starts in Two-Wheeler Segment

IEA says that India is at the cusp of an EV revolution. But it wouldn't start in cars. Rather it would start in two-wheelers and three-wheelers that are financially more affordable in upfront costs as well as maintenance, and that enjoy considerable government subsidies. Incentives are available at both the national and state levels for moving to EVs.

Two and three-wheelers are the most preferred personal transport in India among light duty vehicles (LDVs). A policy mix of financial, behavioural and charging infrastructure incentives has globally proven to be effective to get

EVs off the ground, and India has already started to develop its own tailored approach with the second edition of the FAME.

Tepid Response

However, despite the commencement of this expanded scheme, EV sales in FY 2019–20 were only 1,56,000 units (97% two-wheelers), while under both scenarios, annual EV sales increased to 1.6–2.9 million per year and 13.3 and 42.3 million per year in the next five and ten years respectively, leading to an end of sales of new internal combustion engines by 2035. Policies in China and California in particular could serve as role models here. Both regions have proven that the right policy mix can both support the uptake of EVs, while simultaneously spurring the development of a nascent industry that can bring with it important industrial growth.

High cost, inadequate infrastructure, lack of high performing EVs are main barriers to the fast adoption of EVs. The electric variants of the two-wheelers and four-wheelers are often priced higher than regular fuel options. Capital cost has always been a major factor in the EV purchase decision, with 63% of consumers believing that EVs are beyond their budget. The lack of adequate charging infrastructure in our country is another huge barrier to increased EV penetration. Compared to traditional petrol stations, charging stations are far and few, usually limited by investment costs and difficult infrastructure development.

On 31 March, 2022, Road Transport and Highways Minister Nitin Gadkari told the Lower House of the Parliament, that prices of electric vehicles in India will be at par with those of gasoline-powered vehicles 'within the next two years'. By all assumptions it appears a boast by the minister. But there is no denying the fact that EV prices are becoming increasingly affordable on the back of falling battery prices and government subsidies across the world.

Undoubtedly, the upfront costs of electric cars are 25–30% more than fuel-powered ICE (internal combustion engine) cars. But when operating costs are factored in, the math looks radically different. The relatively high initial outlay cost of buying an EV can be offset by reduced costs in other areas such as running cost and maintenance. The average ICE has a fuel efficiency of only 40%, with 60% lost via heat and friction. As a result, ICEs consume far more energy travelling the same distance as an EV. An EV directly converts electricity into movement. This makes it far more efficient than a conventional car, which has to burn fuel (creating heat) and then convert that heat into motion.

According to an Axis Bank calculation, the running cost of an electric car comes to between Rs 1.2 and Rs 1.4 per km, while petrol prices hover around Rs 9–10 per km. The huge difference is because of the high price of fuel which powers the ICE and the price of electricity which charges the electric car. For example, if 10 units of electricity are required to fully charge a cargo electric three-wheeler sufficient to deliver a range of 100 kms, then at an average cost of Rs 6 a unit, a day's work can be completed for Rs 60. As compared to this, the diesel version with a mileage of 20 km per litre at an average price of Rs 90 per litre would take around Rs 450 to cover the same distance, thus making EVs over 80% cheaper to operate.[11] A 2020 Consumer Reports study found that EV owners, on average, spend 60% less on fuel compared to internal combustion engine vehicles.

Maintenance-wise also, EVs offer greater value for money as there are far fewer moving parts than normal ICE-based cars that require service and maintenance. In fact, electric autos are far more cost efficient and sustainable in the long-run for an average Indian buyer who wishes to go for pocket-friendly variants. Also, the maintenance cost of an EV is lower than an ICE vehicle as it doesn't run on complex combustion engines or moving parts. Road-ready EVs only require infrequent check-ups of electrical systems, including the battery, motor and electronic components, which helps reduce the maintenance cost by approximately 40% as compared to ICE vehicles.

Promoting Domestic Production

The electric vehicle industry in India is at a nascent stage, but is picking pace fast, backed by favourable government policies, growing popular environmental awareness and falling battery prices. New manufacturing hubs, and charging infrastructure are being created across the country, and more investors, both Indian and foreign, are increasingly participating in the development. The government allows 100% FDI in EV industry and makes no distinction between local and foreign investors in giving subsidies.

The government is following a two-fold approach through the FAME scheme, which aims to benefit the Indian industry and citizens. The second phase of the scheme offers US$ 1.4 billion in incentives to spur electric vehicle growth in the country. Work is already under way on setting up 2,636 electric vehicle charging stations across 62 cities in 24 states and union territories by

2025. Real estate developers have been directed to set aside 20% of parking space for EVs in all residential and office projects to facilitate setting up of charging infrastructure for EV owners. The government has set a target of 30% EV penetration in the country by 2030.

The FAME II stimulus has been helpful in the growth of organised three-wheeler EVs as it reduces their high sticker-price that run on Li-ion batteries. The cost difference between the commonly-in-use lead-acid battery and the more advanced Lithium-ion is usually between Rs 1,00,000 to Rs 2,00,000 for a 6 kWh-12 kWh battery. But the incentives under FAME II on Li-ion battery EVs reduce this price difference quite effectively.

Purchase price parity with ICE vehicles, coupled with the benefits of long-term operational costs advantages of EVs, are being promoted among potential buyers to boost the latter's adoption rate. In addition to financial reasons, the rise of conscious Indian buyers who are aware of their environmental responsibilities is also driving the growth of EVs in India. The government has also mandated Energy Efficiency Services Ltd (EESL) to procure 3 lakh electric three-wheelers for different uses. These decisions will drastically help the manufacturers to cut the cost of electric models and will make them achieve more parity with petrol/diesel vehicles, and in some cases, even cheaper than them!

The growing popularity of EVs is prompting the leading automotive manufacturers to launch electric vehicles in India. For instance, in October 2019, Maruti Suzuki, a leader in the conventional vehicle market, announced plans to launch electric vehicles for personal use for the Indian market in the following years. Similarly, in August 2021, Tata Motors launched the Tata Tigor EV in the Indian market. As the market continues to evolve and the consumer preference continues to shift from conventional vehicles to electric vehicles, more and more conventional vehicle manufacturers are expected to launch EVs in the Indian market, thereby driving the growth of the market over the forecast period.

A report released by strategy consulting firm, Redseer Strategy Consultants, in July 2022 indicated that sales penetration of electric two-wheelers is expected to increase by 78% by 2030, on the back of government policies, technology, infrastructure and consumer acceptance. The report suggests that the top reasons for choosing electric two-wheelers included better features (such as interactive dashboards, connectivity and driving features), and superior economics (running cost and price). Other reasons included the fact that it is more environment-friendly, and offers better performance (instant acceleration). In comparison to ICE vehicles, the cost-of-ownership for electric two wheelers is 20–70% less, with the cost savings increasing with increased usage. Interestingly, the negligible need for maintenance and minimal fuel costs is also attracting B2B players to explore electric two-wheeler adoption as a clean mode of commercial operations. "Although emerging strongly, it is not without its challenges—long charging time and poor charging infrastructure are the two main pain points for both users and non-users," says Mukesh Kumar, Engagement Manager at Redseer Strategy Consultants. However, because of government incentives and growth in the segment, several start-ups along with government bodies are building a better charging infrastructure in India. India currently has 3,000 EV charging stations, with 6 charging stations available per 1,000 EVs.[12]

According to an independent study by CEEW Centre for Energy Finance (CEEW-CEF), the EV market in India will be a US$ 206 billion opportunity by 2030 if India maintains steady progress to meet its ambitious 2030 target. This would require a cumulative investment of over US$ 180 billion in vehicle production and charging infrastructure. Another report by India Energy Storage Alliance (IESA) projects that the Indian EV market will grow at a CAGR of 36% till 2026. The EV battery market is also projected to grow at a CAGR of 30% during the same period.

To promote the Indian EV industry, the government has launch e-AMRIT portal, a one-stop platform for information on electric vehicles. It addresses key concerns about the adoption of EVs and their purchase, such as charging facility locations and EV financing options as well as information about investment opportunities, government policies and available subsidies for drivers and manufacturers. In addition, multiple production-linked incentive schemes intend to create a local manufacturing ecosystem to support goals around greater adoption of electric mobility transport. This is sought to be achieved by incentivising fresh investments into developing indigenous supply chains for key technologies, products and auto components.

On 15 September, 2021, the government approved a PLI scheme for the automobile and drone industry, which intends to incentivise high value advanced automotive technology vehicles and products, including 'green automotive manufacturing'. This will support the EV industry with the requisite infrastructure and will significantly cause a reduction in cost of EVs. The scheme for the auto sector is open to existing automotive companies as well as new investors who are currently not in the automobile or auto component manufacturing business.

III. BATTERIES ARE 'NEW OIL' FOR EVS

Battery is the core of an electric vehicle. It is the energy accumulator that stores electricity for transmission to an alternating or continuous current engine. Batteries are a one-time upfront investment for EVs, serving as an asset (with potential for additional revenue streams through secondary use in stationary applications in India) and contrast with ongoing operating expenses for fuel needed for petrol or diesel vehicles. Every battery purchased will reduce oil imports for many years to come, improving future years' trade balance and reducing India's exposure to oil price shocks. There are four types of batteries that are used as energy storage in electric vehicles—Lithium-ion (Li-ion), Lead-acid, Nickel-Metal Hydride and Ultracapacitors. The use of basic lead-acid batteries goes back to the second half of the nineteenth century. But lithium-ion remains the mainstay of the auto industry. It is most commonly used because of its high power-to-weight ratio, good high-temperature performance, excellent specific energy and low self-discharge rate. Lithium is the lightest of metals that provides the basis for rechargeable batteries.

But batteries cost a fortune. In EVs they account for 40–50% of the cost. According to a Benchmark report, between 2016 and 2018, the cost of lithium, the metal which is used for making Li-ion batteries, increased three-fold, and the cost of cobalt rose four-folds. Further, a study by researchers at the University of Freiberg, Germany, highlighted that even the most optimistic scenario projects a shortage of these metals by 2023. In such a scenario, the production cost of the advanced chemistry cell will automatically shoot up.

But latest studies by the IEA and institutions point to the falling trend of lithium-ion battery prices as electric mobility revolution is gaining momentum. According to the IEA, the average cost of batteries declined 13% to a global average price of US$ 137 per kWh per battery pack, while BNEF reports that the price of Li-ion batteries fell from US$ 1,100 per kWh in 2010 to US$ 156 dollars in 2019 (87%) and is expected to dip as low as US$ 100 by 2024. This has been possible due to the rapid increase in sales of EVs globally—3 million electric cars were sold in 2020, up 40% from 2019. Of these, 74% are BEV and the remaining 26% are PHEV. To meet the demand for batteries, automotive battery production, according to the IEA, rose 33% year-on-year to 160 GWh in 2020. Battery production continues to be dominated by China, which holds over 70% of global cell production capacity and produces about half of all batteries for light-duty vehicles. China also accounts for the largest share of demand at almost 80 GWh, but in 2020 Europe had the greatest increase of 110% to reach 52 GWh.

Status of Batteries in India

Currently, lithium-ion batteries are imported in the form of fully readymade packs or battery components are imported and assembled in India. In both cases, India has to depend on neighbouring countries like China, Japan and Korea for EV batteries, semiconductor components, battery management systems (BMS), magnets used in electric vehicle motors, and other electrical equipment. Lithium and cobalt are the two raw materials that provide the basis for rechargeable batteries. Today, China, which is known as the EV capital of the world, it also dominates the lithium-ion battery market. At the moment, India's electric vehicle industry is largely dependent on Chinese imports for batteries and other powertrain components.

In order to reduce the cost of EVs, India must promote local manufacturing of Li-ion batteries aggressively. At present, imported battery packs cost US$ 275 per kWh in India. This combined with the GST of 18% and the lack of lithium in India, further increase the cost of batteries. In 2019–20, India imported about Rs 8,500 crore worth of Li-ion batteries. Same was the case in 2018–19. This was a six-fold rise from 2014–15. India almost entirely depends on global (especially Chinese) resources and technology for this energy transition. Recent tensions with China have made the country even more aware of this dependency.

Still Miles to Go For Full E-Mobility

However, India's goal to a fully-electric transport ecosystem has miles to go. High cost, inadequate infrastructure, lack of high performing EVs are main barriers to their adoption. The electric variants of the two-wheelers and four-wheelers are often priced much higher than regular fuel options. Capital cost has always been a major factor in the EV purchase decision, with 63% of consumers believing that an EV is beyond their budget. The lack of adequate charging infrastructure in our country is a huge barrier to increased EV penetration. Compared to traditional petrol stations, charging stations are harder to find, normally limited by investment costs and difficult infrastructure development enabling people to charge where they usually park, at home or at work, which presents its own challenges, such as dealing with multi-tenant buildings, grid-connection management and charging slot availability. It is anticipated that there will be a shortage of nickel, and scaling up lithium production would be a challenge, leading to supply shortage that may cause manufacturers to use lower-quality mineral inputs, adversely affecting battery performance.

References

1. Top Best Selling Electric Car Brands In India (April 2022) - EV Cars Sales Grow By 260% Y-o-Y; html https://www.drivespark.com/four-wheelers/2022/top-best-selling-electric-car-brands-april-india-036044.html.
2. IEA, 2020; Ministry of Environment Forest and Climate Change, 2018.
3. UNECE. Sustainable Goals: Climate Change and Sustainable Transport, www.unece.org.
4. Council on Energy, Environment and Water (CEEW).
5. IEA, 2021.
6. IEA, 2016.
7. IEA, 2021.
8. E-Amrit, NITI Aayog; e-amrit.niti.gov.in.
9. Ibid.
10. Ibid.
11. 'What Will It Take To Make Price-Conscious Indians Switch to Electric Vehicles?' by Amitabh Saran, *The Economic Times*, 16 September, 2021.
12. Redseer: Sales Penetration of Electric Two Wheelers (EV) to Increase by 78 percent in 2030, 20 July, 2022.

SECTION IV

THE EMERGING ERA OF ENERGY

Chapter 13
CLIMATE CHANGE

I. OVERVIEW

Carbon dioxide (CO_2) and other greenhouse gases (GHG), such as methane and nitrous oxide, are normal part of the atmosphere. They arise naturally and are part of the make-up of our atmosphere. They form the 62-mile-high blanket of gases that separates the emptiness of the outer space from the atmosphere, which is 98% composed of just two elements—oxygen and nitrogen. Greenhouse gases act as balancers when the short-wave ultraviolet radiation of sunlight passes through all atmospheric gases on way to the Earth's surface, and the Earth sends back the long-wave infrared rays towards the sky after converting the short-wave ultraviolet radiation into long-wave infrared rays. CO_2 and other GHG trap the heat of the infrared rays and redistribute it through the atmosphere to keep temperatures within a band. Without them, the departing infrared rays would flow back into the vastness of space, and the air would freeze at night, leaving the Earth a cold and lifeless place.[1] Part of what makes Earth a unique planet that it is neither too hot nor too cold that keeps the planet at a friendly 15°C on average to allow life to grow and flourish.

The heat-trapping nature of CO_2 and other GHG was demonstrated in the mid-nineteenth century. In 1824, French scientist Joseph Fourier calculated that an Earth-sized planet, at our distance from the Sun, ought to be much colder. He suggested something in the atmosphere must be acting like an insulating blanket. In 1856, Eunice Foote discovered that blanket, showing that CO_2 and water vapor in Earth's atmosphere trap escaping infrared (heat) radiation. In 1938, Guy Callendar connected CO_2 increases in Earth's atmosphere to global warming. In 1941, Milutin Milankovic linked ice ages to Earth's orbital characteristics. Gilbert Plass formulated the Carbon Dioxide Theory of Climate Change in 1956. Their ability to affect the transfer of infrared energy through the atmosphere is the scientific basis of many instruments flown by NASA. There is no question that increased levels of GHG must cause Earth to warm in response.

Ice cores drawn from Greenland, Antarctica and tropical mountain glaciers show that Earth's climate responds to changes in greenhouse gas levels. Ancient evidence can also be found in tree rings, ocean sediments, coral reefs and layers of sedimentary rocks. This ancient, or paleoclimate, evidence reveals that current warming is occurring roughly ten times faster than the average rate of Ice Age recovery warming. Carbon dioxide from human activity is increasing more than 250 times faster than it did from natural sources after the last Ice Age.

But if the concentrations of CO_2 and other greenhouse gases grow too large, too much heat would be retained, and the atmosphere would become too hot, with the possibility of violent changes in climate. It is feared that a rise of just two or three Celsius in average temperature would wreak havoc, like melting the ice caps, submerging large swaths of coastlines under water, transforming fertile lands into dying deserts and unleashing frequent violent storms. Estimates vary, but if emissions increase, humanity could experience up to eight feet of sea level rise by the end of the century. Many parts of the US East Coast are already experiencing some of the world's fastest rates of sea level rise. Elsewhere, entire island nations face the possibility of going underwater.

Seven Glacial Changes in past 6,50,000 Years: NASA

Earth's climate has changed throughout history. Just in the last 6,50,000 years there have been seven cycles of glacial advance and retreat, with the abrupt end of the last Ice Age about 11,700 years ago marking the beginning of the modern climate era—and of human civilisation. Most of these climate changes are attributed to very small variations in the Earth's orbit that change the amount of solar energy our planet receives.

The current warming trend is of particular significance because it is unequivocally the result of human activity since the mid-twentieth century and proceeding at a rate that is unprecedented over millennia.[2]

It is undeniable that human activities have warmed the atmosphere, ocean and land and that widespread and rapid changes in the atmosphere, ocean, cryosphere and biosphere have occurred. Earth-orbiting satellites and other technological advances have enabled scientists to see the big picture, collecting many different types of information about our planet and its climate on a global scale. This body of data, collected over many years, reveals the signals of a changing climate.

For over 200 years, humanity has powered itself with fossil fuels like oil and coal. We've seen an enormous amount of development and progress—but at an incredible cost. Since the pre-industrial period, the Earth's global average temperature has risen relentlessly, primarily driven by human activity, particularly fossil fuel burning, but also due to natural processes like cyclical ocean patterns, volcanic activity, changes in the Sun's energy output and variations in Earth's orbit. According to readings from the Scripps Institution of Oceanography and the National Oceanic and Atmospheric Administration (NOAA), atmospheric CO_2 levels have risen from 283 ppm (parts per million) in 1800 to 285 ppm in 1850, to 296 ppm in 1900, to 310 ppm in 1950, and to 369.55 in 2000.

The rising CO_2 levels have sounded alarms for urgent action to limit the rise in Earth's temperature 'well below' 2°C (3.6°F), ideally 1.5 °C, compared with pre-industrial levels, to prevent the marching global warming. In 2015, leaders from 197 countries, party to the United Nation's Framework Convention on Climate Change (UNFCCC) met in Paris and signed an agreement under which they committed to a set of climate action goals, called nationally determined contributions (NDC), to reduce emissions. During this Conference of Parties (COP 21), the countries also agreed to make NDCs progressively stricter every five years to reach a net zero level by 2050.

But far from declining, the average CO_2 emissions has been consistently rising since 2015. The year 2020 registered the record high in CO_2 level when it hit 417 ppm. This was higher than at any point in the past 8,00,000 years, says NOAA. The annual rate of increase in atmospheric carbon dioxide over the past 60 years has been about 100 times faster than the previous natural increases, such as those that occurred at the end of the last Ice Age 11,000–17,000 years ago, according to it. The Mauna Loa Observatory in Hawaii, which has been tracking atmospheric CO_2 levels since the late 1950, has noted that the Earth's atmosphere contained so much CO_2 more than three million years ago, when global sea levels were several metres higher and parts of Antarctica were blanketed in a forest.

The Earth's temperature has been rising in line with the spurt in CO_2 level. Globally, 2020 was the hottest year on record, effectively tying with 2016, the previous record. Overall, Earth's average temperature has risen more than 1.2°C (2°F) since the pre-industrial baseline (1850–1900). According to NOAA's 2020 Annual Climate Report the combined land and ocean temperature has increased at an average rate of 0.08 °C (0.13°F) per decade since 1880; however, the average rate of increase since 1981 (0.18°C/0.32°F) has been more than twice that rate. Over the last century, the average surface temperature of the Earth has increased by about 0.67°C (1.0F). The eleven warmest years in this century have all occurred since 1980, with 1995 the warmest on record. Averaged as a whole, the global land and ocean surface temperature for March 2020 was 1.16°C (2.09°F) above the twentieth century average of 12.7°C (54.9°F) and the second highest in the 141-year record. March 2016 was warmer at 1.31°C (2.36°F).

In January 2023, the European Union's Copernicus Climate Change Service (C3S) said that 2022 was the fifth warmest year on record, and "The planet is now 1.2°C warmer than in the pre-industrial times, as a result of human-caused climate change. CO_2 concentrations in the atmosphere averaged around 417 ppm in 2022—the highest level for over two million years. Temperatures in Europe have increased by more than twice the global average over the last three decades."[3]

Unequivocal Evidence of Human Activity in Climate Change

Scientific evidence indicates increasing temperatures are a direct result of anthropogenic activities like combustion of fossil fuels, industrial processes, deforestation and emission of greenhouse gases into atmosphere. Changes observed in Earth's climate since the early twentieth century are primarily driven by human activities, particularly fossil fuel burning, which increases heat-trapping greenhouse gas levels in Earth's atmosphere, raising Earth's average surface temperature. These human-produced temperature increases are commonly referred to as global warming.

But more people doesn't necessarily mean more emissions. However, more fossil fuel burning does mean more emissions. And more affluence has historically meant more fossil fuel burning. Take a look at the United States and India—25 per person tonnes-equivalent versus 10 per person tonnes-equivalent. By 2030, India's population is projected to be more than four times that of the United States. Yet India's total emissions are still expected to be lower than those of the United States. And the average Indian's emissions are expected to be just one-fifth of an American's.

This reflects a global fact. Countries that represent 12% of the population account for 50% of the emissions that have warmed the planet over the last

170 years. Oxfam has concluded that the world's richest 1%, about 63 million people, account for double the carbon dioxide emissions of the world's poorest 3 billion. For most of the last two centuries fossil fuels, coal, oil and gas, configured the international energy geopolitical landscape. They were the foundation of the global energy system, economic growth and modern lifestyles. The exploitation of fossil fuels lifted global energy use fifty-fold in the last two centuries, shaping the geopolitical environment of the modern world. The geographic concentration of fossil fuels has had a significant impact on the wealth and security of nations. The main story of the energy transition is the rise of renewables, particularly solar and wind, and the future decline of fossil fuels.[4]

Natural processes can also contribute to climate change, including internal variabilities like cyclical ocean patterns, El Niño, La Niña and the Pacific Decadal Oscillation, and external forces like volcanic activity, changes in the Sun's energy output, variations in the Earth's orbit.

Inter-governmental Panel on Climate Change (IPCC) defines global warming as an increase in combined surface air and sea surface temperatures averaged over the globe over a period of 30 years. Unless otherwise specified, warming is expressed relative to the period 1850–1900, used as an approximation of pre-industrial temperatures. For periods shorter than 30 years, warming is estimated at an average temperature over the 30 years centred on that shorter period, accounting for the impact of any temperature fluctuations or trend within those years. Accordingly, warming from pre-industrial levels to the decade 2006–2015 is assessed to be 0.87°C (likely between 0.75°C and 0.99°C). Since 2000, the estimated level of human-induced warming has been equal to the level of observed warming with a likely range of ±20% accounting for uncertainty due to contributions from solar and volcanic activity over the historical period.[5]

A most recent study by scientists at NASA have found that the amount of heat trapped by the Earth's land, ocean and atmosphere has doubled over the 14-year period from 2005 to 2019, thanks to a mix of anthropogenic forcing and internal variability which are causing warming and leading to a fairly large change in the Earth's energy imbalance.[6]

Anthropogenic forcings have contributed more to climatic changes than natural processes. The situation has reached such an extent that even if we stop emitting greenhouse gases today, global warming would continue to happen for several decades, if not centuries; for, it takes a long time for the planet, especially the oceans, to respond, and the heat-trapping carbon dioxide lingers in the atmosphere for hundreds of years. In the absence of major actions to reduce the emissions, global temperature is on track to rise by 2.5°C to 4.5°C (4.5°F to 8°F) by 2100, according to the latest estimates by climatologists.

Rising temperatures are causing phenomena such as loss of sea ice and ice sheet mass, sea level rise, longer and more intense heat waves, and shifts in plant and animal habitats. While the long-term trend of warming continues, a variety of events and factors contribute to any particular year's average temperature. Two separate events changed the amount of sunlight reaching the Earth's surface. The Australian bush fires during the first half of the year burned 46 million acres of land, releasing smoke and other particles more than 18 miles high in the atmosphere, blocking sunlight and likely cooling the atmosphere slightly. In contrast, global shutdowns related to the ongoing Covid-19 pandemic reduced particulate air pollution in many areas, allowing more sunlight to reach the surface and producing a small but potentially significant warming effect. These shutdowns also appear to have reduced the amount of carbon dioxide (CO_2) emissions last year, but overall CO_2 concentrations continued to increase, and since warming is related to cumulative emissions, the overall amount of avoided warming will be minimal.

Earth's warming trends are most pronounced in the Arctic, which the NASA's Goddard Institute for Space Studies Surface Temperature Analysis (GISTEMP) analysis shows is warming more than three times as fast as the rest of the globe over the past 30 years, according to scientists at Goddard Institute for Space Studies (GISS). The loss of Arctic sea ice, whose annual minimum area is declining by about 13% per decade, makes the region less reflective, meaning more sunlight is absorbed by the oceans and temperatures rise further still. This phenomenon, known as Arctic amplification, is driving further sea ice loss, ice sheet melt and sea level rise, more intense Arctic fire seasons and permafrost melt. The higher latitudes have warmed more than the equatorial regions.

II. STORY OF CLIMATE CHANGE

The study about climate change began in the Swiss Alps and its glaciers as a matter of sheer curiosity in the eighteenth century. Horace Benedict de

Saussure, a scientist at the Academy of Geneva and a keen alpinist, was troubled by the question as to why did not all the Earth's heat escape into space at night. To find an answer, he built in the 1770s a 'mini greenhouse' what became known as the 'hot box'. Its sides and bottom were covered with darkened cork and the top was glass. As heat and light flowed into the box, heat was trapped, and the temperature rose. Saussure surmised the atmosphere covering the Earth did the same thing what glass did to the box. He likened the atmosphere as a lid over the Earth's surface, a giant greenhouse, letting the light in but retaining some of the heat, keeping the Earth warm even when the Sun had disappeared from the sky.[7] He showed non-luminous warm objects emit infrared heat. In 1838, physicist Claude Pouillet proposed hot water vapour and carbon dioxide might trap infrared and warm the atmosphere, but there was still no experimental evidence of these gases absorbing heat from thermal radiation.

French mathematician Joseph Fourier, a friend of Napoleon, and sometime a governor of Egypt, was fascinated by the experiments of Saussure and tried to develop a mathematical formula to prove it. He wrote, "The temperature (of the Earth) can be augmented by the interposition of the atmosphere, because heat in the state of light finds less resistance in penetrating the air, than in re-passing into the air when converted into non-luminous heat."[8] But he could find, 'no regular mathematical theory' to explain it.

Swiss scientist Louis Agassiz was obsessed with glaciers. He even built a hut on the Aar glacier and moved into it so that he might more closely monitor the glacier's movement. In 1837 he propounded a theory that there had been something once before the present age, which he called an Ice Age, when much of Europe must have been covered by massive glaciers. The ice, Agassiz maintained, came about due to a sudden, mysterious drop in temperature that was part of a cyclical pattern stretching back to the beginning of the Earth's history. As the glaciers had retreated to the north, they had left behind in their wake the valleys, mountains, gorges, lakes, fjords, boulders and gravel that documented their movement.[9]

In 1859, Irish physicist John Tyndall took Saussure's and Fourier's works one step further when he investigated the absorption of infrared radiation in different gases. To find an answer to whether and how the atmosphere could trap and the climate could change, he built a new machine in his basement laboratory in the Royal Institution on Albert Street in London. This was his spectrophotometer, a device that enabled him to measure whether gases could trap heat and light. If the gases were transparent, they would not trap heat, and he would have to find some other explanation. He first experimented with the most plentiful atmospheric gases, nitrogen and oxygen. To his disappointment, they were transparent, and light passed right through them. Then he tried with carbon-bearing gas, primarily methane made by hearing coal, that was pumped into his laboratory by the local London lighting company. When Tyndall put the coal gas into his spectrophotometer, he found that gas, though invisible to the eye, was opaque to the infrared light; it darkened. Here was his proof. It was trapping infrared light. He then tried water and carbon dioxide. They too were opaque. That meant that they too trapped heat. By this point, Tyndall was close to collapsing due to his continuous ten-hour long days in the laboratory and from his inhalation of fumes. But that did not matter. He was elated. "The subject is completely in my hands," he wrote in his journal on May 1859.[10]

Global Cooling or Global Warming?

One year after Tyndall's death in 1893, a Swedish chemist Svante Arrhenius picked up the story. He was curious as to what effects increasing or decreasing of carbon dioxide, or carbonic acid, as it was called at the time, would have on the climate. He threw himself deep into work, month after month of tedious calculations by hand to calculate the effect of changes in carbon, and showed that cutting atmospheric temperature in half would lower the world's temperature by about 4–5°C, and doubling of carbon would increase temperature by 5–6°C. Arrhenius did not have the benefit of supercomputers and advanced computation. Nonetheless, his results are in the range of contemporary models.[11] Although Arrhenius was the first to predict global warming, he was not worried about its possibility in the near future. He thought it would take 3,000 years for CO_2 to double in the atmosphere, and in any event that would be a good thing, because an increased CO_2 concentration would not only prevent a new Ice Age but would also allow mankind to enjoy a better climate and bring forth much abundant crops.

After Arrhenius study, the debate drifted away from the subject of carbon and climate, until the British steam engineer Guy Stewart Callendar had collected more elaborate data from 147 weather stations around the world and showed in 1938 that CO_2 had indeed risen in the atmosphere from the previous century and was going to lead to a change in the climate, more specifically global warming. But, like Arrhenius, Callendar was not worried and thought that an increased CO_2 concentration in the air would make a better world for mankind to live and enjoy. Meteorologists of that time dismissed the steam engineer's findings. But it came to be known as the 'Callendar Effect'.

Two decades later, Callendar's findings were eventually confirmed by a series of systematic measurements of atmospheric CO_2 at Mauna Loa in Hawaii and in Antarctica by Charles David Keeling that atmospheric concentration was, indeed, rising. In 1959 the average concentration was 316 ppm. By 1970 it had risen to 325 ppm, and by 1990 it would reach 354 ppm. Fitted on a graph, the rising line became known as the 'Keeling Curve'. Based on the trend established by Keeling's pioneering research, the carbon dioxide in the atmosphere would double around the middle of the twenty first century. Keeling's work marked a great transition in climate science, and became 'the central icon of greenhouse effect'. Pursuing his research further in 1969 Keeling warned of risks from rising carbon. In 30 years, he said, "Mankind's world, I judge, will be in greater immediate danger than it is today."[12]

During the 1970s there was much discussion about whether the climate change was going to be in the form of global cooling or global warming. Some feared that glaciers would return. Others warned that the increasing concentrations of aerosols in the atmosphere could be sufficient to trigger an Ice Age. The CIA was investigating the geopolitical impact of global cooling, including the 'megadeaths and social upheaval' that would ensue. By the early 1980s, discussion about global cooling took a new form, the harsh nuclear winter that could be set off by a nuclear war between the US and the Soviet Union.

By the mid-1980s the focus on climate change research shifted from nuclear winter or cooling to global warming. Environmental biologist and climate scientist at Stanford University professor Stephen Henry Schneider had first predicted global warming in 1976. In 1988, it was finally acknowledged that the climate was warmer than any period since 1880. Environmental NGOs started to press for global environmental protection to prevent further global warming. In 1988, IPCC was founded by the United Nations Environmental Programme (UNEP) and the World Meteorological Organisation (WMO) to predict the impact of the greenhouse effect according to existing climate models and literature information. The IPCC consists of more than 2,500 scientific and technical experts from more than 60 countries all over the world. The scientists are from widely divergent research fields including climatology, ecology, economics, medicine and oceanography. The Panel is referred to as the largest peer-reviewed scientific cooperation project in history. It releases climate change reports ever four years, the first was released in 1992.

In the 1990s, scientists started to question the greenhouse effect theory, because of major uncertainties in the data sets and model outcomes. They protested the basis of the theory, which was data of global annual mean temperatures. They believed that the measurements were not carried out correctly and that data from oceans was missing. Cooling trends were not explained by the global warming data and satellites showed completely different temperature records from the initial ones. The idea began to grow that global warming models had overestimated the warming trend of the past 100 years. This caused the IPCC to review their initial data on global warming, but this did not make them reconsider whether the trend actually exists. We now know that 1998 was globally the warmest year on record, followed by 2002, 2003, 2001 and 1997. The ten warmest years on record have all occurred since 1990.[13]

However, though climate change is a global phenomenon, no concrete measures had been collectively taken at the international level to do something about it. It was only in 1998 that the first international measure— the Kyoto Protocol—was adopted in the Japanese city of Kyoto. The Protocol requires participating countries to reduce their anthropogenic greenhouse gas emissions (CO_2, CH_4, N_2O, HFCs, PFCs and SF_6) by at least 5% below the 1990 levels in the commitment period of 2008 to 2012. The Kyoto Protocol was eventually signed in Bonn in 2001 by 186 countries, but several countries such as the United States and Australia have not ratified the treaty.

The Keeling Curves showed a downward trend of global annual temperature from the 1940s to the 1970s. At the same time ocean sediment research showed that there had been no less than 32 cold-warm cycles in the last 2.5 million years, rather than only 4. Therefore, fear began to develop that a new Ice Age might be nearby. The media and many scientists ignored scientific data of the 1950s and 1960s in favour of global cooling.

III. MONTREAL PACT

In 1985, British Antarctic Survey researchers, using data from NASA, saw something that stunned them, a 'hole' was opening up in the ozone over the Antarctica. This was caused by a group of man-made greenhouse gases called chlorofluorocarbons (CFC) that were eating at the ozone, which absorbed the deadly concentrations of ultraviolet radiation, and thinning out and depleting the layer in the atmosphere. CFCs are potent in trapping heat, and estimated to be ten thousand times more potent than CO_2. It was first developed in the 1920s. Its use had multiplied over the years, from propellants in aerosol cans to coolant in refrigerators. The loss of ozone threatened massive epidemic of skin cancer around the world as well as devastating effects on animal and plant life on Earth. The fear was so strong that in less than two years 24 countries met in Montreal, Canada, and signed a protocol to curb the CFCs. At that time there were fewer than forty companies in the world manufacturing CFCs in the world and just two half the market.

In the 1980s, finally, the global annual mean temperature curve started to rise. People began to question the theory of an upcoming new Ice Age. In the late 1980s, the curve began to increase so steeply that the global warming theory began to win terrain fast. Environmental NGOs started to advocate global environmental protection to prevent further global warming. The press also gained an interest in global warming. It soon became a hot news topic that was repeated on a global scale. Pictures of smoke stags were put next to pictures of melting ice caps and flood events. A complete media circus evolved that convinced many people we are on the edge of a significant climate change that has many negative impacts on our world today. Stephen Schneider had first predicted global warming in 1976. This made him one of the world's leading global warming experts.

The IPCC is considered as the largest peer-reviewed scientific cooperation project in history. It released its first Climate Assessment Report to the United Nations in 1990. The report answered the basic question by stating unequivocally that the Earth was warming and that temperatures have risen by over 0.3–0.6°C over the last century. It said that humanity's emissions were adding to the atmosphere's natural complement greenhouse gases and that the addition would be expected to result in warming.

The climate records of the IPCC are still contested by many other scientists, causing new research and frequent responses to sceptics by them. This global warming discussion is still continuing today and data is constantly checked and renewed. Models are also updated and adjusted to new discoveries and new theory.

UN Conference on Environment and Development

Responding to the IPCC report, the United Nations General Assembly called for an international agreement, a 'convention', to limit greenhouse gases, primarily CO_2. So, an Earth Summit, officially known as the United Nations Conference on Environment and Development, was convened. Held in Rio de Janeiro in June 1992, the conference saw massive gathering of more than 160 heads of state and governments and international organisations; 10,000 other government officials; and 25,000 people—activists, NGOs, business leaders and journalists. The event was described at the time as a 'fractious 12 days of diplomatic free-for-all'. It also saw intense fireworks between the developed and the developing nations, with developing countries holding the developed ones responsible for the release of most of the carbon in the atmosphere and consequent global warming as they had had been burning coal, oil and natural gas for a very long time. They argued that it was their carbon; they were responsible for the problem, and they should be the ones to pay for fixing it. Why should the developing countries be denied their chance to grow? The developed countries were divided. European countries sought specific timetables and targets to reduce emissions. Others wanted to proceed, but more slowly, and not with specific targets. However, on the last day of the Earth Summit, the United Nations Framework Convention on Climate was signed on by US President George HW Bush (the first signatory) and 153 other leaders.

The key objective of this Framework Convention was, "Stabilisation of greenhouse gas concentrations in the atmosphere, a level that would prevent dangerous anthropogenic interference with the climate system." Developed countries agreed to return their emissions to 1990 level. Developing countries had no obligation other than monitoring. In addition, the developed countries agreed to provide financial resources to help developing countries reduce their emissions.

IV. KYOTO PROTOCOL

In 1995, the IPCC presented its Second Assessment Report that set the framework for a major international to work out mechanism for implementing the pledges made at Rio de Janeiro Earth Summit in 1992. This was held at Kyoto, the ancient capital of Japan, in 1997. Like the Rio's 1992 Earth Summit, the Kyoto event was a big 'circus', with 10,000 people, including officials, experts, NGOs, industry representatives and journalists rubbing shoulders, among the main negotiators. Kyoto event was meant for securing global binding commitments on reducing emissions. But it was not an auspicious time for that. Asian markets were in turmoil because of the Asian financial crisis which had also impacted other markets. Developing countries bitterly opposed to taking any binding commitment about reducing emissions. However, at the end of the day, the United States, Europe and Japan ended up agreeing on a binding protocol targeting CO_2 emissions reduction, with variations for individual countries, of between 6–8% by 2008–12 compared with 1990. The Kyoto Protocol had to be ratified by 55 countries to go into effect. But the US Senate refused to ratify it, leaving President George W Bush with no option but to remove his country from it. However, the protocol was saved by Russian President Vladimir Putin, who signed it, making Russia the fifty-fifth signatory to sign the treaty. In 2005, the Kyoto Protocol became international law for the countries who had signed on to it.

Meanwhile, in 2001, the IPCC had come out with the Third Assessment Report, with 'new and stronger evidence' that held human beings the main producer of emissions of greenhouse gases and warming seen in the second half of the twentieth century. In 2005, British Prime Minister Tony Blair, who was also chair of the G8 and President of the European Union, appointed a committee, led by economist Nicholas Stern, to study the economics of climate change. In 2006, the Stern Review of the Economics of Climate Change, came out with the conclusion that the costs of inaction on climate change would be enormous and that the costs of mitigating climate change would not be prohibitive by comparison. The study concluded that climate change could damage global GDP by up to 20% if left unchecked, but curbing it would cost about 1% of global GDP.

Carbon emissions in 2006 from fossil fuel burning and industry reached 8 bt per year. The IPCC's Fourth Assessment Report in 2007 concluded that it was more than 90% likely that humanity's emissions of greenhouse gases were responsible for modern-day climate change. At UN negotiations in Bali in that year, governments agreed on a two-year 'Bali Roadmap' aimed at hammering out a new global treaty by the end of 2009. Half a century after beginning observations at Mauna Loa, the Keeling project showed that CO_2 concentrations in the atmosphere had risen from 315 ppm in 1958 to 380 ppm in 2008.

'Major Emitters' or 'Major Economies'

Around the same time, the US President George W Bush, who had pulled out his country from the Kyoto Treaty in 2005 following the refusal by the Senate to ratify it, was forced to bring climate change back on the political agenda. In his 2007 State of the Union Address, he declared that the United States should 'confront the serious challenge of global climate change'. But it would not go through the cumbersome route of Kyoto and the United Nations. Instead, Bush brought together a new grouping of 17 countries that produced the bulk of the man-induced CO_2 emissions, terming them as, 'Major Emitters'. However, when the invitations were sent out, messages came back from the other countries that they didn't really like being called 'Emitters'.[14] 'Major Emitters' then became 'Major Economies' that collectively represented 80% of world GDP, consumed 80% of world energy and produced 80% of the world's CO_2. These included countries like China, India and Brazil which in due course provided a way to manage the contentious divide between the developed and developing countries.[15]

China Overtakes the US as Biggest CO_2 Emitter

By 2006, China had overtaken the US as the biggest producer of CO_2 in the world, and it was expected that by 2030 the Chinese output of CO_2 could exceed that of the all 28 member-countries of the Organisation for Economic Cooperation and Development (OECD) combined, if unchecked. China had come under severe international criticism over this increase, to which it replied thus: first, measured on a per capita basis, its energy use and CO_2 emissions were only a fraction of that of the US and Europe; second, China was still a relatively poor country making a transition that Europe, North America and Japan had made decades ago, and, hence, it should not be denied the same opportunities and standards of living as the developed countries; and the third, it argued that another reason for the increasing energy use and emissions in China was that Europe and North America have in effect outsourced a significant of their energy-intensive production to China, as their own economies continue to shift to services and consumption.

India's stance at international climate change negotiations has been to reiterate even more strongly that it is a developing country in need of a rapid economic growth to raise the living standards of its billion-plus people. It insisted that it must not be penalised for emissions spewed by the industrial countries into the atmosphere for over two centuries. Like China, it uses coal to produce most of its electricity and also burns a great deal of biomass. But it produces only about 5% of the world's CO_2, compared with China's 23%. On the per capita basis, India's CO_2 emissions had increased from 1.1 tonnes in 2001 to 1.9 tonnes in 2019, compared with China's 7.38 tonnes and United States 15.52 tonnes.

V. COPENHAGEN CONFERENCE—COP 15

The Copenhagen Climate Change Conference was a crucial event in the negotiating process. It was supposed to be the successor to Kyoto and has aroused much hope for a new global agreement. Around 113 heads of state or government attended the conference, making it one of the largest gatherings of world leaders ever outside the UN headquarters in New York. According to the UNFCC secretariate more than 40,000 people, representing governments, NGOs, inter-governmental organisations, faith-based organisations, media and UN agencies had applied for accreditation. But the conference ended with only a simple political statement, the Copenhagen Accord, affirming the need to limit the global average temperature increase to no more than 2°C above pre-industrial levels. There was, however, no agreement on how to do this in practical terms. In particular, it failed to agree on limiting greenhouse gas emissions and the question of forming a global environmental agency was sidelined.

This failure was related to many developed countries refusing to adopt restrictive targets on limiting emissions by 2020 and to developing countries insisting on their right to develop their economies. The lack of success in Copenhagen also highlighted the limitations of inter-governmental procedures when trying to agree on the management of public assets globally. Nor did the new economic context, characterised by the financial and then the economic crisis, facilitate the negotiations. For a face-saver, however, the developed countries promised to fund actions to reduce greenhouse gas emissions and to adapt to the inevitable effects of climate change in developing countries. A sum of US$ 30 billion was promised for a period of three years 2010–12 as 'Fast Star Finance', and further to mobilise long-term finance of US$ 100 billion a year by 2020 to help them 'green' their economies and adapt to climate impacts.

Since the Copenhagen Summit, conferences have been held annually (Cancun 2010, Durban 2011, Doha 2012, Warsaw 2013 and Lima 2014) in an attempt to reach a global agreement in Paris in late 2015 that could become effective from 2020 as the successor to the 1997 Kyoto Protocol. There are two key negotiating points—agreeing on voluntary national targets consistent with an effective global response to climate change and resolving the question of how to finance the efforts of developing countries.

In 2011, data showed concentrations of greenhouse gases were rising faster than in previous years. Arctic sea ice reached a minimum extent of 3.41 million sq km (1.32 million sq mi), a record for the lowest summer cover since satellite measurements began in 1979. In 2013, the Mauna Loa Observatory in Hawaii reported that the daily mean concentration of CO_2 in the atmosphere had surpassed 400 ppm for the first time since measurements began in 1958. In the same year, IPCC came out with its Fifth Assessment Report which concluded that scientists were 95% certain that humans had been the 'dominant cause' of global warming since the 1950s.

VI. PARIS ACCORD—UNFCCC

Fearing catastrophic consequences of increasing surface temperatures of the Earth, leaders of about 200 countries convened in the French capital of Paris in 2015 to deliberate on mechanism needed for mitigating climate change. The central aim of the conference was to strengthen global response to the threat of climate change by keeping the global temperature rise this century well below 2°C, and if possible, 1.5°C above the pre-industrial levels (pre-1850). To tackle the negative impacts of climate change and reach the goal, the world leaders at the UN Climate Change Conference (COP 21) in Paris reached a breakthrough deal, better known as the historic Paris Agreement. The Agreement is a legally binding international treaty, signed by 192 Parties, including 191 countries and the European Union. It entered into force on 4 November, 2016.

The language of the agreement was negotiated by representatives of 197 parties at the 21st Conference of the Parties of the UNFCCC in Paris and adopted by consensus on 12 December, 2015. The Agreement was open for signature by States and regional economic integration organisations that are Parties to the UNFCCC (the Convention) from 22 April, 2016 to 21 April, 2017 at the UN Headquarters in New York. The agreement stated that it would enter into force (and thus become fully effective) only if 55 countries that produce at least 55% of the world's greenhouse gas emissions (according to a list produced in 2015) ratify, accept, approve or accede to the agreement. On 1 April, 2016, United States and China, which together represent almost 40% of global emissions, issued a joint statement confirming that both countries would sign the Paris Climate Agreement. On the first date it was open for signature, 175 Parties (174 states and the European Union) signed the agreement, on the same day, more than 20 countries issued a statement of their intent to join as soon as possible in 2016. With ratification by the European Union, the Agreement obtained enough parties to enter into effect as of 4 November, 2016. As of November 2021, 194 states and the European Union had signed, ratified and ratified or acceded to the Agreement. They accounted for over 98% of the global greenhouse gas emissions, including those of China and the United States, the countries with the first and second largest CO_2 emissions among UNFCC members.

The Agreement includes commitments from all countries to reduce their emissions and calls on countries to strengthen their commitments over time. It provides a pathway for developed nations to assist developing nations in their climate mitigation and adaptation efforts while creating a framework for the transparent monitoring and reporting of countries' climate goals. The Paris Agreement works on a five-year cycle of increasingly ambitious climate action carried out by countries. Every five years, each country is expected to submit an updated national climate action plan, known as the Nationally Determined Contribution (NDC). In their NDCs, countries communicate actions they take to reduce their greenhouse gas emissions in order to reach the goals of the Paris Agreement. Countries also communicate in the NDCs actions they propose to take to build resilience to adapt to the impacts of rising temperatures. The operational details for the practical implementation of the Paris Agreement were agreed on at the UN Climate Change Conference

(COP 24) in Katowice, Poland, in December, 2018, in what is called the Paris Rulebook, and finalised at COP 26 in Glasgow, Scotland, in November, 2021.

VII. GLASGOW CONVENTION—COP 26

In August 2021, the IPCC came out with a new climate report warning of devastating consequences of a spurt in global warming in the next 20 years if the global average temperature rose beyond 1.5°C of the pre-industrial level. At present, it's already 1.1°C, and has been rising by 0.1–0.3 each decade above the pre-industrial levels. Coastal areas will see continued sea level rise throughout twentieth century, contributing to more frequent and severe coastal flooding in low-lying areas. Extreme sea level events that previously occurred once in 100 years could happen every year by the end of this century. Climate change is affecting rainfall patterns. In high latitudes, precipitation is likely to increase, while it is projected to decrease over large parts of the subtropics. Changes to monsoon precipitation are expected, which will vary by region. There will be increasing heat waves, longer warm seasons and shorter cold seasons globally at 1.5°C of global warming. Dangerous thresholds are closer than once thought—Earth will cross the critical temperature rise limit in next 20 years, and all regions will have to face disastrous consequences, said the report.

Taking note of the IPCC's stark warning, leaders and representatives of 197 parties to the UN Framework Convention on Climate Change (UNFCCC) convened in Glasgow from 29 October to 13 November, 2021 with one task to decide on measures to limit global warming to 1.5°C above pre-industrial levels a common goal. Though the agreement reached in 2015 Paris conference had set the target of keeping global warming 'well below 2°C', it also urged countries to 'pursue efforts' to keep warming down to 1.5°C. There was general acknowledgment that the Paris Agreement was not delivering fast enough decarbonisation to bring the temperatures down to 1.5°C. Modelling carried out by number-crunchers within the Glasgow halls showed that, even if all the NDCs made by countries at the Paris conference were delivered, there would be a 68% chance of temperatures rising to between 1.9°C and 3.0°C, with a median value of 2.4°C. So, the delegates agreed to go back and do their maths to come up with better pledges for 2030. This means finding the measures to eliminate roughly 20 bt of emissions from national projections before the decade end.

The delegates talked of various ways to shoot the target. According to *The Economist* correspondent, who covered the conference, "Week one delivered a flurry of sectoral deals on forests, finance, cash and more. Some of that continued into week two, before giving way to the main job of UN negotiations among nearly 200 countries and parties. They argued over rules for trading carbon credits between countries, issues around transparency, finance to help poor countries decarbonise, finance to help them adapt and yet more financial provisions to help nations recover from damage done by extreme weather. There was a surprise joining of hands between America and China, and there were politically charged discussions over whether or not the final text should mention 'phasing out' or 'phasing down' unabated coal, and whether to remove the mention of fossil fuels entirely. Delegates disagreed over whether 'urges' or 'requests' bore more weight, and bits of text mysteriously disappeared overnight on at least one occasion."

In the end, however, a series of measures were agreed to move closer to the goal of containing the global temperatures to 1.5°C. The first came in the form of a 'request' to members to increase their pledges for substantial emissions cuts by 2030 before the 27th COP was held in Egyptian city of Sharm el-Sheikh in November, 2022. The second was financial and facilitation of new cash flows. In 2009 rich countries promised to mobilise US$ 100 billion of climate finance each year for poor countries by 2020. By 2019 the annual flow had only reached US$ 80 billion, according to the OECD, a club of mostly rich countries. The shortfall was a major sore point, repeatedly pointed out by poor countries at Glasgow.

Developing countries insisted that they did not have the means to decarbonise without financial assistance. India said it needed US$ 1 trillion over the next decade if it were to cut carbon and boost resilience more than it was already doing. African countries demanded US$ 700 billion each year. The V20, a group founded by 20 vulnerable countries in 2015 and which now has a membership of 48, appealed for rich countries to meet the annual US$ 100 billion goal and fill the gap left from previous years. Other emerging markets called for a higher annual target to be in place after 2025. The 'G77 plus China' group of developing countries lobbied for a fund to pay for such 'loss and damage'. But nothing of all this formed part of the Glasgow Pact. Plans for a loss-and-damage fund were strongly torpedoed by rich countries, particularly America, the world's largest cumulative emitter, which was worried that such moves may open the door to enormous liabilities. However, the rich countries yielded some ground on financing for climate adaptation, such as building sea walls. It was promised by the rich countries in the Paris Agreement to finance mitigation and adaptation in roughly equal measure, yet only a quarter of the US\$ 80 billion raised in 2019 went to adaptation. In the Glasgow Agreement, rich countries pledged to at least double the amount given to adaptation by 2025. But in itself it doesn't take the world anywhere closer to 1.5°C target.

Outside the UN process, some groups of countries, companies and cities came up with their own projects to help climate targets. For instance, US, Britain, European Union, France and Germany agreed to raise US\$ 8.5 billion over a period of three to five years to help South Africa to decarbonise its coal-dependent power sector while protecting the livelihoods of over 1,00,000 people who work in the industry. Progress on this approach will be monitored over the next year. If the results are promising, proponents hope it could be a template for other countries. Projects announced by such groupings (called Coalition of the Willing) at Glasgow included one on phasing out coal power, another on reducing methane emissions, third on greening the financial services industry and the fourth on ending deforestation. In every case some big countries and companies were involved. But in every case some big nations were missing—for instance, the coal pledge did not include the world's five biggest consumers of coal—China, India, United States, Russia and Japan.

The agreement on coal came after an intense wrangling between the advocates of 'phasing out' of coal and ending fossil fuel subsidies, and those favouring 'phasing down'. With its strong intervention India had the wording changed to 'phasing down' coal and accepted, albeit grudgingly, by the Parties to the conference. However, the change in wording hardly changed anything in substance, as without a timeline both formulations were merely symbolic—not binding. The agreement did not please many countries. China, the world's biggest consumer of coal and emitter of greenhouse gases, called it 'by no means perfect'; New Zealand described it as the 'least-worst agreement' and Bolivia said, 'we still have issues and deep concerns'. India felt that the agreement was unfairly calling for developing countries to take actions that could threaten their development. But almost every country affirmed that while the outcome was far from perfect, the alternative, walking away with no agreement, would be worse.

UN Secretary General António Guterres called the outcome of COP 26 a 'compromise'. It reflected the interests, the contradictions and the state of political will in the world today. He said it was an important step, but it was not enough. Guterres intends to set up a body to examine net zero pledges made by companies and to develop standards, according to press reports.

India's Commitments at Glasgow

Addressing the Glasgow summit Prime Minister Narendra Modi announced a five-point action plan, which he called 'Panchamrit' (Five Elixir), to combat climate change. The first component of the Panchamrit targets at raising non-fossil fuel-based energy capacity to 500 GW by 2030, up 25% from the earlier target of 400 GW set by the prime minister. India expects to meet 50% of its projected power demand of 1,100 GW in 2030 by increasing the production capacity of solar to 280 GW and wind to 140 GW, with hydropower, nuclear biofuel supplying the remainder. The government's main thrust is on renewable energy, which is expected to not only reduce the emissions of greenhouse gases relative to fossil fuels and create more employment but also cut oil and gas imports. A drastic reduction in solar and wind energy prices over the years has made investment in renewable energy attractive.

What Do These Goals Mean?

India's electricity demand is set to increase much more rapidly than its overall energy demand. After more than 2% decline in electricity demand in 2020 due to the Covid-19 pandemic, 2021 saw a strong rebound with growth of estimated 10%. This took demand to levels higher than before the pandemic, despite the outbreak of new Covid-19 variants in March-June 2021. Over 2022–2024, the IEA expects annual demand growth to remain above the pre-pandemic levels at around 6.5% per year, mainly driven by growth in the industrial and residential sectors. The 'Make in India' government initiative will continue to propel electricity demand growth in the industrial sector by promoting local manufacturing, and by end uses such as cooking, cooling and mobility in the residential and transport sectors.

The IEA expects 48% of new demand to be met by coal-fired generation and about half of the additional supply to be provided by low-carbon energy sources, principally wind and solar PV, which are set to see new records for renewable capacity addition in 2021 and 2022. The agency expects renewables to provide 35% of the incremental demand, with nuclear largely accounting for the balance. Driven by state and central auctions, as well as the new target of 500 GW of installed renewable capacity by 2030, renewable generation is expected to increase by 30% by 2024 relative to 2021, according to the IEA.[16]

The country has seen a remarkable growth in renewable energy capacity addition among all large economies since 2014, with solar expanding by over 18 times, particularly. Now, in line with Prime Minister Modi's commitment at COP 26 for India to have 500 GW of non-fossil energy capacity by 2030, efforts have been intensified in both private and public sector to set up new renewable energy projects to raise the non-fossil fuel capacity. Some of the country's major energy companies—Reliance Industries Ltd, Adani Group and NTPC Ltd—have announced massive investments in renewable energy, mostly solar, to herald their transition to a low-carbon future. According to the Council for Energy, Environment and Water (CEEW), Indian renewable energy companies raised a record US$ 5.9 billion through 'green bonds' in 2021 from the overseas debt markets. According to the REN21 Renewables 2020 Global Status Report, India attracted an investment of US$ 64.4 billion in renewable programmes and projects during 2014–19, of which US$ 11.2 billion was invested in 2019 alone.

The Central Electricity Authority (CEA) has projected India's overall installed power capacity to reach 817 GW by 2030, of which 63%, or 522 GW, would come from non-fossil fuel sources—solar, wind, hydro, natural gas and nuclear—and the remainder from coal and natural gas. Solar and wind would be major contributors, with 280 GW and 140 GW respectively. The CEA is confident that India would achieve its target of having an installed non-fossil fuel capacity of 500 GW much before 2030.

A new study by researchers at the Lawrence Berkeley National Laboratory (Berkeley Lab) of the US has echoed CEA's projection and also forecasted that India can leapfrog to a more sustainable power system by 2030, thanks to dramatic cost reductions in battery storage and wind and solar energy. According to the study titled, 'Least Cost Pathway for India's Power System Investments', the researchers examined a least-cost investment pathway to meet India's electricity demand through 2030, and found that if India achieves its goal of installing 500 GW of non-fossil electricity capacity by 2030, it could reduce electricity costs by 8–10%, provided that the price of renewable energy and batteries continue to fall.[17]

If we look at the pace at which India's renewable energy capacity (including hydro and nuclear) has been growing for the past eight years (2014–22), there is no doubt that the achieving mission 500 GW is not an impossible task. Over the last eight years the renewable energy capacity had risen by 40% to 220 GW by 2022 and was set to reach 400 GW by 2025, according to the Ministry of New and Renewable Energy. Solar and wind will be the principal contributor to the increased capacity.

According to the CEA's Optimal Generation Capacity Mix projections for 2029–30, India's total electricity generation requirement would be 2,518 BU, which would come from the total installed energy capacity, including both fossil and non-fossil fuels. More than 60% of the electricity generation will come from the non-fossil fuel-based energy sources (solar, wind, biomass, hydro and nuclear), while the share of coal would go down to 36% by 2030, according to Minister of Power and New and Renewable Energy RK Singh and the CEA.

Carbon Emissions Will Be Reduced by One Billion Tonnes by 2030

One of India's pledges at the COP 26 was to reduce its carbon emission by 1 bt between 2021 and 2030. Currently, India's CO_2 emissions are 2.88 bt. Based on the median annual rate of change from 2010 to 2019, the Centre for Science and Environment (CSE) has projected the volume of emissions to double to 4.48 bt by 2030 in the business-as-usual scenario. This means a 22% reduction in the projected emissions to 3.48 bt in 2030, relatively a small 8.4% of the total global emissions, while China and the US will continue to be the two biggest carbon emitters in the world. For India to reduce its emissions by 1 bt in the next nine years is not a difficult task as system efficiencies are improving rapidly and new technologies are maximising production.

In per capita terms, the emissions of 3.48 bt means 2.7 tonnes per head in 2030, up from 1.98 tonnes in 2021. But if you compare it with other major emitters, the US per capita emissions will be 9.42 tonnes, the European Union's 4.12 tonnes and China's 8.88 tonnes per head in 2030. According to the Inter-governmental Panel on Climate Change (IPCC), global CO_2 emissions must be below 18.22 bt in 2030 to limit the global temperature rise to under 1.5°C. This means that the world's per capita CO_2 emissions should be 2.14 tonnes in 2030. The CSE says it has arrived at this number by dividing the global population in 2030. India is reaching this goal without adding to the cumulative emissions in the atmosphere. Although India's total greenhouse emissions in 2030 will be up from 7% to 8.4% of the total global emissions, it will still be considerably less that China and the US. In per capita terms, it would mean India would emit 2.98 tonnes of CO_2 in a business-as-usual scenario, less than half the world average. As of today, India's per capita emissions is 1.98 tonnes of CO_2. If you compare this to the world, the US per capita emissions will be 9.42 tonnes in 2030, EU 4.12 tonnes in 2030, India's will be 2.7 tonnes in 2030 and China's will be 8.88 tonnes per capita. According to the IPCC, global CO_2 emissions must be 18.22 bt in 2030 for the world to limit the rise in the overall temperature to under 1.5°C.

Reducing Emissions Intensity by 45%

India's commitment to reduce emissions intensity to 45% by 2030 from the 2005 level is a more ambitious target than the previous goal of a 33–35% cut is the fourth pillar of Modi's 'Panchamrit'. Emission intensity measures the total amount of greenhouse gas emitted for every unit of GDP. It counts emissions beyond those related to energy (such as emissions from agriculture), and greenhouse gases beyond carbon dioxide (such as methane). It is different from the energy intensity, which measures only the fuels (of all kinds) to create economic growth. Energy intensity of the economy can be reduced by fuel shift from fossil to non-fossil fuels, energy efficiency measures, new and improved technologies, increased productivity and shifts in overall production from sectors that use a lot of energy (like manufacturing or mineral processing) to others that do not (like services). As per India Energy Outlook 2021 of the International Energy Agency (IEA), India's GDP increased six-fold between 1990 and 2019, whereas final consumption of energy only increased two and a half times, indicating a rapid improvement of energy intensity in these three decades. This was mainly due to a shift away from biomass as primary fuel in the residential sector, the share of which reduced from 48% in 1990 to 18% in 2019, due to enhancement of electrification and liquified petroleum gas (LPG) penetration.

Carbon intensity of the economy is measured as CO_2 emissions per unit of GDP. It is dependent on the fuel mix of the energy sector and energy intensity. Theoretically, the lowest carbon intensity would be of a country that has the least use of fossil energy in its fuel mix and the energy that it uses, and has the best energy intensity—also dependent on the nature of the economy (service versus manufacturing for instance). As per India Energy Outlook 2021 India is the third largest global emitter of CO_2, despite low per capita CO_2 emissions. CO_2 contributes more than 78% of India's total GHG emissions (2016), and the energy sector contributes more than 92% of all CO_2 emissions from the country. The carbon intensity of the Indian power sector in the year 2020 was 725 gCO_2/kWh. Though this was lesser than 830 gCO_2/kWh during 2012–13, it was still well above the global average of 510 gCO_2/kWh. This points to the dominance of inefficient coal power in India.

According to the Biennial Update Report (BUR-3), submitted prior to the COP 26 in 2021, India shows that its GHG emissions were 2,839 mt of CO_2e (equivalent), without land use, land use change and forestry (LULUCF). BUR, submitted by nations to the UNFCC contain updates of national GHG inventories, including a national inventory report and information on mitigation actions, needs and support received. Such reports provide updates on actions undertaken by a party to implement the convention, including the status of its GHG emissions and removals by sinks, as well as on the actions to reduce emissions or enhance sinks. LULUCF remains a net sink. After inclusion of LULUCF, India's GHG emissions were 2,531 mt CO_2e. The energy sector's contribution to total GHG emissions of India is the largest. Agriculture is the second largest contributor with more than 14% share. Agriculture emits methane (CH_4) and nitrous oxides (N_2O) and does not have any CO_2 contribution. Industrial processes and product use (IPPU) contributes 8%, in which CO_2 share of contribution is 73%.

According to India's submission to the UNFCC, its emission intensity has been declining at a rate of 1–2% annually. Emission inventory analysis from three sources—Government of India, Potsdam Institute and WRI-CAIT (World Resources Institute – Climate Analysis Indicators Tool)—shows that India has already reduced emission intensity between 24–25% from 2005 to 2016, and if the current rate of annual decline is extrapolated by a moderate 1%, India may achieve a reduction between 39–40% below 2005 level by 2030. According to the CSE, India had already achieved a reduction of 35% of the emission intensity of its GDP until 35%, and is on track to achieve more than 45% by 2030. However, the rate of growth in emissions in hard-to-decarbonise sectors such as cement, iron and steel and non-metallic plants, which together contribute more than 62% of the emissions from the manufacturing sector, has to be particularly kept in check.

India's National Hydrogen Mission and near-term targets to increase renewable energy installed capacity to 500 GW, meet 50% of the country's electricity demand from non-fossil fuels and reduce the total projected carbon emissions by 1 bt, discussed above, are all pathways to achieve energy intensity reduction of 45% from 2005 in the emission intensity of the country's economy by 2030 and ultimately net zero by 2070.

VIII. NET ZERO BY 2070

Modi's fifth announcement at COP 26 committing India to become carbon neutral nation and achieve net zero emissions by 2070 is an ambitious and bold pledge by a developing country which is at the cusp of a significant economic transformation. IEA's Fatih Birol and India's NITI Aayog's Amitabh Kant call it as a new model of economic development, which India is pioneering, that could avoid the carbon-intensive approaches that many countries have pursued in the past, and provide a blueprint for other developing economies. They deem this scale of transformation in India as stunning. Its economic growth has been among the highest in the world over the past two decades, lifting millions of people out of poverty. The rapid growth in fossil energy consumption has also meant India's annual CO_2 emissions have risen to become the third highest in the world. However, India's CO_2 emissions per person puts it near the bottom of the world's emitters, and they are lower still if you consider historical emissions per person.

A rapid and equitable economic growth is critical for India to meet the lifestyle aspirations of its 1.4 billion people, about 25% of whom live below the poverty line. The manufacturing sector needs to grow faster to supplement the impressive services sector economy and cater to the large population living off the agrarian economy. These developmental aspirations inevitably result in a higher use of energy and rise in emissions. Yet, the per capita energy use of the country, as of 2020, has been less than half the world average, as the manufacturing sector has remained underdeveloped. According to India's 3rd Biennial Update to the United Nations Framework Convention on Climate Change (UNFCCC), it was able to reduce its GDP emissions intensity by 24% during 2005–16. The country's per capita emissions also remained low at 1.94 tonnes CO_2 per capita, less than half the global average of 4.2 tonne CO_2 per capita. Renewable energy—solar, wind, hydro, nuclear and biomass power—accounted for over 40% of India's total installed electricity capacity as of November 2021, which is almost as much as four-fifths of its national commitment announced by Modi at COP 26.

Behind the steady rise of India's total emissions is a big focus on developmental activities over the last two decades. India seeks rapid growth through 2030 for a projected population of about 1.5 billion, with 40% living in urban areas. This incorporates priorities such as poverty eradication, education, Make in India, infrastructure development and electricity, housing and health for all, among others. Inevitably, these priorities result in a net increase in emissions which, India expects to mitigate by implementing the 'Panchamrit' announced by Modi at COP 26. Historically India has never been big contributor to the greenhouse gas emissions, it has added up just 4% to the global emissions from the industrial age 1870 to 2019. However, as the rate of the country's growth picks up steam, so will its GHG footprint. As of 2020, India's total carbon emission was 2.5 bt, according to the Global Carbon Project, making it the third-largest GHG emitter in the world. However, it was nowhere near that of the top two countries, China's 10.7 bt and the United States' 5 bt. A slight dip in 2020 could arguably be due to the pandemic and a prolonged economic slowdown.

Net zero was the most hotly debated subject at the COP 26 talks in Glasgow. Achieving net zero emissions refer to balancing the amount of greenhouse gas we release in the atmosphere being offset by an equivalent amount of greenhouse gas we remove from the air. A country is said to have reached net zero when the quantity of greenhouse gases emitted by it into the atmosphere is offset by absorbing an equivalent amount of greenhouse gases from the atmosphere, cancelling each other out. According to a 'Special Report on Net Zero by 2050', released in May 2021, the number of countries having pledged to achieve net zero emissions by 2050 had grown rapidly over the last year and covered around 70% of global emissions of CO_2. However, most pledges were not underpinned by near-term policies and measures. Moreover, even if successfully fulfilled, the pledges to date would still leave around 22 bt of CO_2 emissions worldwide in 2050. The continuation of that trend would be consistent with a temperature rise in 2100 of around 2.1°C.

The IEA's revelation highlights the fact that while most countries are willing to set ambitious targets at multilateral for the COP, real-world action is a far cry from what it needs to be. This is borne out by a World Meteorological Organisation (WMO) report released to inform the United Nations Secretary General's Climate Action Summit, that the global average temperature has increased by 1.1°C since the pre-industrial period, and by 0.2°C compared to 2011–2015. Accompanying that report on GHG concentrations shows that 2015–2019 has seen a continued increase in CO_2 levels and other key GHG in the atmosphere to new records, with CO_2 growth rates nearly 20% higher than the previous five years. CO_2 remains in the atmosphere for centuries and in the ocean for even longer. Looking ahead, the International Energy Agency estimated that, under current spending plans, the planet's carbon dioxide emissions would be on course to hit record levels in 2023 and continue to grow in the ensuing years. There is, its July 2021 analysis claims, "no clear peak in sight."

Based on IEA's WMO's reports, some climate experts have gone on to term net zero concept as a 'recklessly cavalier burn now, pay later approach', over-reliant on incremental cuts to fossil fuel consumption and carbon dioxide removal techniques. Net zero can indeed distract the focus from an urgent need for deep emissions reductions if 2030 targets and short-term action are inconsistent with steps towards their achievement, thereby allowing governments to hide behind aspirational net zero targets.[18]

The world's third-biggest emitter India joined the net zero bandwagon much later than other countries. It's reluctance to embrace a shorter timetable was understandable. While many western countries have committed to a 2050 net zero deadline, the Indian government rightly pointed out that the western nations have used fossil fuels for decades, if not centuries, to lift living standards, India's millions of rural poor are only just beginning to use. Unlike the developed nations' climate promise which was akin to walking the talk, Modi's announcement, 'to achieve net zero carbon emissions by 2070 is like but running the talk'.[19]

Syncing his 'Panchamrit' targets with energy security, Modi has aggressively pushed a swift shift to green energy and mobility that are seen as building blocks to meet the global commitment of net zero emissions by 2070, or preferably sooner. According to a former vice chairman of now-dissolved Planning Commission, Montek Singh Ahluwalia, who served under former Prime Minister Manmohan Singh (2004–14), India's emissions can peak around 2035 and then move towards net zero sometime between 2065 and 2070. Almost corroborating with Ahluwalia's study (published in October 2021), CEEW says that India will have to peak by 2040 to achieve its target of reaching net zero by 2070. For this to happen, the CEEW says, coal-based power generation must peak by 2040 and then come down.

By 2070, the CEEW says, solar electricity generation will have to go up to 5,630 GW and wind energy 1,792 GW. The share of electric cars and the contribution of biofuels for heavier vehicles will have to reach 84% and the majority of industry have to shift to cleaner biofuels or hydrogen. As of 2019, India installed a capacity to generate about 134 GW of clean energy from solar, wind and nuclear sources, the CSE said. In 2021, India had about 210 GW of coal-based capacity, with 39 GW under construction and another 25 GW in various stages of approval. Reducing the life span of such plants to 25 years can help in achieving net zero, says Ahluwalia. There is unanimity among energy experts that India's dependence on coal will have to be cut drastically in the next 10–15 years to achieve its net zero target, and the country will have to swiftly switch to cleaner fuels.

However, phasing out coal completely is not an option for India, which draws 70% of its electricity from coal. The Indian government bitterly opposed a proposal to phase out coal at COP 26. India cannot afford to disband its coal-fired power plants until it has fully developed alternative energy industry (solar, wind, hydro, nuclear, hydrogen and battery storage) which, it expects, will happen over the next two-three decades. Second, phasing out coal will also have serious economic implications for poor states like Chhattisgarh, Odisha, Jharkhand, West Bengal, Madhya Pradesh and Uttar Pradesh. In Chhattisgarh and Jharkhand close to 15% of the state revenue comes directly from the mining sector. Third, the coal sector provides millions of jobs directly and indirectly. But these reasons are difficult to reconcile with India's evolving energy needs and environmental priorities. The carbon intensity of India's power sector, which is built around coal, in particular, is well above the global average. Additionally, particulate matter emissions are a major factor in air pollution, which has emerged as one of India's most sensitive social and environmental issues. In 2019, there were well over one million premature deaths related to ambient and household air pollution.

India has been well aware of the damaging effects of carbon-intensive coal, and has doubled down for 'green' and renewable energy sources to replace it. It has launched a raft of initiatives to quadruple renewable energy generation capacity to 500 GW by 2030, including 280–300 GW to meet half of its projected energy requirement by 2030. As per the IEA's Sustainable Development Scenario solar power is set to match coal's share in the Indian power generation mix within the next two decades. As of

2019, solar accounted for less than 4% of India's electricity generation, and coal close to 70%. By 2040, they converge in the low 30% in the STEPS, and this switch is even more rapid in other scenarios. This dramatic turnaround is driven by India's policy ambitions, notably the target to reach 500 GW of renewable capacity by 2030, and the extraordinary cost-competitiveness of solar, which out-competes existing coal-fired power by 2030 even when paired with battery storage. The rise of utility-scale renewable projects is underpinned by some innovative regulatory approaches that encourage pairing solar with other generation technologies, and with storage, to offer 'round the clock' supply. Keeping up momentum behind investments in renewables also means tackling risks relating to delayed payments to land generators, acquisition and regulatory and contract uncertainty.

In a pathway to net zero emissions by 2070, India's clean energy transition is already well underway. It has overachieved its commitment made at COP 21 Paris Summit by already meeting 40% of its power capacity from non-fossil fuels, almost nine years ahead of its commitment and the share of solar and wind in India's energy mix have grown phenomenally. Owing to technological developments, steady policy support and a vibrant private sector solar power plants are cheaper to build than coal ones. Renewable electricity is growing at a faster rate in India than any other major economy, with new capacity additions on track to double by 2026. The country is also one of the world's largest producers of modern bioenergy and has big ambitions to scale up its use across the economy. The IEA expects India to overtake Canada and China in the next few years to become the third largest ethanol market worldwide after the United States and Brazil.

India's robust energy efficiency programme has been successful in reducing energy use and emissions from buildings, transport and major industries. Government efforts to provide millions of households with fuel gas for cooking and heating are enabling a steady transition away from the use of traditional biomass such as burning wood. India is also laying the groundwork to scale up important emerging technologies such as hydrogen, battery storage, and low-carbon steel, cement and fertilisers. Green hydrogen will play a major role in achieving the net zero and decarbonising the hard-to-abate sectors. India aims to become a global hub for green hydrogen production and exports. India could easily create 5 mt green hydrogen demand thereby replacing grey hydrogen in the refineries and fertiliser sector. These 5 mt will result in abatement of 28 mt of CO_2. This proportion will grow as we fructify green hydrogen economy and will result in 400 mt of CO_2 abatement by 2050.

IX. CLIMATE CHANGES IN INDIA

In March 2021, India's Ministry of Earth Sciences (MoES) published a Climate Change report entitled, 'Assessment of Climate Change over the Indian Region' covering all aspects of regional climate change, including the climatic extremes across the country. The preparation of this report was led by the Centre for Climate Change Research (CCCR) at the Indian Institute of Tropical Meteorology (IITM), Pune. It is the first of its kind where a comprehensive discussion has been made regarding the impact of human-induced global climate change on the regional climate and the monsoon over the subcontinent, adjoining Indian Ocean and the Himalayas.

Based on the available climate records, the report states that the surface air temperature over India has risen by about 0.7°C during 1901–2018 which is accompanied with an increase in atmospheric moisture content. The sea surface temperatures in the tropical Indian Ocean have also increased by about 1°C during 1951–2015.

The rise in average temperature means the hottest days will be hotter and the warmest nights warmer. In 1986–2015, temperatures of the warmest day and the coldest night in a year increased by 0.63°C and 0.4°C respectively in India. In the high emission pathway, these are expected to increase by 4.7°C and 5.5°C, respectively. The warming is and will be gradual. In the high emissions' 'pathway', the report says, the land surface temperature over India could rise by an average of 2.7°C in the next 50 years, until 2069. In the moderate emissions' 'pathway', temperature could rise by 2°C on average in the same period.

Clear signatures of human-induced changes in climate have emerged over the Indian region on account of anthropogenic GHG and aerosol forcing, and changes in land use and land cover which have contributed to an increase in the climatic extremes. The complex interactions between the Earth system components amidst the warming environment and regional anthropogenic influences have therefore led to a rise in frequency of localised heavy rainfall events, drought and flood occurrences, and increase in the intensity of tropical cyclones, etc., in the last few decades. Future projections of regional climate, performed under different climate change scenarios, too, indicate robust changes in the mean, variability and extremes of several key climatic parameters over the Indian subcontinent and adjoining areas (example, land temperature and precipitation, monsoons, Indian Ocean temperature and sea level, tropical cyclones, Himalayan cryosphere).

Hotter Himalayas

IITM experts have calculated that the mountains of the Hindu Kush Himalayas (HKH) experienced a temperature rise of about 1.3°C between 1951 and 2014. Several areas of HKH experienced a declining level of snowfall and also retreat of glaciers in recent decades, though some glaciers in the high-elevation Karakoram range escaped this retreat, due to more winter snowfall.

Alarmingly, the experts say, "By the end of the twenty-first century, the annual mean surface temperature over HKH is projected to increase by about 5.2°C under the RCP 8.5 scenario." That will accelerate glacier retreat, which means meltwater flows in the rivers of northern India will become more uncertain in non-monsoon months, when such water is crucial for millions of people. People living in the Himalayas are already suffering as springs dry up, and that trend will also accelerate with the average temperature going up by this extent.

Monsoon Connections

The heating over land is mirrored by the heating over the sea. "Sea surface temperature (SST) of the tropical Indian Ocean has risen by 1°C on average during 1951–2015, markedly higher than the global average SST warming of 0.7°C, over the same period," the report says. It forecasts that this trend will continue throughout this century.

All this affects the June-September monsoon on which so many Indian farmers continue to depend. Global climate models forecast a rainfall increase, but "The summer monsoon precipitation (June to September) over India has declined by around 6% from 1951 to 2015, with notable decreases over the Indo-Gangetic Plains and the Western Ghats," as the report points out. The reason, it says, is air pollution.

Not only is it raining less during the rainy season, the rainfall is more uneven. The scientists note, "There has been a shift in the recent period toward more frequent dry spells (27% higher during 1981–2011 relative to 1951–1980) and more intense wet spells during the summer monsoon season… Over central India, the frequency of daily precipitation extremes with rainfall intensities exceeding 150 mm per day increased by about 75% during 1950–2015." The report predicts an increase in this variability.

This means a worsening cycle of droughts and floods. The report records this increase in droughts and predicts that there will be even more droughts in the highest emissions scenario. There is an emerging consensus, based on multiple data sets and climate model simulations, that the radiative effects of anthropogenic aerosol forcing over the Northern Hemisphere have considerably offset the expected precipitation increase from GHG warming and contributed to the observed decline in summer monsoon precipitation.

Land and Sea

The report records that around India the sea has risen 3.3 mm per year between 1993 and 2017. The scientists forecast that even in an RCP 4.5 scenario, by the end of the century the seas around India will rise by 300 mm from the average level between 1986 and 2005, with the corresponding projection for the global mean rise being approximately 180 mm. This means a larger area along the coast will be affected by storms and saltwater intrusion.

Global climate models predict an increase in frequency of storms due to climate change, but the Indian scientists have found no evidence of it. However, they have found that the strong cyclones are getting stronger, as seen recently in the case of Cyclones Amphan, Cyclone Tauktae and Yaas, formed in the Bay of Bengal, which left behind a trail of destruction across several Indian states in Odisha and West Bengal.

Overall, climate change has already made India hotter and drier since the middle of the twentieth century, with more droughts, cloudbursts, floods, rising seas, stronger cyclones and a change in the monsoon pattern. "Human-induced climate change is expected to continue apace during the twenty first century," the scientists fear. With IITM being a part of India's Ministry of

Earth Sciences, which also supervises the India Meteorological Department, the report's immediate recommendation is to have more weather stations across the country.

On a wider scale, the report says, "The rapid changes in India's climate projected by climate models will place increasing stress on the country's natural ecosystems, agricultural output, and fresh water resources, while also causing escalating damage to infrastructure. These portend serious consequences for the country's biodiversity, food, water and energy security, and public health. In the absence of rapid, informed and far-reaching mitigation and adaptation measures, the impacts of climate change are likely to pose profound challenges to sustaining the country's rapid economic growth, and achieving the sustainable development goals (SDGs) adopted by UN Member States in 2015."

Projected Changes in Global Climate

The study's global climate models project a pessimistic future. Even if the current GHG emission rates were sustained, the global average temperature would likely rise by 5°C, or possibly more, by the end of the twenty first century. Even if all the commitments (called the 'Nationally Determined Contributions') made under the 2015 Paris Agreement are met, it is projected that global warming will exceed 3°C by the end of the century. However, temperature rise will not be uniform across the planet; some parts of the world will experience greater warming than the global average. Such large changes in temperature will greatly accelerate other changes that are already underway in the climate system, such as the changing patterns of rainfall and increasing temperature extremes.

Indian Ocean Warming

Sea surface temperature (SST) of the tropical Indian Ocean has risen by 1°C on average during 1951–2015, markedly higher than the global average SST warming of 0.7°C, over the same period. Ocean heat content in the upper 700 m (OHC700) of the tropical Indian Ocean has also exhibited an increasing trend over the past six decades (1955–2015), with the past two decades (1998–2015) having witnessed a notably abrupt rise. During the twenty first century, SST and ocean heat content in the tropical Indian Ocean are projected to continue to rise.

Droughts

The overall decrease of seasonal summer monsoon rainfall during the last six to seven decades has led to an increased propensity for droughts over India. Both the frequency and spatial extent of droughts have increased significantly during 1951–2016. In particular, areas over central India, southwest coast, southern peninsula and north-eastern India have experienced more than two droughts per decade, on average, during this period. The area affected by drought has also increased by 1.3 degree per decade over the same period.

Climate model projections indicate a high likelihood of increase in the frequency, intensity and area under drought conditions in India by the end of the twenty first century under the RCP 8.5 scenario, resulting from the increased variability of monsoon precipitation and increased water vapour demand in a warmer atmosphere.

Sea Level Rise

Sea levels have risen globally because of the continental ice melt and thermal expansion of ocean water in response to global warming. Sea level rise in the North Indian Ocean (NIO) occurred at a rate of 1.06–1.75 mm per year during 1874–2004 and has accelerated to 3.3 mm per year, which is comparable to the current rate of global mean sea level rise.

Overall monsoon precipitation in India, which contributes to more than 75% of the country's annual rainfall, between 1951 and 2015 has declined by 6%, especially in the densely populated Indo-Gangetic plains and the Western Ghats.

However, in future, India is to expect more rainfall every year, both monsoonal and non-monsoonal. The monsoon season is also likely to become longer due to climate change, according to the report, and the frequency of extreme precipitation events is likely to increase further, especially in India's central and southern parts.

This will in turn lead to increased flooding, mirroring the steady hike in decadal flood events since 1951. Flood propensity is expected to rise particularly in Himalayan river basins of the Indus, the Ganga and the Brahmaputra. While on the one hand the frequency of floods is predicted to rise, drought severity and frequency too are also expected to become more common.

This seems counterintuitive, but only because, as the report clarifies, the number of consecutive dry days is expected to increase because the annual rainfall will be spread over fewer days. In the high emissions pathway, India's northwest, the Gangetic plains and central India could experience more than two drought events every decade. The area that will be affected by droughts is also likely to increase by 150% by 2100. According to the report, more tropical cyclones are going to be born in the northern Indian Ocean and with greater intensity, in the decades to come due to climate change.

Unpredictable Calamities

Since the middle of the twentieth century, India has witnessed a rise in average temperature; a decrease in monsoon precipitation; a rise in extreme temperature and rainfall events, droughts, and sea levels; and an increase in the intensity of severe cyclones, alongside other changes in the monsoon system. There is compelling scientific evidence that human activities have influenced these changes in regional climate.

Human-induced climate change is expected to continue apace during the twenty-first century. To improve the accuracy of future climate projections, particularly in the context of regional forecasts, it is essential to develop strategic approaches for improving the knowledge of Earth system processes, and to continue enhancing observation systems and climate models.

India's Policy Response to Climate Change

India's climate change policy has been articulated through two key documents—National Action Plan on Climate Change (NAPCC) and the Intended Nationally Determined Commitments (NDC). The NAPCC is essentially a domestic focus, which seeks to make a strategic shift from its current reliance on fossil fuels to a pattern of economic activity based on renewable sources of energy like wind, solar and nuclear energy. It underlines what Shyam Saran, former secretary of India, call a 'co-benefit' approach based on India's own resources to enhance the country's energy security while dealing with the threat of climate change. The NAPCC incorporates India's vision of ecologically sustainable development and steps to be taken to implement it. It is based on the awareness that climate change action must proceed simultaneously on several intimately inter-related domains, such as energy, industry, agriculture, water, forests, urban spaces and the fragile mountain environment.

The NDC is a statement of intent on climate change action submitted to the UNFCCC in 2015. It commits to cut the growth of energy intensity of

India's growth by 33–35% by 2030 compared to 2005 base year, which means that for every additional dollar of GDP India will be using progressively and significantly lesser amount of energy. This is a very ambitious target by one of the world's largest emerging economies, which already has a large energy footprint globally, to tackle global climate change. The Modi government has set a target of achieving 40% of power from renewable sources, particularly solar and wind, by 2030, which is likely to be achieved at least five years in advance. Encouraged by the splendid performance of the sector, Modi has raised the target of achieving renewable energy capacity of 450 GW by 2030, which can be expected to meet three quarters of the country electricity demand by that year. The installation of increased renewable energy capacity will go a long way in enabling to cut the share of coal-based thermal power it its energy mix. Already, coal's share has declined to 55% in 2021 from 77% in 2014. Coal has been very heavily taxed in India, carrying a coal cess of Rs 400 per tonne, proceeds from which go into a clean energy fund. India is also committed to not building any new thermal plants which are not of the most efficient ultra-supercritical category. The increased component of renewable power in the energy mix will also help India to considerably reduce the oil and gas import bills.

Downpours and Storms

Torrential downpours and devastating storms will increase large-scale damage to fields, homes, businesses, transportation and power systems and industry in countries without the financial or human capital resources to respond.

Heatwaves and Droughts

Heatwaves and droughts will increase pressure on already fragile power, healthcare, water and sewage systems, as well as reducing countries' ability to feed themselves or export agricultural products.

Heat will also become an increasingly important killer, especially of the very young and the old. The handful of deaths during the European heatwave of 2003 resulted in a storm of press outrage that this could happen in the developed world.

In 2016, sections of North Thailand suffered two straight months of temperatures of 44°C (105°F) without air conditioning, cooling centres, public health or hospital support. No one counted the dead, but there is no question that across the tropical developing world, heat will become a major killer.

Changing Ecosystems

In the developing world, changing ecosystems seem to result almost exclusively in the loss of important food species, for example, fish and staple crops, and the increase of malign species such as disease vectors.

A study published in *Nature*, a leading scientific journal, provides data that suggest that climate change related phenomena have killed 1,50,000 people annually for the past 30 years, and that numbers will increase. The authors contend that included in the death count should be those killed by, for example, heat induced cardiovascular attacks, as well as those killed by malnutrition resulting from climate change induced crop failures, most of them, needless to say, live in the global South.

Food security, already shaky, is crumbling under rising temperatures and related climate changes. Major staple crops are declining in productivity, while unlike in the developed countries, there are no new, more tropical staples to move in to take their places. Rising population combined with declining productivity, increasing incidence of drought and storms is increasingly leaving developing countries vulnerable of food shortfalls.

Rising temperatures increase the reproduction rates of pests and so shorten the time required for insects and plant pathogens to develop resistance to control regimes. For a review of many of the different ways in which climate change affects pests.[20]

Diseases, like pests, develop more rapidly in the heat and so do their insect vectors. Moreover, with climate change, the range of critical vectors—mosquitos, for example, vectors for dengue, encephalitis, malaria, West Nile and Zika—all expand putting larger and larger populations at risk.

Ongoing ocean acidification threatens more and more small shell fish, which form the broad base of the ocean food chain. Ultimately, this will threaten the entire ocean population and so the critical protein source for one third of the people on Earth and a major industry.

NASA Sounds Alarm Bell for Indian Coastal Cities

The US space agency National Aeronautics and Space Administration (NASA) has warned that 12 Indian coastal cities would be under water by the end of 2050 as the sea levels rise due to global warming. Bhavnagar in Gujarat will be the first city which will submerge as sea level rises to 2.7 ft by 2040, followed by Kochi in Kerala, which is likely to face a sea level rise of 2.32 ft. Other cities that face sea level rise threat are—Mormugao (2.06 ft), Okha (1.96 ft), Paradip (1.93 ft), Mumbai (1.90 ft), Tuticorin (1.9 ft), Kandla (1.87 ft), Mangalore (1.87 ft), Chennai (1.87 ft), Visakhapatnam (1.77 ft) and Khidirpur (0.49 ft).

NASA's findings are based on data provided by IPCC's Sixth Assessment Report, released in August, 2021. They have used their own tool, called the gradient fingerprint mapping (GFM), created by the Jet Propulsion Laboratory scientists, to project the rise in the sea levels across the world.

The IPCC has been providing global scale assessments of Earth's climate every five to seven years since 1988, focusing on changes in temperature and ice cover, greenhouse gas emissions and sea levels across the planet. Their sea level projections are based on by data gathered by satellites and instruments on the ground, as well as analysis and computer simulations.

The IPCC report, 'Climate Change 2021: The Physical Science Basis' approved by 195 member governments, including India, says that the climate change is bringing multiple different changes in different regions, which will all increase with further warming. These include changes to wetness and dryness, to winds, snow and ice, coastal areas and oceans. Extreme changes in sea levels were previously seen once in 100 years, but now it could happen every six to nine years by 2050, and even every year by the end of the century. The rising sea levels will contribute to flooding in low-lying areas and coastal erosion with extreme sea level events. According to estimates made between 2006 and 2018, the global average sea level was rising at a rate of around 3.3 mm per year.

The report says that the climate change is also intensifying the water cycle. This brings more intense rainfall and associated flooding, as well as more intense drought in many regions. Coastal areas will see continued sea level rise throughout the twenty first century, contributing to more frequent and severe coastal flooding in low-lying areas and coastal erosion.

"Further warming will amplify permafrost thawing, and the loss of seasonal snow cover, melting of glaciers and ice sheets, and loss of summer Arctic Sea ice. Changes to the ocean, including warming, more frequent marine heatwaves, ocean acidification and reduced oxygen levels have been clearly linked to human influence. These changes affect both ocean ecosystems and the people that rely on them, and they will continue throughout at least the rest of this century."

While the sea levels rise, the continuous melting of glaciers in the Himalayas is likely to affect over a billion people, who are directly or indirectly dependent on these resources. An earlier report by the Indian Institute of Technology (IIT) Indore on the glacial hydrology of rivers in the Himalayan Karakoram region had shown that glaciers and snowmelt are important components of the Himalayan Karakoram rivers with greater importance for the Indus basin, than the Ganga and Brahmaputra basins. The team projects that the total river runoff, glacier melt and seasonality of flow are set to increase until the 2050s, and then decrease.

References

1. Daniel Yergin, 'The Rise of Carbon', *The Quest*, p.426.
2. IPCC Sixth Assessment Report, Summary for Policymakers, https://www.ipcc.ch/report/ar6/wg1/#SPM.
3. *Reuters*, 10 January, 2023.
4. *New York Times*.
5. IPCC Sixth Assessment Report.
6. 'Earth's Energy Imbalance Doubled in 14 Years: NASA; *IANS*, 19 June, 2021.
7. Daniel Ergin, Glacial Change: The Alpine 'Hot Box', *The Quest*, p.429.
8. *BBC*.
9. Daniel Ergin, Glacial Change (The Alpine 'Hot Box'), *The Quest*, p.430.
10. Daniel Ergin, Glacial Change, *The Quest*, pp.431–2.
11. Julia Uppenbrink, 'Arrhenius and Global Warming', Science 272, no. 5265 (1996), p.1122, quoted in *The Quest*.
12. Daniel Ergin, The Age of Discovery, *The Quest*, pp.444–5.
13. History of the Greenhouse Effect and Global Warming; SM Enzler, www.lenntech.com/greenhouse-effect/global-warming-history.
14. Paula Dobriansky, Undersecretary of State, in an Interview with Samuel Bodman, January 23, 2007, quoted in Daniel Yergin's, *The Quest*, p.508.
15. Daniel Yergin, *The Quest*, p.508.
16. IEA: Electricity Market Report, January, 2022, 'India's Renewable Energy Generation to Rise by 30 percent by 2024.
17. *Wion* web, Washington, 10 December, 2021.
18. India's Road to Net-Zero by Jitendra Bisht and Soumya Singhal, *The Diplomat*, 26 November, 2021.
19. Sunita Narain, Eminent Environmentalist and Director General of Centre for Science and Environment (CSE).
20. JH Porter et al.

Chapter 14

TRANSITION TO THE NEW AGE ENERGY

I. OVERVIEW

This is what the future would look like in the not-too-distant future—electricity will come from wind, solar, water, biomass and nuclear plants, and cars, autos, buses and trucks will run on batteries or hydrogen fuel cells. Green hydrogen will be the main fuel of industry and heavy-duty transportation, and petrol and diesel vehicles will become vintage. Coal, which dominates the global energy space today, will be a vanishing commodity, as green hydrogen and renewables undercut the dominance of fossil fuels, and most households and commercial and office buildings will make their own electricity.

The global energy landscape is undergoing a rapid and profound overhaul. The fast-changing world of clean energy technologies, electric mobility, innovations like hydrogen, batteries, innovations like hydrogen and the emerging environmental imperatives are set to topple the traditional base of thermal energy.

As the energy transition toward low carbon resources are continuing, our dependence on oil, gas and coal are diminishing. There is a greater awareness today than two decades before that burning fossil fuels emits both particulate air pollution and greenhouse gases. The former is strangling cities around the world with smog, and the latter contributes to the climate crisis as the heat-trapping fossil fuel by-products are the single largest contributor to global warming. However, the future looks much different.

A New Energy System Is Taking Shape

Spurred by breakneck innovation, a tide of capital and evolving regulations, companies and investors are placing decarbonisation at the centre of their business strategy. The rise of renewables is leading to profound shifts in the global energy system, which is currently dominated by fossil-fuel molecules. Electrons produced by renewables will be the dominant force in this system. They will provide the lion's share of electricity, fill up massive batteries that will become electricity generators in their own right, power factories, heat and cool buildings and, as electrification emerges as a major fuel for cars, trucks, trains and ships. By 2050, renewables are expected to provide more than 90% of energy, and fossil fuels less than 10%. Biomass and waste will surpass fossil fuels as creators of molecules that will be used to heat buildings and power transport and industry.[1]

Transition Towards Clean Energy

The International Energy Agency (IEA) projects that global demand for the molecules and electrons that power the world will rise by 23% by 2040. In the near term, fossil fuels will continue to account for a large percentage of the molecules that fuel transport and the electrons that provide electricity and heat. As time goes on, carbon free energy sources—chiefly electrons and a rising proportion of molecules—will account for a greater share of production. The IEA now also suggests that oil demand will start to level off by the 2030s as a result of vehicle fuel-efficiency gains and the rise of electric vehicles (EVs), which see passenger car oil demand peak in the late 2020s.

Looking to the decade beyond 2030, renewable energy takes greater market share in the global electricity market, as coal declines and natural gas grows modestly. By 2040, powered by strong growth in wind and solar, renewables will account for about 47% of the electricity market, up from 29% in 2021. In the IEA's STEPS projection for 2030, some 49% of power demand growth would be met by renewables, while gas use is expected to rise rapidly, overtaking coal to become the second-largest source of energy after oil and meeting a third of the rise in overall demand. Oil demand will start to level off by the 2030s as a result of vehicle fuel-efficiency gains and the rise of electric vehicles (EVs), which see passenger car oil demand peak in the 'late 2020s'.[2]

More than 190 countries have committed to the goals of the 2015 Paris Agreement, which include aggressive reductions in emissions. In 2020, investors poured a record US$ 350 billion into sustainable investment funds, more than double the 2019 total. A great deal of capital is going into innovation, R&D, technology and scaling efforts that help bring down the cost of renewable energy production, energy storage, green hydrogen and other low- or no-carbon innovations. The International Renewable Energy Agency (IRENA) expects electrification and efficiency as key drivers of the energy transition, enabled by renewables, hydrogen and sustainable biomass. End-use decarbonisation will take centre-stage with many solutions available through electrification, green hydrogen and the direct use of renewables. Electromobility is expected to help boost the global sales of EVs twenty times the today's volume.

II. WHERE DOES INDIA STAND?

Currently, India's energy mix is skewed towards the use of coal for power generation, oil for transport and industry, and gas and biomass for residential heating and cooking. Since 1990s, over 80% of India's energy needs have been largely met by the three fuels—coal, oil and biomass (COB). Even in 2020, COB met about 82% India's total primary energy demand (880 mtoe), of which coal provided about 44%, oil 25%, traditional biomass 13%, natural gas 6% and renewables merely 3%. But the race is on to replace them with an energy source of the future. Clearly, it is not going to be fossil fuels, and at the same time it is also not likely to be one single source to emerge to take the place of hydrocarbons. Instead, the energy of the future will need to be generated by a patchwork of renewable sources, namely, wind, solar, geothermal, hydro, atoms, green hydrogen and biomass.

Solar is by far the most promising. Why? Because sunlight is by a long shot the most abundant power source on the planet. Enough energy falls on the Earth's surface in the form of sunlight in a single hour to power all of modern civilisation for a year.

Wind power will be nearly as important in coming years. It's perhaps the most established renewable energy source (besides hydro), and is just as cheap as fossil fuels in many markets around the world. Yet as of now, it only meets an estimated 2.5% of the world's power demand. But its share is likely to increase as advances in turbine blade designs are borrowed from aeronautics technology to derive maximum amount of energy from each gust of wind. Wind turbines will also increasingly move offshore, where countries like Denmark are already showing the rest of the world just how effective offshore wind energy can be. Wind power already provides one third of the country's (Denmark's) power and is expected to provide a full 50% by 2030. And because offshore wind resources tend to blow stronger and more consistently than onshore installations, intermittency is less of a problem.

Hydro power, usually generated by dams, where rivers turn mighty turbines within, has been around for ages. It currently supplies around 8.25% of the world's power, and will likely continue to do so. There are also other emerging renewable technologies that can play a significant role—geothermal power, for instance, which harnesses the vast heat rising out of the Earth's crust. The potential for this technology is vast. Google-funded research reveals that geothermal could generate ten times the amount of power than that of all of our currently operating coal plants combined. Some predict that geothermal projects will one day produce as much as one sixth of the world's energy. There are others, too, wave power, which is pretty much exactly what it sounds like, is a nascent technology, but a promising one.[3]

Nuclear power, currently, supplies about 14% of the world's electricity. Since the Fukushima nuclear reactor disaster that hit Japan following a major earthquake in 2011, the nuclear power industry has been working on safer technology solutions. Concepts so far include nuclear reactors dozens or even hundreds of times smaller and more distributed, warehouse-size nuclear plants that power neighbourhoods instead of entire cities. Some of the designs for these modular reactors have passive safety mechanisms built in to reduce the chance of any kind of radiation release that rocked Japan.

Plans are also underway to develop nuclear reactors offshore, like the floating platforms the oil and gas industry already uses. These would be able to withstand a Category 5 hurricane. Moreover, because the reactor cores would actually be submerged beneath the platform, a fresh supply of cold seawater would always be available to cool the reactor core even in a case of power loss.

Biofuels and biomass include fuel from plant and animal sources. They are very promising for small-scale use as they are low on greenhouse gas emission, are an effective waste management system and produce little air pollutants. Oil, or ethanol, obtained from plants such as sugarcane, switchgrass, algae, poplar and corn can be used directly or mixed with other fuels such as commercial diesel and gasoline to provide power. Even plant matter such as dead wood, leaves, wood chips and branches can be burnt to produce energy. This is typically classified as biomass. Biomass also includes any biodegradable waste from plant and animal sources which can be burnt for fuel.

Hydrogen

As a 'versatile energy carrier',[4] hydrogen has a diverse range of applications and can be deployed in sectors such as industry and transport. It can be produced in a number of ways. One method is electrolysis, using electricity to splitting water (H_2O) into oxygen and hydrogen. If the electricity used in the process comes from a renewable source such as wind or solar then it is called 'green' hydrogen. But if the electricity used is from a fossil fuel, usually natural gas, then it is known as 'blue' or 'grey' hydrogen. Most of the 90 mt of hydrogen produced globally or in India annually today comes from fossil fuels, which in turn produces about 830 mt of CO_2 each year. India produces 6 mt per year using steam methane reformation powered by fossil fuels. This hydrogen is consumed as feedstock or process gas in various industrial applications including petroleum refining, ammonia production in fertiliser industry, methanol production in chemical industries, treatment and production of metals and food processing.

The Energy and Resources Institute (TERI), India's think-tank, says that by 2050, nearly 80% of India's hydrogen will be 'green' hydrogen, produced by electrolysis using renewable electricity. It forecasts that the cost of hydrogen produced through renewable energy would drop by over 50% by 2030, enabling it to start to compete with hydrogen produced from fossil fuels. The cost of green hydrogen is determined mostly by the cost of energy. As the cost of electricity procured from solar PV both standalone and hybrid and onshore wind plants are decreasing substantially, the production of green hydrogen is increasingly becoming economical.

With the advancement of new technology, scientists have been able to come up with even more power options. These include fuel cells, geothermal energy and tidal and wave energy, to name a few. Fuel cells are similar to batteries but use reactants from an external source, as opposed to batteries which are self-contained. The efficiency of fuel cells is proportional to the power being drawn from it. They are also lightweight and extremely reliable. Harnessing geothermal energy requires no fuel. The interior of the Earth contains a lot of heat. Shallow regions contain hot water, rock and steam. Deeper inside, the magma is intensely hot. This heat can be harnessed to produce electrical energy and drive various applications. It is relatively cheap and a very sustainable source of energy since the amount of heat contained in the Earth's bed is so vast that even if we harness more energy than we require, it will still suffice for millions of years to come. Mankind can also harness the energy from tides and waves to produce electrical energy. The differences in temperature that occur with varying depths can be used to drive heat engines, which in turn produce electric power. The oceans contain huge amounts of energy in the water currents, and thermal and salinity gradients which can satisfy the mankind's requirement of energy indefinitely. Then, scientists propose that if matter and antimatter were to collide, they would annihilate one another and release vast amounts of energy. However, this is still a theoretical source of energy. Whether anti-matter exists in some part of the universe and can be harnessed in some way is still a mystery to humankind.

There are various ways of extracting energy from the Earth that humankind has discovered and used to its advantage. As the human race evolves, we will continually search for newer, more efficient forms of energy that have the least amount of impact on the environment. At present day, the most economically efficient fuel has proved to be oil.

Impact of the New Technology

Electricity

Power system is the single largest source of CO_2 emissions globally. Approximately 40% of global CO_2 emissions are emitted from electricity generation through the combustion of fossil fuels to generate heat needed to power steam turbines.[5] Burning of these fuels results in the production of CO_2—the primary heat-trapping, 'greenhouse gas' responsible for global warming.

Every kilowatt of electricity produced in India releases 0.85 kg of CO_2, according to the Central Electricity (CEA).[6] Coal-fired power, which is the mainstay of India's electricity system, contributes to nearly 40% of the country's total emissions. The Indian government has decided henceforth to build no more coal-fired power plants to meet future electricity supplies.

So, if not coal, what would be the fuel of the future in the electric power sector to meet the ever-increasing electricity demand arising from the growing population and rapid economic growth. Domestic oil resources are inadequate and output declining, while rising imports continue to stress the financial position of the country. Natural gas, too, is in short supply, and it is too valuable to be burned out in power plants. Rather, it should be saved for higher purposes, banishing carbon-emitting coal, biomass and kerosene and working as a bridge fuel in transition away from fossil fuels.

This leaves us with only one resource, renewables that have the potential to become the mainstay for much of the new capacities in the power sector. They are domestic, they are abundant, they are available for free and they are the ones that can provide security and dependability. India is already moving with focused determination to increase the renewables' share in its energy mix to 50% by 2030, 90% by 2050 and 100% by 2070.

Industry

The industry sector is the largest contributor to global emissions when direct and indirect emissions are included, and the second-largest contributor when only direct emissions are considered.[7] Green hydrogen is going to be the main fuel of industries and heavy-duty transportation in India in the near future, because of its multiple advantages. It is the most abundant element in the universe, almost 90% of the visible universe is composed of hydrogen, according to some estimates, and it can be produced from diverse, domestic resources, including fossil fuels, biomass and water electrolysis with electricity. It is a clean-burning molecule, which can decarbonise a range of sectors including hard-to-abate iron and steel, chemicals and transportation.

High-Temperature Industries

Heavy industry requires high temperature heat for many of its processes, which today is almost exclusively provided by burning fossil fuels. For example, a steam cracker producing high-value chemicals requires temperatures close to 1,000°C or blast furnaces producing iron operate at temperatures even above 1,500°C. Generating high-temperature heat from electricity, especially on a large scale and for electrically non-conductive applications, is impractical and costly with today's technologies; moreover, the availability of sustainable biomass puts a limit on its use as a substitute. Carbon capture utilisation and storage (CCUS) and hydrogen technologies offer means to provide high temperature heat while eliminating most emissions, but, in most cases, industrial applications of these technologies are still at early stages of development.[8]

In the chemicals sector, beyond various applications of carbon capture technologies, the use of electrolytic hydrogen as a feedstock for ammonia and methanol production is currently at demonstration stage. In steelmaking, the hydrogen-based direct reduced iron (DRI) (large prototype stage) and innovative smelting reduction processes (demonstration stage), play a critical role, alongside concepts for new build and retrofit blast furnace carbon capture applications.

Solar heat for industrial processes continues to be an expanding niche market, but due to technical limitations solar thermal energy is only well suited to processes that require low-temperature heat (below 100°C), such as drying, bleaching, cooking and sterilisation, which occur in, for example, the textile and food industries. The development of geothermal systems for industry remains confined to a limited number of countries (14 in 2019), with China, New Zealand, Iceland, Russia and Hungary leading the way. Industrial applications account for less than 2% of total direct geothermal use globally, and include concrete curing, bottling of water and carbonated drinks, milk pasteurisation, leatherworking, chemical extraction, CO_2 extraction, pulp and paper processing, iodine and salt extraction and borate and boric acid production.

Innovation is needed to expand the potential to use renewables and electricity (both directly and indirectly via hydrogen) in a greater portion of industrial processes, particularly for high temperature heat. The steel and cement sectors each generate around 7% of total energy system CO_2 emissions (including industrial process emissions), and the chemical sector a further 4%. Combined, these heavy industries are directly responsible for a similar quantity of emissions as that produced from all road transport, including trucks, cars and two/three wheelers. If these industries are to contribute to a sustainable future pathway for the energy system, their emissions must fall precipitously, despite an increase in demand for their outputs. The heavy industry sectors and long-distance transport modes are areas where emissions are particularly 'hard to abate'. This is in large part because the technologies that will be relied upon to deliver deep reductions in emissions in these sectors are at comparatively early stages of development.[9]

The Indian government considers green hydrogen and green ammonia as the future fuels to replace fossil fuels. Production of these fuels is one of the major priorities to achieve environmentally sustainable energy security for the nation. The government is taking various measures to facilitate the transition from fossil fuel and fossil fuel-based feedstocks to green hydrogen and green ammonia.[10]

Transportation

Electricity will be the transportation fuel of the future. Cars with small onboard generators, advanced batteries or tanks of hydrogen will be the common sight on roads in place of gasoline vehicles of today. This is not a dream. Major automakers around the world are investing heavily in electrification of mass-produced vehicles to meet national fuel efficiency, clean air and energy independence goals. Billions of dollars have been spent developing battery and hydrogen fuel cell technology.

Almost every major automaker around the world is working on battery EVs, which require recharging from the power grid, and cars that produce their own electricity from compressed hydrogen gas. Toyota, Honda and Hyundai already have begun marketing fuel cell vehicles, although a lack of hydrogen fuel stations keeps the initial sales confined to California.

Current Status of EVs in India

The Indian EV ecosystem is currently in the initial stages of development but has been gaining traction. In 2021, EV registrations amounted to 3,30,000 units, a jump of 168% from 2020. The sales were led by two and three-wheelers—48% and 47% respectively, followed by passenger vehicles at 4%. E-rickshaw/e-kart category (top speed less than 25 km/hr) takes the major share among three wheelers with 45%. E-buses are expected to gain traction with state governments inviting tenders to procure e-buses on a large scale. Electric four-wheelers are expected to take more time for large-scale adoption due to issues related to range anxiety, varying duty cycles and sparse charging network. The rise in E2W and E3W sales can be attributed to growing need for personal mobility, increased environmental awareness and rise in prices of gasoline. The second phase of Faster Adoption and Manufacturing of Hybrid and Electric Vehicles (FAME II) incentives have also helped in the increased adoption of EVs, especially two-wheelers.

As of 2021, EVs accounted for 1.1% of total vehicle sales. By 2027, they are expected to account for 39% of total automotive sales, growing at a CAGR of 68% over the next five years. The majority growth in EVs is expected to come from E2W and E3W segment, especially due to e-commerce and groceries shops committing to going completely electric in their last mile deliveries.

In terms of investments, EV industry attracted US\$ 6 billion in 2021 and is expected to gain US\$ 20 billion by 2030. EV market has seen strong attention from PE/VC investors in India with investments increasing from US$ 181million to US$ 1,718 million (recording an annual growth rate of 849%). Ministry of Skill Development and Entrepreneurship has estimated that the EV industry could create one crore direct jobs and five crore indirect jobs by 2030.

Fuel for 'Hard-To-Abate' Sectors

Green hydrogen is going to be the main fuel of heavy industries and heavy-duty transport in India in the near future. It has multiple advantages: one, it is a clean-burning molecule, which can decarbonise a range of sectors including the so-called 'hard-to-abate' iron and steel, chemicals and transportation; two, it has the highest energy content by weight and lowest energy content by volume; energy produced by 1 kg of hydrogen, according to the US Department of Energy (DoE) is the same as the energy in 2.8 kg of gasoline; third, the renewable energy that cannot be stored or used by the grid can be channelled to produce hydrogen, which can be stored in cryo-compressed tanks in gaseous form apart from being kept in liquefied and solid state; fourth, green hydrogen can easily be converted to green ammonia, providing a vast potential for agriculture, fertiliser producing industries and refineries. These industries are some of the major consumers of hydrogen, utilising about 6 mt of hydrogen every year. NITI and TERI predict that the demand for hydrogen will go up to five-folds by 2050, especially in steel and heavy-duty transport industry.

Currently, industry is the largest end-use sector today in India as its share in total final energy consumption (TFEC) is increasing from 28% to 36% between 1990 and 2019 and predicted to rise from 36% in 2019 to 41% by 2040.[11] Coal remains the mainstay of several industries. More than 60% of India's industrial energy demand today is met by the direct use of fossil fuels, more than half in the form of coal. Renewable heating solutions are less prevalent and renewable cooling solutions are even less prevalent. There are instances, where several nations have mandated solar water heating in new buildings, often through building codes at either the national or state level. Space heating and cooling are very important for emerging economies like India. Energy efficiency, material efficiency and electrification are essential strategies for reducing emissions from industrial processes.

The Future Energy Will Come from a Mishmash of Clean Technologies

Nuclear energy, solar energy, hydropower and energy from wind and biofuels are just a few of the promising alternatives for a cleaner and greener future. Other relatively new sources of energy such as fuel cells, geothermal energy and ocean energy are also being explored. Biofuels, hydrogen and batteries will play a key role in India's energy future. Renewables, green hydrogen and other carbon-neutral synthetic fuels will replace gasoline or natural gas as a transport fuel, and coal for power generation. Green hydrogen and synthetic versions of methane, methanol, ammonia and Fisher-Tropsch products (such as gasoline, diesel, kerosene) are being developed for industrial use.

However, demand for the fossil resources will not disappear entirely. On the contrary, the world is experiencing, and will continue to experience, a rapid increase in demand for oil and natural gas as feedstocks for petrochemical products. This is perhaps most clearly seen in the planet's demand for, and production of, plastics—almost all of which are derived from fossil fuels. They would, indeed, continue to play a crucial role in powering economic activity alongside renewables.

Petrochemicals, for instance, which are products of oil refining, would continue to be used for a whole range of chemical products from soaps, detergents, plastics, fertilisers, synthetic fibres, adhesives, foams, gels, tires, paints, digital devices and medical equipment, to explosives. Many industries such as health care, furniture, electronics, clothing, packaging, pharmaceuticals and even electric cars and batteries are dependent on petrochemical products.

The world generates 275 mt of plastic waste every year; over 50% of this plastic that ends up as waste is manufactured for single use packaging. Globally, of all the plastics that have been produced, only 9% has been recycled while about 12% has been incinerated. The rest is simply dumped and finds its way into our environment, including our waterbodies. India reportedly generates 25,940 tonnes of plastic waste on a daily basis, 60% of which is recycled, and the remaining 40% is mismanaged and ends up in dumpsites and on land and in water, adding to pollution.

Methanol is used to make thousands of products used in practically every aspect of our lives, including acrylic plastic, synthetic fabrics and fibres used to make clothing, adhesives, paint, and plywood used in construction and as a chemical agent in pharmaceuticals and agrochemicals. But the production of petrochemicals is not immediately recognisable as a continuing source of carbon emissions, because much of the carbon from the fossil fuel feedstocks is trapped within the petrochemical products. Once disposed of, these highly stable plastic products contribute to perhaps the second greatest environmental catastrophe following climate change—the global plastic waste crisis. It is widely believed that chemical industry is the third largest emitting industry behind the iron/steel and cement industries. According to the IEA, CO_2 emissions in 2018 from the chemical sector were 1.5 gt or 18% of industrial CO_2 emissions. A significant quantity of this CO_2 originates from syngas derived from fossil fuels.

The focus is now on how to reduce the carbon footprint of the chemical industry. Achieving net zero targets and limiting global temperature increases to the 1.5°C recommended by the IPCC is going to be very challenging, and governments and industry will need to deploy a range of technologies to meet these goals. Advanced reforming technology, available and proven at large scale today, can play a key role in the move towards net zero, by enabling the production of syngas with a very low carbon footprint. This syngas, and the hydrogen within it, can help to reduce the carbon footprint of the chemical industry substantially, and will support the decarbonisation of other sectors such as transport and agriculture. And the beauty is that the route to deploy this technology at scale and with very low CO_2 emissions exists today and its deployment will give the world a great head start in the race to net zero.

In the broader context, the products made by the chemical industry contain carbon, and this will continue, so a carbon-free chemical industry isn't possible. However, as outlined above, the industry can, and will, find ways to use the carbon more efficiently, reducing carbon intensity, and reducing CO_2 emissions to very low levels. For example, captured CO_2 and renewable hydrogen can be directly transformed into methanol, or can be converted within the reverse water-gas shift reaction to a syngas containing CO, CO_2 and hydrogen, which can be further processed through well-established Fischer-Tropsch synthesis processes to make chemicals and fuels. This is one route to make drop-in fuels for planes, such as Sustainable Aviation Fuel (SAF) which is regarded as critical to assist the decarbonisation of aviation. In addition, syngas-based technologies can be used to store and transport renewable energy in the form of methanol and ammonia and are being proposed as fuels for sustainable shipping.

References

1. PricewaterhouseCoopers (PwC), 'Inventing Tomorrow's Energy System'.
2. IEA.
3. Brian Merchant, 'What is the Energy Source of the Future?' HowStuffWorks.
4. IEA.
5. International Energy Agency (IEA, 2021).
6. https://cea.nic.in/wp-content/uploads/2021/03/publications_12.07.2021.pdf.
7. IPCC, 2022.
8. IEA, The Challenge of Reaching Zero Emissions in Heavy Industry, 19 September, 2020.
9. IEA, Energy Technology Perspectives, 2020.
10. *Press Information Bureau (PIB)*, Government of India.
11. IEA, 2020.

Chapter 15

EMERGING GEOPOLITICS OF ENERGY

For most of the last two centuries fossil fuels configured the international energy geopolitical landscape. They were the foundation of the global energy system, economic growth and modern lifestyles. The exploitation of fossil fuels lifted global energy use fifty-fold in the last two centuries, shaping the geopolitical environment of the modern world. The geographic concentration of fossil fuels has had a significant impact on the wealth and security of nations.

However, there has always been struggle over secure and affordable access to energy. Any incidence of shortage or embargo of energy has led to geopolitical conflicts between nation-states and to the making and unmaking of alliances. Energy historian Keith Fisher says oil and violence share an intimate relationship. The oil in Baku, Azerbaijan, caused the conflict between the Persian Abbasids and Syrian Umayyad Caliphate. By 1813, the East India Company was drafting reports on the commercial and strategic importance on Persia and Mesopotamia, for their 'exhaustible oil'.[1]

In modern times, the founding of a large-scale petroleum industry in Pennsylvania in 1859, a few decades after the eradication of the native American population, was 'par' for the story of oil, associated with 'conquest and violence', of destroying those who came in the way who were often deemed 'savage' and 'barbaric'. A similar story played out in Russia, which controlled oil from Baku and the Caucasus, subjugating 'untameable' and 'wild' populations, and rivalling American dominance. The British invasion of Egypt in 1882 was only the first of many later wars and coups—all for control over Middle East oil supplies, from Iran to Afghanistan, Iraq to Libya. In British India and Dutch Indonesia, oil and conflict began to mix more. The annexation of Upper Burma was arguably the first war for access to oil. In Aceh, Dutch troops and their scorched Earth policy killed at least a hundred thousand people. The oil company called Royal Dutch Shell had its roots in a 'genocide'. After the First World war, as Lord Curzon said, "The Allies floated to victory on a wave of oil," supplied by the US.[2]

Oil has always been entwined with security and the power and position of nations. The 'special relationship' between the United States and Saudi Arabia goes back to an undisclosed deal struck after a meeting between President Franklin Roosevelt and King Ibn Saud in Suez Canal in February, 1945. From Harry Truman onward, US presidents have made the security of the Middle East, and in particular Saudi Arabia and its oil, a fundamental national interest. Jimmy Carter made this commitment more explicit in response to the 1979 Soviet invasion of Afghanistan, which was seen as a possible 'stepping stone' for the Soviet Union to gain control over the Persian Gulf and 'much of the world's oil supplies'. "An attempt by any outside force to gain control of the Persian Gulf region," said the Carter Doctrine, "will be regarded as an assault on the vital interests of the United States and such an assault will be repelled by any means necessary, including military force." Saudi Arabia, in turn, had tied its long-term security to the United States.[3]

Iraq was an oil country. Its only export was oil, and was of great significance to the global energy markets. But its dictator, Saddam Hussein, was hostile to the US hegemony over the Middle East region. The US felt there was a possibility of a hostile Iraq achieving dominance in the region, and thus over the region's oil, when Iraq conquered Kuwait and was threatening the Saudi oil fields in 1990–91.

In this century, climate change has become a dominant political issue and central to the future of energy. This dire need to limit global warming to 1.5°C above pre-industrial levels has provided a potent rationale for rolling back the supremacy of hydrocarbons and expanding renewables. Today the idea of renewables is deeply appealing as an inexhaustible and environmentally friendly energy source to meet the triple challenges of energy supply, security and climate change. And with this shift, the race and nature of conflicts for energy supply is also changed. The pivot to renewables could reduce the incidence of certain kinds of conflict, and alleviate competition for important natural resources, notably oil, gas, water and food. On the other hand, cybersecurity and access to important minerals may generate increased concern and tension.

Oil exporters will lose global influence, whereas importers will be empowered. Economies that produce oil and gas could lose US$ 7 trillion by 2040.[4] With their huge markets, industry leaders China and the United States will dominate the clean technology sector. And new relationships and allegiances, such as the Global Energy Interconnection Development and

Cooperation Organisation (a platform for companies and enterprises) might replace state-led clubs of old, such as the Organisation of the Petroleum Exporting Countries (OPEC).

Why Renewables Will Transform Geopolitics?

The main story of the energy transition is the rise of renewables, particularly solar and wind, and the future decline of fossil fuels. Renewables differ in many respects from fossil fuels, and these differences will have geopolitical consequences. First, renewable energy resources are available in one form or another in most countries, unlike fossil fuels which are concentrated in specific geographic locations. Renewables enable countries to strengthen their energy security and achieve greater energy independence by harnessing the vast indigenous renewable energy sources that can be found across the planet. The rapid development of renewable technologies and their widespread deployment is certain to have significant long-term effects on geopolitical dynamics. This reduces the importance of current energy choke points, such as the narrow channels on widely used sea routes that are critical to the global supply of oil. Second, most renewables take the form of flows, while fossil fuels are stocks. Energy stocks can be stored, which is useful; but they can be used only once. In contrast, energy flows do not exhaust themselves and are harder to disrupt. Third, renewable energy sources can be deployed at almost any scale and lend themselves better to decentralised forms of energy production and consumption. This adds to the democratising effects of renewable energy. Fourth, renewable energy sources have nearly zero marginal costs, and some of them, like solar and wind, enjoy cost reductions of nearly 20% for every doubling of capacity.[5] This enhances their ability to drive change but requires regulatory solutions to ensure stability and profitability in the power sector.

New Actors

The shift to renewable energy may reshuffle political and economic power, because renewables tend to decentralise and democratise energy systems. Due to the falling cost of solar PV and wind power, as well as smart distribution systems, almost anyone with a rooftop or some land can produce electricity, either for self-consumption or for the grid. These developments will generate a more diverse energy ecosystem. The role of the centralised state in the energy system may change, while many new actors and new business models are likely to emerge and flourish. Local and distributed forms of energy generation give households and communities more autonomy than centralised grid systems.

New Centres of Geopolitical Power

The accelerating deployment of renewables has set in motion a global energy transformation that will have profound geopolitical consequences. Just as fossil fuels have shaped the geopolitical map over the last two centuries, the rapid growth of renewable technologies is now set to transform relations between states, while economies and societies will undergo structural transformations. The energy transformation will be one of the major elements that reshape geopolitics in the twenty first century, alongside trends in demography, inequality, urbanisation, technology, environmental sustainability, military capability and domestic politics in major states.

Historically, most major transitions have proceeded in unexpected ways. Climbing the energy ladder from wood to coal between the eighteenth and nineteenth centuries, for instance, enabled industrialisation. The transition to renewable energy sources will be disruptive, too. Rapidly growing renewables have unquestionably started to transform the global energy landscape in an irreversible way. At the same time, considerable uncertainty that could bring changes just as radical in their scope and impact.

The rise of renewable energy may also create new centres of geopolitical power. As renewable resources become widely distributed, supply-side geopolitics are expected to be less influential than in the fossil fuel era. Instead of focusing on just two major resources, oil and natural gas, low-carbon energy geopolitics may depend on many additional factors, such as access to technology, power lines, rare earth materials, patents, storage and dispatch, not to mention unpredictable government policies. Despite uncertainty, there is no question that the balance of power in energy geopolitics is shifting from fossil fuel owners to countries that are developing low-carbon solutions.[6]

As the world shifts to renewables and the relative importance of fossil fuels declines, a geopolitical shift in the incidence and geographic location of conflicts would follow. Global and local confrontations over contested hydrocarbon reserves, for example in the South China Sea or the Eastern Mediterranean, may diminish or result in fewer conflicts. To this extent, the global energy transformation may generate a peace dividend.[7]

If oil and LNG become less strategic for security, maritime chokepoints—narrow shipping lanes such as the straits of Hormuz or Malacca—may become less critical as a consequence. The Strait of Hormuz is the world's most important oil artery, which links Middle East crude producers to key global markets. At its narrowest point, it is only 21 miles wide and the shipping lane is only 2 miles wide in either direction. Each day, around 30% of all seaborne traded crude oil passes through it, as well as a significant volume of LNG. There have been several military incidents in the Strait. In 2018, Iran hinted it could disrupt oil flows through the Strait in response to the oil sanctions announced by the US.[8]

With renewables set to dominate the energy supply system, most countries, including India, can increase their energy independence by exploiting the vast indigenous renewable energy sources that are found across the planet. This has the potential to change the power structures of regions and states, bringing the promise of energy independence to nations and communities, enhancing energy security and democratic empowerment.[9] Some countries that have historically enjoyed geopolitical influence because of their fossil fuel exports are likely to see a decline in their global reach and influence and will need to adapt to avoid serious economic consequences. IEA has warned that oil and gas producing economies could lose US$ 7 trillion by 2040. The energy transformation is expected to put pressure on fossil fuel prices and their income. If fossil fuel revenues decline, the producing countries will need to rethink their national priorities and strategies.

I. REDUCED OIL AND GAS DEMAND

To the extent that renewable energy reduces demand for oil and gas, there could be significant geopolitical consequences. For oil and gas producers, the decline in revenue generated from fossil fuel energy exports can provide an impetus for political reform and economic diversification. However, a decline in petroleum revenue could also lead to political instability, especially in the short to medium term. Consumer countries would improve their trade balances and their room to manoeuvre in the international system. The development of renewable energy is already a game changer for Chile, Jordan, Morocco and several island states in terms of energy security.

A decline in fossil fuel rents has the potential of profoundly destabilising countries that have not diversified their economies and a life for oil. The loss of oil revenues in such countries could lead to social and political instability. The drop in oil price in the 1980s was one of the factors that contributed to the decline and eventual fall of the Soviet Union, which in turn led to the end of the Cold War, arguably the biggest geopolitical shift since the end of the Second World War.[10] In many oil producing countries, particularly the Middle East, rulers use patronage and handouts to perpetuate their rule. If their oil income falls for a long period, these governments will struggle to provide the socio-economic programmes that citizens have come to expect. Austerity can potentially lead to social unrest, political infighting and even violence. Indeed, the emergence of a power vacuum in petrostates is potentially the biggest geopolitical risk of the energy transition.[11]

For oil importing countries, a high degree of import dependence could generate economic risks. In strategic terms, fossil fuel importing countries are vulnerable to risks of supply disruption and price volatility caused by political instability, terrorist attacks or armed conflicts that may occur in oil- and gas-exporting nations. Smaller energy importing countries may also be subject to pressure or coercion with regard to their energy supply and therefore have less freedom to determine their own strategic priorities and goals.

By contrast, countries that are able to develop their own renewable sources of energy are better placed to achieve energy security. An example is the Brazilian ethanol programme which was put in place after the oil shock of 1973 to reduce the country's oil imports and shield the economy from volatile prices and supply disruptions. This programme has played a vital role in Brazil's efforts to achieve energy self-sufficiency and has helped transform it into the world's second largest producer and largest exporter of ethanol. India, for instance, is expected to overtake China as the largest growth market for energy by the late 2020s.

Developing countries that lack domestic fuel reserves stand to benefit the most from exploiting their renewable energy resources. Small islands developing states (SIDS) rely heavily on imported fuels for their electricity needs.[12] SIDS also sit on the frontline of climate change despite having done the least to cause it.

II. RISE OF NEW ENERGY LEADERS

Countries that are able to take advantage of new renewable energy technologies can expect to enhance their global influence and reach.

Three types of countries have the potential to emerge as new renewable energy leaders.

First, countries with high technical potential for renewable energy generation stand to gain if they are able to become significant exporters of renewable electricity or fuels. Australia's economically demonstrated solar and wind energy resources are estimated to be 75% greater than its combined coal, gas, oil and uranium resources.[13] In the Atacama Desert, Chile has among the world's best solar resources, as well as high potential for wind, hydropower, geothermal and ocean energy. In both cases, however, the remoteness of these locations will probably constrain electricity exports.

Some countries are already net exporters of electricity generated by renewables. Brazil is already a major exporter of renewable electricity from hydro. Norway exports electricity to its neighbours and the Netherlands, and is building new transmission cables to Germany and the United Kingdom. Laos and Bhutan also export electricity generated from hydropower to neighbouring countries. Bhutan's power exports to India raised more than 27% of government revenue and 14% of Bhutan's GDP.[14]

Second, mineral-rich countries such as Bolivia, Mongolia and the Democratic Republic of Congo (DRC) have an opportunity to become part of the global production and value chains necessary for renewable technologies. Doing so will boost their economic development, provided they put the right policies and governance frameworks in place.

Third, leaders in technological innovation are positioned to gain the most from the global energy transformation. No country has put itself in a better position to become the world's renewable energy superpower than China. In aggregate, it is now the world's largest producer, exporter and installer of solar panels, wind turbines, batteries and electric vehicles, placing it at the forefront of the global energy transition.

China is by far the largest global manufacturer of clean energy technologies having excelled in the four technologies—wind turbine components, crystalline silicon PV modules, LED packages and lithium-ion battery cells. In addition, it leads the world in renewable energy patents. China's concerted efforts to research, develop and invest in renewable energy and clean transport offer its industry the opportunity to overtake US and European companies, which have been dominant in sectors such as cars and energy machinery. This will give China a comparative advantage in trade and lend impetus to the country's economic growth.

By taking the lead on renewables, China has improved its geopolitical standing in several respects. By producing more of its own energy, China is reducing its reliance on fuel imports and the risks of energy disruption which could put a brake on its economic ambitions. Its technological expertise in renewables has established it as a leading exporter of clean energy technology, creating a balance of trade advantage.

Concerns Over Security of Supplies

Concerns over energy security have marked the conduct of international relations, the formation of alliances, the protection of national interests and defence planning. Oil interests have shaped the relations between the United States and the Middle East for decades. Evidence of this includes the Eisenhower Doctrine of 1957 and the Carter Doctrine of 1980. Under the Eisenhower Doctrine of 1957, the US offered economic and military aid to Middle Eastern countries if another state threatened them with armed aggression. This was motivated in part by the Soviet Union's growing influence in the region after the Suez crisis of 1956. The Carter Doctrine of 1980 was a response to the Soviet invasion of Afghanistan. It proclaimed, "An attempt by any outside force to gain control of the Persian Gulf region will be regarded as an assault on the vital interests of the United States of America, and such an assault will be repelled by any means necessary, including military force." Similarly, China's need to secure oil supplies and other natural resources to sustain its growth has led it to foster new and deeper ties with countries in Asia, Africa and Latin America, as well as diversify its domestic energy supply with renewables.

In a renewable energy economy, most countries will be able to achieve energy independence as they will have greater energy security and more freedom to take the energy decisions that suit them. Since some form of economically viable renewable energy potential is available in most places, countries that currently depend heavily on fossil fuel imports will be able to use renewables to reap strategic and economic benefits.

In economic terms, a high degree of import dependence also generates costs and risks. Countries that import most of their energy are exposed to currency fluctuations and volatile fuel prices that can result in balance-of-payment problems. The oil price shocks in the 1970s, for example, squeezed many industrial economies and sowed the seeds of a debt crisis that many developing countries suffered in the decade that followed, with serious social and economic consequences. Increasing the share of renewables in the energy mix can mitigate such risks and provide new pulses of economic growth. Countries that switch from imported fossil fuels to domestically generated renewable energy will significantly improve their trade balance.

Changing Relations between States

Renewable energy will not merely influence the balance of power between countries, it will also reconfigure alliances and trade flows, and create new interdependencies around electric grids and new commodities.

If global demand for fossil fuels declines, alliances built on fossil fuels are likely to weaken. Alliances may be maintained for various other reasons, but the energy pillar will become relatively less important. OPEC is a prime example of a fossil fuel-based grouping. It was created in 1960 as a forum for oil-exporting countries to exchange information and coordinate their interactions with the international oil companies that dominated international oil trading at the time. OPEC countries started to coordinate their oil production policies from the early 1980s.

Bilateral relations between states will also undergo change. The alliance between the United States and Saudi Arabia is a prime example of a strategic relationship in which oil plays a key role. This alliance dates back to 1945, when King Abdul Aziz ibn Saud and US President Franklin D Roosevelt came to an understanding that the US would provide military assistance in exchange for access to Saudi oil. Relations between the two states may evolve significantly as economies across the globe become less dependent on oil.

Countries are also beginning to rethink their energy diplomacy. The foreign energy strategy of Japan no longer concentrates exclusively on securing fossil fuel imports but also includes renewables, hydrogen in particular. Germany spearheaded the creation of IRENA in 2009 and has developed bilateral energy partnerships with a number of countries in which renewable energy features prominently.[15] The United Arab Emirates (UAE), a major oil exporting country, has also assumed a leadership position on renewable energy by hosting IRENA, funding renewable energy projects in developing countries via the Abu Dhabi Fund for Development[16] and investing in renewable energy projects in developed countries.

Power Shift

The accelerated growth of renewables is likely to alter the power and influence of some states and regions relative to others, and to redraw the geopolitical map of the twenty first century.

Critical Materials

Lithium is a critical component for light-weight batteries for vehicles. As battery use dominates total lithium use, the foreseen rapid growth of battery manufacturing will require a rapid upscaling of lithium production. Electric cars accounted for around 4% of global car sales in 2020; this share may grow five-fold to ten-fold during the 2020–30 decade, and lithium production needs to grow accordingly.[17]

Cobalt supply is critical for batteries. Its demand may double between 2020 and 2030, and vehicle batteries may account for 60% of total cobalt demand in 2030. However, battery design innovations can reduce this dependency substantially.

Nickel demand may increase substantially due to its widespread use in battery cathodes. Already, producers are considering alternative battery chemistries (notably lithium iron phosphate cathodes), but the product performance is inferior. However, such alternatives can reduce the growth in nickel demand substantially.

Today, around one tenth of all silver is used for solar PV modules. This share may rise further as demand for these grows. To some extent, this can be balanced by more material-efficient cell design.

Demand for other minerals and metals will grow but seems less critical. Such minerals and metals include aluminium, chromium, graphite, indium, iron, lead, manganese, molybdenum, titanium, vanadium and zinc. For some of these, the resource is abundant; for others, alternatives exist, such as substitution of materials and changes in product design that provide similar technical performance.

Increased production of minerals and metals will increase the energy and carbon footprint. However, this effect is dwarfed by the emissions reduction that can be achieved when those minerals and metals are deployed in renewable energy technologies. The deployment of renewable energy in mining and processing operations should be considered.

Copper has a key role in electrical wiring in power production, transportation and use. Electricity demand will increase substantially, and this will raise copper demand. Although the copper resources are adequate, the quality of copper ore resources has been decreasing, it is said.

Neodymium and dysprosium play a critical role in permanent magnets, which are widely used in high performance electric motors (including electric vehicles) and in generators (wind turbines). The key challenge is that mining and processing of these materials is dominated by one country, whereas supply of other critical materials is more diversified. More than 80% of the world's neodymium, used in phones and electric cars, is produced in China. In 2017 alone, China mined 1,05,000 metric tonnes of rare earth metals, while US has only produced about 43,000 metric tonnes in the last 20 years combined.

Geographical Concentration of Critical Mineral

The widespread adoption of renewable energy and related technologies, such as solar panels, wind turbines, electric vehicles and energy storage technologies, will increase the demand for a range of minerals and metals required for their production. In theory, the regions that possess substantial reserves of these minerals should benefit from the energy transformation.

Latin America has huge reserves of copper, iron ore, silver, lithium, aluminium, nickel, manganese and zinc. Africa is rich in platinum, manganese, bauxite and chromium. In the Asia-Pacific region, China has metal reserves, India has iron ore, steel and titanium, Indonesia, Malaysia and the Philippines possess bauxite and nickel and New Caledonia has enormous reserves of nickel.[18]

Advances in prospecting and mining have also made it feasible to exploit minerals located under the seabed, raising thorny issues of sovereignty and governance.[19] As deep-sea mining expands, international norms and standards will be needed to mitigate the risks of environmental damage and conflict.

However, the largest reserves of metals and minerals required for renewable technologies are found in weak states with poor governance records. More than 60% of the world's cobalt supply originates in the Democratic Republic of the Congo (DRC). Unaccountable external factors have sometimes caused or aggravated conditions that have maintained lawlessness and conflict in some of these mineral-rich regions, with devastating social, economic, political and environmental consequences. In

Colombia, a country in which the longest-running internal armed conflict has taken place, various armed groups have controlled and exploited illegal tin, tungsten, tantalum and gold mining resources.

Efforts have been made to address the issue of so-called conflict minerals. Most of these strategies attempt to increase transparency and accountability along the global supply chain. The OECD, for example, has published due diligence guidelines for companies that mine or trade in minerals and the UN Security Council has called for such measures to be applied in Cote d'Ivoire, the DRC, Sudan and other conflict affected states.[20] Well-regulated and transparent exploitation of mineral deposits can make a major contribution to the economic development of these countries.

Growing Competition for Critical Materials

While renewable energy reduces dependence on petroleum resources, it increases dependence on critical materials needed in the production of renewables, and a growing demand for them could intensify international competition that could in turn lead to geopolitical instability. Many scholars think that the world may fracture into two camps in a clean-tech cold war. Technology leaders hold the power. Other countries gravitate towards one of the leaders, reinforcing regional blocs and increasing rivalry. These blocs seek to control the materials needed, such as rare earth metals, cobalt and lithium. They might also withhold access to technologies from nations outside their groups. Thus, conflicts which bedevilled the past will persist during the energy transition.

A new dimension in the geopolitics of energy is the access to critical minerals and metals and to the technology indispensable for this transition. As energy transitions gather pace, security of mineral supply is gaining prominence in the energy security debate, a realm where oil has traditionally occupied a central role. An energy system powered by clean energy technologies differs profoundly from one fuelled by traditional hydrocarbon resources. Solar photovoltaic plants, wind farms and electric vehicles generally require more minerals to build than their fossil fuel-based counterparts. A typical electric car requires six times the mineral inputs of a conventional car and an onshore wind plant requires nine times more mineral resources than a gas-fired plant. Since 2010 the average amount of minerals needed for a new unit of power generation capacity has increased by 50% as the share of renewables in new investment has risen.

The types of mineral resources used vary by technology. Lithium, nickel, cobalt, manganese and graphite are crucial to battery performance, longevity and energy density. Rare earth elements are essential for permanent magnets that are vital for wind turbines and EV motors. Electricity networks need a huge amount of copper and aluminium, with copper being a cornerstone for all electricity-related technologies.

The shift to a clean energy system is set to drive a huge increase in the requirements for these minerals, meaning that the energy sector is emerging as a major force in mineral markets. Until the mid-2010s, for most minerals, the energy sector represented a small part of total demand. However, as energy transitions gather pace, clean energy technologies are becoming the fastest-growing segment of demand. In a scenario that meets the Paris Agreement goals (as in the IEA Sustainable Development Scenario [SDS]), their share of total demand rises significantly over the next two decades to over 40% for copper and rare earth elements, 60–70% for nickel and cobalt, and almost 90% for lithium. EVs and battery storage have already displaced consumer electronics to become the largest consumer of lithium and are set to take over from stainless steel as the largest end user of nickel by 2040. In climate-driven scenarios, mineral demand for use in EVs and battery storage is a major force, growing at least thirty times to 2040. Lithium sees the fastest growth, with demand growing by over 40 times in the SDS by 2040, followed by graphite, cobalt and nickel (around 20–25 times). The expansion of electricity networks means that copper demand for grid lines more than doubles over the same period.[21]

III. RARE EARTH ELEMENTS

Rare earth elements are a group of metals that are critical ingredients for a greener economy, and the location of the reserves for mining are increasingly important and valuable. They are more abundant than their name suggests, but extracting, processing and refining them are fraught with various technical, political and environmental issues. They are mined using extremely energy-intensive processes, spewing carbon emissions into the atmosphere and toxins into the ground. Many of these metals, which include mercury, barium, lead, chromium and cadmium, are extremely damaging to the health of several ecosystems, including humans. A survey done by United Nations University (UNU) and the World Health Organisation (WHO) on the impact e-waste has on child health, raised concerns around chemical burns, cancer and stunted growth. Eradicating these substances from discarded products is difficult and costly, which is why much of the e-waste exported to the developing world under the pretence of being reused or refurbished ends up being dumped.

There are 17 known rare earth elements—lanthanum (La), cerium (Ce), praseodymium (Pr), neodymium (Nd), promethium (Pm), samarium (Sm), europium (Eu), gadolinium (Gd), terbium (Tb), dysprosium (Dy), holmium (Ho), erbium (Er), thulium (Tm), ytterbium (Yb), lutetium (Lu), scandium (Sc), and yttrium (Y).[22]

Until 1948, India and Brazil were the world's primary producers of rare earth metals. The countries with most rare earth metals currently are China, the United States, Brazil, India, Vietnam, Australia, Russia, Myanmar and Indonesia.

China tops the list for mine production and reserves of rare earth elements, with 44 mt in reserves and 140,000 tonnes of annual mine production. Vietnam and Brazil have the second and third largest reserves of rare earth metals, with 22 mt and 21 mt, respectively, but their mine production is among the world's lowest at 1,000 tonnes per year. While the United States has 1.5 mt in reserves, it is largely dependent on imports from China for refined rare earths. India, too, has some light rare earth element reserves of light earths like lanthanum, cerium, neodymium, praseodymium and samarium, but for heavy rare earth elements like dysprosium, terbium and europium, it has to largely depend on imports, mainly from China. India's currently known rare earth element deposits are 6.9 mt.[23]

The 17 rare earth elements are divided into two groups, light and heavy, based on their atomic weights. They exist in natural deposits globally. Heavy rare earths, like dysprosium and terbium, play a critical role in defence equipment, technology and electric vehicles, but they are often harder to source. Neodymium and praseodymium are some of the most sought-after light rare earth elements crucial in products such as motors, turbines and medical devices. Demand for them exploded in recent years with the growth of technology and will continue to climb amid the ongoing race to create a large electric vehicle market.

As China's economy has developed over the last several decades, its leaders have sought to transform the country into a key player in strategically important industries. Toward this end, the state has made China as the dominant global supplier of rare earths, a collection of 17 minerals that are indispensable to the manufacturing of smartphones, electric vehicles, military weapon systems, and countless other advanced technologies. Currently, China produces about 90% of all globally used rare earth metals. Besides its economic dominance, China has also gained unique know-how related to rare earth element processing technologies. While its share in rare earth mining has been declining in recent years, it also produces close to 90% of the world's permanent magnet alloys, and Chinese manufacturing of permanent magnets themselves is on the rise. Based on China's dominant position in rare earth markets, other countries such as Australia, Japan, United States and several across Europe are increasingly concerned about a stable rare earth supply and their increasing dependence on China. Various strategies have been deployed by importing countries to reduce this dependency, so far with limited success.

Ten countries—US, UK, Australia, Canada, Finland, France, Germany, Japan, South Korea, Sweden—and the European Commission have come together to form a Minerals Security Partnership (MSP) to catalyse investment from governments and the private sector to develop supply chains of minerals and the 17 rare earth metal. The grouping is seen as primarily focused on evolving an alternative to China, which has created processing infrastructure in rare earth minerals and has acquired mines in Africa for elements such as Cobalt. India is trying at the diplomatic level to join the group.

Cartelisation of the Supply Chain

Like the cartelisation of oil and gas and the chances of oil embargoes, there are high possibilities of cartels developing in the global rare earth metal reserves and supply chains. Even if these cartels are unable to achieve the kind of impact that OPEC did in the 1970s oil market, they might be able to exert influence over consumers of these materials. Rare earth elements are widely used in clean energy technologies, including solar panels and wind turbines. Today almost all mining, production and processing of rare earth elements takes place in China. This might in some circumstances present opportunities for cartelisation. China's intents of hegemony, non-solidarity with other nations and aims of controlling various sectors and aspects of the world's energy landscape does not augur well for the environment in general, as well as for geopolitics and global renewable energy usage and scenarios. Its intents on doing the same with its vast rare earth reserves will be detrimental.[24]

Recycling of these rare earth metals for continuous usage for various technologies is a good option that can be considered. It is a lengthy process which involves demagnetisation (by heating), crushing and roasting, followed by a leaching process and a separation method before a final roasting to produce a mixed rare earth oxide. Hundreds of thousands of tonnes of rare earth compounds are being produced and manufactured into products each year.

Recycling rare earth materials is challenging because once embedded in devices, they're difficult to take out. Instead of discarding phones or IT equipment after a couple of years, enterprises should aim to get the most out of the technology they have invested in through repairing or refurbishing. Having suitable recycling methods is a valuable contribution towards keeping the costs of the materials low and maximising the use of the rare earth elements.[25]

The usage of these metals in our most advanced technologies and which form a critical part of the renewable energy revolution should be handled with careful, sincere and cleaner measures if the way forward has to be greener and environment-friendly. The three most important materials used in magnets include neodymium, dysprosium and terbium. Terbium is one of the toughest to come by because production, extraction and magnet-making are focused on China. Trade wars and retaliatory tariffs can leave many companies sourcing these crucial materials in limbo, even if they make up just a small portion of a product. Market dynamics can escalate so quickly that companies without a diversified supply chain bid aggressively, materials get scarce and prices go up. In 2011, for example, rare earth prices shot up when China restricted exports to maintain supplies for domestic industries, which was the case again during the 2019 trade war.

IV. INDIA'S CONCERN

India's pledge to reach net zero emissions by 2070 and to meet 50% of its electricity requirements from non-fossil energy sources, especially renewables, by 2030 has been hailed by the IEA as a 'hugely significant moment for the global fight against climate change'.

However, achieving these targets will be an uphill task, fraught with numerous challenges. One of them, and most serious, is a lack or limited availability in India of critical materials, essential for aggregating clean energy technologies. Lithium, for example, is essential for the manufacture of batteries for electric vehicles, while niobium and strontium are needed for steel and aluminium alloys. Most minerals have some degree of substitutability, except for niobium and silver, for which there are no good substitutes. The supply risk is relatively high for yttrium and scandium, followed by niobium and silicon. Silicon is key for the manufacture of solar panels. The rare earth elements of yttrium and scandium have various uses, including alloys, superconductors and battery technologies. India does not have the recycling capacity for most minerals except copper and iron. While there are limited technological options for recycling some minerals, there is scope for increased end-of-life recycling, as demonstrated by higher recycling rates globally.

There will be an increase in the demand for several critical minerals as India transitions towards renewable power generation and electric vehicles. For example, copper, manganese, zinc and indium will be required for renewable electricity generation equipment manufacturing. Likewise, the move to electric vehicles would require increasing quantities of various minerals, including copper, lithium, cobalt and rare earth elements. However, India does not have any known reserves of nickel, cobalt, molybdenum, rare earth elements, neodymium and indium, and the needs for copper and silver are projected to be higher than India's current reserves.

The International Institute for Sustainable Development (IISD) provides a summary of critical material used in renewable energy technologies as cobalt, copper, nickel, lithium, rare earth metals, notably neodymium and dysprosium. A much longer list of critical materials is given in one or more of these studies—aluminium, chromium, gallium, germanium, graphite, indium, iron, lanthanum, lead, manganese, molybdenum, platinum, rhenium, ruthenium, scandium, silver, vanadium, tantalum, titanium, yttrium and zinc.

At present India imports more than 80% of solar panels and modules, primarily from China. Cheap imported panels have contributed to India having one of the lowest solar power tariffs in the world but also raised energy security and geopolitical concerns. Though India has a solar PV cell manufacturing capacity of 3 GW per year and solar PV module manufacturing capacity of 10 GW per year, the country has no manufacturing units for polysilicon, wafer or ingots. To decrease imports and promote local manufacturing of solar panels, the government has offered a number of incentives.

In 2018, a 20% subsidy for capital expenditure in special economic zones (SEZs) was offered to potential manufacturers. In 2021 public procurement of solar components was mandated to be only from Class I suppliers that have local content equal or more than 50%. Solar PV cells and modules must be sourced from domestic manufacturers for central government schemes to promote the use of solar energy such as Pradhan Mantri Kisan Urja Suraksha Evem Utthan (PM KUSUM) for replacing electrical agricultural pumps with solar pumps and for subsidised rooftop solar projects. In addition, the government has also imposed basic customs duty (BCD) on import of solar PV cells and modules effective from April 2022. In 2021, IREDA released a list of 18 bidders for its PLI scheme for setting up fully integrated production of Si solar cells. Four applicants have proposed a 4 GW solar factory each that is fully integrated from polysilicon (highly pure form of crystalline silicon) production through wafer, solar cell and module manufacturing. The PLI scheme is expected to attract a direct investment of around US\$ 2.33 billion. Given the strong response for the PLI scheme for manufacturing solar modules, the scheme outlay has been further increased to US\$ 3.2 billion from US\$ 600 million earlier. This is expected to increase setting up of cell and module manufacturing capacity from 10 GW to 40 GW.

This is not the first time India is trying to establish polysilicon manufacturing capabilities for the semiconductor and solar industries. In 2008 some of the major players announced plans to manufacture polysilicon. The plans did not materialise despite the government's offer of land and other incentives as the cost of electricity proved to be too high and the quality of supply too low. This time may be different not only because the quality of electricity supply has improved but also the market size for solar panels has increased ten-folds. However, self-reliance in the production of wafers, cells and modules may not extend right up to the upstream end of the solar value chain. In 2018, India imported more than 72 mt of Silicon Oxide (SiO2), over 28% of this was from China. Though sources of SiO2 imports were highly diversified it would not count as secure or self-reliance.

To ensure overall mineral security and to acquire equity assets, India has plans to set up a joint venture company namely Khanij Bidesh India Ltd (KABIL) with the participation of three central public sector enterprises namely, National Aluminium Company Ltd (NALCO), Hindustan Copper Ltd (HCL) and Mineral Exploration Company Ltd (MECL). KABIL is expected to carry out identification, acquisition, exploration, development, mining and processing of strategic minerals overseas for commercial use and meeting country's requirement of these minerals. India's experience in acquiring oil and gas equity assets for energy security had only modest success but that experience may enrich India's quest for mineral security.

Cartelisation of Critical Materials

As the transition to renewable energy accelerates, cartels could develop around materials critical to renewable energy technologies. Even if these cartels may not be as powerful as the Organisation of Petroleum Exporting Countries (OPEC), they can exert enough influence from time to time over production and prices of critical materials. According to some scholars who had studied conflict-prone non-fuel minerals it is likely that there will be competition between China and the US over 11 minerals especially over those that cannot be substituted in new technologies, including renewable energy equipment.

Rare earth elements are widely used in clean energy technologies, including solar panels and wind turbines. Although these elements are found in many countries around the world, they are usually found in dilute concentrations and are often difficult to extract. Today almost all mining, production and processing of rare earth elements takes place in China. Lithium, cobalt and indium are also widely used in clean energy technologies and might in some circumstances present opportunities for cartelisation.[26]

References

1. Keith Fisher, 'A Pipeline Runs Through It: The Story of Oil from Ancient Times to the First World War', Allen Lane, 4 August, 2022.
2. 'Why Oil and Blood Mix Very Well', *The Times of India*, New Delhi, 3 September, 2022.
3. Daniel Ergin, The Two Gulf Wars of 1990–91 and 2003 Against Iraq were Logical Corollary of this US Policy, *The Quest*, p.129.
4. International Energy Agency. Outlook for Producer Economies: What Do Changing Energy Dynamics Mean for Major Oil and Gas Exporters? IEA, 2018.
5. DNV-GL, Energy Transition Outlook 2018, DNV-GL, 2018.
6. Massachusetts Institute of Technology (MIT).

7. Goldthau, A, M Keim and K Westphal, The Geopolitics of Energy Transformation: Governing the Shift - Transformation Dividends, Systemic Risks and New Uncertainties, Comment No. 42, German Institute for International and Security Affairs, October 2018.

8. 'Strait of Hormuz: The World's Most Important Oil Artery', *Reuters*, 5 July, 2018.

9. IRENA, A New World: The Geopolitics of Energy Transformation.

10. IRENA.

11. Remark Made by General Tom Middendorp, Former Chief of Defence of the Armed Forces of the Netherlands, Oslo, 24 June, 2018.

12. UNCTAD, The Least Developed Countries Report: Transformational Energy Access, UN Conference on Trade and Development, 2017.

13. Beyond Zero Emissions, Renewable Energy Superpower: Zero Carbon Australia, Beyond Zero Emissions, 2015.

14. IHA, 2016 Hydropower Status Report, International Hydropower Association, 2016.

15. Westphal, K, 'Globalising the German Energy Transition', SWP Comments, Stiftung Wissenschaft und Politik, December, 2012.

16. Weatherby, C, B Eyler and R Burchill, UAE Energy Diplomacy: Exporting Renewable Energy to the Global South, Trends Research and Advisory and the Stimson Centre, 2018.

17. IRENA.

18. World Bank, The Growing Role of Minerals and Metals for a Low-Carbon Future, World Bank, 2017.

19. The 1982 UN Convention on the Law of the Sea (UNCLOS) declared that the seabed area beyond national jurisdiction and its mineral resources are the 'common heritage of mankind'. All mineral exploration and exploitation activities must be approved by the International Seabed Authority, which has begun to develop regulations and guidance to govern the future exploitation of seabed minerals.

20. OECD Due Diligence Guidance for Responsible Supply Chains of Minerals from Conflict-Affected and High-Risk Areas; www.oecd.org/corporate/mne/mining.htm.

21. IEA.

22. Mining: Rare Earth Elements: Where in the World Are They?; Nicholas LePan, 23 November, 2021.

23. US Geological Survey.

24. 'Rare Earth Metals are Used Extensively in Clean Energy Technologies. But How Safe Are They?' By Shourabh Gupta, *Down To Earth*, 18 January, 2021.

25. Ibid.

26. Columbia/SIPA, Centre on Global Energy Policy, Working Paper, The Geopolitics of Renewable Energy, June, 2017.

Unit Symbols

Unit symbols used in the book are listed in an alphabetical order.

barrels per day	(bpd)
billion cubic feet	(bcf)
billion cubic metres	(bcm)
billion tonnes	(bt)
billion tonne per annum	(btpa)
billion units	(BU)
circuit kilometres	(cKm)
degree Centigrade/degree Fahrenheit	(°C/°F)
depletion per tonne	(d/t)
exajoules	(EJ)
gigajoule	(GJ)
gigawatt	(GW)
gigawatts electric	(GWe)
grams of CO_2 per kWh	(gCO_2/kWh)
hectares	(ha)
kilo volt ampere	(kVA)
kilograms of oil equivalent per year	(kgoe per year)
kilowatt-hour	(kw/h)
kilowatts	(kW)
levelised cost of electricity	(LCOE)
mega volt ampere	(MVA)
megavolt ampere reactive power	(MVAr)
megatonnes of coal equivalent	(mtce)
megawatt	(MW)
metre	(m)
metre per second	(m/s)
million barrels per day	(mbpd)
million British thermal units	(mmBtu)
million cubic feet	(mcf)
million cubic meters	(mcm)

million metric tonnes	(mmt)
million metric tonnes oil equivalent	(mmtoe)
million standard cubic meter per day	(mmscmd)
million tonnes	(mt)
million tonnes per annum	(mtpa)
million units	(MU)
normal cubic meter per hour	(Nm3/h)
oil and oil equivalent gas	(o+oeg)
parts per million	(ppm)
petawatts	(PW)
square kilometre	(sq km)
terawatt hour	(TWh)
tonnes of uranium	(tU)
tonne per day	(tpd)
total primary energy supply	(TPES)
trillion cubic feet	(tcf)
trillion cubic meters	(tcm)
volt-amps reactive power	(VAR)
Watt peak	(Wp)

Acknowledgement

Inevitably, a book of this nature draws upon the expertise and insights of very many people and sources.

My first gratitude goes to my fabulous publisher, Manish Purohit, without whose encouragement and support, this book may not have seen the light of the day. He was the one, among many so-called established publishers, (whom I had contacted), who appreciated the fact that energy was no longer a subject limited to the academia or of interest to oil buyers and sellers, but with climate change threatening the very existence of this planet, it has become a major concern for all who inhabit this planet.

The second person I have to thank is my fantastic editor, Vandana Bhagra, who took pains to do a first-class job to turn a rough-hewn first draft into what I hope will be a more polished final product.

It has been my signal good fortune to have a supporting family and children without whose indulgence this volume would not have been completed.

I am also particularly indebted to my son, Rajesh, and his wife, Rupali Sharma, for giving me support to resolve technical glitches and other assistance to complete this work.

This book has profusely relied on multiple sources—books, articles, newspaper reports, government reports and energy agency analyses. It is not possible to mention all the names, but my special acknowledgement goes to International Energy Agency and ETEnergyworld for the data, extensively used in this book. Daniel Yergin deserves special mention as his masterpiece *The Quest*, and Distinguished Professor Emeritus Vaclav Smil of the University of Manitoba (USA), whose outstanding work in *Energy and Civilisation* inspired me to work on *India's Transition from Fossil Fuels to New Age Energy*.

About the Author

 Educated at universities of Allahabad and Lucknow, Kedar Nath Sharma started his journalistic career with *The Times of India*, and served the newspaper as a reporter for fourteen years at Lucknow, Ahmedabad and Delhi. In 1979, he moved on to the Middle East to join *Gulf Times*, a daily, published from Doha (Qatar). After a sixteen-year stint with the *Gulf Times* in various capacities, he moved further on to *Reuters* as a journalist, based in Doha, where his work as a reporter gave him opportunity to study the politics of energy.

In 2004, Sharma returned home, but he continued to work as a contributor to London-based Times *Energy Economist Intelligence Unit (EIU)*, *Financial Times Energy*, *Business Middle East* and *Oxford Analytica*.

He was also the editor of *Energy Today*, a journal dedicated to energy affairs. This is Sharma's second book, after the *Dynastic Ambition: Legacy of Nehru-Gandhis to India's Democracy*, published by TheWritePlace, a unit of Crossword.